One Firm Anchor

One Firm Anchor

The Church and the Merchant Seafarer,
an Introductory History

R.W.H. Miller

The Lutterworth Press

The Lutterworth Press
P.O. Box 60
Cambridge
CB1 2NT

www.lutterworth.com
publishing@lutterworth.com

ISBN: 978 0 7188 9290 6

British Library Cataloguing in Publication Data
A record is available from the British Library

Copyright © R.W.H. Miller, 2012

First Published, 2012

All rights reserved. No part of this edition may be reproduced, stored electronically or in any retrieval system, or transmitted in any form or by any means, electronic, mechanical, photocopying, recording, or otherwise, without prior written permission from the Publisher (permissions@lutterworth.com).

Contents

	Acknowledgements	7
	Abbreviations	9
	Introduction	13
	God Has Spoken by his Prophets	19
1.	The Early Church	21

The Medieval Scene

2.	Where was the Shipping and who was at sea?	35
3.	Devotion to the Saints	58
4.	The Canons and Sea Codes	66
5.	Religious Practice at Sea	81
6.	From the Reformation to the Nineteenth Century	99

The Nineteenth Century

7.	The Nineteenth-Century Revival	118
8.	Early Anglican Societies	133
9.	The Church Congresses	144
10.	The Missions to Seamen	159
11.	St Andrew's Waterside Church Mission	168
12.	The Gibraltar Mission to Seamen	179
13.	American Work	187
14.	The Religious Orders	197
15.	Work among Fishermen	224

Nineteenth-Century Catholic Work

16.	Fr Goldie SJ and the CTS	236
17.	The Work for Catholic Bluejackets	252
18.	The *Œuvres de Mer*	264

Twentieth-Century Catholic Work

19.	Catholic Work 1900-14	280
20.	Peter Anson	292
21.	Catholic Work after Anson	324

Conclusion	334
Bibliography	343
Index	359

Illustrations

Map
Southampton in the later Middle Ages — 34
Figure

1. Faversham: Maison Dieu	55
2. Pevensey Common Seal	63
3. Tenterden Common Seal	63
4. Thirteenth Century Dublin Seal	87
5. W.H.G. Kingston	123
6. Leaf from Lt Cox's diary of ship-visits 1820	125
7. The Rev. Dr John Ashley	136
8. Advertisement for the North Sea Church Mission	156
9. Fr Charles Hopkins	199
10. Ebenezer Mather	226
11. Salvation Navy vessel c. 1900	235
12. The Catholic Sailors' Club in Montreal in the 1920s	247
13. *Œuvres de Mer* Hospital Ship	273
14. Original Apostleship of the Sea membership card 1895	284
15. Peter Anson	293

Acknowledgements

Full lists of acknowledgments appear in the theses which lie behind much of this book. I am grateful to successive supervisors: Dr Tony Mason (Warwick), Dr Alston Kennerley (Plymouth), Dr Norman Tanner SJ and Professor Sean McGrail (London). Additionally I am indebted to Dr Stephen Friend and Dr Roald Kverndal for continuing encouragement and friendship. For access to their archives I must thank: The Missions to Seamen (as it was then), the Apostleship of the Sea (Tilbury, Scotland, Rome), the Augustinians of the Assumption (Rome), Alton Abbey, the SVP, the CTS, but since I consulted them some records have been lost or moved. I have been greatly helped by staff at the British Library, the National Archive (PRO), the Newspaper Library (Colindale), the India Office Library, Plymouth University, Exeter University, Heythrop College, Leicester University, Warwick University, London University, the School of Oriental and African Studies, St Augustine's College Canterbury, the Plume Library (Maldon), Essex County Library (Southend), Glasgow's Mitchell Library (particularly the keeper of the Gartnavel Royal Lunatic Asylum archive), Truro County Records, the Greater London Records Office, and Glasgow Archdiocesan Archive. One of our great national treasures is the inter-library loan service; from the local library staff who are its gatekeepers. I have received much help and more patience, most recently at Dulverton Library, Somerset. Mark Windsor of Tisbury,Wiltshire), and The Rev. Prebendary John Thorogood, Claire Savill, and Mike Bralowski of White Horse Photography in Dulverton, Somerset, have been helpful in technical matters. I thank the Mission to Seafarers (John Ashley), the Faversham Society (Ospringe *Maison Dieu*), the RNMDSF (Ebenezer Mather), and the keeper of the Bible Society Archive at Cambridge University Library (Lt Cox's ship visiting) for providing illustrations. Where I have failed to trace copyright holders this will be corrected in any future edition when they are identified. Anonymous referees made helpful suggestions on two chapters which appeared in the *Mariner's Mirror*; I am grateful to the Hon. Editor for allowing their use. The Abbot of Nunraw kindly gave permission for me to consult the Anson Diaries and to reproduce a picture of the novice Anson. I am indebted to Dr Jan Setterington for listening, reading and commenting. All mistakes are my own.

I thank Fr Bruno Ciceri of the Pontifical Council for the Pastoral Care of Migrants and Itinerant Peoples in Rome for pressing me to publish the material on Anson; my publisher, Adrian Brink, for suggesting additional material; a number of friends who have patiently listened to me over the years; the late Dean Hughes whose bequest helped publication. As much of this material has been accumulated over forty-five years many people who have helped me are not acknowledged here; to them I express my gratitude and offer the excuse of a failing memory.

Abbreviations

AA	Augustinians of the Assumption
AGM	Annual General Meeting
AMIC	Apostolatus Maris International Concilium
ANCL	Ante-Nicene Christian Library
AoP	Apostleship of Prayer
AoS	(sometimes AS in quotations) Apostleship of the Sea
ASFS	American Seamen's Friend Society
Attrib	Attributed
BCM	Bristol Channel Mission
BFBS	British and Foreign Bible Society
BFSFSBU	British and Foreign Seamen's Friend Society and Bethel Union
BFSS	British and Foreign Sailors' Society
BFSSFSBU	British and Foreign Seamen's and Soldiers' Friend Society and Bethel Union
BISS	British and International Sailors' Society
BLFES	British Ladies Female Emigration Society
Borlase	Mss 175/6/Bor/20. J. H. Borlase, *Struggle*, a typescript history of the NSFU
BSS	British Sailors' Society
CBE	Commander of the Order of the British Empire
CCSS	Colonial Church and School Society
CEG	Catholic Evidence Guild
CHR	Catholic Historical Review
CMS	Church Missionary Society
COS	Charity Organisation Society = FWA
cp	compare
CPH	Charles Plomer Hopkins
CRG	Catholic Reading Guild
CRS	Catholic Record Society
CSH	Catholic Sailors' Home
CSI	Catholic Sailors' Institute
CTS	Catholic Truth Society
CYMS	Catholic Young Men's Society
ed(s)	editor(s)
EETS	Early English Text Society
EHR	*English Historical Review*
Fabri	*The Book of the Wanderings of Felix Fabri*, A. Stewart (trans), Palestine Pilgrim Text Society, 1892

F&GP	Finance and General Purposes Committee
Fishermen's Missions	Stephen Friend, *The Rise and Development of Christian Missions amongst British Fishing Communities during the Nineteenth Century,* unpublished MPhil thesis, University of Leeds 1994.
Friedberg	E. Friedberg (ed), *Corpus Iuris Canonici*, 2 vols, (Leipzig 1879, reprinted Graz 1955)
	D = *Decretum Gratiani, Distinctio.*
	C = *Decretum Gratiani, Causa.*
	De Cons = *Decretum Gratiani, De Consecratione.*
	X = *Decretales Gratiani IX.*
FWA	Family Welfare Association
GP	General Purposes
GMS	Gibraltar Mission to Seamen
GoR	Guild of Ransom
GSMV	*Gli Statuti Maritimi Veneziani fino al 1255*, Riccardo Predelli & Adolfo Sacerdoti (eds), Venice, 1903
HBS	Henry Bradshaw Society
HMS	His or Her Majesty's Ship
ICOSU	International Committee of Seamen's Unions
IJMH	*International Journal of Maritime History*
ISF	International Shipping Federation
IT(W)F	International Transport (Workers') Federation
LCL	Licentiate in Canon Law
LEFCS	London Episcopal Floating Church Society
MCS	Mariners' Church Society
MDSF	(Royal National) Mission to Deep Sea Fishermen
MM	*Mariner's Mirror*
MMS	Mersey Mission to Seamen
MN	Merchant Navy
MSABS	Merchant Seamen's Auxiliary Bible Society
MSH	*Messenger of the Sacred Heart*
Mss	This prefix indicates documents in the Modern Records Centre, University of Warwick.
MtS	The Missions to Seamen (now Mission to Seafarers)
n.d.	no date
NMB	National Maritime Board
NMBS	Naval and Military Bible Society
NS	New Series
NSCM	North Sea Church Mission
NSFU	National Sailors' and Firemen's Union
ŒdeM	*Œuvres de Mer*
OMI	Oblates of Mary Immaculate
OS	Old Series
OSB	Order of St Benedict
OSP	Order of St Paul
PBHS	Prayer Book and Homily Society
PECUSA	Protestant Episcopal Church of the United States of America

Abbreviations

PHS	Port of Hull Society
PL	*Patriologiae cursus completus: series Latina*, 221 vols, J. P. Migne (ed), Paris 1844-64.
PLS	Port of London Society
p.p.	privately published
Regesta	*Regesta Regum Anglo-Normannorum*
repr	reprinted
RN	Royal Navy
RNCA	Royal Naval Catholic Association
RNR	Royal Naval Reserve
RS	Rolls Series
RTS	Religious Tract Society
SAMS	South American Missionary Society
SAW(C)M	St Andrew's Waterside (Church) Mission
SCI	Seamen's Church Institute(s)
SFSSP	Seamen's Friendly Society of St Paul
SJ	Society of Jesus
SPCK	Society for the Promotion of Christian Knowledge
SPG	Society for the Propagation of the Gospel
SSP	Society of St Paul
SVP	Society of St Vincent de Paul
TCM	Thames Church Mission
TNA	The National Archive
trans	translator
ts	typescript
Twiss	Sir Travers Twiss (ed), *Black Book of the Admiralty*, 4 vols, RS, 1871
USN	United States Navy
VCH	*Victoria History of the Counties of England*
vol	volume
WCB	Work for Catholic Bluejackets
Wright,1930	R. F. Wright, *Medieval Internationalism*, 1930
Wright,1967	R. F. Wright, The High Seas and the Church in the Middle Ages, *MM*, vol 53, 1967.

Introduction

I possess only a small number of books on the Christian Church and merchant seafarers, for few have written on the subject. Most of these touch on the significance of the call of the first disciples, among them fishermen on the Sea of Galilee, calling them sea apostles; a curious description, unless also the call of Levi indicates an apostolate to the fiscal sector, or Judas Iscariot to nationalist political groups. It overlooks that those fishermen left their nets, left their boats, and were seldom seen on that freshwater lake again. The Gospels offer no evidence of a dedicated ministry to seafarers; the Acts of the Apostles and the Epistles tell us only that the Gospel message was delivered, even by Paul (his intervention when shipwreck threatened no evidence of a sea apostolate but rather a requirement of the Theodosian Code of all on board when faced with danger), to all and sundry rather than specifically to those earning their living on the sea. This book will show that the concept of a mission to seamen is a relatively late one.

Containerization of the shipping industry and the consequent removal of ever larger ships from older dock areas to places allowing their speedy discharge has rendered shipping almost invisible. Many traditional buildings, seamen's clubs among them, have disappeared in consequence. The days, often weeks, once spent in port by ships unloading, have been replaced by hours in all but the smallest ports; today it is usual to be in port only for the twelve hours between tides, rendering the large residential missions redundant. Most Christian maritime activity has become as invisible as the shipping it serves, though the various churches continue to work diligently for the welfare of seafarers, with highly mobile chaplains and lay ship visitors. The Church, in its various manifestations from earliest times has been involved to a greater or lesser extent in the lives of those who travel by sea, and continues to be so.

The Structure of the book

It is difficult to write about seafarers and the Church in any general sense. Among such a vast and disparate crowd of individuals the number of those who are or were Christians cannot be known. If there is any trend for the reader to notice in this book, it is that pre-Reformation the Christian seafarer (I generalise) is perceived as any other member of the Church. There was not the special provision of our own time. Any shipboard chaplaincies were provided more for the crusaders, pilgrims or sponsoring merchants on board, while provisions in port (e.g. *maisons dieu*, churches, lights) were there largely to promote trade by those in whose interest it lay that their ports be used rather than for the benefit of the sailor. After the upheaval of the Reformation, it took three centuries, forming here a period of transition between the two sections of the book, for things to settle down sufficiently for the Church to respond to the seafarer, by the nineteenth century viewing him rather as someone for whom things are done. In every chapter the perceptive reader will want to consider whether the Gospel imperative or the economic imperative is shaping the ministry being described.

The book's emphasis on Great Britain is partly due to access to sources. The nineteenth-century societies dedicated to serving the seafarer coincided with the rise of the British Empire, with London at its heart, and the dominance of the British merchant fleet. There was a mushrooming of societies intended to spread the Gospel, a quick glance at an appropriate encyclopedia revealing for the Church of England alone the Church Missionary Society (1799), Church Mission to the Jews (1809), Intercontinental Church Society (1824), South American Missionary Society (1844), Melanesian Mission (1848), Universities' Mission to Central Africa (1857), to which may be added more for other denominations, their titles indicative of the spread of red across the globe. As the empire spread, so did the British merchant fleet. After the Napoleonic wars, an evangelical revival which had begun in the Royal Navy spilled over into the Merchant Navy. The combination of missionary fervour and revival in the Fleet will be considered for, when peace came, many officers, ashore on half pay, became involved in some of these societies. The post-war effect was felt beyond Britain. The French Church experienced a revival later in the century, not only ashore; many active religious orders were founded, and one, the Augustinians of the Assumption, developed a particular ministry among deep sea fishermen.

The number of footnotes will not be to everyone's taste, but sourcing is important; for those who find them insufficient, I indicate where more can be found. In some chapters named Minutes or contemporary newspaper reports obviate the need for them. Much of the nineteenth-century history survives only in Minutes; tedious reading occasionally spiced with major disagreements. One problem with Peter Anson's work on the sea apostolate was his vagueness about his sources. My footnotes are most abundant in chapters where earlier writers have generalised, been mistaken, or written little. In 1972 Anson asked me to shorten a version of what was intended to be his *Church Maritime*. Additionally I supplied missing material and added sources where I could trace them. He was not pleased with the result and decided to withdraw the book. A couple of decades later I saw in what must have been its final, and much longer, version an acknowledgment of my help, though it seems to have had little effect. In a very real sense, this present book, long in gestation, is a result of what I tried to do to improve his *Church Maritime*. My point about sourcing renders necessary careful thought about a bibliography. A book like this depends on a vast amount of research. I have limited the bibliography to works mentioned in the text in an attempt to preserve a small corner of a distant rain forest; fuller references can be found in the theses listed.

Inclusions and exclusions

My emphasis is on periods and societies which have received little attention; for examples, the Early Church, the beginnings of the modern Catholic sea apostolate, and Charles Hopkins.[1] Hopkins's extraordinary ministry justifies the space allotted him, compared with that given others, Anson excepted, and, when added to the other Anglican chapters, helps balance the Roman Catholic ones. Hopkins has to be seen in the light of the legislation associated with the name of Samuel Plimsoll MP. Remembered as a philanthropist, Plimsoll, a committed member of a Congregational church, was supported in his parliamentary campaigns across the denominations, though seldom mentioned by seamen's missionary societies (SAWCM excepted). His work introduces chapter fourteen.

The name of Peter Anson appears regularly in this book. Little regarded by historians, he was nevertheless the first significant maritime missiologist, probably invented the term, and with the publication of his *Church and the Sailor* paved the way for others to follow. As most who write about the Church and the seafarer refer to Anson's work in establishing the modern Catholic sea apostolate, sometimes calling him its founder, and quarry his book for the early history of the work of the Church among seafarers generally, a serious examination of Anson is justified.[2]

Some omissions reflect an absence of source material. Information for some countries, churches or centuries is hard to find, if it exists at all. The debt to nineteenth-century Methodism needs the attention of someone familiar with Methodist Church history. Kverndal offers some information, but more, surely, remains to be found.[3] The Salvation Army's work among seamen, apart from its Salvation Navy, also deserves more attention; my research has failed to reveal more than scattered records. Even The Missions to Seamen (now The Mission to Seafarers), which occurs in several chapters here, awaits a serious study based on primary documents.

The lack of oriental-rite Christians in the text in modern times is a matter for concern. Relevant sources remain to be found. Orthodoxy reveals a denominational neglect of seafarers, except in the earliest centuries of the Church. The principle that where the ships are, there are the crews, suggests that the size of the nineteenth-century British merchant fleet militated against the presence of many Orthodox at sea, a situation which ought to have changed with the enormous investment in subsequent shipping by Greek families.[4] My only information follows a hint from Anson and can be dealt with briefly here. A room was opened as a 'Greek Church' on Patrick Street, in Cardiff, on 19 December 1873, by The Rev. G. Hatterley (*sic*) 'of Wolverhampton'. The *Cardiff Times* reported the next day that the effect of his sermon and subsequent appeal had not been helped by its

---
1   R.W.H. Miller, *Priest in Deep Water*, 2010.
2   R.W.H. Miller, *Ship of Peter*, unpublished MPhil thesis.
3   Roald Kverndal, *George Charles Smith of Penzance*, 2012, 50ff.
4   Gelina Harlaftis, *A History of Greek-Owned Shipping*.

delivery in English 'while with two or three exceptions, the congregation consisted of Greek sailors who scarcely understood a word'. A dinner at the Windsor Hotel attended by 'a number of Greek residents and captains', followed, though the *Cardiff Shipping and Mercantile Gazette* reported a lack of Greek ships in port. He appeared again on the 5th March 1877, in the *Bristol Daily Post* as The Rev. S. G. Hatherley (correctly), 'senior priest of the Patriarchal Œcumenical Throne of Constantinople . . . a Bristolian by birth', opening a room in Bristol, furnished with the assistance of the captain and crew of the brig *Thessalia*, 'for Greek sailors frequenting the port'. The paper, reporting a ritual more elaborate than 'that of the Roman Church', was otherwise short on detail.[1]

Those who fail to notice that my subject is the merchant seafarer will point to the apparent neglect of the Royal Navy and the standing navies of other nations. Merchant fleets throughout history have outnumbered these other navies; indeed, have often been recruited in times of need to supplement their numbers. To write about the standing navies would take me far from the merchant fleets. A couple of books which deal with religion and the British Navy are those of Taylor and Blake.[2] I notice work among these navies only as it impinges directly on the ministry to mercantile fleets.

Finding the Seafarer

In 1973 Anson wrote to me that 'you never manage to convey the point of view of the average seaman, but view him from a distance and on dry land'. Anson's point was that much of my text was about what the Church was doing for the seafarer, with hardly a whiff of sea air about it. I would argue that to refer to the 'average seaman' is unhelpful, as no such a being exists. Anson, in his final book (untitled, unpublished, and held in Rome in typescript) concluded its introduction by dismissing 'well-meaning landlubbers, who have no personal experience of seafaring life or maritime psychology'. His book *Harbour Head* (145ff) tells of his own deep-sea voyages in the 1920s, his friendships with the crews of the liners on which he travelled, and his trips with the crews of fishing vessels round the British coast, winning their confidence through the medium of his paint brush; experiences qualifying him in ways which those of us who have only sat listening to seafarers in their joys or troubles have to guess. Yet repeatedly in that final typescript he refers to the 'simple sailor' with all the assumptions of those who know little about the sea. Sailors come in great variety, often with a wisdom acquired through travel and the need to work and live, voyage after voyage, in proximity to others not of their choosing; few can be described as 'simple'.

---

1 According to Anson, Stephen Georgeson Hatherley was ordained in Constantinople c. 1870, and later appointed a Proto-Presbyter of the Patriarchal Œcumenical Throne of Constantinople. The British Library Catalogue lists him as author of a number of books, some on Orthodox subjects.
2 Gordon Taylor, *The Sea Chaplains* Richard Blake, *Evangelicals in the Royal Navy 1775-1815*.

Introduction

Finding his religion

As Professor Lewis Fischer, a distinguished maritime economic historian of our own time, has written, 'maritime history is more than the study of ships, sailors and navies but rather a central part of understanding human experience'.[1] Although religious belief is probably the most distinctive part of human experience, it is difficult to find a maritime historian who has given the religious life of the seafarer much attention. The religious life of any traveller, beyond pilgrim or crusader, remains largely unstudied; the difference between others who travel and the sailor is that the latter spends long periods as part of a total community whereas those others, medieval travellers overland or today's passengers on train or plane, do not. The passenger is a relatively free agent, while the sailor is bound to the ship and its master, obliged to work for the benefit of the cargo (passengers are 'human cargo') and lacking the free disposal of his time. Few on a modern cruise ship, apart from the members of the ship's company, know where the crew is and what it is doing. Although crew and passengers were in closer proximity in other periods, large gaps in our knowledge remain for all periods, especially about the sailor's religious beliefs and practice.

The evanescence of faith and practice makes it difficult to fill those large gaps.

> The common pairing of the words 'faith' and 'practice' shows that we find it useful to anchor the ephemeral and personal 'faith' in the more tangible and universal 'practice' when we speak of religion. Unfortunately we cannot measure anyone's religious faith, divorced from symbols and rituals, unless we have access to private thoughts expressed in visual art, in speech, or in writing.[2]

Although most of today's seafarers can write, indeed have a choice of media by which to communicate about their lives, contemporary students of maritime faith and practice find it very difficult to establish how such things are manifested. I cite Alain Cabantous's confirmation of this problem for the 17th-19th centuries in chapter six.[3] When few could write, and what was written has had many centuries in which to perish, the difficulty is compounded. This may explain why the religion of the seafarer is so often ignored.

A second explanation lies in the difficulty of writing about something essentially abstract and highly personal, at least on the experiential level. That is not to say of medieval man, for example, that his religion was the personal preference which religion has become in our own time; the experience would be personal, but the practice corporate, perhaps prescribed by the state or proscribed by the Church. It might be personal in the sense in which the *Hafgerdinga Lay* describes a crew member of a Viking ship as the sole Christian on board.[4] It would be corporate in the sense in which King Olaf required his subjects to adopt the new faith, Christianity. I shall suggest in the text that following the Reformation it became possible to find

1 Reviewing Frank Broeze's Island Nation in MM, vol 85(3), August 1999, 355.
2 Kirsten A. Seaver, *The Frozen Echo*, 96.
3 *Les citoyens du large*, 12.
4 Magnus Magnusson, *Viking Expansion Westwards* 112. *Landnámabók*, 49f. Gwyn Jones (trans), *The Norse Atlantic Saga*, 189.

in crews lone Christians where previously Christianity had been shared. Lynn White Jnr wrote:

professional historians have been taught to read the words of the documents with critical care; yet the sociology of knowledge often involves the study of activities, and of relationships . . . that are so taken for granted, so axiomatic, that they largely elude expression in writing.[1]

That there was nothing remarkable about his religious practice may constitute a third explanation why there should be so little recorded of the religious life of the seafarer. It is seldom wise to argue from silence but here it may be telling us something. My chapter on the medieval seafarer and the saints, for example, adduces from remaining evidence that in this the seafarer was in the mainstream of popular belief.

Technical words

Most subjects have their own language. There are some technical words involved in studying Church work among seafarers. Roman Catholics tend to refer to an *apostolate*. It is derived from the Greek word for 'send', the Latin equivalent giving the words *mission* and *missiology* (the study of mission). The Greek derivation has the more specific connotation of association with the Apostles (the first to be sent) and a church which is apostolic, that is, obedient to Jesus's command to 'go out into all the world to proclaim the Good News' (Mtt 18:19), while the word *mission* has come to have secular uses, as in space missions, or the mission statements of industry. Jesus's command is known as the dominical (of the Lord) command and is binding on all Christians. The sea apostolate is thus a convenient way of referring to those who are active as Christians among seafarers. For the Roman Catholic Church, seafarers comprise 'all those who, by the exercise of the art of sailing or fishing . . . spend their lives continually on ships, and therefore can avail themselves but rarely and with difficulty in the normal care of the Parish Priest . . . ' (*Opus Apostolatus Maris: Leges §2,* Vatican, 1957), a definition with which others are unlikely to quibble.

Protestant and nonconformist are words often used carelessly. I think it is fair to distinguish churches of the Reformation as Protestant. Nonconformists are those who do not conform to the State religion, and thus include Roman Catholics, at least in what is now the United Kingdom. Some may object to Roman Catholics being referred to simply as Catholics. As one for much of his life a member of the Church of England I understand why many prefer to describe even users of oriental rites who are in communion with Rome along with users of the Roman Rite generally as Catholics. I prefer to refer to them as Catholics without differentiation as more accurate and for economy of ink. References to members of the Church of England distinguish between Tractarians, ritualists, Anglo-Catholics and evangelicals, according to the period and the person.

Sailor, seaman, and mariner are used interchangeably of those working on ships; 'seafarer' may include others at sea. Apart from prostitutes servicing

---

1 *Mediaeval Religion and Technology*, 318.

the needs of Crusaders *en route*, an interesting category of supernumerary but undoubtedly at sea, until the arrival in the nineteenth century of large passenger ships, their staffs including stewardesses and similar, females as crew members are difficult to find. Where oars are the driving force, I refer to oarsmen. For those on board but not bound to the ship, using it as a conveyance, the terms traveller, passenger or pilgrim are used as appropriate. The crews of more recent times include men and women, something reflected in the names of today's societies, now altered to avoid being gender-specific.

I hope this book will prompt others to correct what I have written, and add to it. Some of the figures here are inspirational, others not. I couple with the former some of the wonderful chaplains in the ministry to seamen with whom it has been my privilege to work, one having begun his ministry in 1917 as a Church Army officer visiting sailing ships in Lerwick; we are all links in the chain.

God has Spoken by His Prophets[1]

>God has spoken by the prophets,
>Spoken the unchanging Word;
>Each from age to age proclaiming
>God the One, the righteous Lord!
>'Mid the world's despair and turmoil
>One firm anchor holding fast:
>God eternal reigns forever,
>God the first and God the last.

---

[1] Hope Publishing Company gave permission to reproduce 'God Has Spoken by His Prophets' by George W. Briggs, © 1953, Ren.1981 The Hymn Society, Admin. by Hope Publishing Co., Carol Stream, IL, USA. All rights reserved. Used by permission.

1. The Early Church[1]

A number of Christian texts from the first centuries offer glimpses of sea or sailor. Gathered here are some of the more obvious. They offer no uniform picture. The early Church presented a fragmented scene, each grouping convinced of its orthodoxy. Between periods of persecution different groups dominated according to the preference of the Roman emperor. What texts survive were written largely by what are now considered the orthodox at the expense of heterodox material. Other groupings, the Arians, Monophysites and Nestorians, tended to spread eastwards, the latter reaching China,[2] and perhaps Sri Lanka; rendering their writings as they crossed inland Asia unlikely to contain much of maritime interest.[3] What history remains is not for the faint-hearted.[4]

A map of religious expansion combined with the pattern of trade indicates where to look for encounters between seafarer and Church. So, despite 'evidence of early Byzantine trade extending from Ireland in the West to Manchuria in the East',[5] Christian distribution makes the Mediterranean the sea of interest. The first four of the great patriarchal sees (Rome, Alexandria, Antioch, Constantinople, Jerusalem) were important ports. The involvement of Christians in the corn trade is explicit in the texts; the passenger experience, if it appears at all, seldom adds more than references to port of embarkation and destination, sometimes between islands, often to major cities.[6]

---

1 I am grateful to the Hon. Editor of the *Mariner's Mirror* for permission to use in this chapter material previously published in the *MM* in November 2010.
2 Jenkins, *The Lost History of Christianity*, passim.
3 Winstedt, *The Christian Topography of Cosmas Indicopleustes*.
4 See e.g. John, Bishop of Ephesus, *The Third Part of the Ecclesiastical History passim*. John, sixth-century Monophysite bishop of Constantinople, described the appalling treatment of unbelievers and non-Monophysite Christians. His *History* refers throughout to the Monophysites as 'the orthodox'.
   Neil B. McLynn, Christian Controversy and Violence in the Fourth Century, 15-44.
5 Marlia Mundell Mango, Beyond the Amphora . . . , 87.
   For a general introduction to trade see Marlia Mundell Mango,Byzantine trade, 3ff.
6 Tassos Papacostas, *The Economy of Late Antique Cyprus*, 114f offers Epiphanius of Salamis finding a Paphos-bound ship in the fourth-century, and Archbishop Paul of Crete stopping at Crete en route from Egypt to Constantinople in the sixth-century and other examples.

Ships and the clergy

References to ships appearing occasionally in Christian literature add little to the discoveries of maritime archaeology.[1] Imperial galleys feature largely;[2] the work-horse of the merchant fleet, the ΔΡΟΜΩΝ, less so.[3] Kingsley and Decker mention as developments of the period the reduction in the number of mortise-and-tenon joints on 'shell-first' vessels, greater reliance on iron nails, increasing use of pitch rather than lead for sheathing hulls, and 'an overall shift toward frame-first ships', details seldom found in religious texts.[4] Technology sometimes required Church assistance: in the early fifth century, Bishop Silvanus of Troas was called upon to assist in the launch of a ship or raft (πλαντήν) for conveying 'enormous pillars' which was stuck on the shore at Troas. He approached the shore, prayed, touched a rope, and exhorted 'the rest to vigorous exertion', the ship shifting at first pull.[5]

Clergy of one sort or another are easier to spot than lay Christians and appear in a variety of situations. At the quayside, so different from today's secure docks, clergy and ships can be seen together. The Cypriot saint Athanasius Pentaschoinites saved a ship in peril.[6] Athanasius (296 –373), Bishop of Alexandria, 'when the sea rose against the city of Alexandria . . . accompanied by all the priests went forth to the borders of the sea, and holding in his hand the book of the holy Law he raised his hand to heaven', his prayer causing the sea to return to its place.[7] In *The Age of the ΔΡΟΜΩΝ* Pryor and Jeffreys offer a ritual from the time of Leo VI (886-912), here performed with a military expedition, which probably reflects earlier usage, when all the standards of the δρομωνες were blessed during a celebration of the Liturgy by the priests, 'and by a lengthy prayer to God for the successful venture of the *stratos* against the enemy . . .'.[8] There might well have been a nearby chapel. In Constantinople St Daniel the Stylite, down from his pillar, took up residence in the quayside chapel of St Zacharias.[9]

St Melania the Younger (383 – 410), surely in a class of her own, a Roman lady of aristocratic descent and very rich, adopted the ascetic life, founding a monastery on the Mount of Olives. She took her entourage to a nearby ship and informed the captain she was hiring him, his crew and his vessel, insisting, despite adverse winds, they sail for Sicily. The winds presaged a

---

1 Séan McGrail, Renaissance and Romano-Celtic Ship Design . . . , 439ff.
   Lionel Casson, *Ships and Seamanship in The Ancient World,* 148ff. I am grateful to Professor McGrail for these references.
2 Robert Gardiner (ed.), *The Age of the GALLEY*, 90-100, 215f, 218f. I am grateful to Professor McGrail for this reference.
3 John H. Pryor and Elizabeth M. Jeffreys, *The Age of the ΔΡΟΜΩΝ*, passim.
4 'New Rome, New Theories on Inter-Regional Exchange', 13.
5 Socrates, *Ecclesiastical History*, book VII, ch. xxxvii.
6 Tassos Papacostas, The Economy of Late Antique Cyprus, 115.
7 *The Chronicle of John, Bishop of Nikiu,* 84.
8 *op. cit.*, 493.
9 Elizabeth Dawes and Norman H. Baynes (trans.), *Three Byzantine Saints*, 46.

1. The Early Church 23

violent storm; this and the many people on board led to a shortage of water and imminent danger. The crew blamed the wrath of God. Melania, disagreeing, interpreted it as a sign that God wished them to sail elsewhere, and over-ruled the captain. The ship arrived safely at a 'certain island' where the locals were being held to ransom. Melania acceded to the local bishop's plea that she pay the sum outstanding and all were freed, departing for Africa with little more said of ship or crew. The episode illustrates what a large fortune and a strong personality could achieve, her quayside walk and talk to the captain a reminder of the intimacy of fifth-century ports.[1]

Christians and trade

Many early Christians were associated with the sea in some way. Obvious examples were Marcion and Tertullian. Marcion (d. 160), according to Hippolytus a ship owner and son of a bishop, excommunicated for heresy in 144, organised his own church with followers widely spread in such trading cities as Corinth, Lyons, and Rome. Tertullian (c. 160 – c. 220), a native of Carthage, another who in later life veered from orthodoxy, spoke of collections being made at Christian meetings for distribution to the poor and needy, among whom he included the shipwrecked.[2]

There are a number of reasons why there should be an association between Christians and the sea. The Mediterranean in the Roman Empire was a link between its many parts. Paul's Epistles show early Christian communities spreading from port to port. Second, where Christians were landowners they might attract the *munus navicularium*, a legal obligation to contribute ships or money to the shippers' guild (*corpus naviculorum*), effectively a state merchant fleet under the direction of various diocesan (the diocese was an area of secular Roman administration) shippers' guilds.[3] Augustine of Hippo (354 – 430) refused a gift of land because it was burdened with the shipping liturgy or duty.[4] Third, by the third-century Christians had an interest in maritime economic activity, partly because, with its low status, and perhaps fairly low returns, it was an occupation from which they were not excluded; also, because a church, holding members' money in its treasuries, could issue letters of credit to be honoured by the church at the port of destination. Hollerich cited a third-century letter in which a group from Alexandria, probably Christians, contracted with a shipper (ναυκληρος) in Rome for his services to sell grain there.[5]

By the time of Athanasius of Alexandria there was a very heavy

---

1 Elizabeth A. Clark (trans., ed.), *The Life of Melania the Younger*, 42-3.
2 *Against the Heathen*, 81. Cp Lactantius (c. 240 - c 320), *Divine Institutes*, 427f, which lists redemption of captives, protection of destitute widows and children, care for the sick, and burial of strangers and the poor.
3 Michael J. Hollerich, The Alexandrian Bishops and the Grain Trade, 190.
4 Cited in Hollerich, *op. cit.*, 202.
5 Hollerich, *op. cit.*, 189. See also Walter Ashburner (ed), *The Rhodian Sea-Law*, clxxix-clxxx.

involvement of the Alexandrian church's ships in the grain trade.[1] There were serious penalties for any who delayed the delivery of grain, to Rome by more than one year, or Constantinople by two.[2] Behind one of Athanasius's periods of exile, in this instance to Gaul, lay an accusation by enemies swearing to having heard him threaten to prevent the corn supply reaching Byzantium.[3] The Theodosian Code refers to the Alexandrian grain fleet, its maritime expeditions encouraged by the award of four per cent of the grain carried as cargo and a thousand *solidus* paid for each thousand measures.[4] Bulk deliveries received further rewards.

The Theodosian Code mentions the conduct of the industry as overseen by the Guild of Shipmasters.[5] It provided for delay due to bad weather or other disaster. John, Bishop of Nikiu, told of a ship from Alexandria laden with imperial grain which was wrecked, and its cargo lost. The provincial governor, arresting the captain, had him beaten but finding no money on him, concluded that the wreck had not been for personal gain. John recorded a decree of the Emperor Maurice that a captain should not be punished or made to pay compensation in case of shipwreck, the loss to be borne by the imperial revenue.[6] The Roman church, too, was involved and, especially after the collapse of Roman secular authority, needed to import much grain if the citizens were not to starve.[7] The evidence suggests that when Christian congregations were intimate enough for all to know their bishop, and for each bishop to be on corresponding terms with other bishops, the Christian travelling by sea might be passed from congregation to congregation. This is not the same as saying that the bishops had a concern for the maritime apostolate. For example Cyprian (d. 258) wrote: 'Let us know plainly who has been substituted in place of Marcion in Arles, that we may know to whom to direct our brethren and to whom we should write . . .'.[8] The reception of travelling Christians appears in a letter from Celerinus to Lucian: '. . . all the confessors who have come thence from you hither. To meet them, the women themselves went down to the harbour and supported them in the city'.[9] It may be that Christian sailors were received in a similar way.

The corn ships may be glimpsed in contemporary hagiography. John the Almsgiver (560–619), a later Patriarch of Alexandria, received 'news . . . that two of the Church's fast-sailing ships, which he had sent to Sicily for corn, had cast anchor in the harbor . . .' at a time when the population faced famine.[10]

---

1 Hollerich, *op. cit.*, 197f. See also Marlia Mundell Mango, Beyond the Amphora . . . , 96f for details of the fleet and its trade.
2 Section 14.15 and 14.16. *The Theodosian Code*, 416f.
 See also Emin Tengström, *Bread for the People, passim.*
3 Mango & Scott, *The Chronicles of Theophanes Confessor*, 52.
4 Section 13:5:7. *The Theodosian Code*, 392.
5 Section 13:5147. *The Theodosian Code*, 393.
6 *The Chronicle of John of Nikiu* (CIII.2-3),165.
7 Peter Brown, *The Rise of Western Christendom*, 134.
8 Cyprian, *Letters*, Letter 68(5).
9 Cyprian, *Letters*, Letter 21(4).
10 Dawes & Baynes, *Three Byzantine Saints*, 223.

Their fortuitous arrival was credited to his sanctity. The same account records: the ships of the Church of which he was head [Alexandria] met with such a violent storm in the Adriatic that the crew were forced to jettison the whole cargo; and all the ships were there at the same time. And the weight of their freight was exceedingly heavy ... waterproof garments and silver and other valuable goods, so that the weight of what was lost was estimated at thirty-four hundredweight, for there were more than thirteen ships each carrying 10,000 artabes. Directly they reached Alexandria and cast anchor, all the ship masters and captains took refuge in the church ... The next day ... the [Saint said] to them all '... do not be cast down by this mishap to the ships'.[11]

The cause of concern here, prompting the seeking of sanctuary, would be the possibility of attracting those Theodosian penalties for late or non-delivery of the corn. While Christians must have been involved in other maritime business, it is the corn trade which dominates.[12]

Metaphors and their sources as maritime indicators

With such an involvement, and with churches in all the major ports and trading cities, images associated with the sea abound in the writings of the Fathers. Peter Anson, quoting Hippolytus (c. 170 – c. 236): 'The world is a sea in which the Church, like a ship, is beaten by the waves but not submerged', and Clement of Alexandria (c. 150 – c. 215): 'Let the dove, or the fish, or the vessel flying before the winds, or the marine anchor, be our signets', argued that early bishops had a concern for the maritime apostolate, a view unsupported by his quotations.[13] Alain Corbin used the Fathers to illustrate what he perceived to be the view of the sea shared by the ancients.[14] His particular interest seems to have been in their use of language derived from biblical Flood texts, of which there is no shortage, but he missed the theological sense, despite being aware that the Fathers used the ocean as a metaphor ('To attempt to fathom the mysteries of the ocean bordered on sacrilege, like an attempt to penetrate the impenetrable nature of God, as St Augustine, St Ambrose, and St Basil repeatedly pointed out'), offering instead a view of the ocean (its lure) for which it was never intended.[15]

The maritime metaphors of the Fathers derive as much from their classical education, common experience, and the Bible, as from a knowledge of shipping. In some the sea is hardly mentioned. There is no obvious metaphor in Prudentius

---

11 Dawes & Baynes, *Three Byzantine Saints*, 239.
12 The population of Constantinople has been estimated as some three or four hundred thousand requiring 31,200 tons of wheat, the equivalent of 624 annual shipments in merchant ships capable of carrying 50 tons. See Sean Kingsley and Michael Decker, New Rome, New Theories ..., 2, 4. Kingsley and Decker refer to 'far-flung trading interests and activities of the clergy at this time ...'.
13 P.F.Anson, *Church Maritime*, unpublished typescript, copies held by the AoS in and Rome. It was not Anson's practice to give references for his quotations.
14 Alain Corbin, *The Lure of the Sea*.
15 *Ibid.*, 2. Other examples occur throughout the book and seem to derive from a diet of undigested 17th-century authors.

(348 – c. 410), for example, except for a charming phrase in a preface where he wrote that God to the 'port of old age steers my declining days', a contemporary literary convention with no particular Christian association.[1] Tertullian used a metaphor drawn from pagan culture and classical education.

> [Y]et death is much too violent, coming as it does upon us by strange and violent means... That is still a violence to ships: although far away from the Capharean rocks, assailed by no storms, without a billow to shatter them, with favouring gale, in gliding course, with many crews, they founder amidst entire security, suddenly owing to some internal shock. Not dissimilar are the shipwrecks of life... It matters not whether the vessel of the human body goes with unbroken timbers or shattered with storms, if the navigation of the soul be overthrown.[2]

Lactantius (c. 240 – c. 320) referred to the Neptune story[3] and drew on Cicero for another concerning a man on a plank at sea.[4] Clement of Alexandria (c. 150 – c. 215) mentioned Atlas 'the first to build a boat and sail on the sea'.[5] These authors were well-educated in the pagan system before becoming Christians.

Yet some metaphors reflect a general knowledge of ship or sea. Cyril of Jerusalem (c. 315 – 386) wrote:

> Men ought to have been astonished and amazed . . . at the well-ordered movements of the stars . . . how some are signs . . . some indicate . . . the beginning of navigation; and a man, sitting in his ship and sailing amid the boundless waves, guides his ship by observing the stars.[6]

> By faith, seafaring men, entrusting themselves to a tiny wooden craft, exchange the solid element of the land for the unstable motion of the waves, surrendering themselves to uncertain hopes and carrying about with them a faith more sure than any anchor....[7]

His *Catachesis*, aimed generally, may be supposed to use common experience in the interest of intelligibility. Tertullian probably drew from the same well when he wrote, 'Reason . . . is a thing of God . . . voyaging all the universal course of life without the rudder of reason, they know not how to shun the hurricane which is impending over the world'.[8]

The perils of the storm would have been a universal fear. Its concomitant, shipwreck, is used repeatedly, probably prompted by Paul's 'shipwreck of their faith' (1 Tim. 1:19) as much as by the seasonal storms of the Mediterranean; so, Tertullian on Apelles who 'having first fallen from the principles of Marcion . . . afterwards shipwrecked himself, in the spirit, on the virgin Philumene . . .'.[9] Cyprian extended the metaphor:

> For, indeed, if any port on the sea begins to be difficult or dangerous to

---

1 Prudentius, *Poems*.
2 Tertullian, *De Anima*, 52.
3 Lactantius, *Divine Institutes*, 49.
4 *Ibid.* 367f.
5 Clement of Alexandria, *Stromateis*, 1.16.75 (3).
6 *Works of St Cyril of Jerusalem*, Catachesis IX.8.
7 *Ibid, Catachesis*,V (3).
8 *On Repentance*.
9 *On the Flesh of Christ*.

1. The Early Church

ships because of its broken fortifications, do not those sailing direct their ships to other neighbouring ports where the access would be safe and the entrance advantageous and the station secure? . . . It is necessary for this situation . . . that we may receive to ourselves with prompt and benign humanity our brethren who, having avoided the rocks of Marcion, seek the saving gates of the Church.[1]

There may be a hint here of a Christian duty of hospitality to the physically shipwrecked, while the 'gates of the Church' echo the original idea of the walled part of a port, here with 'unbroken fortifications', offering a safe haven. Cyprian's *Letters* contain other examples. Of Nicostratus, removed from the diaconate for fraud, Cyprian wrote to Cornelius, 'a man banished from see and people . . . himself made a shipwreck of truth and faith, is stirring up certain ones like himself to similar shipwrecks'.[2]

Although Cyprian often used maritime imagery, it is probably Tertullian who is the master:[3]

Amid these reefs and inlets, amid these shallows and straits of idolatry, Faith, her sails filled by the Spirit of God, navigates; safe if cautious, secure if intently watchful. But to such as are washed overboard is a deep whence is no out-swimming; to such as are run aground is inextricable shipwreck; to such as are engulphed is a whirlpool, where there is no breathing - in idolatry. All waves thereof whatsoever suffocate; every eddy there sucks down into Hades . . . Let not that be in the Church which was not in the Ark.[4]

Clement of Alexandria refers to heretical baptism as 'crossing a foreign water'.[5] In short, shipwreck may be of the individual or a Church; may consist in heresy or apostasy; and the rescuing vessel may be either the faith of the individual or the Church herself, its debt to the Noah story substantial.

The image of the Church as ship allows the metaphor to be extended. A biblical idea is the casting of the net from the ship to catch bystanders.[6] The ship's captain might be Christ, or Christ its destination, 'the port of Christ'.[7] Equally, the captain might be the bishop, described with pastoral and gubernatorial similes: 'But now no less do we congratulate you . . . that the shepherd might be returned to feed the flock, and the pilot to govern the ship, and the ruler to rule the people'.[8] Faith fills the sails.[9] The destination is the 'anchorage of salvation'.[10] In the meantime, 'The ship which firmly

---

1 Cyprian, *Letters*, 68(3).
2 See also *Ibid*, 4(22), 17(3), 21(2), 52(1), 52(2), 67(8) etc.
3 Despite Tertullian's lapse into Montanism, Cyprian called him 'My Master' - cited from Jerome in Library of the Fathers, *Tertullian*, 1842, i.
4 Tertullian, *On Idolatry*, xxiv.
5 Clement of Alexandria, *Stromateis*, I.19.96(3).
   See also Tertullian, *On Idolatry*, xxiv.
6 Cyprian, *Letters,* 1(4).1 Cf. John 21, 4ff.
7 Cyprian, *Treatises*, XI, 259.
8 Cyprian, *Letters*, 61(1).
9 Tertullian, *On Idolatry*.
10 Cyprian, *Treatises*, I, 10.

rests upon its cable is struck but not broken by the waves'.[1] Tertullian makes an obvious connection between wind and Spirit. His maritime imagery is introduced even to passages of commentary where it finds no natural place.

> 'His glory [is that] of a bull; his horns, the horns of an unicorn . . . '[Deut. 33:17] . . . But Christ was therein signified: a 'bull', by reason of each of his two characters, - to some fierce, as Judge; to others gentle as Saviour; whose 'horns' were to be the extremities of the *cross*. For even in a ship's yard - which is part of a *cross* - this is the name by which the extremities are called; while the central pole of the mast is an 'unicorn'. [Italics original][2]

Other passages relate to baptismal teaching: the Flood, the crossing of the Red Sea, Jonah, and various New Testament texts. Tertullian, in his *De Baptismo* (VIII.12), repeats the ship image, asking if the disciples, with Jesus in Galilee, were baptised, and what the state of the baptised, his answer alluding to the calming of the storm (Lk 8: 22ff) and the walking of Peter on the water (Mtt 14: 22ff):

> Some drop a hint, sufficiently forced surely, that the Apostles supplied the place of Baptism, at the time when they were sprinkled and covered with waves in the ship; and that Peter himself, when walking on the sea, was sufficiently dipped. But to my thinking it is one thing to be sprinkled and caught by the violence of the sea, and another to be washed according to the rite of Religion. Nevertheless that ship set forth a figure of the Church, inasmuch as it is tossed in the sea, that is in the world, by the waves, that is by persecutions and temptations, while the Lord is, as it were, patiently sleeping, until, being awakened in the last extremity by the prayers of the saints, He stilleth the world, and giveth again a *calm* to his own. [Italic original]

There is no shortage in the New Testament of passages from which to cull maritime metaphors.

Some imagery is sourced from experience. It is implicit in Tertullian that he was familiar with terms used within the seafaring community; his home town, Carthage, was a significant port and he had made the journey to Rome and back. Nor was his knowledge superficial. He was aware of the effect of refraction: '. . . it was the water which was the cause of the oar seeming to be inclined or bent; out of the water, it was perfectly straight in appearance . . .', the question of the horizon, 'a vanishing point in the direction of its furthest distance. So the sky blends itself with the sea . . .',[3] and of buoyancy, 'But what, says Soranus [in answer to Tertullian's argument], if men should deny that the sea is a bodily substance, because a ship out of water becomes a heavy and motionless mass?'.[4] Tertullian had a very thorough education, and from Soranus and other classical masters may have derived some of his knowledge of the physics involved. Personal observation better explains his knowledge of ship construction.

> [Y]ou will be bold to maintain that a ship is perfect without her keel, or her bow, or her stern, or without the solidity of her entire frame. And yet

---

1 *Ibid.* VIII, 199.
2 Tertullian, *An Answer to the Jews*, X.
   See also, Hugo Rahner, *Greek Myths*, 328ff, 332, 345, 321, 373, 374 etc.
3 Tertullian, *De Anima*, 17.
4 *Ibid.* 8.

1. The Early Church

how often have we seen the same ship, after being shattered with the storm and broken by decay, with all her timbers repaired and restored, gallantly riding on the waves in all the beauty of a renewed fabric . . . Besides, if a wealthy ship owner . . . thoroughly repairs his ship, and then chooses that she should make no further voyages, will you contend that the old form and finish is still not necessary to the vessel, although she is no longer meant for actual service, when the mere safety of the ship requires such completeness irrespective of service?[1]

If the Christians of Carthage were as involved in maritime economic activity as the Alexandrian and Roman Christians, then Tertullian had not far to look.[2]

Tertullian hints in this passage at the duty of the ship owner to keep his vessel in good repair, a duty obvious in itself, but also a legal obligation found in the oldest sea codes. Indeed, the preservation of the ship, and particularly life, took precedence over everything else, and lay, for example, behind the law permitting jettison, whereby cargo could be thrown overboard to save the ship.[3] The passage hints further at the responsibility of the owner as distinct from that of the κοινωνια or *communitatis navis*, the community of shareholders, the whole body of persons who shared in general average if the ship perished or the cargo was lost.[4] Κοινωνια would hold special meaning for Christians.

Clement of Alexandria used the analogy of a coin paid, 'when one and the same coin is given to a sea-captain we speak of money to pay for the passage, to a tax-collector, tax, to a property owner, rent . . .'.[5] A number of Codes specified what was involved in such a payment, that is, the passenger's entitlement. Clement referred to the corporate responsibility of the crew in the hauling of a boat,[6] or the sole responsibility in case of shipwreck of the 'pilot who has not furled the sail' and is 'punishable by law'.[7] An associated passage pointed to the responsibility of the ship builder for 'the existence of the boat, so the builder for the completion of a house',[8] the comparison making it clear that Clement is referring to a responsibility generally understood, that is, satisfactory completion. That he does not need to explain it to his audience indicates the measure of general understanding of his point.

Cyprian in using the idea of the ship builder touches on the construction of a ship.

[I]f you should say to him whom you are urging to the control over and use of ships: 'Buy your material from the choicest woods, Brother, cover your

---

1 Tertullian, *On the Resurrection of the Flesh*, 60.
  Cp. John Cassian, *Conferences*, 1. *praef.* 3.
2 Peter Brown, *The Rise of Western Christendom*, 134.
3 Evidence of the law of jettison can be found in the Old Testament book of Jonah, though not in the legal portions of Scripture. See S.M. Passamaneck, Traces of Rabbinical Maritime Law and Custom, 527, 536ff (hereafter Passamaneck).
4 Walter Ashburner (ed.), *The Rhodian Sea-Law*, ccxl ff. This sea law was probably written down in the sixth-century AD but incorporated much earlier material. See Passamaneck, 536f.
5 *Stromateis*, 1. 20.98(1).
6 *Ibid*, 1.20.97 (1).
7 *Ibid*. 1.17.82 (1 and 2).
8 *Ibid*, 1.17.82(4).

vessel with very strong and select oak; take pains with the rudder, the ropes, the sails, that the ship may be made and equipped; but when you have done this, you will not see the fruit of its motions or voyages.'

Frame, rudder, ropes and sails are the key parts in the legal definition of a ship at the point of sale.[1] The shipbuilder, unless also owner-operator of the vessel, would receive only what he had been paid for its building.

Early Christians and the sailor

Occasionally Christian involvement in maritime economic activity went beyond the provision of grain ships. Theodoret (c. 393 – c. 458), born in Antioch and subsequently bishop of Cyrrhus in Syria, mentions the fifth-century Theodosius as building a landing stage, creating work, importing and exporting, and claims that he was widely invoked by sailors in distress.[2] Yet those sailors are as hard to find in the texts as the Christians serving them, despite generalisations to the contrary. Kverndal suggests 'the pioneer missionaries of the Early Church would seek to spread the faith whenever they put to sea' but names only 'their great predecessor, Paul' to support his opinion.[3] Seamen tend to be invisible or at best to occupy, as in the case of the crew of Melania's ship, a supporting role; there is no sense of Christians seeking the sailor *qua* sailor.

Theodoret wrote about the joy of the sailors when they see the light marking the harbour entrance on a dark night. He hints at knowledge of crewing issues when he writes, 'When anything happens to the helmsman, either the officer in charge at the bows or the seaman of highest rank, takes his place'.[4] He refers to God as the great Pilot and the bishop as being at the rudder of the local church yet gives nothing that could be understood as maritime ministry in the modern sense; rather, he reveals what may be described as common knowledge of the time, and in that, his writing is typical of the majority of early Christian writers.

Ambrose, in his funeral oration (378) on his brother Satyrus, told of Satyrus travelling by sea while still not 'initiated into the more perfect Mysteries' (i.e. before baptism). Finding himself involved in shipwreck and fearing death 'without the Eucharist' Satyrus asked members of the faithful, whether passengers or crew is unsaid, 'whom he knew were fully initiated, for the Blessed Sacrament, not out of a prying curiosity . . . but to obtain aid and assistance for his faith'. Ambrose says Satyrus wrapped the Host in a napkin, tied it round his neck and jumped into the sea. Safely ashore, his first action was to find a church 'to return thanks for his safe deliverance and to be fully initiated into the eternal Mysteries', Ambrose perhaps echoing Psalm 107, 23-32. Thereafter Satyrus travelled often by sea, not as a crew member (he was a lawyer until appointed prefect of a Roman province), without fear or further danger. Ambrose reveals in this rare instance

---

1 Passamaneck, 530.
2 I am grateful to The Rev. Dr Richard Price for drawing my attention to his translation of Theodoret's *Religious History* (published as Theodoret, *A History of the Monks of Syria*, Cistercian Publications, Kalamazoo, 1985, 89ff.).
3 Roald Kverndal, *The Way of the Sea*, 10.
4 Theodoret, *The Ecclesiastical History* . . . , volume 3, Letters XI (253), CXXIX (301), LXXVIII (274), XXXI (261).

1. The Early Church

that Christians, at least those among the initiated, had access to the Sacrament at sea, and suggests how it might be carried. The translators note the custom, thought to have derived from the days of persecution when imprisoned Christians were brought the Sacrament by co-religionists, of reserving a portion of the Eucharistic Bread in private homes, or to be carried on a journey for special protection, as still widespread in the fourth century.[1] Basil of Caesarea confirms in his *Letter XCIII* (A.D.372?) that the custom was prevalent in Alexandria and Egypt.[2]

Gregory Nazianzen offers a number of opportunities to see Christian sailors. His autobiographical poem, *Concerning his own affairs*, describes a conversion experience when on passage to Athens: winter was close and sailing 'a matter of hardihood and not good sense'. The severe storm which caught his ship was followed by a lack of water, as with Melania's ship, caused by the smashing of a water jar. When mountainous seas swamped the vessel 'a confused clamour arose, cries of sailors, helmsmen, officers, passengers, all calling with one voice upon Christ, even the people who formerly knew not God'.[3] At the end of their ordeal, 'All the ship's passengers and crew went on their way praising the great Christ'.[4]

Christian sailors appear again, in Gregory's poem *On His Own Life*, involved in a late night attempt to replace Gregory in a power struggle. Soon after this unhappy event, a group of Egyptian sailors, passing the many Arian churches in Constantinople, according to Liebeschuetz, while Gregory was acting as the city's orthodox bishop, and the community he served having no church but meeting in a private house, its numbers so small 'the arrival of the corn-fleet from Egypt with its orthodox sailors produced a significant addition to the congregation', to the saint's great encouragement.[5] His Oration 34 seems to have been addressed to a delegation from Alexandria arriving on board the first grain ships of the spring, probably in the year 380. He likens them to the Israelite spies of Joseph's time, coming as they were from Egypt laden with grain.[6] If these were the sailors involved in the late-night attempt to ordain Maximus, Peter of Alexandria's preferred candidate for Constantinople's episcopal throne, against Gregory in the struggle for power, the reference makes sense.[7] Such glimpses of the early Christian sailor in a church building are rare.

Sailors may sometimes be found in contemporary hagiography as the subjects of miracles. Here, as with the church-going sailors in Constantinople, it is the sailors who approach the Church rather than the reverse. Theodore of Sykeon (d. 613) was credited with delivering two sailors from demonic possession. One, a local man, the owner of a small boat, 'had been put

---

1 St Ambrose, First Oration on his Brother Satyrus, 180f.
2 *Basil: Letters and Select Works*, 170.
3 *St Gregory of Nazianzus: Three Poems*, 35, 80ff.
4 *Gregory of Nazianzus: Autobiographical poems*, 21-25.
5 J.H.W.G. Liebeschuetz, *Barbarians and Bishops*, 158-9.
   Brian E. Daley SJ, *Gregory of Nazianzus*, 18f.
6 *Saint Gregory of Nazianzen, Select Orations*, 334ff.
7 J.H.W.G. Liebeschuetz, *Barbarians and Bishops*, 158-9. I have been unable to trace the source from his footnote (n.18).
   Brian E. Daley SJ, *Gregory of Nazianzus*, 18f.

under a spell by someone and was troubled by an unclean spirit'. Trembling limbs combined with other symptoms to prevent his working, reducing him to penury. Theodore prayed over him, blessing oil for the sailor to anoint himself. He returned to the saint some days later, cured and with his affairs improved, to offer in gratitude the tackle of his boat; Theodore 'was only induced to accept it after much insistence'.[1] Another was a sea captain from Kalleoi in Pontus 'afflicted with a demon under his skin, which appeared in the shape of a mouse', a condition difficult to diagnose in modern terms. When the saint touched him he felt the demon 'running about and trying to escape'. Confining it to the man's arm, Theodore prayed, making the sign of the Cross over the arm, after which, the captain had no further trouble.

For hernias, an occupational hazard among seamen, and testicular disease, Artemios was the saint of choice. Perhaps an Arian, martyred in Antioch c. 363, his relics were brought to the church of St John Prodromos in Constantinople before 500, prompting numerous miracles. The sick, sleeping in the north aisle of the church, waited for the saint to appear, usually in a dream, then or subsequently. In miracle five a sailor cured of diseased testicles was discouraged by the crew, expecting a favourable wind, from going ashore to return thanks; he was not only able to do so but found his ship still at anchor on his return. In miracle six Isidore, another sailor similarly afflicted, was cured. Miracle fourteen took place at sea after a sailor had waited in the church for thirty days; crew members witnessed Artemios as a stranger standing next to the steersman, by whom the sick man was lying. The saint made as if to hold the tiller to assist the pilot, and in doing so trod upon the sick man's testicles, effecting a cure. Miracle twenty-seven involved a shipbuilder, Theoteknos, after time spent near the saint's tomb doing carpentry repairs while hoping for his testicles to be cured, and before sailing his own boat for Gaul. Artemios appeared to him in a dream in the guise of the sailing master; he awoke with perfectly restored testicles. Miracle thirty-two concerned the healing of a stevedore ruptured whilst loading jugs of wine. In miracle thirty-five a Rhodian ship owner, George, was cured of a double hernia by an apparition of the saint in the church latrine.[2]

The sixth-century Nicholas of Sion, not to be confused with Nicholas of nearby Myra, was another miracle worker, here associated with the weather. On one occasion he foretold a storm, seeing the devil circling a ship and cutting down the rigging. When the storm arose the crew sought his prayers, which were eventually answered. Nicholas later restored a sailor who had fallen from the mast and been left for dead. The crew, on nearing Egypt, asked the saint to come ashore in the dinghy to bless their houses.[3] Subsequently Nicholas tried to leave Askalon on a Rhodian ship bound for Constantinople; the captain explaining that they had been subject to inexplicable delays, Nicholas prayed and, the impediment lifting, they sailed. Some days later he asked to be landed at his destination. The captain explained that the wind would not permit it, but the wind suddenly preventing the ship from going further, allowed Nicholas to

---

1   Dawes and Baynes (trans), *Three Byzantine Saints*, 170.
2   Virgil S. Crisafulli and John W. Nesbitt, *The Miracles of St Artemios, passim*.
3   Ihor Ševčenko and Nancy Patterson Ševčenko, *The Life of Nicholas of Sion*, 51-57.

1. The Early Church

disembark, prompting the crew again to seek his prayers.[1]

His contemporary, John the Almsgiver, Patriarch of Alexandria, came to the rescue of a 'foreign captain who had fallen upon evil days' with five pounds of gold. The man bought a cargo but shortly 'suffered shipwreck outside the Pharos', but without loss of ship. John, importuned again, spoke critical words, suggesting the man had been remiss in his financial dealings, but gave him ten pounds more. This time the captain managed to lose the ship, though not the crew. John, blaming the event on the ship having been acquired by unjust means, nevertheless handed over one of the church's grain ships laden with twenty thousand bushels of corn. Twenty days and nights of storm followed, the captain explaining their preservation to the steersman having seen 'the Patriarch by his side holding the tiller'. It was claimed they had come to Britain and relieved a famine, before returning with a cargo of tin, some of which through the Patriarch's prayers had turned to silver.[2] A second miracle concerned a man's prayers for the return of his son from Africa. The saint celebrated the Liturgy over the man's generous gift of gold, asking God for the safe return of the son's ship. The lad died three days before the ship, captained by his uncle, returned, when it 'suffered shipwreck', with cargo lost but ship and remaining crew safe. The Patriarch was able to reassure the father in a dream that his son's soul was saved from what would otherwise have been a 'pernicious and unclean' life, adding that, had the ship sunk, his brother also would have been lost, a thought which, when the man awoke, seems to have comforted him. There is no suggestion in the text that anyone associated with a ship might be wise to keep well away from this saint.

Finally, Daniel the Stylite was invoked by one, Sergius, who was, with other passengers, held up by a north wind at a point where demons 'used formerly to hurl stones at the passengers and continually sank their boats'. 'Those in the boat gave thanks to God and made mention of the holy man [Daniel]' and consequently were able to go on their way.[3]

These texts afford a glimpse of two communities, the Christian and the maritime, interacting. To maritime missiologists they should offer enough evidence for a reconsideration, and perhaps modification, of the concept of the early Christians as 'sea apostles'.[4] Instead, once allowance has been made for the agenda of those writing to promote the reputation of particular saints, Christian seafarers can be seen behaving like other members of the Christian community. Priests or bishops are nowhere shown as having more regard for seamen than for church members in other occupations. Instead, the assembled evidence confirms that there were Christians amongst crews, some of whom may have had access to consecrated elements of the Mass whilst at sea, and to be found when in port attending a nearby church. The very normality of this picture is important for placing the Christian seafarer in the regular life of the Church.

---

1   *Ibid*, 63-67.
2   Dawes and Baynes (trans), *Three Byzantine Saints*, 216ff.
3   *Ibid*. 19f.
4   Peter F. Anson, *The Church and the Sailor*, chapter one. Roald Kverndal, *Seamen's Missions . . .* , 5, and Kverndal, *The Way of the Sea*, 10.

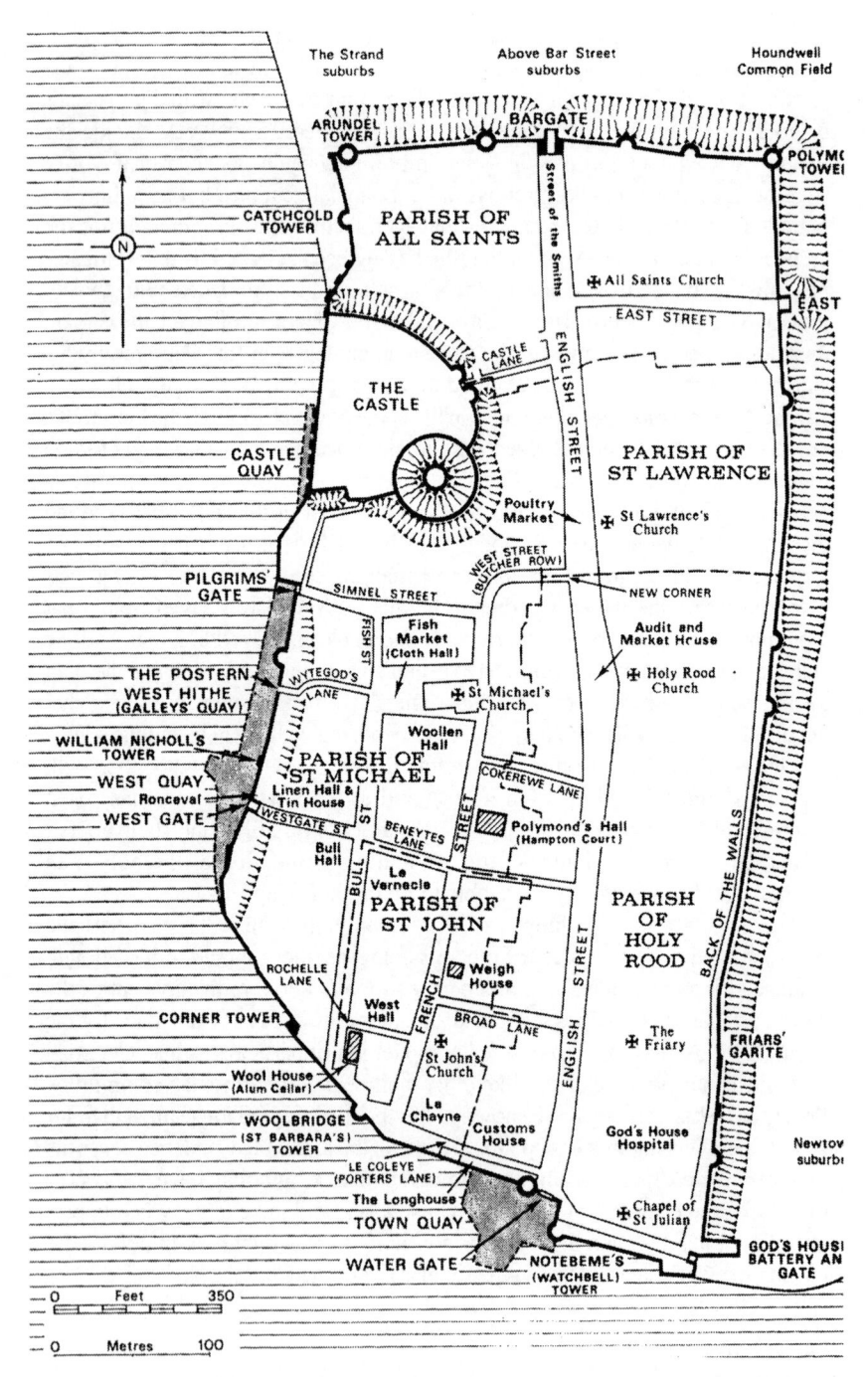

Map: Southampton in the Later Middle Ages
Colin Platt & Richard Coleman-Smith, *Excavations in Medieval Southampton 1953-1969*, Vol 1, Leicester 1975.

The Medieval Scene

2. Where was the Shipping and who was at sea?

The Christians of the Early Church were mainly to be found in the Mediterranean. By the medieval period trade was spreading, and with it the Christian faith. There was some trade with India and China; this further trade passing through Muslim lands to Mediterranean ports and then on Christian vessels to its destination.[1] Mediterranean Africa was in Muslim hands, that continent's further coast awaiting longer voyages, its hinterland barely glimpsed, and its trade largely conducted by the Genoese, even at the height of the crusades.[2] Limited trade with Scandinavia, Greenland and Iceland, and some sort of contact, if not actual trade, with Vinland (America) became more significant as Norsemen became Christian.

Around the year 1000 the conversion of the Vikings to Christianity, hardly an instant event, opened up the Viking world to Christendom (a slightly anachronistic term before the crusades) in a new way, and was remarkable by any measure. Later in the period come the Voyages of Discovery, their name indicating a significant change in seafaring. Abu-Lughod has written:

> By the eleventh and, even more, twelfth century, many parts of the Old World began to become integrated into a system of exchange from which all apparently benefited. The apogee of this cycle came between the end of the thirteenth century and the opening decades of the fourteenth century, by which time even Europe and China had established direct, if decidedly limited, contact with each other.

The subtitle of her book is significant: *Before European Hegemony: The World System AD 1250-1350*, indicating the middle of the 13th century as a point of departure for a major growth in trade, but rooted in the preceding period, which itself had witnessed increasing traffic on the sea.[3] Lopez, in his *Commercial Revolution of the Middle Ages 950-1350*, after describing the early medieval period as a time of depression, saw the period following as that in which the commercial revolution of his title developed.[4] That trade has been detailed by Abulafia, Hutchinson, Abu-Lughod, Lynn White Jnr, Lane and others.

In the same period the rapid expansion of the mendicant orders from the 13th century effected major change in the Church. As the century matured

---

1 George F. Hourani, *Arab Seafaring*, 62ff.
2 S. D. Gotein, *A Mediterranean Society*, vol. i, 45.
3 Janet L. Abu-Lughod, *op cit*, 3.
4 Robert S. Lopez, *op cit*, 56ff.

many Franciscans were to be found at sea, whether as chaplains or passengers a significant presence. Equally or more significant were the crusades, heavily dependent on sea transport. The mid 13th century affords, too, a glimpse of the Gregorian reforms beginning to work through and impinge upon the life of the mariner. The 'great reforming councils', from Lateran III to Lyons II, span the period 1179 – 1274.[1] The canons of Lateran III (1179) and IV (1215) related both to reforms and crusades. For maritime purposes, Lyons II (1274) added nothing new to Lyons I (1245). A council might decree, the bishop take note, and the parish priest try to alter custom accordingly, but, distances being long and communication of all but the most important business slow, the churchman's (and by extension, the sailor's) experience of change in his church would, except in dramatic and exceptional instances (for example, the imposition of clerical celibacy) be a relatively gentle one, and extend into later centuries.

At the beginning of the medieval period, most voyages were local, in the sense that they occupied days away from home rather than weeks. Long distance trade to the north of Europe before 1,000 had been circumscribed by Viking activity, extending from Greenland to Muslim-held parts of the Iberian peninsula, with Vikings to be found in the Mediterranean, reaching Byzantium and the Black Sea via the rivers of present-day Russia.[2] 'Viking', from a word meaning raider or pirate, was used as a catch-all. Their conversion to Christianity, in part a consequence of trade with Christian countries, greatly reduced the threat to maritime trade.[3] Records suggest that formal conversion took place within a relatively short period, though raiding was slow to cease, perhaps because the conversion of hearts takes longer; as late as 1087, the *Annals of Ulster* recorded, 'A sea expedition by the grandsons of Ragnall and by the son of the king of Ulaid into Man, and in it fell the grandsons of Ragnall'; it is implicit that Ragnall was one who had been called upon by Olaf to accept the Christian faith while his grandsons had yet to find it.[4] In the Baltic the Faith took longer to spread, with the peoples of parts of Poland, Lithuania, Latvia, and Estonia subjected to forcible conversion, sometimes simplified to a choice between baptism and death. The decreasing threat to maritime trade which conversion brought allowed an increase in the length and number of voyages. Piracy, an activity not exclusively Viking, continued as it does today, but the spotlight moved from the North Sea and the Baltic to the Mediterranean and the Saracen threat. The North Sea, Irish Sea and Baltic Sea enjoyed increasing traffic, according to Roberts reflected in the distribution of documentary seals along the Baltic and North Sea coasts: 'Their widespread use is an indication of the busy trading links by now re-established throughout northern Europe after the depredations of the Vikings'.[5]

---

1   André Vauchez, *Sainthood in the Later Middle Ages*, 391.
2   Richard Natkiel & Antony Preston, *Atlas of Maritime History*, map, 25.
3   An example of conversion through trade would be that of Ulf the Squint-Eyed's son, Ari, who was baptised whilst delayed in what 'some people call Greater Ireland'. *Landnamabok*, 61, paragraph 122.
4   *Annals of Ulster (to AD 1131)*, pt 1, 523.
5   Owain T. Roberts, Descendents of Viking Boats, 19. For an analysis of Baltic trade: Carl Oloff Cederlund, Explaining a 13th century Cog Wreck, 81ff.
    Gillian Hutchinson *Medieval Ships and Shipping*, chapter 4, especially the post-

2. Where was the Shipping and who was at Sea?

In the south, according to Balard, the Mediterranean

> was a region where landmarks such as promontories and islands, and the enforced use of certain channels, made navigation easy, and sailors were reluctant to let the coast slip from view. The distinction between sea-going and coastal navigation was completely artificial.[1]

Muslim territory in the Iberian peninsula and North Africa limited expansion of trade permitted elsewhere by a Europe beginning to consider itself a Christian whole, but not preventing trade between Christians and Muslims completely. Jews, too, must be written into the equation, Lopez describing their role as that of 'neutral intermediaries'.[2]

Officially Christian vessels were fair game to Muslims, and *vice versa*, especially when a crusade was in progress, but trade, even during crusades, continued, mainly in Muslim ports in Genoese and Venetian vessels.[3] Christian ships would arrive in fleets in Egypt when the season opened. Papal prohibitions against trading with the enemy confirm this; repeated prohibitions indicate its continuation, crusaders negotiating treaties with Muslims despite Papal objections.[4] Sea codes regulating the responsibility of the ship master to his crew when discharging them in Saracen territory are further confirmation, for why else should a Christian ship, with a crew to be discharged rather than enslaved, be in a Saracen port if not for trade? Silks and spices came and continued to come from the eastern Mediterranean and can only have come through Muslim territory. But all was not straightforward. Despite the apparent success of early crusades, which involved Christian ships in long voyages round the Iberian peninsula, Mediterranean trade remained limited; routes across Europe, despite being slow and expensive, were preferred to the perils of the sea and Saracen piracy.[5] Scandinavian pilgrims' choice of an overland route to Rome must indicate reasons other than economy for preferring the land route; among these would be avoidance of Muslim raiders, greater certainty of arrival at the destination, the opportunity to visit other shrines en route, and sometimes a shorter time travelling. Neither route was devoid of perils, but those of the land were, perhaps, more familiar.

All this suggests that, Crusader traffic excepted, the pattern of trade in the Mediterranean was more complicated than popularly supposed. Henri Pirenne in 1965 made the point, still valid, that from the 8th century the Mediterranean, once a link, had become a barrier between Christians and Muslims;[6] from the

---

    millenial growth of Norwegian trade (69f).
1 Michel Balard, Coastal Shipping and Navigation, 131.
2 Lopez, *Commercial Revolution*, 62.
3 For the rise of the Italian States, see Lopez, *Commercial Revolution* . . . , for Venice and Amalfi, 63ff.; for Pisa and Genoa, 65f.
4 Gotein, *A Mediterranean Society*, vol. i, p. 45.
5 M. Magnusson & H. Palsson (trans), *Njal's Saga*, for examples (329, 353, 354) of long-distance pilgrims taking the overland route. Jonathan Sumption, *Pilgrimages*, 115 remarks that following the millennium 'All over Europe the barriers to travel were lifted' but his context indicates that he is referring to overland routes, and he says little of safe conducts required.
6 H. Pirenne, *Economic and Social History of Medieval Europe*, 2.

ninth to the eleventh century Christian maritime traffic was 'bottled up' in the Mediterranean;[1] and from the end of the ninth century as 'the religion of their customers mattered little to the Italians provided they paid' the Italian city states handled the majority of the maritime economic activity.[2] Lopez offered a not dissimilar analysis, describing the Mediterranean memorably as 'the border between three different communities'.[3] Abulafia, whilst stressing the role of faith in the expansion of Italian trade, came to a conclusion similar to Pirenne's as to the largest handler of Mediterranean trade.[4] To understand medieval Church provision for the mariner in the Mediterranean it will be necessary, given this analysis of the trade, to examine the Catholic Church's response to crusader and Saracen traffic.

Then there were the voyages of discovery, many of which sailed with no certainty of a destination to be reached; if such existed, it would certainly have no church. This created a new situation. The most economical response for the Church, though probably made without analysing the cost, was to provide on-board chaplains to serve the long distance seafarer, several travelling with Columbus, for example. As settlements increased, Franciscans, Dominicans, and later Jesuits, were travelling by sea to an extraordinary number of places, and journals indicate that many ministered to the crews with whom they travelled.

Others have written and continue to write about the economic or technical history of the period with great authority and considerable detail, though seldom noticing the activity of the Church or the faith of the seafarer.[5] One author, Abulafia, has written about the place of religion, Jewish, Muslim and Christian, in medieval Mediterranean trade, and in that, he is unusual.[6] Details of that trade form part of the background of this book; for most seafaring is maritime economic activity. Though Abulafia writes of the effect of religion on trade rather than the seafarer or the provisions of the Church, economic history remains the

1   Pirenne, *Economic and Social History*,4.
2   Pirenne, *Economic and Social History*, 18.
3   Lopez, *Commercial Revolution*, 22. The three communities are Islam, Orthodoxy and Catholicism.
4   Abulafia, *Mediterranean Encounters*, § x.
5   Gillian Hutchinson, *Medieval Ships and Shipping*, e.g. notes the monastic records of a shipwreck (3), import of stone (121), tide tables for London Bridge (165), and the use of the compass (168); illustrates seals with religious significance (e.g.154), graffito in church (15, 167), a votive model (34), a map of the waterfront of medieval Southampton (116); refers to the role of monasteries in the fishing industry (121f, 144f), provision by the Church of sailing marks and lights, and church buildings as indicators of navigable channels(171) but says nothing of the religion of the sailor, exemplifying her introductory remark, 'the practical reality of shipping, the ships and the structures and much of the human activity associated with them, has tended to be overlooked'. Ian Friel, *The Good Ship*, concerned only with the medieval ship, has illustrations with religious content, e.g. the seal of Southampton showing moon and stars, and a 15th century carved bench end depicting a crew praying for salvation from a storm. Richard W. Unger, in *The Ship in the Medieval Economy 600-1600*, heads his chapters with seals with similar content. Neither mentions their religious significance.
6   Abulafia, *Mediterranean Encounters*

2. Where was the Shipping and who was at Sea?

best guide to where the seaman may be seen, or his religious practice glimpsed.

The extension of trade by distance and technological change go hand in hand, in turn impacting on religious practices at sea. The increasing use of two masts, like the use of a stern rudder, allowing for more distant voyages, a feature just beginning to appear in the twelfth and thirteenth centuries, explains Fabri's rather late reference to the custom of Venetian seamen on a pilgrim ship gathering round the *main* mast,[1] and Joinville's contemporary reference to pilgrimage round the masts on Louis IX's ship, despite contemporary seals continuing to depict single-masted ships.[2] The liturgical use of the mast will be considered further. Tyndale's sixteenth-century reference to seamen in danger and lacking a priest shriving (confessing) themselves 'unto the mast' surely preserves a custom not later than the thirteenth century.[3] It may hint at the mast as the site of a crucifix or other religious object. In 1215 the Fourth Lateran Council required of the laity the confession of sins at least annually as a preparation for Easter Communion. Before that date confession when in danger of death was the norm, sometimes common, at other times rare, but the interest here is the religious use of the mast.

Lynn White Jr commented that the crusades were preceded by 'a revolution in the art of shipbuilding', a point sometimes overlooked by crusade historians who concentrate on events on shore. Reviewing medieval technology he instanced skeleton-first ship construction (perhaps from the eleventh century), use of fore-and-aft sail, and the development of the mariner's compass.[4] Each of these indicates the exchange of technical ideas between cultures, particularly Muslim-Christian, but East-West in the case of the Chinese-derived compass, for which the Muslims may have been intermediaries.[5] Each contribution to safety and reliability increased the distance a ship could sail, the compass extending the parameters of the sailing season, the others better fitting the ship for longer distances. The further the ship could sail, the further from his parish would be the sailor.

It would be strange to discover, where technology was capable of exchange, that other ideas were transmission-proof. The sea codes and canons indicate that there was no shortage of trade with the Saracens, yet few examples of the

---

1 *The Book of the Wanderings of Felix Fabri* (hereafter Fabri). The reference is not significant in the history of the development of the mast; its interest lies in the area of liturgy.
2 Hutchinson, *Medieval Ships*, chapter 3, indicates that single masts were usual for this period. Her illustrations come from a variety of religious sources: seal, psalter, hagiography, church carving.
3 Tyndale, W., *Doctrinal Treatises*, Parker Society, 1848, 245.
4 Lynn White Jnr, *Medieval Religion and Technology*, xxiii, 7, 8, 81, 287.Emmanuel Poulle, *Les instruments astronomiques. . .* , 27-40. Hutchinson, *Medieval Ships . . .* , 175.
5 For the compass: Julian A. Smith, Precursors to Peregrinus . . . , 21-74. If the compass originated in China, it is hard to see how its transmission was not via Muslims. For trade between Christian and Muslim communities, and the difficulty in identifying the remains of the shipwrecked as Christian or Moslem: George F. Bass and Frederick van Doorninck Jr, An 11th Century Shipwreck . . . , 119-132.

exchange of religious ideas survive, perhaps attributable to the filtering medium of the clerical hand, particularly of such undesirable outcomes as Christians espousing Islam, an outcome more likely to be mentioned by Muslim authors; examples may indeed be found, as in the contemporary *The Rare and Excellent History of Saladin*.[1] Muslims writing were seldom seafarers, and the author of this instance mentions only the conversion of land-based crusaders.

An examination of medieval trade, rather than crusade traffic, requires a focus on maritime activity around the Baltic, Irish and North Seas; from these areas will be drawn most of the evidence for the faith and practice of the medieval seafarer, with an emphasis on English ports. Following the conversion of Iceland, the *Laxdaela Saga* recorded 'England . . . is a good trading centre for Christians now'.[2] Lynn White Jnr wrote, 'in the 8th century the focus of Europe shifted from the shores of the Mediterranean to the great plains around the Channel and the North Sea where it has remained ever since'.[3] Crusade traffic cannot be ignored, nor the importance of Genoese, Pisan and Venetian trade, some of the latter with England, but here the emphasis will be on North European trade, and particularly the English east coast ports. Most of these have lost their importance; indeed, some, like Dunwich, are beneath the sea. By the end of the twelfth century Boston (the outport of Lincoln) was second in importance to London, with Lynn close behind. 'No other port from Newcastle to Fowey, save only Southampton, could stand comparison with either of them'.[4] In the early part of the period the Scandinavian links were especially strong, with Cnut, King of most of England and Scandinavia.[5] Pirenne suggested the twelfth century was when, 'Life began to flow towards the coast, the great rivers, the natural highways. Civilization was purely continental; but it was now becoming maritime'.[6]

The Sources

The search for primary sources presents a major problem. Lynn White Jnr claimed literacy, at least until 'very recently', as the 'perquisite of small ruling groups', and written history as the 'history of the upper classes'.[7] Medieval sailors attract neither description. Chronicles seldom mention abstract experiences, nor do they often record that which everyone knows or does. What is recorded is abnormal, unusual or necessary to remember: national events, grants of land, changes in ecclesiastical office. Belief appears occasionally in contrast to a rival system of belief, frustrating the search for written sources relating to seafarers' beliefs or practice; the evidence is largely indirect. Few medieval western writers encountered belief systems other than Christianity. Most chroniclers were monks whose Rule discouraged travel.

1 Ibn Shaddad, Baha' al-din, *op cit.*
2 *op cit*, 150.
3 *Medieval Religion* . . . , 140.
4 E. Carus-Wilson, The Medieval Trade of the Ports of the Wash, 182-201.
5 Richard of Cirencester, *Speculum Historiale*,156, 166ff.
6 *A History of Europe*, 242.
7 *Medieval Religion*, 133.

2. Where was the Shipping and who was at Sea?

Of other writers, from secular (i.e. non monastic) religious backgrounds, Archdeacon Henry of Huntingdon's *Historia Anglorum* is typical. Henry mentions ships or travel several times, saying only that 'ships came' or somebody crossed the sea. Another source which might be expected to prove fruitful is the medieval sermon, of which thousands survive. In some it is obvious that the preacher, like Herbert de Losinga of Norwich, had travelled by sea, but of custom or practice nothing remains.[1] An exception was Jacques de Vitry, Bishop of Acre, and he will be cited further.

Pirenne in his *Economic and Social History of Medieval Europe* writing 'the [social and economic] historian . . . [of] the Middle Ages, [whose] material is derived as much from annals, chronicles and memoirs, as from public and private acts, cartularies, registers, custumals, etc.' was listing also the sources of the maritime missiologist. Whichever the source the search involves much unproductive reading. Surviving state documents are mainly instructions from the king to his sheriffs. Contemporary wills are almost nonexistent except for the great and the good, particularly bishops; not for those who earned their living at sea. Port lists, so helpful for gauging traffic at a particular port, give valuable evidence for the religious content of ships' names, albeit fairly late. The maritime codes have a religious content. Notarial documents surviving from Italian ports contain small but important details. The problem of fragmented sources is familiar to most medieval and maritime historians.[2] What religious clues remain gain validity when preserved, as they often are, in secular documents, avoiding the tendency to bias of religious sources. Heide Gerstenberger, disparaging the writing of another period, has contrasted '"quayside seafaring historians" [the phrase is Paul van Royen's] who take the wording of maritime codes and other state-controlled sources as descriptions of work and discipline aboard ships' with, in this case, the work of Bolster, erstwhile seaman, whose social history smells of the sea.[3] Unfortunately what Gerstenberger disparages is all that remains for the medieval period. The evidence may be summarised thus: for this chapter, state documents; for chapter three, Church documents, especially hagiography, together with church dedications and their geographical position; for chapter four, medieval sea codes and ecclesiastical Canons; for the fifth, journals and sagas.

Journals and sagas among written sources are exceptions to these generalisations. A few journals from the crusades survive. Crusades caused people to be at sea who might otherwise not have been, among them several chroniclers who mention maritime custom and practice. It may be protested that neither the journal of a crusading knight accompanying his king, nor his record of practice on board the king's ship, is typical. Indeed the very survival of such literature renders the crusade voyages atypical of medieval voyages in general; rarity demands the best possible use be made of it. The sagas are a

---
1 An appeal for material through the journal of the Medieval Sermon Society produced no response.
2 Bolster discusses the problem from an academic point of view in, Roundtable: W. Jeffrey Bolster, *IJMH*, vol X(2), Dec. 1998, 280.
3 See, Roundtable: W. Jeffrey Bolster, 257.

collection of ancient oral stories of a maritime people, Scandinavians, written down by a clerical hand (thought to have filtered out much pre-Christian practice), preserving some of their religious custom and practice. Some contain references to Christians, either from the time that the Norsemen became Christian, or from an earlier and unchurched period. Rune stones and epitaphs confirm the content of what were once dismissed as legend.

As to artefacts, maritime archaeologists have retrieved remarkably little religious material from contemporary wrecks. It is worth asking, what might be expected to have survived that would be of a religious nature? Pilgrims' badges, which have been found, tell little beyond the obvious, namely, that many people of the period went as pilgrims to popular shrines, often travelling by sea. Some Christian objects would perish: evidence that Gospels might be found on board ship, albeit rarely, comes only from written sources. Statues found among Christian maritime remains of the period are rare, though the number of statues, especially of Mary, which have been venerated after being found on the seashore, their finding usually interpreted as miraculous, suggests that statues were taken to sea, to be washed ashore, perhaps after storm or wreck; an explanation incapable of proof. Crucifixes were only becoming a feature of popular devotion in the late medieval period. Rosary beads were found on the *Mary Rose* but the use of the rosary in its present form, like the crucifix, was relatively late.[1] Early rosaries seem to have been undifferentiated strings of beads and difficult to distinguish as aids to devotion rather than for ornamental use.[2]

Maritime historians seeking ship illustrations turn to seals, the graffiti or carvings found in churches, or religious pictures. The same sources inform the missiologist. Town seals were becoming common in this period and port seals, especially from the Cinque Ports, offer considerable religious content relating to the seafarer. Some portray overt religious symbols, such as the church building on Rye's seal, but beyond the obvious, apparently secular surrounding detail on many seals speaks more clearly of contemporary belief. Ship graffiti in church add little beyond indicating the presence in church of people who knew about ships and had opportunity and inclination to deface the building. Church carvings of ships indicate some with a more legitimate intent. Their detail adds little to an understanding of religion at sea but their presence confirms a link between parish church and maritime community which is a valuable, if unquantifiable, contribution. In short, it may be said that, except for the seals, the artifacts which survive add little to our knowledge.

In all these sources, it is hard to find two examples of any one religious practice. Sumption seems to have had the same problem when writing *Pilgrimages*. He picked up instances here and there, often separated by centuries, and drew from them what he could. Given the nature of the evidence, this seems unavoidable, if undesirable. The missiologist is forced to reach a conclusion on grounds as widely spaced as Sumption's. Where only

---

1   *Mary Rose* inventory: The Mary Rose Trust, College Road, HM Naval Base, Portsmouth PO1 3LX.
2   Anne Winston-Allen, *Stories of the Rose*, 14f.

2. Where was the Shipping and who was at Sea?

one example can be given, no conclusion about prevalence is drawn. Two instances, especially when they come from different sources or geographical areas, allow a tentative conclusion. In a few cases, where evidence is abundant an attempt can be made to reach firmer conclusions.

Secondary sources are fewer still; only one published author, Peter F. Anson, has dealt in any detail with the period from the point of view of maritime religion.[1] Anson's view of the medieval period was a romantic one, his writing intended for a popular market, and his professional competence in the field of architecture. In his *Church and the Sailor*, he devoted a chapter to seafaring saints, most like Christopher, Elmo, and perhaps Brendan, saints of legend; others, saints who travelled (e.g. Francis Xavier), serving his purpose in interesting the major religious orders in his attempts to revive the Apostleship of the Sea. His third chapter, 'The Faith of Seafarers', provided a brief but broad tour of *Stella Maris*, coastal shrines, monastic lights and bells, and fraternities. His few dates, absent sources, and little understanding of the economic context point to the need for sourced evidence.

The medieval port[2]

The medieval port town was usually compact and self-contained, fronting on to the wharves, much as in Melania's (chapter one) time.[3] Shipping was seldom more than a short walk from a church. Often there was a nearby hospital or hostel, primitive by today's standards, but allowing a ship's master to provide for sick crew members away from home, as required in contemporary maritime law. Examples are not difficult to find. Dunwich offered a *maison dieu* or hospital on a spur off the nearby Dunwich River which, with the three parish churches (SS. James, Peter and John), was within 200 metres of the shipping at the Town Quay. In Southampton (Map 1) the waterfront was a boundary to four of the city's five parishes (All Saints, St Michael, St John, Holy Rood), suggesting that crews of ships alongside would be considered to be in a clearly defined parish, with clergy responsible for them, and close to St Julian's chapel and a *maison dieu*. Their relationship to parish churches was unlike, for example, that of crews in King's Lynn, where ships could be moored in the river, or alongside in an area served by a chapel of ease (St Nicholas). Church dedications in port areas, especially but not only those of St Nicholas or St Clement of Rome, often signify maritime use. Often, port and parish were indistinguishable, little needing a church set aside for seamen's use.[4]

---

1 *The Church and the Sailor*. His unpublished *Church Maritime* gives rather more detail.
2 I am grateful to the Hon. Editor of the *Mariner's Mirror* for permission to use material in this section previously published in May 2003.
3 For a description of the waterfront, see Detlev Ellmers, Development and Usage of Harbour Cranes, 43ff.
4 Dedications of churches, especially to Nicholas, need to be handled with caution before a maritime connection can be assumed. Miller, *The Man at the Helm*, 73-85.

Church Involvement in Trade

The connection between religious groups and trade is peculiar neither to Christendom, nor the period. Ray might have been writing of the medieval Christian monastery instead of a first-century Buddhist one when saying 'monasteries functioned more in the nature of pioneers in undeveloped areas', and noting the tendency of markets to grow up around them.[1] In many medieval ports the quays were economically associated with the Church, through some sort of ownership, or the payment of dues; indeed may have grown in consequence.[2] Sometimes an abbey's quay was separate from the area of commerce as in the case of Tintern Abbey on the River Severn away from the major port of Gloucester.[3] Abbatial needs for quays reflected the Norman upsurge in ecclesiastical building and the importation of stone, especially from Caen, and the waiving of dues on building materials was no small privilege. Of the Cinque Ports, the borough of Fordwich, together with Hythe and Romney, once busy ports, belonged to St Augustine's Abbey, Canterbury; the prior of Christ Church, Canterbury, controlled Sandwich and the Abbey of Fécamp the ports of Winchelsea and Rye.[4] The 'port' of Evesham, on the River Severn, served the monks of Evesham Abbey, that of Whitby.[5] The Whitby monks, whilst in France Fécamp Abbey had control of a number of seaports.[6] The Abbot of Ramsey had a *litus* or landing place at Reach, Cambridgeshire, its development shared with the prior of Ely.[7] Steyning and neighbouring Beeding, in West Sussex, witnessed considerable disagreement between Saint-Florent and Fécamp Abbeys; the Conqueror arbitrating between them, to settle the dues to be paid by ships passing up the river to St Cuthman's port, Steyning, reveals that control of shipping was no sinecure.[8]

The Abbot of St Augustine's, Canterbury took the customs at Fordwich, receiving 2d for every passenger (Jews paid 4d) touching the port.[9] The prior of Tynemouth had power to exact toll on all imported merchandise landed at North Shields.[10] Fécamp received half the toll for bales and pontage at Winchelsea, with one exception, for '[t]his custom shall be taken from all ships except those of Hastings when they put in from stress of weather'.[11] Such control produced

---

1 Himanshu P. Ray, *Monastery and Guild*, 183.
2 For pre-Conquest abbatial coastal possessions, see D.J. Matthew, *The Norman Monasteries*, 25.
3 A report of the uncovering of this occurs in M.G. Fulford *et al*, 101-27.
4 K.M.E. Murray, *Constitutional History of the Cinque Ports*, 4f.
5 H.W.C. Davis (ed), *Regesta Regum Anglo-Normannorum 1066-1154* (hereafter *Regesta*), vol. 1, xxxiii-iv.
6 H.A. Cronne and R.H.C. Davis (eds) *Regesta*, III, Oxford, 1968, c. 303. '... *que testatur ecclesiie Fiscanni portus maris de Stigas usque ad Leregant, Ideo mando vobis et prohibeo quod vos non ontromittatis de aliqua re que ad portus istos veniat vel sit ...*'.
7 Christopher Taylor, Reach, Cambridgeshire: A Medieval, 271-2.
8 D. J. Matthew, *Norman Monasteries*, 38-40.
9 C. Eveleigh Woodruff, *History of Fordwich*, Canterbury, 32ff.
10 W.H. Knowles, *The Priory Church of St Mary and St Oswin*, 79.
11 *Regesta*, II, 247, c. 1690.

a useful and direct income for abbeys, while monastic exemption from charges indirectly supplemented monastic income when the port was in secular hands, either case demonstrating a link between religious and maritime communities.

The granting of wreck was a further benefit. The monks of Tynemouth were granted '. . . sac, soc and custom, and wreck . . . '.[1] Wreck was given also to, for example, the Abbots of Battle;[2] Ramsey,[3] 'to have his customs of Brancaster and Ringstead [on the Wash, near Hunstanton], including wreck . . .'; and 'the new abbey of St Georges de Bocherville . . . wreckage'.[4] These abbeys may have received these grants as lords of the manor for an Edict of Henry I had laid the responsibility for the administration of recovered goods on the local lord, often either the bishop or an abbey.[5]

Other privileges confirmed abbatial involvement with the waterfront. The Cistercians of St Mary des Dunes, diocese of Bruges, were granted freedom from 'toll and passage [money] and pontage payment for crossing . . . permission to make new ships, sell old ones . . . for their own use'.[6] The monks of Mountebourg received 'all dues wheresoever they go, or buy or sell or convey anything that their men can declare to be for the monks'.[7] The Scottish King David offered similar privileges to the Abbey of Tiron.[8] The Abbey of St Peter's Ghent received '. . . within London, the land which King Edward gave them, namely. . . the wharf [*huevo*] . . . and wharfage [*huervagio*]'.[9] The monks of Abingdon 'have their customs from ships passing on the river [Thames], whether in herrings or in the right to buy goods . . .'.[10] The monks, houses, goods and men of Citeaux were quit of 'toll, passage and pontage', especially in Southampton, Hastings, Dover, Barfleur, Caen, Ouistreham and Dieppe.[11] Much of the trade so advantaged was the import of Caen stone for building purposes, as in the case of St Edmund's.[12] 'Ships of St Paul', London, received privileges for the same purpose,[13] its ships not the only example of ecclesiastical ship-owning; St Mary des Dunes has been mentioned, Fécamp was another, and the sheep-rearing Cistercians of Melrose seem to have had ships to take their wool to the staple in Flanders.[14]

Some responsibilities derived from port involvement; the Archbishops of Canterbury, with such a stake in the Cinque Ports, had to furnish ships and

---

1 *Regesta*, II, cc 882, 918, 1322. Dates: ?1107, 1109, 1122.
2 Regesta, II, cc 1135. K.M.E. Murray, 'Dengemarsh and the Cinque Ports', 664ff.
3 *Regesta*, II, 236, c. 1632a.
4 1115-1129, *Calendar of State Documents Preserved in France*, vol. I, 67f, c. 200.
5 *Regesta*, II, 236, c. 1632a.
6 Round, *Calendar of State Documents*, I, 497, c. 1364
7 Round, *Calendar of State Documents*, I, 319, c. 896.
8 Round, *Calendar of State Documents*, I, 357, c. 1010.
9 *Calendar of State Documents*, I, 502, c. 1375.
10 *Regesta*, II, 91, c. 937. See also J.E. Field, 'The Beginning of Abingdon Abbey', 693ff.
11 *Regesta*, II, 254, c. 1720.
12 *Regesta*, II, 256, c. 1733.
13 *Regesta*, II, 277, c. 1843.
14 R. Miller, The Early Medieval Seaman, 135.

shipmen for military purposes. An example would be the Archbishop at the beginning of the eleventh century who 'granted a ship to the people of Kent and another to Wiltshire' to help them fulfill their obligations to *scipfyrd*, bequeathing also 'to his lord' (perhaps from whom he held certain land) 'his best ship and the sailing tackle with it, and sixty helmets and sixty coats of mail'. Alfwold, Bishop of Crediton, bequeathed '. . . a 64-oared ship; it is all ready except for the rowlocks. . .'.[1] Some time after 1139 there was a dispute between the Archbishop and Battle Abbey regarding a ship which had blown off course on Dunge (Dengie in Essex?) Marsh. The Abbot's men had seized the wreck. The interest here is not the wreck but its ownership.[2] A not dissimilar case arose over a ship owned by the Abbot of St Augustine's, Canterbury, which appears to have been detained, which was ordered to be restored through the agency of the King's Sheriff in Kent.[3] Other examples derive from grants of fisheries to monasteries.[4]

Monasteries were also providers. The Tynemouth monks serviced navigation aids. Quarr, on the Isle of Wight, claimed in its attempts to preserve the abbey from the predations of Henry VIII that its Cistercian monks 'did much to relieve . . . travellers and seamen'.[5] The Trinitarian Friars, whose vocation was the ransoming of captives, seamen among them, received permission to collect, or to go 'beyond the seas' with the Abbot of Westminster at the king's behest.[6] Their activity at this period was probably limited to ransoming seafarers involved in crusading or trade with Saracens. Just occasionally, a mariner is shown becoming a monk: around 1050 the Abbey of Mont St Michel received the 'Charter of Restald formerly ship-master of Rotbert count of Normandy, on receiving at length the long-desired garb of a monk', though this may have had something to do with burial rights.[7]

Lights and landmarks

One form of service to the mariner was the provision of lights. Some medieval lights were maintained by monks or nuns, some by hermits, some perhaps by layfolk employed by a religious order. Others were clearly secular, as at Yarmouth, where a local tax was collected for the maintenance of beacons at the harbour entrance.[8] Stevenson has written:

> The popular impression of old navigation lights is romantic - monks lighting tapers to guide sailors through the storm and fire beacons set ablaze on headlands with flames streaming to the skies.[9]

1   Aelfric, The Will of the Archbishop of Canterbury, 241, 239, 383f.
2   *Regesta*, III, xxvii.
3   *Regesta*, I, 51.
4   R. Miller, The Early Medieval Seaman, 135.
5   David Knowles and R. Neville Hadcock, *Medieval Religious Houses: England and Wales*, 123.
6   *Calendar of Patent Rolls, Henry III*, vol. IV, 215. *Calendar of Liberate Rolls*, vol. IV, 91.
7   *Calendar of Documents*, I, 252, c. 707.
8   Murray, *Constitutional History*, 148.
9   D.A.Stevenson, *The World's Lighthouses before 1820*, xix.

2. Where was the Shipping and who was at Sea?

Monastic lights probably post-dated Viking predation.[1] There cannot have been many, yet Beaver expressed a popular view when he wrote, 'the dissolution of the monasteries was a serious setback to English coastal lights for it swept away many of the men who had devoted their lives to the safety of seafarers'.[2] Stevenson suggested, if this had been the case, chaos would have resulted. The lack of chaos suggests that lights were sold to lay folk, the dues maintaining them facilitating their sale. Confusion about references to lights may derive in some cases through misunderstanding church lanterns as lights rather than architectural features, or the maintenance of lights which were really votive offerings.[3]

Hermit-tended lights attract similar confusion. Some hermits were really solitaries and not necessarily religious. Religious hermits, living under vows of some kind, were recognised by a bishop, and should survive in contemporary records. Clay offers examples both of religious hermits maintaining lights and solitaries maintaining them on behalf of religious orders, among them Tynemouth's lamp and bell, a landmark at Hook (County Wexford, Ireland) built by the monastery of St Saviour, and a chapel of St Nicholas on Lantern Hill above Ilfracombe.[4] Clay's twenty religious lights (of which eight are doubtful) represent a significant proportion of known medieval lights and landmarks. To them may be added a light at Waterford maintained by Augustinian Canons using tolls from ships entering Waterford, and a light at Youghal, also in Ireland, maintained by nuns of St Anne's convent.[5] At Tynemouth the monks kept a light of burning coals. Waltham Abbey supported a light on the River Thames.

In the early thirteenth century 'J, son of Geoffrey, justiciary of Ireland' was commanded to let

> the wardens and chaplains of St Saviour's Rendenan [County Wexford], who are building there a tower as a signal and warning to those at sea . . . [to have] such maintenance in money and other liveries out of the issues of the said land . . . because it is a pious work to help Christians exposed to the dangers of the sea so that they may be brought into the haven out of the waves of the deep.[6]

The reference to 'pious work' equates with endeavours like bridge-building for which the Church encouraged people to offer endowments, often in return for indulgences from the local bishop; Stevenson offers an example from 1522 where the Bishop of Exeter granted 40 days.[7] Often there was more to this matter than piety, for example, the interest of religious orders in the receipt of port dues or the safe arrival of their own ships or cargoes. It

---

1 Emma Cownie, *Religious Patronage in Anglo-Norman England 1066-1135*, 26f.
2 Patrick Beaver, *A History of Lighthouses*, 15.
3 Miller, *The Man at the Helm*, 23f.
4 Rotha Mary Clay, *The Hermits and Anchorites of England*, 49ff.
5 Hague and Christie, *Lighthouses*, 16ff. For more detailed sourcing see Miller, The Early Medieval Seaman, *MM*, 89 (2), May 2003, notes 53-55.
6 Harry Rothwell (ed), *English Historical Documents 1189-1327*, vol. III, 805. *Calendar of Patent Rolls, 1232-47*, 500.
7 Stevenson, *Lighthouses*, 22.

paid them, therefore, to ensure that ships arrived safely, hence, for example, the light on St Mary's Island, barely a mile from Tynemouth Priory, and a burial ground for drowned sailors. Direct evidence of monastic charity extending to the provision of lights on hazards to be avoided, from which no income would be derived, seems not to exist. However, it is possible to understand one of the functions of remotely placed priories in this way, for example one established with 'a lighthouse of sorts' on the Ecré rocks of Jersey by the Abbey of Val-Richer. On the nearby Chausey Islands the Abbey of Mont St Michel established a priory 'on these remote and scanty rocks', presumably for the same purpose.

The Laws of Oleron contained stiff penalties for clergy found burning lights for sinister purposes, implying that some clergy had done so, and that lights round the coast of Europe were not uncommon, if such lights were not to fail as a lure.[1] Of the Eastern Mediterranean, excepting Alexandria's pre-Christian lighthouse, Jacoby has written: 'None of the Crusade harbours seem to have had a lighthouse'.[2] Crusade harbours usually drew a chain across the harbour entrance to prevent entry by vessels at night, hence the lack of lights, for ships forbidden nocturnal entry need no guiding light.

Seamen's Churches

It is extremely difficult to distinguish between churches for seamen and churches used by seamen. Most medieval sailors were parishioners whose voyages took them but a few days from home, obviating the need for anything more than a parish church; a seamen's church would be necessary only in a port far from a parish church, rare in medieval England, more common as the crusades developed, and replaced by a voyage chaplain when longer voyages of discovery increased in frequency. One exception would be where fishing fleets gathered, though even they would return to their markets, with a nearby church, regularly. The need generated by a large expatriate group might also require a church. Three illustrations illustrate the distinction: a Yarmouth church, a chaplaincy at Lynn, and a possible chaplain at Genoa.

Canon 21 of the Fourth Lateran Council (1215) required every Catholic to belong to a parish and do his Easter duty. In the thirteenth century Henry of Susa defined the parish as 'a place with well-defined frontiers whose inhabitants belong to a single church'.[3] Easter duty obliged the parishioner to make confession to the parish priest and to receive Holy Communion at least once a year, at Easter. This new Canon did not mention groups whose absence might be occupational, perhaps because the Church response was both ancient and obvious: that only what is possible can be done. So too with the duty of Sunday church attendance; it was so obvious that a seaman would not be present that his absence goes unmentioned. The designation by a bishop of a

---

1   For maps, see Hague & Christie, *Lighthouses*, Fig. 3 - Europe (11), Fig. 4 - UK (15).
2   D. Jacoby, Crusader Acre in the Thirteenth Century, 9, n 39.
3   Quoted in Sumption, *Pilgrimage*, 11f.

church to be responsible for seafarers 'on the river' (away from home) may be understood as giving the seaman a church in place of his parish church.

The right to designate a church as a parish church lay with the bishop. Other churches were effectively chapels of ease rather than parish churches. A pre-Reformation building described as a chapel implied the lack of font and cemetery.[1] Unfortunately many references lack precision. Baptisms and marriages were limited to parish churches, which were granted the right to have a font for baptisms. The fees or offerings associated with baptisms, marriages and funerals made it a matter of interest whether a particular church had parochial status. Parishioners were further interested if they had far to travel (hence 'chapel of ease') to a church. An example of how this impinged on the life of a seafarer can be found at King's Lynn, once the fourth port in the kingdom.[2] A twelfth-century document appends parochial rights over all sailors on ships mooring at Lynn, the sailors coming at the tail of a grant to the monks of a cure and parts of a demesne tithe.[3] The bishop, William de Turbe (Bishop of Norwich 1146 –74), claimed to be reaffirming an old right:

> We forbid any of the clergy to receive in their church sailors who in their voyaging have reached the port of Lynn, except for their church's own parishioners, and not to exact or receive any benefit from them, and not to provide burial, whereby the church of St Margaret [the parish church] may sustain loss, which has been specially founded for this purpose by Bishop Herbert of blessed memory, that it may grant Christian service to all sailors by chance (*temere*) coming to anchor at Lynn. . . .[4]

It is difficult to know whether the primary concern here was the loss of fees or the care of seamen. Lynn's other two churches at this time were chapels of ease to St Margaret's; one church in this busy seaport now designated for the use of non-resident sailors affords a very early example of a 'specially founded' seamen's chaplaincy.[5] Indirectly, it reveals the necessity for seafarers on the river to be assigned to a particular church; the river bank is in a parish, is usually the parish boundary, but the river is an ecclesiastical no-man's-land.

William de Turbe affirmed Bishop Herbert's grant of St Nicholas's chapel, King's Lynn, to the Norwich Benedictines, distinguishing between the chapel, dedicated to the patron saint of sailors, and the oversight of mariners, showing that the concern for mariners preceded Bishop William and derived from Bishop Herbert. An interest in seamen may have been peculiar to Herbert or it may have been a consequence of his having in his diocese a number of England's busiest ports; the interest of both bishops suggests the latter.[6]

---

1 F.R. Wilson, On Wayside Chapels and Hermitages. . . , 11.
2 Wilfred J. Wren, *Ports of the Eastern Counties*, 39-40 quotes a pre-1204 document describing it as 'much haunted of long tyme with Hollanders, Flemynges and other Nacions of the East Countrye'.
3 Dorothy M Owen, *The Making of King's Lynn*, document 113, 129.
   Christopher Harper-Bill (ed), *English Episcopal Acta: Norwich 1070-1214*, 99.
4 E.M. Goulburn and H. Symonds, *Life, Letters and Sermons of Bishop Herbert de Losinga*, 2 vols. Losinga (d. 1119) was the predecessor referred to here.
5 Harper-Bill, *English Episcopal Acta*, 15.
6 Elizabeth and Paul Rutledge, King's Lynn and Great Yarmouth . . . , 92ff. The grant

Another St Nicholas's church, in Great Yarmouth, was both a chaplaincy and a church dedicated for a particular use. Yarmouth was a major centre for all North Sea fishermen at this time, with its important herring fair, and its beaches used for net repair.[1] The original church had been built by Bishop Herbert, with a licence from Henry I, for seasonal use by local herring fishermen at a place on the seashore with but a handful of houses, offering an unusual example of boats gathered far from a church.[2] Herbert provided a chaplain 'to celebrate divine service always', implying an endowment, 'and found of his own goods the necessary things'. Not only local fishermen gathered, for Cinque Ports fishermen expelled the chaplain and forcibly seized the church, which was only restored by the Sheriff of Norfolk when Herbert petitioned the king. In the ensuing fracas some of the Cinque Ports men were killed. Soon afterwards this church was also given to the Norwich Benedictines.

Distinct from seamen's churches were churches used by seamen. The latter were of two kinds: churches serving expatriate communities and those where evidence remains to suggest that mariners were among the churchgoers. It may seem strange that a Church united by Latin should need within it churches for the service of expatriate communities, but the desire for something from home when abroad is universal. The *Hanse* had churches and chaplains in many ports well beyond this period, not all of them interrupted by the Reformation. Venetians had fraternity meetings and a communal tomb in the chapel of St Nicholas in Southampton.[3] Venetians, Genoese and Pisans, having areas of control and financial advantages in return for their help with military activity and provision of supplies during the crusade period in the eastern Mediterranean ports, formed strong expatriate communities with their own churches, serving also the religious needs of visiting crews.[4] In twelfth-century Acre, the Genoese church of St Lorenzo, and the Venetians' St Mark, were named for the patron saints of their cities of origin. There was also a French church of St Mary.[5] The Pisans at the time were intending to build their own church. Elsewhere there is some evidence that churches dedicated to St Olaf, one at least in London, may have been particularly associated with Scandinavian seamen rather than with Scandinavians generally.[6]

---

appears without mention of sailors in H.W. Saunders (trans), *The First Register of Norwich Cathedral Priory*, 71-3. Vanessa Parker, *The Making of King's Lynn*, 21.

1 Peter Brandon and Brian Short, *The South East from AD 1000*, 83.
2 Murray, *Constitutional History*, 18f. See A.W. Morant, Church of St Nicholas, Great Yarmouth, 226-7 for the original Latin record and English translation.
3 Alwyn A. Ruddock, *Italian Merchants and Shipping in Southampton, 1270-1600*, 9, 132.
4 D. Jacoby, Crusader Acre in the Thirteenth Century, 1-46. For Venetians in Bari and Palermo see David Abulafia, Pisan Commercial Colonies and Consulates in 12th Century Sicily, 71.
5 Jacoby, 'Crusader Acre' Fig. 4 is a map of Acre showing the locations.
6 Birgitte Munch Thye, Early Christian Ship Symbols, 186-96. For a pre-Conquest Olaf church in Waterford, Ireland, see M.F. Hurley, Topography and Development, 19 and map on 7. For Scottish Olaf churches see James Murray. MacKinlay, *Ancient*

2. Where was the Shipping and who was at Sea?

Slessarev has argued that in both northern Europe and the eastern Mediterranean

> the Church formed the centre of merchant colonies; that Church buildings were used as warehouses; that the Church possessed productive plants and, at times, owned the quarters in which resident merchants lived and hostelries for transients; that priests often served as scribes and were the guardians of the correct weights and measures.[1]

A church used in this way was called an *ecclesia mercatorum*. Slessarev cites Baltic examples in Magdeburg, Novgorod, Reval (Talinn), Old Visby, Sigtuna, Lund, Viborg (Denmark), Roskilde and Schleswig. In the eastern Mediterranean his examples are largely those allocated to Venice, Pisa and Genoa, adding information regarding their relations with the Greek Church. His assertion that the Church was part of the trading process rather than the servant of an expatriate community may provide the key to unlock circumstances surrounding the following example of a possible Genoese chaplain.

An ambiguous example of a chaplain, not obviously in charge of a designated seamen's church, survives in a Genoese notarial document of 1254.[2] Opening *In nomine domini amen*, it describes the parties involved in the agreement, of whom the first is *Nos Amines cappelletus*, in the rough Latin of the period. *Cappelletus* is not a surname; this period predates surnames, identity being drawn from place of origin or occupation. *Cappelletus* could derive from *capellarius* (a cap maker), perhaps a man with money to invest in a voyage, or from *capella* (a chapel), referring to a chaplain. Clergy were not supposed to involve themselves in trade (but sometimes did) so involvement here might not be commercial - which begs the question of why a chaplain, if chaplain he be, should be mentioned in a notarial document concerned with a trade agreement between partners. Some trading groups or groups of navigators regularly used local churches for meetings.[3] It is a small step from using a church as a regular meeting place to appointing a chaplain and rewarding his chaplaincy in a variety of ways. If he was one of the clergy of a local church, or the church of the guild, the diminutive might indicate that he was the lesser or least of several clergy. If *Cappelletus* is a nickname, he may not have been an ecclesiastic at all, or at most in minor orders and serving as a *scribarius*, or just possibly the illegitimate child of a priest. The simplest explanation is to see here a priest though the route taken to discover him illustrates the difficulty in finding an example of a chaplain to a group of mariners at this time.

Church Dedications in Scotland: Non Scriptural Dedications vol. 2, 292-6.

1. Vsevolod Slessarev, *Ecclesiae Mercatorum* and the Rise of Merchant Colonies, 177-97.
2. Eugene H. Byrne, *Genoese Shipping in the Twelfth and Thirteenth Centuries*, 125. It is just possible that Byrne's transcription of *Cappelletus* is at fault. I have not been able to see the original document.
3. e.g. *L'Orde Judicien de la Cort dels Consols de la Mar*, probably 14th century, but with earlier material, mentions a Guild of Navigators meeting in the church of St Tecla in Valencia. The earlier (1063?) *Ordinamenta et Consuetudo Maris Edita per Consules Civitatis Trani*, Ordinances . . . of the City of Trani, also refers to a Guild of Navigators. See Miller, The Early Medieval Seaman, 148, nn 83, 84 (which cites an Islamic guild), 85.

Hostels and *maisons dieu*

From earliest times, but blossoming in the Middle Ages, a network of hostels for travellers, pilgrims and seafarers spread throughout Europe. They were known variously as hostels, hospitals, hospices, *domus dei* and *maisons dieu*. Some were dedicated to seafarers' use, others included seafarers amongst their users. Some were for long-term residents, perhaps lepers or the aged. Some provided medical care. All were an extension of the inns which had existed from time immemorial; not all were Christian, though the growth of pilgrimage ensured that many were. Their general usefulness is suggested by their existence in a variety of cultures and periods. The Icelandic *Saga of Grettir the Strong* (twelfth century?) records a group of men

> sitting and drinking. They had made fast in the harbour [in Iceland] where there was a place of shelter set up for men who were travelling about the country, and they had carried in a quantity of straw. There was a huge fire on the ground...

which set fire to the straw and spread 'all through the house', suggesting a building with more than one room.[1]

From the fifth century the Christian bishop was expected to 'look after the needs of the pilgrim',[2] his role later supplied in many cases by monasteries. Knocker has suggested that the great *maison dieu* in Dover was founded to ease the pressure on monastic hospitality.[3] The *Domus Dei* of Osney Abbey on the River Thames may be a similar example. Clay noted that medieval England had 750 such institutions; though many were for lepers, and many inland, the seafarer can sometimes be seen, especially in port areas.[4] In England, apart from the Dover *maison dieu*, others were to be found in Carlisle, Chester, Chichester, Dunwich (supported by a levy on ships entering the port), Ospringe (Fig. 1), Portsmouth, Sandwich, Southampton and Yarmouth; in Scotland: Ardross, Brechin, Dalkeith, Dundee, Dunbar, Leith, North Berwick, St Andrews and more; in Ireland: the sisters who maintained the light at Youghal founded a '*hospitium* or *Maison Dieu*'. Other examples were to be found in Venice; in France: Angers, Barfleur, Fresnay-la-mère; and in Sicily at Messina.[5] Some were hospitals specifically for seafarers. Perhaps the earliest and best English example was St Bartholomew's at Sandwich, which later became a general almshouse. Though Boys thought this was founded in the early thirteenth century, there is some evidence for an earlier date. Leland said that at Sandwich 'ther is a place of White Freres and an hospital withowt the town fyrst ordened for maryners desesid and hurt'. Dugdale's *Monasticon* makes it clear that the White Friars and the hospital were not associated.[6]

---

1 G. A. Hight (trans), *op cit*, 106.
2 James A. Brundage, *Medieval Canon Law and the Crusader*, 14.
3 Edward Knocker, On the Municipal Records of Dover, cxxxivff.
4 Rotha Mary Clay, *Mediaeval Hospitals of England*, xviii.
5 Further details and references can be found in Miller, *The Early Medieval Seaman...*, 142.
6 John Strype, *The Life and Acts of Archbishop Parker*, vol I, Bk II, Ch X, para VII. Hasted, *The History of Kent*, 2nd ed., vol X, 159. William Boys, *Collection for an History of Sandwich, in Kent*, 1, 2, 18 etc. John Leland, *Itinerary*, vol IV, 48. Anon, *Excursions through Kent*, vol I, 121. Anon, *Kentish Traveller's Companion*, 220.

Religious Orders

The involvement of the old orders in the ports has been indicated. The new mendicants, not bound by vows of stability, spread widely and rapidly from the thirteenth century, their friaries, unlike the great abbeys, requiring little imported stone. Their vocation was to spread the Gospel; consequently they, especially the Franciscans, were often to be found at sea. By 1217, a year after the death of Francis, they had six provinces in Italy, two in France, and one each in Spain, Germany and the Near East. Franciscans were established in Britain by 1224, Scandinavia by the 1230s, and Greece by 1247. Apart from the Youghal sisters and their light in Ireland, Franciscans seem seldom to have been found in port areas, except as a point of departure, following which, there are many instances of friars at sea, some with chaplaincy duties, with Columbus for example.

Two orders were of particular interest to the seaman. The Mathurins, or Trinitarians, their full title the Order of the Holy Trinity for the Redemption of Captives, founded by St John of Matha (d. 1213), made their first redemption in 1199, their last in 1855. They were to be found in various ports, responsible for example for hospitals or churches in Dundee, Dunbar and Leith in Scotland, though not specifically for seamen. Their presence is not odd when it is recalled that, for example, Knights Templar held property and many churches in Britain, though associated in the popular mind with the Holy Land, which financed their work abroad. The Mercedarians, or the Order of the Blessed Virgin Mary for the Ransom of Captives, were founded in 1218 for a similar ministry. The ministry of both orders would be welcome to the seafarer at risk of capture from Saracens.

Votives

Little evidence survives to place the seaman in a church building. Exceptions to this include contemporary votive offerings and graffiti.[1] The custom of offering thanks to a deity for favours received is ancient and universal.

Christian thank-offerings vary considerably. What may have been a tomb slab, found in St Hilda's Hartlepool, shows a carved ship of c. 1300, perhaps the *Navis Dei* of Hartlepool, apparently part of a votive offering in a chapel once dedicated to St Nicholas; it may also hint at a sailor burial.[2] Graffiti may have been in part an expression of gratitude, or perhaps a commendation of a voyage to be made, given the number of graffiti and carvings which survive in churches. Graffiti depicting vessels from the thirteenth and fourteenth centuries, perhaps made by crusade-bound sailors, have been found in the cloister of a French Abbey.[3] A particularly fine carving of a sixteenth-century ship survives

---

1 For a discussion on what distinguishes a votive offering from a church ornament, see A.J.H. Prins, *In Peril On The Sea* . . . , 6ff.
2 G.P.B.N., 'The *Navis Dei* of Hartlepool', *MM*, vol 26, 304.
3 Albert Illouze and Philippe Rigaud, Graffiti, *Archéologie Médiévale*, vol XXIV, 418-9. Carpentier, *L'Église de Dives Sur-Mer*, Cabourg, France, 2011, *passim*.

on a pew end in Bishop's Lydeard church, Somerset;[1] others may be found on the exterior stonework of the church of St Peter, Tiverton, Devon, part of an endowment by a man who made his money in exporting wool. The most common type of *ex voto* was probably the ship model. It seems to have been associated more with the traveller than the seaman; the Norman Earl Godwin gave a golden ship as an offering. The French queen, in danger of drowning, counselled by Villehardouin, promised a pilgrimage to the shrine of St Nicholas at Varangeville, but compromised by sending a silver ship in gratitude.[2] These were the gifts of the wealthy, beyond the reach of the ordinary seafarer, whose ship model would probably be of his own manufacture, and using a base medium. An example, probably from the late thirteenth century, may be taken as typical; the crew of a Dunwich fishing boat, grateful for delivery from a storm after asking the intercession of St Edmund, hung a wax anchor in his basilica. Few offerings would survive the Reformation.[3]

The Liturgy

The presence of maritime *ex votis* implies the presence of the seaman in church. It would be strange if he failed to add his prayers to his gift; equally so to find that he had no place in the liturgy when the primary purpose of the church building is to house the faithful at worship. Yet few liturgical documents, surviving mainly in abbey libraries, refer to the sea.

Masses for travellers are recorded, for example in a chapel at Ospringe in Kent, and it may be safely assumed that they benefitted similarly from the ministry of the many bridge chapels, as at Durham, Exeter, on London Bridge, or over the Tyne at Newcastle.[4] It is possible to say, therefore, that the Mass was itself accessible to the majority in the sense that there were chapels aplenty where Mass might be found. It was not otherwise particularly accessible to the laity. Pre-Conquest Bidding Prayers gave the seafarer no place. Twelfth-century commentaries on the Mass were mainly by theologians writing for theologians, or for those who could read and afford a book. Yet the same century's *Lay Folks Mass Book* included those 'upon the sea' in its Bidding Prayers ('and for al land tilland and for al see farand and for the wedir and for the fruyt that is on erthe . . . . And for al pylgrimes and palmers . . . '.), and a further Bidding Prayer asked that they be saved 'fra all maner of parels'.[5] Contemporary texts were hand-written and bulky; inconvenient for the traveller. Nevertheless, as well as the Bidding Prayers there were votive Masses, Masses intended for a particular purpose, perhaps the repose of a soul, for one going on pilgrimage, or for fine weather; some of the bridge Masses would have been votives.

---

1   Adrian J. Webb (ed), *A Maritime History of Somerset*, vol 1, 17.
2   Richard of Cirencester, *Speculum Historiale*, vol II, 189. Joinville & Villehardouin, *Chronicles of the Crusades*, 322.
3   T. Arnold (ed), *Memorial of St Edmund's Abbey*, vol 1, 367. Sumption, *Pilgrimage*, 158.
4   F.R. Wilson, On Wayside Chapels and Hermitages, 15.
5   Mary Martina Schaefer, *Twelfth Century Latin Commentaries*, unpublished PhD thesis, 2.

2. Where was the Shipping and who was at Sea?

Faversham: *Maison Dieu*, Ospringe, part of a complex founded in 1234.
Used by kind permission of The Faversham Society.

Exeter's eleventh-century Leofric Missal contains a *Missa pro navigantibus fidelibus*.[1] The Collect:
> God, who brought our fathers through the Red Sea and conveyed them through abundance of water singing the praise of your name, we humbly pray that you will look upon your servants in this ship [*in hac naui famulos tuos*], drive away [*repulsis*] adversities, and [bring them] by a quiet voyage to the harbour they have always desired. . . .

The Secret prayed 'defend from all dangers those who are celebrating thy mysteries' [*et tua mysteria celebrantes ab omnibus defende periculis*]; the Post Communion Prayer:
> Sanctified by the divine mystery, Lord, we humbly pray and beseech your majesty, by the wood of the holy cross, both to rescue from their sins and in Your mercy to save from all dangers those whom you make to share in heavenly gifts. . . .

The Collect could be understood as belonging to a Mass at sea ('in this ship'), but otherwise the text suggests that it was rather offered for those at sea, perhaps on board before sailing, or in a local church or the cathedral (Exeter cathedral being near the quays), an interpretation encouraged by other evidence suggesting that a Mass at sea was rare. The Roman Missal (1474) understood the harbour of the Collect as that of salvation (*salutis portam*). Instead of the Red Sea it referred to St Peter walking on the water and sought the intercession of the Virgin Mary and the saints. The Secret and Post Communion matched the Leofric Missal. The Sarum Missal followed the Roman, adding a Mass in time of storm and another for those at sea. The absence of anything maritime in the older Irish (eighth century?) missal

---
1 F.E. Warren (ed), *Leofric Missal*, 183.

suggests that maritime material is Norman or Norman-Roman.[1]

In short, the texts, and references to bridge chapels and Masses for travellers confirm that in maritime areas votive Masses for those at sea could be found. It is less clear who might be saying those Masses. Were they like chantry priests, specially appointed, or priests who said votive Masses in response to a Mass offering or to attract an offering from a passing traveller? In some ports and chapels there is the possibility that they were priests attached to early guilds.

The Guilds

By the fourteenth century a significant factor in the sailor's religious life was the guild. Guilds were formed by men with a common craft interest, seamen forming one such craft. Each craft's guild offered various benefits, some specific to the craft, some to the area in which the guild operated. At Lynn, Norfolk, the Shipmen's Guild of the Holy Cross (1368) included Masses and prayers for brethren, with particular attention to funeral rites.[2] This guild, and that of St Leonard at Lynn, offered benefit for loss at sea, as did the Lynn guild for Young Scholars, the latter perhaps for members on pilgrimage.[3] The large York Mariners' Guild took the ninth place in the city's cycle of Corpus Christi mystery plays, appropriately the Noah play, its mariners here associated with the fishermen, as a dispute between them in 1421 led to a division of expenses. Ipswich had a similar but smaller pageant where the 'Fysshers and Marynars' marched under a banner bearing the picture of a ship.[4]

Hull's Shipmen's Guild of the Holy Trinity (1369) seems to have begun as a parish guild. Its Trinitarian dedication was common among mariners. In 1457 it became definitely linked with seamen of the port, supporting a chapel and an almshouse for impotent mariners from c.1461, and taking the Noah play in the local mystery cycle.[5] Its original almsmen numbered thirteen, perhaps in emulation of the Last Supper when Christ gave his *mandatum*,[6] and paralleled in the thirteen almsmen of the Bristol Mariners' Guild (1445).[7] Other Trinity Guilds were to be found at Newcastle upon Tyne,[8] Wisbeach (c.1379), Boston, Sleaford, Wyngale, and the best known

---

1 For full references see Miller, 'The Early Medieval Seaman', 150, nn 139 - 140.
2 H.F. Westlake, *The Parish Guilds of Medieval England*, 193. L.Toulmin Smith, *English Guilds*, 54ff.
3 Westlake, *The Parish Guilds*,197.
4 Westlake, *The Parish Guilds* ... , 51ff. D. Burwash, *English Merchant Shipping 1460-1540*, 71. S. Purvis, *The York Cycle of Mystery Plays*, 49.
5 F.W. Brooks (ed), *The First Order Book of Hull Trinity House*, iiiff.
6 B. Bailey, *Almshouses*, 24.
7 Westlake, *The Parish Guilds*, 88. D. Burwash, *English Merchant Shipping 1460-1540*, 62ff.
8 J. Leland, *Itinerary*, vol V, 59 refers to a *maison dieu* attached to a chapel on the quay (V, 126) near a house of the '*Friers ordinis S Trinitatis*', the Trinitarians involved in ransoming captives.

2. Where was the Shipping and who was at Sea?

'Guild, Fraternity or Brotherhood of the Most Glorious and Undivided Trinity, and of St Clement, in the parish of Deptford Strond, in the County of Kent'. Poor early records make dating the last's foundation difficult. Its various objects were social, religious, charitable, and professional, and it continues to this day, associated in the popular mind with lighthouses, but still with almshouses and other responsibilities.[1]

Almsmen were often required to pray for the traveller or seafarer, as in the case of the guilds at Boston, Bristol, Lincoln and Norwich. The objects of the Guild of the Assumption at Wiggenhall, Norfolk reflect the political situation at the time of its foundation (c. 1384), requiring members to pray for 'the King, the Pope, the Patriarch of Jerusalem, the Holy Land, the fruits of the earth, for shipmen and travellers.'[2] Some guilds provided Mass candles throughout the year, and for Masses to be said for 'all who are in peril on the sea'. A member of the Guild of the Ascension, Great Yarmouth, dying at sea was assured of soul-alms and no less than sixty Masses for the repose of his soul.[3]

When all the evidence is woven together, what appears is not very tidy, but the emerging picture is one which shows the sailor very much as a parishioner not far from home. Where a ship was several nights away, the usual pattern of travel would be from headland to headland, remaining within safe distance of land, its technical name cabotage, and allowing access to a shore-side church when necessary. There the sailor might find a Mass, perhaps a shrine, sometimes a bed for the night, possibly even entertainment as a visiting guest of a guild.

---

1   G.G. Harris, *The History of Trinity House at Deptford 1514-1660*, unpublished MA thesis, 7f, 18.
2   Westlake, *The Parish Guilds*, 157, 174, 216.
3   Miller, *From Shore to Shore*, 12.

3. Devotion to the Saints

Chapter two concluded that the seaman could be placed in the context of normal Church life. If that is correct, it should be possible to see around him other characteristics of the period. An obvious example would be devotion to the saints which flowered in the thirteenth century but continued until the Reformation.[1] A study of the saints at this time reveals both what resonated with the Christian seaman and what some in the Church thought might be appropriate for him. Almost anything written and relating to saints was mediated through clerical hands, surviving largely in the monastic libraries, which explains why the travellers who appear in these sources are usually clergy, yet in the maritime information which survives as a passenger in this material it is possible to glimpse the sailor.

The saints associated with the sailor are not familiar today. Clement of Rome, the earliest of maritime patrons, who died at the end of the first century, supposedly lashed to an anchor and thrown into the sea, prompted a number of what the *Penguin Dictionary of Saints* describes as 'marine dedications', by which it means, dedications of churches in coastal areas. Cited as examples are, St Clement's Isle in Mounts Bay, and the Guild of the Holy Trinity and St Clement (i.e. Trinity House of London). Godric, the hermit of Finchal, erstwhile seafarer, might have been expected to have a certain popularity, but there is no evidence that he did.[2] The Irish Brendan the Navigator had little more appeal than Godric. An examination of church dedications on the English waterfront shows they reflect the continental emphases of succeeding centuries, including saints such as Peter and Paul (a dedication popular after St Augustine's arrival in England), and then Mary. It is possible, however, to identify as favoured by sailors two major saints, Mary and Nicholas; two median, Clement and Julian; and particularly English, Becket and Richard of Chichester.

The Blessed Virgin Mary[3]

Mary's domination of the devotional life of European Christians certainly extended to the life of the seafarer. Eleventh-century rune stones, many with prayers for deceased seafarers, reveal Mary as a favourite within the emerging church of Sweden. Round the English coast places such as Great

---

[1] Vauchez, *Sainthood*, 137f.
[2] J. Stevenson (ed), *Libellus de vita et miraculis S. Godrici*. . . .
[3] References for this section and further details: Miller, *The Man at the Helm*, 57ff.

3. Devotion to the Saints

Yarmouth, Dover, Bradstow (Broadstairs), Scarborough and Southampton offered Marian shrines, acknowledged with *ex voti* from seamen, or the burning of lights; survival of their memory suggests these shrines were popular destinations. Mary was particularly honoured in England under the title of Our Lady of Pity, her image that of the mother holding her dead Son. It is known that seamen could be and were pilgrims, the Laws of Oleron giving pilgrimage as one of the few reasons why a man might be released from his contract by the ship's master.[1]

These places of pious resort served also as landmarks. Passing ships acknowledged the Broadstairs chapel, a church dedicated to St Peter but containing a notable statue of Our Lady, by dipping of sails, more common as a secular salute. Reculver Church was another church to which sails were dipped. Its twin spires (a distinctive landmark) had been erected by an abbess in thanksgiving for deliverance from shipwreck when taking passage to visit the Broadstairs chapel. Chapels at Dover and Southampton, important ports of departure for the continent, afforded travellers the opportunity to pray for a safe Channel crossing or to give thanks for a safe return until well into the reign of Henry VIII.

Contemporary devotions reveal more of the seafarer's response to Mary. The Laws of Oleron, dating from a period well into the Middle Ages, decreed that ships and buoys should bear the ship's name and port of origin so that wreckage might be identified, and the customary Aves and Paternosters said for the souls of those Christians who had died.[2] With the *Credo* and *Gloria Patri*, these were the four things Christians were expected to know. They formed the basic ingredients of the rosary, which was gaining popularity. Though strings of beads had long been used as aids to prayer, not only by the Christian community, few rosaries or other religious artifacts seem to have been recovered from medieval wrecks. Undifferentiated beads and bits of wood offer few clues, though crucifixes and beads were salvaged from the Mary Rose. Time and water would not be kind to such materials.

Few recorded contemporary acts of worship on board ship survive in detail. Though Journals were kept only for journeys of special significance, perhaps a crusade or pilgrimage, rendering them atypical of ordinary voyages, the few that survive are the best evidence remaining. Felix Fabri, writing in the later fifteenth century, described acts of worship on a pilgrim galley between Venice and the Holy Land. At sunrise the captain's servant, blowing a whistle, held up a picture of the Virgin Mary, when all would kneel, say an *Ave*, 'and other prayers if they choose'. Mid-day would be marked with a dry Mass (i.e. without the prayer of consecration). At sunset, crew again before the mast, Mary's picture held aloft, all would recite the *Salve Regina*, and the *Ave* thrice. A litany ended the day, with an *Ave* and a *Paternoster* said for the souls of the parents of St Julian (below), something which puzzled Fabri. The *Ave* would be one of the prayers traditionally said at the 'clearing of the glass' (the changing of the watch at the turn of a sand

---

1   Twiss, *Black Book*, IV, 531, para xi.
2   Twiss, vol II, 477, 479.

timer), a custom post Reformation references recognise as 'according to the old order of England', and found on most ships, pilgrim vessels or not. The *Book of Homilies* of the Church of England, comparing 'St Christopher, St Clement, and divers others' to Neptune and Triton, adds 'specially our Lady, to whom shipmen sing *Ave, maris stella*'.[1]

Marian prayers have a long history and their appeal to the mariner is not far to seek. The *Alma Redemptoris Mater* refers to Mary as 'Star of the deep, and portal of the sky', praying, 'Sinking we strive, and call to thee for aid.' The *Ave Regina* recognises her in the imagery of the dawn, while the Salve Regina asks that she will lead home the one who prays. The appeal of her title of Stella Maris, to those who navigated by the North Star, Chaucer's 'Sterre of the sea, to shipmen light and guide', is self-explanatory.

The increasing contemporary interest in the Holy Places with its emphasis on the earthly Jesus would encourage devotion to his mother. The lives of many saints featured in the very popular *Golden Legend*; Mary's supplemented with a host of legends in other collections, was written that the reader may 'consider in his heart the great mercies she has done for them that adventure in ships upon the sea' (cf. Psalm 107:67).[2] Their legendary nature is emphasised by the absence of date or place. The so-called Mary Legends, particularly, in written form were preserved in monastic circles, suggesting at best a limited circulation among seafarers - but good stories travel by word of mouth. These follow a formula. Invariably, in storm, shipwreck or other trouble at sea, a worthy abbot or prelate who happens to be travelling counsels prayer to Mary, usually after prayers to St Nicholas, St Clare or St Christopher have failed; those who follow his advice are miraculously saved.[3] It is in this context that the devotion to Our Lady's Mantle is presented, a cloak covering her from the shoulders and used to safeguard the drowning or shipwrecked petitioner. It is possible to make much of these legends, but safe to claim only that they confirm the prevalence of Marian prayers and hymns, which might also be heard on board ship.

Traces of this maritime devotion survive in ship names, flags and port seals. The naming of a ship has long been a religious activity, with the ship 'baptised' even in secular ceremonies. It is difficult to know how common religious names were but port lists indicate that many ships carried religious names, with Mary to the fore;[4] difficult too to assess the extent to which Mary and other saints appeared on flags and banners. Flags have a very long history of use on ships, their importance increasing with the heraldic

1   Homily, 'Against the Peril of Idolatry'.David Proctor, *The Music of the Sea*, 17f.
2   References for this section and further details may be found in Miller, *The Man at the Helm*, 66ff.
3   Two examples: the abbot Elsinus returning from Denmark and Guimund and Drogo, pilgrims, on passage to Jerusalem. P. N. Carter, *An Edition of William of Malmesbury's Treatise . . .* , Unpublished DPhil thesis, 163f, 166f.
4   G. and H. Bresc, Les saints protecteurs de bateaux 1200-1460, 161-178. H.and P. Chaunu, Seville et l'Atlantique (1504-1650), vols 2-5 reveals many late medieval religious ship names. Neither book gives comparative figures though Bresc notes: Seul Nicolas paraît avoir joué ce rôle universel d'intercesseur.

developments of the crusades. Waterton gives an unsourced example of the flag of Sir William Weston who, distinguishing himself at Rhodes, was appointed to command 'a great ship *Carrack Of Rhodes*' from which he flew a flag of Our Lady of Pity.[1] The 1515 inventory of the *Mary Rose* included items which point in a similar direction.

The port seal is a more fruitful indicator of Marian devotion, if not of the seafarer, at least where ships and shipmen would be found, and whence crews would be drawn. Seals were adopted by ports from monastic precursors; it is necessary to glance first at the latter. Many monastic seals show Mary. If of Virgin and Child, over the figures a crescent moon (Mary) contains the star (the Holy Child) whereas the Coronation of Mary has the greater light above Christ's head, the lesser over Mary. The Cinque Port seals illustrate the transition from monastic to secular seals. At first glance, of these, only the Rye seal seems to contain overt religious content, showing Virgin and Child imposed upon a church. However, in the background of other Cinque Port seals, and seals from many other ports which portray the secular symbol of a ship, often sun and moon, or crescent moon and star, appear. Good examples can be found from Bridgwater, Lyme Regis, Dunwich, Rye, Pevensey (Fig. 2), Tenterden (Fig. 3), Winchelsea, Ipswich, and Exeter. Heraldic books suggest in explanation an intention to indicate the firmament or a link with the crusades. It cannot simply be to represent the firmament, for space on a seal is limited; no-one needs sun and moon above a ship to confirm that above it is the firmament. Crescent and star on modern Islamic flags might hint at an early crusade link. However, the easiest explanation is that these seals reflect contemporary devotion to Mary and her Son in these seaport areas.[2]

Saint Nicholas [3]

Nicholas, after Mary, attracted much devotion. His name is particularly associated with travellers. Nicholas church dedications from the medieval period plotted on the map of Britain predominate on the east and south coast of England, the Scottish west coast, and in Irish towns with Viking connections. The Viking significance will appear below. Their positioning is such that they can often indicate what was once a navigable waterway.

The legends surrounding Nicholas also circulated in popular legendaries. He was a fourth-century Bishop of Myra in Asia Minor. Many stories link him to the sea. In one, Nicholas appears miraculously to seamen invoking his aid during a storm, adjusts their rigging before the storm abates, and all are saved. In another, a famine was relieved when Nicholas intervened to remedy short measures of corn (preventing those Theodosian Code penalties of chapter one) on ships arriving from Alexandria. In a third, Nicholas

---

1 Edmund Waterton, Pietas Marianna Britannica, vol. 1, 241, n 79. *Carrack Of Rhodes* seems more a description than the name of a ship.
2 Miller, *The Man at the Helm*, offers detailed argument and references, 70-72.
3 Miller, *The Man at the Helm*, 73ff.

(usually portrayed with full beard) appeared on a quayside disguised as a nun, to the wonder of all on board a ship and the conversion of a crew member. Variously he walks upon the sea; saves a crew from shipwreck; revives a drowned boy. When it was claimed Muslims threatened to overrun Myra (1087), Nicholas's relics were liberated or stolen from Myra, and placed in Bari's basilica, newly built and about to be consecrated by Pope Urban II, at the council of Bari (1095); a papal compliment to the new Norman state of Sicily. There are here clues to the popularity of Nicholas.

Among the bishops at the council of Bari was Anselm of Canterbury, a Norman appointee. His prayer to Nicholas, written on his return to England, survives. The Norman connection, William of Normandy sharing a Viking grandfather with Roger of Sicily, explains why Nicholas was the dedication of choice in places with Viking associations, from Greenland's Gardar cathedral (1200) to churches in Constantinople, a city visited early by Vikings. Olaf's conversion to Christianity created among his people a need for saints: the bones of Nicholas, surrounded by suitable maritime legends, were available for the taking.

Other details hint at the Viking-Norman connection. Villehardouin counselled the French queen to promise to make a pilgrimage to the shrine of St Nicholas at Varangeville in return for safety in a storm, testifying, 'St Nicholas has saved us from our present peril for the wind has fallen'.[1] *Orderic Vitalis* has Duke William sailing from Arques to Winchelsea in the wintry season on December 6th, feast day of St Nicholas, 'and all over Normandy prayers were offered for the good Duke'.[2] But *Orderic* also has William sailing to England on the 29th September 1066, under the patronage of Michael the Archangel (patron of Normandy), suggesting either date might be coincidental.

Though Nicholas was a popular dedication for hospitals in England, Scotland and Ireland, it is hard to find anywhere associated with Nicholas described as a *maison dieu*. This may imply that a Nicholas dedication suggests no maritime significance for a hospital, deriving instead from other Nicholas stories of the sick being cured or the burdens of the poor eased. Clay gave twenty-nine Nicholas dedications from the twelfth and thirteenth centuries; of these some were certainly for lepers, and the majority of the remainder for the poor or sick poor, any of whom could be mariners.

Other Maritime Saints

The Early South-English Legendary, a contemporary of *The Golden Legend,* has a cluster of maritime saints.[3] Julian is in company with Nicholas who follows immediately upon Brendan the Navigator; neither matches Brendan for drama, who supposedly spent one Easter with his monks on the back of a whale, but both eclipse him in popularity. The emphasis of The Early

---
1 Joinville & Villehardouin, *Chronicles of the Crusades*, 322.
2 *Orderic* Vitalis, 209.
3 Carl Horstmann (ed), vol I, viii, 240ff, 253, 255ff.

3. Devotion to the Saints 63

Pevensey common seal (obv), early thirteenth century.
Geoffrey Williams, *The Heraldry of the Cinque Ports*, Newton Abbot, 1971.

Tenterden Common Seal (obv), c. 1449
Geoffrey Williams, *The Heraldry of the Cinque Ports*, Newton Abbot 1971.

South-English Legendary, where Becket occupies seventy one pages, Brendan twenty pages, Nicholas fifteen, Clement eighteen and Julian four, reflects terrestrial priorities and confirms the opinion of Vauchez that the first half of the thirteenth century was a period of saint-making in which new saints were replacing the old saints.[1]

Commenting on St Clement in the *Calendar of St Willibrord* (before 750), H. A. Wilson says Clement is 'generally noted in early martyrologies, calendars and sacramentaries'.[2] An Irish source (c. 800), *The Martyrology of Oengus the Culdee*, associates Clement with an undersea convent, on November 23rd including a reference to 'The fair suffering of Clement among the sea's waves: his city is adored under the waves of the wide main'.[3] *The Early South-English Legendary*, more fancifully, has this early Pope 'drowned in the sea, which withdraws and discloses a chapel where his body is enshrined'; adding that he managed to keep a boy alive beneath the waves for a year, miraculously dried up water, resuscitated a drowned boy ('Fair miracle dude seint Clement ofte'), and concluding with the information that Clement's body, on being thrown into the sea, was retrieved and buried in St Clement's church in Rome. This is slender evidence for a devotion within a maritime community. He fared little better in homily form. There is, however, a significant number of Clement dedications on the English coast, including churches in Sandwich, Dartmouth, the former Thames port of Leigh-on-Sea, and Hastings. In London the church of St Clement Danes stands at the east end of the Strand (i.e the medieval waterfront), while St Clement finds a place in the full title of London's Trinity House.

St Julian today, as when Fabri puzzled over sailors' prayers for Julian's parents, is little known. *The Early South-English Legendary* and *The South English Legendary* list two saints named Julian; it is the second, *Sancti Juliani boni hospitis* who has the maritime connection. Neither legendary gives dates, place of origin, or site of the hospice he eventually built, but both offer an entertaining story. The young Julian, out hunting, was warned by a stag that one day he would cause the death of his parents. To avoid this, he moved to a far country, married and settled. His parents, in old age and needing care, made their way to his new home. His wife, prompted by their exhausted state, put them to rest in the marital bed. Julian returned home, saw two heads of differing gender on the pillow and, assuming the worst, killed them before discovering that these were his parents. He set off for Rome on an expiatory pilgrimage, settling by a river where he cared for passing travellers, supported by his faithful wife. One day, not unlike the story of St Christopher, he helped a particularly wretched traveller across the river; the traveller turned out to be an angel who granted him the forgiveness he had previously been unable to accept. Once Julian's story is known, the maritime interest becomes comprehensible, for Julian is seen

---

1   *Sainthood*, 137.
2   *op cit*, HBS, 1918, 13.
3   Whitley Stokes (ed), 234, 236, 245.

3. Devotion to the Saints

as the begetter of many medieval travellers' hostels, some especially for seafarers. Seafarers' hostels with a Julian dedication were to be found in Colchester, Norwich, Thetford, Bordeaux, and Rome; at Southampton the *maison dieu* had a Julian chapel attached to it (map 1). There is a slight possibility of Norman influence. The *Travels of Ibn Jubayr* (1183-85) refers to a Mount St Julian in Norman Sicily, M. Amari noting that it was named in gratitude for St Julian's assistance in its capture.

The Reformation would have its effect upon the position of saints in the religious life of seamen, particularly on Becket, whose name was largely expunged for political expediency under Henry VIII, and this makes it hard today to appreciate the hold that the saints had on medieval religious life; certainly a proper appreciation is essential to an understanding of the *milieu* in which the seafarer moved. Today the dominance of Mary is forgotten by most people, whereas the appeal of Nicholas persists, albeit as Santa Claus. Julian's cult was wider spread and longer lasting than most of the other saints cited; it seems to have been genuinely maritime. It is possible, in an age when saints were of such interest, to find examples of all kinds of saints being invoked by sailors. Martin of Tours, Becket, Richard of Chichester, Edmund Rich, Thomas Cantilupe, and many more from across Europe were often coupled in prayer with St Nicholas. Becket seems to have been extraordinarily prolific in his miracles of rescue if his martyrology is to be believed.[1] A significant number of beneficiaries of his miracles were men on ships sailing round the South East coast of England, perhaps on their way to Becket's shrine. A blind man, on the day of Becket's murder seeking recovery of his sight at the Kent church of St Nicholas (Harbledown?), was warned in a vision to apply to the 'new martyr', thus becoming the subject of Becket's first miracle, and the foundation of what would become a major industry.

---

1 James Craigie Robertson (ed), *Materials for a History of Thomas Becket*, RS, vol I, 1875.

4. The Canons and Sea Codes

The legislative function of the universal Church is known as canon law. Some of medieval canon law related to the seafarer in particular, some to him as part of the Christian community. The medieval period was marked by extensive codification within Christendom, with canon law part of a list including manorial law, feudal law, municipal law, maritime law, merchant law, and Roman law.[1] Of particular interest here is Gratian's *Concordia Discordantium Canonum* ('a harmony of conflicting canons'), usually referred to as his *Decretum*, or the *Decretum Gratiani*, a collection of canon law dating post 1139. It is noticeable that Gratian gives the seafarer little attention, arguably because there was an existing and older code of maritime law. Probably for the same reason, apart from mention of ship service, nothing maritime is found in early English law.[2] The medieval sea codes contain centuries of custom, much predating canon law, sometimes influenced by Church legislation, but codified in the same period.[3] Whereas sea codes served particular areas, canon law covered the whole of Catholic Christendom. The author who has devoted most attention to their relationship is R. F. Wright.[4] To understand that relationship requires an examination of the status of the sea.

Effectively the sea marked the limit of ecclesiastical jurisdiction. In a Church which was essentially territorial, it was the point at which defence was conducted: when Saracens threatened Rome, Leo IV ordered 'our people to gather and go down to the shore'.[5] Key concepts are *mare nullius* and *terra nullius*, no man's sea and no man's land, as opposed to *mare clausum* which refers to an area of sea over which jurisdiction is claimed, and *mare liberum*, which equates roughly with *mare nullius*; there is also the *jus gentium* which gave the rule over adjoining sea to princes.[6] An early example of Church involvement would be the canons forbidding trade with Saracens. A later example of legislation relating to sovereignty was the Bull of Alexander VI in 1494, the Treaty of Tordesillas, which divided the great ocean between Spain

---

1   James A. Brundage, *Mediaeval Canon Law*, 187.
2   Patrick Wormald, *The Making of English Law*, vol I, *passim*.
3   Many sea codes are collected in Travers Twiss, *Black Book of the Admiralty*. (Hereafter: Twiss) See additionally Walter Ashburner (ed), *The Rhodian Sea Law*.
4   *Mediaeval Internationalism*, 1930 (hereafter: Wright, 1930).
5   Aquinas, *Summa*, 2a 2ae 40.2. See also PL 187, C23.8.20 (P) 959,5 and C 23.8.7(T) 955,2
6   I have found very helpful H. G. Knight, *The Law of the Sea*, *passim*. A copy of this is to be found in the Library of Mystic Seaport Museum, CT, USA.

and Portugal.[1] These concepts applied to the developing idea of territorial waters, and the confusing status of a ship within or outside them. Eventually, only water which could be defended (apparently related to the distance of a cannon shot, later extended by the placing of 'castles' on ships) could be regulated by the adjoining state, while, rather after the manner of an embassy abroad, a ship was understood as an extension of another's territory. Some of this legislation related to a bishop's jurisdiction, how is not clear, though the local bishop (below) might be involved, sometimes in the dual roles of local lord and local bishop, for example, in the distribution of the proceeds derived from wreck, the wreck presumably taking place in territorial waters.

The Decretals

By the twelfth century the papacy was claiming for itself considerable authority, whether regulating trade with Saracens, or dividing oceans. The so-called Gregorian Reforms, deriving from a cluster of popes rather than Gregory VII alone, supported this claim. They are relevant here particularly where they relate to the establishment of parishes and the requirement of parishioners to fulfill certain, for example Easter, duties, or with regard to the designation of particular churches for the use of seamen.

Collections of Church law, especially pronouncements of particular councils (canons), were by this century being codified systematically. Rome was also issuing large numbers of decretals (instructions or answers) in response to questions from kings or bishops about local situations. The process by which these were gathered and made generally available was a complicated one; in Gratian's development of a workable structure for this process lies his importance.

The Maritime Codes

The medieval sea codes, a collection of custom, or antecedent practice (*usus*), are difficult to date. Twiss suggested that the principal Church influence lay in the act of codification itself.[2] Gratian's one specific reference is to the Rhodian Sea Law (D. 2.8.27): *Rodiae leges naualium commerciorum sunt, ab insula Rhoodo cognominatae, in qua antiquitius mercatorum usus fuit*, which found its continuing existence in the Mediterranean codes. The existence of these maritime codes meant that there was no vacuum for ecclesiastical lawyers to fill. The Rhodian Law contained nothing of a religious nature, unlike the codes which followed it, though some of its secular requirements, such as the disposition of salvaged goods, could be administered in a religious context, that is, by the local bishop.

The origins of the Rhodian Law, perhaps the oldest, lay in Roman jurisprudence; it survives best in the Amalphitan Table and the *Consolato*

---

1 For a fuller discussion of this subject, see Miller, *The Man at the Helm*, chapter 4.
2 Twiss, IV, xxf.

del Mare, serving the Mediterranean and possibly originating in Barcelona.[1] It strongly influenced the Laws of Oleron (France, Holland, England, and the Baltic) and Islamic practice.[2] With large numbers of ships drawn from many nations gathered for the crusades, and with the establishment of the Kingdom of Jerusalem, it was essential that some sort of maritime code was committed to writing in the Levant.[3] Although particular trading groups, such as Pisans, Genoans and Venetians, had been conceded privileges, including the observance of their own maritime laws, the common origin of these helped the process.[4] The various legal codes of the kingdom of Jerusalem were deposited in the treasury of the church of the Holy Sepulchre, and so were called *lettres du Sepulchre*, mostly lost under Saladin, though the *Maritime Assizes of the Kingdom of Jerusalem* survives. It is plain from the Hebrew scriptures that there were earlier customs than those of Rhodes,[5] for the book of Jonah appears to refer to the law of jettison.[6] All of which led Twiss and others to suggest that the codes of *Jerusalem* and *Amalfi* derive from the tenth century, the Oleron codes from the twelfth century, Wisby perhaps thirteenth century, and the *Customs* from a similar period.

A distinct maritime law was necessary as the requirements of the sea were different from those of the land. The contrast can be illustrated from an English law which, recognising the difficulty of finding twelve neighbours to form a jury in marine cases, perhaps involving people of several countries, allowed such cases to be tried under oath before judges. Terrestrial courts sat at times dictated by the sun, maritime courts according to the tides.[7] Khalilieh's quotation from the Prophet Mahomet ('a day at sea is equivalent to one month on land, and a martyr at sea is like two martyrs on land') emphasises the difference. Twiss argued that through the crusades the clergy became familiar 'with the habits of seafaring men . . . clerks were readily found to reduce into writing the decisions of the maritime tribunals'.[8]

The Sea in Gratian

What maritime information can be gleaned from Gratian? Though most of his references to the sea are scriptural, he revealed some knowledge of the problems of the seafarer, for example the difficulty of fulfilling Easter duties, equating those on 'a difficult sea voyage' with the sick and those on a long journey, for whom desire satisfies such religious obligations.[9] Beyond a brief reference to

---

1 Miller, *The Man at the Helm*, 101.
2 Hassan Salih Khalilieh, *Islamic Maritime Law . . .* , 179.
3 Twiss, IV, 499ff; IV, xviif.
4 Twiss, IV, civ.
5 Samuel Tolkowsky, *They Took to the Sea, passim* gives the Hebrew background.
6 O. R. Constable, The Problem of Jettison . . . , 208.
7 Twiss, I, 252, n 1. Twiss, II, viii says this practice survived from Roman law.
8 Twiss, II, xli.
9 (De con. 4. 13) *Corpus Iuris Canonici*, vol I, 1365-6. Khalilieh, *Islamic Maritime Law*, 165 notes that Islamic prayer obligations were shortened at sea, except for sailors,who were considered well-adjusted physically to the maritime environment.

4. The Canons and Sea Codes

the confiscation of a ship (C.2 q.6, c 26), the remainder of his non scriptural references were to situations *in extremis*. He referred to jettison to illustrate the way a Christian should relieve himself of possessions; his conditions under which jettison may take place are those of the sea codes: a rising storm and the need to save the ship by lightening it (C. 1 q.7, c 16), which is hardly specialist knowledge. In discussing the administration of baptism he indicated shipwreck as an occasion when emergency baptism may rightly be administered by a lay person (*De cons.* 4. 16). If a 'conscientious penitent' died at sea or on a journey (an interesting distinction), the absence of a priest implicit, his soul should be commended with prayers and oblations (C 26 q. 7, c6). That all of this is rather more than common sense is illustrated by what appears in the sea codes, where the secular text makes similar provision, confirming it as the practice of seafarers of the period, for the need to confess in the absence of a priest or bishop appears in at least one Mary-legend, and the custom of 'shriving themselves unto the mast' survived into the sixteenth century.[1]

Religion in the Maritime Codes

Where Gratian mentions maritime practice briefly, religion receives more attention in the sea codes, codified according to Twiss by clerical hands, and apparent from the first words of some codes, especially the later ones. The *Jus Maritimum Lubecense* (the Code of the Osterlings, c.1299) opened:

> In the name of the Holy Trinity, the Father and the Son and the Holy Ghost ... and to those whom these presents shall come ... they send greeting and good wishes for their everlasting salvation in our Lord God.[2]

The *Wisby Stadslag van Sciprecte* (Wisby Town-Law on Shipping, post 1219) opened, 'In the Name of God. Amen', similar words supplemented with 'Omnipotent' appearing in the *Ordinamenta et Consuetudo Maris Edita per Consules Civitatis Trani* (Ordinances ... of the City of Trani, c. 1063).

The international nature of trade and their common origin meant that, although the codes take their titles from particular ports, their contents are often similar. Three examples will illustrate this point while revealing links with the Church. Masters who have sick seamen are required to lodge them in an inn, furnish them with a light, leave a shipmate or hire another person to attend them, and provide such food as they have on board ship. This is drawn from the *Gotland Sea-Laws* but appears also in *Wisby* (with the modification that the disease must not knowingly have been contracted before boarding the ship) and in the *Sea-Laws of Flanders* and the *Purple Book of Bruges*.[3] There is here a Christian-inspired expectation of welfare, but not manifested in the form of *maisons dieu*. A second indicates shared belief, where an earnest (money paid as an instalment) is referred to as 'God's penny'; that the Church should receive it is implicit in the (Oleron) Gotland, Wisby and

---

1 William Tyndale (?1494-1536), *Doctrinal Treatises*, 245.
2 Twiss, IV, 358-9.
3 Twiss IV, respectively 73, para 21; article XIX, 270, article LXII; para 7, 423; article 21, 309.

Dantzig codes.[1] A third example refers to the use of relics in the widespread custom of taking oaths, which was considered a religious activity. The codes of Gotland, Jerusalem, the Osterlings and Wisby required an oath to be taken when testifying to damage caused at sea; anyone refusing to swear on the 'holy relics' being required to pay damages.[2]

It might be expected that the issue of usury would arise, having been specifically condemned by the Third Lateran Council. Ashburner's claim that Church teaching on usury created tension for the sea-going community is hard to see in the sea codes.[3] Gregory IX (d. 1241) had strict words to say on the subject in the decretal *Naviganti* of 1234, but it was generally recognised that maritime commerce had its own special circumstances. The problem was not that the individual sailor might be a usurer; rather, it was the effect of this ruling on trade generally. A man going on a voyage receiving something more than the principal was condemned unless he was paid in kind, in which case it was uncertain if the goods he received would make a profit; nor was a man who bought at one price and sold at a higher price guilty of usury. The Church was forced to recognise that any investment in shipping required recognition of the risk involved. Advance payment was not considered to be usurious.[4] The concern of the period with usury went hand in hand with the rise of commerce.[5] The Gotland Sea-Laws ignored usury, permitting a ship's master to pawn tackle or sails if victuals were needed; it may be significant that money-lending in Christian territory was usually a Jewish activity. That said, there is an example from 1273 from a seaport source of a usurer being refused burial.[6] Refusal of Christian burial, which followed excommunication, might also be attracted by other activities, such as trading with the Saracens or sailing with an excommunicate ship's master.[7]

The Bishop's Role in the Codes

The bishop's role appears most distinctly in the *Rolle of Olayron*. Excommunication, in some cases automatic, in others requiring episcopal authority, was introduced for those who stole from the shipwrecked, but, as Twiss points out, would be imposed by an ecclesiastical rather than a maritime court; it is echoed in the canons of Lateran II. An Edict of Henry I (pre-1135) had tried to increase penalties on such theft, at least in his own dominions, placing responsibility for its administration on the local lord who, often, would be the bishop.[8] Wrecking, a particular kind of theft, was a continuing problem, and one not easy of solution. There are many examples of infringement. In one

---

1 Twiss, IV, respectively para 40 and n 1, 101; ch V, 393; para 40, 337.
2 Twiss, IV, respectively 125, n 7 and para 65; 507, art XIII, 373; ch XVII, 411.
  NB Lateran II, canon 14 which touches on trial by ordeal.
3 Ashburner, *Rhodian Sea-Law*, ccxxi-ccxxiv.
4 J. T. Noonan, *The Scholastic Analysis of Usury*, 91, 114.
5 J. T. Noonan, *The Scholastic Analysis of Usury*, 18.
6 Barbara Dodwell (ed), *Norwich Cathedral Charters*, vol 1, 19 May 1273.
7 Alfred J. Andrea, The Relationship of Sea Travellers . . . , 203-9.
8 *Regesta*, II, 293, cap 1920.

4. The Canons and Sea Codes

case, men of Bristol 'seized and plundered' a ship of the Abbot of Tintern on the River Wye; the outcome of the inquiry is unknown.[1]

Money from salvaged goods, sold publicly to the highest bidder by the lord, was to be devoted 'to have prayer made to God for the dead', 'to marry poor maydes' or to do 'other works of mercy after reason and conscience'.[2] Similar concerns appear as far apart as Anjou and Greenland. When the bones of wrecked sailors were brought back to Greenland to bishop Arnold of Gardar for burial, 'the ship was taken over by the church in payment for the welfare of sailors' souls', while the rest of the salvage was divided among the finders 'according to Greenland's laws'; a dispute concerning this division a year later was dismissed by the bishop. Wreck here was sufficiently common for a corpse-finder to be employed to bring shipwrecked bodies for burial.[3] Gregory VII's Lent Synod of 1078 had decreed that the goods of the shipwrecked should be returned and protection given to survivors. The two positions can be reconciled if Oleron is taken to refer to wrecks where all have perished, while the 1078 Synod refers to wrecks with survivors. Olaus Magnus (1555) suggested that goods from wrecked ships should be kept intact 'unless they are such vessels as follow the wicked practice of piracy, or are hostile to us or the name of Christianity', with a penalty of confiscation - or worse; the same applied to goods washed ashore.[4] Crusaders were encouraged to collect booty without fear of excommunication, presumably because it came from Saracen wreckage.[5]

Wrecking itself, that is, causing a ship to be wrecked, perhaps by the display of misleading lights, or by crew damaging a vessel, was a serious matter, but apparently only wrecking of Christian vessels attracted excommunication; 'bishopes or prelates or clerks' involved in wrecking faced deposition and deprivation. However, in accord with Lateran canons, pirates, sea rovers and 'enemies of our Holy Catholic Faith' (e.g. Turks) were considered fair game, from whom 'every one may take from suche manner of men as from dogs, and may strip them of theyr goodes without any punishment'. Anything else found on the shore was to be treated as wrecked goods and devoted to 'prayers for the dead, and other spiritual goode works', otherwise incurring the maledictions indicated. Found gold and silver were exceptions, and might be kept if the finder was poor, but otherwise made public,

> still further he ought to take counsel of his prelate, or of his curé, or of his confessor, who ought well to consider the indigence and povertie of him who shall have found the silver . . . and give him advice according to God and his conscience.[6]

---

1 *Calendar of Inquisitions Misc (Chancery)*, I, cap 354.
2 Contained also in the *Consolat de Mer*, ch ccvii.
3 Gwynn Jones, *The Norse Atlantic Saga*, 81f, 240f.
   Most religious traditions consider burial of the stranger a 'good work'.
4 Olaus Magnus, *Description of the Northern People*, vol II, Bk 12, ch 24, 609.
5 Joinville & Villehardouin, *Chronicles* . . . , 94.
6 Twiss, II, respectively 463ff, paras 26, 27, 29; 479, para 46; 475, para 41; 477, para 44.

The Taking of Oaths

Oath-taking, found in many contemporary sources, was considered a matter for the Church. The *Black Book* gives a typical form for admiralty jurymen, explicitly religious, concluding 'Soe God my help at the holy doom and by this boke'.[1] The 'boke' is almost certainly the Gospels and, although Twiss wondered if the doom referred to holy relics, it most obviously refers to Judgement day.[2] Crew members were required to give evidence on oath, for example, in the case of jettison, when master and all or some of the crew on arriving ashore, using the 'holy Gospels' would confirm the danger which had led to the jettison; also after collision with a ship at anchor, or to promise future payment. The procedure seems to have been for the witness to place a hand on the book. The most likely place to find Gospels would be the local church, for a copy of the Gospels on board ship risked damage from damp, though the clerk's records, presumably liable to the same damp, were kept on the ship, suggesting that the presence of Gospels on board cannot be dismissed. It is known that oaths could also be taken on relics.[3]

The appointment of the ship's clerk required an oath of fidelity to the master; he faced loss of possessions and branding with a hot iron if found falsifying the records in the ship's book, effectively the ship's inventory and accepted as evidence in case of dispute. The important role of the clerk, and the ability to write (implicit in his other title: *scribarius*), suggest that he could be a cleric (whence the word 'clerk'), perhaps in minor orders, or at least educated in an ecclesiastical context. Venetian clerks, and others in similar positions, to avoid a vessel falling into Saracen ownership would swear to sell the ship only to Venetians, or to honest persons who had taken a similar oath. Venetians loading the ship could be required to swear that the ship was not overladen, Venice having long anticipated Plimsoll's Line. The crew swore faithful service to the ship's master and to make known to him any persons acting against his or the ship's interests.

In short, the whole Venetian, and - presumably - every, maritime enterprise would have collapsed without the taking of oaths, which occupied the place of today's signature. Their ubiquity makes one wonder if the words, 'I swear on the holy Gospels . . .' were in themselves sufficient or if every occasion required the presence of the book (or relics). It is not entirely frivolous to give as an example of an oath not requiring proximity, the one beloved by villains in B movies: 'I swear on my mother's grave . . . '.[4]

---

1   Twiss, I, 43.
2   Twiss, II, 255; II, 319, ch xlvi.
3   Twiss, II, 385, ch lxxxix; II, 211ff; II, 433ff; II, 441, para 8; II, 449, para 14. *Curia Regis Rolls*, 9-10 Henry III, RS, cap 1073 (1225 AD). *Calendar of Documents Preserved in France*, I, 94, cap 278 (dated 1193); I, 1889, 471, cap 1299 (dated 1199); 495, cap 1361 (dated 1197).
4   *Gli Statuti Marittimi Veneziani fino al 1225*, 50, 80, 94, 103, 104, 107, 108, 168, 175.

The Deodand

The *Black Book* gives a further glimpse of religious understanding in its references to *deodands*, items of value found on a dead man at sea, in this case to be taken and administered by the admiral (a word of Arab origin and perhaps indicative of date), one moiety 'for the soul of him who is dead', the other for his relatives.[1] In the *Laws of Oleron*, there is a reference to the working of providence, 'And whan God sendeth the shyppe to dyscharge in saufte ...',[2] but which may indicate little more in the way of religious belief than today's insurers' 'act of God'. The *Charter of Oleron of the Judgements of the Sea* has something similar in the 'adventure of God' where sailors share in the outcome of a particular venture.[3] *The Good Customs of the Sea*, in a section 'of goods found' on the beach, adds that a quarter should be given 'for the love of God ... for the soul of him to whom they belonged'.[4] The Gotland and Danzig Codes refer to God's Penny, either as this charity or the earnest money to be paid on freight when a ship is wrecked, unsaid but probably paid to the Church on God's behalf.

Concern for the dead is also expressed in the *Rolle of Olayron*, which requires anchors and cables (valuable items) found to be returned when possible, but where unidentifiable, the finder should have a *Pater* and an *Ave Maria* said for those presumed dead.

> [I]t has been ordayned, that every mayster of a ship ought to get and have engraved upon the buoys and floats of his ship the name of his said shyp, and of the port or haven from which it is. And this will prevent many souls being damned.[5]

The Barcelona-based *Good Customs of the Sea* refers to the property of passengers ('Every man is called a passenger who pays freight for his person'). Where there has been the possibility of death, if the deceased passenger's property is unclaimed after three years it should be given 'in the presence of the bishop of the territory' for 'the repose of [the deceased's] soul', and the death registered with 'the clergyman who has the care of souls in that place'[6]

Islamic Law offers parallels. Regarding providence, Khalilieh cites the Geniza Letters (1139 CE): 'The pepper was lost completely; God did not save anything of it ...'. The duty to render something from gain by salvage also appears: goods of significant value, in Islamic Law, were required to be kept for a lunar year,

---

1 Twiss, I, para 37, 85. Cp I, 153.
2 Twiss, II, 99.
3 Twiss, III, 1ff.
4 Twiss III, p 439 ch ccvii.
5 Cf. the name and port of origin on today's ships and planes. It may also relate to maritime law treating a ship as an extension of a nation's territory. Twiss, II, 477, para 45.
6 Twiss, III, p 173, ch lxviii; III,, 179, ch lxxii. Three years was also the time prescribed for the safe-keeping of property of one who had gone on crusade, though not in this text; perhaps a common length of time throughout Christendom; if crusader property was protected for three years there must have been some sort of contemporary provision for registration, and the parish priest would have been the logical registrar, as also of deaths.

after which, if no claim was made, or a claim relinquished, 'the salvagor was authorised to keep the goods or to deliver them to religious endowments and indigent people'.[1] It is possible these are older customs held in common in the maritime community, with its universal experience of the seafarer at the mercy of the elements, and by extension, in the hand of the Maker.

Provision for the Sick

The *Customs of Oleron* require that a sick man be put ashore and provided with care and lodgings. The language (*una casa* or *une maison*) implies proper shelter rather than a *maison dieu*, though Twiss says 'hostel was a familiar term amongst mariners for a house where strangers were lodged'. Many but not all hostels were in religious hands. *The Rolle of Olayron* adds that the sick man should be provided with a light as a 'talowe or candell for hym'.[2]

The Concept of Sanctuary

The *Ordinances of the City of Trani* contains a curious provision; forbidding the master to assault a seaman, who, if assaulted, must not immediately retaliate on pain of stiff penalties. Instead, he may escape to the bows and, if still pursued, thence 'to the chain of the rowers, and ought to say, "In the name of my Lord do not touch me", three times', after which he may defend himself without penalty.[3] Olaus Magnus, writing in 1555, was familiar with the idea, 'Those who have committed slight offences run to the forecastle to gain exemption from punishment', but ascribes this rule to *Wisby*.[4] R.F. Wright thought this a maritime equivalent of the concept of sanctuary.[5] It appears in both *Consulato* and *Trani*. Its appearance in both northern and Mediterranean codes is significant.

The idea of a safe zone on board ship is attractive and sits comfortably beside the knowledge that some parts of the ship seem to have been considered sacred. A possible sacred area survives in Tyndale's reference to men shriving themselves to the mast. The custom of saluting the poop or main deck may point to a crucifix or religious picture having been displayed here, or to recognition of the cruciform structure of the mast. There is, however, no evidence that such respect was accorded the bows.

One explanation is that the master is given three chances to calm himself and the sailor, effectively, enjoined to allow this by putting the maximum distance between them. Twiss saw the cry for protection as being less a plea for divine intervention than an equivalent to, 'in the King's name', though Wright pointed out that there would be no lord as the sea codes were a form

---

1   *Islamic Maritime Law*, 110, 114.
2   Twiss, II, 211ff; 433ff; 439, para 7.
3   Twiss, IV, 521ff.
4   *A Description of the Northern Peoples*, vol II, Bk 10, ch 16, p 496 and n 3.
5   Wright 1930, 205.
   Pablo E. Pérez-Mallaína, *Spain's Men of the Sea*, 193 has the same opinion.

of international 'common law'.[1] The triple invocation may be a survival of Roman law, with its required triple admission of guilt before the magistrate, found in the early Christian *Acta* where governors asked Christians three times to affirm their faith before condemnation. There was no religious reason for *where* on the ship the mariner should go, only the practical one of distance on a small vessel. Wright's suggestion of sanctuary on board is echoed in other cultures, especially regarding the bows, hinting at an origin in antiquity. More evidence is necessary before sanctuary underlying the bows as a place of escape can be dismissed.[2] It is just possible that the injunction, if a clerical hand lay behind the code, reflects a monastic hand, for the Rule of St Benedict (chapter 68) considers what should be done 'If a brother be commanded to do impossible things'.

Crusade Influence

The crusade context is apparent in several codes. The reference made in *Good Customs of the Sea* to travel in convoy and the actions of pirates and corsairs, reflecting experiences of Saracen activity, supports Twiss's suggestion of a thirteenth century date. Curiously, the code outlines the master's duty to his crew not only when the ship is being sold in Christian countries (wages to be paid and the crew released, with care until they are placed), but also, despite Church strictures against such trade, being sold 'in the country of the Saracens' (when they must be found food and a vessel). Quite why a ship might be sold in a Saracen port, where there would be no welfare provision, at least for Christians, to match the travellers' hostels in the west, is far from clear,[3] especially as loss of ship through bad weather or action of armed Saracen vessels released the master from the obligation to pay his crew unless he had already received his freight. The question of ransom is discussed.[4] The general context is the Mediterranean, though the *Amalphitan Table* also mentions seizure by pirates, ransom, and the practice of sailing in convoy, implying that lessons learnt were transferred.

During the crusades, the ships of many nations gathered in the ports of the eastern Mediterranean required some means of dealing with their differing customs. The Jerusalem code seems to have supplied this, and from it, variants spread. This is not the place to discuss the matter in detail. However, references may be retrieved from the Jerusalem code to oaths being taken on the 'Holy Relics'; and to general trade with Saracens, with the transfer of such goods as armour and coats of mail described as the action of 'a bad Christian', and specifically forbidden by a Lateran III canon.

---

1 Twiss, IV, 541.
2 Hornell, *Water Transport*, 271ff, 285ff.
3 Twiss, III, p 215, ch cvi and ch cvii.
4 Twiss, III, p 353, ch clxxxv and ch clxxxvi.

The Pilgrim Trade

If crusaders were one form of human cargo, pilgrims formed another. The codes refer to pilgrims in a number of ways. *Oleron* mentions carriers of passengers to 'Compostella, or to any other place, be it Calais, towards Rome, or elsewhere' who were effectively to be registered and inspected, indicating the importance of this trade. Information may be gleaned about the Church and the sailor from what details remain of the pilgrimage business. The *Good Customs of the Sea* offered three reasons why a sailor might be released from his employment after being bound to the ship's master by oath, the first being to fulfill a religious vow, either of pilgrimage or marriage, the other two relating to promotion.[1] Likewise, marriage and the fulfillment of a previously made vow of pilgrimage are two of the four reasons allowing a managing owner not to sail with his ship; similar regulations applied to anybody managing a ship on his behalf.[2] Vows, and the question of who might be a pilgrim, came within the purlieu of the Church and explain the *Oleron* reference to registration. In *Trani* the vow of pilgrimage was qualified by its having been made 'on the present voyage', and to the named destinations of Compostella, Rome or Jerusalem.[3]

Other Religious Content

The question of diet arises in *Good Customs of the Sea*. Meat is to be provided for the crew on Sundays, Tuesdays and Thursdays; Wednesdays and Fridays remain as the universally traditional days of abstinence.[4]

There are fairly late and limited references to Guilds. A Spanish Guild of Navigators met on the eve of the nativity of Our Lady in the church of St Tecla, Valencia, its officers being elected on the 25th December in the church of Our Lady of the Purification, a reminder of the close association between guilds and Church.[5]

Finally, it is worth noticing the use of the Church calendar. For example, *Gotland, Livonia* (article 8), *Wisby* (article VII) and *Osterlings* (chapter XIII) expected ships to be laid up from St Martin's Day (11 November) until Candlemas (2 February), an expectation prompted by concern for winter weather but the naming of the days confirming the calendar in use was an ecclesiastical one.

---

1 Twiss, IV, 531. See Lateran II, canon 11.
2 In other words, a vow could not be made to void a contract. Twiss, III, p 265, ch cxlix. A vow would normally be witnessed, so what is referred to here is not just a pious intention decided privately at some unspecified time. The Church was very keen that vows be kept.
3 Twiss, IV, 521ff; 531 para xi. Cp Twiss, III, 221.
4 Twiss, III, p 211f, ch c. The *Didache* (Andrew Louth (ed), *Early Christian Writings*, 194): 'Do not keep the same fast days as the hypocrites [Jews]. Mondays and Thursdays are their days for fasting, so yours should be Wednesdays and Fridays'.
5 Twiss, IV, 449f; 521ff; 525. Khalilieh, *Islamic Maritime Law*, refers to a 12th century Islamic guild: 29, n 36.

The Canons

Maritime content in the Lateran Canons is dominated by crusade needs, causing the Church to displace the semi-local custom of the sea codes with a series of bans, all very laudable, upon international shipping. Lawyers build on precedent. In these canons Innocent III and succeeding popes created precedent, each being underwritten with an extension of the spiritual benefits accruing to seamen and ship owners from crusade participation.

The First Lateran Council (1123) offered remission of sins to those who set out to Jerusalem in defense of Christian people (canon 10), promising protection to their property. Those who have 'put crosses on their clothes, intending to journey to Jerusalem or Spain, and have later taken them off' are enjoined to restore them and complete their service. Provision of arms, iron, and timber for galleys is condemned, while those who command or govern 'the gallies and piratical ships of the Saracens' attract a penalty, if caught, of excommunication and enslavement; this could be extended to punish those capturing and disposing of goods at second hand, and to Christians employed in Saracen navigation. The robbery of the ship-wrecked was forbidden. Excommunication (canon 14) was the penalty for anyone attacking pilgrims and 'foreigners', which would include seamen.

The Second Lateran Council (1139) required (canon 11) various groups, including pilgrims and merchants, to be allowed to go peacefully about their business; the repetition of canon 14 of Lateran I implies the continuation of attacks on pilgrims. Canon 13 condemned usury in general, unintentionally leading to the adoption of 'various conveyancing devices which cloaked the real nature of the transactions involved'.[1] Of indirect relevance, for it would apply to pirates capturing ships with clergy on board, on pilgrimage or crusade, was canon 15 which excommunicated anyone laying violent hands on clerics and monks.

The Third Lateran Council (1179) repeated the call for travellers, amongst others, to be immune from harassment, the repetition an indication that the Church was failing to bring sufficient pressure to bear on nations to ensure their protection. Canon 24's explicit condemnation of anyone arming Saracens, or offering services as 'captains or pilots in galleys or Saracen pirate vessels', reveals ways in which the enemy was being helped, the necessity for legislation indicating an existing problem. This canon was to be proclaimed 'throughout the churches of the maritime cities', that is, in the communities which provided most seafaring men, implying that seamen or their families were to be found in these churches. Those captured are enjoined to serve rather as slaves (than as pilots for example) of the Saracens. Mention is made of excommunication for any who rob ship-wrecked Christians 'whom by the rule of faith they are bound to help'. As wreck here is in the context of crusading it may reflect the number of vessels gathered in limited areas.

One concern of this canon was when a captain might attract excommunication, and thus put passengers and crew in spiritual peril.[2] The complicated political

---

1   Twiss, III, clxxiii-iv. Robert Sidney Smith, *The Spanish Guild Merchant*, 50.
2   Alfred J. Andrea, The Relationship of Sea Travellers and Excommunicated

relationship between Rome, Venice, Pisa and Genoa made this a real problem, with excommunication sometimes its result.[1] There was a further complication. Mediterranean ports often required pilot services. A pilot's knowledge has limited application, that is, to the port or channel with which he is familiar. Throughout a crusade a port might change hands, now Muslim, now Christian. Between crusades, Saracen and Christian each travelled in the eastern Mediterranean, and who was to inform them that fresh hostilities had arisen during their time at sea? Those in political control might prevent such useful men from leaving a port, while the pilot himself would appreciate all too clearly that his particular knowledge could not be transferred elsewhere, a situation inapplicable to general pilotage or navigational skills in the Mediterranean. Nevertheless the canon was specific, '[T]hose who act as pilots in pirate Saracen ships, or give them any advice . . . are to be punished with deprivation of their possessions and are to become slaves of those who capture them . . .'.

The Fourth Lateran Council (1215) enshrined much of the careful planning which Innocent III invested in the fifth crusade. This more than its predecessors was a maritime crusade. Canon 71 extended the remission of sins 'not only to those who contribute ships of their own but also to those who are zealous enough to build them for this purpose'. Strictures on corsairs and pirates and anyone helping them in any way were strengthened, though as a pirate was already outside the law, adding to the legislation against him made little difference. That both sides employed corsairs to prosecute their war, and that despite all the planning, penalties, and good intentions, trade with Saracens continued, was confirmed in the requirement that if a ship 'be sold in a country of the Saracens, the managing owner of the vessel is bound to find a vessel and food for the mariners until they shall arrive in a Christian land', for unless a ship was in Saracen territory after capture or seeking refuge from a storm, it can only have been there in pursuit of trade. A managing owner was not so required in a Christian country, perhaps because the local church had a duty of care for distressed mariners, and access to hostels, while further employment on another ship was possible.

Canonical Evidence

The canons imply, in calling for greater efforts, not only that crusade success was diminishing but that the maritime community was increasingly being perceived as vital to success, transporting vast numbers of men and quantities of supplies. Consequently, in a way unparalleled in history, terrestrial communities were becoming aware of the importance of the seafaring community and, to an extent, sharing its hazards. Further, the Church was attempting to regulate what might happen upon the ocean, particularly regarding trade, piracy and wrecking of ships from assorted nations, making it possible to see that papal division of the oceans between Spain and Portugal in 1493 was only the flowering of a bud which had demonstrably sprouted more than two centuries earlier.

Captains . . . , 203-9.
1   R.J.C. Broadhurst, *Travels of Ibn Jubayr*, 325 offers an instance.

4. The Canons and Sea Codes

The common interest in the crusades which appears from examining sea codes alongside canons suggests that the codes must largely owe their existence, at least in written form, to this period. The diversity within the codes confirms that each nation had its own customs. It is clear from the canons that popes made no claim to regulate what happened on board ship beyond the ban on allowing assistance to the Saracens. In other words, each ship was still treated as the territory of a particular nation, whilst the sea was recognised as a discrete area, with simple rules for universal application.[1] The concept of *mare liberum* has been discussed. A further distinction now appears; if the vaster part of the ocean was the *mare liberum*, a more limited part of it was the legitimate interest of a particular nation, principally as has been suggested, regarding defense, and by extension, the notion of *mare clausum* begins to appear. In modern terms, the distinction is between the high seas and territorial waters.

Almost nothing from the sea codes found its way into canon law, beyond what related to crusades, because the Church was building upon an existing code. Some canonical material found its way into the codes, the Church lending the force of its judicial system in an attempt to strengthen those parts of the codes with which it had a shared and direct interest: wrecking, crusade transport, pilgrimage, oaths, and the fate of the dead. A useful word, though of another period, to describe the process would be symbiotic.

It is possible to understand the extraordinary situation created by the crusades, at least regarding the sea, by examining some of the contemporary circumstance. The number of people it involved is remarkable. A ship travelling between Acre and Messina in 1184 was said to be carrying over two thousand passengers.[2] Louis IX, returning from crusading in 1254, was accompanied by more than eight hundred. Pilgrims too were measured in thousands. Crusaders and pilgrims would be accompanied by clergy, often bishops, sometimes the papal legate, meaning that sacraments might be available; also, some moral teaching - Jacques de Vitry, travelling from Genoa to Acre, lamented the presence of harlots on board to service the sailors.

Conciliar rulings on trade with the Saracens, on usury, or the need for sacramental confession before receiving Easter Communion could be circumvented; Mackay refers to early fourteenth-century absolutions obtainable by Spaniards trading with the infidel through 'a special royal-ecclesiastical tribunal', perhaps a result of the peculiar history of Spain *vis à vis* the Arab world; Mackay gives no further information.[3]

There are, however, examples of Rome issuing other rulings with maritime impact, related rather to pastoral matters than crusades, for example in

---

1 It was recognised early in English history that the Crown had the right to goods and ships captured at sea, and to bestow them as a reward. In other words, the vessel and its cargo were seen as captured territory. A survival is the continuing practice of arresting a ship. R.G. Marsden, *Documents Relating to the Law and Custom of the Sea*, vol I, section IX.
2 Benjamin Z. Kedar, The Passenger List of a Crusader Ship, 1250, 267ff.
3 A. Mackay, *Spain in the Middle Ages . . .* , 165.

response to an archiepiscopal enquiry whether newly Christian Norwegian fishermen in communities which depended upon their industry for food might fish on days prescribed for rest.[1] Shoals of fish, not observing the ecclesiastical calendar, needed to be caught on the day of their appearing. In summary, Rome permitted work when 'seeking things necessary for food and clothing' rather than 'servile labour', and that a 'suitable distribution' should be made to 'Christ's poor', i.e. that unavoidable labour of the seaman on holy days and consequent absence from Mass was permitted. The offering to the poor has echoes of the deodand. The diet of the seaman on days of fasting or abstinence would depend upon what was available. Nothing of these seems to appear in contemporary homilies or penitentials, perhaps because the matter is one of common sense.

If the seafarer found himself enmeshed in legal codes influenced or promulgated by the Church, this was an experience shared with his brother ashore. The novelty here is two-fold: the direct intervention of the Church and the need for laws or canons to meet the new situation produced by the crusades, where, unusually, if not uniquely (compare the French wine fleet), large and multi-national fleets were gathered in one place for lengthy periods, in many cases provided with chaplains. It is dangerous to argue from silence, but the practical nature of what is said suggests that what is not said, particularly regarding the duty of all Christians at Easter, recognised that the seafarer is a special case who is not excommunicated when prevented by his profession from fulfilling a religious duty which would be required of him were he ashore.

---

[1] I am grateful to Dr Norman Tanner SJ for this reference: X, ii, 9, 3 (Friedberg, ii, col 72).

5. Religious Practice at Sea

While most information available for this period relates to shore-side provision *for* the sailor, something of his religious life at sea can be found in other sources, deriving particularly from the crusades, atypical of contemporary shipping, and the conversion of the Vikings, their absorption into the trade routes of Christendom a major factor. Sagas, journals and notarial documents allow sight of the Christian at sea from Christian and non-Christian perspectives and allow something to be said about such religious activity as prayers, use of Gospels, and the celebration of the Mass.

It has been suggested already that, given the transfer of technology from Muslim to Christian communities in this period, it would be odd if there was no similar exchange in the realm of religious thought. There is evidence that some Christians, when captured, made the spiritual journey from Christ to Mahomet, with some Muslims journeying the other way.[1] Muslim artifacts in Christian churches may have some relevance here; glazed ceramic bowls, *bacini*, originating in the Muslim world and surviving in the walls of churches in Tuscany and other parts of Italy, illustrate ships belonging to both communities.[2]

The importance of high value and readily marketable cargoes essential to the success of a crusade, which put crews at risk, explains why the councils of the Church should be concerned with regulating the conduct of the sea, for the Church was the uniting factor between Christian armies and the instigator of the crusades. Its general concern that travellers, especially pilgrims, should be able to travel in safety was not new. The problem was its enforcement. The crusader was a special kind of pilgrim and the seaman a special kind of crusader. During and after the Second Crusade crusaders were set apart as pilgrims entitled in a special way and with special force to the protection of the Church.[3] One of the functions of the crusader badge was to identify the wearer as such, and its bestowal carried sufficient value, admittedly enhanced by other papal provisions, for the cross to be worn by bogus crusaders. Any man carrying a 'bande of Seint George' would

---

1   John Bryan Williams, The Making of a Crusade, 48.
2   Francesco Gabrieli, *Arab Historians of the Crusades*, 265. For *bacini* see John H. Pryor and Sergio Bellabarba, The Medieval Muslim Ships of the Pisan *Bacini*, 99ff, esp 105. *Bacini* and *graffiti* of contemporary ships from Moslem and Christian sources are illustrated in David Nicolle, Shipping in Islamic Art . . . , 168-189.
3   James A. Brundage, *Medieval Canon Law and the Crusader*, 160ff.

readily be identified as other than Saracen.[1] A canon of Lateran I refers to the wearing of crosses. For those who were captured, a pressing need throughout the period was some means of being ransomed. This was not peculiar to one side. Nor was concern limited to prisoners who had been armed or part of the war machine before capture, Ibn Jubayr referring to 'the distribution of aid to voyagers and to poor pilgrims'.[2] The Mercedarians and Trinitarians have been mentioned as part of the solution to this problem.

Oaths were required of various categories of seafarer: the crew, and particularly the *scribarius* (clerk or scribe of the contract), *nauclerius* (the master), *camerarius* (literally the keeper of the chamber, perhaps a kind of steward, quartermaster or purser), are to swear upon the 'evangels' (Gospels) to maintain the ship, its tackle and its cargoes.[3] Whether access to the Gospels in some form, or possibly relics, was ashore or afloat is not clear, nor are there any hints on how they were used, beyond the taking of oaths, but a Gospel found on board a ship by a Saracen would put a Christian crew at risk.

Crusade Clergy at Sea

The crusades ensured the presence at sea of clergy at every level from legate down. Like other crusaders, though perhaps not seamen, clergy had the benefit of the protection of their estates in their country of origin for three years (cp the preservation of wrecked goods for three years in the Oleron code), necessary if a man was to avoid being deprived of his benefice, which otherwise for absence would have been the case, and removing a major obstacle to his taking the Cross. Since those in Holy Orders were forbidden to fight, his role would have been understood in a pastoral sense, despite exceptions, prompting the question, What would have been expected of him whilst at sea?

It is known that sacramental confession was available. In 1147 Germans, Flemings and English men on 164 vessels assembled at Dartmouth. It is possible to glimpse the role of clergy in a contemporary record:

> Among these people of so many languages [there were] the strongest pledges of harmony and friendship; moreover they imposed as sanctions very severe laws as a death for a death, a tooth for a tooth. Likewise women were not to come out in public; everyone was to keep the peace, except on proof of injury; every week meetings were to be held, separately, by laity and by clergy, unless by chance important matters required a joint meeting of both. Each ship was to have its own priest, and the same things are ordered to be observed as in parishes . . . each man to confess each week and to communicate every Sunday.[4]

The Crusade was understood as an occasion through which grace would be imparted, perhaps accounting for the strict conditions regarding confession and the reception of Holy Communion, which in this form would only be

---

1 Twiss, I, 282ff.
2 Ibn Jubayr, 203: '*la distribtion de secours aux voyageurs at aux pèlerins pauvres* . . .'.
3 Ashburner cxxxvii, cxxxii, clxxxi.
4 Osbemus, *de Expugnatione Lyxbonensis* . . . , vol 1, cxliv.

5. Religious Practise at Sea

required generally after the Fourth Lateran Council (1215). Canons seldom appear overnight, so this may be evidence of a Church beginning to move in this direction. Implicit in this passage is the presence of a number of clergy, which was not always the case; in 1248, when ships left Marseilles, that it was the captain who called upon all to sing, here the *Veni creator spiritus*, in unison, before the sails were unfurled, suggests either a general custom when sails were raised, or the absence clergy.[1]

The passage refers to the presence of women, of whom, other examples can be found. A later example of prostitutes on board can be offered, but those here could have been devout women caught up with crusade fever, or the accompanying spouses of wealthy crusaders, their presence making for a mixed community, more like the parish ashore than that usually found at sea. Whatever the situation, the law on each ship has an Old Testament ring ('an eye for an eye'), beyond normal parish expectation. The requirement of weekly confession and communion, when shore-side practice would have been weekly attendance at Mass but confession and reception of Communion infrequent, suggests a clerical author informing the situation with his own agenda, and perhaps repeated in this passage regarding a storm at sea, when many on board expected death:

> How many there, being penitent, how many confessing with sorrow their sins and negligences, and with groaning washing with a flood of tears the conversion of their pilgrimage, howsoever begun, contrite on the altar of their heart, were offering sacrifices to God.[2]

It is implicit that, while the willingness to confess was a natural response to severe storms, especially in the Bay of Biscay, the times were calling for more frequent confession. The priestly gloss of the writer appears most clearly when he explains the gratitude of the survivors to God for receiving 'the singular privilege of a heavenly benefit, so that it would be a long task to tell one by one, with how many visions the divine wonders opened their sight'. In other words, the storm was God's instrument in bringing the crusaders to their knees and purging their intention in taking up the Cross, just as - ashore - defeats by the Muslims ascribed to Christian sins would lead to demands for the latter to do penance.

The question of the frequency of confession at sea is not susceptible of a straightforward answer. The presence of a priest was not essential; crusaders in danger of death might confess to each other.[3] H.C. Lea, no friend of the Catholic exercise of this sacrament, used the example of a French knight in 1250 confessing on his bed to Joinville to confirm that this was the case.[4] 'Peter Cantor declares that when men in danger of shipwreck confess their sins publicly, they are obliterated from the memory of those who are saved', wrote Lea, discussing the Seal (confidentiality) of the Sacrament and a belief that sins are supernaturally erased from

---

1   Joinville & Villehardouin, 196.
2   Osbemus, *de Expugnatione Lyxbonensis . . .* , cxliv.
3   Joinville & Villehardouin, 253.
4   H.C. Lea, *History of Auricular Confession . . .* , vol 1, 218ff, 228, 274, 283, 422.

the mind of the person hearing them in a quasi-sacramental context. No absolution follows, its need obviated by genuine contrition implicit in an open confession. Before the twelfth century the general agent of absolution had been the bishop, afterwards the parish priest, with the understanding that *in articulo mortis* absolution might be received from any priest; a dangerous voyage, effectively any voyage, would satisfy the canonist as being *in articulo mortis*.

There is no shortage of evidence that storm-engendered piety was soon forgotten. Jacques de Vitry (d.1240), Bishop of Acre, preached eloquently against the vices of crusaders in his See port, reminding them of their calls upon God in a strong storm, who after

> the storm was over, returned to their usual conduct on the very same day, visiting their whores, who had hidden in the bilge and in their usual way stealing the twice cooked food and other victuals of the pilgrims . . . and the wine, and carried off whatever they could . . . with no fear of God.[1]

Again he mentions women on board. There is evidence of at least one shipload of French women, other than these, who sailed with the troops to render them similar comfort; an unusual example of a pious service. In a further homily (CCXII), de Vitry, giving an insight into the contemporary maritime community, castigated 'treacherous men' for robbing pilgrims and selling them as slaves to the Saracens, and 'sailors' for drowning pilgrims and merchants after robbing them in ships hired on terms which despite loss at sea required payment on arrival in port; he called them to repentance. In a third homily, he told of seafarers who had survived one storm, in which they cried to God for mercy, only to find themselves in another.

> But this storm drove the [other] storm from the minds of most sinners: for many, with tears came to confession, who had persisted in their sins for many years. And merchants and important men received the sign of the Cross from my hand, for when they cried to the Lord, the Lord sent us calm weather.[2]

Another remedy for ship-board problems was an adaptation of the church procession. There is liturgical evidence that by the ninth century liturgical processions, originating in Gaul, had spread to Rome, particularly a penitential procession repeated on three days before the feast of the Ascension. These processions, originally accompanied by a litany, an act of petition, were often, over time, reduced to fit the limited space of a church building. Villehardouin in his *Life of St Louis* recorded that when there were problems with navigation, the Dean of Maurupt, who happened to be on board, recommended three processions on successive Saturdays round the ship's two masts.[3] It is tempting to reflect that any problem is likely to have been solved, one way or another, after three Saturdays, but in this instance, one procession sufficed. Villehardouin was so impressed that he advised the same solution to a problem encountered ashore.[4]

---

1   Jacques de Vitry, *Exempla*, homily CCCXI.
2   R.B.C. Huygens, *Lettres de Jacques de Vitry*, Letter 2.
3   Cp Michael Lapidge, *Anglo-Saxon Litanies of the Saints*, 9.
4   Joinville & Villehardouin, 196f, 209.

Non Crusade Clergy and the Sea

It is difficult to imagine quite what the function of a bishop at sea might be when travelling, especially as he would, by definition, be outside his diocese. In the medieval period he was most likely travelling for one of four reasons: to Rome on Church business, thence or elsewhere on State business, on pilgrimage, or on crusade. Bishops, seldom possible to identify by name, appear on enough port seals to allow speculation that their portrayal indicates something more than the idea of the bishop guiding the ship of the Church.[1] It may be that each refers to a port's patron saint, to St Nicholas (the archetypal maritime bishop), or to a particular bishop with a special relationship with the port of the seal. Each bishop is shown on board ship. Each ship, judging by the waves depicted, is meant to be understood to be at sea. In most instances the bishop's hand is raised in blessing, a conventional representation.

Occasionally it is a priest who appears, as on the Lubeck port seal.[2] Succeeding Lubeck seals show two figures on board a ship, one of whom has his hand raised, on at least one of the seals almost certainly in blessing, as waving would be a rather pointless gesture to represent. The ship is at sea but it is hard to guess if the priest is there to calm or bless the waters. The town seals of Dublin, late thirteenth century, show a figure at the foot of a ship's mast (Fig. 4), the density of the waves and the presence of swimming fish confirmation that the ship is to be understood at sea; likewise, the sail is unfurled and the anchor shipped at the bow. Like the Lubeck seal priestly identity is suggested not by the figure's garments but by his action. Here the priest figure is elevating a chalice, presumably as part of a Mass, an interpretation weakened by the proximity of two figures facing away from the elevation but strengthened by fanfaring trumpeters, one on each castle, who might be expected by a liturgist to greet the sacred moment of elevation; it is impossible to be certain for, as Richard of Devizes recorded, an English custom was to drain cups 'to the sound of clarions and the clangour of trumpets', and it may have been the custom of others, too.[3] The Dover seal of 1300 includes two trumpeters on the forecastle as part of assorted activity on board.[4] Whether the seals taken together are enough to indicate that, at least in one tradition, it was known for priests to say Mass at sea at this time is a matter of opinion.

Clergy generally were more likely to be found in port. Here, beyond their parish duties, there are examples of their blessing a vessel or a fleet preparing to sail. The involvement of a religious rite in the building or launch of a ship is peculiar neither to Christianity nor to one country.[5] The Icelander Thorir

---

1 Herbert Ewe, *Schiffe auf Siegeln*: Mardick (59, 152), Calais (59, 113), Gravelines (62, 131f), Dieppe (118), Kaub (141), Sluis (190).
2 Ewe, *Schiffe auf Siegeln*, Lubeck (147, 148), Dublin (119).
3 Richardi Divisensis, *Cronicon De Tempore Regis Richardi Primi*, 73f.
4 Ian Friel, *Ignorant of Nautical Matters?*, 91.
5 L. Blue, E. Kentley, S. McGrail, U. Mishra, 'The Patia Fishing Boat of Orissa . . . , 189ff, esp 201. James Hornell, *Water Transport*, 270ff.

the Sea-Farer 'had a ship built in Sogn to be blessed by Bishop Sigurd'.[1] In *The Saga of Grettir the Strong,* also twelfth century and from Iceland, 'They asked the bishop to consecrate a large sea-going ship . . . and the bishop did so'.[2] It may be this sort of episcopal involvement which led Orlyg, sailing for Iceland from the Hebrides(?), in bad weather, to make a vow to Bishop Patrick of the Hebrides, in which Orlyg promised to name the land at which he might arrive safely after the bishop.[3]

In England, the thirteenth-century Bishop Richard of Chichester blessed a number of things associated with the sea, including nets, and a bridge at Bramber in Sussex.[4] Most records of such blessings tend to be later; a well-known example is the Bishop of Bangor's blessing of the *Grace Dieu* at Southampton in 1418. The blessing seems to have preceded the completion of the ship, possibly at the keel laying, probably at the launching of the hull, before fitting out. When it sailed for the first time it flew among others 'an embroidered streamer of St Nicholas'.[5] The Frenchman Villehardouin wrote of similar decorating of ships preparing to attack Constantinople in 1203.

There is some evidence that sailors carried with them tokens associated with saints, especially Nicholas, and it is likely that many of these had been blessed. Wreck excavations sometimes reveal pilgrim badges, which may mean only that a ship was carrying pilgrims. However, an article on 'Boy Bishop' tokens suggests that a secondary function of the tokens was as 'amulets for sailors'. Nicholas tokens are thought to have been used as coinage for disposable alms during the reign of the Boy Bishop, a ceremony connected with the saint; they are of East Anglian origin, found at Norwich, Dunwich and Bury St Edmunds - where they seem to have been made. They carry various motifs, of three balls (an emblem of St Nicholas), a bishop (a common representation of St Nicholas), and in one example a ship. On the obverse an inscription asks for the saint's prayers.[6]

Religious Life on Board

Religious life on board is hard to picture in any age, principally for lack of evidence. Occasional acts of worship have already been mentioned, together with some evidence for a religious origin in the widespread abstinence from meat on Wednesdays and Fridays. Alternatively, it appears that by the fourteenth century Venetians fasted on Fridays and Saturdays.[7] If there is any evidence of avoiding sailing on Friday, with its association with the Crucifixion, for this period, it has been well hidden: King Louis, for example, sailed on a Friday in 1249.[8]

1 *Landnámabók,* 106 para 250.
2 G.A. Hight (trans), 1965, 104.
3 *Landnámabók,* 24.
4 David Jones (ed), *Saint Richard of Chichester,* 204.
5 Mrs W.J. Carpenter-Turner, The Building of the *GRACE DIEU* . . . , 55-72, esp 68. Ian Friel, Henry V's *Grace Dieu* . . . , 3-19, esp 4.
6 S.E. Rigold, The St Nicholas or "Boy Bishop" Tokens, 87-108 and plates VIII-XIa.
7 Frederic C. Lane, *Venice and History,* 265.
8 Joinville & Villehardouin, *Chronicles,* 201.

5. Religious Practise at Sea

13th century Dublin seal.
Source: Herbert Ewe, Schiffe auf Siegeln, Berlin 1972.

Some customs survived from pre-Christian times. Seamen carrying the escaping Rainier (c. 1143), in the upheaval between Stephen and Maud, 'resorted to the ancient custom of casting lots' to identify the cause when their ship became 'immovable in the midst of the sea'. After casting lots three times (to be certain), Rainier, his wife and their ill-gotten goods, identified by lot, were placed in a small boat and the ship 'immediately gained her power of moving . . . but the skiff sunk'.[9] The use of lots and casting adrift is at least as old as the Jonah story. The weather seems universally to be understood as an indicator of the divine will.

While these meagre examples hint at religious life as lived on board, there are three questions which still remain to be asked, their answers allowing a great deal of disparate material to be brought together. The first relates to the identity of lay Christians at sea, who are most easily seen in contrast with Muslims, or in the case of the Vikings, with those yet to be Christian. Who were these lay Christians and how might they be recognised as Christians? The second examines whether there were Bibles or Gospels at sea. This has nothing to do with the modern idea that a Gospel should be put in every hand

---

9 Joseph Stevenson (ed & trans), 'The History of William of Newburgh', 416. cp the action of a French layman in Fynes Moryson, *Itinerary*, 212.

which, in the case of the seafarer, dates from the foundation of the British and Foreign Bible Society and its maritime offshoot, the Merchant Seamen's Auxiliary Bible Society, following the Napoleonic wars. The presence of a Bible or Gospel may, however, indicate a relationship with the Church. The taking of oaths on the Gospels confirms that Gospels were sometimes available and hints at some sort of belief, for oaths almost invariably started with a Christian formula. At the point of joining his ship, and at other key moments on the voyage, the requirement for a seaman to take an oath has been shown, effectively a quasi-religious ceremony. The third question is whether Mass was permitted at sea. The number of ships, mostly crusade or pilgrim vessels, on which a priest to say Mass would be found was relatively small. However, the answer to this question highlights the way in which the sea was perceived by the Church and will return to the concept of *mare nullius*.

Identity of Christians at Sea

The vast majority of Christians at sea were not clergy. Religious obligations on lay people were few, increasing from the thirteenth century, the principal one relating to Easter duties. Christians as Christians would have been invisible to those around them unless praying in public, or wearing some sort of emblem (perhaps a pilgrim badge or relic), their behaviour or insignia only conspicuous if unusual, rendering them visible particularly when contrasted with Vikings or Muslims.

Ibn Jubayr, travelling in the Mediterranean in the 1180s on a pilgrim ship, noted on All Saints' Day (1st November) that it
> was a festival for Christians, and they celebrated it with lighted candles. Hardly one of them, big or little, male or female, but carried a candle in his hand. Their priests led them in prayers on the ship, then one by one, rose to preach a sermon and recall the articles of their faith. The whole ship, from top to bottom, was luminous with kindled lamps.[1]

It is hard to imagine that the crew was not involved in the ceremony, although the context is clearly a pilgrim ship and cannot suggest that All Saints' was celebrated in this way on ships generally. The sermons referred to may be a Muslim observer's understanding of the homily and Creed. Twelfth-century lay English Christians were required to know at least the Creed, *Pater* and *Ave*.[2] They would also be used to hearing the Gospel in the Mass explained in the vernacular. In this respect the English church was in step with the continent. What Ibn Jubayr describes does not require the leaders to be priests. The combination of being led, with candles and prayers, might easily be a description of the kind of procession referred to by Villehardouin.

It cannot be said with certainty that newly baptised Vikings were required to know the Creed, *Pater* and *Ave*, only that it would be unlikely if conversion was a forced or group event. Accounts of maritime conversions are rare. In 999 AD

---

1   *Ibn Jubayr*, 328.
2   Edgar, The so-called "Canons of . . . ", 322.

5. Religious Practise at Sea

an Icelandic crew converted, under pressure, and 149 of the crew were baptised.[1] No detail is given of the process. It is possible that to seafaring people the Gospel message presented the Christian God as the more powerful protector, as at the end of the tenth century, when a pagan poetess called Steinunn wrote of Thangbrand the missionary, who was drifting out to sea in a gale, that 'Christ did not protect his ship', but rather that he was destroyed by Thor.[2]

That pagans were aware of various levels of commitment among Christians is evidenced by various of the *Sagas*. The principal distinction seems to have been to whom one prayed, especially in time of trouble. One example concerns a poet, 'a Christian from the Hebrides', travelling to Greenland at an unknown date; nothing else is said of his religion beyond his composition of the *Hafgerdinga Lay*, described as the oldest surviving Christian verse-prayer in Icelandic, which has this refrain:

> I beseech the immaculate Master of monks
> To steer my journeys;
> May the Lord of the lofty heavens
> Hold his strong hand over me.[3]

The connection between the Hebrides and the Master of monks is not hard to find, for the first Christians there, as in Iceland, were monks, attested by place names prefixed Papa, and suggesting the primary source of the Christian faith as received by the Vikings. Another who seems to have found faith in the same area was Aud, a formidable woman who built a ship and sailed with twenty freeborn men on the route Caithness-Orkney-Faroes-Iceland, who was said to have 'been baptised and was a devout Christian', but whose one recorded Christian activity seems to have been the erection of crosses.[4]

The saints to whom the seafaring community addressed its prayers, a universal activity confirmed in many sources, and by the common practice of naming ships after saints, have already been considered. In theory clients of a saint would attempt a pilgrimage to their patron's shrine. The *Thómas Saga Erkibyskups*, which concerned Becket, after noting the long history of Church links between England and Iceland, gave as an example the tale of a whaler who invoked Becket in time of need responding to what seems to have been a satisfactory answer to his prayer with a pilgrimage to Canterbury.[5] Although pilgrimage was one reason for which a seafarer might leave his ship, examples of pilgrim-sailors are rare; for it to appear in the sea codes suggests that it cannot have been uncommon, which could explain why no readily available source seems to have thought it noteworthy.

Some rather feeble Christians appear in the *Sagas*, and the record makes clear they are considered so, perhaps because they provide a memorable contrast to robust Vikings. In each case their identity lies in the god to whom prayer was

---
1   *Laxdaela Saga*, 147f. The number converted suggests more than one crew.
2   Dag Strömbäck, *The Conversion of Iceland*, 50.
3   Magnus Magnusson, *Viking Expansion Westwards*, 112. *Landnámabók*, 49f. Gwyn Jones (trans), *The Norse Atlantic Saga*, 189.
4   *Landnámabók*, 51f.
5   *op cit*, E. Magnusson (trans), viiif, xii.

made. An example is Helgi the Lean, apparently twelfth century, who
> went to Iceland with his wife and children . . . Helgi's faith was very much mixed: he believed in Christ but invoked Thor when it came to voyages and difficult times . . . Helgi believed in Christ and called his home after him.

Another was Brodir (c.1000), a Viking raider, along with Ospak lying off the Isle of Man with thirty ships, who, having 'been a Christian had been consecrated a deacon, but he had abandoned his faith and become an apostate' and 'sacrificed to heathen spirits and was deeply skilled in magic'.[1] Viking seafarers who had become Christians were expected no longer to offer sacrifices, replacing them, perhaps as in Aud's case with crosses, perhaps for the majority with Christian prayers and, where possible, Masses.

A peculiar case is that of John de Courtney, an English soldier and a great patron of Ford Abbey; here it was not a question of to whom he prayed, but his understanding of his place in the prayers of the monks. When in danger of shipwreck John 'saved the ship by his confidence in the prayers of "*monachi mei*"' despite his companions arguing that the monks would be asleep in bed. Wood suggests that here is an example of the monks' idea of a good patron's attitude for, on his safe return, John was more generous than ever.[2] He had prayed at length in the storm, asking God to hear the prayers of the monks and to 'bring us safe and sound . . . to the harbour for which we long' with the result that God 'placed the boat on the longed-for shore'.[3]

The Bible at Sea

A question to which there is no easy answer is whether medieval seafarers had access to Bibles; it presents a number of problems. The Bible was unwieldy, hand-copied and in sections, until the advent of printing. Those who could read required a facility in Latin. Of these, few, even among the clergy, would have possessed a Bible in part or in whole. Those who indulged in private devotions were likely to be wealthy people, able to afford a hand-written volume, with the education and the time necessary. Sometimes portions of Scripture might be kept as a kind of 'charm' or talisman, when its principal purpose would not be to be read. Chapter Six will reveal that some English ships carried Bibles, following the invention of the printing press, rendering them of particular interest to the Spanish Inquisition. Only in the nineteenth century, age of cheap printing and increasing literacy levels, would Bibles begin to appear on board ship in the hands of crew members with any frequency.

The usual book for private devotion, a Book of Hours, or Prymer,[4] containing calendar, the Little Office of Our Lady,[5] the Office of the Dead, and a few psalms, prayers and sentences, was intended to be more accessible than the exacting monastic office books. The Book of Hours developed from

---

1 *Njàls Saga*, M. Magnusson and H. Palsson (trans), 345.
2 Susan Wood, *English Monasteries and . . .*, 125.
3 Dugdale, *Monasticon*, vol 5d, 379.
4 *The Annotated Book of Common Prayer*, 14.
5 *Facsimiles of Horae de Beata Maria Virgine*, E.S. Dewick (ed), xv, xvii. *Ave Maris Stella* is one of the hymns.

5. Religious Practise at Sea

the *libelli precum*, pocket-sized books of prayers for daily use by the laity, and associated with the later Middle Ages.[1] No known English copy predates 1400, probably because English copies were ordered to be destroyed in 1549.[2] The *Pilgrim's Sea-Voyage and Sea-Sickness* reveals pilgrims reading on board ship to pass the time:

> 53 Som layde theyr bookys on theyr kne,
> 54 And rad so long they myght nat se

as a distraction from or precaution against a coming storm.[3] Private reading was usually aloud, audible to those around, including crew members. The Prymer or its predecessor was probably the *bookys* referred to here; *bookys* were not for the working seaman, nor improved by the dampness at sea, but this verse confirms that books were to be found on board ship and seamen (the *Pilgrim's Sea Voyage* apparently written by somebody familiar with shipboard life) were aware of them.

There is more to this question, however, than the obvious answer that working seamen lacked the time, resources or skill to use religious books. It has already been noticed that the sea codes required oaths on the Gospels or relics, apparently interchangeable. Relics, and most Christians would possess some sort of relic, were available almost anywhere, portable, and linked usually to a favoured saint. In Christian ports, where the parish church, probably possessed of copies of the Gospels or even a complete Bible, was but a step from the docks or the merchant's office (especially if housed in one of Slessarev's *ecclesiae mercatorum*) where crew would be recruited or business conducted, there was ready access to a copy of the Gospels. The same codes envisaged situations where crews might be discharged, and presumably recruited, in Saracen ports where there would be no nearby church, possession of the Gospels dangerous, and circumstances such that codes allowed the taking of oaths on relics.

Though references in the codes to Gospels are widespread, firmly connected with the taking of oaths, and sometimes accompanied by a form of oath, yet they give no evidence that Gospels were read by seamen.[4] They reveal that at least one person on the ship, the *scribarius*, could read, but the function of the Gospels, as now in a court of law, was to be touched or held rather than read. A notarial document from Genoa (1213) has a dockside contract which makes this clear:

> I will place myself under a bond to no-one nor will I surrender to a pledge without your permission and goodwill until . . . I swear by touching the most holy (sacrosanctis) gospels to pay attention to all the aforesaid matters . . . unless by just impediment of God . . . But if the just impediment of God has intervened. . . .[5]

---

1 Michael S. Driscoll, Penance in Transition: Popular Piety and Practise, 133f.
2 Henry Littlehale (ed), *The Prymer*, pt ii, p ix. Littlehale's *A Layman's Prayer-Book in English*, vi, suggests that though no earlier books survive, there must have been people's prayer books throughout the Middle Ages.
3 *The Stacions of Rome* . . ., Frederick J. Furnivall (ed).
4 *Gli Statuti Marittimi Veneziani fino al 1255*, (hereafter GSMV)109.
5 Eugene H Byrne (ed), *Genoese Shipping* . . ., document X, 76. The text is in dog Latin but the oath was probably in the vernacular.

The saving phrase 'an impediment of God' appears in many contracts, as it does in the maritime codes, and is likely to have as much religious significance as in today's insurance contracts.

Similar documents survive from Venice for the same period.[1] The circumstances requiring an oath vary. The point here is not the content of the oath but that there were numerous occasions when an oath might be required of a seafarer, in each case using a relic or Gospel: not to sell the ship to other than a Venetian, or in case of danger to honest persons who must take an oath 'on the gospels of God'; when loading a ship; joining a ship; to inform the master of anyone acting against his regulations; (to the owner?) when the master does not keep the rules. The master was bound by oath not to sell, cause to be sold, alienate or cause to be alienated, supplies or cargo, or to load his ship above the load line or *cruces*, a name here without religious significance. These oaths, and that required of the *scribarius,* all begin, 'I swear by the holy gospels of God'. In return the Venetian authorities were bound by oath to ensure that the ship had been loaded properly before allowing it to sail. It was to these authorities, 'consuls', that the ship's master was bound by oath.[2]

Does this discussion suggest Gospels were carried on board ship? The absence of references to Gospels in northern literature implies that in the matter of oaths, on Gospels or relics, this was the practice of those countries which had an established Christian presence, suggesting in turn the proximity of churches where Gospels would be found. The custom of maritime groups conducting their affairs in a church prompts a similar conclusion. If it is asked further whether Gospels were to be found outside churches, it seems that parts of the Bible, Gospels especially, were in circulation in the vernacular amongst lay people from fairly early in the medieval period.[3] They were not cheap. By the thirteenth century, according to Wormald, small copies of the Gospels or Psalms were superseding the large volumes of preceding centuries,[4] but he adds that by the end of the twelfth century Gospels were beginning to fall out of fashion, making way for the circulation of the missal.[5] Psalms and missals seem not to have been acceptable substitutes for oaths. Whatever the truth generally, the conclusion that for the seaman it would be unusual for a copy of the Gospels to accompany him at sea seems logical.

The Mass at Sea

If the question of access to the Gospels prompts no clear answer, that relating to whether the Mass could be offered at sea is, if anything, more convoluted. There are surprisingly few references to the Mass at sea, especially in the earlier Middle Ages, indicating either that it was infrequent or too common to be mentioned. Those instructions to the fleet of 1147 leaving Dartmouth could

---

1 GSMV.
2 GSMV, 50, 80, 94, 103, 104, 107, 108, 168, 175.
3 Leonard E. Boyle, Innocent III and Vernacular Versions of Scripture, 98f.
4 Francis Wormald, Bible Illustration in Medieval Manuscripts, 315, 321.
5 Wormald, Bible Illustration . . . , 326.

5. Religious Practise at Sea

not have been clearer, that Mass should be said every Sunday on each ship, but this was a fleet connected with a crusade. Other references to the Mass, a few contemporary, some later, suggest the opposite was the case. Joinville and Villehardouin mention the Sacrament on board the ship of Louis IX (mid thirteenth century).[1] In Joinville's version, the king's ship was in a major storm off Cyprus, when 'the king . . . went and lay with arms outstretched to form a cross before the body of Our Lord on the altar'. Villehardouin seems to be writing of the same event when he says that in the chaos ensuing from the ship's striking, Brother Raymond 'found [the king] lying prostrate on the deck in front of the Body of Our Lord on the altar'. Despite having chaplains on board, this only indicates that on Louis's ship the Sacrament was reserved rather than the Mass celebrated, while Louis went ashore in 1249, when anchored off Limassol Point, for the celebration of the Whitsunday Mass.[2] It may be objected that the royal ship and the response of its (soon to be) canonised royal master was atypical of the period. The point, however, is that if Mass is not celebrated on board for the king, it will hardly be celebrated on board for anyone else. If it is objected further that to say Mass ashore was simply more convenient, neither Villehardouin nor Joinville mention Mass being celebrated on board at any point, despite the presence of chaplains and a chapel relatively large in proportion to the ship (large enough for the king to prostrate himself, and someone else to enter), despite references to the reserved Sacrament.

The king's ship was not unique in the matter of carrying the Sacrament. It seems also to feature in *The Statutes and Ordinances to be Keped in Time of Werre*. Although these statutes are not maritime they appear among the maritime codes, and reflect the attitude of their period (Twiss suggested early fifteenth century).[3] They penalise anyone other than a priest touching 'the sacrament of Goddes body, upon peyne to be drawne and hanged', with the same for touching 'the boxe or vessele, in whiche the precious sacrament is yn'.[4] Laws are seldom made without being occasioned, usually more than once, suggesting here a sensitivity to what was sometimes perceived as a godless attitude among crew or passengers. The fifteenth-century Fabri, as will appear, gave this attitude as one reason for not carrying the sacrament on board. The concern was typical of the period, for Gregory VII in 1080 had used the same reason for forbidding vernacular services in Bohemia.[5]

The *Thómas Saga Erkibyskups* recorded the fleeing Becket in 1164 being

---

1 *Chronicles of the Crusades*, 172, 319.
2 *Ibid*, 201. There is an ambiguity here as the text reads, 'He went ashore on Whitsunday. After we had heard mass, a violent raging wind, coming across the sea . . . '. The *Histoire de S. Louis*, Lille, no date or editor, 72: '*Le roi descendit à terre le jour de la Pentecôte. Quand nous eûmes entendu la messe, un vent violent et fort . . .* '. The most logical explanation is that there was an obligation to attend Mass on a this day. The raging wind may have had a Pentecostal significance for the hagiographer, or, since it came *du côté d'Égypte*, the significance may lay in the Exodus.
3 Twiss I, 282, nn 1 and 2.
4 Twiss 1, 282, para 2.
5 *Gregory VII, Correspondence of*, 148 (Bk VII, 11).

provided by the Prior of Eastry with a small boat to cross the Channel 'and two brisk mass-brothers, to make him fellowship', sailing from Sandwich.[1] If this was to allow the Archbishop to say Mass regularly, it being usual to have at least a minimal congregation to make the responses, then there may be a hint here that Mass could be said at sea, for the Channel crossing could, on occasion, take many days. However, it seems that the custom of Becket's time was not for Mass to be celebrated daily unless by a monastic or chantry priest. Bishop Thomas of Hereford for example, sufficiently devout for popular canonisation, celebrated Mass only on Sundays and holy days.[2]

In the *Chronicle of Henry of Livonia*, which covers forced evangelization in the Baltic area, a missionary bishop in 1214 'abstained from the solemnities of the Mass only with many groans while he was at sea, though he took communion every other day between Sunday services'.[3] This, too, has its ambiguities, perhaps implying that it was the bishop's custom to say Mass on alternate days, when ashore, additional to the Sunday Mass. If Mass at sea was not permitted, the episcopal groans could be understood as pious distress at not being allowed to say Mass; if permitted, the groans could imply seasickness as what prevented his saying Mass.[4] A common method of navigation at this time, in the Baltic or elsewhere, was cabotage, sailing directly from headland to headland, where possible remaining clear but in sight of land, keeping landmarks visible. If the bishop's ship was doing this and spending alternate nights in port, it would allow recovery from seasickness and thus the saying of Mass on alternate days. Equally it would allow the bishop to say Mass ashore on alternate days if Mass at sea was forbidden. A missionary bishop at sea would not be constrained by Fabri's point (below) about knowing to which parish a ship belonged. In short, the position remains unclear, at least for most of this period. To complicate the situation, in place of the Mass *Heinrici Chronicon Lyvoniae* refers to *dominicum officium*, literally 'the Office of Sunday', confused by its *alteris diebus*. If *dominicum officium* is understood as the Lord's Office it might refer to what is more usually called the Divine Office (*divinum officium*), said daily by all clergy; Brundage's translation opts for a Eucharistic sense, which has the precedent of the reserved Sacrament, as found on Louis IX's ship.

A few references from the later medieval period to the saying of Mass at sea may be helpful. One in *The Statutes and Ordinances to be Keped in Time of Werre* to the reserved Sacrament could just imply a preceding Mass on board. It is also known that in the sixteenth century on the galleys of the Order of St John of Malta, Mass would be said before sunrise, presumably before

---

1   *op cit.*, Eiríkr Magnússon (trans and ed), 1875, 245.
2   Vauchez, *Medieval Sainthood*, 296.
3   James A. Brundage (trans), 150-1 (chapter XIX, section 6). *Heinrici Chronicon Lyvoniae*, George Henry Pertz (ed), 124-5. *et multis gemitibus a missarum solemnitatibus in mari abstinebat, licet tamen alteris diebus infra dominicum officium communicaret.*
4   Though *Heinrici Chronicon Lyvoniae* refers to appalling weather, the *gemitibus* (groans) would more likely be *dolor* if seasickness was their cause.

5. Religious Practise at Sea

the start of rowing.[1] Some of the customs on these galleys (e.g. the display on board of a crucifix) are from these later centuries and may not reflect earlier practice. Fynes Morison, writing of a pilgrim ship in 1596, mentioned that some of the ships out of Venice sometimes had Mass on board, but not his own vessel, where the majority of the crew were Orthodox.[2]

Between these later references and the contradictions pre 1250 lies the witness of Felix Fabri, a Dominican friar travelling on a pilgrim ship in the early part of the fifteenth century.[3] His testimony may not apply to every ship, but his reasons for the customs he found are enlightening. He described the celebration of a 'dry Mass', effectively the Mass without the Canon or Eucharistic Prayer, and concluding with the Last Gospel (John 1). If it included the distribution of Holy Communion from the reserved Sacrament, he does not say; more probably those present made a spiritual Communion. He recorded his surprise: 'the sacrifice of the Eucharist is never consummated on shipboard'. He had previously ascribed it to the negligence of prelates in their concern for 'the salvation of the children of God', for he had been aware that since the days of St Gregory (Pope 590-604) 'Masses had been said on board ship, or at least the Host was preserved on board', and that the Sacrament was present on St Louis' ship. His research led him to adduce fifteen reasons why the custom (rather than law) of the Church should in his time prohibit Masses or reservation of the Host on board. In summary the reasons are as follows:

- The Mass is not a sacrament of necessity.
- There is on board ship 'no proper priest whose special duty it is to celebrate Holy Communion as the law directs: for no-one knows to what parish the ship belongs . . . '; effectively that it is not under a bishop's authority, not recognised in Canon Law, and the bishop's name cannot be included.
- Hosts cannot be preserved in damp weather.
- The Eucharist should be reserved only in church, and a ship is not a church.
- It cannot be reserved with a light burning constantly, as the winds at sea would prevent this.
- The celebrating priest might upset everything in bad weather.
- Candles would blow out and the altar linen blow away - both necessary canonically.
- Even in the absence of wind there is a similar danger from waves breaking over the ship.
- There is nowhere suitably reverent on board ship away from the rush of people.
- There may be Jews, Turks, Saracens, schismatics, and heretics on board.
- The presence of sin on board: gambling, swearing etc..
- The 'foul stench and dirtiness of both the galley and the men'.
- The presence of infidels who might not be edified by the disrespect of

---

1 J.M. Wismeyer, The War Galleys of the Order of St John, *Sunday Times*, 8, 15, 22 November 1992. Wismeyer's information is similar to David Allen, A Parish at Sea. . . .
2 Fynes Morison, *Itinerary*, Bk 1, 210f.
3 *Fabri*, vol 1, 141ff.

Christians in the presence of the Sacrament.
- Ignorant Christians might reproach the Sacrament if they were caught in a storm.
- 'The ease and suddenness with which men vomit on board ship.'

Fabri had given the subject careful thought. Most important are his first two reasons, the first having pertained since the Church began and meaning, roughly, that it was possible to be a Christian and not attend Mass when prevented, as the seafarer, by distance, work or infirmity. There was the common practice ashore of not receiving Communion except at Easter, after confession and absolution; those Easter duties ordered by Lateran IV in 1215. Baptism is the sacrament of necessity for a Christian. His second reason reflected thirteenth-century canonical developments. If the proper person, usually the parish priest, was required to say Mass, then on a ship, which had no canonical person, Mass could not be said. A priest at sea was incapable of supervision as he had no bishop, nor could the name of the bishop be included within the Mass, the sea being extra-diocesan. Without this there was a very real sense of no communion, those present being effectively excommunicated, when sailing the *mare nullius*. In that sense it was immaterial whether Mass was sometimes said at sea, as it may have been; rather, the importance lies in this understanding of the seafarer going where the Church did not. It will have been observed that the evidence here is rather thin, beyond the Mass being said on crusade vessels; there is more evidence by the sixteenth century, with more clergy travelling, particularly to the new world, but always, for the Mass, a priest being essential, the absence of clergy placing most seamen far from the formal ministry of the Church.

The lack of access to the Sacrament jars with modern Christians, Catholics especially, who have been, for a century or so, encouraged not only to attend Mass but to receive Communion frequently. In the medieval period this would have been unusual even in normal times. In abnormal times the sacraments would be available to no-one, as when a country was placed under an interdict, an ecclesiastical ban on the celebration of all sacraments. An interdict could last some years. Whilst England was under an interdict, in 1208, the Bishops of Ely and London received from Rome instructions which may illuminate what might have been the practice of the devout traveller by sea. These ordered that for baptisms of infants the 'old chrism' was to be used, and that dying persons be taught 'to make a spiritual communion'.[4] The latter, it can be argued, was therefore not unfamiliar to lay people of the period. It involved uniting oneself spiritually with the action of the Mass from which one was absent, either through distance, infirmity or interdict, and was usually done by rehearsing some of the words familiar from the Mass and using a prayer expressing a desire to receive the sacrament. The relevance of this to the sailor far from home is obvious. In a very real sense, though unprovided with the means of

---

4   *Calendar of Entries in Papal Registers relating to Great Britain and Ireland*, vol 1, 30. The chrism is oil over which the bishop has said the appropriate prayer, usually in Holy week.

5. Religious Practise at Sea

attending Mass, it allowed the seafarer still to fulfill his religious duties and be a part of the Mass. How many seafarers would use this form of devotion is impossible to guess but it makes Fabri's dry Mass more easily understood as something appropriate for a ship at sea.

To write about the lack of sacraments at sea is not to suggest the seaman was neglected by the Church; it would be to misunderstand the effect of the pattern of voyages on the Church's ministry to seafarers.[1] At least until the thirteenth century, and effectively beyond, most voyages were short, the seaman sharing the status of any parishioner away from home for a few days. It is the exceptional and long voyage, on crusade for example, which attracts religious ceremonies at departure and the presence on board of ministering clergy. This was the most economic way of delivering a ministry, as evidenced, when long voyages became more frequent, by clergy, usually friars, accompanying ships. Often it was unknown if some of those voyages had a destination, making them ones of discovery, and necessitating a priest if there was to be a sacramental ministry; later, when there was a destination but with a settlement still to be established, to put it crudely, providing a ship's chaplain was cheaper than providing a settled ministry at the destination. Finally, when sufficient voyages were taking place, it became more economical for the Church to invest in distant buildings, providing the traveller with a settled ministry at the further end of his voyage; a process not apparent at the time, but revealed by the long view, and one interrupted by the Reformation.

If Mass was being said at sea, entire or in part, it may sometimes indicate the type of voyage being undertaken. There is no doubt that as the centuries passed the number of clergy at sea increased. Some accompanied pilgrims; by 1445 some 2,000 pilgrims were travelling to Compostella from England, to instance a single country and destination. Others would be about Church business, between the great monastic houses, or from the thirteenth century, large numbers of preaching friars about their missionary purposes. The latter and other clergy, especially Spaniards and Portuguese, would be travelling with the voyages of discovery, and later to and from the territories newly discovered.

The possible influence of friars, as passengers or ministers, upon seafarers in their travels needs to be acknowledged. That they travelled far is beyond question: William of Rubruck travelled, admittedly overland, to the court of Ghengis Khan, his presence a testimony to the zeal and courage of many friars. Dominicans like Fabri, and Franciscans, were roughly contemporary but it was the latter who were more commonly found at sea. By 1217, within a very few years of their foundation, they had a provincial structure which included Italy, France, Spain, Germany, and the Near East.[2] Vasco da Gama, travelling with a picture of Our Lady in his cabin, and a priest on board to hear confessions, had reached Mozambique

---

1   Miller, *Ship of Peter*, passim
2   J.R.H. Moorman, *A History of the Franciscan Order*, 8, 27, 28, 62, 72, 169. J. S. Brewster (ed), *Monumenta Franciscana*, vol 1, ix.

by 1497. He was joined in 1500 by eight friars on an expedition to India.[1] The first friars in America accompanied Columbus's fourth voyage which sailed in 1502. The presence of such men proves little, but friars usually travelled in pairs, saying their Offices and celebrating Mass where possible, suggesting some sort of ministry to crew could hardly be avoided, given the length of voyages and the intimacy of life on board. That they did other things on board is also known: on his second voyage (1493) Columbus took with him Perzon, a friar interested in astronomy and navigation, plus other volunteer friars.[2]

A formal ceremony often preceded departure. Bartholomew Dias set out from Lisbon, in July 1497, after a night of vigil in the chapel of Our Lady of Bethlehem, on the shore of the River Tagus. A procession to the water's edge, a large crowd accompanying the voyagers, followed Mass. The mariners carried lighted tapers. Priests chanted a litany. Arriving at Dias's ships, all knelt and the chapel priest, after reading a general confession, gave a plenary indulgence to all who should die on the voyage.[3]

Voyaging seafarers would have been aware of the Church calendar; many almanacs included festivals and fasts and a method for calculating the phase of the moon by using the Golden Number 'which would have been posted in churches and offices where mariners congregated'.[4] That such knowledge was carried on board helps in the understanding of what sort of religious observance might be possible, and explains the tendency of discoverers to name islands after the day of the discovery according to the Church calendar, unless the name of the saint under whose patronage the voyage had been undertaken was preferred.

It would be fair to conclude this chapter, with its rag bag of evidence, by saying that it has been possible to indicate some religious practices of some seafarers: Mass, prayer, processions, Gospels, relics, fasts and feasts and a calendar for their observance. While the paucity of evidence makes it possible only to generalise, two statements may be made with certainty; that those whom the Saracens lumped together as Franks, i.e. Western Europeans, would have perceived themselves as they were perceived by the Saracens, as Christians; and that the definitive indication of their commitment would be to whom they prayed in time of danger. By their nature neither would leave traces beyond the kind of passing references adduced here as evidence.

---

1 Moorman, *A History of the Franciscan Order*, 577. H.E.J. Stanley (trans), *The Three Voyages of Vasco da Gama*, 137, n 1.
2 Moorman, *A History of the Franciscan Order*, 578, 579 n 5. Leonard I. Sweet, Christopher Columbus and . . . , 369ff.
3 E. Prestage, *The Portuguese Pioneers*, 252.
4 Derek Howse, Some Early Tidal Diagrams, 27ff, esp 33 and 35. Details of the Golden Number may be found in the *Book of Common Prayer*.

6. From the Reformation to the Nineteenth Century

The extended period of the Reformation did not help the Christian ministry to seamen. Effectively it marks the period of transition between the seaman being essentially a member of a Christian community, if rather far from home, to his becoming a special category in receipt of the ministries of the several churches. Where up to this point there had been an homogeneity in the life of the seaman, fragmentation of the Church meant crews often lacked the uniformity of religious allegiance which formerly prevailed on board, and sacraments ceased to be almost everywhere available. Europe was divided. England lost its monastic hospitality; lights were sold into lay hands, and familiar ecclesiastical landmarks were lost. In many European ports Protestants were unwelcome, while in others Catholics were the strangers. Alain Cabantous wrote well of these centuries:

> With regard to these times, the ambiguity of sources, the absence of plausible responses to certain questions, or the complexity of situations, drives the historian to discount the intimacy that he believes existed between these groups.[1]

The sixteenth century was a time of great change. The majority of voyages remained short-sea, but longer voyages and larger vessels became increasingly common. Longer voyages were dominated by Spaniards and Portuguese travelling to the New World. The religious situation of the seafarer at this time has attracted the attention of Cabantous and Rediker.[2] Theirs is not an easy task for seafarers, like any other industrial group, will include some devout, others not.

> It would be a mistake to forget that seamen were also landsmen, more or less integrated into the towns and villages in which they spend a good portion of their lives . . . sixteenth century Spanish sailors . . . spent only about a third of their active lives aboard ship . . . I calculated that time spent at sea represented between forty-five and sixty percent of the working lives of seafaring people in northwest France during the eighteenth century.[3]

Other factors, of less obvious religious significance, need attention. These three centuries were marked by a series of wars which led to the division of the Low Countries, the emergence of the United Provinces, and the

---

1 *Les citoyens du large*, 12. *A terme portant, l'ambiguïté des sources, l'absence de réponses plausibles à certaines questions ou la complexité des situations conduisent l'historien à en rabattre quant à l'intimité qu'il croit entre tenir avec ces milieux.*
2 *Between the Devil and the Deep Blue Sea.*
3 Cabantous, On the Writing of the Religious History of Seafarers, 215.

eclipse of Antwerp by Amsterdam. Wars had the effect of curtailing Church activity and interrupting trade. In spite of war, however, Europe's population having recovered from the Black Death of the preceding century, the ratio of people to available space introduced pressure to expand. The sharp rise in nineteenth-century populations is already to be glimpsed in this period.[1] Where a state was prevented from expansion, perhaps by water as in England or the United Provinces, increasing pressure to expand coincided with the Industrial Revolution and led to a significant growth in fleet sizes and waves of migration.[2] Religious persecution added to the pressure.

Clergy, sometimes in the formal role of chaplain, but now of various denominations, continued to be found at sea; some of these will be examined. In some ports full Catholic privileges remained available. A few hostels survived the Reformation, in Venice for example, and seafarers still travelled with the prayers of the Church, Protestant or Catholic. While trade and shipping were changing, the Counter Reformation brought a new confidence, albeit to a world in which to restore what had been lost was a struggle; Tridentine reforms gave the Catholic Church a fresh missionary impetus, new religious orders, and new devotional practices. The seventeenth and eighteenth centuries saw more Catholic chaplains, often Franciscans, but now sometimes Jesuits, accompanying the increasing number of longer voyages, a pattern which became less urgent as churches were built at distant destinations, that is, in the developing ports of the colonies. The need to trade surmounted some major religious and political divisions (for example, the ending of confiscation of Protestant ships in Spanish ports and imprisonment of their crews when Bibles were found on board), just as in another era it had overcome the Viking invasions. The Christian seafarer who fell foul of Muslims, with whom some trade persisted, could still hope to be ransomed by the traditional religious orders, both survivals from earlier centuries; reference to them seems less recondite when it is discovered that the Trinitarians, as late as 1795, were invited by Thomas Jefferson to use their influence to obtain the release of twenty-one American sailors captured by Muslims.[3]

If the sixteenth century, the century of the Reformation, is to be described without bias it is probably best described as a century of change. The change spread gradually and not without pain, adding to shores traditionally Islamic, Catholic or Orthodox, those of Lutheran Scandinavia, the Calvinist United Provinces, or a choice of allegiances on the Rhine banks. British shores ceased to be Catholic. France offered a picture of confusion. Italy's various states were Catholic if sometimes anti Papal, but with no fleet specially significant, the Venetian fleet beginning a long decline after the Portuguese discovery of the Cape route.[4] Even so a St Nicholas' Mariners' Guild was founded in Venice in

---

1   Useful tables can be found in Heinz Gollwitzer, *Europe in the Age of Imperialism 1880-1914*, 19f.
2   Simon P. Ville, *Transport & Development of the European Economy 1750-1918*, 69f.
3   Kenneth Fenwick (ed), *Galley Slave*, passim.
4   J.I.Israel, *Dutch Primacy in World Trade 1585-1740*, 3ff.

6. From the Reformation to the Nineteenth Century

1573, with provision of a hospital for sick seamen, while religious services and other forms of welfare, and chaplains were to be found on Venetian galleys - but galleys were not the vessels for long routes to the New World.[1]

Cabantous, writing extensively of the religious dimension in French maritime life, demonstrated that in settled communities, as those of Breton fishers, the outward manifestations of Catholicism remained fairly constant, if gilded by the Counter Reformation. His examples, *mutatis mutandis*, resemble pre-Reformation English ones. It is easy to dismiss the accumulated evidence of everything from graffiti to *ex voto* offerings as the detritus of the religious life of the maritime community but cumulatively it has to be accepted as the most significant evidence available.[2] Surviving religious customs on post Reformation English ships confirm the innate conservatism of the mariner. Protestant and Catholic alike clung to ancient customs; religious festivals survived in almanacs; ancient prayers accompanied the clearing of the glass; ships continued to be given religious names.[3]

Almost the whole of the second half of the sixteenth century was marked by confusion. This is true in matters maritime. What had been one of the largest and wealthiest trading groups, the *Hanse*, or Hanseatic League, was in terminal decline, the Reformation not the primary factor, for the *Hanse* had no uniform religious policy, each member town being left to make its own decision in such matters; by the end of the century Hamburg, for example, had decided to forbid Catholic services.[4] *Hanse* decline was hastened by the growing Dutch trade, the latter ascribed in part to a rejection of sixteenth-century Spanish Catholicism; whatever the truth, the Dutch were prepared to carry for anyone in the late sixteenth and early seventeenth century, becoming by mid seventeenth century the dominant maritime power, and Protestant.[5]

Behind this changing trade pattern lay a more subtle effect of the Reformation than simply the matter of what worship was forbidden or encouraged in a particular port. 'The medieval idea of a universal polity with an ultimately religious purpose was replaced,' wrote Riemersma, 'in Reformed thinking, by a pluralistic conception of numerous independent states'.[6] Seafaring was changing from a way of life to a job, a process almost completed in these centuries, implicit in the way the sailor was paid: 'The share system, as a form of pay, dominant in the Middle Ages, was largely a thing of the past by the early eighteenth century'.[7] Religion, terms of

1 F.C. Lane, *Venice - A Maritime Republic*, 343, 420.
2 Cabantous, *Le Ciel dans la Mer*, is the principal source. His thesis, published as *Dix Mille Marins Face à l'Océan*, contains more tables and details. Cabantous and Hildesheimer (eds), *Foi Chrétienne et Milieux Maritimes*, offers a selection of papers associated with the period.
3 Compare the list of vessels named in H and P Chaunu, *Seville et l'Atlantique (1504-1650)*, vols 2-5. Cabantous, *Le Ciel dans la Mer*, 136ff.
4 Philippe Dollinger, *The German Hanse*, 357.
5 Ralph Davies, *The Rise of the Atlantic Economies*, 76f. Joshua S. Goldstein, *Long Cycles . . .* , 313f.
6 Jelle C. Riemersma, *Religious Factors . . .* , 35.
7 Marcus Rediker, *Between the Devil . . .* , 118, 149.

employment, purpose of voyage, all things giving a crew homogeneity, were changing a way of life into a means of getting a product from one place to another. The triumph of trade over other divisions has already been indicated. Now it was conceivable for a crew member to find himself the only Catholic or Protestant on board. The loss of group identity and the discovery of the individual owes much to the Reformation.[1]

The Inquisition presented the formal face of Catholicism in some ports. The connection between Reformation and printing press meant that an increasing amount of literature was in circulation. Its point of entry was invariably the port. Hakluyt noted the arrest of a ship's crew in Tripoli in 1560 because the master's mate had a Geneva Bible in his hand.[2] In Spain the ports were directly under the Inquisition and, according to Froude, any ships possessing forbidden books were liable to confiscation, and entire crews to incarceration in the Inquisitorial prison;[3] something moderated in the interest of trade towards the end of the sixteenth century when Lord Cobham negotiated an agreement for the interest of the Inquisition against English Protestant merchants in Spain to be limited to a merchant's activities within a Spanish port after his arrival and only the goods of the accused to be confiscated instead of ship and cargo. Searches followed a regular pattern: first, an enquiry whence they came and with what cargo, then whether any books or pictures forbidden by the Holy Office were carried, and if there were any on board 'that hath said or done anything against the catholicke faith of Rome'. By February 1600 searches had been greatly modified and compulsory church attendance abolished.[4]

Such penalties were not limited to the English. Spanish relations with Venice were deteriorating; as early as December 1524, at the Spanish port of Almazarron some officers from Venetian galleys were arrested by the Holy Office for selling Bibles, and conveyed to Murcia. The Venetian Ambassador, Contarini, was assured by the Emperor that he would do everything to preserve the friendship of the Republic but that the Inquisitors had told him that the delinquents had been arrested for selling books against the faith.[5] There are examples the other way. In Cardinal Wolsey's day Hugh Prykness submitted to correction after confessing that a ship's purser had left in his chamber a text from Germany, *Opera quaedam Martini Lutheri*. In 1583 the Catholic John Nutter was executed in London, after examination, for smuggling catechisms and testaments.[6] The trade in literature indicates the religious climate, the peculiar position of the mariner in the transmission of ideas, and the currency

---

1 Matthias van Rossum *et al*, National and International Labour Markets . . . 1600-1850, 47f.
2 Hakluyt, III, 144 quoted in D.M. Palliser, *The Age of Elizabeth 1547-1603*, 387.
3 J..A. Froude, *English Seamen* . . . , 22f.
4 Albert J. Loomis, Religion & Elizabethan Commerce . . . , 27ff.
5 *Calendar of State Papers Relating to English Affairs . . . in Venice etc.*, vol I (1202-1509), xlv; III, (1520-6), xiv. Contarini was Venetian Ambassador to Charles V.
6 Robert Moody, *John Benett of Pythouse*, p.p., Bristol 2003, 16. J.H. Pollen, *The English Martyrs 1584-1603*, 37f.

religious literature was gaining in the maritime community, whether Catholic or Protestant. There were, of course, more obvious manifestations of the tension: it is known that chaplains accompanying the Spanish Armada included three of English origin.[1]

The English Sailor

Of contemporary voyage chaplains, some were missionaries travelling by sea, others appointed as ships' chaplains. Most ships still carried no such person, but an increasing number of clergy was beginning to appear at sea. The Muscovy and the East India Companies sent out ships with chaplains. Accounts become available by or about chaplains accompanying, for example, Edward Fenton, Frobisher and Drake. Most of the companies claimed to set out, like the Muscovy Company, 'for the honour and increase of the revenues of the Crowne' and 'for the glory of God'; aims similar to those sailing from the Iberian peninsula. What divine patronage of a voyage might mean is a moot point. The Muscovy Company despatched its first three ships in 1553 with a 'Minister', John Stafford, for the fleet, to serve a total of 115 people: officers, crew and traders. In theory the East India Company provided chaplains on its large vessels; from 1698 those of 500 tons or more had to carry a chaplain; in practice company tonnage was limited to 499 tons, though the absence of a chaplain cannot have been a great economy. It is tempting to wonder if the economy reflected an old, but still extant, superstition that a priest on board ship is unlucky.[2] Each chaplain had to be approved by the Archbishop of Canterbury or the Bishop of London.[3]

Hakluyt wrote of Frobisher's third voyage that his chaplain Master Wolfall, whilst the *Anna Francis* was grounded awaiting repair,

> on the *WINTER'S FURNACE* preached a godly sermon; which being ended, he celebrated also a communion upon the land, at the partaking whereof was the captain of the *ANNE FRANCIS*, and many other gentlemen and soldiers, mariners, and miners with him. The celebration of the Divine Mystery was the first sign, seal, and confirmation of Christ's name, death, and passion ever known in these quarters. The said Master Wolfall made sermons, and celebrated the communion at sundry other times, in several and sundry ships, because the whole company could never meet together at any one place.[4]

In writing thus, he was recording a problem familiar to every ship's chaplain, especially when travelling in company with other vessels, their crews working in watches.

Captain Edward Fenton in 1582-83 sailed with four ships and two chaplains. The senior chaplain, Richard Madox, given three years' leave of

---

1 Albert J. Loomis SJ, The Armadas and the Catholics of England, 385ff.
2 A.G. Course, *The Merchant Navy - A Social History*, 149.
3 M.R. Kingsford, *Life of W.H.G. Kingston*, Toronto, 124. R.J. Cornewall-Jones, *The British Merchant Service*, 72.
4 Hakluyt, *Voyages of the Elizabethan Seamen*, 178f.

absence from All Souls' College, Oxford, sailed on the *Leicester* (named for the voyage's chief sponsor and Madox's patron, the Earl of Leicester). Madox was evidently familiar with the life of the seafarer and the latest methods of navigation. He appeared in the crew list as Preacher, and was allotted the service of one man. Unlike their Spanish counterparts, English chaplains were not supported by the State. Madox had a senior position as secretary for 'all assemblies and consultations' to keep the minutes, and was one of three men on the voyage provided with a key to the names of succession should the 'Generall governour' of the voyage die. His fellow chaplain, John Walker, sailed on the *Edward,* dispensed by the Queen for three years' absence from his Cornish parish 'untyll I returne from the Indyans'. Both chaplains thought the voyage was intended for trade but soon were faced with Fenton's desire for self-aggrandisement and the crew's piratical designs, which the absolute authority of the commander at sea made it difficult for them to denounce. A chaplain on a similar voyage, with Drake, denouncing immorality as the cause of the ship being driven upon a rock in 1568, had found himself taken on board the *Golden Hind* to be publicly punished and humiliated.

Fenton's voyage had started under the motto, 'Under the conduct of Christe wee forowed the seaze'; its first article required God to be 'syncerely and dayly honoured' with the daily reading of Morning and Evening Prayer, and then that the 'ministers of gods holy word' be accorded due reverence. Records show that the Offices were indeed said daily, and Communion at least quarterly, the custom in the Church of England of the time. Madox taught 'the boys yt wayted' at each meal a verse from Proverbs. Examples of some of his sermons survive. As Fenton had made his ship's master on one occasion accept the punishment of kneeling throughout the Divine Office for some offense, his chaplain showed real courage when speaking out against those purposes of the voyage of which he disapproved. Most of the homilies concerned ethics and conduct, the minority on Christian doctrine, including the affirmation 'yt wee wer bound in duty to spoyl all papists, as enemyes to god & our soverayn, of what cuntry so ever they were'.[1]

Frobisher's voyage instructions were not dissimilar to Fenton's. Captains were to banish swearing, dice, card playing and 'filthy communication . . . and to serve God twice a day, with the services as usual in the Churches of England, and to clear the glass according to the old order of England'.[2] Cabot in 1553 also required of his captains the daily recitation of Morning and Evening Prayer.[3] The clearing of the glass, a pre-Reformation custom, involved reciting a psalm and a short prayer at the end of each watch (four-hourly) when the sand in the glass was running out and the watch preparing to go below.[4] There were other examples of religious practice. Burwash

---
1 E.G. R. Taylor, *The Troublesome Voyage of Captain Edward Fenton,* 582f and *passim.*
2 Hakluyt, *Voyages of the Elizabethan Seamen,* 178f.
3 M.R. Kingsford, *W.H.G. Kingston,* 123.
4 Hakluyt, *Voyages of the Elizabethan Seamen,* 136n. cp. Jaap R. Bruijn, *The Dutch Navy of the Seventeenth . . . ,* 125.

cited an extract from the anonymous *Complaynt of Scotland*, which gives a rhythmical chant used in getting a ship under weigh; the passage concerned with unfurling the mainsail seems to include a simple prayer for fine weather:

> Than ane of the marynalis began to hail and to cry, and al the marynalis began to hail and to cry, and al the marynalis ansuert of that samyn sound. hou hou. pulpela pulpela. boulena boulena. darta darta. hard out steif, hard out steif, afoir the vynd. god send, god send, fayr vedthir, fayr vedthir . . . mak fast and belay.[1]

Frobisher's articles included the watchword to be used for night recognition between his ships. The challenge was, 'Before the world was God', and the reply, 'After God came Christ His Son'.[2] In Captain John Smith's *Seaman's Grammar* of 1652, describing the taking of a prize, the commander orders, 'Boatswain, call up the men to prayer and breakfast'.[3] There is enough evidence to demonstrate that, with or without chaplains (and the majority of ships would have no chaplain), some of the old customs of the sea had survived the Reformation.

The Catholic at Sea

There were chaplains to Catholic fleets. Fra Girolamo da Pistoia, in 1570 appointed head of thirty Capuchins, chaplains to the Papal Navy, died while serving plague-stricken crews after an abortive mission against the Turks. His successor, a one-time soldier of fortune, was Fra Anselmo de Pietramolara.[4] Other chaplains served later and smaller sorties against the Turks by navies from Genoa and Venice. In 1588 the Roman Curia as re-organised by Pope Sixtus V included a Sacred Congregation of the Papal Navy. The same year saw Spain's Armada fleet off the English coast; this too was well supplied with chaplains by Philip II. Indeed, there seem to have been priests on merchant ships, though perhaps travelling to missions ashore in the New World; ships in danger risked Spanish owners' fortunes, and one, Juan de Escalante de Mendoza, listed the priorities when abandoning ship: first should be coinage, pearls and other lightweight items of value; second, women and children, the elderly and the sick, priests and religious; third, passengers and slaves; fourth; the youngest pages and the oldest and weakest sailors; finally, the captain, officers and remaining crew after using any time left to transfer any valuable merchandise to the other ships in the convoy.[5]

Chaplain Madox's interest in navigation was paralleled by that of the Dominican friars, Father Bartolomé de las Casas, who on the strength of his observations during sixteen Atlantic crossings was said to be as good a pilot as the best, and Father Pedro Calvo, a man consulted by pilots, having learnt similarly how the angle of the sun was measured.[6]

---

1 D. Burwash, *English Merchant Shipping 1460-1540*, 80.
2 Hakluyt, *Voyages of the Elizabethan Seamen*, 136f.
3 *op cit.* lxxi.
4 Fr Cuthbert OSFC, *The Capuchins*, vol 1, 189f.
5 Pablo E. Pérez-Mallaína, *Spain's Men of the Sea*, 215.
6 Pérez-Mallaína, *Spain's Men of the Sea*, 213.

Pérez-Mallaína records the kind of religious practice to be found among the sailors as seen by their passengers, though commenting that blasphemies were as common as prayers.[1] His primary evidence, as before the Reformation, lay in the names of ships, most sailing under the patronage of Mary or some other saint, and contrasting, when they joined the armadas with Flemish vessels, with the secular names of the latter, such as *Unicorn* or *Red Lion*. Coupled with this was the concern of the authorities to obtain the 'benediction of heaven', so, to the name of the ship, generals and admirals added a requirement that no sailor should be allowed to join his ship without having confessed his sins and received communion; a provision emphasising, if emphasis were necessary, that there was no guarantee of a safe return.

Once on board, the daily round would be marked, as on the English ships, by prayers and invocations, including psalms and prayers to be said by the pages at the clearing of the sand glass; the same pages being required at night to repeat the principal prayers of the Church (presumably the *Pater*, *Ave*, *Credo*) until all knew them by heart. Pérez-Mallaína says that Mass would be uncommon on board, with only the great war galleons carrying a chaplain; travelling friars would not usually say Mass, presumably because many were lay brothers. Instead, on Saturdays the master would preside over the singing of the *Salve Regina*, followed by litanies, attended by passengers and crew. Prayers would also be said in times of danger and on safe arrival.

One custom, resembling the deodand of the medieval codes, was the adding, on voyages of discovery in the first half of the century, of the names of some saints to the crew lists so that at the distribution of wages a share - apparently modest - would fall to those named, received on their behalf by those who managed their shrines. To supplement this source of income, it appears that religious orders would 'fill the ships with almoners and poor boxes'. The friars would board the ship shortly before it sailed and entrust a money box to a pious sailor to look after on the voyage, a practice the authorities tried to prevent. Sailors in danger of death might leave something, perhaps clothes or a share of wages due, for a few Masses to be said for their souls.[2]

Despite these pious practices, the general opinion seems to have been that seamen were a godless lot, failing to observe holy days, fasts, confession, Easter Communion and all else that was typical of Catholic life ashore; this, despite the inclusion in calendars of moveable religious feasts to remove excuses for non-observance.[3] How it was supposed that sailors at sea might observe most of these things is not said by their critics. Pérez-Mallaína offers examples of irreligion through the witness of Friar Antonio de Guevara:

---

1   Pérez-Mallaína, *Spain's Men of the Sea*, 237ff.
2   Cp the English custom of the 'mortuary', an offering from the estate of the deceased to his parish church. An example of a 'legacy from the galley man', presumably from a Venetian galley, can be found in a letter (1501-2) from Matthew Fox to the Mayor of Southampton, in R.C. Anderson (ed), *Letters of the Fifteenth and Sixteenth Centuries from the Archives of Southampton*, 34.
3   A form of confession and absolution survives in Neptune's visit when crossing the Equator.

Sometimes the oarsmen and sailors on the galley make fun of me when I ask them for their certificates of confession; they show me a deck of cards, saying that in their holy confraternity, they learned not how to confess their sins but to gamble.

Danger from storm or shipwreck would provoke a variety of promises of reform, usually forgotten when calm ensued.

The prayers that marked the passing of the hours were of interest to the religious authorities. The Inquisition in Mexico sent commissioners on board to check the purity of the religious customs, to the extent on occasion of ensuring any pictures of saints, male and female, were decently clad; also, regarding the keeping of vows made on the voyage. Among the saints invoked were Elmo, Nicholas, the Evangelists, Mary under various titles, and Clare, much as the custom of their English pre-Reformation counterparts. Saints might be saluted by gunfire or dipping of sails.

The Reformed Liturgy and the seafarer

While the forms of service on board Spanish ships seem to have changed little, the Mass emerging from the Council of Trent offering little that would have been unfamiliar to a seaman at any point in the medieval period, the same cannot be said for sailors encountering the liturgies of the Reformed churches as offered on English ships, for example, the Offices of Morning and Evening Prayer; instead, it can be said with confidence that although these derived from pre-Reformation Offices their use on board English ships marked a development in liturgical life at sea. They appeared in the *Book of Common Prayer* of 1549, with revisions in 1552, and 1662. Their use on naval vessels was mandatory, voluntary on other ships, their advantage their requiring no priest for recitation. Both Offices included a chapter from Old and New Testaments, use of an official English translation of the Scriptures being ordered. To provide a sermon in the absence of a minister, a *Book of Homilies* was published in 1547, containing sermons written by eminent contemporary Anglican divines, of whom Thomas Becon (below) was one.

Some companies required the saying of the Offices. The East India Company ordered that a religious service be held on board its vessels every Sunday, weather permitting, the master failing to do so without good reason liable to a fine of two guineas, no small sum, though perhaps a small portion of the profit he might make on the voyage.[1] Naval use was made clear in the first of the Articles of War:

> Officers are to cause Public Worship, according to the Liturgy of the Church of England, to be solemnly performed in their ships, and take care that prayers and preaching by the chaplains be performed diligently, and that the Lord's Day be observed.[2]

That the prayers were appreciated in the Royal Navy is suggested by Thomas Carte, though he was writing in the eighteenth century; the same is

---

1 A.G. Course, *The Merchant Navy - A Social History*, 148.
2 *Annotated Book of Common Prayer*, 688.

nowhere indicated for the merchant navy. Carte was defending what might be called the Anglican compromise between the extremes of Catholicism and Protestantism. It is hard to know whether his were the views of sailors; rather, they seem to reflect the views of the divines responsible for shaping the Church of England, following the rejection of the Commonwealth and the restoration of the Stuarts. Referring to the Fleet, in particular to the its revolt in 1648 in favour Charles I, and offering a claim which would be repeated in the nineteenth century, he wrote,

> The English seamen are a singular kind of men. . . . Nothing could be more disagreeable to the taste of these men, than the long winded cant, allegorical phraseology, and unintelligible notions in the sermons and prayers of the Presbyterians; they like the plain rational way of instruction and form of worship used by the Church of England much better.[1]

Before 1662 no special prayers in the Church of England were provided for the use of those at sea, though some prayers could easily be adapted. During the reign of Elizabeth I, several prayers were put forward to supply this lack; that they were mainly for the Navy is explicit. In 1596 a supplement 'for her Majesty's Forces and Navy' was published, followed in 1597 by 'Certain Prayers set forth by Authority, to be used for the prosperous success of her Majesty's Forces and Navy', some of which were apparently from the Queen's own hand.[2] Carte might have said less about 'long winded cant' if he had been familiar with these prayers, which tend to be lengthy, mainly, as most prayers produced in times of national stress, asking for the divine assistance for the English Fleet and Forces, and the undoing of the enemy; little here for the merchant seaman.[3]

Others in the same century were writing similar prayers. Thomas Becon (1513 – 67) had produced a little earlier the *Flower of Godly Prayers*, a collection of prayers of his own composition, dedicated to the Duchess of Somerset, in which he included a 'Prayer for Mariners', typical of its kind, a catena of scriptural texts in praise of God, to be used by 'all such as labour by land or sea, but namely them which for getting and maintenance of their living are compelled to travel the seas, and to commit themselves to the dangers thereof', dangers which Becon may have experienced when going into exile under Queen Mary before returning under Elizabeth I. It asks God to answer the prayers of those at sea, that they be 'delivered out of fear, escape all dangers, and travel a fortunate journey'.[4] Although there is no obvious link between this prayer and that which opens the 'Prayers for Use of Those at Sea', in the 1662 *Book of Common Prayer*, there is a marked similarity, nor does anything obvious remain to indicate whether any seaman saw his prayers.

The 1662 book, a revision prompted by Cromwell and his Commonwealth, followed the Restoration. In 1641, under Cromwell, a *Directory of Public Worship* had been presented to Parliament as *The Service, Discipline, and*

---
1 Thomas Carte, *A General History of England*, bk XXIII, 585.
2 *Liturgical Services of the Reign of Queen Elizabeth*, 665.
3 *Annotated Book of Common Prayer*, 690.
4 Becon, *Works of Thomas*, 33.

6. From the Reformation to the Nineteenth Century

Forme of the Common Prayers and Administration of the Sacraments used in the English Church of Geneva, a necessary step towards replacing the 1552 *Book of Common Prayer* with something more suited to reformed taste. It was followed in 1643 by *The Reformation of the Discipline and Service of the Church according to the best Reformed Churches*, a title finally shortened to *A Directory for Public Worship*, to which was soon added *A Supply of Prayer for the Ships that want Ministers to pray with them*. This supplement was prefaced with 'a reason of this work' which said that

> whereas there are thousands of ships which have not ministers to them to guide them in prayer, and therefore use either the old form of Common Prayer or no prayer at all; the former whereof for many weighty reasons hath been abolished, and the latter is likely to make them heathens rather than Christians: Therefore, to avoid these inconveniences, it has been thought fit to frame some prayers agreeing with the Directory established by Parliament.

'This work' consisted of a prayer, the Our Father, Psalms, a reading from both testaments ('but none out of those books called Apocrypha'), a prayer for the Church universal and 'our united Churches and Kingdoms', and a second prayer for the King which, though composed under the Commonwealth, asks that he might be 'rich in blessings'. The singing of a further psalm was permitted, and 'the conclusion may be with a thanksgiving and a blessing', to which were added a 'prayer particularly fitted for those that travell upon the seas' and a 'prayer in a storm'.[1]

The 'Forms of Prayer to be used at Sea' in the 1662 *Book of Common Prayer* cannot be said definitely to have been prompted by the *Directory*, but the Navy having doubled in size under Cromwell, and with contemporary pressure for Prayer Book revision, this was most probably the case.[2] The *Book of Common Prayer*, it is easy to forget, had been a controversial book in the sixteenth century; long before the rise of Cromwell there were those who disliked its distance from Geneva, while some regretted its lack of proximity to Rome. Seamen in Catholic ports found in possession of the *Book of Common Prayer*, as with the English Bible, were at considerable risk, in Spain involving confiscation and incarceration by the Inquisition.

The restoration of Charles II to the English throne in 1660 brought back the *Book of Common Prayer*, a few revisions delaying its publication until 1662. Its Preface says 'it was thought convenient' that certain prayers should be added for those at sea. These 'Forms of Prayer to be used at Sea' are first mentioned in the records of Convocation (the Church of England's deliberative assembly) on the 5th December, 1661, apparently the work of Bishop Robert Sanderson of Lincoln (d. 1663), a man with a felicitous turn of phrase and moderately Catholic in outlook.[3] Its naval orientation is confirmed by its second rubric, 'These two following prayers are to be used in His Majesty's Navy every day', a context further suggested by 'O Almighty God, the Sovereign Commander of

---
1   F. Proctor & W.H. Frere, *A New History of the Book of Common Prayer*, 162.
2   *Annotated Book of Common Prayer*.
3   G.J. Cuming, *A History of Anglican Liturgy*, 166.

all the world'; its references to battles and enemies at sea would resonate also with seventeenth-century merchantmen who were prey to 'Turkish' pirates and other enemies, but the tenor of the service remains naval. A later, revised, Irish Prayer Book altered the service slightly to make it fit either naval or merchant fleets, true also of the American Prayer Book which would follow.

The first rubric in the Forms of Prayer makes it clear that the regular offices are not to be displaced: 'The Morning and Evening Service to be used daily at Sea shall be the same which is appointed in the Book of Common Prayer'. Two prayers for use in storms precede one for use before 'a Fight at Sea against any Enemy'. Short prayers follow 'for single persons, that cannot meet to join in Prayer with others, by reason of the Fight, or Storm'; for general use; with respect to the enemy; and in event of a storm. A form of general confession for use 'when there shall be imminent danger' and an absolution to be given by the priest 'if there be any in the ship' follow the Lord's Prayer. The expectation of confession and absolution *in extremis*, as in the form ordered for the Visitation of the Sick, is typically Anglican. Two psalms (66 and 107) are given for use in thanksgiving after a storm, followed by two collects of thanksgiving. The Forms of Prayer ends with a hymn of praise for use after a 'dangerous Tempest', a further catena of scriptural texts, and the Grace. An alternative ending offers a similarly composed hymn after 'Victory or Deliverance from an Enemy', an additional collect, and the Grace. Appended is a version of the words of committal from the Burial Service adapted for burial at sea.

The little evidence to suggest how these Forms of Prayer were used implies only that some, mainly Evangelicals, felt it necessary to supplement them. Josiah Woodward, associated with the Societies for the Reformation of Manners, groups of young men meeting to study Scripture and grow in the Christian life, offered a number of prayers of his own composition in response to a 'request of some under my Ministry'. These prayers are more intimate, confessional, asking for a safe return and the care of friends and family. Their existence suggests that some of the young men were seafarers, the prayers apparently published for their use; one can only guess whether they were used.[1]

Sixteenth and Seventeenth Century Welfare in England

This interest in the spiritual seaman at sea was not matched by the sixteenth century attitude towards his physical well-being ashore. Many English gilds,[2] unlike their European counterparts, were disbanded at the Reformation, often their works of charity suffering accordingly. Some new hospitals and almshouses were built, founded by Christian laymen, but without obvious Church connections. At Chatham a hospital was founded by Sir John Hawkins

---

1 Josiah Woodward, *An Account of the Rise and Progress of the Religious Societies in the City of London &c* . . .
2 Older sources tend to use this spelling.

for 'poor decayed mariners and shipwrights' in 1592. Ten pensioners were kept, receiving 3s. 6d each per week, and an annual 'chauldron of coals'. Disability was the qualification for entry.[1] The number of these foundations restricting admission to Navy men was a sign of the times and an indication of how the Navy had grown; by the end of the eighteenth century the famous Royal Hospital at Greenwich was admitting only 'such as had served in the Royal Navy', but since merchant seamen were obliged (from the tenth year of Queen Anne) to pay an annual sixpence to help support the hospital, they too could be admitted on production of an 'authentic certificate' showing that they had received whatever was their complaint or infirmity in the Queen's service.[2]

An increasing number of seafarers received parish assistance at the hands of the churchwardens who had taken over this responsibility from the parish constables, but this was not Church assistance. Contemporary parish records include seamen as recipients. Those of Wye, on the busy route from Kentish ports to London, offer examples. Through Wye seamen would travel, often in bands, usually after the loss of their ship, and would be helped on their way, as shown by such entries as:

to Thos Jenkins and 3 more who lost their ship belonging to Bristol 1s.
given to Thomas Williams and three more of Newport Vectis whose ship founded at Dunghill Ness 1s.
given to seamen cast away in the County of Cardigan, bound for Suffolk 1s 6d.

In some cases assistance was given to the relatives of seamen who had been taken as prisoners of war by the Dutch. Other seamen had been taken as 'slaves of the Turke' from vessels in the Channel.[3]

Naval Chaplains

In France in 1628, Cardinal Richelieu assumed the title of *grand maitre et surintendant de la navigation*, abolishing the office of Admiral of France. Larger French ships at least were provided with chaplains. For the Royal Navy, in 1651 the Council of State in England asked the Navy Committee that 'an able minister should be settled at Chatham to teach seamen and others their duty', recommending the services of The Rev. William Adderley, who was willing to accept the appointment for a hundred pounds a year and certain extra sums. Fifty-one officers wrote to him in testimony of their satisfaction with his abilities, asking him to accept the post with the intention of 'only preaching, expounding of scripture and catechising of youth'.[4] His sabbatarian principles caused him to refuse to be rowed to ships on Sundays, preaching instead in the parish church, while making it his business to board warships at least once before they sailed. Under the Commonwealth (1649 – 60) the navy saw an increase in chaplains; men required to use the *Directory for Public Worship*, to be of sound doctrine

---

1 Anon, *Kentish Traveller's Companion*, 122.
2 Hasted, *The History of Kent*, vol I, 404ff.
3 G.E. Hubbard, *The Old Book of Wye*, 125.
4 *Calendar of State Papers, Domestic*, 1651-2.

and possessed of morals above suspicion, their chief duties to offer prayer twice daily, before dinner, and after a psalm had been sung at 'setting the evening watch, and any man absent was liable to spend twenty-four hours in irons'.[1]

Charles II, replacing the *Directory*'s prayers for seamen, did nothing to maintain the high moral tone prevailing under the Commonwealth. Naval morals soon reflected those of the Court; sailors were allowed to have women on board when in port and in some cases the same women were to be found at sea; a number of women of doubtful morals were killed, for example, in the North Sea when English and Dutch fleets fought in June 1666. Naval morals were in part improved, despite his own amorous proclivities, by Samuel Pepys, who arranged for naval chaplains to be nominated either by the Archbishop of Canterbury or the Bishop of London; in other words, that they should be fit people.

The chaplains appointed discovered something which may have disturbed them more than the presence of the women. This was the spread of the Quaker movement to the navy, which included a number of George Fox's disciples even before his founding of the Society of Friends in 1668. It is not unreasonable to suppose that some of them would also be found in the merchant fleet. It is certainly true that many men in the merchant fleet would have spent time in the Royal Navy. Clergy who had struggled to uphold the Elizabethan Settlement were naturally suspicious of anything which dispensed with the ordered worship of the Church of England. An interesting example of the effect of Quakerism survives from the fourth rate frigate *Bristol* where within a six-month period two boys and twelve men became Quakers; it seems that life on board became exemplary, the Quakers, while not refusing to fight, declining to take the spoils of battle which would rightly have been theirs. In due course Quaker pacifism did become a challenge to the system. Numerically they were never strong, but their presence at sea was, for the maritime missiologist, another fruit of the Reformation.

Sixteenth Century Catholic Provision for the Seafarer

Two Catholic post-Reformation figures, both later canonised, stand out as beacons. The first, Peter Claver, a Spaniard born in 1581 or 1583 in Catalonia, on joining the Jesuits followed at Cartagena Fr Alonso de Sandoval SJ in a ministry to slaves. Claver had shown his concern for those on board on his outward voyage; dining at the captain's table, he would remove food to take to the sick, hoping to create an opening for instruction in the faith. In port he began to meet slave ships with gifts of food, tobacco and clothing, to bathe wounds, care for the sick, and prepare those willing to receive baptism. He extended his ministry to the port of Veracruz. It has been estimated that annually he served between ten and twenty thousand Africans. On occasion he intervened with masters on behalf of slaves. At least one instance is recorded of his dining on board a Spanish flagship, where captured English officers were also guests, hoping to use the occasion for their conversion; his ministry extended beyond the slaves to

---

1 Cited in C.N. Robinson, *The British Tar in Fact and Fiction*, 100.

the crews and others on the ships which brought them. He died in 1654.

Peter Claver's French contemporary, Vincent de Paul, was born c. 1580. He was ordained in 1600. Captured in 1605 he spent two years in Tunisia as a slave, escaping in 1607 to Avalon. From 1613 until 1625 he was chaplain to the household of Emmanuel de Gondi, General of the Galleys, a position giving him access to the prisoners who manned the oars. In 1619 this voluntary ministry to prisons and galleys was recognised in his appointment as Chaplain General of the Galleys. To help him in this work he founded confraternities of charity for men and women, followed in 1625 by the Congregation of the Mission; the latter to give missions (also to serve country people, and to train clergy). Details survive of a 1621 mission to galleys at Bordeaux. These were crewed by condemned criminals and convicted heretics, Protestants among them, and used to pursue Barbary pirates, whose vessels in turn often depended on Christian slaves.[1] By 1639 the missions had been extended to the galley slaves of La Tournelle. As his work became established a pattern emerged: every six months the chain gang would leave for Marseilles, after a short retreat, penance and Communion. Those who died were buried with solemnity. The Company of the Mission and the confraternities were assisted in this work by *La Compagnie du Saint-Sacrément,* and the Sisters of Charity (founded by Vincent in 1633 with St Louise de Marillac). *La Compagnie du Saint-Sacrément* was a charitable group; surviving details are far from clear, partly because a number of other groups used this title, but this one was founded 'for good works' in 1627, recruiting from the wealthy and influential to work among the poor, slaves, and those on the galleys. The Sisters of Charity began working in 1640 with the galley slaves. That a major effort was required may be guessed from the numbers involved: each galley carried eighty soldiers responsible for 275 men, the latter shackled to benches and often scourged. At this time there were usually forty or more galleys stationed at Marseilles.

The involvement of lay followers of Vincent de Paul in the revived Catholic mission to seafarers late in the nineteenth century demands an examination of the work of the man who inspired them. What form would a Vincentian mission take? One mission, led by John Baptist Gault, an Oratorian and Bishop of Marseilles, assisted by Gaspard de Simiane, a *Compagnie du Saint-Sacrément* member, involved a substantial team: Vincent's own missionaries, eight priests of the Most Blessed Sacrament, some Oratorians, while the Jesuits, 'who were chaplains to certain galleys, agreed to look after their own'. Priests were allocated two or three to a galley and ministered on board for twenty days. After covering the principal points of Catholic doctrine and the reception of the sacraments, priests would move to the next galley, intending to finish within two months. The Bishop also went from galley to galley, catechising, preaching and absolving. Good results were reported: it was said that all became communicants,

---

1   Alain Cabantous, *Religion et monde maritime* . . . , 6.

obedient and no longer swearing. Daily morning and evening prayers, and the midday *Angelus*, were said. A few Turks accepted baptism. From 1644 the Chaplaincy General to the Galleys was attached to the office of Superior General of the Mission rather than to Vincent personally, and five extra priests appointed to hear the confessions of Germans, Italians, Irish, Bretons, and converted Turks, a list suggesting that the nationalities present on the galleys included not only Muslims and Protestants. Chaplains now accompanied galleys to sea and said daily prayers and Mass on board. In time a priest of the Mission went as chaplain to the French consul at Tunis to work there among slaves, mostly captured Christian sailors, while Fr le Vacher of the Mission worked from Bizerte on the slave ships.

Increasing French lay involvement

A different *Confrérie du Saint-Sacrèment*, this one for sea captains, pilots and mates, the senior members of the profession, at le Havre was approved in 1662 by the Archbishop of Rouen, apparently to replace an older confraternity with something reflecting better the spirit of the Council of Trent. Its members were fishermen, operating entirely off the coasts of Newfoundland where the number of fishers involved was already substantial, their practice of religion described as *inexistant* by Cabantous, despite the availability of a chaplain to say prayers and attend to sickness. The provision of chaplains was not easy. Bishops and heads of religious orders were reluctant to release men, a situation this *Confrérie du Saint-Sacrèment* was intended to mitigate. Members were encouraged to concentrate on confession and communion, apparently with access to the reserved sacrament at least in some contexts, and to lead daily prayers - at sea is implicit. Saints' and other holy days were to be observed, using the dates for feasts and fasts to be found alongside the tide tables in the almanac. Catechism featured in the instruction of *les mousses*, often youngsters from an orphanage. Here too there were Jesuits, in this instance of the *Missio Navalis de Flandre*. A catechist was paid from confraternity funds. Members were expected at sea to encourage adults, and on shore the clergy, to join in various devotions and to discourage blasphemy and the use of alcohol. The whole venture was placed under the patronage of the Virgin Mary, and the saints: Peter, Paul and Nicholas. Of particular interest is Cabantous' discussion of the literature available to members to supplement the traditional acts of devotion (*Veni Creator*, *Ave Maris Stella*, and *Miserere*), which included the *Introduction to the Devout Life* by Francis de Sales, a *Guide de Pécheurs* by the Spanish Dominican Grenade, and Thomas à Kempis's *Imitation of Christ*. Cabantous reminds us that membership of this confraternity was unusual in its being confined to men; whether any women were to be numbered among the fishers involved is a moot point. This work, and that of Vincent de Paul, foreshadows the French ministry to seafarers which would be part of the late nineteenth-century revival of the Catholic sea apostolate, when it would be an attempt to restore what had been lost in the French Revolution.

Religious life on board British ships

Where church services on board British ships may be cited as examples of Christian activity they say little about the religious beliefs of individual seafarers, rather reflecting the values of the ship's master, which an examination of one captain's voyages and Church contacts illustrates well.

The journal of Captain Charles Bishop, not a particularly religious man, who ended his life insane, gives a glimpse of life on board.[1] In the later eighteenth century he travelled to Australasia, South America and the Far East, recording a wealth of information about the people among whom he travelled, and their customs, including Catholic ceremonies in Rio de Janeiro, of which he disapproved. He seems to have had little to do with the Church of England, beyond conducting his business through a former Church of England priest turned confidence man in Canton. In Tahiti in 1798 he had some contact with the missionaries of the London Missionary Society (founded 1795), an undenominational Protestant organisation, over a question of trade. He subsequently carried some of them on board when natives with firearms proved difficult, his crew refusing to sail until the next day, considering it unlucky to sail on a Friday.

Despite the very mixed nature of his crew Bishop made it his business to read the *Book of Common Prayer* Offices to them: 'Sunday . . . Performed divine service, to which I had the pleasure to see the whole of my crew very attentive'; 'This day being Sunday, Read prayers to the people . . . '. On one occasion, having had cause to give one of the crew a dozen lashes with the 'Catt & nine tails', put him in irons and then release him on payment of a fine, he added 'after which all hands as usual attended Prayers in good order'. Following the funeral of a crew member, 'To dispel the Gloom which such an event naturally raised in the crew, after the ship was cleaned, Prayers were read, which produced the desired effect . . . '.

The crew seem not to have been a very moral bunch, Bishop noting of their encounter with Easter Islanders, 'The sailors . . . urged them to accompany them below' for the purpose of prostitution. The crew were expected to live a life of unrelieved continence while the captain, and occasionally the officers, might be accompanied by wife and family. Bishop noted that women and pubs looked wonderful after confinement on a small ship for a couple of years, an impression that he remarked changed after a few days ashore.[2]

British convict ships were now beginning to appear to transport convicts to the colonies, attracting the attention of Anglicans and Protestants. Transport of convicts to America was sanctioned in 1666. Australian settlement began in 1787.[3] The last transport to Australia was in 1868. To combat boredom on these long voyages, charitable organisations, one organised by the Quaker Elizabeth Fry, and later by the Government, provided sewing materials and small libraries mainly of religious or moral works. Singing and dancing were

---

1   *Journal and Letters of Captain Charles Bishop, passim.*
2   *Journal and Letters of Captain Charles Bishop*, 24f.
3   W.A. Carrothers, *Emigration from the British Isles*, 23.

encouraged and schools were organised on board. Occasionally a clergyman and his family would take passage to a colony, few provisions being made for the spiritual needs of the convicts either on the ship or at their destination, unless a clergyman volunteered and was granted permission to accompany them.[1] The *Church Quarterly Review* commented that it would be hard for the Government to devise a better means of advancing the cause of irreligion among convicts, which it might also have said of provision for the crews,[2] who might all too easily find a welcome among the female convicts.[3]

The undenominational Protestant British and Foreign Bible Society provided Bibles for some ships. Some Bibles came from other sources:

> There was no divine service on board [the *Amphitrite*]. Each woman had a bible given her at Woolwich, by Mrs Fry and two other Quaker ladies . . . [who] came on board at Woolwich four or five times, and read prayers . . . The Newgate [prison] girls wish she might fall overboard and drown.

While the Quaker ladies are best known of those trying to assist the convicts, others should not be forgotten; Archdeacon Broughton of New South Wales was campaigning for more chaplains to the convicts, on the voyages out and at the colonies.[4]

The number of Anglican clergy travelling to the colonies increased in time. Apart from East India Company chaplains, most travelled under the auspices of the two leading missionary societies, the Society for the Propagation of the Gospel in Foreign Parts (SPG) and the Society for Promoting Christian Knowledge (SPCK); both alive to the possibilities presented to these travelling clergy. In 1706 SPG issued 'Instructions for the Clergy employed by the Society . . . ', instructing those 'going on Board the Ship designed for their Passage' to demean themselves inoffensively and prudently 'so as to become remarkable Examples of Piety and Virtue to the Ship's Company'. Whether passengers or chaplains they should 'prevail with the Captain or Commander' to allow the saying of Morning and Evening Prayer daily, together with 'Preaching and Catechizing every Lord's Day'. Throughout the passage they were encouraged to 'Instruct, Exhort, Admonish, and Reprove, as they have occasion . . . with such Seriousness and Prudence as may gain them Reputation and Authority'. SPG's first two missionaries, sailing for Boston in April 1702, so impressed the ship's chaplain (how the ship came to have a chaplain is not said) that he promptly joined the SPG. One of them, The Rev. George Keith, commented in a letter to the Society on the good order on the ship, writing,

> If any of the seamen were complained of to the captain for profane swearing, he caused to punish them according to the usual custom, by causing them to carry a heavy collar about their neck for an hour, that was painful and shameful; and to my observation and knowledge, several of the seamen, as well as the officers joined devoutly with us in our daily prayers according to the Church of England, as did the other gentlemen who were passengers with us.

1   C. Bateson, *The Convict Ships*, 208.
2   *op cit*,1877-8, vol V, 42ff.
3   C. Bateson, *The Convict Ships 1787-1868*, 65, 88, 106.
4   Richard Whately, *Thoughts on Secondary Punishments, passim* .

6. From the Reformation to the Nineteenth Century

Mr Keith omitted to indicate how usual was the 'usual custom' for punishing profane swearing.

The first SPG missionary to South Carolina was less fortunate; during his passage down the Channel he was 'forc'd to lye upon a chest', and only 'after many importunate and humble perswasions' was able to obtain leave to read prayers daily, being 'curs'd and treated very ill on board'. He changed ship at Plymouth, after being desperately seasick, and for the next twelve weeks and two days was able to read prayers, not twice but thrice, daily, and catechize on Sundays.[1] His complaint and those of others led the Society to draw up a letter of recommendation to masters of ships carrying its missionaries, resulting in most missionaries being allowed to conduct services regularly for passengers; to which the crews were encouraged to come.[2]

If the situation was improving for travelling clergy to minister to emigrants and convicts, it may be wondered whether the same applied to ships carrying slaves. It can be said with certainty that the Church of England produced no Peter Claver though it can be proud of its members, William Wilberforce and those who supported him, who campaigned for the abolition of this trade on which so many eighteenth-century fortunes were built. Most people are familiar with the story of the conversion of John Newton (1725 – 1807), slave ship captain turned Church of England minister, Calvinist in theology and a great influence on the Evangelical Revival in England, but his present fame rests more upon the hymns he wrote than his support for Wilberforce's campaign. Recent decades have seen the study of the slave trade become a major industry and to add to it, apart from commenting that, on the one hand the traditional churches provided little in the way of a ministry to sailors on these ships, and on the other, that those who were or had been slaves, often in their turn sailors, had a religious life which was sometimes Christian, would be to wander rather far from the subject.[3]

---

1   C.F. Pascoe, *Two Hundred Years of the SPG*, 10, 12.
2   *The Mission Field*, vol XII, 196.
3   The subject of religion in the lives of African American seamen in the age of sail is covered comprehensively in W. Jeffrey Bolster, *Black Jacks*.

The Nineteenth Century

7. The Nineteenth-Century Revival

The modern sea apostolate really begins with a series of Protestant initiatives. Fr Goldie SJ, a key figure in the revival of Catholic work among seamen, after a careful study of nineteenth-century Protestant efforts, likened his acknowledgment of the Catholic debt to them to Jesus' use of the Samaritan in the parable of the Good Samaritan, offering a good reason, if one was lacking, for examining what the non-Catholic churches were doing for the seafarer before turning to the Catholic sea apostolate.

A recruiting poster from the time of George III, addressed to the 'Royal Tars of England' and seeking men who hated France and would damn the Pope, is reproduced in Kverndal's *Seamen's Missions*, and illustrates the English religious situation well, as does Taylor's being able to cite only two instances of Catholic ministrations in the Royal Navy illustrate the position of Catholics in the RN.[1] Catholic Emancipation in Britain was not achieved until 1829, the hierarchy restored in 1850. Official appointments of Catholic naval chaplains had to wait another fifty years; in 1856 chaplains were appointed at Plymouth and Portsmouth, in 1858 at Chatham and Sheerness. There was a growing awareness among British Catholics, in the early nineteenth century a minority group, possessed of limited resources, and with the privilege of public Catholic worship only on the horizon, of the neglect of Catholics in the RN in contrast with Protestant provision.

The present chapter will examine the long nineteenth century, the effect of the French Revolution and French wars upon navies, and the effect of the cessation of hostilities and consequent reduction in naval fleets on merchant fleets. It is marked by decline of the fleets of traditionally Catholic nations and the rise of others, particularly the British. The seminal role of G. C. Smith and the emergence of the BETHEL movement from what Kverndal has called the 'Naval Awakening', which extended to French and American navies, will be acknowledged. From this naval context would emerge much of the ministry to the merchant seafarers of Britain, France and America.

The principal maritime countries at the opening of the nineteenth century were Britain and France. Its Revolution and successive wars had removed France from the seas as a serious competitor, though its fishing fleet continued in strength. No Catholic country (there was still a Papal navy), nor Germany or America, had a fleet, mercantile or otherwise, to match the British; a priority maintained regardless of indicator - steam, sail, ships built. Spanish

---

1   Gordon Taylor, *The Sea Chaplains*, 1978.

and Portuguese fleets were marginal, as were those from eastern Europe. The post Revolution French Church was paying for its association with the *Ancien Régime*, its collapse so complete, according to Cabantous, after a careful analysis of baptism registers, marriages and similar indicators, that it would take another forty years, many missions to maritime communities and a complete reorganisation of the French littoral parochial structure, to turn the tide. Cabantous described the period between 1800 and 1840 as a time of transition in the French maritime world, with anticlericalism virulent among naval officers, the Catholic minority more extreme in reaction, and parishes only slowly being won back by the devotion of their pastors. The Revolution had led to the replacement of many religious confraternities by revolutionary groups and the cessation of chaplaincy work in the French navy. In the upheaval, many members of religious orders fled to England where a sympathetic reception allowed them to rebuild on British soil. The impact of these exiled religious orders on the British Catholic sea apostolate will become apparent in later chapters.

A Time of Revival

All the nineteenth-century Christian denominations reveal a growing missionary movement, the reasons for which are complex, and, apart from delineation, beyond the scope of this book. The increasing distance between this period and the troubled years of the Reformation may be significant. While it can be argued that a characteristic of this century was a Catholic Church trying to restore in Europe what had been lost, whereas the Protestant churches were seeking new fields to conquer, it can be added with certainty that the rush for empire and the mass migration of working populations meant also that much of the work which extended the Catholic Church at this time, and to a lesser degree the Protestant churches, was actually a ministry to an extended Europe rather than to new peoples, with, in a sense, seamen as part of that extension. After 1815, improved global communications provided by a period of peace became another factor in the rising concern to spread the Gospel, a concern which seems to have been rooted in the period of war.

A time of war is not one that would prompt religious revival as a first thought, yet Kverndal has described a major religious revival in the Royal Navy between 1793 and 1815, calling it the 'Naval Awakening'. With the coming of peace the consequent dispersal of thousands of naval men carried that revival into the merchant fleet and became a significant factor in the succeeding phase, the Thames Revival. A significant factor when considering the Naval Awakening, and what followed in the merchant fleet, was the rise of the Bible and tract societies. Some of these societies, for example the British and Foreign Bible Society (BFBS, founded 1804, undenominational), began distributing tracts during the war among French prisoners as well as to British soldiers and sailors. In addition to the BFBS were the Society for Promoting Christian Knowledge (SPCK, 1698, Church of England), the Naval and Military Bible Society (NMBS, 1779, undenominational), the Religious

Tract Society (RTS, 1799, undenominational), the Prayer Book and Homily Society (PBHS, 1812, Church of England), and the Merchant Seamen's Auxiliary Bible Society (MSABS, 1818, an undenominational offshoot of the BFBS), forming a significant cluster around Kverndal's Naval Awakening. Each was providing tracts, initially to the RN, then to the merchant fleet, and to particular groups such as the men of the revenue cutters, before 1820. Those who distributed the tracts became aware not only that seamen could be brought to religious faith but that an almost exclusively lay-led revival was taking place. Lay leadership would not have been disparaged by these organisations, themselves largely the product of lay leadership: SPCK was founded by The Rev. Dr Thomas Bray and four laymen; the PBHS by lay members of the so-called Clapham Sect;[1] the NMBS by two Methodist laymen, the RTS by a mixture of clergy and laity; the BFBS similarly, but dominated by lay figures. The BFBS began distribution of tracts and Scriptures to the Army and Navy in response to a petition received from a layman. More attention will be given to these societies below.

The Naval Awakening produced the seminal figure of George Charles Smith, a Baptist minister attached to a chapel in Penzance, who had served in the RN before his conversion. In 1809 circumstances led to his conducting a Naval Correspondence Mission, involving an extensive ministry by letter to men of the Navy in the five years following. The dramatic reduction in the size of the Navy on the outbreak of peace was matched by a corresponding growth of the peacetime merchant fleet, numbers of Christian naval officers on half-pay, and older vessels surplus to requirement. With some of these officers, in 1818 Smith bought an old naval vessel for use as a floating church in the port of London, starting the undenominational Port of London Society (PLS) for work among seamen.

Presented thus there appears to be a natural progression in the early years of the nineteenth century from Christian neglect of the seaman to a rapidly developing, if not yet wide-spread, missionary movement for his conversion. With the Thames Revival, groups of men on colliers began meeting in what Kverndal has called 'cells' for the purpose of worship and witness, prompting suspicion similar to that encountered by early Methodist groups in the RN. Enthusiasm in English religion at this time was suspect. Kverndal traced the Thames Revival to Wesleyan Methodists in Rotherhithe, particularly to Zebedee Rogers, a shoe maker and a man familiar with collier brigs, who began regular prayer meetings on board some of these vessels in 1814, following an emotional encounter with a captain after a prayer meeting in the Silver Street Wesleyan Chapel. In his work Rogers was supported particularly by Samuel Jennings, a timber merchant.[2]

Smith's foundation of the PLS followed his engagement with some of these groups. In the following year, a combination of tensions and opportunity led him to found the undenominational British and Foreign Seamen's Friend

---

1 An informal group of wealthy Anglican Evangelicals mostly worshipping at the parish church of Clapham where the influential Rector was J. Venn.
2 Kverndal, *Seamen's Missions*, 151ff. Kverndal, *George Charles Smith . . .* , 50ff.

7. The Nineteenth-Century Revival

Society and Bethel Union (BFSFSBU) to extend PLS work beyond London to meet the men's spiritual and welfare needs. His foundations, mainly due to his character, proved to be fissiparous, seldom remaining within the orbit of their founder. However, the movement grew and Smith encouraged local groups to copy the work of the BFSFSBU. In each case the encouragement came mainly from the central production of a magazine through which local groups maintained contact by correspondence. Recognition that they belonged to the parent society was indicated by the bestowal and display of the BETHEL flag.[1] This had emerged in 1817 as the preferred signal for worship on the Thames colliers, originally with the word 'BETHEL in white sewn on a blue ground, soon with the addition of a white star and dove. This flag, adopted by Smith as, by now, well recognised, was accorded to captains sympathetic to the movement and intending to hold prayer meetings aboard ship and in foreign ports. There was also, at least in London and Liverpool, a parallel effort by the Church of England. Elsewhere, for example in Dublin, were more peripheral societies of uncertain denominational status, of which the barest details have survived, but all part of the general movement.

Despite the fragmentation of Smith's foundations the general trend of the century was for societies to coalesce. A major combination came about in 1856, when the Anglican layman, W.H.G. Kingston (Fig. 6), a prolific author of popular stories for boys, after a rapid tour of several British ports (Dublin, Kingstown, Cork, Queenstown, Waterford, Milford, Liverpool), brought about an amalgamation of Anglican work, The Missions to Seamen (MtS), which would absorb in 1858 the Bristol Channel Mission (founded by The Rev. Dr John Ashley in the 1830s), and later another product of the Evangelical Revival, the Thames Church Mission (TCM), founded in 1844. An exception to this pattern of combination was the 1881-2 foundation of the (Royal National) Mission to Deep Sea Fishermen (MDSF), spawned by the TCM to meet a particular need.

Nineteenth-century foundations were not confined to the British Isles. In large part inspired by Smith's pioneering work, churches in Norway (1864), Denmark (1867),[2] Sweden (1869), Finland (1875), and Germany (1886) established ministries dedicated to seamen. These denominational societies enjoyed an homogeneity which the Bethel Unions lacked, able to claim denominational support, where undenominational ones had to rely largely on private subscriptions. The denominational approach also made for a hitherto absent centralism. If the language of the market, wrested from its usual context, is applied here, these national bodies and denominational societies have about them something of the chain store with its numerous branches and central management, sometimes subsidised from the centre, where Smith's Bethel Unions would better attract the description 'franchise', the financial links being replaced for the Bethel Unions by the BETHEL flag (a common logo), a system of correspondents, and a common method of organisation;

---

1   Kverndal, *Seamen's Missions*, 156ff.
2   Henning Henningsen, *Sømand og Sømandskirke: Dansk Sømandskirke i fremmede Havne 1867-1967*, Christiansfeld, 1967.

effectively a reflection of the Baptist family, to which Smith owed his allegiance, where each gathering was considered a complete church in itself.

This chapter opened by trying to indicate briefly why the nineteenth century should have witnessed this outburst of missionary activity, which was confined neither to work among seamen nor the Anglophone community. Another missionary movement (*Läsare*) had spread from Sweden to America, its roots in the previous century, while Kverndal gives abundant evidence of the 'Great Awakening' as a feature of American religious life generally.[1] If the Naval Awakening is to be given a serious explanation, part of the answer must lie in the rise of standing navies and their better organisation, accompanied increasingly by the appointment of regular chaplains; Kverndal's linking it to the work of Charles Wesley has something to commend it. Despite the lack of strong evidence here it may be significant that Kverndal has been able to chronicle a lesser awakening in the US navy. The work of G.C. Smith needs to be set against the background of both the Awakening, and the rise of the Bible and tract societies, which will be considered below. Smith receives a full measure of attention in Kverndal's monumental work, *Seamen's Missions: their Origin and Early Growth.*

The Bible and Tract Societies

In considering the various societies which paved the way for dedicated work among seamen it is necessary to return to the eighteenth century. SPCK and SPG found their place in chapter six, their work among emigrants significant and spilling over into contact with the crews, but the work of both was limited by charter. Evangelical dissatisfaction with this led to the founding of the Society for Missions to Africa and the East in 1799, renamed the Church Missionary Society (CMS) in 1812. Its foundation came in a roundabout sort of way: in 1786, the year the first convicts were transported to Botany Bay, members of the Eclectic Society (founded 1783), among their number some of the leading Evangelicals in the Church of England, began to consider how best the Gospel might be spread in New South Wales. Pressure from Evangelicals like Wilberforce and John Thornton on Prime Minister Pitt resulted in the sending of a chaplain to the convicts and, incidentally, the foundation of the CMS.[2]

The foundation of the CMS reflects the rise at this time of the Evangelical movement, responsible also for other foundations, directly or indirectly involved with the sea, as, for example, a Bible Society (1779) which initially provided Bibles to the Army, then shortly after 1779 changing its name to the Naval and Military Bible Society (NMBS),[3] eventually to be incorporated into the Scripture Gift Mission (1888), both undenominational. The NMBS, with a Council of Anglican bishops and Evangelical worthies drawn from the senior ranks of the RN, had among its objects the dissemination of the Scriptures to sailors and soldiers of His Majesty's Service and in the service

---

1 Henry C Whyman, *The Hedstroms and the Bethel Ship Saga*, 40ff.
2 F.W.B. Bullock, *Voluntary Religious Societies 1520-1799*, 243f.
3 Kverndal, *Seamen's Missions*, 71ff.

7. The Nineteenth-Century Revival

Obituary picture of W.H.G. Kingston, *The Boy's Own Paper*, 1880.

of the Honourable the East India Company, and to fishermen and all mariners, whether connected with inland or general navigation; objects to be achieved through a network of auxiliary societies.

The 1826 NMBS Report (in the chair, Admiral Lord Gambier), its 48th, gave a breakdown of ships and corporations supplied with Bibles or Testaments, including bargemen and others at Weedon, the Seamen's Friend Society at Edinburgh, merchant seamen at Lynn, merchant seamen and fishermen at Norwich, the Mariners' Church Society, and mariners at Torquay. Its list of auxiliaries indicates how such groups multiplied in this period, for this and other societies: Dublin (1817), Edinburgh, Portsmouth (1819), Cork, Stirling (1820), Deptford, Greenwich, Woolwich (1824), Blakeney (1825), Bath, Bristol (1826), Plymouth, Devonport, Stonehouse (1826), Torbay (1826), plus Cove and Fermoy. The 1827 Report added Southampton, Sheerness, Chatham, Gloucester, Witham, Braintree, Halsted and Sudbury. Of these places some served ports, some canals, and, presumably, some were supporters' groups.[1]

A similar society, the Religious Tract Society (RTS), was founded in 1799 at a time when the Anglican body for tract dissemination, SPCK, was at a low ebb, with a committee consisting of equal numbers of Anglicans and Nonconformists.[2] Details surviving from its foundation confirm that seamen were soon recipients of its tracts. By 1817 it was supplying the Navy, as was the NMBS, plus the hulks moored at Sheerness on the River Thames, and in 1818 'colliers on the Thames, the crews of four ships proceeding towards the North

---
1 Miller, *From Shore to Shore*, 48.
2 I follow custom in referring to Protestants outside the Church of England as Nonconformists, but am aware that Catholics are among those who do not conform to the State religion.

Pole, to the convict ships, . . . to the Committee for the Relief of Poor Seamen.' Succeeding copies of the *Missionary Register* offer more details, including that its most popular tracts, *Conversation in a Boat between Two Seamen* and *The Swearer's Prayer*, sometimes prompted remarkable conversions after even casual reading.[1] From 1819 the RTS had a regular ship visitor distributing tracts in the Port of London, the success in his work soon leading to the formation of smaller tract societies in Aberdeen, Sunderland and the Isles of Scilly, which were likewise printing and distributing tracts especially for seamen. The Port of London agent reported visiting between eleven and twelve hundred ships during 1821, where, usually, his tracts were well received.

The SPCK began providing Bibles and copies of the *Book of Common Prayer*, in 1814 to six quarantine vessels at Milford Haven, and various convict and prison ships, in 1816 adding two bound volumes of Bishop Wilson's sermons to its distribution of Bibles, Testaments, and Prayer Books to each of the 62 Revenue Boats established around the British coast for the prevention of smuggling. The sermons were given without charge because the men's work on the revenue boats prevented their Sunday church attendance, this generous gift prompting an appeal for a similar grant from the Inspecting Commanders of H.M. Revenue Cutters (42 being supplied), who expressed their intention not only to read the 'Church Service' (presumably Morning or Evening Prayer) on Sundays for the crews, but also to include one of Bishop Wilson's sermons.[2]

The British and Foreign Bible Society (BFBS), like the RTS having a committee of Anglicans and Nonconformists (fifteen of each), was founded in 1812, in part because of SPCK's failure to print a Welsh Bible.[3] By 1816 it was providing Scriptures to bargees on the Grand Junction and other canals.[4] By 1818 its work among seamen had grown sufficiently to create the Merchant Seamen's Auxiliary Bible Society (MSABS), which relieved the BFBS of Bible distribution to seafarers, the MSABS intending to 'provide Bibles for at least 120,000 British Seamen, now destitute of them'. In its first two months a total of 1,721 men on 133 outward-bound ships were visited at Gravesend by the MSABS agent, Lieutenant Cox, who distributed 580 Bibles and Testaments.[5] To extend Bible distribution to seamen four depositories followed in Liverpool, adding a year later, another BFBS auxiliary, the Hull Marine Bible Society.

Statistics were beginning to be kept by the Bible and missionary societies, principally for circulation to encourage supporters. The first year's report of Lieutenant Cox (Fig. 15) showed him to have supplied Scriptures to '1,681 vessels, having on board 24,765 men, of whom 21,671 are reported able to

---

1 *Missionary Register*, 1818, 403ff. Tracts were not always well received. Charles Hopkins was scathing about what he called tract mongers.
2 *Missionary Register*, 1816, 348..
3 Bullock, *Voluntary Religious Societies 1520-1799*, 232.
4 *Missionary Register*, 1816, 278.
5 *Missionary Register*, 1816, 175; 1818, 503; 1819 etc. In early 1818 SPCK referred an application from the Society for the Aid of Destitute Seamen in London for a supply of 'suitable books' to the MSABS which responded with a hundred each of Bibles and Testaments in assorted languages. Godron C. Cook, *Disease in the Merchant Navy*, 81.

7. The Nineteenth-Century Revival

Date of issue.	Ships' Names.	Captain.	Ships' Owner or Husband.	Port to which she belongs.	Voyage.	No. of Men.	No. that can read	Supply found on board B. | T.	Supplied gratuitously. B. | T.	Sold B. | T.	Amount for what sold.
March 26.	A Boat with four people from Gravelines, with apples, to Gravesend.										s. d.
	Pallas,	Peter Clemont,	Philip Mitchel,	Jersey,	Newfoundland.	10	9	.. ..	1 2	.. ..	.. ..
	Corvo,	George White,	George White,	London,	Rio Janeiro.	10	9	.. 1	1 2	.. ..	.. ..
	Elizabeth and Mary,	James Chipperton,	Philip Cleyston,	Harwich,	Orkneys.	8	8	.. ..	1 2	.. ..	.. ..
	Tiger,	William L. Powel,	Ranson and Saltmash,	London,	Constantinople.	16	16	1 1	1 3	.. ..	.. ..
	Thalia,	John Head,	Joel Foster,	London,	Barbadoes.	18	16	.. ..	2 4	.. ..	.. ..
	Dugay Trowen,	Joseph Lorand,		La Rochelle,	Normandy.	7	7	.. ..	1 1	.. ..	.. ..
	Inverness,	Thomas Potts,		London,	Greenland.	28	26	1 ..	3 6	.. ..	.. ..
March 27.	Sprightly,	David Rogers,	David Rogers,	Arbroath,	Memel.	8	7	.. ..	1 2	.. ..	.. ..
	Samuel,	Ralph Barrel,	Samuel Barber,	N. Yarmouth,	Baltic.	9	8	would receive no supply.			
	Sisters Providence,	George Greenslade,	George Payton,	London,	Seville.	7	7	.. 3/4	1 2	.. ..	.. ..
	William,	Charles Duncan,	Moses Duncan and Co.	Scarborough,	Restoff.	7	7	1 1/4	1 2	.. ..	.. ..
	Mary,	Alexander Craig,	Henry Oliphant,	Kirkaldy,	Stettin.	8	8	every man possessing a Bible.			
	Venus,	Thomas Ellison,	Mate did not know.	Hull,	Riga.	11	10	.. 1	1 2	.. ..	.. ..
	Adventure,	John Gaterell,	John Savage,	Greenwich,	Orkneys.	9	8	1 ..	.. 2	.. ..	.. ..
March 28.	Industry, (Smack)	James Frize,	John Ludekker,	London,	Greenland.	28	26	1 ..	3 6	3 ..	10 1
	Fortitude,	Thomas Thompson,	James Argo,	Peterhead,	Oporto.	8	8	1 ..	.. 2	.. ..	.. ..
	Nancy,	John Rowe,	John Rowe,	London,	North Sea.	9	5	.. 1	1 1	.. ..	.. ..
	Amity, (Smack)	Philip Magott,	Ann Sanders,	Harwich,	North Sea.	9	4	2 ..	.. 1	.. ..	.. ..
March 29.	Prince of Orange,	Peter Lambton,	Robert Scurfield,	Sunderland,	Stettin.	9	9	.. ..	1 2	1 1	7 1
	Anacreon,	Robert Surtees,	Robert Nicholson,	Newcastle,	N. Brunswick.	20	20	.. ..	2 4	2 ..	7 5
	Swallow,	Thomas Ford,	Messrs. Newman & Hunt,	London,	Oporto.	12	12	.. ..	1 3	.. 1	1 7 1/2
March 30.	Pomona,	John Gay,	John Gay,	London,	Demerara.	8	8	2 ..	.. 2	.. ..	.. ..
	John,	William Padley,	William Padley,	Hull,	Rotterdam.	8	8	.. ..	.. 1	.. ..	.. ..
	Wharfe,	Thomas Haglewood,	William Heand,	Hull,	St. Domingo.	10	9	.. ..	1 2	.. ..	.. ..
	Pacific,	Alexander Sim,	Englis and Co.	London,	Demerara.	14	12	1 ..	1 3	.. ..	.. ..
	Admiral Nelson,	Richard Appleton,	Richard Appleton,	Harwich,	North Sea.	9	5	1 ..	.. 2	.. ..	.. ..
	Princess, (Smack)	James Fothem,	Matthew Saunders,	Harwich,	North Sea.	8	7	.. ..	1 2	.. ..	.. ..
	Timanda, (Smack)	James Baiguie,	John Dingwall,	London,	Bombay.	18	16	.. ..	2 4	7 ..	15 2
	Newbiggen,	John Wright,	William Herring,	Sunderland,	Hamburo.	9	9	.. ..	1 2	.. ..	.. ..
	Byrdon,	Charles Richardson,	Robert Oskew,	London,	Quebec.	16	16	.. ..	2 4	1 ..	5 9

March 31.	Shakespear,	William Jackson,	Thomas Gillispie,	London,	North America.	10	10	2 ..	.. 2	.. ..	.. ..
	Hannah,	George Dickson,	Willbank and Co.	London,	North America.	13	12	1 1	1 2	.. ..	.. ..
	Rambler,	James Cummings,	J. and W. Gowans,	Leith,	Meloel.	13	11	.. ..	1 3	.. ..	.. ..
	Hebe,	John Sugden,	J. S. Bivnt and Co.	London,	Bengal.	20	16	2 2	1 3	.. ..	.. ..
	Clio,	William Richardson,	George Miller,	London,	Demerara.	15	14	.. ..	1 2	.. ..	.. ..
	Orion,	Charles Smith,	Gordon and Co.	London,	North Sea.	32	29	1 1	3 6	.. ..	.. ..
	Julius Cæsar,	David Laikie,	Perry and Co.	London,	Demerara.	16	10	.. ..	2 4	.. ..	.. ..
April 1.	Freedom,	Andrew Black,	Alexander Duncanson,	Alloa,	Dangie.	9	9	.. ..	.. 2	.. ..	.. ..
	Duncan Forbes,	Blando Wilson,	Wilson and Co.	Aberdeen,	Leghorn.	9	9	well supplied from Aberdeen.			
	Constellation,	Thomas Feil,	Brookleband and Co.	Whitehaven,	St. Domingo.	11	10	.. ..	1 3	1 ..	2 2
	41 Vessels.					**499**	**456**	**22 6**	**42 102**	**15 2**	.. ..

GENERAL OBSERVATIONS.

A very old man in the French boat acknowledged, with much politeness, the Testament to be a grand present, and earnestly wished me to take its value in apples; he said he would read it very much.

The Captain of the *Dugay Trouen*, when a prisoner in England, possessed a French Testament, but unhappily lost it: he greedily received the present of another, and promised to read the good Book to all under his authority.

James Smith, Mate of the *Sprightly*, has permission of the Captain to assemble the people aft, every evening, to hear the Scriptures read.

I find it is a common practice in several small vessels that I have visited, for those who can read, to teach those who cannot; indeed, I have met with here and there a larger vessel, where the same good practice is adopted.

Captain Baignie, of the *Timanda*, teaches the people himself to read and write; at least, he did in the last ship he commanded; and tells me, every man, under his command, shall learn to read the Scriptures, on his way to Bombay. I sold seven Bibles to this ship.

The Mate of the *William* brought to me his Bible to look at, being almost thumbed to pieces, pleaded hard to have it re-placed; from his conversation, I believe he knew something of the value of that best of Books. This ship's cabin was half occupied with a large case of Scriptures, directed to the Secretary of the Russian Bible Society.

(Signed)   JOHN COX, Lieut. R. N. *Agent.*

Extract from Lt Cox's Log of ships visited - BFBS *Monthly Extracts*, 1820.

read'; his statistics rare indications of scripture ownership and literacy levels. On these vessels he found 1,475 Bibles and 725 Testaments, all in private ownership and not for common use. They were unevenly distributed: as many as 590 ships, having 6,149 men on board, of whom 5,490 were literate, were without Bible or Testament. The MSABS was able to issue free 1,075 Bibles and 4,068 Testaments to foreign-bound vessels, selling a further 390 Bibles and 207 Testaments at half price, yielding £89. 4s.10d.

Cox reported his approaches being 'contumeliously rejected' on only four occasions. More often his offers were met with pious responses, usefully brought to the attention of BFBS supporters in its reports. Many, but not all, of the vessels he boarded were smacks with small crews. A Dutch ship with a crew of twelve held on board daily prayers and singing, with grace said at meals, and every crew member in possession of a Bible.[1] The Mate of the *Sprightly* from Arbroath (eight crew), with his Captain's permission, gathered

1   *Missionary Register*, 1819, 167f.

men aft every evening to hear the Scriptures read, while Captain Baignie of the *Timanda* of London (eighteen on board), concerned that his men could read and write, promised they 'shall learn to read the Scriptures' on their voyage to Bombay. The MSABS was encouraged sufficiently to produce a sample letter for captains, offering Bibles at a subsidised price, and suggesting for crews of eight or nine, 1 Bible and 3 testaments, and for larger crews, a Bible for each watch, and a testament for every three or four men. As an inducement the letter continued, 'The Committee beg to call your special attention to this subject, as suggesting the best means of improving the moral character of seamen, and promoting among them the habits of regularity and subordination'.[1]

In 1820 the *Missionary Register* reported that 7,803 seamen on 789 ships had been saved from sailing without Bibles by the MSABS. The National Bible Society of America, perhaps encouraged by such statistics, called upon its coastal auxiliaries to become Marine Bible Societies providing Scriptures to seamen. In 1824 it drew attention to the Calcutta Bible Association's second annual report, which announced the formation of a Marine Sub-Committee to help establish Bible associations actually on board ships. The success of the MSABS allowed the NMBS to direct its work to the armed forces. Initially financed by the BFBS, money for the MSABS came from many different sources, including a donation of 100 guineas from Trinity House. After seven years' existence, the MSABS claimed to have provided 9,275 Bibles and 10, 647 Testaments. Its income for the year was £911. 4s. 7d and expenditure £860 .8s .6d; a happy state of affairs.

The 1826 MSABS Annual Meeting, presided over by Admiral Viscount Exmouth, heard that a further 1,555 Bibles and 893 Testaments had been distributed. Annual meetings ran to a pattern, reporting similar statistics. A point of interest is the names which appear, overlapping frequently with other Anglican or Nonconformist meetings concerned with seamen: The Rev. Andrew Brandram,[2] Captain Colin Campbell C.B., RN, John Petty Muspratt Esq., W. Parker Esq., Captain G. Gambier RN,[3] The Rev. Professor Shedd of New Orleans, Captain Edward Parry RN, and Captain Bazalgette RN. The work of the society continued for many years; as late as 1849 its Liverpool Auxiliary engaged a colporteur to work with local shipping. He reported distributing 2,471 Bibles in his first year, only seven in English, suggesting that the pattern of this ministry had broadened; of these Bibles, 928 were sold to Catholics and 1,543 to Protestants. No indication of the languages of Bibles sold is given; of more interest to supporters would be sales to Catholics.[4]

The specifically Anglican society in the field of tract and Bible distribution was the Prayer Book and Homily Society (PBHS); founded in 1812, it too appeared regularly in the *Missionary Register*'s pages. It began disseminating tracts, Prayer Books and the *Book of Homilies* at reduced prices among seafarers

1 BFBS Annual Report, 1818, 251. BFBS archives are held at Cambridge University Library.
2 Newly appointed Master of the Queen's Chapel of the Savoy.
3 Son of Admiral Lord Gambier, a Methodist, whose ship, the *Defence*, in 1793 suspected of being a 'prayer ship' had proved itself also a fighting ship.
4 W. Canton, *The History of the BFBS*, vol. II, 164.

in 1825, largely through the efforts of individual committee members. Its agent was sick for its first six months, limiting sales, but a fourteen month distribution total was announced to 1,261 ships visited, of 1,614 Prayer Books, nineteen copies of the complete *Book of Homilies*, and almost 1,500 canvas-bound copies of the shorter *Book of Select Homilies*, some given free for the use of ships' crews at a total cost to the PBHS of about £100. It was reported that the visits of committee members and agents had prompted some masters to resume the practice of reading Divine Service (Morning and Evening Prayer from the *Book of Common Prayer*) for crews on Sundays. The *Book of Select Homilies* was considered sufficiently admirable a medium for Church teaching that in 1827 its distribution was extended to include Naval vessels, allowing the society to report that all H.M. Ships in ordinary at Sheerness, Chatham, Portsmouth and Devonport had been supplied with the 'Formularies of the Church', and all prison hulks visited and their chaplains given free volumes of the *Book of Select Homilies* to offer to the prisoners. The same report drew attention to the neglect of fishermen, particularly of river fishermen. Expansion continued, with forty representatives being appointed in various ports in 1828, amongst whom were seven clergy, the remainder laymen under clerical supervision (as supporters would wish to be assured, and guaranteeing the PBHS its cloak of ecclesiastical respectability), most new to the work and functioning in an honorary capacity. These representatives were able to report Bibles, testaments and '8,788 Homily Tracts, and Festival Services in the same form, principally in Foreign Languages, distributed among sailors who have visited English ports'.[1] It is possible that the PBHS was the earliest agency working among seamen to make a serious attempt to respond to the presence of non-English speakers.

Cox's statistics for Bibles and literacy levels on board merchant ships visited are supplemented in the 1828 PBHS Report by figures relating to religious observance on board 590 ships visited in the Port of London, where 891 Prayer Books were sold, and 1,500 copies of the *Book of Select Homilies* given.[2] On these 590 ships, Divine Service was held regularly when at sea (weather permitting) on 207, occasionally on five, and never on the remainder.

The books and tracts of the PBHS sound unappealing to present-day ears. Cheap printing and increasing levels of literacy had allowed the tract to become a popular medium for Gospel sharing. Sailors, with little to fill their leisure time at sea, welcomed reading material. The tract could go where ministers could not, passing from hand to hand, and continuing its ministry until discarded, worn out or washed away. It avoided the whim of the ship's master and could impart sound teaching; well-written, it could even be exciting. Equally, tract scattering could be a hindrance to the Gospel; there are hints that these early agents of the PBHS had to discriminate when placing tracts.[3] Dissemination of tracts got visitors on board ships, and these were the men who started the early societies.

1   *Missionary Register*, 1828, 372ff.
2   The extraordinary figure for the *Homilies,* which required considerable concentration, may be explained if it is understood to refer to the homily tracts of the preceding paragraph.
3   Cp Basil Lubbock, *Round the Horn before the Mast*, 22f. See also, Miller, *Priest in Deep Water*, 92.

G.C. Smith[1]

It was an agent of the RTS who remarked in 1821 upon 'the active zeal of the Port of London Society for preaching the Gospel among seamen in a noble chapel on their own element', adding that when he observed 'The British and Foreign Seamen's Friend Society and Bethel Union' holding prayer meetings on the River Thames he detected the hand of the Lord at work. The Lord's hand was working through George Charles Smith, born in London in 1782, raised an Independent Christian, and, aged fourteen, apprenticed to Captain Clark of the brig *Betsey* of Salem, Massachusetts, sailing for Boston, until pressed by HMS *Ariadne*. This experience did not deter Smith from returning to the RN, voluntarily joining HMS *Agamemnon*, on which he served five years; he witnessed the Nore Mutiny, served under Duncan at the Battle of Camperdown (1797), and Nelson at the Battle of Copenhagen (1801). He led a disparate life until an illness, followed by the death of his mother, ended in a conversion experience in 1803. Now twenty-one, and returned to London, he was drawn to a Baptist Chapel, then began preaching in the Plymouth Dock at Devonport among his former naval mates while undergoing training for the Baptist ministry. In 1807 he was called to be pastor of the Octagon Chapel, Penzance, his base for the next seventeen years, while he preached widely among seamen in West Country ports.

Smith's oratory was not without effect, while his ministry was continued in the printed word when he was asked to correspond with some sailors, in 1809 founding the Naval Correspondence Mission after an invitation to preach on board a ship at Penzance; effectively his first mission to sailors.[2] Then, in 1812, he was called to London where he preached in the open air.[3] London, seat of empire and busy port, was notorious for the conditions in which its sailors had to live; press gangs, brothels, crimps and much else made their lives very hard. The *Weekly Dispatch* carried an item on 30th April, 1837 which could have been written in 1812:

> It is really heart-rending to hear of the various ways in which the 'British Tar' is imposed upon as soon as he is paid off. The harlots and a variety of other wretches in the vicinity of Wapping, &c., pounce upon him like so many hyenas. It is a pity so little protection is shown to that noble body of men.

The paper printed details of seamen being flogged, kept up the mast or on the poop almost to the point of death from exposure, bound and trailed overboard until nearly senseless, clapped in irons, given the cat-o'nine tails, swindled by boarding house keepers, involved in drunken debauches and murders, pressed and carried aboard ship, and more. There were opium dens in Limehouse, brothels on the Ratcliffe Highway, and gin palaces and public houses at every turn, waiting to

---

1 Kverndal, *Seamen's Missions*, deals comprehensively with Smith: 113ff. His book, *George Charles Smith of Penzance*, 2012 adds little.
2 Kverndal, *Seamen's Missions*, 121f.
3 In addition to Kverndal, a useful source of information was the *Soldiers' and Sailors' Magazine*, 1862.

7. The Nineteenth-Century Revival

welcome the returning sailor, newly paid off and carrying large sums of money.

The evidence suggests prayer meetings began on vessels in the Port of London early in the nineteenth century, the first apparently organised by the master of a Tyne collier for his crews and those on neighbouring vessels in 1812.[1] Soon a BETHEL flag would be hoisted when a service was about to be held. Smith's main ministry, a preaching tour on the Continent excepted, remained in Penzance, but he was making his name as a fiery preacher in London; it is hard to imagine that he was not involved in the steps which led to the increase of such services. The 1819 formation of the undenominational Protestant PLS followed, soon associated with the MSABS and similar societies, and the obtaining of a floating chapel for which plans had been laid in 1817; the work of Smith and R. Marten Esquire.

By 1825, according to the Annual Report, as in the *Missionary Register*, 'this Meeting rejoice[s] . . . in those zealous exertions at Liverpool, Leith, Dublin, and other out-ports - at Gibraltar, Calcutta, and other of our Foreign Dependencies - and in America'. The floating chapel flourished at its mooring off Wapping.[2] It is illustrative of the overlapping of early kindred societies that here a Mr Sherriff Brown moved a motion, doing so again at the London Episcopal Floating Church Society meeting; the Gambiers, last seen at the MSABS Annual Meeting, were also present. There was the perennial concern about money (1826: income £375. 15s. 5d; expenditure £539. 3s. 5d) and more support desired from owners and insurers of ships, in whose interest it was claimed that seamen be better behaved; a result expected if more could be led to faith.

Smith's work increased as need unfolded. In 1819 he founded the British and Foreign Seamen's and Soldiers' Friend Society and Bethel Union (BFSSFSBU), in 1820 the first *Sailors' Magazine*; in 1825 claiming the first mariner's church in England, meanwhile continuing to conduct a number of preaching missions. The BFSSFSBU was supported by most of the people who supported the PLS and seems to have grown in a similar way. In 1826 a motion was approved 'to give every possible stimulus to the Foreign Operations of the Institution by, among others, the Gambiers, Professor Shedd, The Rev. Mr Crosbie of Dublin, and The Rev. John Jack 'missionary from Astrachan'. In 1822 Smith founded the Watermen's Friend Society for giving religious instruction to watermen, bargemen and coal-whippers; in 1824 the Shipwrecked and Distressed Sailors' Family Fund (which coincided with the start of the undenominational London City Mission and the opening, according to one source, of a Mariner's Church in Wellclose Square); in 1826 the first Shipwrecked and Destitute Sailors' Asylum and Sailors' Home.[3] In 1829 he was responsible for the first temperance mission to sailors and the foundation of the Maritime Penitent Female Refuge. Although a Baptist, Smith attracted support from other denominations including the Established Church.

The PLS and the BFSSFSBU, sharing a common president and working

---

1 M.R. Kingsford, *Life of W.H.G. Kingston*, 125.
 See also Smith's tract, *Bethel or The Flag Unfurled*, 1819.
2 *Missionary Register*, 1825, 251.
3 *Missionary Register*, 1826, 233.

harmoniously, merged in 1827, to form 'The Port-of-London and Bethel Union Society, for Promoting Religion among British and Foreign Seamen', to become in 1925 the British Sailors' Society, and since 1995 the British and International Sailors' Society. It is implicit in its early annual reports that all went well; they would hardly suggest otherwise. The 1828 meeting heard of another of Smith's foundations, the Merchant Seamen's Orphan Asylum. The society's school in Wapping was commended for its aid to 'the numerous and destitute children of Seamen and Rivermen' with 180 boys and 90 girls in attendance. The Floating Chapel, also at Wapping, reported two services every Sunday and a monthly Communion service, an annual attendance of 17,585 at services, 9,014 of these being seamen; there were 135 seamen attendances at Communion.[1]

If these developments were not enough, it was at this time that the next important foundation took place, the Mariners' Church Society (MCS). At various times there were several societies using this name. This one, of either 1825 or 1827, merged with the BFSFSBU in January 1846 to form the Seamen's and Soldiers' Evangelical Friend Society, from 1848 the Seaman's Christian Friend Society, a markedly protestant organisation, and particularly given to tract dissemination.[2] This MCS can be traced to Smith.[3] It was based in the old and disused Danish church in Wellclose Square, London, perhaps to be associated with the Home opened there at No. 19 by George Gambier and Captain R. Elliott. They financed this Home from November 1827, appointing a mate to issue relief, and allowed Smith to use it as an operational base. On the 1st January, 1828 a warehouse was opened offering straw beds for sailors, the 'donkey's breakfast' of the sailor's bunk; then, when the Brunswick Theatre collapsed on the 28th February 1828, its site was obtained and replaced with a Home in 1829. At this point Smith resigned, perhaps to initiate other work; opinion is divided on whether the parting was amicable. Gambier withdrew at the same time, Elliott remaining, together with an unnamed Captain RN mentioned only as a supporter. Elliott at this time was involved with the Church of England, starting in January 1828 a Home in Dock Street under its auspices, its foundation stone laid by Prince Albert.

The Wellclose Square MCS assumed in 1827 the title of British and Foreign Seamen's Friend Society and Bethel Union, which had been discarded by the earlier BFSSFSBU on its amalgamation with the PLS. This MCS had a monthly magazine called the *Steam Packet*, renamed the *New Sailor's Magazine*, which resembled very closely the *Sailors' Magazine* of the BFSSFSBU.[4] To add to

1   *Missionary Register*, 1828, 227.
2   C.H. Milsom, *Guide to the Merchant Navy*, 132.
3   Kverndal, *Seamen's Missions*, 266ff.
    Stephen Friend, *The Rise and Development of Christian Missions amongst British Fishing Communities during the Nineteenth Century*, (hereafter, *Fishermen's Missions*) 85 suggests that this was intended to be an auxiliary of the BFSFSBU, that the relationship was soon fraught, Smith being forced to resign in 1826 when he was in the process of founding a third seamen's mission in London. I have rather dodged the complicated issue of Smith's many foundations and fallings-out but the message is clear enough.
4   *Missionary Register*, 1827, 236.

7. The Nineteenth-Century Revival

the confusion, its first Annual Meeting was held under the name of the British and Foreign Seamen's and Soldiers' Friendly Society, but the contemporary *Missionary Register* makes it clear that this was indeed the MCS renamed. This meeting was well attended (requiring a second room), not least by Anglicans, some involved with the Episcopal Floating Church. The Report for this MCS in 1829 is further confused in the *Missionary Register* by being indexed under 'Episcopal Floating Church Society', and claiming as its achievements 'The Sailors' Home' or Royal Brunswick Maritime Establishment, with its Receiving and Shipping Depot, Distressed Sailors' Refuge and a Sea Boys' Rendezvous; The Sea and River Tract Society and Thames Mission; and The Sailors' Orphan House Establishment for fifty boys and fifty girls.[1]

There is much confusion here with a number of the works overlapping. Apparently Smith, Gambier and Elliott remained on good terms, despite Elliott's move towards the Established Church. Indeed, Elliott seems to have moved to ease pressure on Smith's existing work, going at Smith's suggestion to found the Dock Street Home. Little has been said of rivalry and disagreement, but much of the confusion between these early Protestant societies derived from the character of Smith. *The New Sailor's Magazine* of 1829 reveals that Smith's relations with the committee of his original Bethel foundation had reached a stage where one committee member, named only as 'Philo-veritas', took it upon himself to precede Smith's preachments about the country with letters to people of influence accusing Smith of dishonesty in his direction of the society's funds.[2] Despite the Port Society's disclaimer of Philo-veritas it advertised a meeting to examine the state of the trust, proposing that all monies coming through Smith or the Seamen's Friend Society might be returned to donors. Smith fulminated in print, likening himself to the apostle John on Patmos, reminding readers what his labours of twenty years had achieved among seamen, and drawing attention to the circulation of his *New Sailor's Magazine* (its foundation surely confirming earlier troubles) which was treble the circulation of the magazine of which he had been deprived. His new 'Sailors' Guardian Society' would be firmly allied to the British and Foreign Seamen's and Soldiers' Friend Society, 'lashed, yard-arm and yard-arm'. Smith convened a meeting of ministers to arbitrate. According to Kverndal, these accusations were found to be unfounded and Smith received a public apology from his

---

1 *Missionary Register*, 1829, 212, 216. There were a number of foundations for orphaned or destitute children of seamen around this time The Port of Hull Society for the Religious Instruction of Seamen, founded 1821, initially opened a floating chapel, followed by a school to teach men to read, then in 1837 by its Sailors' Orphan Institution (Milsom, *Guide to the Merchant Navy*, 166f). On the Thames was the Sailors' Orphan Girls Episcopal School and Asylum, of 1829, among its patrons, Captain R.J. Elliott. The children were 'ministered to by the Rev. C.B. Gribble, Chaplain of the newly erected Church for Seamen'. Children to be admitted were required to show evidence of baptism and vaccination and to attend the Established Church twice on Sundays. On leaving each received a copy of the *Book of Common Prayer*. These details survive in its 20th Annual Report (1848). Miller, *From Shore to Shore*, 48-49.

2 *New Sailor's Magazine*, 1829, 384ff, 406ff, 464ff.

calumniator. Since more accusations and fallings-out followed, either Smith was trampling on egos, cutting corners, or over-working.[1] It is hard not to think of ruffled feathers and broken egg shells. The original slander seems to have originated with an assistant secretary of the British Reformation Society, whose name was coupled with that of Lieutenant Brown, Secretary of the Episcopal Floating Church Society, the two bodies having offices under a shared roof.

A comprehensive unravelling of Smith's foundations appears in Kverndal's *Seamen's Missions*. Once the confusion has been acknowledged, the reader grasps with relief the bits which can be understood. For example, the straw bed asylum which replaced 19, Wellclose Square was a warehouse in Dock Street. The Royal Brunswick Theatre was in Well Street, now Ensign Street. The Royal Brunswick Maritime Establishment, to allay suspicions of heterodoxy, was placed under the auspices of the Bishop of London in 1831, though continuing its association with Smith's work, and its Chaplain, Mr Gribble, was the incumbent of St Paul's Church, Dock Street. Perhaps in 1829, certainly before 1835, Elliott set up his own 'crewing office' to try to avoid some of the evils of the crimping system.[2] The Home was extended with the support of Queen Adelaide in 1848, and enlarged in 1865, retaining its royal patronage. This refuge for destitute seamen became a model for other, albeit smaller, institutions serving sailors around the globe. By 1890 it included the adjacent St Paul's Church for Seamen, had a staff of more than forty people, and provided four meals a day, hot baths, a tailor's shop, over 500 beds in individual cabins, a savings bank, a barber, a daily visit from a surgeon, reading and smoking rooms, a library, and more. It also housed a Navigation School.[3]

The confusion of titles and many organisations of the first half of the nineteenth century, of which Kverndal lists many more, hides a firm foundation being laid for a style of sea apostolate in which the Church went to the seafarer. Smith, virtually alone, had woken the denominations, even the Church of England, from somnolence. His was the first sailors' home of modern times, and his the hand which lay behind so many groups working among seafarers around the world. At another time this might not have been so, but London's position made a better time hard to find; most modern missionary activity on behalf of the seafarer in the churches can be traced directly or indirectly to Smith, an achievement undiminished by his imprisonment for debt in 1836, and on three subsequent occasions.[4] The fissiparous nature of his foundations reflects something of the character of the man; now, in the second half of the century these societies would begin to coalesce, most of the undenominational ones into the British Sailors' Society, and the Anglican ventures into The Missions to Seamen.

---

1   Kverndal, *Seamen's Missions*, 275f.
2   Kingsford, *W.H.G. Kingston*, 125ff. See also the Annual Reports for these years.
3   Alston Kennerley, *British Seamen's Missions and Sailors' Homes, passim*.
    Alston Kennerley, Joseph Conrad at the London Sailors' Home, 70-102.
4   Friend's *Fishermen's Missions*, offers more detail of these difficulties. Kverndal, *George Charles Smith of Penzance*, 104.

8. Nineteenth-Century Early Anglican Societies

Floating Churches

The work of the undenominational societies among seamen, especially in London, stirred members of the Church of England into action, beginning with the formation of the London Episcopal Floating Church Society (LEFCS). There was an element of competition, but there was also the view that undenominational work lacked the episcopally-ordained ministry and sound teaching of the established Church. Hulks and former naval vessels were to be found on the Thames, used as prisons, for coal storage, sea schools, and other purposes, but none yet as a church. Supposing there was space to build in a dock area, to build a church was not cheap. Smith had shown the economy involved in acquiring an old naval ship for conversion as a floating church. There might also have been a thought that sailors would feel more at home worshipping on board a ship.

The LEFCS held its first meeting on the 20th July 1825 at the City of London Tavern, with the Lord Mayor in the chair. Among those present were Lord Bexley,[1] Mr Alderman and Sheriff Brown, Lord Calthorpe, Robert H. Marten Esq.,[2] Admiral Sir Richard Keates,[3] the Hon. Captain Waldegrave RN,[4] Zachary Macaulay Esq.,[5] E.H. Locker Esq.,[6] John Pynder Esq., The Rev. W.A. Evanson, the Earl of Clarendon, W.T. Money Esq., and The Rev. T. Webster, a list which illustrates the kind of people the Church of England was able to draw upon, some of whom have already been encountered and others will follow, all indicative of Evangelical and Establishment networks.

The meeting resolved that:
the instruction of British seamen, on principles which shall introduce them to an acquaintance with the Doctrines and Precepts of the Christian

---

[1] Nicholas Vansittart, sometime Chancellor of the Exchequer, a Director of the Greenwich Seamen's Hospital, whose father had been lost at sea.
[2] Despite being the man of influence here Robert Humphrey Marten was a Congregational deacon.
[3] Sometime Governor of Greenwich Hospital.
[4] Later Earl Waldegrave and from a distinguished naval family.
[5] Governor of Sierra Leone and one of the Clapham Sect. Kverndal, *Seamen's Missions*, 31.
[6] William Hawke Locker, a civilian layman, a 'staunch supporter of the new piety in the navy' (R. Blake, *Evangelicals in the Royal Navy 1775-1815*, 182 n12) had been secretary to Admiral Sir Edward Pellew

Religion, to be a duty of solemn national obligation, and eminently entitled to the support of as many as would desire to combine the universal diffusion of true Christianity, with the moral exaltation and commercial prosperity of the British Empire.

[L]ong experience having proved the general ignorance of Seamen on the subject of Religion, and their disinclination to join in the Worship of a Congregation on Shore, to be insuperable difficulties in the way of their deriving advantage from the existing Parochial Churches . . . that the establishment of Floating Chapels, in connection with the Church of England, offers the only practicable form in which the benefit of her Worship may be generally extended to the seafaring part of the community.

[A]n Institution now be formed . . . The Episcopal Floating Church Society, for promoting the diffusion of Religion among the Seamen of the Empire, agreeably to . . . the Church of England.

[B]y aiding in the institution of Floating Churches and Schools, for the Religious and Professional Improvement of Apprentices; . . . the establishment of Depositories for the Scriptures, Prayer Books, Homilies, and Tracts, and the provision of Circulating Libraries.[1]

The use of the plural throughout suggests ambitious plans. Only some of the resolutions were achieved; others were soon obviated by the rise of the PBHS, the difference between them that the PBHS had no intention of providing churches and the other settled arrangements here proposed.

The LEFCS established itself at 32, Sackville Street, Picadilly, the London House of the Religious and Charitable Societies, a facility which seems to have been founded in 1832 under the trusteeship of the Earls of Roden and Rocksavage, Viscount Lorton, and Lords Calthorpe, Farnham, Barham, and Bexley.[2] The treasurer of the house was Henry Drummond, its secretary, a Mr Lamprey.[3] The societies using this address had their own rooms but shared such facilities as waiting and committee rooms. The principal work of the LEFCS was the floating church, moored off the Tower in the Pool of London, the erstwhile HMS *Brazen*, lent by the Admiralty as were most of the floating churches. Its position was ideal as, at this time, all merchandise had to enter London via the legal quays, situated on the north side of the Pool of London; only later were London's large, enclosed docks built to ease the pressure caused by increasing trade and larger ships. A former Naval lieutenant, The Rev. Horatio Montague, was appointed to visit ships from London Bridge to the Pool.[4] The *Brazen*'s first service was held on Good Friday, 1826, with Divine Service (Morning and Evening Prayer) held regularly thereafter until 1845 when the work had declined to the extent of being no longer practicable; the *Brazen* had capsized in 1831 and continued to deteriorate thereafter.

Contemporary with the LEFCS was the Liverpool Mariners' Church Society, formed in 1825 when a group of local people, after careful thought, approached

---

1 *Missionary Register*, 1825, 309f.
2 *Missionary Register*, 1823, 517.
3 *Missionary register*, 1825, 220.
4 M.R. Kingsford, *Life of W.H.G. Kingston*, 125.

8. Early Anglican Societies

The Rev. Dr William Scoresby with a plan for a floating chapel, perhaps stimulated by the Nonconformists' two decker, the *William*, moored in the King's Dock since 1820. The Admiralty made HM frigate *Tees* available. It was moored in a corner of the George's Dock, where it was managed by the Liverpool MCS, properly founded in 1826, with the Bishop of Chester as patron. It had seating for some thousand people. Scoresby had been a whaling ship captain and Arctic scientist. After a conversion experience in 1817 he began to hold religious services on his ship; his move to Liverpool in 1819 had led him to join G.C. Smith and others in 1821 in founding the Liverpool Seamen's Friend Society and Bethel Union.[1] In 1823 he felt called to seek ordination in the Church of England, which took place in 1825, to an assistant curacy at Bridlington. He came to the Mariners' Church in May, 1827. Scoresby served as Chaplain until 1832, when his wife's declining health determined their departure. His successor died in office in 1875. Sizeable congregations attracted by the novelty soon began to dwindle. When W.H.G. Kingston visited it in 1856 he found few seamen in a congregation drawn from the shore-side population. It offered two Sunday services, taken by duly licensed clergymen. By the time the Trustees handed the vessel over to the Mersey Mission to Seamen in 1879, it had been moved to Birkenhead, probably following its sinking in the George's Dock in 1872.

The Rev. John Ashley

In 1835 The Rev. John Ashley (Fig. 5) and his small son, on holiday at Clevedon, near Bristol, were looking out at the islands of Flat Holm and Steep Holm in the Bristol Channel. His son asked how the islanders went to church. Ashley, having no answer, went to see for himself and, finding fishermen and light-house keepers untended by any church, used the remaining three months of his holiday to continue his visits, holding services for them. From the islands he could see large fleets of wind-bound ships waiting in the Bristol Channel. On his farewell visit to the islanders, preparatory to taking up a benefice, he asked how the crews of these vessels lived and what were the conditions of their ship-board life; the number of vessels and their neglect revealed in his question's answer determined Ashley to turn down the proffered living and instead try to do something for these men.

Ashley was fortunate in having family money made in the West Indies. He purchased a cutter, the *Eirene*, and began visiting the wind-bound crews. His work proved so necessary that by 1837 it had reached the point when it could not be continued by private enterprise alone. Despite the LEFCS's ambitious plan to set up institutions 'in all situations where they may be of service to the object' neither it nor any other Anglican society was able to offer him assistance. Ashley turned to the Archbishop of Canterbury for advice. It seems the Archbishop suggested that Ashley form a local society, the Bristol Channel Mission (BCM), becoming in 1845 the Bristol Channel Seamen's Mission, a change to clarify its purpose.

Two of Ashley's logs survived in the archives of The Mission to Seamen,

1   Kverndal, *Seamen's Missions*, 287ff.

The Rev. John Ashley. Courtesy of the Mission to Seafarers.

8. Early Anglican Societies

volume I covering his work from the 12th November 1841 to the 11th February 1843, and the second continuing until 22nd July, 1843. They give a glimpse of his extraordinary work in the Bristol Channel visiting wind-bound vessels in all weathers and at all hours. They show a kindly man concerned for his own crew. Sometimes Mrs Ashley accompanied him. The *Eirene* carried Bibles, tracts and a medicine chest. It was fitted out to allow the holding of services on board. An extract from the first log (1:13) gives an idea of his industry. On the Thursday he visited twelve vessels, giving away nine Bibles and Testaments, and three Prayer Books. On the Friday he visited another eleven ships. On the Sunday:

> Newport River - Torrents of rain - Weather wild and uncertain - Wind shifting about. At eight o'C: hoisted signals for Service at Eleven being the best state of the tide. The morning so very bad did not expect anyone. However men came across from several vessels, and one Woman, the wife of one of the Captains - several came who purchased Bibles yesterday. One of the seamen led in that beautiful hymn, 'When I survey the wondrous cross', and the singing was very sweet and delightful. Preached from Isaiah 56: 6,7. Still raining heavily, and blowing fresh from the S.W. In consequence of the very unfavourable state of the Weather I did not like to hoist signals for the Evening Service.
>
> Did not go out in the boat to visit any vessels, being anxious that our crew should have rest, as they had a severe day in the boat with me yesterday, and all hands had been up through whole of the night in consequence of the gale, as well as the whole of the night but one before, when we were in Penarth Roads.

Nothing seemed to daunt Ashley. The same log (1: 23):

> Nov 26th. Got under way from Newport River at 3 o'Clock a.m. Wind down from the Eastward. The whole fleet sailing at the same time there was scarcely room to keep clear of each other - ran down to Cardiff Roads between the Sands - reached them before day - Lead going repeatedly.

The financial state of the BCM was never good. Ashley had to spend valuable time away from visiting his ships to attend meetings and raise funds, a side of his work illustrated by an extract for part of February 1843.

> From this day [7th] to the 11th was engaged in Bristol and Bath on committee business, and endeavouring to raise funds for the Society. Thus again my time taken away from the duties of the Mission through our not having a Secretary for Bristol. Besides other annual Subscribers which I obtained these few days I got two Subscribers (annual) of *Five guineas* each, and one of these has promised to assist in raising a sum for *endowing* the Society. I did not return home before Saturday the 11th at **1/2** past 5 in the Evening when I found many letters to be answered. At 9 o'Clock the same evening I went down the river in one of our boats to join the Eirene at Kingsroad. Wind East, blowing fresh, and very cold. Arrived on board at 1/4 past 10 at night, when we met for Prayers, and arranged to get under weigh soon after four in the morning for Flat Holm Island.[Ashley's emphasis]

To help raise funds the *Eirene* was taken to a number of ports for public viewing, for example in 1842 to Newport on the 17th August, Weston-super-Mare on the 4th September, and Tenby on the 27th September. At the same time Ashley was pursuing new money further afield; on the 22nd June he was preaching an appeal at Brighton, going on the 25th to Cheltenham via London for the same purpose. In 1843 in one four-day period:

> Our sails being sent to be repaired I visited Taunton, Exeter, Torquay, Brixham, Dartmouth, Plymouth, Devonport, Bridgwater, and Bath for the purpose of attending meetings and preaching sermons for the Society.

The second log ended shortly after this entry. There is little mention of sums raised. The logs record mostly his work afloat, but other statistics survive. Ashley noted that for the period 1837 to February 1843, he had visited 6,990 ships, all ships afloat, their visitation involving climbing from one moving vessel to another, often in the dark or the rain. He had sold 1,005 Bibles and 189 Prayer Books. His ship-visiting continued until 1850, by which time the number of ships visited had reached fourteen thousand, with some five thousand Bibles and Prayer Books sold.

The BCM's financial position made the last five years of his ministry the most difficult; though Ashley himself received no pay, his crew and the vessel's maintenance required funding. His financial worries, long hours, late nights and the energy required for his ship-visiting brought him to the point where ill health forced his retirement. The wonder is that he was able to keep going for so long, a marvel of energy and diligence. When he did retire the work fell into abeyance for five years, to be revived as the Bristol Missions to Seamen. It was hoped that a spin-off from this revival would be a ministry to vessels off the Isle of Wight. The Rev. T.C. Childs, working among emigrants at Plymouth, resigned his living in that port and attempted to get the new venture going. Lack of money rendering the exercise nugatory, the Bristol work tentatively joined The Missions to Seamen on its formation in 1856. The BCM soon withdrew, one may guess in part because of different styles of work, but with lack of funding the problem as stated by The Missions to Seamen; an amalgamation between the two was finally achieved on St Peter's Day, the 29th June, 1857. Indeed, the financial situation of the BCM was so bad that The Missions to Seamen Committee had to state that it could not claim the BCM's foundation date as its own (1837 otherwise being more impressive on its letter headings than 1856) lest this render it liable for the BCM's debts. Nevertheless, Ashley soon became the father figure of The Missions to Seamen, and for many, wishfully, the founder. For example, on the 125th anniversary of Ashley's death (30 March 2011), The Mission to Seafarers' General Secretary, The Rev. Tom Heffer, was quoted on the MtS website as saying that the 'Mission to Seafarers . . . carries on his important legacy to care for those on whom we depend to keep the world afloat (*sic*)'. It was Childs, following Ashley and inspired by him, who had so impressed W.H.G. Kingston by his work at Plymouth, which prompted Kingston to form The Missions to Seamen from an amalgamation of the various Anglican works for seamen which he had been able to discover. For the brief period when the two societies drifted apart, 1855, Childs's assistant was The Rev. C.D. Strong, with Childs working off the Isle of Wight, and Strong based at Bristol to continue Ashley's work. Strong came with the BCM into The Missions to Seamen and stayed to work among seamen for twenty-three years.[1]

---

1   BCM material, apart from Ashley's logs, comes from Kingsford's book on W.H.G.

8. Early Anglican Societies

The Thames Church Mission

Two primary founders of the Thames Church Mission (TCM), influenced by Ashley's work in the Bristol Channel, were disquieted at the moribund state of the LEFCS. Shipping was moving away from the LEFCS's floating church in the Pool of London, while the effectiveness of the LEFCS can hardly have been helped by the capsizing of HMS *Brazen* in 1831.[1] In consequence the TCM was inaugurated at a meeting in London's King William Street on the 23rd February, 1844; its prospectus, soon following, was issued from 32, Sackville Street, where the LEFCS offices were accommodated. Captain Waldegrave, who had been present at the founding of the LEFCS, took the Chair. Others present included Captain Henry Hope CB, Captain R. Elliott RN, and four Trinity House Captains. The meeting was followed by a visit to Bristol where Ashley's work offered a vision of what might be possible on the River Thames and led to a sailing vessel, the *Swan*, being obtained for the Thames. Despite some of the committee being linked to Smith, the TCM was a Church of England society, albeit in the evangelical mold, and soon enjoying episcopal patronage.

The first resolution of the committee was the name, Thames Church Mission Society. It gave itself the power to co-opt, adding Henry Blanchard Esq., Captain Vernon Harcourt RN, Lord Henry Cholmondley, Captain Alfred Chapman, Thomas Chapman Esq., The Hon. Captain Francis Maude RN,[2] and The Rev. C.A.J. Smith (unrelated to G.C. Smith). Elliott was the active member, tasked with investigating statistics of vessels on the Thames. The Archbishop of Canterbury agreed to become Patron, at the invitation of the Bishop of London, and the Lord Mayor of London, as Conservator of the River Thames, a Vice President, with the Bishops of Rochester and Winchester.

The appointment of a chaplain was addressed in May 1844. It was agreed that the chaplaincy should cover the Thames between the Pool of London and Gravesend. The chaplain would be expected to hold Sunday services, and to visit shipping on weekdays. He was to be a clergyman of the Established Church, nominated by the committee and approved by the Bishop. Two weeks later, the Admiralty transferred the cutter *Swan* (140 tons) to the TCM. Captain Elliott reported on its poor condition and the Admiralty's willingness to caulk and paint the hull. It arrived, jury rigged, at Blackwall where Messrs Wigram offered to fit it out at cost. Donations followed advertisements placed in the Press. J.W. Hancock, ex-coxswain of HMS *St. Vincent*, was appointed master of the *Swan*, his salary £4 per month with rations. Thus, within four months the new society had vessel, master, committee, eminent Patronage, and £381 in the bank. Painting and rigging the *Swan* was overseen by Trinity House. Nevertheless, the master-designate of the *Swan* enquired into 'the

---

Kingston or from The Missions to Seamen's 1935 publication, *From the Bristol Channel to the Seven Seas*, by C.A.J. Nibbs.
1   TCM Minute books and other papers were inherited by the MtS and provide the information which follows.
2   Erstwhile NMBS secretary.

Permanency of the Institution' before accepting his appointment.

The TCM adopted the BCM flag and pennant, omitting the word *Eirene*, for use on the *Swan*. The Admiralty granted two boats for use with the *Swan*. The search for a suitable and willing chaplain proved less straightforward. In September 1844, Elliott rejected a well-recommended curate, a former officer of the East India Company, for he:

> felt himself conscientiously bound to say, that on the score of Power in his Preaching, and the Entire Absence of Energy of Manner, the Minister he went to hear, would not be likely to sufficiently interest the Seamen.

While the search for the right man continued, the *Swan* wintered without charge in the East India Dock, where it was fitted out, its chapel including seating for a hundred, pulpit, communion table, creed, commandments and Lord's Prayer, everything as in a parish church. The Rev. Thomas Morton of Plymouth was appointed chaplain to start on the 25th March 1845. Meanwhile, the TCM had an offer to conduct services from a clergyman, the Bishop being agreeable, but the Rector of Poplar, in whose parish the dock was situated, refused to countenance any services, an insurmountable obstacle, behind which almost certainly lay the question of churchmanship.

Funds were raised mainly by subscription; to encourage subscribers, small subscription books were to 'be laid on the Bankers' tables, Lloyd's Coffee House, the Jerusalem Coffee House, &c., &c.'. The appointment of a Collector, receiving 10% on all new subscriptions and donations that he could obtain, and 5% on such other monies as he was able to collect, reveals how societies set about raising money at this time. Tracts for the vessel were supplied by the RTS and the PBHS, the Secretary of the latter expressing a willingness to co-operate with the TCM.

The opening service on the *Swan*, at Trinity Moorings in the Thames off Blackwall, took place on the afternoon of Monday, the 21st April, 1845, with almost everyone from the Trinity Yard attending. The chaplain was now in residence and about to begin visiting ships. Aft, with Admiralty permission, flew the White Ensign, surmounted by the adapted TCM flag. Hopes were high that The Rev. Mr Morton would earn his £300 a year. He was in sole command, subject to the TCM committee, which provided detailed bye-laws to govern chaplain and master. One for the chaplain was headed 'Immorality':

> He will reprove and check every immoral act which he may have the pain to witness, remembering never to speak to a Drunken Person, during the time of his intoxication, but carefully to avoid him, seizing the first opportunity when the offender is sober, quietly to point out the wickedness of the act.

Twenty days later the committee heard of the *Swan*'s first accident; whilst on the buoys it had been run into by the *Duke of Portland*, on tow and attempting to avoid another vessel. Despite the bustle of the Thames accidents were not to be frequent.

The next year proved a poor one for the Society. The chaplain left, despite being expected to serve for three years, on his appointment to a living by the Simeon Trustees, a markedly low church patronage society. He was allowed to read himself into his new parish, appointing an assistant curate to look

8. Early Anglican Societies

after it, while he remained with the TCM until a successor was appointed.[1] A sharp decline in income prompted economies; the crew was reduced in number with the salary of the new chaplain, The Rev. W. Holderness from Lancaster, appointed in July, reduced to £200 a year. He seems to have been a man of enthusiasm, undaunted by warnings about the BCM's finances and taking up his appointment in a flurry of activity, buying a small organ for the *Swan*, and arranging for the words THAMES CHURCH to be painted on the ship's side in large letters. For its part, the TCM approached (unsuccessfully) the Church Pastoral Aid Society, an organisation not dissimilar to the Simeon Trustees, for a grant. Holderness was able to report some healthy statistics at the end of his first quarter's work:

- Services held   61
- Ships visited   956
- Tracts disseminated   3,049
- Bibles sold   63
- Testaments sold   184
- Prayer Books sold   71
- Congregations   about 2,646

On his own initiative he had done some preaching on the TCM's behalf, for example in Hull.

The TCM committee expressed its satisfaction with Holderness's work through the award of a bonus. Others were less pleased. Although the MSABS had offered him Bibles, he obtained them usually from the NMBS and sold them at the usual rate, apparently 8d. whereas 10d. was the MSABS's rate. Reference to the NMBS allowed the matter to be resolved; a slight matter but allowing insight into life on a church ship and relations between the evangelical societies. The SPCK provided books for the *Swan*, making a lending library possible. Under the chaplain's instruction, three crew members became Scripture Readers, and the captain was appointed a sub-agent of the PBHS. Generally Mr Holderness had brought improvement. Funds were sufficient to permit investment of a modest surplus. By the end of 1848 it could be said that the TCM was running as envisaged by its founders.

New work was initiated. At the request of the Marine Society, fifty of its boys were allowed to attend Divine Service on Sundays. The attendance of boys preparing for a sea-going profession would be welcome. An essay competition was started. The essay was symbolic of the TCM's pioneering spirit; the first essay, a 'Life' of St Paul, was so successful that another, on 'The Sailor's Sabbath', was advertised, open to 'sailors, the crews of steamboats, barges, canal-boats, fishermen and watermen, in all cases to be "men before the mast" or apprentices', with a prize for the winner.

The TCM was casting its net wide upon the waters. It began to work among the emigrants whose ships could be found waiting in the Thames.

---

1   An incumbent took hold of his benefice by reading the Thirty-nine Articles, assenting to the Prayer Book and Book of Homilies, and taking the Oath of Allegiance to the Sovereign; only then could he enjoy its fruits.

Emigrants were not among the original TCM objects; though in 1849 the TCM had received a grant of £50 from the British Ladies Female Emigration Society (BLFES) towards the stipend of a lay assistant, only in 1851 did the objects include visitation of 'Emigrants, Convicts, Passengers'. The warning of the secretary of the PBHS that he saw here a potential clash of interests between the PBHS and the TCM was ignored and no avoiding action taken, though the visitation of emigrants fell into abeyance, to be renewed at the end of the year, perhaps with an eye on the BLFES grant. This proved too much for the PBHS, which demanded the appointment of two sub committees, one from each society, to resolve matters. This was done in early 1852 by agreeing four rules: prior invitation would give the invited society precedence on board; such invitations would be communicated between societies; in the absence of an invitation precedence would go to the first society to board; failing these rulings, agents were to remember that the good of the emigrant was the deciding factor. These rules prompted the BFLES to withdraw its grant in 1853, but brought peace between the PBHS and TCM, perhaps brought together in opposition to the Government Emigration Agent's objection to the TCM Scripture Reader addressing emigrants. Meanwhile, the chaplain went about his work, on 28th February, 1855, noting that, 'In consequence of the River having been covered with large masses of Ice, for the last fortnight, the Chaplain has been prevented from visiting the Ships.'

W.H.G. Kingston addressed the Committee Meeting of 7th March, 1856 on the possibility of the TCM joining his proposed amalgamation, here described as 'The Central Society for Missions to British Seamen Afloat and Ashore . . . through forming part of *One Great Scheme* without losing in any way its individual character'. The committee declined his offer, turning instead to complaints from the master of the *Swan* and similar domestic issues. Others, however, would heed Kingston's words.

By the mid nineteenth century, the Church of England's growing awareness of its responsibility towards seamen was paralleled by a massive expansion in dock building, which increased the need for such Church work, as in London where The Rev. A.W. Mason was writing of a proposed Plaistow and Victoria Dock Mission to 'bring its clergy into direct communication with sailors and emigrants'.[1] Nor were such efforts restricted to London. Among other initiatives, in Yarmouth the Vicar, The Rev. George Hills, at his appointment in 1848, began a ministry among fishermen and seamen which continued until his departure in 1859 to inaugurate the Anglican see of Columbia. His labours resulted in a Beach and Harbour Mission.[2] In Worcester, SPCK gave grants to The Rev. J. Davies, Rector of St Clement's, for work among seamen on the River Severn in 1848 and 1849.[3]

In Ireland, attempts were being made to reach the seafarer in Dublin, Queenstown, Cork, and Kingstown. At Dublin an independent church and

---

1   *Colonial Church Chronicle*, IX, 1857, 51.
2   Kingsford, *Life of W.H.G. Kingston*, 130.
3   Kingsford, *Life of W.H.G. Kingston*, 130. See also SPCK *Reports*, 1848, 14; 1849, 29.

8. Early Anglican Societies

seamen's institute under the charge of The Rev. A. Campbell became part of the MtS amalgamation in 1856. A reference to a mariner's church here dated from 1828. It is not clear if the two are the same; the date of 1828 suggests a connection with Smith's Bethel movement.[1] At Queenstown, the Cove of Cork, then an important port of call for ocean liners, a convicts' chaplain, The Rev. J. Bouchier, extended his ministry to visit ships in 1856. His main work was among the convicts of Spike Island, but he had an assistant paid for by the Island and Coast Society of Ireland. There seems to have been a good deal of interest in the town at this time in seamen's ministry for he, together with the incumbent, and others, formed a Corresponding Society of The Missions to Seamen, probably following the visit of Kingston, and having the assistance of his missionary, a Mr Wenham, and two assistants, one acting as colporteur, and a whale boat.[2] At Cork a George White had been evangelising before 1856, mentioned by Kingston in *A Cruise on the Mersey*, who in that year formed with a Mr J.C. Hall and six other gentlemen a Corresponding Society of The Missions to Seamen; between them they divided the docks in such a way that ships could be visited regularly and services held on board. Perhaps in a supervisory role, the Queenstown missionary visited them twice weekly. Kingston also noted a poorly attended Mariners' Church at Kingstown under the chaplaincy of The Rev. B. Brooks.

W.H.G. Kingston (1814 - 1880), after a tour of ports (his income from publishing enabled the luxury of his own yacht), brought about the amalgamation of a number of the Anglican works referred to, creating the MtS, and using as the enabling platform his fame as the author of stirring stories for boys, his editorship of the *Colonial Magazine* (1849 - 52) and *Kingston's Magazine* (1859 - 62), and the contacts made through his many efforts to improve the lot of the emigrant. He became its first secretary, giving a great deal of his time to what was, for him, a labour of love. This centralisation was not a complete solution; though it simplified the work of historians of the nineteenth-century societies at work among seafarers, some contemporary churchmen continued to feel the need for outreach through local organisations, particularly through parochial agencies (the St Andrew's Waterside Church Mission came about as a reaction to the Evangelical nature of existing Church work among seamen and its disregard for parish structures), but it went a long way to meeting many of them. Subsequent developments would show whether Kingston's advocacy of *one* society contained wisdom. How the TCM came to be part of the one society will appear in Chapter Ten.

---

1 M.R. Kingsford, *The Mersey Mission to Seamen 1856-1956*, Abingdon, 1957. *Missionary Register*, 1828, 372ff.
2 Kingsford, *The Mersey Mission* . . . , Appendix A.
 Kingsford, *Life of W.H.G. Kingston*, 131.

9. The Church Congresses

The nineteenth-century societies in the United Kingdom tended to view the seaman as an object of charity, often debauched, a second-class citizen to be rescued from perceived extravagances of sin through the distribution of tracts, sale of Bibles, temperance preaching, teas in the Bethel, and shipboard or quayside religious services. An added danger for the man sailing in Mediterranean waters, or in mixed crews, was possible contact with Catholicism; tracts of the period suggest this was a major concern. Zealous missionaries in ports like Dublin were snatching the men from the teeth of the enemy. The passage of time brought a mellowing, with maturing national societies settling into a more balanced pattern of ministry.

To avoid duplication in the account of each society, reveal the relationships between them, and their place in English Church life, it is necessary to see how this change came about before examining the establishment of The Missions to Seamen (MtS) and the St Andrew's Waterside Church Mission (SAWCM) in detail, and the merging of the various societies. The main forum for this, for Anglican societies, was the Church Congress. Annual Congress reports reveal that the main division among societies was not between *High* and *Low* churchmanship in any liturgical sense, but whether the work among seamen might best be carried out through local initiative and the parochial structure or through a national or supranational agency. A subsidiary question, also related to church order, was whether an episcopal church should have a *Bishop of the Seas*. Protagonists were many, most prominently Commander W. Dawson RN, Secretary of MtS, and Canon John Scarth for SAWCM. Chronological examination of the Congresses reveals both the unfolding of their disagreements and the growth in number and geographical spread of the societies and individuals involved in the maritime apostolate.

History seems to have answered, at least in part, what kind of society is best able to minister to seamen. In the mid and later nineteenth century this was not so clear. Canon Scarth brought to the question much heat while fighting hard for a cause close to his heart, the seafarer. His argument that work be done through SAWCM's linking of parishes had much in its favour. It was, though Scarth might not have seen it so, in some ways paralleled by the British and Foreign Sailors' Society's role in linking local Bethels. Equally, it could be defended on grounds of Church order, economy and labour. The seaman considered in the context of his home and family would most easily be reached through the local parish. But the seaman's mobility meant that

9. The Church Congresses

this was often not the case, making the seafaring life particularly attractive to men with neither home nor family. Dock areas tended to straddle a number of parochial units and ships moved between docks and parishes. Incumbents displaying any interest in their transient parishioners often lacked funds to reach out to the ships on which these were found, allowing Commander Dawson to argue that a national organisation was required, something which the existence of SAWCM as an agency linking assorted parish work implicitly confirmed, a point overlooked by both men.

Church Congresses provided a national platform for debate within the Church of England, moving annually to a different diocese and taking a theme usually linked to that year's venue. The first Church Congress was held in 1861. That seafarers were not considered until 1869 may indicate that Congress had other priorities, or that the societies concerned with seamen's welfare were slow to grasp the opportunity afforded by the Congresses. In October 1869 the Congress meeting at Liverpool included in its programme Church of England work among seamen. Earl Nelson, a regular speaker, outlining the work of 'the society for Church Missions to Seamen', SPG, SAWCM, and some isolated work conducted among fishermen on parochial lines at Yarmouth, Cromer, and Bridport, concluded that the need was for a Bishop with over-all responsibility for maritime work. Bishop Ryan, lately Bishop of Mauritius, following him, added flesh by giving more details of the societies working among seamen: TCM, MtS, SAWCM, the Royal Naval Scripture Readers' Society; parish work among fishermen in Yarmouth and Lowestoft, and chaplaincy work on training ships at Spithead and Gorey (Jersey). After noting the rapid rise of this work, he told of his own experience in Port Louis, where he had established a Floating Church and Sailors' Home, ordaining a man specially for this ministry. He commended those shipping companies, P & O by name, which provided religious services at sea. He concluded with three points: that there was need for more work sponsored at parish and diocesan levels, for greater publicity, and for more authorised services at sea.

Henry Duckworth drew attention to the missionary potential of the individual seaman. He described the MtS, largest of the Church societies, employing 36 chaplains and Scripture Readers, and its kindred society, the Mersey Mission to Seamen (MMS). His contribution then became rather muddled. After commending the work of SAWCM for what he considered its correct approach, viz. through the parishes, he then called, not for a parochial response, but for a separate work for seamen in Liverpool to replace the 'cheerless looking black hulk in George's Dock, pretentiously labelled the "Mariners' Church", with its two stereotyped services on Sunday', with a permanent church with special services - in the manner of the Nonconformists. Christopher Bushell enlarged on the Liverpool work, and the foundation of the Mariners' Church and its Society, which had a reading room ashore for the distribution of tracts and libraries. The Mersey Mission, according to Bushell, with its two chaplains and five Readers, visited ships, homes, the sick, and some 700 seamen's boarding houses. One of its Readers was supported by the Liverpool Scripture Readers' Society, and another by local ship-owners. Despite this the MMS was at a financial disadvantage compared with the local Bethel Society, the latter drawing its income from many inland chapels whereas the MMS's catchment area was limited by diocesan boundaries. The four speakers' overview of the contemporary scene in the host port allowed sight of current tensions.

Congress returned to the subject of seafarers in 1874, when meeting at Brighton. Again the speakers were drawn from the Societies. Canon Scarth, head of SAWCM and Vicar of Holy Trinity, Milton-next-Gravesend, referred to the absence of seamen from the congress agenda since 1868 (*sic*) 'when a system of parochial missions to seamen was so strongly advocated'; a statement coloured in SAWCM's favour. He drew attention to the continuing growth of Waterside Missions (i.e. SAWCM); to the recent restoration of the floating church at Shields, 'but the Mariners' Church at Liverpool has sunk at its moorings and no-one seems to care'. Worse,

> The 'Sailor Church' on the Thames is little disturbed by chaplain or by congregation, and the venerable lay missionary in charge thinks that sailors prefer extempore petitions to the beautiful prayers which the Church provides.[1]

He disapproved of the increasing use of laymen, and of mission rooms apart from parish churches, giving the example of the London Sailors' Home which, although beside a lovely church (St Paul's, Dock Street), had set apart one of its rooms as a mission hall, installing a lay missioner to work among its residents. In Liverpool, too, such a room had been opened opposite another lovely church. In his view the character of seamen had stagnated in the last ten years, marked by a church slackness at sea, in port, and on the training ships. He called on Congress to do for seafarers in matters religious, in a rare reference to Plimsoll, what the latter was doing in matters Parliamentary.

The Rev. E.L. Salisbury, following, pointed out that it was a matter of concern to the missionary societies overseas that seamen should be Christian, drew attention to the Report of the Royal Commission on Seamen,[2] and called for a church ship to be sent among the fishing fleets. In the discussion which followed, Commander Dawson took the opportunity afforded to give a survey of the work of his own society. He too remarked upon Church neglect of seamen:

> When sailors reach the shore . . . they are warmly welcomed by publicans, brothel-keepers, and other parishioners, with difficulty they find the Church open, and then idle pew-closers are stationed at every door, to tell them that 'nothing common or unclean' could enter there.[3]

His rejoinder to Scarth's emphasis on parochial agencies at the expense of a national society was followed, predictably, by an appeal for support for the MtS.

---

1 The distinction between High and Low churchmanship in the Church of England originally derived from either a high or low regard for the *Book of Common Prayer*. High churchmen were associated successively with the Tractarians and the Ritualists; it will be seen that SAWCM was definitely High.

2 Scarth and Dawson had sat on the committee which produced the *Report of the Society for Improving the Condition of Merchant Seamen* (London 1867); there was also a series of Merchant Shipping Acts over these decades. David M. Williams, Mid-Victorian Attitudes to Seamen and Maritime Reform . . . , 101ff.

3 The issue of rented pews was a contemporary one, with a campaign for free pews for all.

9. The Church Congresses

Three appendices to this conference's Report contain contemporary statistics presented to the Congress.[1] Appendix A listed staff numbers, places where societies were at work, and the approximate annual income of each. The MtS supported twelve clergy, and twenty-six lay agents, (income £6,500); the MMS two clergy, seven lay agents (income £1,600); SAWCM, three clergy and one lay agent (income £600); Yarmouth Beach and Harbour Mission, two clergy, one lay agent (income £600); Brixham, a parish mission to fishermen, one clergyman; St Paul's Dock Street, one clergyman, one lay agent assisted by three city missionaries (no income given); TCM, one clergyman, five lay agents (£1,600). Also listed were societies working with the RN, and undenominational or Protestant societies: BFSS, Liverpool Seamen's and Emigrants' Friend Society, Glasgow Seamen's Friend Society and Scottish Coast Mission, Leith Mariners' Church, the Hull Fishermen's Apprentices' Bethel, and the Seamen's Christian Friend Society of Bath ('Tracts and letters to men in RN. Conducted by a lady').

Appendix B listed training ships with numbers on board as of the 1st January 1871; numbers sent to sea in 1873; the number of those confirmed since 1871; whether there was a chaplain, and additional remarks. These were variously reformatories, for orphans or the poor, or training ships. Six ships were listed for the Thames, four on the Mersey, two on the Severn, and one each for the Clyde, Humber, Tyne and Tay. That on the Clyde was Presbyterian and two, on the Mersey and Tyne, were Catholic.

Appendix C, on the 'Influence of Seamen in Missionary Work Abroad' was presented by the Mersey Mission's chaplain and quoted various bishops and others concerned with work overseas.

The 1875 Congress, held at Stoke-on-Trent, examined the work of the MtS among bargees.[2] The 1876 Congress, in Plymouth considered 'The Church in the Army and Navy and Among the Seafaring Population', its emphasis on the armed forces. The Rev. C.E.R. Robinson, founder of SAWCM and now the Vicar of St John's, Torquay, read a paper justifying SAWCM's approach. He recognised that parish clergy were sometimes too busy to meet the needs of the seaman, or unwilling to have a community within the parish community, but suggested a remedy lay in the employment of a missionary curate. He touched on the importance of the seaman to the overseas church (where a bad example could do much damage). He indicated that, in his view, a national society was necessary only to raise funds to support missionary curates who, on appointment, being licensed as missionary curates, would owe their allegiance solely to the bishop, rather than to a society.

Commander Dawson in his account of MtS work abroad and afloat mentioned a chaplain at work in the Singapore roadsteads, Readers at Malta and Lisbon, and work in twelve British roadsteads.[3] His refutation of the

---

1 Most of the text of these is reprinted in Miller, *From Shore to Shore*, 69ff.
2 Details in Miller, *From Shore to Shore*, 69ff. It covered, for example, the work of the American Seamen's Friend Society on a large number of American canals. I offer little detail here as it is about brown rather than blue water.
3 Kingroad off Bristol, Penarth off Cardiff, Milford Haven, Falmouth Roads,

popular belief that the MtS worked afloat where the SAWCM worked ashore carried by implication the failure of Robinson's parochial outreach to meet the sailor's needs at sea. When church work in the docks was left to the parishes, an incumbent was seldom willing to accept that these were part of his parish, a state of affairs Dawson was certain would not pertain if a box of gold was found in the dock marked 'for the parish church'. He emphasised four points: ship visitation, especially before services; lodging house visitation, particularly at weekends; a welcome at the doors of the church, with good seats to which men would be shown and provided with marked prayer and hymn books; and cheerful services with lots of singing.[1] He offered St Paul's Dock Street, London as an example of what might be achieved by a busy incumbent. St Paul's had welcomed some 7,000 seamen in 1875, averaging seventy seamen per Sunday service despite the Vicar being responsible also for a parochial population of 8,000. He inclined to the view that mission rooms were not a perfect answer because seamen would always prefer the real thing, the parish church, if only it were made possible. He concluded with a call for the 22nd October 1876, to be observed as a National Seamen's Sunday, the date chosen because Psalm 107 ('they that go down to the sea in ships') was appointed in the *Book of Common Prayer* for use on that day.

Canon Scarth spoke briefly of overseas work, especially in the diocese of Gibraltar. Referring obliquely to the position of the two societies, he mentioned that two ships could run safely in the same channel if they showed their correct lights. Perhaps to deflect any damage from Dawson's views on the effectiveness of parish-based ministries, he indicated the MtS's lavish distribution of papers to Congress, SAWCM not having done so lest it be seen as an act of opposition 'when my desire is that we should act cordially together'.

The 1879 Swansea Congress returned to 'Our Seafaring population'. The Bishop suffragan of Nottingham opened with platitudes about the duty of the National Church to its seamen. He commended the example of most Scandinavian (Lutheran) captains in the matter of religious observance on board ship and bewailed the passing of those days in British history when godly merchants employed godly captains, and godly captains employed godly crews, to the benefit of all concerned, but without indicating when that period of history might have been. He referred to work among seamen at the host town, and at nearby Cardiff where there was a church built on the upper deck of a frigate, with a young deacon sailing daily from Cardiff to visit ships in the roads. He concluded with general thoughts about the two main societies.

Canon Scarth, recognising the importance of Welsh steam coal to the economy of the conference host port, examined the changes brought about at sea by the use of steam, before drawing attention to the improved behaviour of seamen, the result, he thought, of the efforts of the several societies. He touched

---

Plymouth Sound, Portland Roads, the Solent, the Downs, Great Yarmouth, Tyne, Passage off Waterford, and the Cork River.

1   Bibles and prayer books with numbered pages were a novelty in the nineteenth century, their order previously learnt by rote; this development seems obvious but at the time was not everywhere welcomed.

9. The Church Congresses

on what could be achieved by a society overseas, instancing the SAWCM-affiliated Sailors' Mission in Demerara, with its mission and boarding house, for which there was hope of a grant from the local government of $10,000 towards the cost of providing a proper sailors' home. After suggesting the great need for a Church ship among the British fishing fleets might be aided in a similar way, he reverted to his usual topics: that there was world-wide work to be done among seamen; it ought to be done through parishes; work afloat reflects work ashore and *vice versa*; the Home Church should help the Church overseas. He commented on improved arrangements by the Board of Trade for seamen to send their pay home. He wondered if the appointment of a Bishop of the Seas might tend to decrease interest taken in seafarers by seaboard diocesan bishops, and to overlook the importance to the seaman of a shore connection. He concluded: 'Is it not contrary to Church practice to consecrate a bishop for a *class*?'. This was an unusually thoughtful speech for Scarth, offering a reflection on changes in the industry rarely found in Congress speeches.

Admiral A. P. Ryder spoke of Naval work, referring to the growing demand for and general approval of a bishop for the Navy. The Rev. J.J. Stevenson Moore pointed to the neglect of fishermen, bargees, lighthouse men, and foreign-going sailors; indicated the need for a church in every port offering plenty of short and hearty services; and suggested seamen be taught clearly about the Communion of Saints to lessen their sense of isolation at sea. The Rev. G. Venables, Vicar of Great Yarmouth, spoke of work among fishermen and commended to Congress a form of prayer for those afloat put out by the MtS. In the discussion which followed, the tendency of 'fashionable people' to edge out seamen was raised by the Vicar of Blakeney in Gloucestershire, a parish bordering the River Severn. Commander Dawson offered statistics for MtS work in the host port, Swansea. His figures for international work included enrolment of 2,418 men in 1878 into the Church of England Temperance Society, reflecting the temperance movement's steady growth at this time.[1]

Seamen next featured at the 1881 Congress in Newcastle when the work of the Diocese of Durham was presented. Here Dawson opened: the MtS had ministered on the Tyne for twenty-four years, Sunderland twenty years, the Hartlepools for six years, and encouraged the work of parish clergy in Seaham and Berwick. He reminded conference that merchant ships - unlike naval vessels - were without chaplains, that the provision of churches for seamen in these ports was difficult, and that a mariners' church not only required endowment but usually came with pastoral oversight of a parish ashore to reduce the time a chaplain could give to seamen. He was followed by E.J. Mather of the TCM, speaking on behalf of a small society, claimed as the oldest in the Church of England, on its first platform at a Church Congress. He described its work afloat and ashore; his presence at this Congress a result of the number of colliers from the Durham diocese frequenting the Thames. He mentioned that seamen had originally resisted the work of the TCM's

---

[1] Temperance lodges were spreading, with quasi masonic ritual, e.g. the International Order of Good Templars, and appear in the literature of the time, e.g. F. T. Bullen's *With Christ at Sea*, 206ff.

Swan, thinking it a Government attempt to force religion upon them, and fearing they might be taxed for the *Swan*'s maintenance.[1] In giving details of the TCM's ministry, he referred to the training ships on the Thames.

In 1885 the Congress, surrounded by the Navy in Portsmouth, concentrating on the 'Spiritual and Moral welfare of Soldiers and Sailors', heard papers by the Chaplain of the Fleet and Miss Agnes Weston.[2] In the discussion which followed, The Rev. T.S. Treanor, MtS chaplain at the Downs, reminded Congress that while only the army and navy had been considered, the MN - its more than 360,000 men exceeding those of the army and the RN combined - had been passed over in silence; this he proceeded to remedy.

'The Duty of the Church to the Seaman' was next raised at the 1888 Manchester Congress. The Bishop of Newcastle, chairing the session, remarked on the importance of the subject when fifty per cent of the world's shipping was British. He made several disconnected points: there was in Liverpool a 'Great Sailors' Institute' within 150 yards of 46 public houses; the seaman was peculiarly isolated by his distance from home; many seamen had no home (only 25% of the Tyne collier crews were married). He condemned undenominational work as 'emasculated Christianity' before mentioning the work of the Church societies, and commending the MtS for leading 70,000 men to sign the pledge in the preceding nine years. He touched on the need for a 'paged Prayer-book' to help seamen follow the service. It was his experience that many parish priests were too busy to help seamen, their extra parochial work requiring a missionary curate. Finally, after saying all that each society would wish to hear him say, he advised the MtS to widen the membership of its executive committee by including representatives of each seaboard diocese, ship-owners, and members of the commercial classes, to 'exercise a far wider influence'.

Canon Scarth again reminded Congress of the changes taking place at sea, where engineers and stokers formed a new category of seafarer. He touched on the good work being done among fishermen; then, seizing his opportunity, he turned to a consideration of the British and Foreign Sailors' Society, in its seventieth year, which, despite its nonconformity, enjoyed a large measure of episcopal and archiepiscopal support.

> But there are professing Churchmen, who, in defiance of Church discipline and order, send paid agents into parishes, ignore the efforts of the responsible

---

1   Mather did not say if this misapprehension was prompted by the flying of the White Ensign, nor whether the *Swan*, now alongside as a mission room and library off East Greenwich, still flew it.
2   Miss Weston's undenominational Seamen's Rests were largely used by the RN though supposedly also open to the MN. She had written in 1868 to a soldier on the troopship *Crocodile*; he had shown her letter to a sailor, who wondered if she would write to him also; soon she was writing 4,000 letters to men of the RN, then given permission to visit HM ships, largely in the temperance cause. She hired halls for Sunday afternoon meetings, transferring them for lack of numbers to a friend's house for tea and cake. The work prospering in its new context, she opened her first Sailors' Rest, where attendance at religious services was voluntary. Her autobiography: *My Life Among the Blue Jackets*.

clergy, and introduce the bitterness of party spirit . . . When these men are allowed to have the advantage of any Episcopal patronage, they should come under Episcopal control in the parishes where they intrude . . .

adding more in the same vein. He was concerned about publicity: 'It is not in accord with the parochial plan to make the pastoral intercourse with individual souls a subject of sensational publicity'. He warmed to his subject.

I have before me the Reports of three irresponsible Sailors' Missions that have their head offices in London, an aggregate income of £59,000 a year. To secure this they spend in advertisements, publications, printing, postages, travelling, office expenses, and deputations, more than £17,000 a year! (This is £4,000 more than the SPG, and only £6,000 less than the CMS.) If only half the sum left over for the work were expended on curates to take up the work of the Church among seamen, in direct combination with the responsible clergy on shore, it would provide more than a hundred clergy at £200 a year in waterside parishes for this special work, and other help too, to 140 curates at £150, and thus enable the Church to fulfill her duty to seamen at home and leave £21,000 for work abroad in the same cause!

He condemned the use of 'lay agents' for 'ministerial work', asking if it was 'right to delegate to so many irresponsible agents the duty' of Church clergy? He thought it improper for beneficed clergy to appear on society lists as 'Honorary Chaplains of the Mission', omitting to say that SAWCM produced similar lists, often naming the same clergy, but calling them 'Correspondents'. With a final flourish he pointed out that SAWCM's entire working expenses for the previous year (£800) were less than the expenditure on postage of any two of the three societies named.

Perhaps those present wondered what would follow when Canon Scarth sat down. Commander Dawson rose and remarked how little *un-aided* parishes had done for seamen, the little that had been done usually prompted by newly-opened non-sectarian work. He promised to say no more on the subject, but to let the facts speak for themselves. He instanced Bilbao, where work among seamen allowed the Catholic population to see that not all Protestant seamen were drunks; implicit here was the difficulty for a parish-based effort to extend to seamen in foreign countries. He reminded Congress that 36,000 British merchant vessels, and countless yachts, barges, lighthouses, and islands claimed its attention. All lacked chaplains, and 20,000 of the ships, at least, had no Sunday service. Some 136 ports were used annually by more than 2,000 seamen under the British flag, few with any Church provision ashore for seamen, and none with provision afloat. The appointment in 109 ports of MtS Honorary Chaplains was at least a step forward; something to be compared with provision for Scandinavian seamen, who were actually provided with chaplains.[1] A major hindrance to Church work was Sunday labour; in the heathen ports of China, Christian sailors were forbidden to work cargo or coals on the Lord's Day, whereas in British Colonial Waters (e.g. Hong Kong) they were compelled to work. There was more: 28,970

1 The situation of the Scandinavian churches meant that effectively, this was State provision, whereas the English Church, though by law established, received no State aid except consular chaplaincy provision.

registered British fishing vessels also had need of the care of the Church. His society had been labouring at this problem for years and now had

> twenty volunteer mission-smacks on the east coast which cost the public nothing, flying its flag on the Dogger Bank, and bearing a helpful and noble witness to Christ among their comrades in the trawling fleets of the North Sea.[1]

He reminded his audience that the Church's outreach was to seamen of any creed or nationality, in doing which, except in Scandinavia, it was following a way paved by 'nonconformists'.

> The Church, hidebound in its parochial system, ignored the water and its dwellers . . . It was not till ten years since the late Archbishop Tait devised a way of licensing the chaplain of the fleets in the Downs directly to his hazardous work on the waters. And it was only three years ago that the bishop of Durham found, in the Private Chapels' Act, a means of licensing seamen's chaplains. Before then Missions to Seamen chaplains working afloat had to be licensed to sham Curacies for landsfolk.

As seamen moved from parish to parish, ship to ship, dock to dock, even diocese to diocese, and there had been 'utter failure' by parishes to cope with this mobility, all this was required.

Dawson made a number of other points which appear disconnected in summary form but give a glimpse of his society about its business. He referred to its work for purity in the merchant fleet; in the absence of a special agency, his chaplains were encouraged instead to enroll men in the White Cross Society. White Cross work was conducted in 48 churches or missions, with the men enrolled intending to continue afloat what the MtS was trying to do ashore. He touched on the debate about a Bishop of the Seas, suggesting such an appointment might isolate men further from their dioceses. Of the bishops generally, the Bishop of Gloucester and Bristol was the only one of the society's episcopal Vice Patrons notable for his attempts to encourage activity among mariners in his diocese. Bishops of London, despite having responsibility for the largest port in the world, had done nothing, Bishop Jackson excepted, who had tried to start a scheme of unpaid lay readership among captains at sea, but his clergy had produced no captains; of the two who had been licensed, both had been brought forward by laymen.[2] He referred briefly to work among emigrants. In short, he had gently responded to each of Scarth's points but referred neither to societies nor personalities. Many of the points at issue between the two reveal tractarian rubbing against evangelical, less in doctrinal terms than in understanding of

---

1   A system whereby Churchmen promised to hold services on board and were issued with a Flying Angel flag at a solemn service. The flag was to be surrendered to any chaplain on request.

2   The question of lay readers at sea is of interest. The Diocese of Newfoundland tried, at one time, the experiment of licensing a crew member (usually the skipper) to hold services on the larger fishing vessels, a report to be presented to the priest on return to the shore. The 1885 SAWCM Report quotes the Rector of Rotherhithe: 'We believe that the Bishop of London is willing to license captains to conduct public services on board their own ships, on what conditions we would like to know. We have never heard if any of these licences have been granted, and with what results.'

parochial and episcopal authority, and finding the surface rough.

The Sunderland MtS chaplain gave details of the steps followed by the Bishop of Durham in licensing as chaplain a man who had been a lay reader for sixteen years until local clergy liaised to finance a chaplain, himself, in 1883. He argued strongly that the 'professedly Church societies [should] confer together with a view to *amalgamation*' and with other societies to promote better relationships. He thought that every port should have chaplain, readers and institute. The Church should give of its best to seamen, particularly in the matter of literature for ship-use, as seamen were not stupid. As to a Bishop of the Seas, he reminded Congress of a resolution to this effect at the end of the May 1888 Meeting of the Central Council of Diocesan Conferences: 'There is good reason to believe that their lordships would earnestly consider the practicability of the scheme.' Such a Bishop's duties would include organising work at foreign stations, acting as a rallying point for the scattered work among seamen, holding (with the permission of the diocesans) additional confirmations, and ensuring that everywhere sacraments were properly administered. His title might be *Bishop of the High Seas*; his proposed appointment presciently akin to the Provincial Episcopal Visitors of the late twentieth-century Church of England.[1] Finally, he suggested that problems over Sunday labour might be overcome through a campaign of attrition, in which chaplains and others would work on local merchants, and parish clergy on seafaring residents.

The Under Secretary of State, Sir James Fergusson, spoke for the National Mission to Deep Sea Fishermen. Responding to the suggestion that money would be better spent on missionary curates, he pointed out that the MDSF's annual income of £25,000 had to maintain twenty Mission vessels, with two further hospital ships being built.[2] He felt that, though this was not a Church work, it was a very necessary work and that everyone would get along much better if unnecessary friction was avoided.

A long discussion followed. The Bishop of Calcutta, known to be willing to administer Confirmation as necessary either in Mission or cathedral, reported that seamen's work in Calcutta was connected with the parish, 'not swamping the one in the other, but linking the two together'.[3] The Bishop of Sodor and Man suggested his own work was not unlike that proposed for the Bishop of the Seas. A MtS speaker thought that seamen were very shy and that the appointment of such a Bishop, even if only a suffragan to the seaboard bishops, would bring home to them the concern of the Church. A Vicar from Bootle thought that a compromise could be achieved between MtS and SAWCM if the work of the former afloat and the latter's work ashore could be encouraged. The Bristol Seamen's Institute chaplain drew attention to the material needs of the seafarer: his poverty; his poor working

---

1 The MtS for may years would have a department with a Senior Chaplain of the Church on the High Seas largely concerned with co-ordinating cruise chaplaincies.
2 For a summary of MDSF work: Stephen Friend, Social and Spiritual Work Amongst Fishing Communities, 138ff. This summarises much of Friend's MPhil thesis.
3 Chapter 14 details the moribund state of the Calcutta port chaplaincy around this time.

conditions in the forecastle, especially the firemen's quarters; his average expectancy of working life just twelve years, often ending in a watery grave. He called upon the Church to lend its voice in support of a Government Bill then being considered to create a seamen's pension fund.

The 1889 Congress at Cardiff considered 'Missions to Seamen', adding little beyond fresh statistics to the bones of 1888. Seamen reappeared in 1892 at Folkestone in a discussion on 'The Church of England on the Continent', giving the spotlight to the Gibraltar Mission; some of the information given was inaccurate (see chapter twelve). A corrected summary would reveal that the Bishop of Gibraltar, Bishop Sandford, had drawn together, on a diocesan basis, work which preceded his episcopate, and had received support from the BFSS, SAWCM, and the MtS. Canon Scarth used the opportunity to repeat his views on the use of lay readers.

The last Congress of the century to consider the ministry of the Church to the seafarer took place in Norwich in 1895. Canon Scarth opened, reminding those present that the state of national commerce, which amounted to £1,000,000,000, was directly related to the labours of seamen. He looked for more Government legislation to improve the lot of seamen, his particular concern being seamen on 'ocean tramps', who sailed without any idea of destination or duration of voyage. He commended the efforts of the Bishop of Gibraltar who, having more ports than any other Anglican Bishop, his diocese covering the whole of Europe, yet managed 'to help chaplains in almost every port between Lisbon and Odessa'. Seamen were the most isolated class of men and needed integration into the local community. His closing points were rather more combative. 'The parochial clergy need not much mind when their work is ignored by the managers of independent and irresponsible agencies that think of no other work than their own.' Rather than heed the advice given at the Manchester Congress that the societies should amalgamate, he argued that it would be better if they all went parochial, adding a strong condemnation of episcopal patronage for any work which was not definitely of the Established Church.

The Archdeacon of Macclesfield observed that twenty years earlier it would have been unusual to see a *bona fide* seaman in church. To indicate how things had improved he gave figures for communicants in a number of MtS ports, where the Church had paid attention to their special needs and provided for their ministry 'special men with special qualifications' who 'have been found to give their whole time and special attention to this most special work'.

> I am fully alive to the fact that there are a few like the reader of the last Paper who would prefer to bring the seaman to the parish church, and to make this branch of the Church's work a branch of the parochial work; but I cannot shut my eyes to the well-tried experience of the special clergy for this special work, and the great appreciation of the sailor for his own church.

He suggested the large number of donations sent by parochial clergy to the MtS indicated their overwhelming support.

> I would not wish to imply for one moment that much good work has not been done in some sea-board parishes by the assistance of SAWCM in helping to provide a curate in such populous parishes to try and reach the sailor.

He complimented the work of the TCM before arguing for a coalition between

the societies, giving four reasons: the first,
> that seamen may recognise in the Church's work amongst them a unity of spirit and action; a mission flag the same symbol in each port; a close communication of sympathy and effort in each port; commending from one port to another the communicants as they sail from sea to sea;

the second, that it would be more economical; then, that it would overcome wrong feelings of rivalry and competition; finally, that stronger pressure could be exerted on ship owners by a single society. He concluded by turning to secular matters: the improvement in Board of Trade provisions for the transmission of wages, and possible ways of remedying the custom of encouraging men to desert in certain ports, notably San Francisco.

Sir George Baden-Powell MP told Congress that if clergy were provided for seamen in the same ratio as in the parochial system, there would be 2,500 chaplains at work among seamen. He instanced the Gibraltar Mission's Seamen's Guild (with its rules of daily prayer and Bible reading, attendance at public worship where possible, observance of the Lord's Day, and the intention to lead a moral life) as a means of linking men. The MtS had also some 10,000 'voluntary associates' bound to a similar rule. He concluded with remarks on Sunday labour, calling for parliamentary action and suggesting that no ship ought to be allowed to fly the British flag if it hoisted no church flag on Sundays!

The final speaker was The Rev. Forbes A. Phillips, Vicar of Gorleston, Chairman-Founder of the North Sea Church Mission (NSCM), who turned the attention of Congress to the need of North Sea fishermen for Church work and a Church ship. His efforts had made it possible for the NSCM, with a grant from the Additional Curates' Society, to maintain at sea with the fleet a small smack fitted out as a church ship (Fig. 7).

If it is asked what value these Church Congresses had, several answers are possible. The historian will see the development of the various societies, their statistics presented regularly to succeeding Congresses, and the relationship between them illustrated in their competition for funding for differing types of ministry. The sociologist will observe that Canon Scarth, almost alone, spoke of the physical needs of the sailor and the effect of technological developments on his daily life. Incarnational theologians will recognise his churchmanship, and understand what lay behind his comments on stokers and firemen, tramp ship crews, and the impact of steam and other technical developments on the industry. The Congresses brought pressure on the Church establishment to find ways of supporting the ministry to seafarers, and to the contemporary church member, news of what the Church was or should be doing in his or her name for the seafarer. Congress reports found their way into the Church press, and at least one monthly magazine, *Mission Life - or the Emigrant and the Heathen*, ran a series of articles throughout the 1870s written by secretaries of the societies or port chaplains. No Bishop of the Seas emerged.

One result of importance, not directly from the Church Congresses but surely prompted by them, was an agreement that a *Report* should be compiled for Convocation on the spiritual provision being made for seafarers.[1] The 'First

---
1 Convocation was the nearest thing to a governing body possessed by the Church of England at this time. See *Chronicle of Convocation*, 1876, 91f. The Report is

228 THE GT. YARMOUTH PRINTING CO.'S ANNUAL.

North Sea Church Mission

WATERSIDE, GORLESTON, GT. YARMOUTH.

PRESIDENT:
The Right Rev. the LORD BISHOP OF THETFORD.

VICE-PRESIDENT:
The Right Rev. BISHOP HORNBY.

The ONLY Church of England Society working **Summer & Winter** among the NORTH SEA FISHING FLEETS which employ over **13,000** MEN AND BOYS.

TRAWLING.

The North Sea Church Mission, in addition to providing a Permanent Church and Clergy for work on the Fishing Grounds, supplies gratuitously **Medical and Surgical aid and appliances,** Books, Papers, and Magazines, warm Woollens, and (by permission of H.M. Customs) Tobacco free of duty.

ANY CONTRIBUTIONS OF

Money; or of Literature, Woollens, or other useful articles,

Will be gratefully received and acknowledged.

Full particulars of the Mission, and how to help it, may be obtained on application to JOHN H. EASTERBROOK, Esq., *Chairman of Committee and Managing Director, at the Offices of the Mission, Waterside, Gorleston, Gt. Yarmouth.*

An advertisement for the North Sea Church Mission, 1899

Report of the Committee on the Spiritual Provision for Seamen at Home and Foreign Ports' was brought before Convocation in 1877, a result of a debate in its Upper House, raised by the Archbishop of Canterbury as early as June 1874 and produced by a committee consisting of the Prolocutor, and an assortment of archdeacons, canons and prebendaries chaired by the suffragan Bishop of Nottingham. It concluded that the Church owed much to seamen and that seamen in port had as much claim upon the attentions of the Church as other Church members; each time a seaman was in port might be the last opportunity for the Church to offer him salvation. Despite this, the MN had attracted only private attempts at Church work whereas the RN had official provision, points considered at some length, as were the services provided for use of those at sea. Among its resolutions, the third was 'That the supply and support of additional Sailors' Homes in Foreign Ports is most desirable'.

Subsequently more sections were presented to Convocation, the full *Report* being adopted in 1878. It drew a detailed and panoramic picture: mortality rates, number of ships, number of men, percentage of Lascars employed, conditions of work, needs, and the duty of the Church towards the sailor, together with Church provision in sixty-four Home ports. In short, it was the most comprehensive examination of the subject to be made by an official body of the Church of England. One or two passages may interest the general reader; the serious student will want to consult the *Chronicle of Convocation* 1878 for the full Report.

> The most devout of all [were the Norwegians] . . . the captains of their trading ships acting as chaplains to their crews, conducting prayer and reading sermons to them, besides taking care that they are provided with bibles, prayer and other devotional books. The Scandinavian Church provides pastors and churches for their seamen in many of the foreign ports frequented by them.

The *Report* observed that Welsh seamen had a strong devotional feeling but were generally Methodist; the Irish feared the Bible as a 'forbidden book'; and Italian seamen 'stand low in the religious scale', usually ignorant and superstitious.

The *Report* noted that on only one ship of 666 sailing out of Sunderland were Sunday services to be found board, with similar figures for Hull and Bristol. In other ports: at the Downs one in 122 had services, Falmouth Roads one in 134, Swansea one in 43, Poole one in 35. The introduction of steam had greatly increased Sunday labour in port with a consequent effect on church attendance. The *Report* called for 'Unanimity of Work' regardless of whether Church work was being conducted on parochial or other lines. It observed in the section 'Mode of Worship' that seamen did not seek segregation in their own chapel ashore, 'nor do they care for any attempts to imitate their particular phraseology on the part of those seeking to serve them.' As most seamen were at least nominally Church of England members from a parochial background it was important that they should not be looked on as 'sea-going aliens'. Those who complained of the seaman's unwillingness to go to church were reminded that others, such as agricultural workers in rural areas, were equally unwilling. The seaman's life

---

appended to the 1877 *Chronicle of Convocation*; some copies lack the appendix.

was not conducive to forming the church-going habit, nor to getting to know the local church and its people. Seamen in general complained about seating arrangements in most churches; there was encouraging progress where free seating had been provided and a welcome extended, with an example given.

Sections followed on the MtS (which 'in every way stands first on the list'), the TCM, and SAWCM. One, on 'Seamen in Port', suggested that the best place to minister was at sea where temptations were few and there was time for serious thought, failing which, the Church could arrange for services to coincide with the start and finish of every trip.

> When least able to bear temptation on shore, it comes upon them with full power, for no sooner does a ship enter port and her crew is in a state of excitement and exuberant joy at their freedom, and the expectation of their forthcoming pay, than they are assailed by male and female harpies, eager to despoil them of their hardly earned gains, and, still worse, of their character as Christian men. Runners and crimps from public-houses, bad boarding-houses and from clothiers &c. . . .

The importance of providing decent sailors' homes was stressed, a recommendation suggesting these offer religious instruction for any who desired it, rather than to all regardless of desire. Parochial clergy should aim to visit boarding houses at least weekly.

Worship at sea received much attention. 'Through want of privacy on shipboard, even the most godly men cannot substitute private prayer or [due performance of Divine Service] with any comfort'. 'Forms of daily prayer are greatly needed'. To aid Divine Worship the *Nautical Almanac* ought to give the 'proper designation to each Sunday . . . as a guide to its Collect and Lessons'. The committee's First Report (1877) suggested prayers be provided 'to be used in time of great danger', and a service of thanksgiving; the first time for two hundred years that the Prayer Book services for seamen had received attention from an official body. The committee considered replacing Morning and Evening Prayer with a special Office for normal use at sea but did little beyond suggesting for the absolution, prescribed in the Forms of Prayer for Use of those at Sea when a priest was present, instead a declamatory form of words, perhaps reflecting contemporary disquiet about the use of sacramental confession. This section of the 1877 Report suffered the fate of most reports; no action followed.

Other reports which followed added little to what has been gleaned from the Congresses. The Third Report, of 1879, concentrated on foreign ports, consular support, the need for mission rooms and boats, and, of particular interest, recommended the use of *Certificate Cards* for issue by MtS and SAWCM agents to religious seamen as cards of commendation, a suggestion prompted by cards produced by SPCK for emigrants to present to clergy on arrival; effectively an ecclesiastical passport.

10. The Missions to Seamen[1]

The publisher and prolific author, W.H.G. Kingston took up the cause of emigration in the 1840s, as Secretary of the Colonization Society in 1848 publishing a treatise, *A system of General Emigration and for the disposal of Convicts in the Colonies*. Another of his works was *How to Emigrate*. Touring ports to investigate provision for emigrants, Kingston was impressed by what he saw of Church work among seamen, particularly in Plymouth and Bristol, where chaplains were visiting seamen and emigrants. His *Kingston's Miscellany* brought his thoughts on their work to a wide audience. In an address made at Southampton in 1850, he described meeting The Rev. T. Cave Childs at Plymouth and seeing, for example, how he organised emigrants into classes, allowing those who could read to teach those who could not, and so providing occupation during the tedious weeks at sea.

There is no particular evidence to show how The Missions to Seamen came into being, beyond Kingston's interest.[2] By 1856, the work of his Colonization Society having been taken over by the SPG, he found himself free to concentrate on achieving an amalgamation of Church of England groups working among seamen, for which purpose he called a preliminary meeting on the 20th February 1856.[3] According to Kingston, Childs had attempted to attract his interest in those BCM debts which had led John Ashley to cease working in the Bristol Channel.[4] Kingston visited a number of ports, noted what he saw, and began trying to bring the various agencies together, initially through a committee recruited from the great and the good, particularly naval men. The recruitment of senior naval officers was a feature of the century; they had useful networks, often came from influential families, usually had a regular income, perhaps private means or half pay to support their leisure, and, it may be guessed, were thought to understand life at sea.

Nothing survives in MtS history to parallel, for example, the retrospective comments which show how the TCM grew out of the Episcopal Floating Church Mission following prayerful consideration for a Thames ministry afloat. What do remain are Minutes of committee meetings preliminary to a

---

1 The Society *Minutes* provide the material in this chapter unless otherwise indicated.
2 The only biography of Kingston seems to be M.R. Kingsford, *The Work and Influence of William Henry Giles Kingston*.
3 M.R. Kingsford, *The Work and Influence.*, 122ff.
4 There are other versions which suggest Ashley gave up his BCM work through ill-health.

Public Meeting; apparently, out of a few small and only gradually absorbed groups grew quickly a busy society. While it seems never to have had large sums of money, nor was it plagued with the financial difficulties of the earlier societies or of SAWCM. It did not have to create work; appeals for its help came quickly enough, as the picture given at the Church Congresses confirms. Kingston had discovered and responded to a real need.

Kingston did not seek to dominate meetings. At a first meeting, February 20th, in the chair was Captain Scott, accompanied by Kingston, Captain Waugh, J. Richardson Esq., W. Benson Esq., and J. H. Tate, laymen all. They formed a provisional committee which would include the Duke of Manchester, and Captains Caffin, Fishbourne, and Sullivan, to start a society in London to support missions to seamen.

At a second meeting, February 28th, it was agreed to form a central association to work on the lines of the BCM, which it was hoped would become a member while continuing its work as before, explaining the choice of 'Association' to describe the venture. A March approach to the TCM was rebuffed. On April 5th, the committee drew up working guidelines. The first section, *Laws and Regulations*, decreed that the title of the society should be, 'The Society for the Promotion of Missions to Seamen afloat, at home and abroad'; the 'afloat' in this title lying behind Church Congress speeches suggesting work among seamen ashore would fall to others. It would have Patron(s), Vice Patron(s), President, Vice President(s), and a committee of twenty-four. Other paragraphs dealt with subscriptions, General Meetings, and regulations to govern the committee. Kingston and The Rev. T.A. Walrond were named as Honorary Secretaries and the Hon. A. Kinnaird and Admiral W.B. Hamilton as Treasurers.

A week later *Bye Laws* were drawn up and accepted. There were ten of these, placing operations of the society under the central committee in London, but allowing for provincial committees, corresponding members, and Foreign and Colonial Port Committees. The central committee was to organise other committees, select and appoint staff, communicate with the Government, receive chaplains' reports, and handle subscriptions and other monies. The provincial committees were to create interest and raise money; the Port Committees to oversee vessels and boats employed in the work of the society and assist port chaplains, with Colonial and Foreign Port Committees having a similar function. Chaplains and other agents were to keep journals of their work for submission to the central committee. The central committee would pay stipends quarterly.

Negotiations with the Bristol Channel Mission

Details of those stumbling negotiations with the BCM now begin to appear. The MtS committee asked for the objections of the BCM (25 April 1856) in the hope that the two societies could move closer. The Minutes of the 2nd May reveal that the BCM was highly suspicious of the London committee, fearing an attempt to encroach upon its Bristol activity, something 'indignantly

10. The Missions to Seamen

repudiated' by the MtS. London instead disowned the BCM debts, to which it was unable to give 'undefined aid and assistance'. Further investigation (13 May) into the income and expenditure of BCM stations at Bristol and Ryde prompted, five days later, a compromise proposal, effectively for the Bristol work to become a provincial committee. This was unacceptable to the BCM. The next meeting (28 May) of the central committee, considering an apparent BCM debt of £1,000, concluded that to give more than ten per cent of its income towards removing the debt was impossible.

In an attempt to overcome the impasse, for the BCM The Rev. D. Coper and its Hon. Secretary, Henry Grant, travelled to London to meet the central committee and supervise the transfer of all papers. London agreed to liquidate by instalments the BCM debt, now revealed as £450, by an agreed percentage of its income. A month later Mr Grant wrote to say that the Bristol Committee was now dissolved; the national society accepting the dissolution, appointed Walrond as Secretary of the society, agreed to pay him £200 a year, and ordered him to obtain office premises. In early July an office was taken in Fenchurch Street, in the City of London. Plans were made to launch a major appeal for funds. Dr Ashley was contacted regarding his handing over the *Eirene*. The Rev. C.B. Gribble was approached about the possibility of absorbing the Wells Street Sailors' Home and St Paul's Church. This proved a step too far.

In August 1856 the *Eirene* became a bone of contention, partly over ownership, partly because it was felt to be economically prudent for the cutter to be laid up, causing the BCM to show signs of independence. These hardened in October when changes to the running of the Ryde station were threatened. Otherwise, the London committee was making progress. On the 29th October its first appeal for assistance came from Odessa. The Archbishop of Canterbury agreed to serve as a Vice Patron as did the Bishop of London, though the Archbishop of York deferred his decision. Sir James Duke MP and Captain Gambier became Vice Presidents.

The committee entered 1857 concerned with more practical matters. A large Public Meeting was planned which Lord Shaftesbury agreed to chair.[1] It amended the Constitution to clarify that the society belonged to the Church of England. The Public Meeting, booked for the 10th March, and to be held at Willis's Rooms, a venue favoured by the TCM for meetings, recognised the neglect of its seamen by the Established Church, commended the work of the new society, and replaced what had been a provisional committee with a regular one.[2]

This new committee met on the 11th March 1857 and appointed The Rev. J.N. Gilman as Travelling Secretary. From this date, it may be said, the

---

1 *Minutes*, 18.2.57, 25.2.57.
2 Captain Caffin RN, CB; J.C. Colquhoun Esq.; The Rev. W.B. Daubeny; Montagu Gore Esq.; Captain W.H. Hall RN, CB; Kingston; The Rev. W. Light; Captain Nolloth RN; Captain Scott; Admiral Sir William Carroll KCB; H.D.P. Cunningham Esq.; Captain Fishbourne RN; The Rev. C.B. Gribble; The Rev. E. Kingston; Captain Liardet RN; Captain Mangles; J. Richardson Esq.; Captain Waugh.

society 'got under weigh'. Grants were made to several ports and others were investigated. Gilman travelled widely to publicise the work. He seems to have been involved in some way when the (by now) totally separate BCM re-opened negotiations with London at the end of May 1857. The existence of two societies with Missions to Seamen in their titles caused public confusion, compounded when it was discovered that the Bishop of London was connected with both. Despite slow progress in bringing the two societies together, Ashley was elected a Vice President of the MtS in September 1857. His role in discussions is nowhere made clear; he had retired to a parish and was in poor health and it may be guessed that his election was important as a symbol.

The London committee's first report, for 1856 – 57, indicated considerable progress. It had established a first permanent station on the Cork River and Queenstown Harbour; a missioner was working on the part of the Thames not served by the TCM; chaplains represented the society on the Mersey, the Bristol Channel, the Isle of Wight, Milford and Swansea, Cork, the Sussex Coast, Great Yarmouth, Plymouth, the Tyne, Malta, Leghorn, and the Elbe, while readers served the Tyne, Yarmouth, Brighton, Plymouth, Portsmouth, Swansea and Madras.

In contrast, the BCM had little to report. In 1858 another move was made to bring the two societies together under the *Missions to Seamen* title as being 'more free and open'. Four points emerged - that question of the title, the combining of committees, the pooling of resources, and the honouring of engagements already entered into by the BCM. The London committee drew up a circular by the end of April 1858, circulating it to the Archbishop of Canterbury, Lord Shaftesbury and the Duke of Marlborough for their consideration, which proposed that both committees resign and a new committee be formed; two representatives from each society would select a committee mutually agreeable; the Vice Patrons of both societies who were Prelates, Peers or Admirals to be retained; the General Committee to meet quarterly in London with two standing sub-committees, one in London, the other in Bristol (in effect a local committee). The first three of these points were agreed and the remainder left for consideration by the new committee. On this basis the MtS and the BCM achieved union on the 19th May 1858.

The MtS continued to grow from this time, following the pattern indicated in successive Church Congresses. Its expansion was rapid and world-wide. There was no doubt about its primacy. At the same time, attempts continued to be made, from time to time, to absorb the other Anglican societies. Where absorption was not possible, a policy of mutual co-operation was proposed but not always achieved, as Congress skirmishes with SAWCM have demonstrated. Problems with the TCM remained.

Negotiations with the Thames Church Mission

The TCM continued its work on the Thames. Here it acted also as the agent for the NMBS until that society stopped supplying merchant seamen at the end of 1857, the TCM turning instead to the BFBS, which was, at the

10. The Missions to Seamen

beginning of 1858, looking for a society to relieve it of its two colporteurs on the Thames. This the TCM would do, as it involved hiring another man and a boat, only if the BFBS was willing to pay the £135 necessary for the first year of operation. The BFBS declined, preferring to continue its work with the 'New Metropolitan Agency about to be called into Existence', perhaps but not certainly the MtS. At the same time, the TCM was having problems with the PBHS, which objected to the TCM's failure to use the 'Ritual of the Church of England', conducting instead extempore services on board ship, an indication that the TCM identified itself with the Low Church party within the Church of England.

In April 1865, the TCM received a letter from Walrond suggesting a closer relationship. A sub-committee was appointed to consider this. By May, after considerable discussion, it was clear that the TCM was unhappy with the idea of a merger. Nevertheless, a public meeting on June 1st came out in favour, suggesting points which might allow union to be achieved:
- That the society be designated the Thames Church Mission in union with The Missions to Seamen;
- 'that the present arrangements, appointments and management of the Mission [TCM] remain as before';
- that any extension of work on the Thames be considered jointly;
- the future appointment of a chaplain to the *Swan* to be in the hands of the TCM committee;
- the TCM to report quarterly to the MtS, its report to be printed in the MtS journal, *The Word on the Waters*;
- the MtS committee to guarantee £680 *per annum* to the TCM and the TCM to hand over surplus collections, etc., to the MtS;
- such surplus to be devoted to TCM work;
- the TCM to incur no extra expenses without sanction from the MtS; the MtS Secretary to be an *ex officio* member of the TCM committee;
- the TCM accounts to be audited and sent to the MtS annually.

The TCM committee was informed on June 16th that Walrond had made a river trip on the *Swan*, and found great alterations to be necessary to the structure of the ministry. A sub-committee was formed to examine changes in the shipping pattern to see how they related to the work of the TCM. By December total amalgamation or reversion to the original position was the choice to be faced. Two motions regarding salaries and committees were passed, which if rejected by the MtS would be followed by the *status quo ante*, with the TCM forced to draw on its contingency fund. Though this suggested that shortage of funds lay behind the TCM's willingness to talk to the MtS, the TCM committee ignored Walrond's call for immediate and total amalgamation. On failing to achieve satisfaction from the MtS, a General Meeting of the TCM was called for 22nd February 1866. This dissolved the 'union' and was followed by a committee meeting to consider the situation; the TCM reverted to independence, perhaps as a gesture of defiance extending its work by appointing an additional two workers, and obtaining an office and a secretary.

Reconstituted and newly invigorated, TCM made good progress in the short term, receiving help from the Evangelization Society, the Pure Literature Society, and the Dock Street Sailors' Home, where The Rev. Dan Greatorex, a TCM committee member, was chaplain. In 1868, despite its evangelical tradition, there was some question of the chaplain of the *Swan* using the surplice and the Litany at weeknight services, to the annoyance of nonconformist captains and others; a matter resolved by directing the chaplain to use short extempore services, with the Litany at his discretion, and without the surplice, a garment seen here more as a red rag than as the white over-garment of actuality. Partly in reaction to the TCM and its churchmanship (as evidenced by those extempore prayers, dislike of the surplice, and disregard of local incumbents), in 1864 SAWCM (Chapter Eleven) began its work at Gravesend where shortly a dispute arose with the TCM over the ship-board baptism of an emigrant's child. The TCM chaplain informed his committee he had seen the Vicar of Gravesend, Robinson, who had been co-operative, over the matter of registering the baptism. Robinson 'seemed disposed to leave to [TCM] the undisputed control of the highway of the River', a disposition of short duration.

Problems were not slow to re-emerge. In February 1867, Mr Robinson protested that he, as incumbent, had not been informed of a TCM meeting to be held in his parish. He enclosed details of his society, the SAWCM, to show that it was not antipathetic to the TCM's aims, and suggested - perhaps mischievously - the amalgamation of TCM and SAWCM; a suggestion the TCM committee declined. Robinson's next ploy was to reply, deploring the overlapping of the work of the two societies and suggesting that the TCM should make a grant to SAWCM to do its work at Gravesend or hand that work over to SAWCM in its entirety. This too was declined.

TCM also clashed briefly with the MtS in the mid 1870s when the MtS appointed a lay reader to visit ships on the Thames. Since his work was limited to a portion of the Thames that fell in the parish of The Rev. Dan Greatorex, presumably with his approval, the TCM could do nothing except protest. TCM's work on the rest of the Thames remained unaltered. It struggled on despite a worsening financial situation. In 1875 – 76 it sub-let part of its office to the National Truss Society.[1] In 1876 it moved to new offices at 31, New Bridge Street, Blackfriars. In 1877, Captain Maude's influence with the Admiralty on behalf of TCM was enough to stop the Admiralty acceding to a SAWCM request for a launch.

In 1878, pressure from the committee which produced the Convocation report on Church work for seamen produced a slight thaw in relations with the MtS. It was agreed that the MtS could appoint chaplains and readers to Thames-side parishes as funds allowed, something to which the TCM could hardly object. Despite TCM staff problems (Chapter Fifteen), otherwise good relations continued to operate at those points where the societies

---

1   The prevalence of hernias among seamen has been noted in connection with St Artemios. It is not clear whether these industrial injuries explain the TCM's connection with the National Truss Society.

overlapped, it was not until July 1903 that another serious meeting between the two societies took place to look again at the possibility of amalgamation; a special meeting for this purpose was arranged for the September. TCM's ministry to people who were not seamen was an obstacle. Other points considered were the relation to the Church of England of its staff of chaplain and eight laymen; the maintenance of TCM's river work; an examination of the four halls run by TCM at Tilbury, Radcliffe, Leigh and Erith; the state of its finances; and the retention of its name. It was agreed to retain the TCM staff, replacing them gradually with Anglicans. The relationship between the TCM halls and the parishes in which they lay being considered somewhat tenuous, it was agreed to maintain them for the time being, provided their use would be for seamen only.

Little could be done about the TCM finances; in 1902 it had a working deficit of £1,239 and investments, mainly its pension fund, of £4,781. The Bishops, by October 1903, had expressed themselves in favour of an amalgamation; this was agreed subject to use of the Prayer Book, emphasis on use by seamen of the TCM halls, continued employment of TCM staff, and the incorporation of the TCM name in the MtS title. Financial and episcopal pressure combined to ensure acceptance of these terms by the TCM on November 3rd, subscribers being informed that they were to take effect from 31st March 1904. For many years, though long since dropped, the title of the Thames Church Mission appeared below the title of The Missions to Seamen. In this way the MtS could be said to have perpetuated work begun in 1825 by the Episcopal Floating Church Society.

Although W.H.G. Kingston had intended that the MtS should act as the central body for church missions he did not intend it to be the only one. During his feverish round of activity in 1856 he had visited many parts of England and Ireland. On his way to Ireland he spent the weekend of November 22nd-24th in Liverpool with The Rev. J.N. Gilman, newly appointed MtS Travelling Secretary. His Saturday morning was given to forming a provisional committee, the Sunday ship-visiting in the port with Gilman, the Monday morning to a second committee meeting, effectively the first formal meeting of what would become the Mersey Mission to Seamen (MMS). Kingston hoped it would become a self-supporting organisation, and possibly able to contribute to a mission he hoped to found at Milford Haven. Gilman was to become the first MtS chaplain to South Wales.

The Mersey Mission to Seamen

Liverpool had the Mariners' Church Society (see chapter eight), founded back in the 1820s, and a Seamen's Christian Friend Society, a nonconformist society, dating back to Smith. However, a large and fast growing port needed more to be done for the seaman. It had many ships, much crimping, countless sailors' boarding houses and bars of the worst kind. Against this background Kingston made his semi-autonomous foundation, the MMS, which despite an optimistic start, soon began to show the familiar signs of financial insecurity. Consequently only in 1874 did it became an independent society, with an understanding with the MtS that its financial catchment area should be the dioceses of Liverpool and Chester. It retained close connections with the parent society, flying the MtS (Flying Angel) flag, but having its own Chaplain Superintendent. In 1879 it absorbed the work of the Mariners' Church Society. The various centres from which it worked in Liverpool crossed nine parish boundaries, and employed two chaplains and four lay readers - all members of the Church of England, though the 1878 *Report* to Convocation commented on their failure to adhere to *The Book of Common Prayer*. From 1892 it provided chaplaincy services to the training ships on the Mersey. The gift of a launch in 1897 permitted work on the river to be renewed. From its beginning the MMS had had a number of links with SAWCM. SAWCM's main interest in Liverpool had been emigrants, which interest it became increasingly keen to hand over to the MMS because of its financial problems. This was achieved in January 1895, and from this point the MMS had the monopoly of Church of England work on the Mersey, by 1900 with rooms in Runcorn, Ellesmere Port and Birkenhead.

By the end of the nineteenth century a number of well-established Anglican societies were working among seamen. When the Church Congress met in Northampton in 1902, and returned to the subject of 'Church Work among Sailors', the situation was outlined by the Chaplain Superintendent of the MMS. He explained that while the MtS was undoubtedly the largest society, there were others at work: the TCM, the Gibraltar Mission to Seamen in the Mediterranean, the Order of St Paul

(which by means of a monastic system, closely following the medieval plan, ministers to a number of destitute seamen at Barry and Greenwich and maintains a small house for aged seamen at Alton, Hampshire),

the Lichfield Diocesan Barge Mission, the NSCM, Miss Weston's work for the RN, the BFBS, the (Royal National) MDSF, and the undenominational Liverpool Seamen's Friend Society. Indeed, so many were labouring among seamen that he though something ought to be done to align them.

I plead once more, as I did at the Manchester Congress for a Sailors' Bishop. He would be given grace at his consecration to lay hands on the men the Church wants for this ministry; co-operating with all the territorial Bishops, and serving, as he saw opportunity, under the flag of each of our Seamen's Societies in turn.

In this way the work would have a unifying factor. The precedent for such an appointment could be found in the Bishop of North and Central Europe; seamen's missionaries wanted such a man; chaplains would have a legal status above that of licensed preacher. It says much for the nineteenth century that the twentieth could open with such a confident appeal; more about the twentieth that such a man was never appointed.

The MtS remains the dominant society at work among seafarers in the name of the Anglican Communion. At other times, other bodies have been at work. Early in its history the South American Missionary Society

10. The Missions to Seamen

(SAMS) had reached out to the crews of ships arriving in its sphere of influence. Although thus far the MtS has been shown as swallowing, or merging with, the TCM or SAWCM, in the twentieth century it has neither sought nor achieved a monopoly. In the case of SAMS, the two societies worked in harness until, the specialised nature of the ministry to seafarers and the value of a world-wide network being recognised, early in the twentieth century the SAMS began to hand over its work among seamen to the MtS, which in its Jubilee Year demonstrated the world-wide nature of its work by opening ten new stations, the South American ports of Buenos Aires, Iquique and Callao among them.[1] Other agencies came and went; during the 1914 – 18 war the Church Army extended its work to include seamen, withdrawing at the war's end.

---

[1] E. F. Every, *The Anglican Church in South America*, 1915, 118ff. Robert Young, *From Cape Horn to Panama*, 1905, *passim*. SAWCM Reports, 1875, 1876, 1885, 1886, 1898 etc. SAMS had been working in a sporadic way for two decades, in some cases benefitting from SAWCM grants.

11. St Andrew's Waterside Church Mission[1]

The St Andrew's Waterside (Church) Mission, its full title not always used, was founded in 1864 by The Rev. C.E. Robinson, incumbent of the parish of Holy Trinity, Milton-next-Gravesend. Some idea of the work of SAWCM has been given in chapter nine through the voice of Canon Scarth. It may be wondered why, with so many societies working on the River Thames, another was thought necessary. Though the amount of shipping on the river at this time, when London lay at the heart of an expanding Empire, meant that there was always more work to be done, it was the factional nature of the Established Church which led to SAWCM's foundation. The evangelical stance of the TCM and the MtS was inimical to Tractarians and their Anglo-Catholic successors, with their emphasis on Church order and its parochial system which was intended to ensure pastoral care for all.

At first SAWCM's work was confined to Gravesend, its name taken from the dedication of a Gravesend waterside chapel. From its beginning it was subject to financial problems, but seems to have enjoyed the favour of the Bishop of Rochester, the Gravesend diocesan, who advised continuance for a further year in spite of its financial uncertainty. His advice was apparently justified, for SAWCM reported an improvement in 1868, though its income was always dwarfed by that of TCM or MtS. Bibles and Prayer Books were distributed, together with vast quantities of books and magazines, contributed by the public and freighted free of charge by the local railway company. Its 1868 *Report* quoted *The Monthly Packet* of October 1868, describing the 'Waterside Mission' as housed in Gravesend's former Spread Eagle Tavern, facing the river and with its own quay, its lower floor converted into a chapel, and, above, a Mission House with reading room, library and night school. The clergy worked on the principle that if sailors came not to them, to the sailors they must go, including in their ministry from January 1864 the crews of passenger and cargo vessels, anyone connected with these, and fishermen. Outward bound steamers coaled at Gravesend from twelve coal hulks, on board each hulk a family which SAWCM staff visited. A Mothers' Meeting was begun for the many families of seamen in Gravesend. These families provided much work for SAWCM to do, its attentions apparently surprising the poor for whom such attention was a novelty.

SAWCM's improved income was maintained in 1869, with over £100 cash in hand, a deposit account of £200, and £200 put aside towards the purchase of

---

[1] Material in this chapter is drawn from SAWCM *Reports* and Minutes unless sourced otherwise.

11. St Andrew's Waterside Church Mission

a Mission House. Money was raised mainly through deputations and increased as the work became more widely known. There were no office expenses. A donation of £1,000 in 1870 to the chapel fund allowed the laying of a foundation stone on St Peter's Day, and consecration on St Andrew's Day, a year later. The local yacht club offered the use of a steam yacht to facilitate ship-visiting, a Ladies' Committee supported the work, and small grants for books were received from SPCK. All this was timely. Gravesend was a coaling station and the place where ships changed pilots. Following the opening of the Suez Canal, a marked increase in the number of ships required SAWCM's attention. The building of a Sailors' Home was contemplated though never achieved.

By 1872 SAWCM could boast a staff of two chaplains, two honorary chaplains, one Reverend Treasurer, and a lay reader. The Archbishop of Canterbury agreed to become Patron. An organist was appointed for the newly acquired chapel organ. Chapel windows were installed, a significant advance in any Victorian building programme, and, perhaps more in accord with modern taste, a day school started for fishermen's children. A new boat was presented in the following year. Improved finances allowed the opening of a branch to serve London's Victoria Dock, in St Mark's (later, on the division of the parish, St Matthew's) parish, where ship-visiting was begun, 130 libraries issued, and an anonymous donation received towards the cost of a missionary curate. At Gravesend, for ship-board services, a portable Holy Table and linen were acquired. SPG gave £25 towards the visitation of emigrants and £10 was received from the Pure Literature Society.

In 1874 the SAWCM *Report* mentioned a first contact with the MtS, following the receipt of 'some gifts'. Its work in London's growing dockland area was extended when a grant was made to the Vicar of St Luke's, Millwall towards a missionary curate to visit ships in the Millwall and West India Docks, while in the Victoria Dock, the Victoria Docks Company had provided a permanent church for seamen. Appeals for help were beginning to come from abroad. An Honorary SAWCM chaplain had been appointed at Corfu, and SAWCM was arranging to supply him with a safe boat from Malta, while parcels of books were being sent to Yokohama, Naples and Algiers for seamen, to Jamaica for the seamen's hospital, and Odessa for the sailors' home. At this time Odessa was being visited by some 7,000 British sailors annually, prompting SAWCM to appeal for £200 a year for room rental, and an additional £25 for furnishings.

Most requests for assistance from SAWCM were for small things, and repetitious (books, boats and missionary curates), but giving an idea of how the society was growing and its method appreciated. In 1875 its Secretary visited Rotterdam, Hamburg, Copenhagen and Gothenburg to investigate possibilities. It was aware that the Bishop of Gibraltar was doing the same in his diocese and opened a fund to assist him. An appeal for Naples had born fruit to the extent of establishing a flourishing sailors' home. At Grimsby SAWCM was committed to provide half the stipend of a missionary curate. There were plans, too, to place a curate at Tilbury, just across the river from Gravesend, where the railway company was developing docks. Annual gifts were received from

SPCK (£150), SPG (£25), and the MtS (hymn books). Appended to the annual report was an impressive list of ports receiving books, or honorary chaplains appointed. Although the 1876 *Report* to Convocation showed the SAWCM income for the year as no more than £600, its increasing presence in the ports makes it possible to see why Canon Scarth was able to speak with confidence at Church Congresses. A small but interesting detail in this year's report indicated ships wishing to exchange libraries could fly the code flag for M from the mizzen, while those holding a service on board were encouraged to fly the same flag from below the ensign. That this system could operate with the expectation of being understood suggests that SAWCM was beginning to make an impression among seafarers.

Perhaps with the Convocation *Report* in mind, in June 1876 the SAWCM Constitution was confirmed at a General Meeting. Essentially it was

1. 'to advance the influence and teaching of the Church of England among Sailors, Fishermen, and Emigrants, on board ships and elsewhere, through the agency of the parochial clergy at home, and the responsible clergy abroad'.

2. 'governed by a Council consisting of 25 Members, and the Presidents and the Vice-Presidents of Local Committees who shall be ex-officio Members of the Council. The Council shall appoint the Chairman, Secretary and Treasurer, and fill up vacancies in the three Trustees, if need be . . . '.

3. 'The Council shall meet annually . . . '.

4. Any station may have a local committee.

5. The Annual General Meeting to be held in London. Those entitled to vote at an AGM are Council Members, donors of £5 or more; all clergy and churchwardens who have given offertory collections in the last twelve months, all local committee members.

7. A Standing Committee shall meet at least quarterly.

8. Officers of the Society are the Honorary Treasurer and Secretary.

9. Any supporting parish may have a Local Association.

10. (This item is taken up with Accounts.)

11. 'There shall be a commemoration service on the day of the AGM. All meetings are to begin with prayer.'

12. 'A Quarterly Paper relating to the affairs of the Mission shall be prepared and published'.

13. 'The Standing Committee and Local Committees shall have power to make bye-laws to be approved by the Council at the next Annual Meeting'.

This Report shows how SAWCM went about its work in these early years. There were its *Corresponding Members*, that is, usually chaplains who had little, in many cases, to do with SAWCM beyond sending it an annual account of their work, but liked to feel that they were allied with it in some way. Sometimes they received a SAWCM grant towards their work. Meanwhile Gravesend, a parish mission with an unequalled amount of shipping, was showing what an ambitious and imaginative parish could do. It had depots

11. St Andrew's Waterside Church Mission

for the reception of books at Gravesend and London, the latter providing also waiting rooms for captains and officers attending to correspondence or receiving guests, a facility illustrating rather well the difference between those amidships and those in the fo'c'stle. A small but helpful innovation was the production for distribution of maps of dock areas in Gravesend, London, Genoa, Naples and Bordeaux marked with places of importance to the seafarer, including places of worship provided by the Church of England.

In 1877 SAWCM took over the emigrant work of the SPG and SPCK in Liverpool in return for financial aid from both societies. In London its attention seems to have turned to lightship crews. At Gravesend, its report noted the combination of salt and freshwater men using the reading room was not making for harmony. In 1878, a major society, probably the MtS, though this is not named, launched an appeal for £5,000 for work in London's dockland, which SAWCM saw as an invasion of its territory. Indeed, the Honorary Secretary worked so hard in his attempt to remedy the damage this caused to SAWCM's funds that he required a Mediterranean holiday for his health. The campaign for a Bishop of the Seas added to his troubles; SAWCM, committed to working through existing parochial structures, argued that such an appointment would discourage even the little attention work among seamen received from bishops and clergy. Meanwhile, it was extending its operation to work among troops at Gravesend, Dartmouth and Madeira, presumably on troopships.

To view a society from its annual reports is not sufficient. Another picture comes from the appendix to the 1878 *Chronicle of Convocation*, which describes SAWCM as 'excellent but smaller' than the MtS, its office address 36, City Chambers, Railway Place, Fenchurch Street, London, in the heart of the city, and by the railway station which was the terminus of its supportive railway company; probably too the address of its waiting rooms for officers. It mentions Scarth's succession as Secretary, his extension of SAWCM work generally, and confirms the primacy of work at Gravesend where two curates assist in 'the arduous and important duty of visiting the numerous . . . ships passing in ceaseless succession'. Additionally the stipends of three other curates are provided for the Port of London; some 25,000 books are dispensed to seafarers annually; mention is also made of the society's many correspondents and its North Sea work.

Increasing commitments stretched the SAWCM's budget. A Minute of the 12th August 1881 authorised the Treasurer to discharge liabilities as cash came in, a hand to mouth existence. The recruitment of more clergy, even a bishop or two, to preach appeals, particularly at St Andrew's tide, on SAWCM's behalf helped, and support continued to come from sources, lost to the historian, if not the archivist of dusty reports, such as the £10 from the 'Canterbury Mission Society for promoting Missions to Seafaring and Waterside Populations, upon closing that Society, which now leaves the field open for contributions to this Mission'. The charitable Baroness Burdett-Coutts, builder of better housing for the poor and giver of endowments for significant Anglican Sees in the Colonies, limited her support in 1879 to sending SAWCM an abundance of copies of 'A Service for Use at Sea' as used 'on board her ladyship's steam yacht *Walrus*'.

In 1881 SAWCM opened its first major foreign work. An anonymous lady offered SAWCM £100 for its funds if Canon Scarth would go out to organise a permanent chaplaincy in Port Said.[1] Scarth, taking a holiday abroad for his health, undertook temporary chaplaincy work there. Providence favoured the society; in a very short time P & O had offered him a free return passage, and at the recommendation of *M*. de Lesseps, President of the Suez Canal Company, the Administrators of the Canal made a grant of some sixty square yards of land (then worth about £3,000). The Canal Company promised all possible assistance. An English Church, Hospital and Sailors' Home were planned, subject to the permission of His Royal Highness the Khedive. The Rev. F.W. Strange left chaplaincy work at London's Victoria Dock to become the Port Said chaplain.

SAWCM at this time was fostering work among Lascar crews using the Port of London. Indeed, the whole of its London enterprise was prospering. In 1882 an anonymous, Liverpool-sourced, donation of £1,000 allowed SAWCM to extend considerably its work in Liverpool. By 1885 'Grants for the Year' were being made:

to the Port of London	£1,050
Other Home Ports and the North Sea Fleet	395
Port Said	100
Genoa	50
Constantinople, Hong Kong, Rangoon New Brunswick, Hastings £25 each	125
Other small grants	445
	£2,165

The Hastings grant is of interest; once a MtS port, it was now to be run on parochial lines following the resignation of the MtS chaplain. Some of the shipping companies were generous to SAWCM; British India, P & O, Allan, and Orient Lines carried its parcels of books and associated goods free of charge. In 1886 SPCK donated £250 worth of its books and continued to make similar grants annually.

SAWCM was beginning to extend its ministry to the fishing industry. In 1886 Brixham fishermen asked SAWCM to help their curate to accompany them in a mission ship, to which end they subscribed £60, no mean sum. SAWCM had so far maintained that it worked ashore whilst the MtS worked afloat, a distinction not recognised here, and one further eroded in 1889 when the SAWCM was given three vessels to extend its work afloat. These were the small steamer *Kestrel* for use at Gravesend, the RTS yacht *Sapper* to be a church ship, and the *Water Kelpie* (54 tons) for use as a floating church.[2] Hopes that one of these might serve the Dover-Lydd-Rye area came to nothing. However, in 1891 a petition, perhaps circulated to all the societies because it noted gratefully the work of the MtS ashore and afloat, was received from thirty-six East Coast clergy asking for a church ship in the North Sea to serve the fishing fleet. These clergy envisaged a ship 'perhaps partly paying her own expenses by working as a trawler with the fishing fleets, when not otherwise

1 For the context see Freda Harcourt, The High Road to India, 19-72
2 A floating church was not intended to put to sea.

11. St Andrew's Waterside Church Mission

engaged', a model favoured by the TCM/MDSF, and with a chaplain on board. The 1894 Report made it clear that lack of funds had prevented the *Sapper* from being sent to sea. Instead, the *Goshawk*, lent by J.R. West Esq. RYS, after fitting out as a church ship, made a trip among the fishing fleets under the SAWCM flag of St Andrew.[1] The opening service on board took place at Gosport on 3rd July, 1893. It was crewed mainly by Brixham fisherman, and carried a surgeon and chaplain, its first trip not to the North Sea but to the Shambles lightship, Dartmouth, Brixham, Torquay, Milford Haven, Cardigan Bay lightship, Ramsey (IoM), Oban and Aberdeen. A second trip was made in 1896. However, it proved too expensive to run, though when the Vicar of Gorleston set about raising the money to purchase a vessel locally it seems that SAWCM was shamed into running it again among the North Sea fleets.

The following year the society decided to change its name to the more general 'Saint Andrew's Church of England Mission to Sailors, Emigrants and Fishermen', though it was felt that the old name would die hard, as proved to be the case. Other societies might have preferred a change of attitude. In 1888 there was a spat between SAWCM and TCM following a TCM advertisement in the *Guardian* and other national papers, which Canon Scarth maintained misrepresented the work among sailors in the Port of London; perhaps TCM's response to SAWCM's placing the *Kestrel* on the Thames. TCM's advertisement quoted the Bishop of London. Canon Scarth, wanting to protest against this apparent episcopal sanctioning of TCM claims, had a Statement drawn up, signed by all London incumbents in receipt of SAWCM aid, to be laid before the Bishop by the Archdeacons of Essex and Rochester. The Archdeacons, unhappy with this, suggested instead that the Bishop be asked to chair the next SAWCM AGM, when his attention might be drawn to the Statement. How the matter was finally resolved does not appear; things rumbled on for a year or two, the 1892 and 1893 Reports strongly refuting an unspecified claim that seamen in the Port of London lacked Church provision. Despite this, the 1893 Report, giving thanks for the improvements since the foundation of SAWCM in the lot and behaviour of the merchant seaman, yet coupled SAWCM's efforts with those of the TCM, MtS, and BFSS, perhaps intending an olive branch, but adding:

> The distinction between these and the SAWCM is, that the latter works purely on Church principles, acting simply as a helper of the Church, passing all her grants through parochial and responsible Clergy, without regard to any special views.

Church principles were sufficiently elastic for the 1894 Report to reveal that SAWCM had begun distributing Miss Weston's (undenominational) literature.

In 1896 the society was incorporated, its income rose, and it initiated a number of works. One was among seal fishers in the Pacific, through the agency of the Victoria (British Columbia) Harbour Mission; another the provision of a Mission

---

1   A picture may be found in the 1894 Report, 55. Stephen Friend, in his thesis, says that *Sapper* was used in the North Sea, Holland and France in 1890 but was unsuitable for North Sea work. *Water Kelpie* was lent to the Grimsby mission in 1891 but, proving unsuitable, was moored in Grimsby fish docks as a reading room, with occasional Church services on board, attracting local and visiting fishermen.

House for the pearl fishers, almost exclusively Japanese, off Thursday Island, North Queensland. Naval work in the Mediterranean was increasing, which may explain SAWCM's distribution of Miss Weston's tracts. By 1898, income had risen to £4,227, plus £1,000 allotted to the society by the Bishop of London for work in the Port of London, but then began to fall, as charitable donations generally were affected by the South African War, a famine in India, and a fire in Ottawa. By the turn of the century SAWCM claimed correspondents in

America (including the West Indies and Canada)	12
China (including the Bishop of Corea[sic])	5
Japan (the Bishop of Osaka)	1
India (including the Bishop of Rangoon)	4
Persian Gulf	2
Australia	4
New Zealand	4
New Guinea	2

The financial effects of the South African War persisted for some years beyond its conclusion (1902), but SAWCM's expansion continued. In 1905 it supported the first of the Annual Seafarers' Services in St Paul's Cathedral. In 1906 it accepted responsibility for chaplaincy work on the Thames training ship *Warspite*. By 1907 it was providing grants to some fifty stations: nine in the Port of London, twenty on the British Coast, and twenty-one abroad. In 1909 it absorbed the work of the North Sea Church Mission at Gorleston, off the Norfolk coast, with which it had been associated since 1895, when The Rev. Forbes A. Phillips, Vicar of Gorleston, Chairman-Founder of the NSCM, had turned the attention of Congress to the need of North Sea fishermen for Church work afloat. A grant from the Additional Curates' Society had helped maintain a small smack, fitted out as a church ship, at sea with the fleet. In 1903 the *Kestrel* was replaced with the *St Andrew*, which seems to be identical with the *St Andrew The Fisherman* (YH 1018), built in 1885. Its name, the St Andrew's flag on its bows,[1] and the Gorleston church dedication to St Andrew, imply a close association between the NSCM and SAWCM, perhaps the NSCM being a rather ambitious SAWCM Local Committee. In Grimsby, north of Gorleston, the missionary curate visited the local lightship, served a fishermen's church and mission room near the parish church, and, from 1898, an orphanage for the daughters of fishermen and sailors. It is not always clear in the records which of the fishing ports the SAWCM vessels were serving. The general picture suffices; those who want more detail can find it elsewhere.[2]

Before the 1914 – 18 war, SAWCM aided the North and Central European Sailors' Mission, about which little is known. The 1913 Report describes this as one of the 'two important Continental Missions for sailors', the other being the Gibraltar Mission. The North and Central European Sailors' Mission seems to have consisted of some sort of work in the ports of Libau

---

1   I am indebted to Mr L.Hawkins of Norwich, author of 'The Mission Boats', for this information, based on a photograph in his possession, and conveyed in a private letter.
2   Stephen Friend, *Fishermen's Missions*.

and Neufahrwasser, which came to an end on the outbreak of war.

War usually prompts a rise in the income of seamen's missionary societies, the public responding generously to appeals for work among sailors in a time of increased danger. Grants were received from the British Sailors' Relief Fund of Canada and the King George's Fund for Sailors. The outbreak of war coincided with SAWCM's Jubilee year. Its continued work among fishermen, many of whom donned the blue uniform of the Navy to man mine sweepers in the North Sea, may lie behind reports of 'parade services, work amongst soldiers as well as sailors, hospital visitation of both'. Port chaplaincy work, however, decreased, as an increasing number of clergy chose to serve with the armed forces, while many docks were made secure areas. In June 1917 the SAWCM London office was bombed in an early Zeppelin raid; no SAWCM staff member was injured.

War's end coincided with a number of retirements of long-serving office staff. Changes were inevitable. Finances were returning to their pre War state; by 1920, despite the recruitment by a new Clerical Organising Secretary of a further thirty local associations, income was little increased. The general decline of SAWCM may date from this period. Apart from its work in London and Liverpool, its attention was devoted to fishermen around the British Coast, but the 1920s saw many fishing boats laid up. Small initiatives continued, for example, the provision of libraries to all Trinity House lighthouses and ships. In 1922 a Ladies' Committee was formed to encourage fund-raising on a national scale, its target £400 a year. The Ladies had a disused jewelry sale in 1923. There was an appeal for 'a million magazines' and 'nearly as many novels' for the despatch of which, on receipt of a postcard, SAWCM would send sack, label and packing needle. But these things were whistling in the dark; SAWCM's finances continued to flounder, Reports became shorter, and by 1927, when a service of thanksgiving for fifty years' work on the Thames was announced, a deficit was carried forward for the first time. Grants were reduced to six for London, Tilbury and Gravesend, fifteen to other home ports (Liverpool reduced to one), and sixteen for overseas work.

A BBC appeal by the Bishop of Chelmsford and grants from Trinity House and Lloyd's failed to improve the situation, which was exacerbated by the nationwide depression. In 1932, money had to be transferred from the legacy account to the current account. Most missionary societies, their cash flow irregular, have to juggle accounts, balancing them at the year's end after Christmas generosity; here the juggling emphasised the continuing trend. The 1935 Report literally <u>underlined</u> the bad financial situation. Grants were further reduced: five to London, twelve to other home ports, eight sent overseas. A welcome donation came from Cunard-White Star from the proceeds of a public viewing of the newly-launched *Queen Mary*.

In 1937 an augmented Ladies' Committee under a new President organised a special matinee 'shared with another well-known Sailors' Organisation' (unspecified) which netted SAWCM over £800. The SAWCM Minutes tell a darker tale. Debts had risen from £500 to £2,000 in the decade to 1937, offset in October 1937 by sale of stock to the value of £1,700. The appointment of a new Organising Secretary in April 1938 brought no improvement. The SAWCM's Chairman, the Bishop of Exeter, in the next annual Report, announced by letter:

It was Resolved that the Offer of The Missions to Seamen as set out in their Offer dated 29th April, 1939, to take over and continue the work of St Andrew's Waterside Church Mission for Sailors be and is hereby accepted AND that the Executive Committee be and is hereby authorised to notify The Missions to Seamen accordingly. . . .

As Chairman of the SAWCM since 1928, I am convinced that this step is a wise one. The proposal was first made to the Executive Committee on my initiative. . . .

This was accompanied by a letter from the Archbishop of Canterbury commending the Bishop's action, perhaps to deflect any suggestion that Jonah was being swallowed by the whale, and emphasising his responsibility for all decisions made.

Hindsight reveals SAWCM's financial position had for long been insecure, while speeches at Church Congress and elsewhere encouraging the societies to work more closely give this amalgamation a longer history than at first appears. In 1922 a letter dated November 22nd had arrived from Lambeth Palace addressed to The Rev. B.S. Mercer, then Organising Secretary, Archbishop Randall Davidson writing:

Dear Mr Mercer,

. . . I am not quite clear as to what I ought to do with regard to your request that I should send a message of encouragement in order to give a new stimulus to the work of S.A.W.M. I have, as perhaps you know, been for a long time wondering, and sometimes enquiring, whether it would not be possible for the work of the Mission to be incorporated with that of the Missions to Seamen. I know the value of the work of the SAWM during these many years, but it does not seem to me that it now differs in any marked way from the work of the Missions to Seamen, and I should like to know whether the subject is under consideration of a possible amalgamation of the two agencies. The idea of amalgamation is not due to any thought of deficiency or inadequacy on the part of either. . . .

Mercer had replied on November 30th, St Andrew's Day:[1]

Yr Grace,

. . . I am replying unofficially because this will enable me to write more freely. The 3 outstanding reasons why we do not become absorbed in the Missions to Seamen are these:

1. We do different work
2. We tap a different source of income
3. We feel that the advantages of amalgamation are less than the disadvantage of losing our identity.

I regret all three reasons; and that not as a novice. . . .

But the reasons remain intact.

– I understand that the Missions to Seamen set up an independent organisation in whatever parish or port where they work ([crossed out] some keen [illegible] Incumbents resent the erection of a local Bethel) whereas we work exclusively on parochial lines, making grants to Incumbents. . . . Not a few Incumbents and Chaplains gladly welcome our form of assistance whereas they would resent independent ministrations and the erection of an

---

1 The text of is taken from Mercer's copy on the back of the Archbishop's letter.

11. St Andrew's Waterside Church Mission

independent Bethel. Your Grace will understand this is no adverse criticism of the Missions to Seamen for which I have the greatest respect.

– In my vagabond life of preaching, from Lancashire to Kent and from Yorkshire to Devon I found not a few churches which welcome us but which would not welcome the Missions to Seamen and vice versa. We are reputed Catholic, and they are reputed Protestant.[1] The distinction is unreal, but the opinion still survives. And what influences certain churches also influences certain donors.

– Your Grace will probably know about the meeting held this month of *representatives of societies* doing home work . . . The spirit of the meeting was acutely in favour of friendliness and acutely inimical to [illegible] amalgamations . . . and the same was urged re the Missions to Seamen and ourselves.

A Minute of 10 February 1926 reveals no progress:

3. The unauthorised correspondence that had passed between the Rev. B.S. Mercer, former Organising Secretary of the Mission and the Archbishop of Canterbury was considered and after full discussion it was Proposed . . . that the correspondence be allowed to remain on the table, as it was felt no good purpose could be attained by the re-opening of the matter - carried unanimously.

The MtS and SAWCM continued as uneasy bed fellows, but now without the public invective of early Church Congresses, hinted at in Mercer's letter. A Minute of 16th October, 1930 records a Conference convened by the MtS, attended by representatives of sailors' societies working in London, SAWCM among them, which agreed to continue to meet quarterly. Despite this positive sign, when later in the same year the MtS asked SAWCM to match funding for a chaplain in Freemantle (SAWCM £100, MtS £100, SPCK £125), SAWCM declined 'as it would be against the principle of the working of the Mission, in addition to no funds being available'.[2]

In 1931 SAWCM refused to sign a 'Resolution of the United Seamen's Missions and Sailors' Homes' to avoid overlapping of members' work because its committee had no jurisdiction over parishes and could not in any way bind the clergy in their work on behalf of sailors, a matter in which it was, technically, correct.[3] In 1932 SAWCM refused a grant to Townsville *because* it was a MtS port.[4] Yet the pressure for a thaw was increasing, though this Minute of 31st October, 1934, raising hope of an early Spring, was followed by no recorded action:

Careful consideration was given to the position of the Mission and the Representative Council of Seamen's Missions and Sailors' Homes. The Memorandum submitted by the Missions to Seamen to the Representative Council was reviewed . . . the Chairman should communicate with the Archdeacon of London with a view to co-operative action between the Missions to Seamen and S. Andrew's in future.

Until 9 February 1939, when a Special Sub-Committee's Report was

---

1 Various SAWCM Reports show pictures (Sharpness being a good example) of churches displaying all the signs of advanced Churchmanship, whereas the MtS *Word on the Waters* from this period does nothing to dispel the impression of Low Churchmanship.
2 SAWCM Minute, 11 Dec 1930.
3 SAWCM Minute 24 March 1931; see also 16 July 1931.
4 SAWCM Minute 18 Feb 1932.

presented, confirming that deliberations had been taking place in the months preceding, nothing of their content had been minuted:

> In the absence of the Secretaries, the Executive Committee discussed the recommendation contained in the Sub-committee's Report that Mr G. N. Croucher, the General secretary, be retired on a pension of £200 per annum. The Committee then proceeded to discuss the suggestion of the Chairman that the time had arisen for further negotiations with the Missions to Seamen. It was then decided to appoint the Rev. W.C. Brown and the Rev. G.C. Moore, to open talks with the Representatives of the Missions to Seamen, and to report back. . . .

A week later, following the report of these two gentlemen, it was noted that the MtS 'seemed anxious to re-open discussions'; peaceful talks following the strained relations of the past, and the MtS willing to consider amalgamation with a society as stretched financially as SAWCM; a circumstance which, in 1856, had prevented MtS amalgamation with the BCM.

On 16 March the Bishop of Exeter chaired a meeting of the two societies at the office of the MtS. Here the SAWCM conditions for a merger were laid out:

- All grants to be maintained while present incumbents remained in grant-aided parishes.
- The book department to remain whilst there is a need for it.
- If possible, grants to parishes to be maintained on change of incumbents, and in the spirit of SAWCM.
- All monies to be used in the spirit of SAWCM.
- Incumbents of grantee parishes shall, as before, be free in their work save for sending an annual report of their work.
- The Missions to Seamen shall have the right, in consultation with the Bishop of the Diocese, to discontinue grants where they are no longer required or the work is not being done.
- Pension rights of SAWCM General Secretary.
- Employment of the Assistant Secretary.
- Hope was expressed for the continued employment of the SAWCM Book Packer.
- SAWCM Representatives to be on the Missions to Seamen Committee.

A supplementary memorandum explaining these conditions was added. It emphasised the desire for continued employment for former SAWCM staff. It agreed to grants to parishes being subject to annual review, asking that they should not be withdrawn on grounds of grantee's churchmanship. It was hoped that SAWCM's aid to seaside parishes, considered a 'good work', might continue. The desire was expressed that this would be a true amalgamation rather than the continuation of two societies under one roof; the evidence for this would be the appearance of the SAWCM name on all publications of the MtS in the same way as 'The Thames Mission' (*sic*), that is, beneath that of The Missions to Seamen.[1] The desire to unite, it said, comes 'in the interest of true religion and in the face of the increasing secularization of the appeal for Sailors', revealing that the merger had come about with a surprising degree of skill and charity.

---

1   This has not been the practice for many years.

12. The Gibraltar Mission to Seamen

Several chapters have already referred in passing to the SPG and its assistance of work among seamen on the continent. Some of its earliest work, before it began aiding the Diocese of Gibraltar, lay in its provision of a number of churches for English congregations in Europe at various times since its foundation in 1701. Indeed, this was one of its objects, the other being to carry the Gospel to the heathen. Most large European ports have an English church with a history going back several hundred years. One example will suffice: the first Report of the SPG gave information that an English church had been founded at Amsterdam.

> For the interest of the English nation, the honour of its Establish'd Church, and comfort of its members residing here in peace and war, as gentlemen, merchants, soldiers, seamen &c. The Burgomasters have given a piece of ground for building an English Church: till that can be compass'd a private Chapel is made use of. . . .

That would have been in 1702. The SPG provided £50 a year for two years towards the salary of the chaplain, Dr Cockburn.[1]

SPG may have been the earliest Anglican work, but a number of European churches, in what might be deemed a second wave, can trace their work among seamen, more or less directly, to the efforts of G.C. Smith, if not to his several preaching tours across the English Channel, which seem more aimed at landfolk. Anglican work among seamen in Europe, not a direct part of his legacy, made particular progress in the ports of Mediterranean Europe, especially those with consular chaplains, always members of the Church of England, and paid by the State. Though the warmer coasts of the Mediterranean attracted large numbers of British a significant factor was the trading pattern of contemporary British shipping resulting from the increasing use of steam.[2] Another was the interest of the RN in the Mediterranean. Kverndal's reference to a Gibraltar Seamen's Bethel Society dating from 1821, with a 'Resident Agent for Transports' points to the military importance of Gibraltar. This Agent seems to have had particular support from a local Methodist minister. A Methodist minister also kindled the interest which led to the foundation of a Malta Bethel Union in 1824, followed in 1825 by an

---

1 *Anderson's History of the Colonial Church*, 1848, II, 767.
2 The rise of the GMS coincides with the changed pattern of shipping, and British shipping in particular, in the Mediterranean. David M. Williams & John Armstrong, Changing Voyage Patterns in the Nineteenth Century, esp. 164ff.

attempt to obtain a floating chapel for Valletta.[1] These may have gone some way towards prompting the earliest Anglican work.

The Anglican diocese of Gibraltar was formed in 1824. Covering most Mediterranean countries, it supervised the work of embassy and consular chaplains, chaplains to English churches among those sizeable communities of expatriates, and seasonal holiday chaplaincies. Many of the latter were financed by SPG or the Colonial Church and School Society (CCSS).[2] The thousands of British seamen present in the Mediterranean ports convinced successive Bishops of Gibraltar that they could not be ignored. The repeal in 1873 of the 1825 Consular Advances Act meant that, if most of the consular chaplains were not to be lost, the diocese would have to finance them, prompting Bishop Harris in 1872 to launch the 'Gibraltar Diocesan Spiritual Aid Fund'.[3] His successor, Bishop Sandford, appealed widely for support for this fund, using it mostly to support seamen's work. In 1884 an increase of interest and subscriptions allowed the Bishop to found 'The Bishop of Gibraltar's Mission to Seamen', from 1889 the 'Gibraltar Mission to Seamen in the Mediterranean' (GMS), building on earlier work among seamen in the diocese.[4]

The first major work had begun in Marseilles, though there had been other outposts. In a letter of May 1855, The Rev. M.J. Mayers, Her Britannic Majesty's chaplain at Marseilles, wrote of the large number of British seamen and his attempts to produce 'on a small scale' a Sailors' Home which 'gives promise of great usefulness, and of proving a nursery, so to speak, to the Church'.[5] His work prospered and was continued by his successor, The Rev. J. B. Hawkins, aided by a grant from SPG, its journal, *The Mission Field*, describing it as 'a most useful work among nine thousand sailors who visit that port annually. He requests help for the Sailors' Club and Reading Room' where he held Sunday evening services for sailors.[6] He was assisted by a 'Scripture Reader for Sailors' who visited ships by boat. Hawkins, on leave in Britain in 1867, used the opportunity to view work among seamen in London, Newcastle, North Shields, Greenock, Glasgow, Southampton and Liverpool, a series of visits assisted by a growing railway network. His services in Marseilles attracted congregations of between forty and seventy seamen, and his success prompted Lisbon, Genoa and 'other places' to request the establishment of similar clubs.[7] Hawkins was moved to Baden Baden in 1869,[8] but his work was continued, for Bishop Harris on his second Visitation Tour of the diocese wrote, 'at Marseilles I was rejoiced to find the Sailors' Club in increasing favour, but the Sailors' Home is still a desideratum'.[9]

1   Kverndal, *Seamen's Missions*, 245.
2   Founded 1824, in the Evangelical tradition, later renamed the Colonial and Continental Church Society, now the Intercontinental Church Society.
3   H.J.C. Knight, *The Diocese of Gibraltar*, 89f.
    Colonial Church Chronicle, 1872, 260.
4   *Colonial Church Chronicle*, 1872, 126ff.
5   *Colonial Church Chronicle*, 1854-5, 464f.
6   *op cit.*, 1868, 24.
7   *Mission Field*, 1868, 103.
8   *Mission Field*, 1869, 120.
9   *Colonial Church Chronicle*, 1870, 174, 217, 295.

12. The Gibraltar Mission to Seamen

The same state of affairs pertained on his 1872 Visitation, when he commended particularly the Sunday evening service at the Sailors' Club.[1]

Shortly after Mayers began his work in Marseilles, in March 1855, SPG provided for the erection of a Memorial Chapel in Constantinople, resolving in the November to send two chaplains. It appointed in February 1856 The Rev. E. Pyddocke and The Rev. C. G. Curtis, charged to care for those British sailors, shipping agents, store-keepers, and other residents, in and about Galata and Tophana, who were beyond the reach of the Embassy Chaplains. It was hoped that they would be able to obtain a room ashore to use for Divine Service and, if possible, 'a hulk to serve as a Chapel for the crews of the ships in the harbour'.[2] A fund was launched for the Memorial Chapel in 1856. This was consecrated by the Bishop of Gibraltar on 22nd October 1868,[3] the delay caused by the stone being brought from England.[4] The chaplains laboured under some difficulty; in 1864, after the Bishop had confirmed ten Turks, their work was almost brought to a standstill by wild rumours of proselytising, but, the local Muslim leader ruling that Turks could adopt what religion they chose, the chaplains spent but a short time in prison.[5] It may have been this incident which attracted the financial support of the CCCS.[6]

There were other, smaller, efforts. There is some evidence that there was a Sailors' Club at Messina by 1871,[7] apparently following a very thorough visitation of ships there by Bishop Harris on his Visitation Tour of 1869.[8] By 1871 a chaplain, a Mr Addison, was visiting ships and holding services on them.[9] At Corfu the English Chaplain started to visit ships regularly, around 1873.[10] SAWCM provided him with a boat, and an annual grant of £10 towards its maintenance.[11]

A significant step forward was the founding of the Diocesan Spiritual Aid Fund in 1874. It grew in part from 'The Church of England Mission to the English in Spain, and English Sailors in Spanish Ports', founded in January 1860, but now moribund, partly through English apathy and probably a meed of Spanish resistance; indeed, continental sensitivity to Protestant activity may have played a part in encouraging chaplains to minister primarily to British seamen.[12] Another factor was the increasing number of SPG grants being made for continental work following the repeal of the Consular Advances Act. Government grants

---

1 *Colonial Church Chronicle*, 1872, 123, 254.
2 *Colonial Church Chronicle*, 1855-6, 346.
3 *Mission Field*, 1868, 333 gives details of the service.
4 C.F. Pascoe, *Two Hundred Years of the S.P.G.*, 736.
5 *The Missionary Intelligencer*, XV, 1864, 206-8.
6 H.J.C. Knight, *The Diocese of Gibraltar*, 96.
   Colonial Church Chronicle, 1870, 174, 217, 295.
   Mission Field, 1861, 37, 175; 1862, 97, 204.
7 *Mission Field*, 1871, 18.
8 *Colonial Church Chronicle*, 1870, 174, 217, 295.
9 *Mission Field*, 1871, 18.
10 SAWCM *Report*, 1875.
11 SAWCM *Report*, 1874.
12 Knight, *Diocese of Gibraltar*, 62.

ceased in 1874 for chaplains in Genoa, Madeira, Nice, Lisbon and Oporto; 1881, for Corfu and Leghorn; 1890, Smyrna; c. 1893, Malaga; 1905, Trieste; and in 1909, Marseilles.[1] The diocese reviewed the situation, examined its finances and published its various needs, creating the Spiritual Aid Fund to raise money for places which could not afford a chaplain. Among the main areas of need were the ports, the Fund becoming the Bishop of Gibraltar's Mission to Seamen in 1884, incorporating a number of works already in existence.

At Gibraltar, a Seamen's Home and Sailors' Rest (a home was residential, a rest recreational) already existed by 1881 though the civil chaplain had little time to devote to either.[2] At Marseilles in 1876 The Rev. H. S. Brooks was at work in the Sailors' Club, now used by over 5,000 men a year (one hundred or so a week does not sound many, but sufficed to ensure the Club's viability). He had some relationship with SAWCM, in 1878 SAWCM providing him with a harmonium, and in 1879 launching a major appeal for a Sailors' Home. This raised much local money and attracted the patronage of the Duke and Duchess of Edinburgh and the Duke of Westminster.[3] The Home was opened in 1880.[4]

A SAWCM grant to Constantinople supported a missionary curate to work seasonally, in summer in Galatz, Sulina and Odessa, and in winter in Constantinople. The ministry to seamen in Constantinople included afternoon services in the hospital and prison. A new Sailors' home was being built, and sufficient progress had been made by 1884 for attempts to be made to obtain a hulk to extend the work.[5] In Corfu, ship-visiting continued, with tracts received from SPG and books from SAWCM. The chaplain, although part-time, in 1877 visited 57 ships on 160 occasions; distributed 3,780 tracts; made 25 hospital visits; and conducted four free burials of seamen. He forecast that his work among yacht crews would increase when the Turko-Greek troubles had been resolved and the area became once more fashionable.[6] The British chaplain in Athens also began ship-visiting in 1877, holding a service for sailors on the Piraeus on Sunday afternoons. He too received a grant from SPG, and books from SAWCM.[7]

Work with seamen in Barcelona may have been part of the Mission to English Seamen in Spanish Ports, about which, little information seems to have survived. A Mr Cannay started to minister there to seamen in 1856, aided by the MtS's first grant (£1), which society listed him as a Corresponding Chaplain.[8] An earlier reference suggests he was building on foundations already laid:

> We should not omit to notice, that in these, as in all other sea-port towns of any importance in the Mediterranean, great opportunities may be found for usefulness amongst the crews of English merchant vessels, many of which remain in port three or even four months at a time; a consideration which furnishes an additional reason for placing Chaplains at the principal ports on

1 Knight, *Diocese of Gibraltar*, 110.
2 SAWCM, *Report*, 1878, 1881.
3 SAWCM, *Report*, 1876, 1878, 1879.
4 SAWCM, *Report*, 1880.
5 SAWCM, *Report*, 1884.
6 SAWCM, *Report*, 1877, 1880.
7 *Mission Field*, 1877, 359; 1884, 63. SAWCM *Report*, 1878.
8 Kingston, *A Cruise on the Mersey*, ii, xxii.

12. The Gibraltar Mission to Seamen

the eastern coast of Spain ... This branch of duty is one that has heretofore been overlooked; in most instances unavoidably, from deficiency of time or strength, the want of a suitable place in which to assemble the seamen, the unwillingness of the masters to allow their crews to come ashore, and other similar causes. The subject has, we know, engaged much of the Bishop [of Gibraltar]'s attention, and he has already, in some instances, been successful in devising means to remedy the deficiency.[1]

A 'workmen's and sailors' reading room' at Seville, dating from 1869, whether connected with the same Mission to English Seamen not said, was revived by another civil chaplain, a Mr Tugwell in 1877, with the hope of extending it by the establishment of a Home.[2] In Cartagena in 1878 a resident offered £100 towards a chaplain's salary if SAWCM could find a chaplain. SAWCM invited interested clergy to write for details, apparently with a negative response, for in 1880 a local family, the Barringtons, with their small son, started working among the ships on Sundays, visiting, holding services on board, giving tracts. In 1882 Mrs Barrington asked SAWCM for a signal flag (perhaps the international code for *M*) to advertise the ship-board services. They continued in this ministry for some years.[3]

Italy was little different. In 1875 SAWCM was grant-aiding Leghorn, where there were hopes of opening a 'sort of Sailors' Home, or at any rate a reading room and house of call for sailors'. An appeal fund was launched. The public was informed that the chaplain was visiting ships by boat, and employing a boatman to ferry without charge sailors wishing to attend the English church. An SPG grant supported this work.[4] SAWCM established a chaplaincy fund for Genoa in 1876, reporting a Mission and some ship-visiting. In 1878, 834 ship-visits, a service on board a ship nearly every Sunday, and visits to seamen in the local hospital, suggest no small effort. By 1883 the Bishop was making plans for a Sailors' Institute to be attached to the English church.[5]

At Lisbon the Embassy Chaplain appears to have started work among seamen in 1876, establishing a Reading Room, ship and hospital-visitation, with the assistance of a MtS-supported Scripture Reader.[6] It was hoped shortly to appoint a chaplain specifically for this work. A note added that the men before the mast took more readily to a Reader than a chaplain; also that on board ship the *Book of Common Prayer* was better appreciated than extempore prayer, which many, it was claimed, found difficult.[7] The port received a grant from SPG's Continental Chaplaincies Committee.[8]

---

1 *Colonial Church Chronicle*, 1847-8, 208.
2 *Colonial Church Chronicle*, 1869, 84ff, 252ff.
3 SAWCM, *Report*, 1878, 1880, 1882. The Barringtons, as a family, may have been especially welcome to men far from their own families.
4 Pascoe, *Two Hundred Years of the SPG*, 741f.
  SAWCM *Report, 1875, 1877, 1879*.
5 SAWCM *Report*, 1875, 1876, 1878, 1883.
6 A Scripture Reader was paid, a Lay Reader not, a distinction which no longer applies.
7 *Mission Life or The Emigrant and the Heathen*, 1876, 40. *Mission Field*, 1877, 359.
8 *Mission Field*, 63.

In Naples, the welfare of seamen forming part of his daily work, the consul appealed to SAWCM in 1874 for the establishment of a Sailors' Home for the six or seven thousand seamen he estimated to use the port annually. He suggested a Home could be opened in rented rooms for about £200 a year, with an initial £25 for furnishings. The Bishop, encouraging the scheme in 1875, called at least for the provision of a Reading Room. SAWCM noted in 1876 that the Sailors' Home (probably not the Reading Room) was ill-attended. Its grant was returned in 1877, the 1878 SAWCM *Report* revealing that the consul, its driving force, had died and the Mission shut in consequence. In its place there was to be found a floating chapel, once the *Victoria*, in the harbour, seating a hundred and locally funded but the detail necessary to bridge the gap between Mission closed and floating chapel opened is not available.[1]

Another early Sailors' Home in the diocese was at Odessa, in 1856 the source of an early appeal to the nascent MtS. It seems not to have been denominational, for on Sundays the Anglican chaplain and a Presbyterian minister provided services in its large hall by turn. It had come to fruition slowly, one source dating it to 1884,[2] another to 1874.[3] In January 1880 the Bishop to appoint a chaplain: 'Last year I held a service there in the Seamen's Home; . . . I have asked for the support of the Saint Andrew's Waterside Mission; the Gibraltar Fund will give £50 a year; can SPG give £50?' supporting his request with the claim that 14,000 seamen visited the port of Odessa in 1878.[4] The SAWCM *Report* (1880) described the British Chaplain holding services in the Sailors' Home and a temporary chapel in the town. The Home occupied a large villa and offered three reading rooms, a library, and sleeping accommodation. A lay manager and his wife ran the Home.[5] It was unusual in that it was self-supporting, a feat achieved by few apart from Miss Weston's Sailors' Rests. The Anglican chaplain spent some of his time on board ships. It was his hope to be able to provide additional recreation at the Home to try to draw men away from the 'Vodka Shops'.[6]

In Palermo a British Chaplain was visiting ships by 1875; by 1884 there were plans for an Institute. SAWCM provided the chaplain with a boat for ship-visiting; likewise for the chaplain at Patras from 1879 where SPG added a grant for him to ship-visit[7]. In Savona, which was beginning to eclipse Genoa in the coal trade, the Bishop counted on one day seventeen British steamers in port in 1879. SAWCM could not afford a grant here, prompting the Bishop to approach SPG. By 1884 the Genoa chaplain had obtained rooms in Savona in the British vice-consulate to serve as a 'Church of England Sailors' Rest'.[8] SAWCM Reports offer a confused picture for Trieste, with news of the foundation of a Sailors' Home in 1876, a committee

---

1 SAWCM *Report* 1874-8.
   The Bishop of Gibraltar's Pastoral Letter in *Mission Field*, 1876.
2 Knight, *Diocese of Gibraltar*, 138.
3 SAWCM *Report* 1874.
4 *Wants of the Colonial and Missionary Church*, SPG leaflet, May 1880, 28f.
5 SAWCM *Report*, 1881.
6 SAWCM *Report*, 1883.
7 SAWCM *Report*, 1875, 1884.
8 SAWCM *Report*, 1877, 1879, 1884.*Mission Field*, 1884, 63; 1877, 359.

12. The Gibraltar Mission to Seamen

formed for the 'proposed home' in 1877, and plans to use a former Maritime Police building in 1878. According to Bishop Knight success followed only in 1888.[1] All these ventures were eclipsed by the ministry to seamen in Malta where the RN had its base and provided the primary field of work for three laymen: a nonconformist, a member of the Royal Navy Scripture Readers' Society, and a MtS appointee to assist the Archdeacon of Malta.[2]

The Gibraltar Mission to Seamen came into formal existence in 1884. From this year most advertisements for seaport chaplains included ship visitation among their duties. The GMS and the Diocesan Spiritual Aid Fund received increasing prominence. In an 1885 memorandum to the SPG Standing Committee the Bishop wrote, 'We have also a Diocesan Spiritual Aid Fund ... [which] also supplies British Sailors in the Mediterranean and neighbouring seas with chaplains, lay-helpers, sailors' homes and institutes ....' He explained the new emphasis in diocesan priorities by giving numbers for British seamen in various ports: Bilbao, 63,000 *per annum*; Genoa, 19,000; Marseilles, 17,000; Odessa, 10,000; and in the Lower Danube, 8,000.[3] His statistics supported his call for a concerted effort to bring the Gospel to these men which would unite the diocese in a new sense of purpose and mission.

The GMS grew rapidly, initially with continuing support from SAWCM, SPG and CCCS. A committee in Liverpool (aiming at the pockets of ship-owners with Mediterranean interests) aided by the Mersey Mission raised further sums. As a measure of progress it was said, whereas in 1880 there had been four (Anglican) Homes for seamen in the whole continent, there were now seven in the Gibraltar diocese alone: Naples, Bilbao, Gibraltar, Malta, Marseilles, Lisbon and Constantinople. To these should be added Odessa (1874?), Genoa, Savona, Messina, and Palermo (1884 – 85), Trieste (1888), Seville and Venice (1889), Piraeus (1891), Barcelona (1892), Algiers (1893), Fiume, Nice and Cannes (1898). As the list of ports grew, the GMS became increasingly independent of aid from SPG, SAWCM and CCCS.[4]

The Diocese of Gibraltar, with more coastline than any other Anglican diocese at the time, was peculiarly situated for work among seamen, but its strength was also its weakness, for it was spread across many countries, and worked almost exclusively among expatriates. The First World War delayed plans for rebuilding the mission at Messina (flattened by an earthquake in 1908). At Nicolaieff in Southern Russia, a large sum had been collected pre-war to build a mission on a Russian Government granted site, something prevented by the Revolution, which similarly ended episcopal plans for a mission at Novorossisk.[5] Closure of Institutes at Sulina and Odessa followed the closure of the Dardanelles. Smyrna was shut. The clubs at Trieste and Fiume were lost, and those at Catania and Piraeus closed. Conversely, work increased in some ports, the GMS extending its activity in Marseilles, Savona,

---

1 Knight, *Diocese of Gibraltar*, 138.
2 *Mission Life or the Emigrant and the Heathen*, 1876, 43.
3 *Mission Field*, 1885, 240ff.
4 Knight, *Diocese of Gibraltar*, 134ff.
5 Knight, *Diocese of Gibraltar*, 186.

Genoa and Venice, whilst submarine crews received care at Palermo. In 1916 the MtS had to rescue the work at Marseilles with cash and staff, from which date the relationship between the two societies became increasingly close.[1] The GMS never really recovered from the First World War, and its decline was compounded by the spread of Communism throughout Eastern Europe, loss of British influence generally in the Mediterranean, and a dearth of British shipping, most of the lines once famous gone for ever. In 1970 only three GMS works were listed: Gibraltar, Barcelona, and Leixoes, the GMS appearing as one of the MtS's 'kindred societies'.

The British and Foreign Sailors' Society was also active on the continent, some of its work appearing in association with the American Seamen's Friend Society, its American partner. It seems to have helped some GMS work financially. In some ports it had been long established, in Malta, for example, since 1865. It is difficult to establish which were its own works, and which it was aiding for, like SAWCM, it tended to assist local work with grants and other forms of encouragement. By the end of the nineteenth century it was associated with work in Antwerp, Bilbao, Bremerhaven (where there was a small Sailors' Rest for English and Scandinavian seamen), Constantinople, Dunkirk, Flushing, Genoa (particularly well equipped), Gibraltar, Havre, Hamburg, Leghorn, Messina, Malta, Naples, Odessa, Rouen (represented by a French Methodist minister working from a local church), Rotterdam (1878), St Petersburg, and Venice, all ports mentioned in the BFSS magazine, the *Chart & Compass*.

This work may be contrasted with what is known of contemporary Catholic efforts. In some ports clergy and sisters would be working unsung with all in need, but specifically may be noted Catholics in the Navy being served from 1875 onwards by the English College, Lisbon when the Fleet was to be found in the Tagus.[2] In 1895, according to the same source, priests were appointed to visit seamen in hospital in Brindisi and Genoa, and there is a hint that something similar was being done in some Spanish ports in 1896. A little more detail for Catholic efforts to work in Europe will appear in Chapter Sixteen.

That Christian Europe did not care more for its sailors in the nineteenth century may be a cause for wonder. The political upheavals of the century may form part of an explanation. Those countries which did care for the needs of seamen would cater for the needs of those nearest their principal source of income, at least initially. Scandinavian missions, with State funding, tended to care for Scandinavian seafarers. Similarly, the German church served mainly German seafarers. The size of the British Royal and Merchant Navies and the rise of its empire explains why Britain supported more Institutes, Bethels and Rests than other European countries, a situation extended by the advent of the GMS, if the diocese of Gibraltar is understood as an arm of empire. By date of foundation of its various continental provisions for seamen, the GMS has no claim to precedence, but by numbers of foundation it had a majority between 1884 and 1914.

---

1   Knight, *Diocese of Gibraltar*, 246ff.
2   P.F. Anson, *The Church and the Sailor*, 61.

13. American work

The sea apostolate in the United States began in a way very similar to that in the United Kingdom, and quite as early. The two principal American organisations were the undenominational American Seamen's Friend Society (ASFS), equating with the BFSSBU, and the Seamen's Church Institutes (SCI) of the Protestant Episcopal or Anglican Church, the American equivalent of the MtS. In addition there were a number of Scandinavian Homes and churches where Scandinavian seamen and Scandinavians settling in America were welcomed.[1] Catholic work, its beginnings post-dating these societies by many years, will appear in later chapters.

The first American foundation of a religious nature was the Sailors' Snug Harbour on Staten Island, the result of an 1801 bequest by Captain Robert Richard Randall of the income from a Manhattan farm to found and support a 'snug harbour' for aged or enfeebled sailors. The original Snug Harbour opened only in 1833 with thirty inmates under a Governor answerable to Trustees; its long delay, according to Kverndal, the result of protracted litigation. Occupants were expected to attend all services. Meals commenced with a grace. The Snug Harbour was to grow to an enormous size, with chapel, gardens, workshops aplenty, and the many things necessary to support daily life: accommodation, kitchens, public rooms, infirmary and more, housed in fine neo-classical buildings. The Sailors' Snug Harbour, effectively a *maison dieu* resurrected, was served by chaplains from various denominations. Captain Randall's generosity benefitted thousands of seamen, though the visitor to Staten Island today finds these vast and impressive buildings devoted to aged seamen no longer.

The first organised outreach to serving seamen seems to have been through the undenominational Boston Society for the Religious and Moral Improvement of Seamen. Supported by the Boston Marine Society and the interest of Unitarian clergymen,[2] this Society began placing tracts, and holding services, on board ships in May 1812. Among its intentions was 'a school for the instruction of lads for the sea', which Kverndal suggests may indicate the London Marine Society as the source of its inspiration.[3] The

---
1 Kverndal's *Seamen's Missions*, 407ff gives a very detailed history of the early American sea apostolate.
2 Congregationalism in America often veered towards Unitarianism, which may allow the quibble that Unitarian work for sailors is not what is generally understood as Christian.
3 Kverndal's *Seamen's Missions*, 409f.

Boston Society's failure seems in part to have been due to contemporary politics, its early demise being blamed on problematic relations between the colony and its colonial masters. Kverndal suggests further that inexperience, dependence on tract distribution without ship-visitation, and the breakdown of health of a key member were other important factors. It seems to have published its last tract in 1817.

Less dependent on tract-distribution was the outreach of New York's Brick Presbyterian Church, begun around 1816 following seamen present at its services asking for their own prayer meetings, much as led to contemporary Thames meetings. Several members of the church would be among the founders of the American Seamen's Friend Society. The following year, on 14 March, the Marine Bible Society of New York, later merged with the New York Bible Society, came into being at the instigation of The Rev. Ward Stafford. At his proposal a meeting was held in the house of Jonathan Little Esq., 16 April 1816, to discuss the building of a Mariner's Church. As a result, on 5 June 1816, 'The Society for the Propagation of the Gospel Among Seamen in the Port of New York' was organised, and incorporated in April 1819. When built, the church was claimed as the world's first Mariners' Church (i.e. exclusively for seamen). Built on Roosevelt Street, near East River, it was dedicated on 4th June 1820, by Methodist, Reformed Dutch and Protestant Episcopal clergy. From its inception an interdenominational policy was followed, and continued on its merging with the ASFS.

Separate Bethel meetings were held in New York for some years. A Bethel Union was formed on 4 June 1821, in association with the Bethel Union of England, intending to spread the Bethel movement beyond New York. A BETHEL flag was provided by the English society, flown for the first time on 22 June 1821, on the *Cadmus*, at the foot of Pine Street. There is evidence that these various agencies were beginning to work more closely. Merging Bethel meetings prompted the Mariners' Church pastor (The Rev. John Truair) to appeal for the formation of a national society which might be called 'The American Seamen's Friend Society and Bethel Union'; something suggested to him in a letter from G.C. Smith in 1823.[1]

Truair edited *The Mariners' Magazine*, published by the New York Mariner's Church, and issued jointly by the New York Port Society and the New York Bethel Union. In September 1825 it carried a letter, signed by 114 masters and mates, appealing for the formation of a national society. This issue reported the existence world-wide of seventy Bethel Unions, thirty-three marine Bible Societies, and fifteen Seamen's Churches and Floating Bethels. It prompted much interest, including a public meeting in New York City on 25 October 1825, when a constitution was drawn up and officers appointed for the embryonic organisation, achieving fruition in 1828 when, on 5 May, the ASFS was inaugurated with, at its helm, the following officers: President, the

---

1 Details of the ASFS have largely been taken from G.S. Webster, *The Seamen's Friend*. I am grateful to Roald Kverndal for drawing my attention to this useful book. It seems not to be available in the UK. Its American Library of Congress number is HV 3034.W4. See also Kverndal, *Seamen's Missions*, 454ff.

13. American work

Hon. Smith Thompson (an Associate Justice of the Supreme Court, and former Secretary of the US Navy); Corresponding Secretary, The Rev. Charles P. McIlvaine; Recording Secretary, Philip Flagler; Treasurer, Silas Holmes; and General Agent, The Rev. Joshua Leavitt. Leavitt, a Congregationalist, became the first Executive Secretary of the ASFS.[1] A number of independent societies were brought into association with the ASFS, including the remnants of the Boston Society (above), together with work begun in 1819 in Charleston and Philadelphia; Savannah (1821); Portland, Maine and New Orleans (1823); New Bedford (1825); and Baltimore (1826).[2] In 1828 provision of libraries at sea begun in the US by the Port of London and Bethel Union Society was adopted by the ASFS in the following year.

The ASFS sent out its first chaplain in response to a call from a local minister in Whampoa, the port of Canton (16th February 1830). Then, in November 1832, The Rev. John Diell was sent to the Sandwich Islands; arriving in Honolulu in 1833, he organised in 1836 what was claimed to be the first ASFS foundation in a foreign port, the Oahu Bethel Church. The appointment of a chaplain in Cronstadt, Russia in association with the BFSS in the same year was followed shortly by an appointment in Gothenburg of a Baptist minister, Frederick O. Nelson. Nelson, eventually forced to leave by Swedish State Law, continued his ministry in Bornholm, and then Copenhagen (1851). Of the many developments which followed, one of interest was in Yokohama, where the ASFS was represented by the MtS chaplain.

The bulk of ASFS work remained in America, not only in the ports but among the bargees on the inland waterways. The *Soldiers' and Sailors' Magazine* reported in 1862 that the ASFS was supporting sixteen workers in this inland ministry, although some of what it supported was work of an associated nature; listed were Pittsburgh, Cleveland, Cincinnati, Detroit, Sandusky, Lake Shore, Toledo, Milwaukee, Chicago, St Louis, Upper and Lower Mississippi, Cairo, Upper and Lower Ohio, Illinois River, Saginaw Bay, Illinois Canal, Wabash and Erie Canal, and the Miami. An estimated 5,000 contacts per worker was reported, presumably for the year, with much relief given to widows and orphans. One example, the work on the Welland Canal, commenced June 1867, was handed over to the Upper Canada Tract Society on the death of the ASFS missioner. The number of local societies doing similar work must have been considerable. The canal work of the ASFS is outside the focus of this book.

The ASFS closed its New York office and retired the chaplain in 1976. Rather than allowing the ASFS to limp on, a shadow of what had been, a brave decision was taken to wind up the ASFS; it ceased completely in 1986. Shipping patterns had changed, the US merchant fleet was increasingly flagged out, and ministerial patterns had evolved; what once had been can now be seen at the Mystic Seaport Museum, at Mystic CT, which benefitted from the ASFS demise, holds its records, and displays a perfect example of a nineteenth-century Reading Room, perhaps the last in existence.

1 *The Seaman*, April 1908, carried an article on the start of the ASFS.
2 Comprehensive details of these are given in Kverndal, *Seamen's Missions, passim.*

The Protestant Episcopal Church of America, the American version of the Church of England, began its work among seamen rather later, perhaps prompted by ASFS activity, or intelligence of G. C. Smith's work; possibly even by that of the London Episcopal Floating Church Society.[1] However, as its first properly organised work only began in New York on 6 March 1834, as the 'Young Men's Auxiliary and Missionary Society', a subsidiary of the New York Episcopal City Mission Society, it may have been self-generating. Its first President, The Rev. B.I. Haight, was Rector of St Peter's Church. Its intention was to minister to the thousands of seamen on the New York waterfront. The group of young men assumed a more definite form in March 1842 as 'The Young Men's Church and Missionary Society in the City and Port of New York'; its first chaplain, The Rev. B.C.C. Parker, appointed on 3 July, 1843, ascribing his call to work among seamen to an occasion when he was becalmed among fifty other ships off Fall River on passage from Boston to New York, at which time he offered to hold services for passengers and crews in a hotel ashore.

Following his appointment a church afloat on two barges was moored at the foot of Pike Street, on the East River, and consecrated by the Bishop of New York on 20 February 1844, as the 'Floating Church of Our Saviour for Seamen'. In 1844, too, when it was decided to separate from the Episcopal City Mission, a new title was adopted, and the 'Young Men' incorporated as the 'Protestant Episcopal Missionary Society for Seamen in the City and Port of New York' on the 12th April. Its new President was The Rev. Smith Pyne, Rector of Calvary Church, New York. The object of the society was to

> provide by building, purchase, hiring or otherwise so many floating and other churches for seamen, at different points in the City and Port of New York as they may deem proper, in which churches the seats shall be free; and to provide suitable clergymen to act as missionaries in the said churches.

Despite the floating church sinking on several occasions, once from the weight of snow, the ministry was sufficiently successful to prompt a new venture on the West Side in 1846; at a cost of $2,800, the 'Floating Church of the Holy Comforter' was built and moored at the foot of Day Street. Its designer, Richard Upjohn, was the architect of the famous Trinity Church of New York. The Rev. Daniel Van Meter Johnson was appointed Chaplain, a post he occupied until 1855.

Johnson and three members of his Board, soon recognising a very basic need of seamen for clean and cheap lodging, organised and ran a Home at 2 Carlyle Street until 1854; necessarily a private venture since they had no charter for such an action by the Society. A burial plot for indigent seamen was donated at the Evergreen Cemetery in 1851, which when full was succeeded by a plot at Cedar Grove Cemetery, both on Long Island. Its expanding ministry encouraged the Society in 1852 to appoint a missionary-at-large, The Rev. E.R. Remington, who was based at 31 Coeties Slip. He held services in the open air or under canvas as weather dictated until it became possible to rent an old store ashore. His successor, The Rev. Robert J. Walker, was credited with beginning the visitation of seamen in hospital.

---

1   H.H. Kelley, The Early History etc., *Historical Magazine*, IX, 1940, 349ff.

13. American work

In 1854, the State Legislature authorised an amendment to the Charter which allowed the Society to

> build, purchase, hire, take or hold one or more houses or lots, and the requisite furniture thereof, for the boarding, lodging and entertaining of seamen or boatmen in the City and Port of New York, to an amount not exceeding the sum of one hundred thousand dollars, and to lease or demise the same.

Accordingly, in October 1854, 'The New Sailors' Home' was opened at 338, Pearl Street, at a cost of $22,000, replacing the Home in Carlyle Street, and with room for seventy-five men. It remained in use until 1893. The work prospered, despite the early death of its first chaplain in 1859, the sale of the Floating Church of Our Saviour after condemnation as 'unseaworthy', and the similar demise of the West Side Church in 1868. That year a house was bought at 34 Pike Street and fitted out as a Mission House and chaplain's flat. The Floating Church of Our Saviour was replaced at the foot of Pike Street by another with the same dedication, until towed away to Staten Island in 1910 to be put aground as the church of All Saints. On the West Side a temporary church was in use until 1879, replaced in 1880 by a Mission House built on land bought at Houston and West Streets; replaced in 1888 with a fine set of brick buildings comprising Church of the Holy Comforter, Mission House and Rectory, enabled by a $50,000 legacy from William H. Vanderbilt. This remained in use until 1913. Four further centres at different times served the seaman: a Sailors' Home at 52 Market Street (1894 – 1907), Battery Station at 1, State Street (1902 – 13), a Brooklyn branch at 22, First Avenue (1904 – 07), and the Breakwater Hotel in Brooklyn (1908 – 13) offering accommodation for 120 men.

An important figure in the New York Society was The Rev. Archibald R. Mansfield, ordained to a ministry among seamen on leaving the General Theological Seminary in 1896, and remembered for his battle against the crimping system. A steam launch, the *Sentinel*, presented to him in 1903 by the women of the Seamen's Benefit Society, led by a Miss Augusta de Peyster, enabled him to board ships as they entered port, ahead of the crimps, to encourage crews to use the Mission lodgings and warn them against crimps and their boarding houses.[1] As part of this battle he undertook to provide ships with decent, sober crews at a lower price than the crimps. In 1904, Mansfield became Chaplain Superintendent of the East Side stations.

In 1906 the society's name was changed to 'The Seamen's Church Institute of New York'. As the work prospered its charter was altered to allow it to raise capital from $100,000 to $6,000,000. This was a bold step; more difficult was to find such a sum. Chaplain Mansfield and a lawyer, Edmund L. Baylies, raised the money to provide a thirteen-storey building at 25 South Street, opened in 1913, replacing the other stations, sold to raise capital, were with a Chapel of Our Saviour, and accommodation and ancillary facilities

---

1 Crimps would induce men to desert ship with all kinds of promises, ideally to accept their accommodation, where they would get them drunk or drug them, steal their goods and ship them out, paid by another ship seeking a crew, before the men could recover. It was a battle fought in many ports.

to serve five hundred men. A marine school was added in 1916. In 1921 the lodgings were extended to accommodate 1,200 men. When Mansfield died in 1934, he had the satisfaction of seeing a building and mission exceeding by far anything which might have been dreamt of at his appointment in 1896.

All Seamen's Church Institute chaplains were authorised by the Protestant Episcopal Church (PECUSA) and a regular part of its ministry.[1] In the same tradition, and next in foundation after New York, came Philadelphia. In 1847 a Churchmen's Missionary Society of Philadelphia was formed, in 1848 sending a delegation to the New York society to see the work of the floating church, before commissioning C.L. Dennington to design a floating Chapel of the Redeemer, to be built at Bordentown, and moored at Philadelphia's Dock Street Wharf. It was consecrated by the Bishop of Pennsylvania on 11th January, 1849. The service was attended by the New York Chaplain, Mr Parker, who went away impressed by what he had seen, presaging the future close association of the two societies. Regular services were held in the floating church until 1854, when it was put ashore as the church St John, Camden, New Jersey. The work for sailors continued at first in a sail loft,[2] then in purpose-built premises in Catherine Street, South Philadelphia; later in a larger stone Church of the Redeemer (consecrated in January1879) with a parish hall, and situated at Front and Queen Streets until shifting patterns in dock usage (larger, steam-powered ships) prompted a further move to better buildings and a proper Institute in 1920, incorporated as the SCI of Philadelphia.[3]

In Charleston, South Carolina about 1853, a Miss Harriett Pinckney gave her garden on East Bay and Market Street as a site for an Episcopal Church for Seamen; this was formed and incorporated as the Church of the Redeemer. Buildings on the site were leased until a building fund of $50,000 accumulated. In 1878 the Charleston Port Society, an undenominational society, united with the PECUSA corporation, allowing to be erected the Church of the Redeemer and the Harriett Pinckney Home for Seamen. The Port Society dated from 1818, from 1828 running a mariners' church until it was destroyed by earthquake in 1886. The amalgamated societies became undenominational, on condition that the Episcopal Rector of the church should be superintendent of the Home, giving PECUSA oversight of the chaplaincy but not excluding the major denominations from the governing Board.[4]

Ship-visiting in Honolulu was mentioned in a SAWCM Report of 1877, under Church of England auspices, and in *The Mission Field* in 1889.[5] The Hawaiian Islands were annexed by the United States in 1898, and four years later the Presiding Bishop of PECUSA appointed Bishop Nichols to visit the islands and effect the transfer of local church work from English to American hands. During his stay as Provisional Bishop of Honolulu, Nichols took steps

---

1　PECUSA, *Journal and Canons, 1871*, Hartford, 1872, appendix I, 462; appendix XIX, 690, 692f.
2　Unlike many lofts, one thing a sail loft did not lack was a large open space.
3　H.H. Kelley, The Early History etc., *Historical Magazine*, IX, 1940, 356f.
4　H.H. Kelley, The Early History etc., *Historical Magazine*, IX, 1940, 358.
5　*op cit*, 1889, 60.

to organise a Seamen's Institute. Local interest aroused, and with many English people in the community, the work was placed in the hands of the MtS, which sent an experienced lay worker from England. The first rented rooms were soon outgrown, and with the arrival of the first American Missionary Bishop, a larger building, already a Sailors' Home (whether secular or deriving from the Bethel Movement is unsaid), was obtained, providing chapel, reading and recreation rooms, and lodgings for thirty seamen.[1]

In Boston, PECUSA's work among seamen had been the responsibility of the Episcopal City Mission. In 1890, after a service on board the USS *Wabash* conducted by people from St John's Episcopal Church, Charleston, the ship's executive officer, pleased with the improvement among his men which resulted, joined one of the laymen involved, George E. Neal, in renting rooms ashore at 46 Water Street, near the Charlestown Navy Yard gate to form the Sailors' Haven. St John's provided books and magazines, and a small cabinet organ was given. John Allan, an experienced YMCA director, was engaged. At this juncture the Superintendent of the Episcopal City Mission became interested, accepting the Sailors' Haven as a unit of the City Mission. John Allan singled out a man from the *Wabash* who had responded well: Stanton H. King. King, granted a discharge from the US Navy, was sent to Mount Hermon School, Massachusetts, for religious training, during vacations assisting Allan until 1893, then returned to work full-time. The Sailors' Haven prospered, and was enlarged in 1896. King succeeded Allan as superintendent in 1899. The Haven's need for further expansion led to an offer of funds from a Miss Marian Lawrence. It was decided that an extension would be wasteful; a new building was required. Miss Lawrence directed the appeal for funds. The Haven moved to temporary quarters in 1903 until a new three-storey building was opened in 1905.

A second church centre for seamen in Boston was opened by Mr and Mrs James Monroe Battles, aided by The Rev. F.B. Allen and Bishop Phillips Brooks, as another unit of the Episcopal City Mission in 1891. This was St Mary's House for Sailors on Cottage and Marginal Streets, East Boston; to it was added in the same year 'St Mary's Free Church for Sailors' (i.e. with free seating). The Vicar of St Mary's was assisted in his work for seamen by students from the Episcopal Theological School in Cambridge, Mass. An important feature of ministry here was the visitation of ocean liners.[2] The late start of episcopal work in Boston, where Protestants had been working since 1812, a date almost certainly linking it with G. C. Smith, is unexplained.[3]

For a period San Francisco was one of the best known missions in the world, New York notwithstanding. The Rev. James Fell started as chaplain here on 2 February 1893. San Francisco had been a quiet Franciscan mission settlement when R.H. Dana called there in 1832. Dana's book, *Two Years Before the Mast*, did much to stir American interest in seamen's welfare. When a gold rush hit the town, it quickly turned the quiet mission settlement

---

1 H.H. Kelley, The Early History etc., *Historical Magazine*, IX, 349.
2 H.H. Kelley, The Early History etc., *Historical Magazine*, IX, 349ff.
3 *The Encyclopedia of Missions*.

into one of the most notorious ports in the world.[1] Before Fell arrived
some previous effort had been made by the San Francisco clergy and Church people to look after the boatmen and deep seamen, at the city front [but] no organised, well-sustained work on their behalf had been undertaken.[2]
This he would change.

Fell, erstwhile chaplain with the MMS at Liverpool, alarmed by accounts of conditions in San Francisco, especially of young apprentices disappearing in the port, went out to investigate, financed jointly by the MMS and the MtS. He found a good friend in his new diocesan, Bishop Nichols, whose help in obtaining funds and interest from merchants and ship owners in the city got things moving quickly. In April 1893, after the Bishop preached in St Luke's church, appealing for the city to do its duty by the seafaring community, a group of citizens met with the Bishop and, under his presidency, formed a Committee to open an Institute. The upper floors of a three-storey building at 33 Steuart Street, were rented for $1,500 a year and opened for seamen on the 3rd June with a chapel, and books, magazines, writing materials, billiards tables, bagatelle, and similar games.

Sailing ships remained in San Francisco for extended periods, often after long voyages, many arriving via the Cape experiencing appalling weather conditions.[3] In these circumstances sailors, seeking diversion in the town, were offered every kind of vice, accompanied by a vicious crimping system.[4] Crews were often forbidden shore leave as captains feared losing them and having to pay crimps dearly for their replacement.[5] Accounts of Fell's battles against the system are many, varied and colourful, perhaps improved in the telling, but in his first year the number of disappearing apprentices dropped from sixty to twelve.

To combat vice and keep seamen from the bars where many were drugged and shanghaied, to awake at sea, with aching heads and empty pockets, on a different ship, Fell began weekly 'chantey' sessions, and holiday picnics at Golden Gate Park and Alameda. The picnics were popular, attracting two hundred or more men. The crimps, boarding masters and saloon keepers, noticing the loss of business, put Fell's person on several occasions seriously at risk. Despite being 'jumped' and shot at, he continued his work, and the Institute, so near the docks, was well used. Captain A.G. Course told a famous story which he ascribed to Shalimar (the pen-name of Captain F.C. Hendry) of:

an Irish bar keeper in San Francisco who was a notorious crimp as well as a prize fighter. When Fell went to see him about some apprentices who had been doped and sent to sea, he was given two minutes to leave or be thrown out of the bar. At the end of two minutes it was the bar keeper who had been knocked out and the Rev. Fell was bathing his face with iced water to bring him round. The Irishman was so impressed by being knocked out by a padre that he gave up crimping and joined Fell in the rescue of those

---

1   Many accounts exist by seamen. See e.g. Sir Bertram Hayes, *Hull Down*, 54-9. Also J. Havelock Wilson, *My Stormy Voyage Through Life*, vol I.
2   D.O. Kelley, *History of the Diocese of California 1849-1914*, 138.
3   Cf. *Sea Breezes*, vol 44, no 297 (September 1970), 582ff.
4   For lavish detail see Stan Hugill, *Sailortown*, 207ff.; *Shanties from the Seven Seas*, 45ff.
5   A.G. Course, *The Merchant Navy . . .* , 242ff.

who were about to be doped and shipped off to sea ... The Irishman joined the Missions to Seamen and founded the Mission sports section where he assisted in teaching sea-apprentices the art of self defence.

The Institute had small auxiliaries across the Bay at Oakland, and up the Bay at the sugar and grain docks of Port Esta, Eckley, and Crocket, staffed by volunteer lay workers as required; as shipping declined, these centres became redundant. Additionally, seamen were visited in hospital, where eventually it became possible to provide a chapel and recreation hut, the latter developed as a Government-approved occupational therapy unit.

Fell left San Francisco in 1899, writing a book on his return to Britain, *British Merchant Shipping in San Francisco* (1899), which made an appeal to public opinion. It listed the evils he had found in chapters covering 'Ships' Tailors', 'Tailors and Pocket Money', 'Crimping', '"Running Men Out" of Ships', 'Allotment Notes', 'Paying Men Off', 'Apprentices and Desertion', all sailor-language for means of separating the sailor from his money. Fell wrote generously of the parish clergy in San Francisco, suggesting that the evils found there were beyond them, busy as they were with their congregations; their invitations to the men to join them in church on Sundays almost useless. Like Charles Hopkins, he asked, 'Why should sailors of all men be offered tracts and continual invitations on most weekdays as well as Sundays to church? Landspeople are not much troubled in this way; why should sailors be?'

None of his successors stayed long in post. In 1906 the San Francisco Institute was destroyed in the great earthquake and subsequent fire. The then chaplain, Frank Stone, contemplated a mobile mission, a hut on wheels, as a short term solution, and this was done; perhaps the first of its kind, and a century ahead of today's response to fast turn-arounds. A floating institute was considered and a decommissioned ferry given for the purpose, but the idea failed to find favour. Eventually, the Bishop and Mr Stone decided to buy a plot on Steuart Street, built an institute with borrowed money, vesting it in the Bishop as a corporation sole, allowing a substantial two-storeyed, reinforced concrete building to be erected in 1907. It was handed over to the Diocese of California in 1914 and renamed the SCI of San Francisco; financial backing came from the Women's Auxiliary to the Board of Missions.[1]

Given the American love of large corporations, it is not surprising to find a growing desire for SCIs to affiliate. In 1889 PECUSA's General Convention had appointed a commission to examine the needs of seamen. Its report was given to the Convention in 1892, and the matter referred to the Domestic and Foreign Missionary Society. At the annual conference of the Eighth Missionary Department, held in Los Angeles in 1904, Rev. S. H. Wingfield Digby of the San Francisco Institute proposed that the Board of Missions make a more comprehensive and systematic provision for work among seamen, prompting Bishop Potter of New York to invite the bishops of seaport cities to join him in Boston on 20 October 1904, before the

---

1   H.H. Kelley, The Early History etc., 349ff. D.O. Kelley, *History of the Diocese of California etc.* 138ff.

General Convention met, to consider a general commission of the Church. A joint commission of three bishops, three priests and three laymen, was appointed to enter a Report at the next General Convention.

What follows in this paragraph is not for the faint-hearted. After meetings in 1904, 1905 and 1906 a Report was presented to the 1907 Convention at Richmond, Virginia, recommending the appointment of a central Church board for work among seamen. This was duly accepted by the Convention, which required it to consist of five each of bishops, priests and laymen, and to be organised under the Board of Missions, with provision for study of the existing work and the need for extension. Bishop Nichols, following Bishop Potter as its Chairman in 1908, presented the Board's Report in 1910 to the General Convention. This resolved that the Board of Missions should proceed with the organisation of seamen's work on a national scale; a report in 1913 to the General Convention stated that Bishop Nichols was now the elected President of the Board of the SCI of America, and authorised to complete the organisation required by the 1907 Commission. As the Board of Missions could offer no financial assistance(!) the newly integrated SCIs could not be considered its subsidiary. This was confirmed in 1916 and a Joint Board established; in 1919 it became 'The Joint Commission on Seamen's Work', incorporated under New York State Law in 1920.

A number of Institutes followed this national foundation, for example, Newport, Port Arthur (1920); Los Angeles, Houston, New Orleans (1922); Tampa, Mobile (1923); Manila (1924), demonstrating a fresh impetus given by the national body. Over time changing shipping patterns have reduced the number of SCIs considerably. The New York SCI claims on its website (2011) to be the 'largest, most comprehensive mariner's service agency in North America', and can certainly be said to have progressed since the 'Young Men's Auxiliary and Missionary Society' started work there in 1834. Much of its work is now educational.

There have been a number of smaller societies in America involved with seamen in a variety of ways, many of these meticulously recorded in Kverndal's *Seamen's Missions*. One of the more unusual, and little remembered, was the New York Altar Guild, a society of ladies formed in 1903. It began maintaining altars on passenger ships in 1933, particularly those of the United States Lines. It provided the altars for the old SS *Washington* and the *America*; the completion in 1933 of the *Washington* perhaps prompting the interest of the guild to this specialized work. When a new *United States* was commissioned the Guild was invited by the United States Lines to provide an altar, a request declined with regret as the necessary fireproof materials were beyond the means of the Guild; instead, portable altars, complete with linen, were provided for the *United States* and the *America*, and subsequently maintained, the ships being furnished with the necessary candles and wafers; a quiet but valuable service.[1]

---

[1] *Forth*, official organ of the PECUSA, vol 118(11), 23.

14. The Religious Orders

From Celtic onwards times tales survive of monks, like St Brendan the Navigator, taking to the sea. Many of these were listed in Anson's Church and the Sailor. None seem to have been directly involved with seamen before the Middle Ages. Medieval religious ran *maisons dieu*, lights, ships; ransomed captives, and did the many other things identified earlier in this book. Later still the foundations of St Vincent de Paul and the heroic work of St Peter Claver stand out. However, the connection between seafarer and religious orders was a diminishing one. This is strange, given the similarities in their lives: a communal existence, a day ruled by bells, chosen or unavoidable celibacy, and until recently life lived in a single sex context.

Though many religious were travelling by sea at this time, this chapter will concentrate on those directly concerned with a ministry to the seafarer. Of Catholic orders the Scalabrinians and their work with emigrants has some relevance.[1] The Augustinians of the Assumption at work among French fishermen off Newfoundland and Iceland will appear in chapter eighteen. In this chapter the work of Miss Sellon will be mentioned, and the Order of St Paul (OSP) and its founder Charles Hopkins covered in detail. Neither is particularly well-known; both the product of the Catholic revival in the Church of England.

Priscilla Lydia Sellon

The nineteenth-century Catholic revival in the Church of England produced a number of religious orders, many ephemeral, some which survive.[2] An early founder was Priscilla Lydia Sellon (Mother Lydia), daughter of a naval Commander.[3] Responding to a general appeal by Bishop Phillpotts of Exeter for something to be done about the appalling conditions and spiritual destitution to be found in Plymouth and Devonport, with his approval she began work in this naval heartland in 1848, at first alone, then laying the foundation for a Sisterhood with his guidance, with her few companions doing heroic work in this poverty-stricken neighbourhood at a time when

---

1 Marco Caliaro and Mario Francesconi, *John Baptist Scalabrini: Apostle to Emigrants*.
2 P.F. Anson, *Call of the Cloister* .... He recycled much of his material in *Building Up the Waste Places*.
3 Margaret Goodman's books: *Experience of an English Sister of Mercy* and *Sisterhoods in the Church of England*. Anson's *Call of the Cloister* (259ff) gives an extended history of Miss Sellon's Society of the Most Holy Trinity, and cites contemporary sources regarding her difficulties.

Sisterhoods were a novelty in the Church of England. Of their various works, a home for the orphan daughters of British soldiers and sailors, St George's College for Sailor Boys, and a home for old sailors and their wives relate directly to seamen. Opposition from Protestants and publicity from a disgruntled former Sister (Miss Goodman) followed, peaking in the 1860s, and losing her a significant number of patrons. Among the Sisterhood's original objects were 'the education of female children of Soldiers and Sailors ... Visiting of female immigrants aboard vessels ... '. Miss Goodman related that in the house for old sailors 'they were encouraged to make their old age as cheerful and comfortable as their infirmities would admit', being expected to attend some Church services.

According to Miss Goodman, the St George's College for Sailor Boys was in the care of a Sister Amelia, assisted by an 'old man-of-war's man; who also took charge of the flogging department, under her immediate superintendence ... '. The lads swabbed floors, learnt to wash and mend their clothes, and slept in hammocks. Knot-tying, climbing ladders, and other sailor-like activities filled the rest of the day. They were given religious instruction. 'The Sisters' boys were well-known, and much sought after for the Royal Navy and their promotion was rapid'. Their training would certainly have fitted them for the RN, their placement perhaps aided by Miss Sellon's father's connections. Miss Goodman's willingness to criticize much of Miss Sellon's other work adds value to her opinion here. This College had to be closed in 1862 for lack of funds. Of her other efforts for the sailor, or his children, little more is heard.

Charles Plomer Hopkins [1]

Hopkins is unique in the history of the sea apostolate, particularly for his close association with the development of seamen's trade unionism. He survives in Peter Anson's *Call of the Cloister*.[2] Anson initially wrote about him in the 1920s, more interested in his religious foundation than his work for the sailor.

Charles Plomer Hopkins was born in the United States in 1861, then taken via Cornwall, his mother's home, to Burma, where his American father was employed as a River Pilot. Aged eight, he was sent from Burma to England on the *Geologist*, to be educated at Falmouth. Later he would write in his book, *Altering Plimsoll's Mark*:

> My personal introduction to the load-line controversy took place on board the sailing ship *GEOLOGIST* in or about 1870, on my passage from India

---

1 Material in this chapter comes from three main sources: *The Messenger*, various issues; local newspapers; and the Family Welfare Association (Charity Organisation Society) files kept in the Greater London Records Office. I am indebted to Dr Stephen Friend for pointing me to the latter. Contemporary descriptions of Abbey life show the influence of its Indian origins. The Anglo-Catholic response to it can be found in Compton MacKenzie, *My Life and Times: Octave Two*, 190f, 203f, 219f.

2 Anson wrote this book uncritically, with material supplied by his subjects. In the case of Hopkins he made mistakes, as did I when following him in my *From Shore to Shore*. For more details Miller, *Priest in Deep Water*.

Charles Hopkins
(obituary picture, *Seamen's Chronicle*, 1922)

> to England to school. The sailors called her a 'death-trap' and she all but drowned me on the main deck. . . .

His father, familiar with visiting sailing ships, is unlikely to have consigned his eldest son to a coffin ship, though its logs reveal the *Geologist* to have been a 'hard' ship. The concept of coffin ships is closely associated with Samuel Plimsoll's campaign for greater safety at sea, in and out of the British Parliament, and Hopkins's work for seamen must be seen against Plimsoll's legislation.

After schooling in Falmouth, Hopkins studied music in London, before returning to Burma as Rangoon's cathedral organist, becoming increasingly involved there in a ministry to seafarers, particularly the apprentices. Ordination and appointment as Port Chaplain followed. Almost at once he was caught up in the case of a ship overloaded:

> My next personal experience . . . took place in Rangoon, Burma, in or about 1884, when the load-line disc of the sailing ship *CASSIOPE* was raised by the captain's orders to enable more cargo to be taken aboard. She was lost with all hands. . . .

The father of a lost apprentice wrote to Hopkins for evidence. Hopkins, trying to respond, found his efforts rebuffed by bishop and shipping community alike, both advising him to concentrate on spiritual matters. His willingness to publicise injustices made him unpopular with the shipping worthies and led to his removal to the small, seasonal, rice port of Akyab. Though there as parish priest he soon started a seamen's club. Staffing problems turned his thoughts to the religious life as a means of providing a committed ministry to seamen. His time in Akyab was ended by malaria, which permanently damaged his health, and forced his return to England.

Hopkins's brief stay in London, principally for medical attention, coincided with the growing unrest which culminated in the Dock Strike of 1889. He stayed with a colourful and remarkable clergyman, The Rev. A. Osborne Jay, Vicar of Holy Trinity, Shoreditch, whose very deprived London parish responded well to its vicar's unusual methods, some of which Hopkins adopted in his next appointment as Port Chaplain in Calcutta. Jay, and surrounding clergy who were Christian Socialists, cast a little light on the thinking of the time, though Hopkins cannot be directly associated with Christian Socialism. Jay had founded a small and ephemeral religious community (the Society of St Paul), its members bound by an annual promise, in which Hopkins made his profession just before departure; no more is heard of his membership after arrival in Calcutta, where, as River Chaplain, he began to attract large numbers of seamen to the Seamen's Church, assisted by several men in his own foundation, the Order of St Paul.

Hopkins and the Shipping Acts

It is necessary to examine Hopkins and his work in the light of the various Merchant Shipping Acts if his ministry in Calcutta and then England is to be understood. Of religious groups, only Hopkins and his Seamen's Friendly Society of St Paul became directly involved in applying the legislation, principally the Merchant Shipping Acts of 1854, 1876 and 1894. Although Hopkins had to become familiar with local variations in the Indian Merchant Shipping Acts, it is these three which were of prime importance to him, to the Union and to the seaman. The Act of 1854, as those that followed, in face of considerable owner opposition, attempted to introduce minimum conditions under which men sailed, including ship registration, basic provisions, training, and safety.[1] Steamships, especially passenger vessels, were to be subject to inspection, with fines imposed if regulations were infringed. Seamen were to be discharged with an indication of character. Those discharged abroad for medical reasons were no longer simply to be cast adrift. Complaints could be made and fines imposed for bad stores. The Act's short-comings are evidenced by the need for Samuel Plimsoll's campaign which followed.

Of particular interest in the 1854 Act was the section on discipline. Any seaman deserting or failing to join his ship after signing-on was liable to a

---

1 P. G. Parkhurst, *Ships of Peace*, vol. 1 covers the period to 1885, giving an inside picture of the Board of Trade.

14. The Religious Orders

maximum of twelve weeks' imprisonment with hard labour and the forfeiture of any possessions left on board ship. Plimsoll was to bring such injustices to public attention in 1873, graphically illustrating his book *Our Seamen - an appeal* with photographs of overloaded or otherwise unseaworthy 'coffin ships', the crews of which could be imprisoned, under this Act, for refusing to sail in them. Such severe penalties suggest that masters had difficulty obtaining crews, which in turn reflects the harshness of life at sea at this time. Owing much to Plimsoll's pressure, a Royal Commission reported in 1873 on unseaworthy ships.[1] Its findings were mixed. It led the Government to introduce an Unseaworthy Ships Act in 1875 which required a load line but, through the pressure of shipowners, placed at the owner's discretion.

Improvements followed in 1876 and 1894, largely through Plimsoll's efforts. Plimsoll, familiar with the men who carried the cargoes of coal which were his father's business, stood at Derby as a Liberal on the reform of the 1854 Act, being returned as its Member of Parliament in 1868.[2] Plimsoll, an active member of the Congregational Church, attracted support from across the denominational spectrum. He proposed legislation for the proper measurement and registration of ships, their inspection before putting to sea, and adequate insurance, together with strict rules regarding loading. In the resulting parliamentary debate he withdrew his bill in favour of one sponsored by a government aware of the depth of feeling in the country aroused by his book.[3] This became the 1876 Act, somewhat emasculated by opposition from shipowners in parliament.

The 1876 Act permitted the positioning on each ship of a line, 'Plimsoll's mark', at the shipowner's discretion though forbidding its subsequent adjustment.[4] This was the problem when Hopkins heard the master of the *Cassiope* proposing to move his mark to take on more cargo. The 1876 Act also dealt in detail with the matter of ships' provisions. Hopkins was to prosecute in a number of cases in Calcutta where poor provisions were involved, one involving six-month-old pork in the cask, open in the tropics for weeks with only the brine changed, and responsible for the death of several seamen. Plimsoll cited seven-year-old meat being returned to naval dockyards for sale to parties who put it in fresh pickle to sell as stores for merchant ships. He asked for the Board of Trade (BoT) to check provisions.[5] Plimsoll was to continue his fight for better conditions for many years.

The 1876 Act included many items on which Hopkins and the president of the nascent seamen's union, Havelock Wilson, would campaign. In it,

---

1 British Parliamentary Papers, 1873, XXXVI and 1874, XXXIV. See also P. G. Parkhurst, *Ships of Peace*, 216.
2 P. G. Parkhurst, *Ships of Peace*, 208-226 gives the Board of Trade's view of Plimsoll and notes some of his inexactitudes.
3 George Peters, *The Plimsoll Line*, 97ff gives the progress of Plimsoll's bill in Parliament, describing his passionate appeal to the House and his expulsion for unparliamentary behaviour. His campaign greatly affected his health.
4 P. G. Parkhurst, *Ships of Peace*, 223.
5 J. H. Wilson, *My Stormy Voyage Through Life*, 33.

sending an unseaworthy ship to sea became punishable in a Crown Court rather than before magistrates. A survey could be ordered by the BoT and business conducted in open court, with costs against a guilty owner 'recoverable as salvage is recoverable'. It gave power to require of complainants security against frivolous complaints, but with no deposit required if a quarter of the crew (not less than three) complained. These regulations applied even to foreign ships in British waters. It takes little imagination to see that a seaman remained in a peculiar position if he did complain, risking owners closing ranks if he sought further employment, and why he would need the support of people like Hopkins. Although the 1876 Act included many improvements, a comparison with Plimsoll's book revealing the measure of his success, Plimsoll continued campaigning, believing that the best protection for seamen lay in fair legislation. Havelock Wilson, seamen's union founder, was to assist him in his later years, and, to an extent, assumed his parliamentary mantle.[1]

The 1876 Act tied up many loose ends but, as shown by Hopkins's articles in *The Messenger*, his community magazine, in 1893, work remained to be done, especially in the matter of the men's protection, both ashore and at sea. Their financial position was little improved: a man setting out on a two-year voyage needed some means of getting money to his dependents during his absence, while accumulated sums in his pocket when paid off at the end of a voyage making him an easy prey for land sharks.[2] Seafarers' industrial mortality rate was another problem area. While the physical conditions under which seamen laboured were always harsh, and some aspects of life at sea, such as storm or ice, could not be altered, others could. *The Seamen's Chronicle*, the official organ of the National Amalgamated Sailors' and Firemen's Union, gave figures for industrial fatalities during the first six months of 1894:[3]

Month	Railway Servants	Miners	Factory & workshop operatives	Seamen
January	63	82	55	359
February	31	60	33	316
March	39	53	36	195
April	32	63	35	242
May	41	78	46	120
June	36	349	29	139

Industrial fatalities January-June 1894
Source: *Seamen's Chronicle*, 25 August 1894

---

1   *Ibid*, 162ff
2   Alston Kennerley, *British Seamen's Missions and Sailors' Homes 1815-1970*, 112ff.
3   Cf P. G. Parkhurst, *Ships of Peace*, 406 where fatalities are given for 1867-82.

14. The Religious Orders

Two further areas affected by contemporary legislation need attention. The toughness of life at sea has been indicated above. That it affected all equally is only partly true; the most vulnerable group was the apprentices. Hopkins's ministry to sailors, at least in its early years, was especially to these boys. They are also significant for the special legislation which related to them. A second connected area concerns the wider issue of training seafarers.[1]

Throughout the nineteenth century a debate persisted whether government or owners should be responsible for training apprentices, young men training to be officers. In the early part of the century there was no requirement that an officer should be certificated. Government's interest in this came about because of the need for the RN to have access to a pool of trained men. The Merchant Navy needed its supply of officers to be constantly replenished too. An Act of 1835 required ships to carry apprentices in proportion to tonnage. In 1845 there were 15,704 apprentices. From 1849 when compulsory apprenticeship was abolished and the onus put on owners, numbers of apprentices began to dwindle alarmingly: by 1894 the Registrar General's Returns recorded only 2,164. The 1876 Act required that apprentices be boys aged at least twelve who should be healthy and strong. Hugh Falkus summarised some of the changes affecting apprentices:

> In the second half of the century a more rigorous approach was adopted towards the training of ship's officers. By 1888, for example, the Board of Trade standards required that a second mate be no younger than seventeen, but with four years at sea - so that sea-going at the age of thirteen was envisaged! The second mate, furthermore, had to be capable of finding his latitude from meridian altitude, and his longitude from sun sights and chronometer.[2]

A boy was to be bound to a master who 'is to be a proper person for the purpose', and must be brought before him at the time of the crew's engagement. Parents would usually pay £50 for his indentures; of this, he would receive, as pay, £8 for the first year, £9 for the second, £10 for the third, and £13 for the final year. If his money restricted his activity, the indentures did so further. Either seaman or officer, his hours of work, free time, instruction, welfare, all depended upon the master. In a less than gentle age, the poor ship's apprentice was often the subject of great brutality. His only escape might be a few hours ashore, at the whim of the master, without friends, and prey to people willing to take the little money he had. Hopkins's Indian priories were full of apprentices glad of a haven.[3] His initial efforts seem to have been entirely independent of Plimsoll's campaign in Parliament, though Rangoon and Calcutta, well supplied with English newspapers, would have had ships with crews abuzz with news of attempts at home to improve conditions of life at sea. Hopkins would surely have been encouraged, even prompted by this news. There were exceptional shipowners, many of whom put by what

---

1   Alston Kennerley, Ratings for the Mercantile Marine . . . , 31-51.
2   H. Falkus, *Master of Cape Horn,* 1982, 66.
3   D.R. MacGregor, *The China Bird,* 85.
    P.G. Parkhurst, *Ships of Peace,* 180, 187, 235. See also V.C. Burton, Apprenticeship Regulation and Maritime Labour. . . , 29ff.

they would have spent on insurance to maintain their vessels, but for many, maximum profit remained the driving force.

The 1894 Act was a consolidation bill, an amalgamation of many Acts into one tidier Act.[1] It was the subject of much discussion in Parliament through 1893 and into 1894. A glance at the index in Hansard reveals many horror stories brought forward during its passage, even in the final days. One will suffice to show that, despite the progress made since Plimsoll's original Bill, much remained to be done. On 10 July 1894 the House of Commons heard of the case of the *Helvetia*. Three days earlier the Cardiff Stipendiary Magistrate had condemned its captain for prematurely abandoning his ship, suspended his certificate for two years and censured the ship's owner. The ship, twenty-nine years old, had been bought for £5,000. After being laid up for twelve months she was insured for 'a sum much in excess of her cost and value' and sent to sea without survey or repair. Within five days of sailing she was in great danger off Cornwall, signalling for tugs. Her owner and agents were telegraphed repeatedly, the telegrams ignored. After twelve hours she was towed into Cardiff with fifteen feet of water in her hold. She was surveyed, repaired (superficially in the court's opinion) and, insured for a larger sum, and put to sea again, only to be abandoned 'under suspicious circumstances' three days later and 'is supposed to have ultimately foundered', the evidence at the bottom of the sea.

Hopkins's Response

In Calcutta Hopkins did not confine himself to a spiritual ministry. Using his religious community, the Order of St Paul (OSP), he fought some thirty cases defending seamen through the courts, and got involved with Havelock Wilson's seamen's union. When his bishop refused him permission to be its president, Hopkins started a seamen's guild, the Seamen's Friendly Society of St Paul (SFSSP), to offer religious support and legal representation where necessary - hence those thirty cases, most concerned with appalling conditions on ships or bad treatment of crews. The Calcutta period was interrupted twice by Hopkins's need to tour England in pursuit of recruits and financial support. A talk to an 1893 Hastings audience impressed two Jesuits, Fr Goldie and Eugene Grosjean, present sufficiently for what they heard to help shape Catholic work among seafarers.

His court cases and general agitation made enemies: he left Calcutta in 1894 to return to the United Kingdom surrounded by rumours of sexual impropriety following a court case which seems to have been arranged to blacken his name; those who had most to gain by his removal were members of the Calcutta shipping community. His reputation was upheld by the court. Had there been a shred of evidence against him the Shipping Federation would not have hesitated to use it when Hopkins, returned to England, joined the Federation's arch enemy, the seamen's union - but rumour cast a blight on his

---

1 Alston Kennerley, The Shore Management of British Seafarers in the Twentieth Century.

14. The Religious Orders

ministry. The years following his return were spent consolidating the life of his community, which continued its maritime work through priories established in Barry and Greenwich, while the Indian work was allowed to run down and the Diocese of Calcutta to buy its property. In England Hopkins's lack of tact, combining with the requirements of the Colonial Clergy Act, and episcopal willingness to listen to the rumours which followed his return, placed him in an ecclesiastical limbo. The seamen's union, however, welcomed him.

The years between Hopkins's meeting Havelock Wilson in the late 1890s and becoming secretary of the International Committee of Seamen's Unions in 1910 are dimly lit. As secretary he was privy to the plans for the strike which, in 1911, it was his privilege to announce, before bringing it to a reasonable conclusion by a series of negotiations, mostly led by him. Strikes of other workers associated with the industry prolonged the dispute. Industrial unrest is usually controversial and any interpretation of Hopkins's and Wilson's roles, and the subsequent relationship of the seamen's union with the main body of trade unionism, depends much upon who is viewing it.

References to the 'Union', hide three successive manifestations of the same organisation. It began as the National Amalgamated Sailors' and Firemen's Union of Great Britain and Ireland, founded at a public meeting on 18th August, 1887; today it is part of a larger transport union. It started in the North East of England when Havelock Wilson, after a spell at sea, became very active within a Sunderland union which, due to contemporary attitudes and legislation, was more of a protection and benefit society than one which campaigned. Havelock Wilson extended the number of its branches, trying to bring them and some of the other few existing unions into one organisation, eventually forming a national union for seamen, with the lengthy title given above.[1]

It was just at this time that Hopkins was starting his seamen's guild in Calcutta. That is to say, his organisation and the Union were developing concurrently, which may have given them much in common. The problems which beset the infant Union were, and are, peculiar to seamen who, likely to disappear at any time and remain away, sometimes for years, were difficult to organise. There was also the problem of who could be a member in an hierarchical industry: might the Union include the officers? The shipowners conceding no right of membership, it took a brave supporter to carry the Union message to his shipmates when his job might be lost in consequence. If recruitment was difficult, the exercise of control was harder yet. The seamen's Union was forced to rely more than any other on the paid official, creating a constant drain on its hard-to-collect finances. It was effectively as a local organiser that Hopkins first contacted Havelock Wilson, writing from Calcutta; at their first meeting in London some five or six years later Havelock Wilson hoped to recruit Hopkins to this similar role, which Hopkins seems at first to have accepted.

Responding to the 1889 Dock Strike the owners formed the Shipping Federation as a 'fighting machine' to counter the increasing Union power. It

---

1 Marsh V and Ryan A, *The Seamen*, 17f.

began to bring considerable pressure to bear upon the Union by, for example, getting creditors to call in debts or question the lack of accounts, methods which served it well over the years.[1] It used its influence throughout the docks and in allied industries where its members were the principal employers, introducing restrictive conditions, such as the requirement to sign-on at the Federation office and undergo Federation medical tests, which in 1911 would become negotiating points. It had sufficient members in Parliament to hamper Plimsoll's attempts to improve conditions for seamen through the legislative process.[2] It issued its own ticket, which became a powerful means of control, carrying with it various benefits to the man who sold, the Union's word, himself to the Federation. It imported where necessary blacklegs to circumvent strikes and retained the threat to employ cheap labour from abroad. It was quick to take Havelock Wilson to court, his first appearance being in April 1889, charged with attempting to persuade two seamen to desert. Havelock Wilson was to sue and be sued on many occasions. His litigious disposition - he was not always wise in the cases he initiated - strained Union finances though, in his defense, it may be said that in many of those cases he was a man sorely provoked. He was doing the same thing at the same time as Hopkins in Calcutta. There is no doubt that the Federation was out to 'get' Havelock Wilson. His reluctance to publish accounts was partly because of lack of membership income, but also, it would seem, poor book-keeping. Young unions' lack of financial expertise often provided easy targets.

Hopkins in India

Hopkins described his methods of work among seamen in an article for the *Indian Church Quarterly Review* of April 1890, shortly after arriving in Calcutta. The article, entitled 'The Church and Our Sailors', outlined the general condition of sailors:

> our sailors are neglected by governments, politicians and ship-owners alike . . . their condition today is little better in many instances than it was half a century ago. And the same may be said for the sailor's spiritual condition. . . .

a statement which upset his bishop. He drew attention briefly to the appropriation of sailors' earnings, overloading, under-manning, poor accommodation, poor food, and more, to emphasise the need for Church concern with spiritual and temporal welfare. He denigrated the preaching of uninvited sermons and tract-scattering on board, arguing that the men should be approached cautiously, with time to talk and hear of their circumstances.[3] This could best be done overseas (where men stayed with their ships) rather than in home ports (where they were paid-off), and was being done by MtS and the SAWCM. In colonial ports, crews often remained for weeks, sometimes months, usually working in tropical temperatures, often fleeced of their wages, and sometimes hounded in

---

1 See e.g. Mss 367/TSF/1/4/1, GP Committee *Minutes*, 12 June 1891. Mss 367/TSF/1/1/1, *Minutes* of the SF, 26 October 1906.
2 Marsh & Ryan, 30f.
3 He disliked 'tractmongers'.

14. The Religious Orders

sickness to the point of deserting ship. In such conditions they would welcome any sign of friendship and give the Church its opportunity.

Hopkins argued that opportunity was best seized by treating the sailor, not as something apart, but as a fellow Christian. Port chaplains, he suggested, should not be segregated but parish staffs should be strengthened and the work among seamen firmly based in a parochial context.[1] The work would fall into two parts: afloat and ashore. Afloat, chaplains could visit ships between 8.00 a.m. and 9.00 a.m. when the men were breakfasting, or after 6:00 p.m. when work was finished for the day. Hopkins stressed the need to visit both officers and men to avoid the implication that the 'men' were somehow more in need of the Gospel, and to obtain more readily, if desired, the object of holding a service on board. The captain could press the crew to attend but Hopkins thought it better for attendance to be obtained freely and willingly. Services afloat were best kept simple, perhaps supplemented with Bible classes; ashore they were better sacramental. Ashore, provision for the men should recognise that they had been cooped up, perhaps for months. Many seamen would have signed articles offering 'no liberty abroad', intended to prevent their jumping ship, and meaning that time ashore could not be claimed as a right. In what liberty they were permitted they sought 'a bright and cheerful Club or Home', preferably furnished with a piano, ideally frequented by other parishioners willing to make friends, and perhaps offering access to sleeping accommodation. Sunday, the great liberty day for crews, should not be marked by a strict sabbatarianism; simple board games and amusements would keep many from sin. Given all this, those who did seek Christian ministrations should find a decently and solemnly (the ambiguity is probably deliberate) celebrated Communion service.

Contemporary reports confirm that Hopkins practiced this pattern of ministry. He returned frequently to the theme of Sunday as a 'day of temptation ... when there were plenty of places open ... for vice and sin' and his references to cricket and swimming caused one reporter to mistake him for 'an advocate of the "muscular Christianity" method of missionary labour as contrasted with the evangelical style.'[2] Different weeknight evenings at The Priory in Calcutta were set aside to receive the various groups of men (ratings, apprentices, officers), with Sundays open to all comers. At special times of the year, such as Christmas, an extra effort was made; he might have as many as a thousand, in two sittings, for the dinner accompanying the New Year Sports (high jump, shot, long jump, obstacle race, three-legged race, sack race, tug of war) at the Sailors' Home. Catering was done by the Great Eastern Hotel, its Secretary a member of Hopkins's management committee.[3] Donations for these events came from a variety of sources, including the Viceroy, the Lieutenant Governor

---

1 Working in a parochial context was what distinguished the High Church SAWCM, with its grants for missionary assistant curates, from the MtS, which pursued a policy of appointing port chaplains usually unattached to parishes. Hopkins received a SAWCM grant for some years.
2 *Hastings & St Leonards News*, 1 Sept 1893.
3 See e.g. *The Englishman (Weekly Summary)*, 11 Jan 1893.

of Bengal, and the Commander in Chief. Police Commissioner Lambert, another committee member, wrote at the end of 1889 that his men had had nothing to do on the streets of Calcutta over Christmas where in previous years sailors had kept them very busy, ascribing this happy state of affairs directly to Hopkins's work. Similar success began to be found in the church, and the twenty communicant sailors found on Hopkins's arrival in 1890 had become 1,450 by 1892, though how this figure was constituted is not explained.

To achieve these things Hopkins had the help of his brethren. These belonged to the Order of St Paul, which the bishop had insisted must not look to the diocese for financial support. Two received the salaries intended for his two assistants; other money came from donations, some raised by Hopkins on his preaching tours of England. Their good works were supported by and channelled through the Seamen's Friendly Society of St Paul.[1] His emphasis on his Friendly Society, which clearly has echoes of the friendly societies that preceded the trade unions, may have a further and provocative significance when placed alongside the title of the older, undenominational protestant, British and Foreign Seamen's Friend Society and Bethel Union, a society inimical in its beliefs to a High Church member of the Church of England.[2] The 'objects' of the SFSSP were fully given:

- To provide Religious Instruction, Worship, and the means of Grace[3] at 'the Seamen's Church;
- To provide Healthy Recreation and Intercourse for Men and Lads at its 'Recreation Rooms';
- Offers the Hospitality and Advantages of 'Home' at the Priory or Mission House;
- Shelters the Homeless and Destitute;
- Defends the Weak against imposition and wrong;
- Cares for the Sick and Dying on board and on shore;
- Guards and tends the Graves of the Dead.

Employers would have hesitated at the fifth object. Taken together, these objects combine seamen's missionary work, much of what old-style trade unionism offered, and legal representation.

Hopkins intended to work beyond Calcutta, envisaging a network of seamen's homes world-wide.

[I]t is not my wish or intention that we should confine ourselves to this local effort. We desire in addition to organise a body of men to go forth, and undertake the charge and work of Seamen's Missions in other places . . .

In India, his work began to spread, to Chittagong and to Budge Budge, downriver from Calcutta, where petroleum was unloaded. In 1894, too, Brother Alban began work in Bombay.

In 1893 a house was opened in Barry, South Wales, carefully chosen as a port where no other society was at work. Hopkins wrote, 'If we are to occupy Foreign Ports in other parts of the world (as we are certainly now called to do) we must establish a Mother House of the whole Society in England.' Barry was

---

1   C. P. Hopkins, *Altering Plimsoll's Mark*, 65f.
2   The BFSFSBU may well have founded the original Calcutta Seamen's Home.
3   The means of Grace would be the administration of the Sacraments.

a step on the way. As early as May 1892, Hopkins had written in *The Messenger*:
> It may be as well for me here to state the lines on which our Society works in connection with outports. We desire to see each port with its own well organised and firmly established 'Seamen's Mission and Friendly Society', we ourselves constituting a society or community of men ready to go to these different ports to manage and work these different Missions. We do not seek to absorb into our own Society existing organisations; but seeing the past failures of the Missions to Seamen in certain parts of the world, through the absence of trained, qualified, and devoted workers in the persons of members of our own Society. . . .

Hopkins, aged all of thirty, addressed his guildsmen as 'My Dear Sons'. There is a description of him at home in The Priory with some of his members:
> It astonished me to see sailors comfortably seated in big easy chairs and smoking like steam boat funnels. 'There's Father', and suddenly the piano sounds and a dozen lads rush to it. 'Good evening, Father', I hear them say, and 'Good evening to you, you bad boys' is the answer given in a merry and hearty tone.

His rule was firm. He would defend members where necessary, but offered no legal redress for lads who had deserted, for example, and if a Friday meeting found them guilty miscreants would find their names in the magazine as being expelled. A member summoned for insubordinate conduct on board ship was not expelled because he was willing to apologise. In this case, Hopkins wrote to the captain concerned, of the Rahane, asking if he would accept the man's written and public apology but saying that he would arrange for the man's defense if he would not. The captain declined to reply. The magistrate agreed with Hopkins that an apology would be sufficient. In another case,
> Louis Edwards of the *CASTOR* was called upon . . . to send in his resignation on account of his refusal of duty and absence without leave. He was on this account refused the services of the Guild Solicitor when charged by his Captain. . . .

But there were benefits beyond legal privileges. Men who died in membership were given impressive and solemn funerals with guildsmen and brethren watching at the bier until the funeral. Hopkins's experience, when a small boy on his voyage to England, of the funeral of a sailor may have influenced him in the making of this provision. Funeral rites also provide an echo of the medieval guilds on the one hand, and on the other, of the earliest trade unions which were largely benefit and burial societies. That the guild stood at least in the latter light Hopkins was quite sure:
> The Bishop of Calcutta holds . . . very pronounced views as to the advisability of the Clergy of the English Church having anything to do with Trade Unions. Our Guild is not the harmless association usually understood by the term 'Guild' in these 'reformed' days of ours, but is of the nature of the old world and Catholic Trades Guild for the mutual help and protection of its members in the temporal relationships and work of this life, as well as for mutual help and protection in preparation for the life to come . . . our Guild undertakes, by the very nature of its Constitution, many of the functions of a Trades Union. . . .[1]

---

1 *The Messenger*, Jan 1897.

This was not everywhere well received. The captains and ship owners, as well as boycotting the Sailors' Home, declined to employ any of Hopkins's known associates, prevented crews from using The Priory, and withheld subscriptions. They used the Press; nor did they confine their Press campaign to writing letters, according to Shipmates (July 1894), which gives details of a conspiracy against Hopkins where a boy said to be aged thirteen apparently threatened to publish in the *Sunday Times* 'a very offensive accusation'. The editor of the *Sunday Times* was prosecuted for obscenity in 1894 for his coverage of this case before the district magistrate's court. According to the *Indian Daily News Overland Summary:*

> The report of the case of the Revd Father Hopkins was not a report at all, but was unadulterated filth, revolting garbage which had been prepared by putting these questions to Father Hopkins in order that all this dirt might find its way into the paper. . . .

The *Sunday Times* was a sensational paper and the accusation here is that it rigged the case so that sensational questions could be asked, and published, for the titillation of readers. Robert Smallman, the boy, had charged Hopkins with an offense under Section 511 of the Indian Penal Code. Hopkins retaliated by pursuing the boy in court, the subsequent case occupying many columns in the *Indian Daily News Overland Summary* and the *Englishman*. Section 511 of the Indian Penal Code applied in cases which would otherwise attract a penalty of transportation or imprisonment,[1] its use implying that Hopkins had 'tried it on', rather than achieved his alleged immoral purpose. Hopkins demanded the 'fullest investigation' for his name to be cleared, the affair progressing beyond the magistrates' court in which it had started. The boy was convicted of 'criminally intimidating' Hopkins and Hopkins's 'excellent character' upheld. The *Sunday Times*' editor received four months' rigorous imprisonment and a fine of Rs600, non-payment of which led to his paper's press, type, printing materials and furniture being seized, from which the paper seems never to have recovered.[2]

It is not hard to believe that someone, or several people, had an interest in undermining Hopkins in Calcutta, nor is the suggestion that this was the work of a section of the shipping community implausible. Whoever was responsible, despite failing in court, succeeded in besmirching Hopkins's reputation, and made his bishop's position *vis à vis* Hopkins's future employment difficult. It came at a very inconvenient time, for the brother dispatched in early 1894 from Calcutta to open the new house at Barry died suddenly in the June. Replacing him reduced community numbers to the point where it became imperative for Hopkins to return to the UK. Though his decision to return to the UK predated the court case, it and the pressure of significant officials in Calcutta's mercantile community explain his bishop's willingness to release him, not without reluctance, in September 1894. Hopkins arrived in the UK in late October, by November planning to take a larger cottage, apparently with the approval of the Bishop of Llandaff, in whose diocese Barry was situated.

---

1 So, for example, where a burglar might find a safe empty, his intention though unsuccessful would make him liable to prosecution under Section 511.
2 *Indian Daily News*, 16 August 1894.

14. The Religious Orders

Hopkins returns to England

The priory at Barry doubled as mother house and seamen's mission until mid 1895 when Hopkins found and bought land at Medstead, three miles outside the modest Hampshire town of Alton, with the intention of building what was called, even then, The Abbey, though it was to have no abbot until Hopkins was long dead. For the next five years his main work seems to have been the building of The Abbey, first in corrugated iron, then in stone; an inspiring story but, for the most part, peripheral to Hopkins's maritime ministry.

He began to tour the country preaching for funds and recruits. In 1899 an additional house at Greenwich was opened, handy for the Dreadnought Seamen's Hospital, and London's dockland. The attraction of a London base is an obvious one. The SFSSP Guild magazine *Shipmates* was merged with the OSP magazine *The Messenger* in November 1896. Hopkins continued to use this as a crusading platform. Some Indian work remained as did the Guild, its thousandth member being enrolled in February 1897 in Calcutta. Membership numbering was continuous so that it would be unlikely to discover a thousand members at any one time. There were, however, problems with the Calcutta work. In 1896 Hopkins found it necessary to return to Calcutta, explaining in a letter in *The Messenger*, dated 31st August, that in effect the Bishop of Calcutta wished to take over the work of the OSP, Hopkins seeking the contrary. An impasse, followed by arbitration, was resolved by OSP withdrawing from all Indian ports except Bombay (though Bombay was shut by 1900), which was in another diocese; this withdrawal to take place on condition that the bishop should take over the OSP's property and pay Rs 4,000 for it.

Rumour now began to play its part. It was said that Hopkins had got the OSP so heavily into debt (his mortgage on the properties in India) that the bishop had had to intervene to the tune of £4,000 (the Rs 4,000 mentioned above). Regarding the court case rumour failed to recall that Hopkins had been cleared, but fed on the nature of a case which had been discussed with periphrasis and, at a time when Oscar Wilde was making headlines, turning it into something quite sinister. This caused ecclesiastical and financial problems, without which, it is unlikely Hopkins would have found himself in the arms of the NSFU and, some years later, leading an international strike.

The Abbey lay in the diocese of Winchester. Following protocol, Hopkins wrote to his diocesan, the Bishop of Winchester, Randall Davidson, in September 1895 saying that he hoped to be able to place before him his various Church documents, to seek Randall Davidson's approval to establish at Alton 'the Noviciate or Training College . . . ' at which there would be no public services, on land 'which has been presented to us', and requesting permission to celebrate Holy Communion at The Abbey as it was three miles from Alton Church.

Hopkins's letter appears to have met with no encouragement.[1] This was not helpful. Davidson, closely associated with Queen Victoria, was bishop of the third most senior See in the Church of England after London and Durham, and a

---

1 Most of the Davidson material comes from the Davidson papers in Lambeth Palace Library. Full details are given in Miller, *Charles Plomer Hopkins etc.*

man of influence. The Vicar of Alton wrote to Davidson (10th December, 1895) to say that he had no objection to Hopkins's celebrating in his own chapel for the OSP '[b]ut clergy who take the strong individual line which he does are apt to be eccentric and are sometimes carried forward into practices which they did not at first intend', an opinion the vicar failed to explain.

By March 1899 Hopkins was writing to Randall Davidson in confidence begging for the renewal of his licence: 'You can afford to be generous, and remove the unjustifiable suspicion which hangs over me that the withdrawal of your licence implies more than it really did' (Hopkins's emphasis). The bishop, temporising, asked for more information. In April the Archbishop of Canterbury's chaplain wrote asking Hopkins to obtain a letter from Bishop Davidson undertaking to renew Hopkins's licence if Canterbury renewed his Permission to Officiate. On the 17th April 1899, Davidson wrote to Hopkins:

> I am afraid it is not possible for me to write such a letter as you desire, undertaking to license you in this diocese in the event of the Archbishop's renewing your Permission to Officiate in England. I write this after fully considering the circumstances of the case.

That Randall Davidson could not have been less helpful becomes clear in a copy of a letter which he wrote, dated 31 October 1899, in response to enquiries made to him about Hopkins. It merits quotation almost in its entirety:

> I was compelled to withdraw from Father Hopkins the 'Leave to Officiate' ... not on the grounds of his doctrine or ecclesiastical usages, but on account of some grave indiscretions which he himself admitted, although he regarded them as less serious than I do myself or than others in whom I have confidence. I investigated the matter to the best of my power. Father Hopkins resigned the headship of his little Order, becoming an ordinary member under a clergyman [*sic*] who came from India to take the lead. After a few weeks or months this clergyman severed his connection with the Order, and I am myself unable to say of whom it now consists besides Father Hopkins himself. I have no reason whatever to doubt his probity in financial matters, but I cannot regard him as one entitled to confidence as a worker with young men and boys. I say this after very full enquiry both as to his work in India and his work in England. Bishop Mylne, late of Bombay, who at first supported Father Hopkins, has I believe now declined to allow his name to be used in connection with the Association.

Careful reading of this letter reveals that the 'indiscretions' are separate from the reference to 'young men and boys', the latter sufficient to kill his career stone dead. The indiscretions of which Hopkins made light were a public spat with the Bishop of Hereford. Additionally, at this time, the Charity Organisation Society was gathering and spreading similar innuendo about Hopkins to any who asked.

It was Hopkins's misfortune that Randall Davidson became Archbishop of Canterbury in 1903, closing any avenue for appeal which might have remained to him. His last letter to Davidson was written in 1907 when he sought to marry a niece to a Merchant Navy officer. His letter met with no success. Hopkins wrote:

> I have often felt that I should like to meet Your Grace again face to face; but that is never likely now to be. However, although I have often felt deeply angered at your treatment of me, I realise that perhaps it was all for the best.

> You were in a difficulty - with a tremendous responsibility on you - and you did at the time what you considered was best. [Hopkins's emphasis]

This trouble with his bishop made raising money to build his Abbey and recruiting members very difficult. Without a Licence, he could appeal neither for finance nor vocations in any church in England, nor would a potential recruit arriving at The Abbey find the superior recognised either by his own parish priest or the incumbent of the parish in which The Abbey was situated.

Hopkins continued to campaign for seamen. He wrote in *The Messenger* (March 1900),

> Father Hopkins has been accused of being a dangerous agitator; ecclesiastical circles have been disquieted because he has flung into their midst a wrathful shipowner or two; he has not been asked to preach a second time in certain Churches because he upset the congregation so by his harrowing tales of the sea - people wept, it is said, and remarked 'How awful!' - and what of that? I can, at any rate, look sailors straight in the face today and not feel ashamed . . . A Parliamentary Committee has reported, since these days of which I write, that our English ships <u>have been</u> sent to sea undermanned; and steps have been taken to improve matters somewhat; but not yet enough in my opinion . . . A Priest <u>must</u> take up such matters if he is to represent, and reproduce the work of Christ, who is the Saviour of the whole man - his body as well as of his soul. [Hopkins's emphasis]

To this end he made sure that he publicised the working of the 1894 Merchant Shipping Act and Havelock Wilson's work in Parliament. Hopkins was no longer directly concerned with his own Guild but could claim it as a power base when necessary. He seems at this time to be more convinced of the need for changes to be effected by legislation; persuasion and publicity no longer sufficed. There are several references in The Messenger to his having written to Havelock Wilson and, subsequently, he met him. There is no date for this meeting nor any hint of explanation for its delay, but it was probably before 1900. Havelock Wilson saw that here was just the sort of man he could work with.

Hopkins's association with the Union was not the only thing to occupy him at this time. The OSP published in 1903 a *Prayer Book for Catholic Seamen*. A copy survives in the British Library. How many copies were published is unknown. It is a reminder that Hopkins was still very much the seamen's chaplain. He spent most of his time at the Greenwich Priory, the OSP's main point of contact with seamen after the closure of its Indian houses. The *Prayer Book for Catholic Seamen* was

> compiled . . . mainly for the use of those merchant seamen and firemen who, in seeking either hospitality or shelter in one or other of the Houses of our Brotherhood, are moved by the HOLY SPIRIT through us, with a desire and determination to try to live a Godly, righteous, and sober life; and to look to the Order of St Paul for help and guidance in their spiritual endeavours and duties.

Despite its title the book was clearly from an Anglican stable, and steeped in the *Book of Common Prayer*, though it had a Catholic equivalent, *A Guide to Heaven*, produced in the early 1890s by the Catholic Truth Society.[1]

---

1 Miller, *Ship of Peter*, 67.

In 1906 a proposed revision of the Plimsoll line, a subject on which Hopkins had become an authority, would have altered the carrying capacity of a ship at a stroke if the line was allowed to be adjusted in the owner's favour. Hopkins believed this revision to be dictated by the desire for greater profitability rather than increased safety. His continuing work on the Plimsoll line was published as *Altering Plimsoll's Mark* in 1913.

Towards a strike

In early 1910 Hopkins intervened at Southampton, where a strike was threatened, claiming that he did so as one without official Union connections. A local history has only this to say of the strike:

> In 1910 the Southampton branch of the S&FU, whose members had been discontented for some time, struck for an increase of ten shillings a week, though their strike was not recognised by the union's central headquarters. A settlement was soon arrived at, although in the meantime the White Star liner ADRIATIC had had to sail (slightly late) with the engineers and other members of the crew stoking and pick up in Southampton Water a scratch collection of temporary firemen . . . eighty-nine of whom had never been to sea before.[1]

Hopkins's claim not to be officially involved with the Union at this time was disingenuous, though he lacked a clearly defined or official role. It is now that mention begins to be made of journeys at the turn of the year to speak at meetings of seamen in Cardiff and Newport, both important coal ports.

> The fact is that the 'unrest' among seamen at the refusal of the Shipowners' Federation to consent to the formation of a Conciliation Board for the settlement of disputes has not been allayed; and I cannot escape the responsibility to take counsel with the men as to 'what's best to be done'. All this extra work is teaching me that I am not as young as I was!

His writings begin to envisage some sort of popular uprising, coinciding with the foundation in September 1909 of the International Committee of Seamen's Unions (ICOSU), a response to the Shipping Federation's initiative in establishing the International Shipping Federation (ISF).[2] Membership of both organisations came from Belgium, Denmark, Germany, Holland, Sweden and the United Kingdom. With ICOSU behind it, the NSFU was able to demand with rather more confidence in July 1910 a national negotiating and wages board to consider, among other things:

---

1   A. Temple Patterson, *A History of Southampton 1700-1914*, vol iii, 126f. I have failed to find further details. Patterson seems to be using as his source a local newspaper. Nowhere is Hopkins referred to. Did this event cause Hopkins to start work in Southampton, and provide his link with ICOSU, or did Hopkins prompt this strike?
2   Mss 367/ISF/1/1 *Minutes* of the ISF gives date of first meeting as 24 May 1909 and the primary (article 12) purpose as dealing with strikes and lock-outs. See also Mss 367/TSF/1/4/1, General Purposes Committee, *Minutes*, 23 Aug 1909. Mss 367/TSF/1/1/1, *Minutes*, 24th April, 1908 refers to an International Federation to be formed following a conference, with a draft scheme approved on 23 October 1908. Mss 367/TSF/1/4/2, General Purposes Committee *Minutes*, 14 Feb 1908, refers to the conference.

14. The Religious Orders

- a uniform sliding scale of wages for all ports and with a minimum wage;
- a scale of manning;
- the right of a union representative to be present at signing on;
- the abolition of all Shipping Federation offices, with ships' officers only being empowered to engage crews;
- the abolition of all Federation medical tests.[1]

On 7 July 1910, the NSFU addressed a circular to British shipowners asking for a conciliation board. The ICOSU unions of Belgium, Denmark, Holland and Norway did the same in their respective countries. This was a well-trodden path which led to refusal. The principal excuses given were that the Union was neither representative of the profession nor a registered union.[2] ICOSU meetings seem to have been held in February (Copenhagen) and November (Antwerp) 1910, and in March 1911 (Antwerp). A further meeting took place at the Greenwich Priory on 1 May 1911 when Hopkins drew attention to the ISF's refusal to establish a conciliation board because the demand was not made by representative persons and there were no grievances requiring adjustment. He proposed a letter to the ISF asking if it would meet with the ICOSU. He
> stated that the International Strike Committee ought to be kept distinct from the permanent International Committee of Seafarers Unions. He hoped that an International Strike Committee would be formed

and this was agreed. He was invited to be the secretary.

The Messenger of January 1911 refers to the SFSSP starting a branch of its work in Southampton to relieve hardship among liner crews and others, strengthening the link between Hopkins and Southampton. The same *Messenger* reveals him visiting Cardiff, Newport, Shields, Middlesbrough, Manchester, Liverpool, Glasgow and Leith to speak and listen to seamen. Nor was Hopkins the only person addressing seamen at this time. At the beginning of February Havelock Wilson wrote to Hermann Jochade of the ITWF, 'During the past two weeks I have addressed over 150 meetings'.

Hopkins had accepted the position of international secretary on condition that he should have such paid assistance as might be necessary, with his own position an honorary one. Together with Havelock Wilson and general secretary Cathery, he was appointed to a subcommittee to act for ICOSU on this and other matters which might arise. He was to have full voting rights as an *ex officio* member of the International Strike Committee. It was further agreed that, while the press might be allowed to attend public meetings, no official statements would be made to the press on behalf of the International Strike Committee unless signed by Hopkins.

On Tuesday evening, 13th June, a large meeting at Southampton took place in Kingsland Square, with Councillor T. Lewis presiding. Wilson spoke first, saying that he had come to Southampton as the men had insisted on a

---

1 Mss 175/6/Bor/20. J. H. Borlase, *Struggle*, a typescript history of the NSFU, hereafter referred to as 'Borlase'.
2 Mss 367/TSF/1/1/1 *Minutes*, 18/11/1910, 19/5/1911, 29/6/1911 etc. for the Shipping Federation view.

strike.[1] Hopkins had the star role, announcing that the strike would begin the following day (14th June). According to the *Liverpool Echo*:

> At the big mass meeting of seamen in Southampton last night the men threw down the gauntlet . . . Father Hopkins made an impassioned speech. He drew on his experience as chaplain to missions to seamen in India and elsewhere, described his efforts to better the lot of sailormen, and gave the history of the movement to internationalise the cause of seafarers. He complained bitterly that although he represented the seamen of many nations as secretary of the International Strike Committee, the Shipping Federation had treated his representation with indifference. 'The time,' he continued, ' has come to draw the sword and use it to obtain for seamen the just conditions of life to which they are entitled.' He then read an official notice declaring the international strike.

Over the next few weeks Hopkins addressed groups of thousands of striking men. A mass meeting in Hull seems to have been a turning point. He moved on to negotiating groups in Manchester and then South Shields. Here he was met by some 500 men who carried him in a chair shoulder-high, escorted by the police, to Mill Dam, where the local official, Mr R. F. Bell, introduced him to a mass meeting and where 'he had a reception which he is not likely to forget'. 'Father Hopkins said he was very anxious to be among the chaps on Tyneside, but, as they all knew, he had been busy elsewhere'. He listed the victories won by the strike so far, hoping the same could be achieved on Tyneside. The *Shields Daily Gazette* noted that Hopkins was going to take charge of the strike committee. 'Father Hopkins stated . . . that his mission to Tyneside was not to widen the breach . . . but to heal it.' He continued to Newcastle and Middlesbrough, with midnight talks, and a fair amount of drama, where talks with the North East Ship-Owners reached an agreement, made final, according to ITWF records on the 28th July.[2]

The effect of the 1911 strike upon the NSFU was dramatic. For a union which had limped along with a membership of a thousand, many behind in their payment of union dues because of absence abroad, a massive increase in members was a novel situation.[3] Tupper, strike organiser in South Wales, claimed when Havelock Wilson had recruited him just before the 1911 strike the Union had £6. 13s in the bank.[4] General secretary Cathery, estimating new members since the start of the strike on 14 June 1911, suggests 35,000, increasing weekly income from £150 to over £1,000. He could also argue that the strike had increased sailors' wages, a state of affairs which some would dispute and which failed to persist into 1912.[5] *The Seaman* (January 1912) quoted Cathery at the NSFU Annual Meeting as saying 'I am closing the year without any financial worry and with a substantial balance at our bankers'.

However, the strike was principally aimed at getting the Federation to agree

1 *Justice*, 24 June 1911; *Liverpool Echo*, 14 June 1911; *Southampton Times*, 17 June 1911.
2 Mss 159/3/B/91.
3 Tom Mann, *Memoirs*, 1923, 225. Mann has nothing to say of Hopkins.
4 *Seamen's Torch*, 19.
5 *The Seaman*, January 1912, 205, 207.

to recognise the Union and grant a conciliation board. The Federation refused to grant recognition, a response often repeated since Havelock Wilson's earliest approach in 1891.[1] A united workforce was not to its liking. By the time of Hopkins's death in 1922, a quasi-conciliation board had been achieved.

After the strike

Hopkins became a trustee of the NSFU, an elected delegate, increasingly involved in Union affairs. Better Union records reveal his duties as trustee and delegate. He seems to have been, to use modern jargon, its number cruncher and trouble shooter, roles which were to become of considerable importance nationally, the First World War adding demands for increasing numbers of crews and complicating the issues surrounding recruitment; issues which became meat and drink to Hopkins.

Tribute to Hopkins's strike role was paid at the dinner which followed the NSFU's 1911 AGM. Present was Walter Runciman, according to *The Messenger*, seated on Havelock Wilson's right, making the first attendance by a shipowner, and one of whom Hopkins had been scathing in Calcutta days. Hopkins was on Havelock Wilson's left, with Mr Devitt, Chairman of the Shipping Federation on his left. Runciman reflected on recent events in his speech, saying:

> We have emerged from one of the most bitter fights that has taken place during my time. I never suspected six weeks ago that to-night I should be a guest at your festive board . . . I venture to say that there is not an owner at this table who is not pleased you have got [10s. a week more] . . . [M]any of the shipowners had been converted to the view that it was the proper thing to recognize the men's union. . . .

Havelock Wilson said:

> In every port those responsible for the conduct of the campaign did splendidly. There are, however, a few conspicuous figures whom I must mention, as they are to some extent outside our movement. First I shall refer to Tom Mann, who did for our cause magnificent work in Liverpool . . . our good friend Father Hopkins rendered yeoman service - first at Southampton, then at Hull - afterwards Manchester - finally at the North East coast. Without his help victory would have been uncertain. . . .[2]

If Hopkins had looked at any stage to see what was said of his efforts in the Church press, he would have looked in vain. Throughout the strike the *Church Times* kept silent. In his own paper in October 1911 he wrote:

> Twenty-two years ago I was urged - commanded in fact - by my Ecclesiastical Superiors not to identify myself with the Labour Movement and Trade Unionism; I obeyed for a time; but was soon constrained by 'a voice within' to readjust relationships so as to enable me to become free to do what conviction told me I ought to do in the matter. Although my persistence lost me the help of some friends and has plunged me from time to time in much 'hot water', I do not regret my persistence. I much appreciate that title 'Banner-bearer' [bestowed by the *Frankfurter Zeitung*].

---

1   Mss 367/TSF/1/4/1. *Minutes*, General Purposes Committee, 6 March 1891.
2   Mss 159/3/B/63, General Correspondence of ITF and NSFU 1907-11.

If I am a Banner-bearer today in the great Labour Movement of the people they know that on that banner is blazoned the Cross of my Master Christ, with the words written large beneath it '*in hoc vinces*'. That has been and always will be my justification.

After the strike, Hopkins disappeared from the wider press, appearing instead in NSFU records, and in its weekly, *The Seaman*. *The Seaman's* editorial address was given as Alton Abbey, its secretariat in the Abbey Gatehouse. At the AGM on 25 September 1911 Hopkins was appointed a trustee of the Union. He remained a trustee until his death in 1922. Trustees attended the Executive, and the Finance and General Purposes (F&GP), Committee meetings. Indeed, the latter could not meet without a trustee present, as one of the trustees' functions was approval of expenditure. Hopkins appears to have been a conscientious trustee. In the absence of Havelock Wilson usually he took the chair. The Union occupied him in other ways; producing various of its publications, necessary research, speaking at public meetings, attending AGMs, and generally being about Union business took much of his time.

In 1912 and 1913 he was occupied in campaigning for a National Wages Board, but including in that campaign improvements to the load line, seamen's accommodation, and working hours.[1] This involved letters to the press, visits to the Board of Trade, and more speeches to men. He wrote to Jochade in early 1912 suggesting that the International Committee of Seafarers' Unions, formed on 11 March 1911, might be reconvened to consider its dissolution or its continuance as the Marine Section of the ITWF.[2] Later in the year he wrote to Jochade, 'although not much sought after or consulted in normal times - I am nearly always at once called to the front & given responsible work to do when labour <u>trouble</u> is being experienced' (Hopkins's emphasis). In February 1912 he was made secretary of the Union's Manning Campaign.[3]

In 1913 a Union handbook, *Official Wages - Agreements*, was issued, embodying all the agreements made in 1911, 1912 and 1913. The handbook contained the kind of details associated with Hopkins's work and listed agreements made in ports around the globe.

> It must be understood that in those days we had won no Maritime Board with its national wages scale and agreement. There were dozens and dozens of different agreements. In some places like London there were even different agreements for different docks. The rates of pay for different ratings and different departments, on different classes of ships, varied everywhere; only overtime, at 9d per hour, appears as a figure almost universal . . . Some of these agreements are quoted as made, not with a port, but with individual shipowners. There are even some in which rates and conditions vary in different ships belonging to the same owner! Agreement had to be reached not only on the question of Monthly and Weekly Pay, Sabbath and Overtime Pay, but on Tides Work, Boating and Running Lines, and Shore Work. For some ports half a dozen technical movements to do with shifting

---

1 *The Seaman*, 27th Dec, 1912; 10th Jan, 7th Feb, 7th Mar, 21st Mar, 13th June, and 17th Oct, 1913.
2 Mss 159/3/B/91, 9th Feb, 1912.
3 Mss 175/1/2/1, NSFU, F&GP Committee *Minutes*, 17th Feb, 1912.

14. The Religious Orders

ships in harbour are itemised with rates of remuneration under Tides Work - and another half dozen to do with tying up, kedging, and letting go, etc., under Boating and Running Lines.[1]

Minutes of the F&GP Committee reveal more of Hopkins's tasks. Sorting out relations with the breakaway British Sailors' Union took him to Glasgow (to remove Emmanuel Shinwell), Southampton, and probably Liverpool. Disputes, for example between the crew and owners of the *Holmwood* (12th February 1913), came his way for resolution. It was he who was asked to obtain the services of a full-time agent in Fowey, the small china clay port in Cornwall. Irregularities in the NSFU Leith office required his attention. For all these activities, often with much travelling, he received his expenses. Occasionally, too, he was involved in the various property deals of the Union; more so during the war with the purchase of properties for the internment of alien seamen, though property was really another trustee's area of responsibility. While Havelock Wilson was in America Hopkins led the Union's position over a threatened strike in 1912.

At this time, Hopkins was working on his book, *Altering Plimsoll's Mark*, its publication financed largely through Union purchase. To fight the BoT's proposed changes to the load line, perhaps under pressure from owners, required evidence; the accumulation of evidence was Hopkins's strength. His campaign is revealed in his book. Its prefatory note, headed 'St Mawes Priory, October 1913', dates publication with some precision; the St Mawes Priory was a cottage purchased by the OSP in the hope that Hopkins could use it for respite as his health deteriorated. It had the advantage of being near members of his family. The book is not easy to find today; it details the history of the load line and the significance of the changes. Hopkins's introduction was pungent: 'while Capital remains avaricious, while self-interest is on the grasp for more, while officialism hates the trouble and the added responsibility of reform, the natural tendency will be ever backward'.

On the outbreak of the War in 1914, disputes fell into abeyance in the interest of national unity. The Greenwich Priory became a receiving centre, and The Abbey a camp, for alien seamen. As most of the brethren were called up, the 'staff' was severely limited. Guards were declined at The Abbey, its two hundred aliens cared for by three brethren. Two at the Greenwich Priory supervised another sixty. When the aliens' camp closed, remaining brethren who were eligible joined the army, of whom four died subsequently.[2] Closure of the camps followed the sinking of the *Lusitania*. Seamen generally were appalled by the submarine war which destroyed forever the idea of the brotherhood of the sea; the Union withdrew from staffing the aliens' camps in its care and those associated with Hopkins's community followed suit.

During 1917 Hopkins was contributing a regular column to *The Seaman* entitled, 'Extracts from the Reports of Admiralty Cases', a densely written series, consisting of court judgments relating to wages and other, especially manning, agreements. There is no indication that Hopkins had help with

---
1   E. Tupper, *Seamen's Torch*, 100-101. It does not mention Hopkins.
2   Mss 175/3/4/3, NSFU Correspondence with SFSSP.

these and every likelihood that he was trawling his many files of collected information. Agreements in wartime could easily become muddied, one of the reasons for establishing the National Maritime Board, and this series clearly indicated the rights of the seaman. His readers would be better equipped to defend themselves, as had been his intention when publishing similar material for his Guild members during his time in Calcutta. The series may also reflect Union pressure on management and government to come together to negotiate conditions.

The Union was not blind to the massive profits which wartime brought shipowners. Figures relating to these profits were another part of Hopkins's stock in trade. The Union built up its strike fund with an eye to the post war years. For its part, the Federation continued to demand that all seamen carry a Federation ticket. In mid 1916, when the Union was becoming increasingly aware of crewing problems, it extended a hand to the Federation, receiving no response.[1] Unrest among seamen was caused not only by owners' excessive profits but also by the threat of conscription, while the issue of wage differentials between British and American ships drew many British seamen to serve under the Stars and Stripes, exacerbating the difficulty in crewing British ships. The Munitions of War Act of July 1915 had allowed the government to impose arbitrated settlements upon unwilling employers. Hopkins later dated the first sign of movement towards a conciliation board to June 1917 when the Union and the Federation met informally, the Union suggesting district committees be set up to resolve overtime issues on weekly vessels (always a special category). As this would involve a Standing Joint Central Committee, it was passed back by representatives to the main body of each for formal consideration. Events were overtaken when Lloyd George's newly established Ministry of Shipping invited both parties to confer with government representatives on the supply of seamen, wages, and delays. In August 1917 industrial discontent led the Government to establish joint meetings between the Ministry of Shipping (a wartime creation), the Union and the Federation, from which evolved what became the National Maritime Board (NMB).[2] Speaking in 1921, Jim Cotter, a militant, and member of the BSU, said, 'the National Maritime Board was formed in 1917 during the War because the government and the original Maritime Board could not carry on themselves as far as the working of the seamen were concerned'.[3]

The Union supported the idea of a national wage for seafarers determined by a joint committee but proposed that it - the Union - should supply labour, to which the Federation objected. A solution was devised by the Ministry of Shipping through the independent Liverpool Shipowners. The process is described in detail elsewhere.[4] This was to be a body, effectively the

1 A. Ryan & V. Marsh, *The Seamen*, 73, 78.
2 John Chatham, *British Seafarers: from opposition to collaboration* . . . , 39ff gives considerable detail of the NMB.
3 Mss 175/3/17/5, iii and iv, NSFU Correspondence 1912-21.
4 A. Ryan & V. Marsh, *The Seamen*, 80ff. C. P. Hopkins, *National Service of*

14. The Religious Orders

NMB, drawn from both sides which would recruit and supply and which was formally announced on 23rd November, 1917.[1] The NMB had four main panels: deck officers, engineers, sailors and firemen, and cooks and stewards.[2] Hopkins's panel involvement was primarily with the sailors and firemen, minutes for which show that he usually fielded a substitute. A network of port offices was established. Hopkins and Cuthbert Laws (of the Federation) were appointed joint secretaries. By 1918 the Shipping Federation had accepted the need to work with the NSFU sufficiently to resist attempts by the Ministry of Reconstruction to form a single National Council rather than something distinct to deal with seamen and questions affecting dock labour and to argue that it should consist of an equal number of shipowners and seamen.[3] The structure was not a perfect one. In 1920 Hopkins wrote to a Mr Brett:

> The patience (& forbearance) of Shipowners & officers & officials with some of these men surprises me. So 'sick' am I, at the moment, with the majority of the seamen's representation on the N.M.B. that it would be a relief to resign my Joint Secretaryship. But I doubt if it would do any good. Possibly Borlase or Mr [Vey?] might be appointed in my place.[4]

Until his death, Hopkins's signature was appended with that of Laws to every official document circulated to the Merchant Navy, one such circular, on accommodation, being issued on 22 March 1922, the day of his death.[5] A conciliation board had finally been achieved with Hopkins a joint secretary. It had taken many years to reach this goal.

There were other issues during the war years. The Union had to decide how to react to the German submarine campaign. Injuries, wreck and death brought to its emergency fund many requests for aid. Hopkins was usually involved in its disbursement, at least to the extent of agreement; sometimes he was asked to investigate claims. Immediately a ship was sunk the pay of crew members ceased and this caused much hardship. Two general examples of welfare work will suffice in illustration. At the F&GP Committee of the 26th July, 1916, Hopkins reported on the Seamen's Orphan Homes (*sic*) at Newlands, Hull. At the same meeting he had referred to him for investigation 'dispensaries for seamen in (*sic*) special diseases', effectively sexually transmitted diseases. Concurrently he was busy with a pamphlet on the accommodation of crews. In the 1916 Honours List Havelock Wilson was awarded the CBE for his war recruitment work and Hopkins the OBE; when the final list of war honours was published in 1920, the Union was proud to announce that Hopkins, Cathery, Chambers (general treasurer), and Henson (of the Bristol Channel) had been appointed CBE.

In 1920 Hopkins published a comprehensive account of the role of the

British Seamen 1914-18, 41. Records in the National Archive give details of panel meetings but little information about Hopkins.
1 Mss 367/TSF/1/4/2, General Purposes Committee *Minutes*, 13th September, 1917.
2 Alston Kennerley, The Seamen's Union, the National Maritime Board and Firemen . . . , 15-28.
3 Mss 367/TSF/1/4/2, 5 December 1918. Mss 367/TSF/1/4/2, 4 December 1919.
4 Mss 367/TSF/3/4/5.
5 Mss 175/6/NMB/1. NMB *Circulars*.

Merchant Navy, *The National Service of British Seamen 1914-1918*, its sales helped by Union purchase. It is a well-documented guide to the prejudice and discrimination against the men then to be found in the Merchant Navy, and to the owners' wartime profits. It was followed by another project, a *Seafarer's Annual*, issued in 1921 with further volumes dependent on demand. This was a departure from his campaigning works and, priced at 6d, intended for the popular market. It was obtainable from the SFSSP. Its annual nature was emphasised by Hopkins's recording seamen-related events of the preceding year; his chronology dealing with the reduction of wages, the new engine-room union, and the new union for cooks and stewards. A chapter on organisation explained the Seafarers' Joint Council (of which Hopkins was the treasurer), and which union to join, according to rank and profession. Another explained the structure of the NMB with its various panels. All pay scales and leave entitlements were listed. Further chapters dealt, some heavily, with Union history, and others, usefully, with such issues as rates of exchange. The final chapter, on revolution, reflecting the concerns of the time, took an anti-Bolshevist line.

His friends had become accustomed to Hopkins's recurring ill-health. The Priory at Greenwich was supposed to provide him with better air than the woods of Alton Abbey, as was the cottage at St Mawes, near Falmouth. Sister Frances, last survivor of the sisters who had been early to join his work, remained at Greenwich, welcoming the few seamen who came, dealing with queries and orders to the SFSSP. At Alton, departures of brethren in protest at Hopkins's part in the 1911 strike, and losses among those called up to serve in the war, left but two brethren at The Abbey to care for the shellbacks (retired seamen) there.[1] In March 1922 Hopkins, at St Mawes, was taken seriously ill. On 24th March, five days after Sister Frances wrote to Cathery explaining that Hopkins would not be able to attend the next finance meeting because 'he is dangerously ill and the doctor holds out little hope of his recovery', he was dead. He died at the Priory Cottage. The primary cause of death was listed as a cerebral haemorrhage of fourteen days earlier, and the secondary, cardiac failure, by Dr John Llewellyn, the attending doctor. Hopkins's occupation appeared as 'Priest'.

His body was taken to Alton Abbey. The local newspaper, the *Hampshire Express*, of Saturday, the 8th April, carried a full report of the funeral, which took place 'on Thursday afternoon last week in the beautiful little cemetery at The Abbey'. Apart from members of OSP and a few relatives, there were representatives from the NMB, the NSFU, the Shipping Federation, the Hull Seamen's Union, the Marine Engineers' Association, the Seafarers' Joint Council, the Imperial Merchant Service Guild, the International Seafarers' Federation, the Thames District Maritime Board, the Gravesend Sea School, the Alton Union, the local council, and others yet, together with local residents and 'many typical British seamen, weather-worn and stern-visaged, who had come to pay their last tribute to a man who had done so

---

1   Mss 175/3/4/3, NSFU Correspondence with SFSSP. Few details survive beyond this brief reference.

much for their betterment'; an attendance unparalleled at the funeral of any other person in this book - or since.

Hopkins's coffin, covered with the Union flag and surrounded by a wealth of floral tributes, bore his cross as Superior General of the OSP and his insignia as a Commander of the Order of the British Empire. Years before, Hopkins printed in his community magazine an extra verse for the hymn, 'Eternal Father', possibly his own work, which seems to have been used for the funerals of seafarers in Calcutta. If it was among the verses when the hymn was sung at his burial, it made an apt conclusion:

> And for our brethren called away
> by death's swift summons, Lord, we pray;
> O grant them rest and peace and light,
> their sin-stained souls make pure and white;
> so at Thy Coming they may be
> raised up triumphant from the sea.

Hopkins remains a unique figure in the maritime apostolate. His functions within the Union: the statistics, the trouble-shooting, the speeches, the wise counsel, all the duties of a trustee, the essential back room work, leave a feeling after examining all the available evidence that Hopkins, rather than being a shadow cast by Havelock Wilson, was more the Grey Eminence. His influence over Havelock Wilson was at the least substantial. His legacy is less obvious; the OSP continued its work for retired seamen for some years before turning itself into a Benedictine community.

15. Work among fishermen

The work pattern of nineteenth and early twentieth century fishermen was very different from that of other groups at sea, with whom they had little in common, whether inshore or deep-sea, beyond being at sea. Fishermen tended to come from fairly closed communities. Often their vessels were locally owned. The perishable nature of their harvest required a regular return to port and home or to a mother ship. Two major societies served their particular needs. One, that of the Augustinians of the Assumption, working through the *Œuvres de Mer*, is left to chapter eighteen. This chapter concentrates on the (Royal National) Mission to Deep Sea Fishermen before briefly noticing the Salvation Navy.

A number of early Bible and tract societies, mainly in ports where fishing was the local activity, set out to serve the relatively local fisherman. The Hull Marine Bible Society of 1817, influenced by the ministry of G.C. Smith, becoming in 1821 the Port of Hull Society (PHS) on the opening of its floating chapel, extended along the Yorkshire coast, by 1832 reaching Grimsby, to create what was hoped would become a chain of missions ministering principally to fishers. Various auxiliaries merged with the PHS, so that by 1845 its missionary arms stretched from the Humber to the Tees. Friend chronicles a number of similar societies, including the Scottish Coast Missions (1850) and the Portsmouth and Gosport Seamen's Mission (1869), both supported by the British and Foreign Sailors' Society.[1] These were numerically successful; in 1861, for example, the Scottish Coast Missions employed ten missionaries, serving twenty-nine stations between Cockenzie and Arbroath. Its missionaries visited sailors as well as fishermen and their families. Overlap between fishers and mariners was common in traditional fishing ports, as in Hull, where the work of the PHS, followed in 1828 by an Anglican foundation, the Episcopal Mariners' Church Society, served both communities.

Work among deep-sea fishermen from the earliest days was recognised as being more effective when done afloat. A Vicar of Yarmouth, who began a mission among fishermen in 1848 (it passed to the MtS in 1862) had plans for a full-time chaplain with the fleet. There are other scattered examples. The Brighton Church Congress of 1874 heard an appeal for a boat to work among the fishing fleets, and the Swansea Congress of 1879 was reminded by Canon

1 Stephen Friend, *The Rise and Development of Christian Missions amongst British Fishing Communities during the Nineteenth Century*. Dr Friend has made E. J. Mather and the MDSF his special subject. I have drawn heavily on his work. See also, Stephen Friend, Social and Spiritual Work amongst Fishing Communities, 138-145. Stephen Friend, The North Sea Liquor Trade, c.1850-1893, 43-71.

Scarth that a boat-owning incumbent of his acquaintance had for twenty years been using it to visit fishermen at the mouth of the Thames. SAWCM had further been able to offer vessels for use in the North Sea and off Brixham.

The Mission to Deep Sea Fishermen

The Mission to Deep Sea Fishermen (MDSF) came about through the efforts of Ebenezer Joseph Mather (Fig. 9). His book, *Nor'ard of the Dogger* (1888), reveals him as familiar with the *Book of Common Prayer*, clearly an Evangelical, but as will appear, only from 1883 a member of the Church of England. This was no obstacle to his being appointed Secretary of the Thames Church Mission for a probationary period of three months from 9th February, 1880. He was to receive £105 per annum, together with 10% of any commissions or subscriptions which he might be instrumental in obtaining for the TCM, and allowed 'to have full liberty to continue his private business', the nature of which was not specified. The provisional nature of his appointment may have been the result of the TCM Committee's experiences of his immediate predecessors, none of whom stayed for long. He seems to have given satisfaction for, within a month, it was agreed to increase his pay to £155 per annum.[1] Two months later he was confirmed in his post.[2] His initiation period was not an easy time. An early problem came before the TCM Committee in July 1880, when The Rev. Anton Tien was dismissed on discovery that, before his appointment by the TCM, he had professed 'Mahomedanism' at the Sublime Porte, a fact supported by papers from the Foreign Office, the Archbishop of Canterbury, and the Ambassador at the time in Constantinople.[3] Then, Mather had to dismiss a long-serving collector for embezzling funds, and then a missionary, absent without permission, who had also misappropriated money. Though staff problems continued throughout the 1880s, Mather appeared to give the TCM a sense of direction, of which the interest of the owner of the 'Short Blue' fleet, Mr Hewett, a new work among the navvies extending Tilbury Docks, and the opening of a 'Sailors' Rest and Reading Room' at Poplar were promising signs. The Tilbury development prompted the incumbent of Chadwell St Mary to write to the Archbishop of Canterbury in March 1883 that he was not prepared to work with the TCM; he was already doing Church work among the Tilbury navvies, with support from SAWCM, while Mather was 'an avowed Plymouth Brother and that their tenets largely if not exclusively prevail in the Thames Church Mission Society'.[4] It is Friend's opinion that this prompted Mather and his wife to join the Church of England in 1883.

In the autumn of 1881, Mather stumbled upon what was to be his life's work. He reported to the General Committee of the TCM 'at Messrs Hewett and Co's earnest request' that he had visited Hewett's fleet of fishing smacks

---
1   TCM Minutes 10.3.1880.
2   TCM Minutes 21.5.1880.
3   TCM Minutes 1.7.1880.
4   A copy of the letter is included in Friend's thesis as Appendix 11.

Ebenezer Mather. Courtesy of the RNMDSF.

at the Dogger Bank.[1] Hewetts of Billingsgate and Barking ran the 'Short Blue' fleet which dominated the industry. The owner, Samuel Hewett, had offered to convey and feed a missionary, at his company's expense, to work among his fleet in the summer months.[2] The company was already a subscriber to the work of the TCM, adding to its generosity permission for TCM vessels to coal at Hewett's Rainham depot at a preferential rate. Mather seized the offer and made good use of his summer trip, according to a colourful account in his book, assessing the possibilities, and distributing a thousand scripture portions, as many illustrated tracts, and half as many hymn sheets among the twelve hundred smacksmen working in the fleet. The well-established fleeting system was served regularly by a steam ship to ferry the catches, well iced, back to Billingsgate, for dispersion round the country by the rapidly expanding railway system, allowing the smacks to remain at sea for longer periods. Mather reported that, 'The men as a whole are wild and godless' although it is clear from his book that he found Christians among them. The TCM Committee postponed making a decision about adopting this extension to its work to allow a time for mature consideration.

Mather's vision of how the men in the North Sea might be served had still to

[1] TCM Minutes 18.11.1881.
[2] Stephen Friend, The North Sea Liquor Trade, c.1850-1893, 45.

15. Work among fishermen

be worked out. Although Hewett's operated from the Thames, Mather having started his visit to the fleet by taking a train from Fenchurch Street Station to Rainham and walking across the marshes to join an iron steamer built specially for the fish-carrying trade, to ask a Thames-based society to extend its work into the North Sea was a serious step calling for careful thought; something emphasised when Samuel Hewitt decided to move his company base to Gorleston in Norfolk. The Committee continued to pray about the matter, temporizing by agreeing to allow any staff member an extra fortnight's holiday each year to be spent at sea among the fishing fleets.[1] Mather reported in May that a Scripture Reader had been out to the Dogger Fleet, supplied with woollen cuffs, comforters, tracts, and bibles for distribution and carrying a modest medicine chest.[2] By June a desire for a 'specially equipped Mission Smack' became clear and further prayer was asked to this end.[3]

On June 23rd, the General Committee called a Special Meeting to hear from Mather that an anonymous friend (probably Samuel Hewitt) had placed the sum of £1,000 in his hand towards a Mission Smack, to be registered in the name of E. J. Mather as managing owner. The Committee felt 'the offer was so distinctly an interposition of the Divine hand in answer to prayer, that it would be wrong not to accept it'; a thousand pounds on the table making it difficult to do otherwise. The secretary was reminded, or perhaps he reminded the Committee, of the Minute of 9th February, 1880, allowing him to transact any private business 'provided it was not detrimental to the Society'.[4] By the end of July Mather was able to inform the Committee that a 56-ton smack, the *Ensign*, a Hewett vessel, had been purchased, fitted, and victualled for £1,000. A Captain had been appointed who would represent the TCM as its Honorary Agent, as also the Shipwrecked Mariners' Society, the BFBS, and CETS, and to run the mission when at sea. Of the vessel's fittings, '[t]he large lending library, the Medicine Chest and harmonium are specially appreciated'.[5] The speed of events suggests that Mather was leading, rather than following, the Committee. At the end of the year Hewett's increased its subscription, and several of its directors became individual annual subscribers, in recognition of what was being achieved among its crews.[6] In a further gesture, it gave the TCM free access to its stores, workshops and dry-dock for use of the *Ensign*.

Mather's book claims that what lay behind Hewett's satisfaction was its crews' access to first aid, their increased sobriety, and the owners' consequent avoidance of loss of equipment. The sobriety and loss of equipment require explanation. The North Sea fishing fleets employed some 12,000 or 15,000 men and boys, kept at sea without entertainment, and few comforts. Into their tough life a little relief was brought by the copers, which according to Friend, were especially active between 1878 and 1893. These were trading boats operating

---

1 TCM Minutes 20.1.1882.
2 TCM Minutes 19.5.1882.
3 TCM Minutes 16.6.1882.
4 TCM Minutes 23.61882.
5 TCM Minutes 28.7.1882.
6 TCM Minutes 15.12.1882.

out of Dutch and German ports to bring to the fleets cheap tobacco, made possible by the tax differential, and, in increasing quantities, and for which tobacco was the gateway, cheap alcohol. Copers were fitted out attractively and stocked with a variety of goods, including toiletries, patent medicine, dice, cards, silks and satins, musical boxes, and pornography, as well as tobacco and alcohol in various forms. The appalling conditions which often prevailed in the North Sea made cheap alcohol particularly welcome. Mather's book, published in 1888, described at length the effects of the alcohol, including increased accidents, raised mortality rates, and the loss of income to wives and families when wages were diverted to the copers. The company was well aware that much equipment and some fish found its way to the copers, bartered for goods when cash had been exhausted. Mather's descriptions would have registered with, as Friend says, 'Victorian moral concerns over drink, gambling and sex, all three of which were associated with the copers'.

A further indication of the way things were going was to be found in the proposal of The Rev. Cecil M. Bevan and Mr George Lionel Dashwood 'in concert with other gentlemen' to purchase 'at least two more smacks', to be registered in Mather's name, the Committee accepting the proposal unanimously.[1] Admiral Fishbourne (his real name), who seems to have been the chairman of the railway company involved in building Tilbury Docks, gave notice that he would move at the next General Meeting that a special fund be formed to meet the expenses of a ministry in the North Sea. Although implicit in this notice is a recognition that this new work was straying from TCM's remit, the General Meeting established a 'Fishermen's Fund' with Bevan and Dashwood elected to Committee membership.[2]

By 1884 the pressure on the TCM was beginning to tell. Its Fishermen's Fund was transferred to a separate account. Mather was beginning to show signs of strain, a recurring illness plaguing his next five years. Increasingly the fishing side required his attention at the expense of other duties. TCM finances were not good, the bank in May 1884 reporting an overdraft of £456. In the succeeding months the situation failed to improve while Mather's health worsened, making it obvious, by the end of 1884, that the fishery work required more attention than his TCM duties allowed. His solution was to remain the TCM Secretary at least in name, but withdrawing his loan of the vessels registered in his name to start a Fishermen's Mission which would occupy part of the TCM offices. Any expense caused to the TCM could be set against its Fishermen's Fund, an arrangement Mather estimated would save the TCM a sum of £353 a year.[3] With certain financial provisos his proposals were accepted for a six-month trial period, with TCM's shorthand clerk deputed to keep fishery books and accounts separate from those of the TCM.[4]

---

1 Special Committee Meeting, TCM Minutes 21.2 1883.
2 Details of these mission vessels and those which succeeded them can be found in L. W. Hawkins, The Mission Boats, 34ff. See also Answers 20 (1951), *MM*, 38(1), February 1952, 72f.
3 TCM Minute 21.11.1884.
4 Special Committee Meeting, TCM Minute 28.11.1884.

15. Work among fishermen

It was moved that Mather's resignation be accepted, whilst he continued as Honorary Secretary, and he was elected to membership of the General and Finance Committees. Although the latter rejected his membership, the rest was carried *nem con*.[1] He did join the Finance Committee, only to resign in June 1886, parting amicably with a donation, allowing his departure to be seen as an easing out to allow him more time with the fisheries' mission.[2]

The North Sea work appealed to the public imagination, and to the owners of the fleet, but clearly required more vessels. Mather arranged the loan of three vessels, which remained in the ownership of Dashwood, Bevan, James Morton Bell and William Frederick Alphonse Archibald, to add to the two already purchased. The idea was that the mission ships would be self-financing (by sales and some fishing) as they worked among the fleets, with Mather sharing in the disbursement of the profits. The great enthusiasm engendered in 1883 by the International Fisheries Exhibition in London can only have helped the cause.

Unfortunately, an unforeseen downturn in the industry began around 1883; more boats meant over-fishing and decrease of stocks, leading in turn to the suspension of several fleets, perhaps reflected in the availability of vessels for Mather to receive on loan. Mather can now be seen to have taken an enormous risk. His choice had been between selling his vessels for what he could get in a recession and risk having to pay his creditors from his own pocket or establishing a new organisation, the MDSF, with funds raised from the public; and his decision had had to be taken when there were other urgent calls upon his time. The publicity attracted by using the mission vessels to fight the business of the copers by selling tobacco, in an attempt to close the gateway to the purchase of liquor, helped. Mather had found a short cut to avoid tobacco duty, allowing cheap sales until in 1887 permission was granted for the mission ships to sell tobacco out of bond.[3] He was greatly assisted by the support of the Wills tobacco family. The MDSF publicised this work in a monthly magazine, *Toilers of the Deep*, which was launched in January 1886. The final triumph over the copers came in November 1887 with the signing of a Convention at The Hague banning the sale or barter of spirits in the North Sea.

MDSF Minutes start from 18th June, 1886, when Mather is recorded as Founder and Director; others present were R. M. Ballantine Esq., James Curtis Esq. (Hon. Solicitor), G.A. Hutchinson Esq., T. B. Miller Esq., Dr A. T. Schofield and D. W. Wales Esq. By November the Committee was making decisions on staff salaries, committee structure,[4] and religious character: 'The Committee considered that the Institution was distinctly undenominational in its character, and that this fact was at present sufficiently indicated in the various publications

---

1   TCM Minute 20.11.1885, 1.12.1886.
2   TCM Minute 18.2.1886, 18.6.1886.
3   The copers were successfully driven from the North Sea. Stephen Friend, The North Sea Liquor Trade, c.1850-1893, 43-71, gives comprehensive details.
4   MDSF Minutes 5.11.1886.

of the Mission'.[1] The RTS and BFBS provided literature at half price. Initially it distributed Miss Weston's 'Blue Backs' (tracts) before switching to the RTS tract *Friendly Greetings*.[2] In June 1886 the MDSF Council had a Deed of Covenant drawn up specifying that all ships, stores and belongings now lay with the committee as a whole rather than with Mather alone. It agreed that his salary should be £800 a year, rising to £1,000 when funds permitted.

The appointment of a Finance Committee in February 1887, and the growth of the MDSF, made it necessary to clarify the relationship between the MDSF and the TCM.

> The Director reminded the Committee that the Mission to Deep Sea Fishermen resulted from a visit which he paid to the Short Blue Fleet in August 1881. After that he had resolved, God helping him, to do something towards meeting . . . the needs . . . He mentioned the matter to the Committee of the Thames Church Mission (of which Society he was at the time Secretary) but they were decidedly unwilling to become responsible for any mission work beyond the limits of the River Thames. . . .

This was not entirely fair to the TCM. In his version, Mather recounted the events leading to the purchase of the *Ensign*. This was for 'spiritual and philanthropic purposes and in the summer of 1883 a special Fishermen's Fund was instituted in connection with that Society'. Two other vessels had been added in the name of Mr Dashwood and as they were failing to pay their way after twelve months, the TCM and MDSF parted company on the 23rd November, 1884. The MDSF dated its first Committee Meeting to the 24th November, 1884.[3] Having reviewed the past, this meeting turned to the future, establishing a sub committee to examine medical matters, soon to become an important part of its mission. The members were Dr Gilbart Smith, Dr A.T. Schofield, Frederick (later Sir Frederick) Treves, and Mather himself.

A cloud appearing at this time was generated by the relationship between Mather and Dashwood, the latter making many 'erroneous statements' about the MDSF and Mather.[4] It was not resolved until 1888. Refutations show Dashwood claiming to be the original founder, and the entire monetary founder in three of the first four vessels; had sold the smack *Edward Auriel* to the Mission as a memorial ship,[5] leaving a sum of money in the hands of the Society; that the Society was now little more than a tobacconist's business (a reference to the battle with the copers); and accusing that the affairs of the Society were 'scandalously and extravagantly mismanaged, and the accounts ill-kept'. The MDSF responded that in the matter of foundation, Mather had been the founder, others apart from Dashwood had donated money for the vessels, the *Edward Auriel* had been accepted without obligations, any money of Dashwood's had been repaid, and the Society continued in its first

---

1   MDSF Minutes 12.11.1886. Friend suggests this may have distanced it further from the 'Church' TCM.
2   MDSF Minutes 3.12.1886.
3   MDSF Minutes 4.2.1887.
4   MDSF Minutes 1.4.1887, 4.11.87, 2.3.1888.
5   Friend says that it was added to the fleet in January 1884, provided by Dashwood in memory of an un-named clergyman.

15. Work among fishermen

principles. A small quibble about donations directed to the TCM which had been intended for the MDSF was soon attended.[1]

Dashwood refused to let the business of the *Edward Auriel* rest, alienating Committee members to the point where his resignation was requested, and continuing to air his grievances in public, particularly in *The Record*, a protestant paper. Still not satisfied, he wrote anonymously in December 1888 to Sir Henry Ponsonby, equerry to Queen Victoria, accusing the MDSF of misleading the public. On his handwriting being recognised, prosecution was only avoided by his admission of wrongdoing. At this point, January 1889, just before Dashwood's apology was read, Mather suddenly announced his intention of serving in an honorary capacity; an offer, after legal advice, declined by the Committee. More unpleasantness was to follow. According to Friend, Mather now had to face charges brought by Committee members; charges which included unauthorised expenditure, failure to account for expenditure, deception (e.g. travelling third class but charging first class expenses), forgery, and untruthfulness when challenged. Mather's offer of to resign was overtaken by a Committee decision, published in the November 1889 *Toilers of the Deep*, of 15th October, to sever Mather's connection with the MDSF.

> Complaints of a serious nature having been made with regard to Mr Mather's conduct in certain matters connected with the Mission, the Council felt bound to call upon him ... for explanations. These explanations being unsatisfactory ... certain specific charges ... should be referred to an independent Arbitrator. This Mr Mather refused.

This was a sad end for the man who had been instrumental in founding the MDSF. His chief failing seems to have been one which remained unsaid, that he was effectively a one-man band.

In Mather's time the MDSF had brought a number of significant benefits to the men the mission was founded to serve. His successful battle against the copers, and the publicity it brought, had served it well, but the MDSF is probably better remembered for its pioneering work in the matter of fishermen's health. In 1886 a Committee member, Dr Schofield, had begun training mission skippers in first aid. Schofield attracted the interest of the surgeon, Frederick Treves, who accepted an invitation to visit the North Sea fishermen, before recommending that the MDSF develop its medical work. By 1887 plans were being aired for a hospital ship to accompany the fleet. Mather happily rebutted the suggestion this would be at the expense of the spiritual purpose of the MDSF. The medical committee was not idle. It had been thought when the fishing smacks were acquired that trawling to pay for their running of the mission would be detrimental either to the trawling or the missionary work. The MDSF's trawling activity certainly hampered its tobacco sales, allowing copers to maintain their ascendancy. Treves advocated dropping the trawling and devoting the space gained to hospital accommodation. It was his plan that each mission smack, accompanied by a resident medical officer, be staffed by his medical students at the London

---

1   MDSF Minutes 6.5.1887.

Hospital, each serving for two or three months. And so it came to be. The medical side of the MDSF's work became very important. One of Treves's students, Wilfred Grenfell, became a household name after being sent to the coast of Labrador to explore opportunities to serve fishermen, where he extended his brief to the needs of those who lived ashore.[1]

Imitation is a sure indication that a work is useful. The work of the French *Œuvres de Mer* (chapter eighteen) followed. A Dutch hospital ship was launched, apparently suggested in 1897 by a Lieutenant Sluyterman, captain of the Dutch cruiser *Dolfijn*, who had seen MDSF vessels at work when about his fishery protection duties; his suggestion being put to Domine Van der Valk of the Reformed Church, a committee was formed. The Domine had worked at Lerwick, perhaps there meeting The Rev. J. Chambers, an Episcopalian clergyman, who came to Amsterdam to advise on the setting up of a society to manage a hospital and church ship, to be named *De Hoop*.[2] The 'Dutch Committee for the Benefit of Fishermen of Every Nationality' was supported by a nation-wide committee of ladies. The first *De Hoop*, a wooden sailing vessel, originally a pilot schooner, sailed for the first time from Vlaardingen on 17th June 1898, following an interdenominational service. A second vessel, initially under sail but later converted, lasted from 1912 until 1954, when it was succeeded by another *De Hoop*. The Dutch society supporting it enjoyed royal patronage, as the MDSF was to do.

Chapter eighteen on the *Œuvres de Mer* and its work among French fishermen will show that the French withdrew from an active apostolate among fishermen after the Second World War, when the fleeting system had virtually disappeared, communications improved, and needs changed. The (by now Royal National) MDSF responded similarly to the same changes in the fleeting system, when radio communication, air-sea rescue and similar developments rendered much of its work obsolete. Its last vessel, *Sir Edward P. Willis II*, was withdrawn from service at the end of 1949, ending a long process of replacing the work afloat with institutes for fishermen and their families ashore which had started around 1900, a boom time for the Society, and four years after it had been granted the Royal prefix. Although it is easy to see the need for such facilities for crews in foreign ports, a question mark has long hung over their purpose in home ports, where crews are able to enjoy the benefits of hearth, home and local church.

The Salvation Navy

A ministry to fishermen which has received little attention is that of the Salvation Navy.[3] Its parent body, the Salvation Army, founded in 1865 by William Booth, and organised on military lines, with a General at its head, began to respond to conversions among fishermen which seem to have

---

1   Many Grenfell books were published in the twentieth century. His autobiography, *A Labrador Doctor*, was reprinted several times. Other examples: Fullerton L. Waldo, *With Grenfell on the Labrador*; Basil Mathews, *Wilfred Grenfell, the Master Mariner*.
2   *Anglican Sphere*, St Mary's Church, Rotterdam, May 1973. A picture of the ship appeared in *Toilers of the Deep*, XLIX, 209.
3   Robert Miller, The Salvation Navy, 91-94.

15. Work among fishermen

followed the opening of an Army *corps* in Grimsby in January 1880. Some of these fishers, following the well-established custom of flying a flag to indicate a service on board, advertised their meetings at sea by hoisting large flags bearing the word SALVATION. The name 'Salvation Navy 'had certainly been coined by 1885, for the Army's 1886 *Orders and Regulations for Officers* included a page regulating the Salvation Navy.[1] The name went out of use after the 1914-18 war, to be revived briefly in the 1950s as a local ministry to canal folk.

In May 1885, Booth's son Bramwell wrote to his father that the Cardiff coal owner, John Cory, wished to give a vessel in which Mrs Booth might cruise for her health. This vessel, the *Iole*, appears to have been Cory's own pleasure yacht.[2] It was a three-masted, iron-framed, wooden steam vessel with a hold deep enough to accommodate three hundred people as a congregation, and with a good piano already in place. It is not clear if Mrs Booth used the yacht for pleasure. It was certainly taken in a programme of evangelization and encouragement in the summer of 1885 to Brixham, Mevagissey, Mousehole, Plymouth (two weeks), Exeter, Topsham and Exmouth.[3] In 1886 the *Iole* sank after running on a sandbank in the Humber, and was replaced by the yacht *Vestal*.[4] The *Vestal* was taken to Sweden in the spring of 1890 where its captain seems to have worked among dockers in Goteborg.[5] It was referred to as a 'Salvation gunboat'.[6]

The Grimsby fishermen were not the only seafarers who desired to meet for worship and witness. In 1885 Salvation Army sailors from three ships visiting Buenos Aires met for worship. In the same year a Brigade was recorded in New South Wales.[7] An article, 'Our Sea Soldiers. Our Navy Brigades at Work', noted that the Salvation Navy consisted of

> fishermen, seamen, and naval servicemen . . . they rarely congregate in greater numbers than three or four, and are scattered over the deep amongst numbers of ungodly mates . . . .

It explained that Salvationist meetings at sea took place beneath the Salvationist flag, claiming that these meetings were well known among coastal men. It added that some thirty or forty fishing boats 'out of Lowestoft alone' flew the Salvationist colours.[8] In 1886 a Salvation Naval Brigade was formed at East Hartlepool.[9] Its uniform included a cap band with silver lettering on a navy blue ribbon, distinguishing it from the regular Army uniform. 'Steps were at this time taken to enrol all sea-going Salvationists

---

1   *op cit*, 569.
2   *All the World*, January 1886; *War Cry*, 17 June 1885; *Year Book*, 1977, 7ff. All Salvation Army publications.
3   Robert Sandall, *History of the Salvation Army*, vol II, 99 (hereafter Sandall); *War Cry*, 6 March, 19 June 1886.
4   Sandall, vol II, 99; *War Cry*, 12 March 1887.
5   Sandall, vol III, 73.
6   *War Cry*, 5 January 1890.
7   *War Cry*, 16 May 1885.
8   *War Cry*, 9 April 1887.
9   *War Cry*, 30 October 1886.

in naval brigades'.[1] Brigades of 'sea-going soldiers', which were linked to *Corps*, would, according to *Regulations*, consist of two or more sailors.

The visit of the *Iole* to naval ports, such as Plymouth, suggests that it was attempting to recruit naval men, following a route taken by Agnes Weston and her Royal Sailors' Rests. The Army's naval work, eventually to become part of its Red Shield Services, which ministered to service personnel in the Army's name (officially so from 1914 when the Army was recognised as a religion), was called the Naval and Military League in 1894, and operated under Salvation Navy regulations.[2] Its rules required of members total abstinence, purity, non-gambling, daily Bible reading, and a commitment to encourage comrades to come to Christ. The League opened rooms for seamen in Gibraltar (September 1895), Chatham (November 1895) and Malta (July 1896). By 1899 Devonport, Portsmouth, Yokohama, Hong Kong and Barbados had been added, by which time fishers, indeed merchantmen as a whole, had ceased to be the Salvation Navy's primary focus, though it continued to include other sea-based ministries. By 1900 it listed in its official statistics four ships, none large, but widely scattered. One, the *Salvationist*, almost certainly a sailing vessel, was reported in 1895 to be working off the Labrador coast among fishers, though it seems to have escaped mention by Wilfred Grenfell and others working in the area.[3] Another, the *William Booth*, a steam yacht was reported to be evangelizing in the Great Lakes.[4] A third was the *Vestal*, operating in Sweden. By 1900, the Salvation Navy was running a lifeboat, the *Catherine Booth*, off the Swedish coast (Fig. 10). The *Regulations* governing the Salvation Navy mention the hire or purchase of further vessels, implying that the Army intended to extend its Navy. Whatever its intentions, they were overtaken, perhaps like the maritime ministry of others working among fishers, by the need to adapt to changes in fleeting systems and the consequences of the 1914 – 18 war. It is a curiosity, but a curiosity which met a contemporary need.

Today's ministry to fishermen is little different from that to seafarers generally. Indeed, in the Catholic Church both groups are cared for by the same body; nor does the Church of England make a distinction, The Mission to Seafarers responding to the needs of both, though its chaplains are generally found in fishing ports only where there is an overlap with general port facilities. Although the RNMDSF enjoys the patronage of senior figures across the denominations, and an emotional appeal for the many supporters who know little of today's fishing industry, it is likely that the RNMDSF will share the fate of the Salvation Navy and the *Œuvres de Mer*.

---

1 Sandall, vol II, 101.
2 Sandall, vol III, 288ff.
3 *All the World*, 318ff.
4 *The Officer*, July 1895, 196.

15. Work among fishermen

The *Catherine Booth*, Salvation Navy vessel c. 1900

The Nineteenth Century Catholic Sea Apostolate

16. Fr Goldie SJ and the CTS[1]

Catholic Concern for the Seafarer

The naval awakening of the early nineteenth century had significance for the development of Catholic work among seamen. There is some evidence that a similar awakening was to be found in the French navy which has been overlooked in recent times but finds a hint in the final chapter of Cabantous's book, *Le Ciel dans la Mer*, and would account for the number of naval officers who would serve on the committee of, or be associated with, the *Œuvres de Mer* and its concern for Newfoundland fishermen towards the end of the century. The Catholic Truth Society (CTS), equally late in the century, attempting to establish Catholic work among British seafarers, published short lives of two French naval officers who were part of the Catholic awakening, written by a member of the CTS Seamen's Sub Committee, Lady Amabel Kerr, wife of a British (Catholic) admiral.

Auguste Marceau, born in 1806 in Paris, joined the French navy in 1826, serving on the corvette *Bayonnaise*, and in 1836 promoted lieutenant commanding the steam vessel *Minos*. Despite his reputation as something of, to use a nautical term, a 'hell-raiser', he was converted to Catholicism and began to witness publicly in the navy. The Marist Fathers inviting him to run a mission ship serving Central Oceania, in August 1845 he took command of the *Arche D'Alliance* ('Ark of the Covenant') with its flag bearing a Cross, and a figurehead of Our Lady of Compassion. There was nothing unusual about missionary activity in the area; Protestants were active through the London Missionary Society.[2] The significance lay in his being a naval officer. He spent the next four years with the Marists, with regular Masses on board, and daily prayers, before returning to France and a Marist vocation, in the event prevented by terminal illness. Lady Amabel wrote in 1902:

> Men like Clerc, Joubert, de Plas and Bernaert, with whom their faith was the first object, came after [Marceau], and following in his footsteps infused a new and Catholic spirit in the Navy, which, it is to be hoped, endures to this day.

Lady Amabel wrote also about the Clerc mentioned in this passage, a slightly later figure, born in 1819 to a Catholic mother and an unbelieving father. He joined the French navy at the age of twenty-two and spent four years in the Pacific where he met missionary priests in the Gambier Islands. The gift of a catechism by two missionaries sailing for Gaboon in his ship *Caiman* changed his life. He made his confession at St Mary's Church, Gaboon, in December

---

1 Detailed sourcing for the Catholic chapters can be found in R. W. H. Miller, *Ship of Peter* 1995.
2 Hugh Laracy, Marists as Mariners: . . . , 59ff.

16. Fr Goldie SJ and the CTS

1846, remaining in the Navy, but now joining the Society of St Vincent de Paul (SVP), and starting classes for sailors. His request to join the Jesuits in 1850 was refused. Instead he sailed on the *Cassini* to check French missions, carrying a number of clergy, holding daily prayers and classes for boys, and enjoying the privilege of chapel and Blessed Sacrament. After four more years a second attempt to join the Jesuits succeeded in 1855; he was subsequently ordained priest, taken hostage in April 1871 under the *Commune*, imprisoned, and killed on 26 May 1871, as Paris was being relieved.

The details of these two officers not only illustrate how the CTS went about its campaign to reach the British Navy. They indicate a growing importance of Catholicism in the French navy, which when added to a brief record at this time of French Catholic concern for the Icelandic fishing fleets (where in 1860 the *Abbés* Bernard and Beaudoin ministered to fishermen from Normandy and Brittany), and to the earlier ministrations to Newfoundland fishermen already touched upon in chapter six, show that, in spite of the troubled nature of French politics, there were attempts in the French Catholic Church to meet the needs of its sailors. Post-Revolutionary France might seem infertile ground; equally so the Catholic situation in Victorian England. However, the Church is most active when it is in a missionary situation. When the missionary situation is combined, (as in France) with the blood of martyrs, much follows.

Because it is devoted to a particular industry the nineteenth-century approach to seafarers of the BFSS and the MtS may be described as 'new style' missionary work. The wave of new style Catholic activity among seamen between 1890 and 1920 is to an extent a mirror image of the Protestant work which preceded it; each starting with a literature campaign and naval correspondence, followed by increasing concern for the general welfare of mariners. The time span between naval correspondence and dedicated Catholic Sailors' Clubs primarily for the Merchant Navy parallels the thirty or so years between similar stages in the earlier development of Protestant work.

It is not clear if the primacy for this new Catholic concern lay with the British or the French, for there is evidence to indicate an early start to French work. Anson (and everyone so far has followed him) is quite clear that a letter from The Rev. Lord Archibald Douglas in the *Messenger of the Sacred Heart* (*MSH*) of January 1890, set in motion the revival of the Catholic sea apostolate.[1] The role of the *MSH* and its editors will be considered in chapter seventeen. The *MSH* was an English-language publication of the Apostleship of Prayer (AoP), a French-founded confraternity. In his letter Douglas wrote that a group of clergy and laity was already (i.e. before January 1890) meeting to discuss how to respond to the needs of seafarers. Each month the AoP published a

---

1   An anonymous article 'Sailors' Homes and Refuges' in SVP's *English Bulletin* XLVI(3), 80-94, which reviews work in the UK and France, says that 'In 1891, the Apostleship of Catholic Sailors was begun in English seaports.' 'The Rev. Father Goldie earnestly pleaded the cause of sailors at a large number of the General Meetings of our Society.'(87) A reference to 'one of the best historians of the Apostleship of the Sea' (F. M. Harms, *die Seemansmission*, Gotha 1890, 7), which I have failed to trace, confirms that the AoS title was being used widely for work among seamen in 1901, if not in 1890.

prayer intention chosen by the Pope; coincidentally in May 1890 the Papal choice was 'Sailors'. The editor of the *MSH* emphasised that the proximity of Douglas's letter and the Papal intention was fortuitous, the intention being chosen for the AoP internationally rather than for English-speaking members. The combination of prayer and a desire to accommodate the Papal interest may go some way towards explaining why at this point in both countries Catholic activity aimed at seafarers began to take a definite shape.

It was Anson's opinion, one formed in 1920, that despite his reference to Douglas's letter, primacy lay with France. Another opinion, nearer the event, suggests the French initiative followed one by the British Fr Goldie SJ.[1] The Hon Mrs Georgina Fraser,[2] Secretary of the CTS Seamen's Sub Committee, reporting for the year 1896 on her committee's achievements to the 1897 Catholic Congress, wrote:

> From the beginning we realised the need for English-speaking priests at foreign seaports, frequented by English and Irish seamen; and Fr Goldie SJ lost no opportunity of inviting the assistance of the Fathers of the Society [of Jesus], and other friends on the Continent, and of drawing their attention to the immense amount of money and energy expended by English Protestant Societies for seamen, and the absence of any effort by Catholics. A well-timed article in *Études* [a French Jesuit publication], aided no doubt by other causes, fell upon good ground in France, and a Society was founded in Paris in 1894, whose primary object is the care of French fishermen off the coast of Newfoundland and Iceland.

There is no doubt that the French society referred to here is the *Œuvres de Mer*. The involvement of the Augustinians of the Assumption (AA) in its foundation, featured prominently by Anson in his maritime writing, will be shown almost certainly to have derived from British inspiration. The AA was at this period in the process of buying a British ship for pilgrimage use. One of its editors, M. Bailly, was aware of the work of the MDSF, and through Eugène Grosjean (chapter seventeen), a French Jesuit novice, of the Church of England's Order of St Paul among seamen. Some of Mrs Fraser's 'other causes', such as the example of the French naval officers, and the implied if modest revival in the French navy, providing in France 'good ground', encouraged British Catholics through Lady Amabel's pen. In this way was knowledge shared.

Fr Goldie's work on behalf of seamen, especially merchant seamen, mentioned by Mrs Fraser will unfold in the next few chapters. His time in

---

1   Francis Goldie, according to SJ records, born Shrewsbury 20 Oct 1836; educated Ampleforth, Ushaw and English College, Rome; joined SJ 1868, Louvain 1869, returned UK 1872; attached to Farm Street, London from 1874 with various appointments. In 1884 for health reasons, forbidden to read, took chaplaincy on troopship *Euphrates* on return trip to India, repeated 1888, 1889. 'In 1895 [*sic*] at Manresa, *excurrens* [i.e. based there and conducting other work] when he took up the work for Catholic Sailors . . . ' Died Dec 1913. 1895 is a mistake.
2   The Hon Georgina Mary Fraser, only daughter of George F. Heneage of Hainton Hall, Lincolnshire, married Lt Col The Hon Alexander Fraser, 2nd son of the 12th Baron Lovat. She died in March 1928. Her Lovat marriage gave her a connection with Miss Scott Murray (of the WCB), a Lovat grand-daughter.

16. Fr Goldie SJ and the CTS

Rome and Louvain, and his troopship chaplaincies, gave him a network of connections, as had his near contemporary and fellow Jesuit, Fr Dignam, editor of the *MSH*, who had spent eighteen months serving English-speaking Catholics in Boulogne c. 1871.[1] French Jesuits had been pressed very hard by their government as one of its principal targets. The noviciate for the Paris Jesuit province was in exile from 1880, situated first in Aberdovey in Wales, and then more conveniently at Slough. One of its novices was Eugène Grosjean. Goldie's name can be linked with three particular efforts. His immediate involvement was with the CTS Seamen's Branch. He was closely associated with the Jesuit-promoted Work for Catholic Bluejackets (WCB), and connected through Grosjean with much French work for sailors, particularly, but not only, through the *Œuvres de Mer* (chapter eighteen).

Goldie's connection with the sea apostolate among French and British merchant navies, and work for the RN, prompts the question, Why Goldie? Goldie was one of a fairly small circle of high profile Catholics concerned to further the conversion of England. Catholic groups from this period overlap extensively. To these Goldie turned for support, recruiting members of the Guild of Ransom (GoR) and the Society of St Vincent de Paul (SVP) to start ship-visiting, and then to run a Sailors' Home, in London. At the SVP Superior Council he was clearly among friends. He was a life member of the CTS and on its main committee. Here he met with society ladies like the Hon Mrs Fraser, who would hold drawing room gatherings to extend CTS work. His chaplaincy to the troopship *Euphrates*, accompanying troops to India, perhaps one result of the Catholic Bishop of Portsmouth's successful pressure in the 1880s for the presence of Catholic chaplains on the troopships to serve what were often substantial numbers of Catholic men.

As a Jesuit he was part of a world-wide and influential order. Contemporary groups featuring in this story at this time were the Scots Jesuits, concentrated in Glasgow, English Jesuits with an important house in London, and French Jesuits in Slough, all of which would work to his advantage. Goldie would have had access to Jesuit publications, in particular, the *MSH*, its wide and popular circulation affording him a means of informing Catholics of the CTS's work for seafarers. It was the *MSH* which published the letter of Lord Archibald Douglas appealing for something to be done for seafarers. It is probable that Goldie was one of the clergy Douglas's letter hinted were already considering the problem.

Goldie, followed by Anson, believed one of the first Catholics, if not the first, to express concern for seafarers in print was The Rev. Lord Archibald Douglas. Whether Douglas recruited Goldie to the sea apostolate, or Goldie Douglas, is not clear; either way, Douglas as the titled member of the group of clergy and laymen mentioned in his letter would be the signatory to

---

1   Jesuit records give Augustus Dignam as born London 8 May 1833, joined SJ 1856, ordained 1867, Boulogne 1870-1. 1882 Director of AoP, giving 'new life to a work which had been languishing for fourteen years'. 1885 Editor of *MSH*, giving it popular form, and increasing circulation from 4,000 to 27,000, and with it, membership of AoP. Died 1894.

attract maximum attention. His letter, in the January 1890 *MSH*, told of a conversation one day in his sacristy after Mass with a Catholic bluejacket (a rating in the RN). The sailor had spoken of the Church's neglect of seafarers. Douglas wondered what could be done to remedy this. His letter was published under the heading JACK WRECKED AT SEA. He asked for the prayers of AoP members, indicating that his letter referred to spiritual shipwreck. 'The talk I had with the sailor has borne fruit. Some priests and laymen, in the service [RN] and out of it, are putting their heads together, to see what can be done . . .'.

AoP members were required to pray for the Pope's monthly intention, quite unknown in advance by such as Douglas. The May 1890 intention, 'sailors', appeared with a sympathetic explanation by the editor and Promoter of the AoP, Fr Dignam SJ, who drew attention to the zeal of Protestants in the sea apostolate, the naturally religious inclination of the sailor, and as an instance of the need, the lack of Catholic chaplains RN in a navy where many of the men were Irish Catholics. Dignam kept the subject open, publishing a couple of months later an account of a remarkable rescue from shipwreck of the husband of an AoP member, then with a letter from a seaman on HMS *Curaçoa*, writing from New Zealand to the *MSH*, signing himself 'Bluejacket', in which he explained that his sister regularly sent him her copy of the *MSH*, which was greatly appreciated on board ship, where reading material was scarce, particularly Catholic reading material. His suggestion that Catholics might consider sending their magazines to HM ships received editorial support. Dignam, confident of readers' response, wondered how to discover where to send material, until a reader wrote that Whittaker's *Almanac* provided a list of ships on station and that the *MSH* office could act as a clearing house for whatever Catholic literature might be forthcoming. From this grew the WCB (chapter seventeen).

While the editor of the *MSH* was still wondering what to do, the CTS had formed a Seamen's Sub Committee (sometimes called the Seamen's Branch) to consider the problem. The principal work of the CTS was to produce informational Catholic literature. CTS archives contain no details of this committee but it probably consisted of the CTS people who had already shown an interest in the sea by sending, from 1889, libraries of CTS publications to troopships and emigrant ships, perhaps another Goldie initiative and one confirming the interest of the CTS before the Sub Committee was formed. By 13 March 1891, James Britten (CTS Secretary) was speaking of the CTS work for these ships at one of Mrs Fraser's drawing rooms. Anson claimed in a tract of 1928 that Britten had sent a copy of the January 1891 *MSH*, for its article JACK AT SEA, to Mrs Fraser (soon to be the Sub Committee's Secretary), 'whom he knew to take a special interest in all that concerned the sea', and had then secured the services of Fr Goldie. It is probable that Douglas approached the CTS through Britten to obtain its interest, but Goldie's position as the story unfolds makes it more likely that Goldie was the initiator rather than the initiated, though he and Mrs Fraser could have been made aware of the need by Secretary Britten's bringing it to the attention of the main CTS Committee, of which both were members.

16. Fr Goldie SJ and the CTS

MSH readers were told of the recent formation of this CTS Sub Committee 'for the purpose of supplying Catholic literature to ships'. The date of its formation is unclear. It *could* have derived from the group of clergy and laity referred to in Douglas's 1890 letter. Its first meeting, according to Mrs Fraser, took place on 23 June 1891, a week before the annual CTS Conference - at Westminster - 'at which Fr Goldie SJ said a few words about the work for Catholic seamen', though its formation was announced in *The Tablet* of 6 June 1891, which added that the CTS was hoping to work among troop and emigrant ships, the 'RN, the Merchant Service, Deep Sea Fishermen, &c'. The *Tablet* named the Bishop of Portsmouth as Chairman and Mrs Fraser as Honorary Secretary *pro tem*.

The Sub Committee, if not at its inception, soon included Goldie, Mrs Fraser, Lady Amabel Kerr (announced as Treasurer by Mrs Fraser at a CTS meeting on 14th November 1892), James Britten, Miss Mary Scott Murray, Miss Margaret Stewart, and Edward Lucas, together, at some stage, with the Director of the AoP, Fr Dignam SJ. Mrs Fraser's version is that they were later joined by Bishop Vertue of Portsmouth, Admiral Whyte RN, Captain J. Burke RN, and Count Moore. Lady Amabel, Mrs Fraser and Fr Goldie were also members of the main CTS committee. Miss Mary Scott Murray and Miss Margaret Stewart were invited to join, as AoP members, indeed Promoters, associated with the WCB, to avoid confusion between CTS and WCB work. Plans were made to distribute literature to ships and coastguards. It is very difficult to follow the activities of the Sub Committee; if records were kept, they are no longer to be found, and references to its work in the Minutes of the main CTS Committee are minimal.

Goldie's presentations to CTS Conferences and his writing, like Grosjean's *Études* article (chapter eighteen), which almost certainly derived its information from Goldie, began by reviewing non Catholic work for seamen. His paper at the 1892 CTS Conference appeared at some length in *The Tablet* Conference supplement of 22 October 1892. Here he referred to the Douglas letter, the Papal intention, and the AoP's response in supplying HM ships with literature. The emphasis on HM ships at this point is significant, for it is only clarified some time later, in correspondence which survives in the AoP archive, that the CTS was to concern itself with the Merchant Navy. Goldie indicated the formation of the Sub Committee, and the invitation to membership of the AoP secretaries. All 122 of HM ships in commission now received monthly packets of Catholic papers, while Catholics on board HM troopships had 'for many years' received CTS publications, and the ministry of a chaplain on each voyage, of which he could speak from experience. The 'many years' probably meant 'for as long as the present committee can remember' for the CTS itself had only recently been revived, and records show Catholic voyage chaplains only from the 1880s.

Goldie approached the challenge of reaching the merchant seafarer with a care unusual in the history of the sea apostolate. Most pioneers, like Smith, Ashley, Agnes Weston, non-Catholics all, had responded to an observed and immediate need, whereas Goldie tried to discover how many Catholics were in the British Merchant Navy. Research took him to the London Docks where discussions with 'old and intelligent seamen' persuaded him that Catholics in the Merchant Navy were roughly in the proportion: of the sailors, 5%; of the firemen, 20%; of the officers, 1%; and of the whole, 16%. He referred to Catholic laymen visiting ships in the London Docks, and commented favorably on a local Committee of Literature for Catholic Seamen, started by GoR members, in London's East End, encouraged by the Archbishop of Westminster. It almost certainly owed its existence to Goldie's prompting. Its members visited incoming ships and distributed polyglot leaflets advertising local churches for Mass and priests able to hear confessions in languages other than English. As this work was clearly beyond the parish clergy his article called for the

> formation of confraternities, or sodalities, or guilds of longshoremen, or officials, or old sailors, or any with leisure or zeal, who for the love of God would do for their poor brethren in Christ what the Society of St Vincent de Paul does . . . in bringing the men to their duties and in putting Catholic books and literature in their way. Another of their tasks would be to guide them to respectable lodgings till such times as Catholic homes can be established.

This *Tablet* article of October 1892 is one of the earliest references to SVP activity in the sea apostolate. It is significant for the breadth of its thought: literature, guilds, polyglot literature, and Catholic sailors' homes; the concern for respectable lodgings it shared with others.

Fr Goldie was to return to the idea of 'binding all seafaring men together in some confraternity'. It was an aim which was achieved by sailors joining the AoS from 1895, and receiving a membership card which continued to have validity beyond 1922, from which date the AoS claimed Papal recognition. It was a matter which occupied the Sub Committee. One source of Goldie's continuing interest may be found in Charles Hopkins's SFSSP. Goldie, with the Jesuit novice Grosjean, heard Hopkins speak at Hastings on 28th August during Hopkins's 1893 tour of England. Grosjean described Hopkins's platform manner, habit, and appearance in an 1894 *Études* article, *Les Missions Protestantes d'Angleterre en Façeur des Marins*, to which Goldie responded in *The Month*. It would be entirely likely that Jesuits going to hear a member of the Church of England should go as a pair, Goldie, as the professed Jesuit, taking the initiative, and presumably taking Grosjean as part of his plan to encourage a French interest in the maritime apostolate, as well as furthering Goldie's researches into what other Christian denominations were doing for the sailor. Grosjean's 1894 *Études* article was a summary of the results of Goldie's research, which Peter Anson would later use, though without crediting his source. Goldie noted the inspirational role of Hopkins and his religious community in the *MSH* of July 1894:

> Note - The Ritualist *Father* Hopkins, in his *Priory* at Calcutta, has daily Communion Services for sailors living and dead! Might we not imitate his misplaced zeal? [Goldie's emphasis]

In Goldie's 1892 *Tablet* article the distinction between work for Bluejackets and the Merchant Navy was far from clear. Importantly, it showed in how many directions Goldie was exploring. Some of his thought was born of his personal experience: he reminded readers that there was an acute need for chaplains RN, mindful of which, the Sub Committee had co-opted the Catholic naval chaplains from Portsmouth and Plymouth *ex officio*. Partly with the Mediterranean fleet in mind, he reminisced of being summoned in Barcelona by an officer who had found Goldie, only after much searching, to minister to a dying seaman in need of an English-speaking priest, an experience which prompted the Sub Committee almost from its inception to produce and circulate lists of English-speaking priests abroad. Another spiritual need was met in the committee's production of a CTS prayer book for seamen. Goldie mentioned grants of books to various ports, work amongst fisher lads at Grimsby, and the establishment of local committees in Liverpool and London. He expressed the hope that, perhaps inspired by the example of Captain Marceau (mentioned by name but yet to appear in Lady Amabel's tract), Catholic France would soon be emulating the MDSF by sending floating hospitals and chapels to its fishing fleets, a hope which prompts the question, given that he was writing in 1892, whether he might already have been in touch with *M.* Bailly (chapter eighteen). He suggested Germany too might play its part, perhaps through the German-founded Society of St Raphael's port chaplains, placed to work among emigrants, and well positioned to help seamen. Goldie was under no illusion about the amount of labour required: it 'needs the zeal almost of a St Peter Claver . . .', topical because canonied just four years earlier, his heroic work among slaves and sailors already noted.

Goldie's study of non Catholic work had a utility beyond providing the stimulus to get something Catholic started, for it shaped his views on *how* Catholic work might be organised and showed him *what* could be possible. Apart from his debt to Hopkins and the OSP, he was also impressed by SAWCM. This Church of England Society (chapter eleven), with its grants to parishes for the provision of missionary curates, assistant clergy within parish structures, to work among seamen and its encouragement of Sailors' Chapels on quaysides as chapels of ease to the parish churches, seemed to Goldie to offer a way forward, he and SAWCM sharing a Catholic understanding of Church order. Perhaps from SAWCM he derived his idea of uniting all Catholic works for seamen internationally, not within a monolithic structure like the MtS, but federally, taking account of the autonomy of each bishop in his diocese.

This structure is of more than academic interest. The BFBSS, consisting of independent Bethels, had been forced, *nolens volens*, in the face of an ecclesiology which emphasised the completeness of the local church, to discover for itself an understanding of the wider Church through federation. That is to say, the mobility of the seaman required an extended ministry which went beyond the competence of a local gathering of Christians. The dispersed authority of the BFSFSBU protected that local autonomy but provided the necessary link with others, perhaps derived from the Baptist Union, which had developed in a similar way, uniting local independent congregations whilst respecting their autonomy. By contrast the MtS operated a centralised structure. Its institutions tended to be separate from the parish. While obtaining a licence from the local bishop for its chaplains it remained the appointing body. SAWCM's alternative to this created a role for the bishop and a link with the Church family as expressed through the parish; a model, in turn, which allowed Goldie to see how a Catholic structure could be set up which would take account both of episcopacy and the needs of the seafarer.

Throughout the 1890s the CTS Sub Committee was fortunate in its advocates. Mrs Fraser spoke at several CTS Conferences, her subject usually seamen, and much of the information which survives does so because of her annual reports. Her diligence, the vision of Fr Goldie, his contacts, and the pen of Lady Amabel, gave the Sub Committee a very productive decade, before dwindling away in the 1900s. The details of its demise are far from clear but seem due to the increasing age of its members and to the Cardinal's handing some of its work to the Royal Naval Catholic Association (RNCA), a group about which little information survives, but which will be considered in chapter nineteen.

The wide publicity which Goldie's 1892 speech received was maintained by a leader in *The Tablet* (5th November 1892). The author had given thought to the relationship between Goldie's campaign, and the state of the contemporary Church. Additionally, it suggested why such a campaign should emerge in the Catholic Church in England at this time.

> It is one of the disabilities of a missionary Church that it is so busied with building chapels and the carrying on of parish work that its efforts have to be limited to the beaten paths . . . It is only when a settled and ordered system has been evolved . . . that there is leisure to think of those whose lives are not along the highroads . . . It is pleasant to think that one result of all these Protestant agencies has been to quicken in Catholics a sense of their own duties and responsibilities . . .

Initially the work of the Sub Committee was what the CTS itself did best, as a Church publisher. Local groups were urged to distribute polyglot leaflets and take parcels of good, mainly Catholic, reading matter, rosaries, medals and similar aids to devotion, on board ship. Then, its high Catholic profile and the lack of any other organised body involved with seamen meant that it provided a focus for others, such as Fr Hawkins and his work among the Grimsby Fisher lads, mentioned at the Catholic Conference. A third aspect of its work became the provision of sailors' clubs and homes. These three areas need examination.

Literature is an omnibus word which includes production and distribution. Mention has been made of its distribution. Regarding production, of primary importance was the prayer book for Catholic seamen. Prayers for seamen as a class predate the Reformation (chapter two); the idea of a prayer book was a development. The Commonwealth's *Directory of Public Worship*, with its supplement for ships (chapter six) offered a precedent, but the CTS Catholic book seems to have been the first ever for Catholic seamen; perhaps, in its turn, the inspiration for the *Prayer Book for Catholic Seamen* produced in 1903 by the Anglican OSP. References to the Catholic book are not uncommon, but of its conception or birth tell nothing. Its production post-dated the formation of the Sub Committee (June 1891) but this need not be true of its conception. CTS *Minutes* seldom refer to it. The earliest reference is dated 11th January 1892: 'A report was given by Mrs Fraser as to the Sailor's Prayerbook: and it was agreed on the motion of the chairman that £50 out of the Special Fund should be devoted towards printing it'.

Its *Imprimatur* in 1892 suggests the work involved in its production could have been what created the need for a Seamen's Sub Committee. It was early announced in the *MSH*, where it was described as 'small, but complete', and concern expressed as to the means of its distribution; word of it seems to have travelled without difficulty. It contained the usual prayers (Our Father, Hail Mary, Glory be and *Credo*), to which were added an outline of the days of obligation, devotion, fasting and abstinence; a summary of Christian doctrine; an explanation of lay Baptism; prayers for morning and night; the Way of the Cross; Litanies, a Sunday morning service for use at sea; the text of Holy Mass (with a short instruction); how to serve at Mass; the Rosary; a section on the sacraments; prayers for the dying; prayers for Holy Communion; burial of the dead; Epistles and Gospels; and assorted hymns. Its adoption by the Admiralty as the official Catholic prayer book helped distribution and finance and gave the book status, and hinted at improving conditions for Catholics in the RN. It was published as *The Guide to Heaven* and remained popular until Fr Martindale SJ at the behest of the SVP produced a replacement in the late 1920s. It was widely used, and by 1902 14,000 copies were in circulation. A new edition followed in 1904. A 1926 edition carried the information that 33,000 copies had been printed, claiming the first edition - perhaps in that format - had been produced in 1904.

The second function of the Sub Committee, to become a focus for the work of others, is illustrated by the work in Grimsby among fisher lads by Canon Hawkins. Anson, giving details in *Harbour Head*, used *The Tablet* report of 1893 and, although Hawkins's work had disappeared, probably by the turn of the century, perhaps with the change of fleeting patterns or the departure or retirement of Canon Hawkins, he seems to have been able in the 1920s to see Hawkins's fisher lads' confraternity registers, though without saying where he had seen them. Young boys were apprenticed to the fishing fleets without serious spiritual formation. Many were orphans. Hawkins tried to identify which were Catholic, to keep in touch with them, and encourage them to use local rooms which he had made available. The CTS Conferences, held in a different town each year, provided a useful means of making this work known. By becoming the umbrella organisation for a variety of disparate Catholic works such as in Grimsby the Sub Committee became aware that the need for its interest in the maritime community was both great and wide.

The CTS Sub Committee having followed a similar route to Protestants in the matter of literature distribution, a natural development would be, like theirs, to provide some sort of sailors' home. The first and most enduring success of the Sub Committee was in Canada. According to Dr W.H. Atherton, Montreal had had a Sailors' Institute since 1862 following earlier work by the local (undenominational) Young Men's Christian Association. Catholic work for seamen in Montreal began after someone, spotting the *Tablet* article advocating that something be done for seamen, brought it to the attention of a small group of Catholic converts who 'about 1891-2' had formed an English Catholic Association, before becoming the Montreal branch of the CTS. The article was a resumé of Mrs Fraser's paper delivered in Liverpool to the 1892 CTS

Conference, 'How are we to help our seamen?', placing the Montreal group clearly in the CTS/Goldie context. Because of its primacy, the institute deserves more than passing attention. The group proved ephemeral, ceasing around 1896.

Montreal is a seasonal port. Its closed season was soon to end. With some urgency a meeting of the group was called to form a small committee to begin something quickly for Catholic sailors. Credit for this has been placed incorrectly at Dr Atherton's door, for Atherton did not arrive in Montreal until 1907. It met for the first time on Good Friday 1893. After several abortive attempts to find suitable premises a room was obtained, handy for the wharf front but in a garret up three flights of stairs. Though predated by Canon Hawkins's fisher lads' institute, it was claimed to be the first modern club for Catholic seafarers, established on 18 May 1893, with a formal opening on the 30th May. Its financial position was precarious. Responsibility for it passed from the small founding committee to the local Catholic Ladies' Committee which soon gathered about it an influential group of men, allowing the opening of a newer and better club for the 1896 season; in the early years of the new century, a purpose-built Sailors' Home was erected (Fig. 12). This was no mean achievement for a group using a property which had the financial drain of seasonal usage, though the months when it was closed may have been convenient for fund-raising activities.

The Montreal club was followed shortly by one in London. In this case Goldie got together several friends and persuaded them to rally their organisations, particularly the converts Fr Philip Fletcher, founder of the Guild of Ransom (GoR), and Fletcher's friend Lister Drummond, CTS member, active Ransomer, and later a London magistrate. Fletcher's GoR members, who undertook open air preaching on Tower Hill, were soon involved in literature distribution to Catholic seafarers, Fletcher describing their mission in *Faith of Our Fathers* (May 1893), where he mentioned that this distribution, and the printing of a prayer book and other 'special literature' for seamen, were among the latest efforts of the CTS on behalf of the seafarer. Mr Blenzberg, Tower Hill's District Ransomer, aided by fellow Ransomers, had reportedly placed Catholic literature on 23 ships in the Port of London. Fletcher told his Ransomers that each should have a 'sailor's box' for literature collection; the box, when full, to be sent 'to the port which Ransomers have decided to help ... '. There were few ports at this stage able to accept what was collected but Fr Fletcher expected his Ransomers to be ambitious.

A letter from Blenzberg in *Faith of Our Fathers* (June 1893) calling for more volunteer distributors, revealed that his committee, the Catholic Sailors' Literature Committee, elsewhere referred to as the Committee for Literature for Catholic Seamen, had been established in March 1893, under the presidency of The Rev. J. O'Reilly OMI (who in 1893 did a tour of duty as a troopship chaplain), with Blenzberg assisted in his secretarial duties by a Mr J. Riordan. Its purpose was to encourage

> good sound reading by the distribution of suitable books and literature ... on board the vessels ... to afford the sailors every information as to the nearest churches and hours of service ... the best and safest lodging for sailors ....

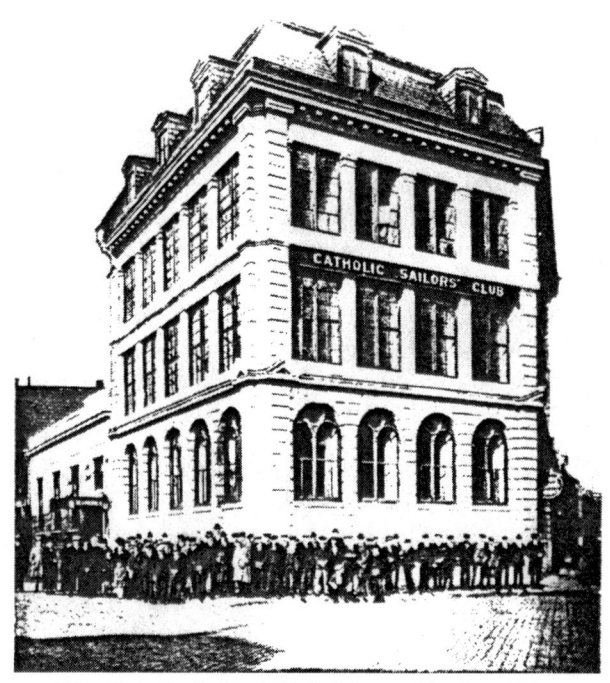

The Catholic Sailors' Club, Montreal in the 1920s.

In this a dozen men were involved, at least in the first months, visiting, every second Sunday afternoon (reflecting the slow turn around of nineteenth-century ships), in pairs. Fr Goldie attending a meeting of this group on 16 June 1893, was welcomed by Fr Fletcher in typical Ransom language as 'preaching a crusade on behalf of the sailors'. Goldie's message was consistent, speaking in similar vein to the SVP in December, that he hoped their work would extend to both sides of the river ('in Westminster and Southwark dioceses'). The Ransomers sought advice from Commander FitzGerald of Greenwich 'who for many years has been harbour master'.

Ransomers continued to visit ships, recording numbers visited and Catholics encountered, but initial enthusiasm began to wane in the face of what was proving a major commitment - a familiar problem. Volunteers visited in spare time, usually on Saturday or Sunday afternoons after a week's hard work and with family commitments to be included. FitzGerald suggested that opening a Catholic Sailors' Home or Depot in the Tower Hill Mission might ease the situation. In the event, Ransomers were able to obtain premises in nearby Wellclose Square, opened by Cardinal Vaughan on 20th September 1893, some four months behind Montreal. A triumphant Fr Fletcher wrote in *The Ransomer*,

> ... the Jesuit ... to whose zeal and love Catholic seamen in great measure owe their first club in London ... Fr Goldie ... has preached indefatigably ever since the last Catholic Conference ... the co-operation of two ladies, who have been inspired with equal zeal and love for the same cause. The Hon Mrs Fraser and Lady Amabel Kerr ... to the former lady is due ... the first year's rent.

Since their initiation, Tower Hill Ransomers had visited 300 ships. A Ransomer (and SVP supporter),

> Mr White of Tower Hill League Guards [part of the GoR structure] . . . has taken over command of the Catholic Seamen's Club . . . What has begun on Tower Hill . . . it is hoped may be attempted at the Regent, East and West India, Millwall, Victoria and Albert Docks . . . We ransomed an old beer shop in Well-close Square for our Seamen's Club.

Wellclose Square was chosen, though shipping was moving down river to these docks, most of them newly built or building, because it was close to the BoT offices 'where Jack has to come to draw his pay'. When a move became possible, the club, or more correctly Home, moved from 14 to 18 Wellclose Square. In 1913 a new Home was opened near the Victoria Dock, which in July 1922 Cardinal Bourne placed in the care of SVP. The SVP-run Home survived into the 1960s.

Other clubs and homes followed. It is difficult to chart this side of the Sub Committee's work. Lists really begin around the turn of the century and they lack consistency. One list, from the 1901 *Stella Maris*, has Genoa, Ghent, Glasgow, Isle of Dogs [London], Liverpool, London [Wellclose Square], Maryport, Middlesbrough, Montreal, New York, North Shields and Ostend, together with some French ports which will be considered in chapter nineteen. Added to the list of ports was another of English-speaking clergy overseas. A later list in a Goldie article published in 1906 mentioned New York, Philadelphia and 'possibly Liverpool' alongside London and Montreal. A name on a list is no guarantee that anything beyond the name existed, an observation which is as true of Catholic lists as it is of the long lists of correspondents offered by protestant societies of the period.

The wide variety represented in these lists is illustrated if each is examined in turn. American work may not derive directly from Goldie and the CTS though the dates are suggestive.[1] Philadelphia, with SVP and Jesuit involvement, would seem to have a fairly direct link. Its information is confusing. One source says in 1893 Fr John Scully SJ gathered a group of SVP men to serve the 'apostolate of the wharves' but that clubhouse and reading rooms were not obtained until 1919. A second says that sailor work began in Philadelphia in 1906. A third offers 1889 as the starting date, with SVP involvement. It is the 1893 date which suggests the likelihood of a link with Fr Goldie and the CTS. A possible interpretation is that 1893 was the starting date for typical SVP literature distribution by ship-visitors, with subsequent attempts to develop the work by obtaining premises.

In New York, Fr Charles N. Parks USN, mentioned as a US naval chaplain in 1890 in the *Glasgow Observer,* asked Archbishop Corrigan in June 1894 to establish a seafarers' centre. A committee was appointed and reading rooms, financed by a diocesan collection, opened on 27th December, 1894

1 *Glasgow Observer,* 10 January, 1891 quotes the *New York Catholic Review*: 'for nearly a year now in the Navy there has been an attempt to establish the means for regular worship on board ship . . . '. The *Stella Maris* of March 1901, 35-37, included an article, 'Madame Bayer and the Catholic Bluejackets of America', which said that *Mme* Bayer's visiting of Catholic seamen in Brooklyn's City Hospital had led to the appointment of Fr Parks as the first chaplain in the US Navy in 1888.

at 296 West 10th Street. In 1898 Fr William F. Dougherty was appointed chaplain. The reading rooms were moved first to 178 Christopher Street, then to 422 West Street. Dougherty, full-time from 1903, was said to be the first in the United States. In 1907 he was followed by the legendary Fr McGrath, famous for a very muscular approach to the problem of crimps preying upon seafarers. Underfunding seems to have been a perennial problem; in 1922 Dr Atherton described this work in New York as 'the Cinderella of all the institutions I saw there'.

Few sources in English give details of the work in Genoa, Ghent and Ostend. Evidence of AoP and Jesuit involvement implies a link to Goldie or the *MSH*, or both, in the cases of Ghent and Ostend. In Ghent, after lady promoters of the AoP successfully invited, on 29th August, 1893, bargees to the Jesuit residence for Mass for a boatman's wife who had died of cholera, the *Œuvre des Bateliers* was founded, on the last Sunday of each month opening the Jesuit chapel to barge families; apparently the two-mile walk was no disincentive. The lady promoters boarded barges, gathered the children and offered them instruction, assisted by Fr Beck SJ. In December 1894 a Sodality of Our Lady Star of the Sea was started with 44 members and 48 candidates. Two retreats were given in February 1895, when all navigation had been halted by severe frost, the first for eighty-four bargees, the second for forty women, presumably wives. This success led to a pilgrimage for some 150 bargees and their families in the summer of 1895. By 1899 a house of call had been built at Dock 31 where Fr Beck could be found, alongside an information centre, entertainments, newspapers, a library, and with a chapel planned, if not realised. The Ostend work was an extension of the Ghent work by the AoP ladies, with similar openings at Antwerp. All three ports had considerable barge traffic, often delayed by bad weather.

In Genoa a mission of sorts opened in January 1889. One report says that by 1901 the chaplain had visited more than 700 ships and met 2,000 sailors. If 1889 is correct his ship-visiting average was roughly one ship a week. The early starting date seems to predate Goldie's interest and may have been associated with large numbers of naval personnel or the increasing number of British merchant ships as steam replaced sail in the Mediterranean.[1] The Archbishop of Genoa gave an annual donation of £20 conditional upon its being matched by English donations. The chaplain had reading rooms at 73 via Milano, with twice-weekly concerts, a pattern familiar to sailors visiting protestant clubs, which he may have been emulating. The long-serving chaplain was Canon Hay, an English priest attached to a local church in a capacity not specified. Advertisements in the Catholic press offering places to three or four Catholic clergy to winter, presumably for their health (numbers of English people visiting the area for the same reason), imply that his means were private but inadequate. Hay's ministry opens a window on what was then considered a modern and attractive programme. On Saturday evenings he offered a phonograph entertainment, his sixteen tunes (each costing 2s. 6d) proving very popular. Sunday nights were devoted to magic lantern shows on

[1] David M. Williams & John Armstrong, Changing Voyage Patterns . . . , esp. 164ff.

sacred subjects. By 1901 he was also trying to fix up a chapel; a delay of twelve years before providing a chapel seems rather long, rendering 1889 as a starting date suspect. Hay suggested, writing in *Stella Maris* in 1901, that such a ministry 'would afford a very suitable occupation for convert clergymen with families'.

It is easier to examine the British ports listed. London has been referred to. In Liverpool it is doubtful that there was any Catholic provision at this time beyond access to one or two parish clubs despite its listing in the 1901 *Stella Maris*. Maryport, Middlesbrough and North Shields received the attention of the SVP. By 1905 North Shields' St Cuthbert's parish SVP was visiting a local Sailors' Home, apparently one of the secular homes to be found around the UK, and giving regular spiritual instruction to the eighty Catholic boys on board the training ship *Wellesley*, with support from the SVP's Sunderland Particular Council. The 1901 Glasgow reference will be considered in chapter seventeen. In short, Goldie's various initiatives had led by the turn of the century to the establishment of nearly a dozen ventures for seamen, involvement of the SVP and the GoR, and a fruitful liaison with the WCB. His advocacy of the seamen's cause continued almost to his death in 1913. Effectively his ministry fell into two phases, here stimulating direct work among seamen, and then, post 1900, publicising their cause in fairly substantial papers presented at conferences or published in the Catholic press.

There was one other area of CTS Sub Committee work, its provision of literature to coastguards. Handed over in 1896 to the WCB, it illustrates how CTS and WCB ran concurrently, and reveals how differences were handled between the two committees. Like Protestant literature societies, the CTS early extended its literature distribution to these men, apparently from the autumn of 1893. This was easily done, for they were in home waters, station addresses easy to obtain. It was organised by Edward Lucas, originally from the London area, later from Boscombe, Hampshire. The Sub Committee found itself in difficulties with coastguard work in 1896, perhaps because of the temper or health of Lucas.

This coastguard 'problem' survives in correspondence in the Jesuits' London archive. In August 1896, with more than a tinge of irony, Lucas wrote to Fr Gretton saying that he had been pleased to learn from the *MSH* that the AoP was taking over (his) coastguard work, a matter which had been discussed by the Sub Committee in June without resolution. He said that he had always worked under the CTS but 'how I became a member of the Committee whose meetings were held at Mrs Fraser's I never knew'. Nor was he clear who had decided which would be responsible for Merchant and Royal Navies. The division of labour between the two will be returned to in the next chapter. What Lucas did know was that his work had been taken over by the AoP's Miss Petre. His letter was copied in abbreviated form to the AoP Secretary, Miss Scott Murray, in October. A further letter from Lucas to Fr Gretton demanded to know why his name had been omitted from the list of those nominated to receive contributions 'towards supplying 37 Coast Guard Stations (to say nothing of 4 ships and 3 hospitals)'. However, he promised

16. Fr Goldie SJ and the CTS

to continue to collect private donations. In the same letter he complained of eye trouble. A letter of the following day enclosed his expenses. Fr Gretton's reply has not survived but appears to have been sufficiently emollient, for Lucas replied to it on 15th October with a pleasantness lacking in earlier letters. In this letter he agreed to send Miss Petre a list of all coastguard stations, promising that he would continue to send them papers until the end of the year (and to three or four stations thereafter), but he would no longer be able to supply the hospitals.

This coastguard incident is the only disagreement surviving from the period. The evidence is one sided. Though a small storm in a large teacup, it contains significant points, providing useful insight into the working of the two committees. It illustrates the attachment to a cause which can be formed in a short time, the informality of recruitment of committee members and supporters, and the need for clear lines of demarcation. It shows, too, how the work of the two agencies (CTS and AoP) overlapped in membership and intention. Its resolution, for which details are sparse, allowed Mrs Fraser to write in her 1896 *Report*:

The problem 'How to help our Coast Guardsmen' has been happily solved at last. After much time, thought and money had been spent by Mr Lucas in developing this part of our work, he found that owing to ill health and removal to a distance from London, he was unable to continue his exertions; the work was taken over by the Director of the Apostleship of Prayer and is now carried on most successfully by Miss Margaret Petre, as Secretary for coast-guardsmen, on the same lines as the work for bluejackets.

By the beginning of the twentieth century the CTS Sub Committee had made useful progress, despite its informal procedure (no *Minutes*) and fluid membership. Its primary role of literature distribution had diminished but the number of clubs, reading rooms and homes with which it was associated had increased. The real link here was as part of the Goldie network, for homes and clubs were not really part of the CTS purpose. How much Goldie would have achieved without the contacts and support of Mrs Fraser and Lady Amabel is probably not a question to which there is an answer but their contribution was significant. The prominence of women in the sea apostolate, repeated through Miss Scott Murray and others in the WCB, and Mrs Howden on Glasgow, finds little equivalence in protestant work, beyond Agnes Weston and her Royal Sailors' Rests. Now, the CTS Sub Committee was almost exclusively occupied with the Merchant Navy, which had become possible because of the parallel developments for the RN through the work of the WCB.

17. The Work for Catholic Bluejackets

The purpose of this chapter is to consider the role of the Apostleship of Prayer in the Catholic ministry to seamen. It will return to the lack of a Catholic naval chaplaincy service before making its principal concern the naval seaman following Bluejacket's letter to the *MSH* in January 1891, whence the development of the Work for Catholic Bluejackets. The development of the Apostleship of the Sea, following the recruitment of sailors of the RN into the AoP, what their membership meant, and its 1898 extension to the Merchant Navy in Glasgow will be described. The various contributions to the sea apostolate of the AoS, the CTS and the SVP will be considered, setting the important role of the St Aloysius' Working Boys, responsible for ship-visiting in Glasgow, in context. With London limping and Montreal seasonal, by the end of the nineteenth century the Catholic sea apostolate in Glasgow was arguably the most developed Catholic port work of the period. Its decline into dormancy around 1909 and its role as a bridge between pre and post war Catholic work among seafarers will be postponed until chapter twenty.

All nineteenth-century English Catholic thinking about the sea apostolate began with the RN. Its role in the development of empire was both operational (without its ships there would have been no empire) and symbolic (where naval ships were, there was the empire). It was easily defined and highly organised. The kind of people working to develop the Catholic sea apostolate were people with leisure, and more likely, for reasons of class, to have relatives in the RN than in the Merchant Navy. The Kerr family, Lady Amabel and husband Admiral Lord Walter Kerr having sons in the RN, offers an example. Of the other names associated with the apostolate, only Mrs Howden in Glasgow is known to have had connections with the Merchant Navy; her father and her husband had been master mariners.[1] It was not

[1] Her *Glasgow Observer* obituary said she was the widow of Captain J. L. Howden of Shawlands and late of 46 Dudley Drive. Her death certificate adds that she was a daughter of James Young, Master Mariner. As her husband died in April 1896 when his steamer, the *Siddons*, was in collision in fog in the North Sea, her AoS recruitment was less than two years into widowhood, and in her late thirties. Her death, on 15 March 1919, aged 61, followed three days of pneumonia, in the Gartnavel Royal Lunatic Asylum, to which she had been admitted in 1912 as a private patient at the request of her brother-in-law, John A. Warren of Partick, after certification by two doctors, her symptoms including religious mania, depression, paranoia, auditory and visual hallucinations, and aggression; latterly she required feeding by tube, a sad end to a remarkable woman. Full details can be found in the hospital archive in Glasgow's Mitchell Library (HB13/5/168, pp 234ff).

17. The Work for Catholic Bluejackets

difficult to discover where the ships of the RN were stationed, or to establish the approximate number of Catholics in the RN, estimated by one source as 10%, mostly men from Ireland, and its few Catholic officers well-known as being from the relatively small circle of the Catholic upper classes. The official chaplaincy of the Established Church contrasted with the provision for non-conformity, in which Catholicism must be included.

Before the nineteenth century there was no official Catholic ministry to the RN beyond a priest at Havant from 1733 who must have exercised a very limited ministry; Catholic chaplains at Chatham and Haslar from 1797, and at Gosport from 1799 probably had more scope, while Catholic chapels were to be found at Chatham, Portsmouth and Plymouth by c. 1800. In 1856 William Woollett was appointed to serve at Portsmouth, Henry Woollett at Plymouth, Henry Lea at Chatham, and in 1867 a priest was appointed at Malta. Not until 1859 were Catholics in the RN excused attendance at Church of England worship. In 1876 the English Catholic hierarchy formally requested that Catholic chaplains in the RN be appointed on the same basis as those of the Church of England, a matter which remained unresolved until 1943; they had to be content with a gesture, a token increase in the salaries of the chaplains at Portsmouth and Plymouth. The pressure for Catholic equality brought slow but steady progress. The first Catholic priest at sea in the RN sailed in 1887. The first Mass on board ship was in 1905. In 1901 the matter was raised in Parliament, by which date there were 148 ports with full or part-time Catholic chaplains, but none with the status of Chaplain RN. A partial solution considered was for priests to serve as Naval Instructors but the matter was not pursued; the time involved in becoming an Instructor militated against it, and the potential relationship between Instructor and instructed was thought inappropriate for a priest with a pastoral ministry to exercise. The neglect of Catholic 'bluejackets', a word which always referred to ratings of the RN, was well understood by the 1890s when the attention of Catholics was drawn to it in the pages of the *Messenger of the Sacred Heart* (*MSH*).

The Rev. Lord Archibald Douglas's letter in the January 1890 *MSH* asked 'that some means may be devised for helping Jack', a paternalistic approach entirely consistent with the period, 'Jack' being a term for a rating. While little more is heard of Douglas, the letter resonated with *MSH* readers. Fr Dignam SJ, editor of the *MSH* and Director of the AoP, reminded them of the sums available to aid Protestant sailors, writing that 'No one class of our people is, perhaps, so destitute of spiritual aid; none more in need of it'. Soldiers, even convicts, received better provision than sailors. 'The difficulty is great, no doubt, even to devise a means, still more to provide one. But prayer and charity can accomplish all things . . .'. The means was suggested by 'Bluejacket', a sailor on HMS *Curaçoa*, who wrote suggesting that literature would be welcome on board if sent to HM ships. His letter, written in January, appeared in May 1891, the slow response to Douglas's letter due to a different pace of life, Bluejacket's distance on station, and the time lapse involved in publishing a monthly magazine.

Bluejacket's suggestion simply and economically offered a means of countering the mass of protestant literature provided on board ship. The need for such a solution was pressing, for the resources of the Church were limited. Fr Dignam told his readers:

> ... if it were a want of the Church of England men, the thing would be easy. The Lord Mayor would call a meeting in the Egyptian Hall; several noblemen and charitable people would make speeches; a committee of admirals would be appointed, with an office in Pall Mall, and a secretary at three, four or five hundred [pounds] a year. He would soon have every information at his fingers' ends.

Readers would have recognised this witty caricature of the methods of the Church of England's missionary and philanthropic societies, their own organisations sufficiently outside the Establishment for the *Catholic Directory* to include annual lists of Catholics in the peerage and other significant groups. The caricature allowed Dignam to highlight the slenderness of Catholic resources, consisting in the AoP office and the thousands of the Associates of the League of the Sacred Heart (members of the AoP). 'Subscriber' solved the problem of knowing where to send donated literature with the information that ships on station were listed in Whitaker's *Almanac*.

Subsequent issues of the *MSH* revealed the willingness of readers to send literature for the WCB, the CTS Sub Committee's early pressure for distribution to be made through 'one department of this great work' apparently unheeded. By limiting the distribution of literature to the RN, *MSH* readers were given a clear target. For them a small leaflet of advice was available. People initiating this work were called promoters. The term has an ambiguity which requires attention to context. They might be members of the AoP, or organisers of the WCB. The first of the latter was Miss Mary Scott Murray,[1] assisted by a colleague, Miss Margaret Stewart. Later, with the development of the AoS, promoters were those who had authority to enrol others into the AoS. Miss Scott Murray's form of address to Fr Gretton SJ, who followed in the work after Dignam's death in 1894, suggests that she may have been one of his penitents, making her recruitment from the circle of AoP promoters as someone known to the Director, and as a lady with time to spare, entirely natural.

The leaflet produced for readers contained a general letter explaining that senders of literature were required to dispatch parcels monthly. Each, provided with an address, had to send literature in the way specified to avoid liability of the recipient to pay duty. Correspondence between sender and sent was forbidden. The Secretaries (or Promoters) had sole responsibility for correspondence. Their work related only to the RN; coastguard work was separate and passed through several hands. Literature sent would differ in quantity according to ship size but would include newspapers, magazines and tracts. A list of possible Catholic magazines and papers was included with the *caveat* that the Catholic weekly *The Universe* was not allowed on board ships of the RN.[2] Although the AoP was in this work treading a path well trodden by Protestant agencies, it was doing so in a novel and highly efficient way. The

---

1   Scott Murray is sometimes hyphenated.
2   I have failed to find an explanation for this prohibition.

17. The Work for Catholic Bluejackets

advantage of having the *MSH* as a medium for publicity cannot be ignored. In succeeding issues, letters from grateful sailor-recipients were published. In January 1892, for example, letters were included from bluejackets serving in China, the Mediterranean, Australia and Africa, reminding readers of the size and distribution of the contemporary Navy. These letters raised issues hitherto unconsidered: funding, instruction, and particularly the unsuitability of the rule of the AoP to the maritime life.

Funding for the WCB came from various sources. Seamen who wrote in often enclosed donations which, since the enterprise was run on a very small budget, were welcome, as were the donations from other sources. The shoestring budget is confirmed by the few accounts which survive; those of 1899, for example, showed an income of £37. 2s. 11d, and an expenditure of £41. 13s. 11d, the balance being covered by the proceeds of a Cake and Apron Fair. Some donations came from people asking for inclusions in the Memento Book, kept at the Jesuit church of the Sacred Heart, Wimbledon, where the AoP had its offices. A small income derived from the sale of publications. Expenses were confined almost entirely to postage and printing. As early as 1894 a petition to his Rector was made by the 'Central Director' for permission to use alms offered for unspecified good works for the benefit of the 'Apostleship for Sailors Work', as he called the Work for Catholic Bluejackets, foreshadowing of the AoS title. At this stage titles of the various works were still fluid.

On 26 March 1895 Fr Gretton wrote to his Rector (his superior in the SJ) to clarify financial matters:

> 1. . . . The Secretary of the Apostleship Work for Catholic Sailors (Miss Scott Murray) collects funds for that work and has asked my permission to subscribe towards the forming of a library for a Seamen's Home [London?], which does not come under <u>our</u> work but under the Catholic Truth Society's Work for Catholic Seamen. The CTS take the Merchant Service and we the HMS. Our funds are quite distinct and so are our Secretaries, though the Secretaries and I belong to the CTS Sailors' Committee. May I use my discretion in similar cases to allow the Secretary to then dispose of what she can afford out of her funds.
>
> 2. The sailors on HMS often send the Secretaries money for charities to be chosen by them . . . [I] have suggested that they sometimes apply the money to the Sailors' Work as a good charity. [Gretton's emphasis]

The Rector, Fr Bampton SJ, required further information. A day later Gretton was replying to his queries, assuring the Rector that any money given to a Sailors' Home would not come out of AoP funds, but out of money collected by Miss Scott Murray for sailor-work; the subscription which prompted this exchange was unlikely to exceed a pound and was not intended as a subsidy. Perhaps there is a hint of the Rector's real fears in this part of Gretton's reply:

> I don't think there is the slightest chance of the CTS ever asking us to take over any part of their work. Perhaps an occasional charity of the sort proposed would emphasise that the CTS funds and ours are quite distinct . . . a subscription given now and again...would tend to promote a kindly

feeling . . . not that there has been opposition, but a tendency in the CTS to take the whole kudos themselves . . .

The Rector was probably only exercising his office in ensuring that the SJ was not to become heir to a series of unpredictable liabilities.

Additionally, the correspondence reveals for the first time the possibility of tension between the two agencies, which the appointment of AoP members to the CTS Sub Committee had been intended to forestall. There is here a very clear indication of the two spheres of influence, RN and MN. It was not a new distinction, for Gretton's predecessor, Fr Dignam, had been aware of it, writing in the *MSH* in 1893:

> Meantime, let us not forget that a far larger, a far more difficult and ungrateful work is being undertaken by the CTS, which is endeavouring to cope with the religious destitution of the merchant service. . . .

Though problems were eased by good will on both sides they did not cease; mostly they related to areas of responsibility. In 1896, James Britten, CTS General Secretary, replying to a letter from Fr Dignam, responded to difficulties which the latter seems to have raised, which are unspecified in the reply:

> I quite agree with you that it will be easy to keep our special interests apart, and yet to co-operate; and I confess that it never occurred to me until you brought the matter forward . . . that there could be any difficulty . . . or that any complication had arisen. It had certainly seemed to me that things were working most harmoniously and with perfect understanding, and I should be surprised to learn . . . that any - still less many - should have thought that this was exclusively a CTS work; for we have always been careful to mention the Apostleship in all our Reports . . .

The date suggests that the 'difficulty' concerned coastguard work and the role of Mr Lucas. The letter continued by mentioning subscriptions which might have been sent wrongly to CTS, Britten giving the assurance that 'we should be very sorry to appropriate anything which was intended for the Apostleship'. Whatever the truth here, harmony between the two agencies was maintained. A discussion about differences is not the same as a discussion about tensions.

Britten's letter went on to consider the subject of literature. Both CTS and AoP were involved in the business of publishing, an area in which contention might have arisen. A second topic was the question of instruction. It was related to the first, money, as publishing instructional material required capital, and to the third, the suitability of the AoP to the maritime life, as Christian support to the sailor was largely delivered through the printed word. The CTS had assumed responsibility for, and financed entirely, the publication of the sailors' prayer book, *Guide to Heaven*. Its adoption by the RN had ameliorated considerably the book's financial implications. But a new question had arisen. Regular letters of Christian instruction for seamen, begun in 1896 at the suggestion of a warrant officer, were published quarterly (by 1901 seventeen were available, indicating gaps in publication) under the title *Letters of Christian Doctrine*, and circulated to 6,000 Catholic seamen. Additionally an article from the 1897 *MSH* was reproduced as a very small leaflet, *How to Help Dying Seamen*, containing a letter from Bishop Grant to

17. The Work for Catholic Bluejackets

Henry Schomberg Kerr 'then a young naval officer' (later a priest SJ), which included simple prayers and guidance. When *Stella Maris* was introduced for sailors as a monthly magazine in 1901 the *Letters* were included in that, continuing after it had become a magazine intended for families. They were the product of various Jesuit pens. Britten wrote:

> If you think it would be better that the Apostleship should undertake the printing and all responsibility for the letter, my own feeling would be strongly in favour of its doing so. I cannot help being afraid that complications may arise in the future which may interfere with our joint work, and it is desirable if possible to forestall so undesirable a contingency.

The *Letters on Christian Doctrine* will be returned to in connection with the 1901 *Stella Maris*. Their significance in the context of the history of the maritime apostolate is apparent if it is recalled that G. C. Smith and Agnes Weston had begun their work for sailors through naval correspondence. Additionally, in 1898 the AoP published a small hymn book for seamen.

The considerable number of parcels and leaflets despatched, particularly channelled through Catholic officers on board ship, brought to the AoP secretaries a wide knowledge about Catholics in the RN. In 1897 a *List of Roman Catholic Officers on the Active List of the RN, RM, and RNR* was produced for circulation, updated from time to time, and eventually handed by Miss Scott Murray to the young Peter Anson as his first assignment in 1917. The production of such lists was not uncommon. They prevented a man's religion from being a private matter.

The entire work of the AoP was undergirt with prayer. A Mass was said monthly for supporters, and another for sailors, at the altar of the 'Sacred Heart Pleading' at the Sacred Heart church, Wimbledon. AoP members were encouraged to offer masses, prayers and other acts of devotion for sailor-work, and many convents and religious orders had agreed to add their prayers. Thus very large numbers of people were being made aware in a very particular way of the needs of Catholic seamen, a route followed by Peter Anson, on assuming the Secretaryship of the AoS in 1920, in seeking the prayers of convents and religious orders.

It is appropriate at this point to recall the still considerable overlap between the various English Catholic organisations for seafarers. The *MSH* regularly drew attention to the work of the CTS. The AoP had taken over from the CTS in 1896 the dispatch of literature to coastguards, in 1897, beginning a correspondence with a Fr Cullen who wanted to extend the work of the WCB to Wexford and the Irish coastguard. The *MSH* gave publicity to an attempt to form a literature distribution committee in Liverpool. Co-operation most evident in the various attempts to start a sailors' home in Glasgow where the CTS, AoP and SVP worked in conjunction. Before the latter can be considered it is necessary to examine the development of the Sailors' Branch of the AoP: the Apostleship of the Sea (AoS).

The third topic in the letters received by the *MSH* concerned the suitability of the AoP to life at sea, and led to the emergence of the AoS. Many letters to the *MSH* from bluejackets were written either collectively or on behalf of a group, for example, the letter which said, 'We have [on board] a St Vincent de Paul Society - not a real one, but slightly on those lines'. Sailors joining the AoP as members promoted its work on board. Numbers involved in membership, seldom declared, were never large; in 1899 there were 157 members on ships in commission, and fifty coastguards (including families). Members were committed to 1) the daily offering of prayers, good works and suffering; 2) the daily recitation of the Rosary for the Pope's monthly intention; 3) the reception of Holy Communion.

In 1893 a sailor on *HMS Dreadnought* wrote to the *MSH*:

> I am sorry I have not got any names for you (for the Apostleship). The men say they don't think they could manage to keep up the forms. Hoping you will not be angry with any of us for not sending our names, as I have to say we all try to be as good as we can . . . .

Fr Dignam gave the matter his attention. Although men had joined the AoP, and it is implicit that prayer groups existed on some ships, there was a resistance to the AoP Rule. The difficulties, nowhere spelt out, are suggested in the alterations which Dignam began to outline in a version of the AoP for seamen, to be called the Apostleship of the Sea. He died on 26 September 1894, before this could be given effect, leaving his successor, Fr Gretton, to launch the AoS on 23 April 1895 (Fig. 11). AoP conditions of membership were simplified. Members were required to be enrolled by a Promoter, to make the Morning offering ('At the beginning of every day to offer to the Sacred Heart of Jesus, for all its Intentions, the Prayers, Actions, and Sufferings of that day . . .'), and say some short morning prayer; to exceed this minimum when possible, to avoid alcohol, and to encourage each other in their Christian duty. Following enrolment a white badge of the Sacred Heart was sewn into the shirt. Within a year some 225 men had been admitted to the AoS.

The emphasis on simple prayers and acts of self-denial originates in the Rule of the AoP. This had been founded in France in 1844 by a French Jesuit. Thus the prayer-side of the AoS was a product of the French piety which had already produced in the eighteenth century a revival of the guild system for the purposes of devotion. This makes its other feature, that it had to be *joined*, of particular significance. Other religious groupings for sailors, almost entirely non-Catholic, were either temperance bodies (from which the attitude of the AoS to alcoholic drink is drawn) or religious fellowships associated with the major missionary societies, pietistic all except for Fr Hopkins's SFSSP, which had its roots in the labour movement and the medieval guilds. The AoS shared with the SFSSP an understanding that members enjoyed a co-operative relationship. Where the MtS and the BFSS did things *for* seafarers, the AoS (and the SFSSP) *was* its seafaring members. At this stage the difference is not very important, nor is its mild divergence from the AoP Rule. Its importance was psychological and lay in its name, to be assumed in 1920 as the umbrella for the world-wide apostolate, which was thus originally intended, not to be one which did things for seafarers, but rather to consist in its seafaring members; an

17. The Work for Catholic Bluejackets

approach which in the later 1920s began to disappear as the AoS ministry was increasingly to be found in buildings and chaplains for the seafarer.

Having established how the AoS was created, it remains to be seen how its membership was translated from being British and Naval to one drawn from the merchant fleets of the world. The point of transition was Glasgow, where the AoP was administered by the Jesuits of St Aloysius' Church, Garnethill. Fr Joseph Egger SJ, a priest there from 1892, had as one of his responsibilities the AoP. Contemporary reports add to those responsibilities the CTS and SVP. Newly arrived in Glasgow in 1895 from Ireland, aged eighteen, was a future Jesuit lay brother, Daniel Shields, employed as a tram driver before forced by illness into the Western Infirmary for three months, an experience which turned his thoughts to religion. In 1898 he joined the Catholic Young Men's Society (CYMS) a popular Catholic youth grouping of its time, meeting Fr Egger at St Aloysius. Although both were to feature largely in the Glasgow sea apostolate, they were not the first to be associated with it, and their names appear but seldom at this stage.

As early as March 1895 the *Glasgow Observer* carried an article, 'Home for Catholic Seamen, Glasgow', reporting that:

> A movement which was set on foot some time ago to provide Glasgow with a place of resort for Catholic seamen . . . such as in existence in London, or other maritime centres of England, is rapidly reaching accomplishment. His Grace the Archbishop of Glasgow . . . encouraged the promoters in the kindest way . . . premises are about to be rented . . . at the corner of Carrick Street and Broomielaw . . . a house containing a suite of rooms . . . to transform into a club for Catholic seamen . . . £200 is necessary, and of this sufficient has been received to warrant renting . . . and a partial refurnishing . . . gifts, furniture . . . to the Secretary, Mr St John Tully, 257 Renfrew Street . . . .

The date and reference to London indicate that this attempt drew its inspiration from Fr Goldie and the London CTS committee. There is no mention of Fr Egger; rather, the prominent name is that of St John Tully, described as an active SVP member, but Secretary also of the Seamen's Branch of the London CTS (not to be confused with its national secretary, Mrs Fraser). The CTS interest is confirmed by the speech of Lt Bateman (a Glasgow Committee member) to the annual CTS Scottish Conference on 'Work Among Catholic Seamen', a speech mainly devoted to RN work and AoP literature distribution, but hoping 'they would soon have a depot by the Broomielaw . . .'; in other words, modelled on distribution of literature in the London docks. Tully seconded the vote of thanks. Concerts were held to raise funds for the projected seamen's club, their intervals providing opportunities to publicise the aims, the Catholics of Glasgow spurred on by references to the homes in London and Liverpool. It is not known how long Tully remained in Glasgow.

The Glasgow club proposed in 1895, said in March 1897 to be 'proceeding apace', was ambitiously referred to as a Catholic Sailors' Home (CSH), a grand title masking plans to obtain a flat in York Street. The SVP Central Council added its weight to the venture. Then, in January 1898, a letter appeared in the *Glasgow Observer* from Mrs Kate (Katherine) Howden, headed, 'Spiritual Destitution of the Catholic Seaman'. It revealed her familiarity with the work of the GoR in London's Docks, describing its campaign of literature distribution, and mentioned that there was already in Glasgow a committee of ladies concerned to collect literature, only lacking the males deemed necessary for its distribution. Addresses for literature or offers to distribute it were appended. Her letter was concerned specifically with merchant seafarers. While no mention of affiliation to any group was made, a surviving copy of a contemporary leaflet describing the AoS listed as its Promoters an SVP member from Manchester; Mr White of the London Sailors' Home; and Mrs Howden as one of four at Glasgow, under the care of Fr Egger. The implication here is that Glasgow was the primary, though not the only, port where AoS enrolment was available to members of the MN.

In May 1898 the *Glasgow Observer* published another letter, also headed 'Spiritual Destitution of the Catholic Seaman'. This letter mentioned the Apostleship of the Sea. It described the inability of seamen to go to church and the necessity of obtaining for them a 'place of meeting'. The anonymous writer is identified only as a Promoter of the AoS, the letter giving Mrs Howden and another lady as contact points. The two letters combined to circumvent the hiatus in the campaign for a CSH. Mrs Howden as the daughter of one and the widow of another Master Mariner was probably well known in the maritime community. The anonymity of the second letter leaves a question mark over her authorship. Anson always refers to Egger, Shields and Howden as key figures at this time, though Shields had yet to be a Promoter. Egger and Shields met initially through the youth work of St Aloysius, their ship visiting beginning only in July of the following year, using a group referred to either as 'Working Boys' or 'Boy Associates' which seems to have replaced the parish branch of the Catholic Young Men's Society (CYMS) in 1898 or 1899. Shields himself coupled the name of Mrs Howden with that of the Boy Associates as the founders of the work for Catholic sailors in the port.

Attempts to start a CSH were such that the *Glasgow Observer* reported in April 1899, with unusual caution, 'the first steps in connection with the beginning of what may ultimately develop into a Catholic Home for Sailors'. Readers were reminded that the matter had been before a committee of CTS 'and others' for 'almost seven years', with nothing done owing to the 'difficulty of obtaining suitable premises'. Now, rooms had been taken on the south side of the river at 33 Plantation Street from early August, with a formal opening in September. The same article coupled an appeal for literature with one for donations, implying that the AoS and CSH committees overlapped. Donations for the CSH were to be received by the priest at St John's, Portugal Street.

The overlap is further illustrated by the Boy Associates. Their recruitment is nowhere explicitly explained but they had begun to distribute literature to the ships and to what is described as the Protestant Home (probably a secular one if Catholic visitors were welcome) by July 1899. They met on Friday evenings, using the weekend to visit ships, when they would direct men to church and advise on service times, and if possible enroll them in the AoS.

17. The Work for Catholic Bluejackets

They also directed men to what was now called the Catholic Sailors' Institute (CSI). The *Glasgow Observer* carried a regular paragraph giving the number of ships visited, parcels of literature distributed, and AoS members enrolled, invariably in the name of the Working Boys, the work of ship-visitation apparently theirs alone. Fr Egger is sometimes mentioned as attending their meetings. They made a monthly corporate communion at St Aloysius.

The CSI finally developed from premises taken in May 1899 by SVP members. It had three objects: to allow the committee to look after Catholic seamen, widows and families, provide a centre, and supply Catholic literature - this latter in conjunction with the Working Boys. The Archbishop of Glasgow agreed to be its patron and gave a donation of ten pounds. Glasgow now had two strands: the CSI, and the Boys' ship-visiting on behalf of the AoS.

Mrs Howden's name remained as a collector of literature, her house used as a repository and to store the AoS Sacred Heart badges. From there parcels of books were sent abroad, especially to Genoa, Italian books being received in exchange. Other links were made with London, New York and elsewhere. *Glasgow Observer* paragraphs show that the numbers of people associated with her fluctuated. The ship-visiting increasingly depended upon one or two regular and dependable Promoters. They distributed enormous amounts of literature and enrolled many sailors in the AoS. It was on their initiative that AoS forms were translated into languages other than English. No evidence remains to suggest that any other Catholic port was recruiting for the AoS at this time.

It is difficult to calculate the AoS achievement in Glasgow, for the *Glasgow Observer* sometimes had weeks when the AoS paragraph was missing, or where published figures were an aggregate of several weeks, rendering totals incomplete and unclear. Nevertheless, some assessment is possible. The most detailed figures survive for the year 1900, a year atypical because for a number of weeks the Boy Associates of Pollokshaws were assisting those of St Aloysius in ship-visiting. Their involvement from January 1900, with eighty keen members, lasted until the summer, in which time they distributed thirty-eight parcels of literature on thirty-eight ships. These figures are included in the year's total of 538 ships visited, 620 parcels of literature given (including to the unidentified sailors' home), and 232 AoS members recruited. It is necessary to remember that ship-visiting was the leisure activity of young working men; also, that most ships would be alongside for quite long periods, their crews having more leisure at weekends. In the early 1900s visitation and literature were extended to troops stationed nearby. Anson's obituary of Shields claimed a total of more than 20,000 AoS enrolments. If the annual figure for enrolments is rounded up to 250 as a plausible average, and multiplied by eleven (the number of years of enrolment pre-Anson), and then generously doubled to account for enrolments in Anson's four years as AoS Secretary, it only accounts for roughly 25% of Anson's estimate of 20,000 as Shields's number of enrolments in the AoS, suggesting that Anson was the victim of a nought too many.

Who were the Working Boys? The groups working among seamen in earlier chapters were drawn largely from the middle or upper classes, people with leisure, and the drawing rooms in which to spend it. The people involved as ship visitors in Glasgow, and to a lesser degree in London, offer a contrast, being drawn from the sort of nineteenth-century Catholics who lived or worked in the dock area, their leisure confined to weekends. Industrialization and increasing urbanization combined to introduce a change in attitude to leisure. Leisure, defined as 'time at one's disposal', was a relatively new concept. In earlier times the distinction had been between exertion and repose, the idea of a holiday having little meaning for most people, for whom the seasons marked the passage of the year and dictated the amount and type of labour. The arrival of the factory, with its set hours and monitory clock, brought a distinction between work and leisure to the many, and an accompanying concern for the proper use of that leisure, reflected in the rise of Young Men's Institutes, particularly from the 1880s onwards.

The Working Boys in Glasgow were part of this movement. Shields's recruitment to sailor-work followed his involvement in this new group at St Aloysius. It seems not to have displaced the CYMS in every parish, for the CYMS was important enough in Glasgow in the 1920s for Anson to seek its support for the revived AoS, but at Garnethill the Working Boys apparently did displace the CYMS. *Glasgow Observer* references suggest the movement was not widespread, perhaps confined to the industrial parishes of Glasgow. The Pollokshaws members were rather younger than the ones at St Aloysius. Activities included football: Glasgow's famous football teams grew from religious groups like these. Both CYMS and Working Boys were aimed at young men ('teenagers' had yet to be discovered), the latter involved in classes of work like Shields's tram driving.

The relationship of the Boys to the CSI is an example of how the AoS might relate to the CTS and SVP. The SVP usually acknowledged the efforts of the Boys but sometimes claimed the literature distribution and ship-visiting as its own. The problems which flowed from this did so after 1900 and will be considered in chapter nineteen. At this point a distinction can be drawn between two kinds of ministry: the static ministry of the CSI and the peripatetic one of the ship-visitors. The CSI had its measure of misfortune. It disappears suddenly from the SVP *Report* of 1903. Its first superintendent, John McNichol, had died suddenly. His successor, Captain Burke, moved after three months, being succeeded by a Magnus Boyle. New managers rubbing against established Associates may have contributed to the looming *débâcle* .

It is now possible to begin to summarise the achievements of the AoP's interest in seamen which had sprung from that 1890 letter of Lord Archibald Douglas, which referred to a recently formed group of priests and laymen. It had taken three forms. There had been a fruitful association with the CTS, and the AoP members on the CTS Seamen's Sub Committee. Second, the WCB, a result of the letter's publication in the *MSH*, continued as a separate literature-sending agency, which Miss Scott Murray was still organising at the end of the 1914- – 18 war and maintaining the *List* of

17. The Work for Catholic Bluejackets

Catholic officers in the RN, though by the end of 1901 AoP production of other literature for the seaman had effectively ceased. However, its third and most important contribution to the sea apostolate had happened almost by accident, for by 1900 local effort in Glasgow had transmuted the AoS from a pious association of RN personnel into a mercantile-dominated religious grouping which, in turn, would have consequences for the post-war revival of the Catholic sea apostolate. Part of the transmutation involved reaching men who were not, nor would aspire to be, officers, a process extended by the fortuitous association by Mrs Howden and Fr Egger of Shields and the Working Boys with the AoS.

The involvement of the Working Boys with the CSI would have its effect upon Shields's personal story too. Anson, in his various accounts of this period, gives to Shields a dominant role, whereas the surviving facts leave a slightly different, if hard to verify, impression, that in the background it was Mrs Howden who was supplying the motivation; that one of those to whom she applied pressure was Fr Egger; and that Egger recruited and encouraged Shields for the ship-work whilst Mrs Howden provided the logistical support. It was her letter, not one from Fr Egger, which originally called for ship-visitation in Glasgow. She did this, not in imitation of the Protestant sea apostolate, but from her knowledge of the CTS and GoR ministry in London.

18. The *Œuvres de Mer*

French Work in the Fisheries from 1894[1]

Chapter sixteen linked Fr Goldie with the establishment in France of the *Œuvres de Mer* (ŒdeM), an organisation which would greatly impress Peter Anson. Whereas the AoS, like the major non-Catholic missionary societies, has traditionally not distinguished between fishers and other mariners, the ŒdeM followed the undenominational protestant MDSF as a mission dedicated to fishers, effectively the sea apostolate in microcosm, serving an industry with a clear spatial and temporal definition. The spatial came from the fishing grounds, the temporal (some thirty years) from the technology which determined the rise and fall of the fleeting system.

This chapter will follow the history of the ŒdeM from its foundation to its becoming a constituent of the revived AoS. Its distinctive structure, a secular organisation alongside a chaplaincy, provided by the Augustinians of the Assumption (AA) derives from the unusual contemporary French political situation. Anson, misunderstanding or overlooking this, pointed to the document *Jam Inde*, issued by Rome to regulate the ŒdeM, and claiming it gave the AA responsibility for the world-wide Catholic sea apostolate. Its implications for ecclesiastical authority will be discussed. The AA derived a vertically structured system of line management, unequalled elsewhere in the Catholic sea apostolate, from *Jam Inde,* devising a highly effective chaplaincy system to serve the thousands of French fishers. The ŒdeM's foundation, and the role of the AA, was dictated further by the spiritual needs of the French fishery, and shaped by developments in contemporary medicine. It is no accident that medical missions to fishers should appear within a decade of each other in several countries. The chapter will conclude by considering whether the ŒdeM owed its foundation to Fr Goldie or to others. This will be helpful in explaining the role of the ŒdeM when revisiting it in chapter twenty-one in the context of the formation of the *Apostolatus Maris International Concilium* (AMIC).

Grosjean's *Études* article of February 1894 suggested what little was being done in France by way of a maritime apostolate was both scattered and sporadic. In a subsequent article, he recalled the *initiative Chrétienne française* of the admirals Mathieu and Gicquel des Touches. The latter had opened an early *maison de famille* for seamen in Havre in 1884, the *Hôtel Saint-Martin*, which had had predecessors from as early as 1868 in Marseilles, Nantes and Toulon,

---

1 Full references are given in chapter 7 of Miller, *Ship of Peter*.

all ephemeral and all founded to combat a *problème social*.¹ All three were in French naval ports, their foundation perhaps a response to the religious revival in the French navy. The religious nature of these attempts is at best ambiguous for in the French political climate a work might fare better if perceived as social rather than religious. Grosjean also mentioned a local priest's attempt to serve fishers at Croisie, involving a trade association, with similar work at Brest and Saint-Servan. In 1894, perhaps prompted by the *Études* article, a library for Newfoundland fishermen was started at Concale, and in Marseilles in April a *hôtel de marins* was opened where *l'Œuvre du Fourneau de famille* made a room available. These ventures appear to be the only formal provision for seafarers at this time by members of the French Church though other limited efforts attempted informally on a local basis cannot be excluded.

The ambiguous nature of French Church involvement in social work resulted from the French political situation, which certainly dictated the relationship between the ŒdeM and the AA. The position of the French Church was a peculiar one. Many in the Third Republic associated the Church with conservatism, often with the possibility of a royalist revival, making the State wary. Church/State relations were governed by the *Concordat* of 1801 between Napoleon and Pope Pius VII, which later governments sought to define and control. The State attacked the Church through education: a series of education bills promoted by government minister *M*. Ferry required religious orders involved in teaching to be recognised by the State. Ferry admitted that this was a battle between lay government and theocracy, the extreme nature of his terms reflecting the tension of the period. The Jesuits were the first Order in his sights. Initially, religious superiors showed solidarity with them by refusing to register for State recognition, but papal pressure in the interest of compromise led them to register, lest in a Church-State confrontation the Church lost its State subsidy. The Jesuits could not be saved; their Paris noviciate was moved to England where the novice Grosjean met Fr Goldie. Despite the Pope's instruction to Orders to make a declaration of loyalty to the Republic, negotiations collapsed, and 262 men's religious houses were closed, involving between five and six thousand men, many of whom left France. No action was taken against female religious at this time. The new legislation caused some two hundred law officers to resign in protest. To avoid confiscation or closure the affairs of many congregations were placed in the hands of Catholic laymen, hence the foundation of the ŒdeM.

Orders unwilling to accept the State's action, especially the newer ones, mostly, like the AA, ultramontanists (those who looked 'over the mountains' to Rome), favoured a policy of *Ralliement*. Older Orders had learnt to trim their sails to the prevailing wind, but not these 'noisy and foolish priests of the Order of Assumptionists'.² In 1886 the AA lost all its schools. Its particular

---

1 Anon, Sailors' Homes and Refuges, *English Bulletin* XLVI(3) (published by SVP), dates work in Havre from 1867 and gives details of foundations with State support in Dunkerque (1895), Bordeaux (1896), Nantes, Marseilles (1897), La Rochelle, Rochefort, Havre (1898), all with 'the omission of religious influence'.
2 D. W. Brogan, *The Development of Modern France*, 358.

enemies, if not the only ones, in the government were Ferry, Combes and Waldeck-Rousseau. The Church was faced with the State annually reducing the Public Worship Budget, leading to a final separation in 1905. The AA was suppressed on French territory as part of a supposed royalist movement.

The AA made an ideal target. Added to its ultramontanism, which may be guessed from its date of foundation, and its object to 'fight the Church's enemies under the revolutionary flag . . . ', there was its influence derived from its newspapers, *La Croix* and *Le Pelerin*, their circulation of some three million large for the period. Publishing had been one of the AA's objects at the time of its foundation. Assumptionist newspapers supported the right-wing of the French Church in the *Affaire Dreyfus*, where the AA view seems to have been that those who were anti-semitic might in short time become pro-Catholic. Mixed up in the feelings engendered by the Dreyfus case was the perceived role of major, mostly Jewish, financiers in the financial collapse of the de Lesseps' Panama Canal venture of the late 1880s and early 1890s. In a country which had so recently undergone violent revolution, the presence of strong feeling and polarised opinion is no cause for wonder. Some were fighting hard for the revolution, others for the Church; the century producing in government Ferry and Combes, and in the Church Catholics like Ozanam, founder of the Society of St Vincent de Paul (SVP), and d'Alzon, his friend and AA founder.

Although the British merchant fleet far outstripped the French in size, the latter had kept an importance, alongside its navy, in maintaining links with the French colonies, though in maritime terms its most significant aspect lay in its fishing fleet which, overall, was second to that of the UK. It is not easy to find a satisfactory and contemporary table of countries ranked either by tonnage of fish caught, size of fleet, or number of men, and usually it was men, but one source noted that of 90,000 French sailors, 65,000 were fishermen, and that in 1866, 448 ships crewed by ten or twelve thousand men were involved in the Atlantic cod fishery. Suffice it to say that the French cod fishery was extremely large, its nature easier to describe than its statistics.

The harsh conditions and technological developments of the French cod fishery are well-documented. The majority of those involved came from the traditionally Catholic areas of France such as Normandy and Brittany, fishing for cod mainly off Iceland and the Newfoundland Banks, away from home for many months of the year, particularly the summer months: the fishing season started around March and closed in September, depending upon the ice. From the continual fogs and storms of the fishing season the men returned to winter in France. Those fishing off Iceland were drawn mainly from around Dunkirk, Gravelines and Pampol; those off Newfoundland from Fécamp, Granville, St Malo and Concale. A few stayed as residents at St Pierre et Miquelon. The bonds uniting them lay in their religion, places of origin, and the profit-sharing system, things which the medieval seafarer would have found familiar. As in the North Sea, so in the Newfoundland and Icelandic fisheries, the harsh weather, hard work and isolation often led to dependence upon alcohol, in turn contributing to injury and mortality rates.

Fishing involved schooners using nets, but line fishing was also practised.

18. The Œuvres de Mer

The lines, perhaps with a thousand hooks, would be served by a couple of men in a small boat, or dory, who might drift and get lost in the fog, never to return. There were many *graviers*, inshore fishermen. As to numbers, in 1895 the AA-chartered *Massilia* had returned to France at the end of the season with 950 on board; in 1897, the *Notre-Dame De Salut* carried between 1,200 and 1,500 men to Newfoundland.[1] Along the French Shore, where the British had ceded the French certain rights, fishermen were accommodated on land, in barracks, or *chaffauds*, simple wooden huts brought from France by the men using them; men who would venture out daily, returning at night to a monotonous diet in an isolated spot where the sole occupation was the necessary salting down of the cod.

Many aspects of the fishing industry had survived the passage of centuries little changed. The *Encyclopedia Britannica* described the Grand Banks schooners as the 'peak of development', their rigging requiring fewer crew than a square-rigged vessel. The end of the nineteenth century witnessed the increasing use of steam power in many areas, like the North Sea, in these isolated waters dependence upon the wind remained in the absence of a cheap and reliable source of coal. Because of the limited area in which at any time fish were to be caught, and for reasons of safety, fishing vessels tended to gather in fleets, returning to harbour when holds were full of fish or fresh water needed. The North Sea fleeting system, where British sailing vessels caught their fish and packed them in cases of ice to be rowed to the mother ship, a steamer unaffected by the vagaries of the wind, and sped to the home port where the fish would be unloaded and sold, usually to be freighted by the rapidly expanding rail network to provide urban markets with the freshest fish possible, pertained neither to men fishing off Newfoundland nor Iceland; by the time the economies of improved steam power became feasible for these French fleets, the 1914 – 18 war had intervened, and things would be very different. The peak period for this French fishery was much as that for the British, roughly between 1885 and 1910, but for the French the ancient technology of sail continued, accompanied by the equally ancient drying or sometimes salting of cod. Photographs remain of acres of cod gutted and left to dry in the cold winds when, as stockfish, it would keep for years, a product light and easily transportable.[2] Much of the cod waste would feature in the universal soup of the evening, a stew simply prepared, capable of being cooked by anyone, but always having the advantage of being warm.

This was the context to which Grosjean's *Études* article of February 1894 brought news of British work among seamen and fishermen, dwelling upon Charles Hopkins and the OSP's work among seamen and the MDSF's with North Sea fishermen. By 1892 the MDSF had sent a staff member, Wilfred Grenfell, who had pioneered medical work in the North Sea, to Labrador to see if it might be extended to that lonely part of the world. His enthusiasm

---

1 AA ship-ownership and chartering came about through their organisation of pilgrimages.
2 Ronald Rompkey, *Terre-Neuve: Anthologie des vayageurs français, 1814-1914*, has early photographs of cod stretched out to dry.

for the modern, scientific form of medicine, represented by such giants as Pasteur and Lister, the early anaesthetics, and the almost evangelical zeal of the doctors trained in this new medicine, suggests that the stage through which medicine was passing may have had as much to do with the development of this ministry to fishermen, as the technological and economic developments which so happily coincided with a rising missionary fervour in the churches, and a spirit of philanthropy among men of good will; a concatenation which explains satisfactorily why this should be the time when fishermen should begin to benefit from the efforts of medical missions.

The present chapter opened by indicating sporadic French attempts to serve its seamen. The French Church had already shown a concern for fishermen, at least in Iceland where two names survive: the *abbé* Bernard, who ministered there from 1857 to 1862, and the *abbé* Jean-Baptiste Baudoin from 1858 to 1874. The liberalization which permitted Catholic worship in Iceland from 1874 was thought by Dalbard to be due in no small part to Baudoin's ministry.[1] The French navy had maintained an Iceland station for fishery protection which had offered very limited medical aid, and where naval officers had seen conditions at first hand.

Grosjean wrote his article in late 1893 for the French public to see in February 1894. The principal founder of the ŒdeM, *M*. Bernard Bailly, almost certainly, as editor of *Cosmos*, part of the French maritime and literary world, would have seen Grosjean's article before publication, but he may already have been aware of the work of the MDSF in 1893, if not through Grosjean then from his own experience as one who had visited England, for a 1925 article using a contemporary source revealed that Bailly had, in September 1893, an idea for the benefit of fishers in Iceland and Newfoundland.[2] If Bailly was one of those influential people Mrs Fraser reported Fr Goldie as contacting in France then his thoughts on a ministry to French fishers may have been fired as early as 1892. That Grosjean was the link between Goldie and Bailly is not certain. Whatever the situation, it took the whole of 1894 for Bailly's vision to be sufficiently shared to bring about the formation of the ŒdeM; in the process Grosjean's article, with its emphasis on the work of the MDSF, was reprinted as a tract, *Ét nos marins?* The link between the two will be considered further.

The influence of the MDSF is important. Bailly's name is coupled as ŒdeM's founder with that of Dr Bonnafy. Bonnafy, little mentioned, had served on the Newfoundland station and, according to Dalbard, had studied *les réalisations anglaises*, which may be understood as the MDSF. Bailly probably needed his expert advice, though their connection may equally have been naval friendship, as both had been in the French navy. Dalbard noted that Bailly had made several trips to England and familiarised himself with the *fonctionnement des Missions* . . . If Dalbard is correct, then both men were familiar with the work of the MDSF before the Grosjean article. Two other sources, from 1895 and 1899, link the founding of the ŒdeM, in the one instance specifically with the MDSF, and the other, less specifically but in a clear reference to the MDSF,

---

1   J Dalbard, *La Societé des Œuvres de Mer de 1894 à 1939.*
2   *Lettre à la Dispersion,* No 129, 7 March 1925, 421.

18. The Œuvres de Mer

with *Les Protestants anglaises [qui] construit les bateaux-missions* . . .[1] There is, however, a difference between knowing about something and realising that in that knowledge lies the answer to a particular problem. It would be quite in accord with the facts to credit Bailly and Bonnafy with prior knowledge of the MDSF and their inspiration to Grosjean's prompting. This will become clearer as Bailly's role is considered.

Two things from this period may indicate a wider French concern to do something for seamen. In 1893, inspired by the seventeenth-century Confraternity of the Blessed Sacrament for sea captains, pilots and mates in Le Havre,[2] the *abbé* Théodore Garnier and his Confraternity of *Notre Dame de la Mer* opened *foyers* (clubs) at various points along the coast which seem not to have out-lived their founder. About the same time the AA launched a modest journal *Croix des Marins*. The AA had a number of specialized publications: one for the pilgrimage business; another, *Cosmos*, a weekly naval journal. *Croix des Marins* was dedicated to Our Lady, Star of the Sea, and first published probably in April, certainly in 1894. It was offered specifically for those who worked at sea or on the rivers, their families and their friends. Its conception must coincide with the Études article and the gestation period of the ŒdeM. By September 1895 it claimed a circulation of seven thousand. If it was seen as an interim measure pending the launch of the ŒdeM, it would suggest that the first meeting of the ŒdeM in December 1894 was a culmination rather than a point of departure.

Bernard Bailly and the AA were closely linked. His father had been a devout Catholic, associated like d'Alzon in the early part of the century with Ozanam, founder of the SVP. *M.* Bernard, the middle of three brothers, at first a naval officer, resigned his commission to look after the family estate, as both of his brothers were professed members of the AA. The elder, *Père* Vincent de Paul, founder and director of *La Bonne Presse*, appointed Bernard editor of *Cosmos* in 1885. *Père* Vincent would have been aware of his chosen name-saint's ministry to the French galleys (chapter six). The younger brother, *Père* Emmanuel, became the AA's third Superior. A sister became Superior of the Dames of St Clothilde.

In 1893 the AA had purchased the British *Dunrobin Castle* to ease transport difficulties encountered in connection with the Jerusalem eucharistic conference. *M.* Bernard, present on 24 September 1893 when members of the AA were considering a name for the ship, one reflecting religious ownership, suggested that it should be one that would not need changing in the future, one of a series with their smaller vessels, so that *vos missions de mer* might compliment the Assumptionist missions on the land. He indicated Iceland and Newfoundland, claiming 16,000 fishers went there annually, as being in need of religious aid, and subject to the attentions of *les Protestants*, and called upon the AA to bridge the gap. His words received general approval. Their being spoken four months *before* the publication of the Études article suggests his prior knowledge of Grosjean's work.

1 References are given in Miller, *Ship of Peter*, note 26, chapter 7.
2 Alain Cabantous, *Religion et monde maritime au Havre* . . ., in *Annales de Normande*.

The idea sown by *M.* Bernard took hold of the group during 1894, leading to a meeting on the 3rd December of several admirals, various dignitaries, the editors of *Croix* and other AA papers, some twenty people, in the office of the AA Superior, *Père* Picard, which agreed that an urgent need existed and should be tackled. The next day a central council was formed under the presidency of Vice Admiral Lafont, with *MM* Augustin Normand and Le Maréchal as vice presidents, together with *MM* Raoul Ancel, the *abbé* Belin, de la Bigne, de Cuverville, Fournier, Admiral Lauge, Admiral Mathieu, *Père* Picard, and Commandant Riondel. *M.* Bernard Bailly, as secretary, had his office at the *Maison de la Bonne Presse*, 5 Rue Bayard, Paris, an AA address.

The council initially circulated all who might be interested with the intention of raising the money necessary to buy and support a hospital ship, which would be sent to the fishermen off Iceland and Newfoundland, to bring spiritual, moral and physical aid. A generous response allowed a ship, the *Saint-Pierre*, to be ordered for the 1896 season. In the meantime, 1895 was to be used for the establishment of a land-based ministry; *Pere* Yves Hamon and the *abbé* Belin (parish priest of the fishing port of Saint-Servan) were sent to St Pierre and Miquelon to investigate the potential. This speedy response may reflect the freedom enjoyed by religious Orders in the deployment of personnel, while Belin's availability may indicate the reduction in parish work at Saint-Servan during the fishing season.

The pair left St Malo, each on a steamer, accompanying 2,500 fishermen bound for St Pierre. Their peculiar canonical position (a seasonal chaplaincy in another diocese to men drawn from yet other dioceses, where one chaplain was a regular priest, the other a secular) had required special permissions from Rome. At St Pierre, to establish their mission, they rented with the approval of Mgr Tiberi, the apostolic prefect, a former boarding school from the Sisters of St Joseph of Cluny. The reason for careful mention of permissions and religious Orders will become apparent. Here they set up a shelter (*abri des marins*) for the fishermen. The term *abri* seems to denote a club with the implication that it lacked chapel and accommodation. The building was referred to as a *maison de famille*, which became the usual designation after the ŒdeM bought the school and, from 1898, began its development.

The *maison* provided fishermen with a welcome alternative to the local, mostly alcohol-related, attractions. Over the next quarter century the battle against strong drink, waged with cider, cordials, cocoa, and eucalyptus tea, reduced the number of suppliers from thirty-six to five, the resulting loss of income perhaps causing the bad feeling towards the ŒdeM among local people, a story paralleled in the annals of most contemporary seafarers' agencies. The *maison* served fishermen based ashore (*graviers*); those ashore whilst their vessels were unloading, replenishing supplies or undertaking repairs; and the many convalescent. By its second year the *maison* was receiving 28,000 visits, an average of 122 men per day throughout the season, a figure which would rise to 122,000 visits. Eventually, it was able to offer a thirty-bed dormitory for convalescents, the ship-wrecked, or others obliged to be ashore; a chapel with a movable partition between it and the main hall; a library with lecture and writing rooms; a printing works producing the monthly newsletter *Terre-Neuva*; a room for billiards and quiet games; a large covered court with space for more active games and a gymnastic beam; a bar serving cider and cordials; and a shop. The description reveals the *maison* to be well within the pattern of homes and institutes of the period, if on the ambitious side.

As to the ministry of chaplains, considerable detail of *Père* Yve's work survives. Its sacramental emphasis sets it apart from all but the OSP in India, but in other respects differences from Anglican and protestant contemporaries are few. *Père* Yves spent his afternoons visiting, listening, comforting, encouraging, and reminding the men that the *maison* would be open (7 - 10 p.m.). The evenings would find him about the *maison*, often hearing confessions, perhaps helping men with their letters, or arranging some entertainment. The evening would close with an act of worship and a short address, if numbers merited with a magic lantern show, usually on the Catechism, much as, for example, Canon Hay was doing in Genoa. The magic lantern had the advantage of not requiring electricity.

Père Yves spent five years based at St Pierre, sometimes at sea on the hospital ship, sometimes visiting other isolated settlements, with the help of the navy if visiting French Shore. Second and third chaplains were as often Assumptionists as secular clergy. His assistant at St Pierre from 1896 was *Frère* Eugène whose twenty-six years of ministry would receive the award of the *Legion d'Honneur*. *Père* Yves opened another *maison* at Faskrudsfjord, Iceland, in 1901 on similar lines to that at St Pierre. It differed in having nearby a seasonal hospital, apparently opened in 1897 following a visit there by the *abbé* Pitte who had made several visits to Iceland to see his parishioners, and run by Sisters of St Joseph de Chambery, the first of a never realised series of land-based hospitals planned by the ŒdeM. Faskrudsfjord was also distinguished by a small French cemetery graced with what was described as a fine bronze Calvary.

In its early years, the primary emphasis of the ŒdeM was the ministry afloat, something shared with the early years of the MDSF. This was its principal attraction to the public, and the support committees, mostly hard-working ladies, who ran fêtes, concerts, flag days and similar ventures to fund the vessels. It was this, too, which attracted Press interest, the ships open to the French public before departure for the fishing season among the *braves marins*. And it was this rather than the chaplaincy which the French Government recognised as a Public Utility on 7 December 1898, allowing the ŒdeM to receive from the Government valuable subventions of money, either directly or indirectly, even at the height of the anti clericalist movement.

The first hospital ship, the *Saint-Pierre*, was a sailing vessel. Sail was chosen for reasons of economy and expediency, being cheap to build, cheaper to run, and requiring coal only for cooking or heating. It was ordered in 1895, launched on 16 March 1896, and blessed on April 6th. Described as a graceful three-masted schooner, it had a chapel complete with Reserved Sacrament, wards for the sick, and an operating room. It sailed on April 20th from St Malo for the Banks with the *abbé* Belin on board. On its first cruise it communicated with eleven fishing boats, distributed provisions and coal (for stoves), gave news, consultations, first aid, received ten men from a shipwreck, comforted and encouraged everyone, and returned on the 19th May to St Pierre to take on water. This pattern of activity was typical and the welcome nature of the link that it brought in the days before radio may be imagined; so too, in the face of the 'paper doctor'or medicine chest, would be its medical attentions.[1] The ship was received back in port by Mgr Tiberi, who came on board on the Sunday to say Mass.

When there were two clergy on station it became the custom to take *maison* and *bateau* by turn. *Père* Yves, chaplain on the second cruise of the *Saint-Pierre* on the Banks, was returning in thick fog and with a strong and unusual current after an eight day trip. A sharp jolt at 0100 awoke the crew who feared an iceberg. Instantly all hands were on deck, except *Père* Yves, who had gone below to consume the Host. Daylight revealed the vessel to be aground at the foot of a 150 metre cliff, Cap St Marie. Distress signals went unanswered. About to abandon ship, they were discovered by an American who demanded a large sum of money for their rescue, giving way, however, in face of the captain's gun. In due course all twenty-one men were landed safely at Placentia. By chance an English artist was on board, to paint scenes from the voyage, as he had done in the previous year on board a MDSF vessel, his written account of events published in an issue of the ŒdeM's *Lettre à la Dispersion*. The *Saint-Pierre* was a total loss.

In Paris *Père* Picard rallied *M*. Bailly, proposing the lost ship should be replaced, not with a single vessel, but with two. *Croix* opened an appeal which Picard headed with a donation of Fr 1,000. The new ships, *Saint-Pierre 2* and *Saint-Paul*, were ready for the 1897 season. The *Saint-Paul* became a total loss off Iceland in 1899 and was not replaced, the ŒdeM building instead, in 1900, on receipt of an anonymous gift of Fr 75,000, the *Saint-François D'Assise*, with sail and an auxiliary engine. It proved expensive to run and was altered in the following year, becoming from 1904 the sole vessel, its increased efficiency allowing it to do the work of two, until joined in 1911 by the *Notre-Dame De Le Mer*, which lasted eleven years; to this was added in 1914 the *Saint-Jehanne*. Both vessels spent the war in the service of the Ministry of Marine. At its end, only the *Saint-Jehanne* was worth patching and returning to its former duties, renamed *Ste Jeanne D'Arc* on that saint's canonisation, and surviving until 1933 (Fig. 13). Another ship, the *Saint-Yves*, served from 1935 until 1939 when changes in the industry and the outbreak of war led the ŒdeM, like the MDSF, to switch to a shore-based ministry.

How did the ŒdeM see the role of the hospital ship? A summary printed in 1925 by the AA naturally put the first purpose as bringing to the fishing fleets the encouragement and comfort of a priest; then, to aid men not seriously sick or injured with medicine, advice and dressings; to receive on board the seriously ill for treatment, delivering them to the colony for specialist attention; finally, to

1   The 'paper doctor': the numbered list of medicines to be given for a matching number on a list of ailments.

The *Œuvres de Mer* Hospital Ship. *Missions Benedictines*, 1923, 431.

transport the shipwrecked, the convalescent, and the crews of the dories which had drifted or got lost. The delivery and collection of mail and the general transmission of news served to encourage men far from home and family.

It might be supposed that such work would not attract criticism. The ŒdeM itself seems to have avoided the difficulties of the AA; the original purpose of having a secular group to run the venture. Its primary function was raising sufficient income to maintain ships and *maisons*. Even at times of extreme political difficulty the recognition of Public Utility ensured State assistance in some form, and the decoration of *Frère* Eugène by the State demonstrated that this approval continued. Strangely, the principal opposition came from some Church authorities, particularly at St Pierre, perhaps as a result of local pressure, and clearly aimed at the Assumptionists.

The problem of Church authority was to occupy the AA for some years, finally resolved by Rome issuing the Instruction *Jam Inde*. It was, moreover, a problem which Peter Anson had to consider twenty years later when reviving the AoS; his romantic understanding of the Instruction prompts consideration of *Jam Inde*. Initially the AA had applied to Rome for the necessary faculties (permissions) for chaplains at St Pierre to function as priests; necessary because they were going to minister in the administrative areas of others. Rome granted permission for the first season. At St Pierre, Mgr Tiberi, prefect apostolic and Rome's man on the spot, authorised the renting of the former boarding school. Tiberi was no stranger to the AA, having been its guest in Paris for some months over 1896 – 97. However, as early as April 1895 *Père* Yves wrote to *Père* Picard, a week after his arrival in St Pierre, that Mgr Tiberi was not being totally helpful, that *Il n'aime pas les religieux, c'est un fait*,[1] although three-quarters of the population in Tiberi's area of responsibility were served by the Holy Ghost Fathers. Matters seemed to come to a head with the opening of a new chapel at St Pierre as part of the *maison*. Its purpose was to serve the

---

1 'he does not like the religious, that is certain'.

fishermen who could not because of working hours, or would not because of the formality (perhaps meaning their working clothes were unwelcome), attend the parish church. Tiberi regarded this as uncanonical, against the intention of the *Concordat*, without his approval, and a misunderstanding of his authority. In 1895, Rome had granted the AA approval for the season, in 1896 for the year. When in 1898 Rome was petitioned by Picard for the chapel a reply (21st February, 1899) granted faculties for five years permitting a variety of services in the chapel for fishermen and authorising the director of the *maison* to allow priests designated by him to hear confessions and to preach. The matter was reinforced in April 1900 in the document *DECRETUM quoad facultatem excipiendi confessiones fidelium navigantium*.[1] In addition, a faculty to allow confessions to be heard by duly approved priests was granted to the director general of the ŒdeM, *ex officio*. It was probably for this reason that Picard was put on the council of the ŒdeM in January 1902 *ex officio*, with a renewal of that council's invitation from a meeting of 12th November, 1896 to Picard to be also its spiritual director, responsible for the choice of chaplains *et de toutes les questions qui peuvent se rattacher à leur ministère*.[2] In short the ŒdeM now had a clear and officially recognised line of authority: ashore the chaplain was responsible; at sea, the captain, then the chaplain, thirdly the doctor.

The Sacred Congregation for Extraordinary Affairs in Rome in April 1898 generalised the permissions already given to relate to all existing situations, and to those yet to be founded, allowing *Père* Yves every reason to believe that he could proceed with his work in peace. The opening of the chapel for the 1899 season was for Mgr Tiberi, apparently in France for his health, a step too far. As the *Lettre à la Dispersion* delicately put it:

> Mal instruit, sans doute, et mal conseillé, il prit la brusque décision de supprimer la chappelle, d'interdire le P. Yves et de lui ordonner de quitter Saint-Pierre.[3]

Père Yves, armed with the correct authority but forbidden by Tiberi, wondered what to do. His Superior ordered him to stay at his post. Considerable activity followed between the various authorities and Rome, which was displeased with its apostolic prefect, invited the AA to assume the prefecture, something which, with implications for the *Concordat*, although supported by the French Ambassador to the Holy See, was quashed at the objection of the French Colonial Minister. The AA detected the hand of freemasonry, perhaps shorthand for anticlericalism, but not necessarily so. The matter was resolved at the end of the 1899 season by *Père* Yves, on his return to France, being sent on a voyage to China, before starting the 1901 season in Iceland, opening a *maison* on the lines of the one in Newfoundland. Meanwhile, Tiberi resigned in 1899, being replaced by Mgr Legasse, who retained the approval of his superiors and the French authorities sufficiently to become Bishop, first of Oran and then of Perigeux. The chapel at St Pierre remained closed until

---

1 *Acta Sancta Sedis*, Rome 1899-1900, vol XXXII, 760.
2 'And all the questions relating to their ministry'.
3 'Not understanding, without doubt, and badly advised he quickly decided to forbid Fr Yves access to the chapel and ordered him to leave St Pierre.'

1908, well after the end of the *Concordat*. The whole episode may have been a reflection of the pressure being brought upon the AA in France, a view reinforced by a letter from the *abbé* d'Auvigny to Picard in 1902. d'Auvigny was a secular priest, so that his experience of the new prefect should not have been muddied by any view that prelate might have about religious, unless there is guilt by association, but he reported that the apostolic prefect was going round the ŒdeM's suppliers and staff to discover their grievances. It is implicit in the mention of local suppliers that added to any political problems regarding the AA there was hostility from local businesses caused by their substantial loss of income, resulting from the AA battle against alcohol.

This forms the background to *Jam Inde*. Propaganda in Rome issued it on 21 December 1905 to regularise the AA position with more precision, with validity for ten years. It was extended verbally in 1915, and renewed on 3 April 1919 for a further decade, before being allowed to lapse. Anson wrote later in both *Harbour Head* and *The Church and the Sailor* that *Jam Inde*

> In effect . . . gave the Assumptionists spiritual jurisdiction over seafarers of every nation in any part of the world . . . Had the *Œuvres de Mer* been able to commission a fleet of Mission Ships, each provided with a chaplain, they could have developed their maritime apostolate on the high seas with all the liberty of an exempt religious order. To all intents and purposes . . . Propaganda had entrusted the Assumptionists with the spiritual welfare of seafarers throughout the world. The year 1905 which saw the issuing of the Instruction *Jam Inde*, stands out as one of the most important dates in the history of the Catholic Sea Apostolate. Never before had such privileges and faculties been granted by the Holy See to any organisation devoting itself to the spiritual welfare of sailors.

Disregarding the point that the ŒdeM's 'Mission Ships' served only a fleeting system, by Anson's time almost obsolete, was his assessment of *Jam Inde* justified? Modest allowance must be made for his fascination with shipowners which recurs in his autobiographical books. It is also pertinent to recall that Aelred Carlyle's Benedictines, with whom Anson found his home, had moved to extra-diocesan Caldey Island to avoid episcopal authority, leaving the Church of England for the Church of Rome when challenged by Bishop Gore on their understanding of authority; Anson had been privy to those discussions and one of those received into the Catholic Church. The question of authority, at least in the matter of jurisdiction, exercised him when having to consider the position of the AoS, for canonically (i.e. in the law of the Church) the position of the sea was far from clear. His research had shown that as early as the fifteenth century the Dominican Felix Fabri gave as one of the reasons that Mass was not celebrated at sea the impossibility of knowing with certainty the name of the bishop in whose diocese the ship might be at any time. Anson, as will appear later, had had to find a means of uniting various organisations which crossed diocesan boundaries and overlapped each other. Father Goldie, facing the same problem, thought he had found at least part of his answer in the model provided by the SAWCM. Anson, having petitioned Rome for recognition of the AoS, after seeking Jesuit consent for the adoption of its name, saw *Jam Inde* through the lens of his own concerns.

If it is asked whether Anson's view of *Jam Inde* was correct, the answer is that it was not. He seems to have overlooked the situation which created the need for *Jam Inde*, namely the misunderstanding between the AA and Tiberi and his successor, and all that lay behind that. He seems, too, to have ignored the peculiar position of the French Church and the *Concordat*, despite being aware of what had forced exile on many French religious orders. Finally, he seems to have missed the real relationship of the AA to the ŒdeM, where the former were promoters of the latter, not directors; their responsibility the spiritual side of the ŒdeM's work. Never before had such faculties been granted because never before had a situation required them.

With the context in mind, it is possible to approach *Jam Inde* with a reasonable expectation of assessing it fairly. It opens with a paragraph to the effect that now the ŒdeM has been in existence for a decade, the functions of its chaplains should be defined. Four sections deal with I) the houses and chapels of the ŒdeM, II) faculties and privileges, III) their use, and IV) duties and laws. These gave chaplains afloat had an almost free hand, provided that they were approved by the Spiritual Director of the ŒdeM, a situation which could hardly be otherwise. In other words, the necessarily free hand of the priest at sea was tempered by a clearly defined hierarchical link with someone ashore. The Instruction recognised that peculiar hours of work might affect the hours at which Mass needed to be said, or in the fulfilment of Easter duties. The situation was quite different ashore, or if a ship was in harbour for any length of time, or in harbour in respect of, for example, a funeral. Here the authority of the Ordinary[1] had to be obtained, or at least acknowledged by showing him the necessary permissions. Similarly, houses might be set up with chapels, two being approved in Newfoundland, with the agreement of the Ordinary and the approval of Propaganda. Within them, priests of the ŒdeM 'shall be free to direct matters', their ministry, however, to be confined to fishermen, mariners and passengers, but not to local people except ŒdeM staff. They were to behave in a reverent and compliant manner towards the Ordinary, to keep the laws and customs of the local parish, and allow the Ordinary to inspect the chapel. If the Ordinary was dissatisfied, his usual recourse would be to the ŒdeM Spiritual Director unless matters were of such moment as to permit no delay, in which case the Ordinary must act first but then justify his action to Propaganda. The priests of the ŒdeM are to live 'in the bond of peace' with the local clergy. It will be observed that this document acknowledged the possibility of problems on either side and offered a remedy for both. It excluded no other agency from ministry to seamen but regulated the actions of the clergy attached to the ŒdeM, who need not, as references to chaplains in the present chapter have demonstrated, be members of the AA, or, indeed, religious of any other Congregation, but could be secular clergy. In short, nothing supports Anson's understanding of *Jam Inde*, or suggests that he had read the original.

Jam Inde contains a few clues to illuminate the problems at St Pierre, for

---

1   The local bishop, parish priest or other authority.

example, the reference to providing a ministry to seafarers only, and not to local people. It is possible, too, that Mgr Tiberi was trying to avoid playing into the hands of the anticlericalists, or nodding gently in their direction in an attempt to further his career. He may have received complaints from local businesses. It is even possible that his action was no more sinister than the product of the illness which had taken him to France. Whatever the reason, it is primarily his action which lay behind the need for *Jam Inde*, although it would have been entirely appropriate for such a document to have been sought at any time; it is unlikely that the Superior of the AA would have wanted to apply often for faculties when one application of the right kind would secure such a document obviating the need for repeated applications.

Though *Jam Inde* may hint at further expansion, its immediate purpose was to avoid the kind of unpleasantness which has been described. Subsequent history reveals that *Jam Inde* was not immediately successful. A document from 1908 suggests a clash between secular and regular clergy. Another of 1910 has the apostolic prefect at St Pierre accusing *Père* Benoit of giving scandal by his language (speaking to illiterates in 'familiar and popular language') and his behaviour (accepting dinner invitations, if he was guilty of which, he said, he was not alone, for he had dined six times in the company of the ship's captain and doctor; and of dancing, which he denied, though happily admitting to having organised dances). A letter of 1911 from Mgr Legasse to *Père* Emmanuel Bailly (i.e. between apostolic prefect and AA Superior, successors to the original protagonists) suggests that the resident clergy, who stayed permanently at St Pierre, might have substance in their complaints against those who came and went according to season, for a resident population of some four thousand would surely feel invaded when the fishing season brought its sudden influx of ten thousand visitors, almost exclusively men. The AA was among those visitors. Yet, that the apostolic prefect should write thus to the Superior suggests that *Jam Inde* could be made to work and the passage of time proved it so. It lasted until 1929, by which time the ministry of the ŒdeM had changed considerably: it had joined the federation of French Catholic maritime welfare organisations in the *Apostolatus Maris International Concilium*. It was this which led to a decision not to renew *Jam Inde* , the ŒdeM choosing to take its place in the ordinary life of the Church.

In 1925, in the context of a review of the life of *Père* Yves Hamon, a series about the work of the ŒdeM was printed in the AA's house magazine, *Lettre à la Dispersion*, and an attempt made to assess the achievements of twenty-five years of work. The conclusion was that it had been impressive, in spite of the interruption of war years:
- 414 rescued from shipwreck
- 1,582 hospitalised
- 23,626 hospital-days
- 7,587 consultations made at sea
- 4,333 gifts of medicine
- 620,218 letters received or sent

The anonymous author, finding it hard to quantify the spiritual achievements, pointed to the continuing ministry of the priest, the large numbers of men at acts of worship, making their confessions, spending time in good company instead of getting drunk, and returning safely to their wives and families; each illustrating the effectiveness of the chaplaincy.

Each year the ŒdeM sent out a number of clergy to Iceland and Newfoundland, except between 1915 and 1918 when *Frère* Eugène ran the *maison* at St Pierre alone. The full list reveals that of almost one hundred chaplain-seasons (often the same people each year), there was a slight majority of AA priests over secular clergy. The significance of this statistic lies in its indication of how closely bound together were the AA and the ŒdeM, while remaining independent of each other. French politics ensured that that independence remained a reality.

By 1919 staffing with chaplains had become a problem. The end of the war meant that religious orders, often seriously depleted in membership, were being invited to undertake new tasks. Fishermen's numbers, and the fishery generally, were much reduced. Catholic involvement with fishermen now reflected these changed circumstances. The earliest reduction had been attributable to politics: in 1902 a secular French Hospital Society for Iceland was founded at Dunkirk, resulting in the closure of the small Catholic hospital at Faskrudsfjord. The same society sent an ambulance-ship, *France*, in 1909 to coincide with the ŒdeM's own *Saint-Françoise D'Assise*, and gave an edge to the contention of anti-Catholics in Government that the ŒdeM was no longer a public utility, its subvention being better spent elsewhere. The needs afloat were changing.

Change was not confined to the sea. It had been the custom of *Père* Yves to continue his ministry outside the fishing season among the fishermen and their families back in France. The hospital-ship doctors used the same opportunity to give instruction in first aid. There was thus a precedent for a shore-based ministry. Improved conditions at sea and reduced numbers of fishermen meant that the ŒdeM ministry had to change. Increasing costs reinforced the point. The fact that it survived to become a member of AMIC, and beyond, is testimony to the hard work and devotion of ŒdeM members.

Two other works need to be mentioned in connection with ŒdeM. Both were to become members of AMIC. As early as 1897 it had become apparent that the fishing community contained many children who had lost one or both parents. Admiral Gicquel de Touches (of the Havre *Maison* of 1884), with the help of *Père* Picard founded an orphanage, the *Orphelins de la Mer*, its successive bulletins revealing the numbers involved and thus the need met. In its first year, nineteen orphans were admitted, then: 62 in 1898, 124 in 1899, 144 in 1900, increasing to 271 in 1905. By 1927 a total of 3,294 children had been aided. The rise in numbers in the early years may suggest an increasing number of orphans but more likely results from an increasing awareness within the fishing community of this good and necessary work.

The other AA-derived work was the *L'Œuvre du 'Livre du Marin'*, founded in 1910 by *Frère* Eugène Bergé to circulate good reading material throughout the French navy. The idea was that books could go where people could not. It is surprising to discover that it was founded so late, for the WCB had started literature distribution in the 1890s and protestant distribution earlier still. The surprise increases when the heavy involvement of the AA in publishing is considered. The number of *L'Œuvre du 'Livre du Marin'* beneficiaries increased steadily, with tracts and calendars being sent to the fishermen in Newfoundland as well as the '*navires de guerre*'. In 1916 this literature distribution was constituted as a separate organisation, renamed *Le Livre du Marin*. Its origin in Newfoundland echoed a need discovered by Wilfred Grenfell, who organised an ambitious system for the distribution of books along the Newfoundland coast, albeit for the benefit of lonely settlements ashore. *Livre du Marin* published a journal called *Au Large*, and an annual *Le Livre du Marin*. Books were issued free to members, who paid a fee for membership, which was set at a minimum of Fr1.00 *per annum*. The costs were underwritten by benefactors.

The influence of the ŒdeM and the AA cannot be overestimated. Together with that of Thézac's *Abris* it formed the bulk of French Catholic maritime work. It will be considered later how that influence was used to arrange the conferences which culminated in the AMIC. Its role as an inspiration to Peter Anson of what a sea apostolate might be, needs emphasis. It also needs to be emphasised that the ŒdeM was a curious development of two English ministries: the MDSF and the OSP. The details of its ministry to fishermen, with clubs, chaplains, and groups of supporters, though remarkable for its efficiency, was to be seen in the maritime ministry of other denominations. Its significance here derives from its role in the development of the maritime apostolate in the authority structure of the Catholic Church.

Was the ŒdeM another of Goldie's inspirations, as implied by Mrs Fraser, or solely ascribable to the French as Anson, and to a lesser extent Dalbard, seem to imply? The facts suggest that Bernard Bailly conceived of a French equivalent to the MDSF in part from his own experience, in part from direct communication with Fr Goldie, a connection suggested by Mrs Fraser but lacking a paper trail. The AA involvement, as distinct from Bailly's inspiration, is likely to have come about, not just because of its close links with the Bailly family, nor because of the AA's status as shipowners, but because of his knowledge of the Grosjean Études article, with the MDSF alongside the OSP and its SFSSP, a fortunate juxtaposition. The article would have shown Bailly not what could be achieved - the ŒdeM - but rather, how it could be achieved, given the very peculiar relations between Church and State. The ŒdeM is precisely the kind of hybrid which might be expected to result from such a cross-breeding: work among fishermen afloat (MDSF) staffed by a religious Order (OSP). There is even the similarity in the choice of a neutral name, Œuvres on the one hand, SFSSP on the other, which allowed the work of each to appear at some distance from the religious Order involved in its activities. The credit for the idea of French work among fishermen, as well as much of its achievement, must go to Bailly, but the MDSF-OSP inspiration indicates a fine but real thread leading back to Fr Goldie and the CTS.

19. Catholic Work 1900 – 1914

The turn of the nineteenth century ended the first decade of what might be called the 'modern' period of the Catholic sea apostolate, but the great watershed of the 1914 – 18 war, given its effect upon the nations involved, offers a better *terminus ad quem*, with two further factors encouraging this division: the death of Fr Goldie in 1913, and the existence of two lists, dated 1910 and 1911, of ports where Catholics were serving the maritime community. There is no sense in which the year 1900 was the beginning or end of any aspect of the sea apostolate.

These lists allow a comparison, with each other and with non-Catholic work. It would be unreasonable to compare the relatively recently founded Catholic ventures with the longer established Anglican and protestant societies. The first twenty years of the Catholic apostolate is better compared with the first twenty years of protestant work (c. 1840), and with Anglicans rather later; something made possible by Dr Kennerley's statistics.[1] The comparison will be attempted at the end of the chapter. It is complicated by the lack of homogeneity in Goldie-derived work. Several attempts throughout the decade tried to bring the disparate Catholic works together, a new development in the Catholic apostolate.

The rest of the chapter will examine what survived of the initial enthusiasm of the 1890s. It will consider the work of the two main agencies, the WCB and the CTS Sub Committee, and indicate their changing roles. It will examine work in the ports in some detail before considering the lists of clubs and homes, illustrating what was being done, and by whom and consider the role of Glasgow as the cradle of the post war sea apostolate, before comparing the port lists of Toll and Anson with those revealed by other, especially SVP, sources.

The WCB continued its work of sending literature, and arranging for its being sent. A decision was taken in June 1900 to include in a monthly magazine format the hitherto quarterly *Letters on Christian Doctrine*, distributed to the RN and coast guards and by 'zealous persons in seaports to Catholic Seamen in the merchant service'; a decision effected in January 1901 with the publication of *Stella Maris*.[2] It was Fr Gretton's intention, as editor, that the magazine should act both as a forum and a link - a new idea - between the various Catholic clubs and homes, including inside its front cover a list of all the Catholic clubs so far

---

1 Alston Kennerley, *British Seamen's Missions and Sailors' Homes 1815-1970*.
2 I refer to two quite distinct *Stella Maris* magazines. They can be distinguished by their publication dates, 1901 and 1911.

mentioned. The lack of information beyond an address should not detract from the significance of this list, that someone was now in touch with all the places given, these now appearing together for general circulation. Some were SVP initiatives. French ones were largely Catholic-supported secular organisations for reasons already explained (chapter eighteen). A list of English-speaking priests in thirteen European countries was also given.

Stella Maris's parent magazine, the *MSH*, described it as a new monthly magazine for Catholic seamen. In advertising all the items which the AoP had traditionally produced for sailors, the AoS admission certificates, leaflets, *Letters on Christian Doctrine* reprinted, and the sailors' hymn book, it illustrated continuity of intention, though its short existence suggests that it failed to become the link uniting existing work for which its editor had hoped. His other wish, that it should be a forum, was certainly fulfilled, for a number of sailor-related organisations appeared on its pages. Some proved ephemeral, the 'St Joseph's RN Fund' started in Cork as an attempt to train boys for naval chaplaincy being one example. More significant would be the Catholic Newspaper Guild, though unappreciated at the time; founded in 1900, with a Mercantile Marine section perhaps prompted by GoR members, it supplied seamen's hospitals and homes with Catholic newspapers. From 1903 it was known as the Catholic Reading Guild (CRG), a name indicating a wider purpose. The editor of *Stella Maris* suggested as an extension of the CRG ministry, couched in rather limited terms, the dispatch of newspapers to various liners, allowing three parcels per liner, one each for crew, engine and stoking staff, and stewards, with a fourth category on cable ships, of, not officers but, cable hands. *Stella Maris* featured specific Homes and Institutes, like the Bordeaux *Maison du Marin*, and the Glasgow CSI, together with articles on Catholic chaplains in the RN and the first Catholic chaplaincy in the US Navy. The bias was towards the RN, as might be expected of something connected with the WCB.

This *Stella Maris* survived for a year as a magazine dedicated to sailors. Then, in January 1902, Fr Gretton wrote:

> As many of our readers are aware, this magazine started twelve months ago for Catholic seamen, with whom it has been a great success. Today we present you with an edition especially adapted for the use of families and schools . . .

It continued to be advertised in the *MSH*, which in May 1902 suggested a wide use by schools and colleges, which had their own supplement. But in July 1902 it was being described as a supplement of the *MSH* in which more up-to-date material could be printed as the *MSH* went to press so early. The *Letters on Christian Doctrine* survived, though for a new audience, and all those taking *Stella Maris*

> will thus have an opportunity of supporting good Catholic literature, and, indirectly, of helping the work for Catholic Sailors - for whose benefit a special edition of *Stella Maris* is published monthly.

It was not explained how taking *Stella Maris* helped seamen. Copies of the special edition, some sort of printed newsletter for inclusion with parcels of literature for HM Ships, seem not to have survived. Its future, following a 1904 policy declaration to use it 'in propagating devotion to Our Blessed Lady and the Saints', was revealed in an article, '*Stella Maris* for 1905':

> We are about to make this greatly appreciated magazine more attractive than ever to our younger readers. After December next it will be no longer connected in any way with the work for Catholic Seamen - though we hope never to give up the task of supplying our Sailors with good reading. *Stella Maris* will be, in every sense of the word, a FAMILY MAGAZINE.
> [original emphasis]

From this point it ceased to have any maritime interest. What remained of the work of the WCB and the AoP consisted in the faithful ministry of Miss Scott Murray, who maintained the distribution of more general literature to the RN and updated the naval *Lists*, which in 1919 she handed to Peter Anson. The *MSH* continued to provide literature, occasional publicity, and have Masses said at Wimbledon for seamen.

The WCB became effectively redundant at some point in the decade, when Cardinal Bourne became involved to the extent of establishing the Royal Naval Catholic Association (RNCA), perhaps prompted by the more settled position of Catholic chaplains in the RN; probably in 1908, as it first appeared in the 1909 *Catholic Directory*. This showed it as having two chaplains entitled to pensions, twenty chaplains on fixed allowances, and 130 priests in receipt of capitation grants. The Cardinal, who would act through his Vicar Capitular, was listed as President of the RNCA, signifying his approval, and the Vice President was Admiral of the Fleet, the Right Honourable Walter T Kerr GCB, widower of Lady Amabel (who had died in 1906). Its Secretary was Fr Hamilton Macdonald, a former Anglican chaplain, appointed in 1897 to HMS *Victory* and the Royal Naval Barracks at Portsmouth. He continued as Secretary for many years, his role apparently as the link between priests doing chaplaincy work with the RN. Macdonald was also to be the connection between Miss Scott Murray and Peter Anson, which suggests that the WCB and its *Lists* had become part of the RNCA.

The vagueness surrounding the establishment of the RNCA is precision compared with any attempt to determine the last days of the CTS Sub Committee. It continued, as far as is known, to keep no records. Notes of its work appear in different places, which reported gifts of books, or money as start-up grants. Its principal offspring, the Montreal Club (Fig. 12), prospered and was self-supporting, whereas the London Home was regularly reported by its chairman, Count de Torre Diaz, to be under financial pressure. de Torre Diaz, a keen member of SVP, depended increasingly on SVP help. Recognising that changes in the London Docks had overtaken it, in 1911 his committee, among a number of economies necessarily taken, decided not to renew its lease on the Home, taking instead a quarterly tenancy, to reduce the rent and allow it to move when an opportunity might arise, which it did in 1913 to Lambert Road, beside London's Victoria Docks, where new premises were opened by the Cardinal. In Genoa, Canon Hay's Home, which had rented rooms from the Canons Regular of the Lateran, passed to their care in 1910 when Hay died. Statistics are rare for establishments of the period, adding value to Hay's. In 1902 he reported:

- attendance at club   6-7,000
- chaplain's ship visits   2,500
- prayer books, rosaries etc. 500
- religious instruction given 90
- dinners to distressed seamen 900+

His thoughts on the maritime apostolate were not confined to Genoa. In April 1904 he appealed for lay missionaries or superintendents who might open, first a mission at Stettin on the Baltic, for which he had £50 donated, and then at Constantinople, Gibraltar and Alexandria. None of these materialised.

Other work for seafarers appears in contemporary Catholic literature. In 1901 rented rooms were opened in Charlestown Docks, Boston, USA, with a superintendent visiting ships daily, supported by a Catholic Alumni Sodality; the rooms mainly for the US Navy and used by 12,544 men in the first year. In Falmouth, England, the parish priest appealed regularly (1903-5) for assistance towards the hire of a boat to visit the many ships calling at the port for orders. He received foreign literature from the ŒdeM. In Port Said some Franciscans opened a club in August 1902, apparently with an annual CTS grant of £40. A club in London to cater for the needs of Goanese seamen from the P & O liners 'and the very poor seafaring men whose work lies in the docks' was opened at St Anne's Church, Custom House, near the Royal Docks.

Fr Goldie, in his seventies, continued to foster interest in sailors' welfare. His paper for the Second Australian Catholic Congress, 1902, was published in the Australian SVP Superior Council's 1904 *Report*, and reprinted in SVP's *English Bulletin* in 1906. He exhorted the Australians to set up a Committee for Sailors in each port for the distribution of literature, touched on the need for temperance, and explained how that could be encouraged through the AoS. More significant was his suggestion to Australian Catholics that they might find a model in the SAWCM in its appointment of extra curates to work solely among seamen in waterside parishes from quayside chapels devoted to their use. He concluded with an appeal:

> Why should we not, in spite of the boundary walls of national dislikes, federate our work, and interchange with all countries in the world our plans and methods for the sailor's good? Efforts have been made in that direction, circulars sent to the Bishops whose dioceses contained ports, personal appeals made in Spain and other countries, but the scheme has met with the fate of all things new and untried. But cannot well-wishers combine, and ask, and seek, and knock? Endeavour has been made to enlist the sympathy of the world-wide SVP, and its President-General has given his cordial approval.

Perhaps to encourage action, the *English Bulletin* followed with an account of the work of the Melbourne SVP, giving statistics of its ship-visiting and details of its Christmas Dinner for 'some 250 jolly light-hearted seamen'. A search has failed to trace the circulars mentioned by Goldie, or find details

> **APOSTLESHIP OF THE SEA,**
> SEAMEN'S BRANCH OF
> **The Apostleship of Prayer,**
> THE HOLY LEAGUE OF THE SACRED HEART OF JESUS.
> (Under the Patronage of Our Lady Star of the Sea and St. Peter.)
>
> **CERTIFICATE OF ADMISSION**
> *(Which every Person who wishes to be a Member must receive).*
>
> ....
>
> has been enrolled in the Apostleship of Prayer, the Holy League of the Sacred Heart of Jesus, the Seamen's Branch called the Apostleship of the Sea, this .... day of ...., 189......
>
> EMILE RÉGNAULT, S.J.,
> *Director-General.*
> JOHN GEORGE GRETTON, S.J.,
> *Central Director for Great Britain.*

An original Apostleship of the Sea membership card, 1895.

of his scheme, but his clearly expressed intention here is that it be federal and international - and perhaps built on the foundation of the SVP. This is a subject which will be returned to in chapter twenty-one.

In Glasgow, where the CTS, AoP and SVP, had come together in sailor-work so early, the century opened with the Boy Associates and the CSI on a collision course. The *Glasgow Observer* continued its regular paragraph of statistics, revealing the lack of people willing to be ship-visitors as a real problem; for a period the whole venture hung on one visitor, with the continuing and devoted support of Mrs Howden. The absence of a priest in the docks received comment. The call for multilingual literature implied its use had fallen into abeyance. To these difficulties, the paper gave a positive spin, suggesting that the results were encouraging, with seamen, especially 'Portuguese Catholics from Goa' attending church services. The solitary visitor, provider of statistics, enroller of AoS members, is not named but may have been Daniel Shields, at least until 1905. He was so rarely mentioned by name at a time when his interest is known that the only explanation for the omission is that he wished not to be named.

A 1904 letter from Shields reveals that at Glasgow everything was not as a reader of the *Glasgow Observer* might suppose. It contains what little is known about the relatively young Shields and his AoS work. Dated 1st March, 1904, and circulated to all members of the CSI Committee, it survives as a copy, now in the diocesan archive, sent to the Archbishop of Glasgow in March 1905, after Shields's 1904 circulation of the Committee produced no result. In it he mentioned the AoS origins and the continuing support of Mrs Howden, explaining that his letter was prompted by news of the impending dissolution of the CSI. It was Shields's opinion 'it was bound to come to that'. He summarised the history of the CSI: that sailor work had started six years before, since when the work and the people had changed. 'To a lady is due the founding of the scheme - Mrs Howden . . . and with her . . . the "Boy Association"'. He credited McNichol, first manager, with starting the CSI, its ship-visitation, distribution of literature, daily invitations to seamen, and a kindly welcome, in conjunction with the 'Boy Association' and the AoS. Shields hinted that the manager's work was restricted by the committee which had, on the manager's death, rejected a young man's proposal to take his place. His description of that young man, 'Filled with the desire to spread the work and make the Institute a central place of work', raises the question, whether this was Shields himself; a question which will be returned to in chapter twenty, where an affirmative answer would afford one reason why Shields might be identified with the pseudonymous Jarl Higg-Cameron, author of several public letters written in a similarly combative style.

Shields's letter complained the CSI was no longer run for the sailor and co-operation with the Boy Associates had ceased.

> I saw that there was no help to be obtained from the Committee . . . so I had to begin again and appeal for literature etc., for the visitation of ships, and thus it continued up to the present time [March 1904]. For the last four years there has not been a single seaman enrolled in the AoS in the Institute, nor has there been half a dozen ships supplied with literature from there, while the work of the AoS went on and the Committee and the Institute took all the credit. This I never noticed but always endeavoured to induce seamen to go to the Institute which visiting once, they never visited again . . .

His own workers were not asked to help in any way and this he thought was because the committee

> thought that they were of a certain 'CLASS' whilst most of the workers were labouring 'Boys'. The Spirit Trade was largely represented on the Committee and this I blame for some of its apathy.

He appealed that more might be done for sailors, saying that he and Mrs Howden, who both had worked for so many years under the direction of Fr Egger, felt the matter keenly. In his covering letter of 13th March, 1905 to Archbishop McGuire he added:

> The work for Catholic sailors still goes on in connection with the 'AoS' but much more, very much more could be done for our Catholic Seamen if there was a right spirit of zeal among those able in time or otherwise to help.

His imminent departure may have prompted the letter; in 1905 he went to try his vocation as a Jesuit lay brother, perhaps because not offered the CSI role.[1] If his letter was to ensure the survival of AoS work, rather than the CSI, in Glasgow he was successful to the extent that the *Glasgow Observer* was still reporting ships visited, books given, and AoS enrollments made, two years after his departure. In the two weeks preceding 9 March 1907, for example, seventy ships were visited and supplied with literature, and thirteen men enrolled in the AoS; numbers implying more than one ship-visitor and a new impetus. The *Glasgow Observer* had been a great supporter of seamen's work in the city. That it gave more space to the AoS, less to the CSI, might only reflect the amount of information sent to the editor. Its report (23 January 1904) on the closure of the CSI shows that the CSI was suffering from the same problems as the London CSH, where funds were short and interest flagging:

> The CSI seems to have fallen upon evil days, and for a time the subscriptions necessary for the upkeep of the Institute have not been sufficient . . . A meeting was held [19 January 1904] in St John's Library to consider the position of the Institute, but unfortunately the attendance was so small as to indicate a lack of interest on the part of the large number of Catholics invited. The meeting [decided] . . . that the Superintendent should cease to solicit subscriptions, and the affairs of the Institute be wound up as soon as possible. It is to be regretted . . . but there is something to be grateful for, since members of the AoS have undertaken very successfully most of the work of the committee in charge of the Institute had to do, such as the visitation of ships and the distribution of Catholic literature among Catholic sailors.

Though it had withdrawn its support from the Glasgow CSI, the SVP was increasingly involved in the sea apostolate, encouraged by Fr Goldie from its platforms to share his vision; his recruitment of SVP support in London kept the CSH going. SVP Brethren were reported visiting secular clubs in French ports. In America, Philadelphia and New Orleans were served by the SVP, the latter with a St Vincent's Seamen's Haven by 1908.[2] In Australia, it was busy in Melbourne and Sydney by 1911. Articles on a range of maritime work, one of 1908 describing an imaginative project among French river and canal folk, in SVP literature encouraged a breadth of thought in members, and indicate support for the sea apostolate at SVP's upper levels. Its involvement in the maritime apostolate is of particular significance, for the SVP had an international and vertical structure which the AoS lacked at this time. The CTS published a *Life* of St Vincent de Paul by Goldie in 1909.

Where possible Fr Goldie met with SVP members at the local level. For example, in 1901 he was at Olympia, Newcastle-upon-Tyne, encouraging SVP interest in Sunderland and Tyneside, where 'Brothers of the Tyneside conferences of SVP have been for several years working with success among seamen frequenting the various parts of the diocese of Hexham

---

1 Jesuit records give the date of his entry as 7th December, 1905.
2 Is a Haven to be distinguished from a Home, Club or Institute? As an American term it has echoes of the Seamen's Snug Harbour, a retirement home for seamen on Long Island. Here it seems to be an institute, in 1908 with an average daily attendance of 45 men. No ship-visiting figures survive but among goods distributed were 4,519 clay pipes (for Smoking Concerts?) and 2,373 hand rags (for stokers?).

and Newcastle', and where enthusiasm led to talk of a sailors' home and chaplain. By 1903 until the outbreak of war, St Cuthbert's, North Shields was maintaining sailor-work; from 1904 supported by the Sunderland Particular Council; in 1906 extending its ministry to Catholic boys on the training ship *Wellesley*. The parish of St Philip Neri, Dunston, took responsibility for ship-visiting at Dunston Staithes, bringing foreign seamen to Mass. Men from both parishes took an interest in the local sailors' home. St Patrick's, Sunderland, had two SVP brothers visiting ships in 1912. The north east was traditionally a Catholic stronghold.

Other English ports occurring in *SVP Reports* are few. The Jesuit church of the Sacred Heart, Bournemouth, collected and sent to Poole literature for distribution, probably because the WCB's Miss Scott Murray worshipped there. London SVP Conferences are mentioned: Our Lady, Kentish Town, gave an annual concert at the CSH for several years, probably from 1898; St Thomas, Wandsworth, had a member on the CSH committee; the Rotherhithe Conference was involved in literature distribution.

In Ireland SVP sailor-work was more ambitious, opening the CSI in Belfast on Dock Street in March 1909, SVP members in their first year visiting 919 ships, and bringing 429 men to Mass. In February 1910 the SVP opened a building large enough to include both a Home and an Institute on Sir John Rogerson's Quay in Dublin, where, by the end of the year, 447 ships had been visited and 13,179 men used the Institute, a healthy daily attendance helped by the building's proximity to the dock area.

Catholic work apart from the clubs, homes and other activities connected with the CTS Sub Committee, the Glasgow AoS, and the SVP, was slight until 1910, when a new venture for sailors, apparently unconnected with any of these, opened at 14 via Marina, Naples. Very little is known about its founder, Dr Toll, a German priest of the diocese of Osnabruck. Gannon followed Anson in reporting that Toll had the blessing of the Holy See, dated 14th June, 1910, for a scheme to link all existing CSIs. Anson derived this information from a German-English magazine called *Stella Maris*, not to be confused with the 1901 magazine of the same name, his only issue that of October-December 1911, fourth issue of a quarterly production, obtained from Fr Macdonald at Portsmouth.[1] It is important because it listed all the Catholic clubs known to Toll, which Anson thought the first 'serious attempt . . . made to combine all these ideas and put them into practice'. There is no evidence that Toll's plan for unity by federation had more success than Goldie's or, indeed, any success at all. Anson thought the Toll list of clubs sufficiently important to reproduce, though the list he offered introduced variants, adducing fourteen clubs from Toll's longer list; notably absent is any reference to French work; nor are Dublin and Belfast included, probably because started too recently.[2] Whichever total

---

1 I have failed to trace any copies beyond this one of Anson's which I saw in the AoS archives. Even that seems to have disappeared.
2 *Aden, Amsterdam, Baltimore,* MD; *Boston, Mass*; (Catholic Sailors' Club, Water Street); *Bremerhaven,* Ecke Donnen & Schiffer Streets); *Bruges* Dar-es-Salaam

is accepted, Anson's or Toll's, the spread of Catholic works for seamen in twenty years is not to be dismissed lightly. Strangely, Anson placed no significance on Toll's papal recognition.

A view of this assessment is available from another source. Fr Goldie, in the *Catholic Social Year Book* of 1911, offered a broad account of the contemporary scene, first distinguishing between work for the RN and MN; the former well provided for by the AoP and the RNCA (' . . . recently formed [and] gaining ground and recognition, which should open the way for real social work in the service') but less optimistic about work for the MN:

> The best helpers in the various ports used to be the local Brothers of the SVP, but fewness of their number and the vastness of their work ashore made it well-nigh impossible to do efficiently and continuously the work of visiting ships in port and of interesting themselves in the sailor ashore.

In his opinion:

> The only way to find some remedy seems to be to set on foot in London a fresh Central Committee which would rally old workers and new, and would restore and strengthen, if still in existence, whatever work is required in our numerous ports. A strong effort was formerly made to give a Catholic and international character to the work, to encourage foreign Catholics to begin Sailors' Homes, and other good works for seamen.

Goldie's implicit confirmation of the demise of the CTS Sub Committee and the recent establishment of the RNCA is helpful. The article appears to be the work of a tired man. He had little to say on the state of the contemporary French sea apostolate beyond suggesting that SJ and AA work had perished in the anti-Christian persecution, and nothing about French naval chaplaincy work. The secular structure of the ŒdeM ensured its ministry to fishermen survived the AA's expulsion from France. In his list of Catholic work for seafarers, Goldie listed homes or institutes established in Belgium at Antwerp and Bruges, in Italy at Genoa; elsewhere in Montreal, Sydney, New York and New Orleans. 'Spain was approached,' he wrote, 'but the Spanish American War came to stay any development.' His concluded by hoping that the cause might find publicity at a future Catholic Congress. To his seven institutions may be added known ones omitted: London, Belfast, Dublin, Melbourne and Philadelphia, giving a total of twelve, almost that of Anson's fourteen, but less than Toll's. The naming of different ports makes reconciliation between lists impossible.

What then of Anson's claim that Dr Toll's 1910 effort in Naples was the first 'serious attempt . . . made to combine all these ideas . . . '? The 1901 *Stella Maris* had been started to bring together Catholic clubs world-wide. There

(Reading Room); *Genoa* (Sailors' Institute, via Venezia, 1); *Hamburg* (Hopfen Street, 31); London (Seamen's Home and Institute, 16 Wellclose Square E); *Malta* (St. Joseph's Institute, 17 Piazza Britannica, Floriana); *Melbourne*; *Montreal* (Catholic Sailors' Club, Corner St Peter & Common Streets) *Naples* (Seamen's Home "Stella Maris", 14 via Marina); *New Orleans*, La. (St. Vincent's Seamen's Haven, 2057 Tchoupitoulas Street); *New York City* (Catholic Seamen's Mission, 422 West Street); *Philadelphia, Pa.*; *Port Said*; *Rotterdam* ("De Volksvriend", Oranjeboomstraat, 40); *Sydney*, N.S.W.; *Tanga*. [Italics and punctuation as in Toll's original]. Anson's version of this list appears as a footnote in *The Church and the Sailor*, 85.

19. Catholic Work 1900 - 14

were, too, Goldie's appeals for unity: his Australian SVP paper (1901), and the *Catholic Social Year Book* article, suggesting a revived Central Committee in London; both with the implication that he had beaten the same drum elsewhere. Anson knew of the 1901 *Stella Maris*, and can hardly have been unaware of Goldie's 1911 appeal, for it is easily found in *The Tablet*, back issues of which Anson spent time examining at Fort Augustus Abbey in his search for examples of work among seamen; his notes of *Tablet* extracts survive in the AoS archives. The same may be said about SVP publications; it would have been odd had he not acquainted himself with these before turning post war to recruit SVP support in reviving the AoS. He was dismissive of SVP in general and equally so of his hosts (in 1920 he was to write to Fr Macdonald, 'In most places I am stopping with laymen of the SVP type (publicans, pawnbrokers and fishmongers!!)', though happy to accept their hospitality, making it difficult to believe that his attention was not drawn to SVP publications or their maritime content. To say that he was writing as a journalist, rather than as an historian, would diminish the importance of his *Church and the Sailor*, intended as the first serious attempt at a history of the Catholic sea apostolate. His claim that the Assumptionists had been poised to take over the entire Catholic sea apostolate, and his failure to consider that Goldie's vision and that of the 1901 *Stella Maris* preceded by almost a decade this claimed 'first serious attempt . . . to combine all these ideas' cannot be satisfactorily explained.

Goldie, Toll and Anson agree roughly that by 1913 there were some fourteen established institutions for seafarers, the total less in dispute than the detail. It is likely that about ten of the fourteen had some sort of sleeping accommodation and may properly be described as Homes. Ports where the SVP was visiting ships without the provision of Home or Institute probably total four, with perhaps doubled at its peak. In Glasgow, Dublin and Belfast, for example, ship-visiting as a sole work had preceded the acquisition of a dedicated building. If it is assumed that each Home employed at least one lay person to supervise the institution, disregarding the seasonality of Montreal, a further figure, one for employees, may be estimated. New York, Genoa and Naples seem each to have had a designated chaplain, and the ŒdeM employed an average of three chaplains a year. If Catholic naval chaplaincies are disregarded (i.e counting only agencies concerned with the MN) a tentative and very conservative summary of Catholic work might look like this:

- Ports served from a building   18+
- Chaplains (full or part-time)   7+
- Salaried lay staff   c10
- Volunteers (say 5 per institution)   90
- Ports served without a building   c4+

Kennerley gives statistics of non-Catholic organisations at the same stage in their development. His statistics for MtS and BFSS are mostly drawn from publications produced by the societies concerned, statistics sometimes presented in the best possible light, to be balanced against the caution used in these Catholic figures. For the MtS at a similar stage in its development (i.e. 1869) equivalent statistics might be

- Ports served 29
- chaplains (full or part-time) 47
- salaried lay staff 25

Its 1856 foundation ignores the earlier work of the institutions it incorporated by a significant number of years, giving MtS a base denied Catholic work at its 1889 start.

Figures for the BFSS are less easy to provide. The looser federal structure of its early days, like Catholic work, make it hard to assess statistically. Kennerley, forced to estimate figures, was unable to provide satisfactory ones before 1860. His estimate of ports served in 1860 was nineteen, of which sixteen were in the United Kingdom. His comparison with Catholic work depended upon Anson's list of ports.

Catholic work in 1914 compared with the total of Protestant work among seamen in the same year appears insignificant. Indeed, Catholics like Goldie, Grosjean and Anson emphasised in their speeches and articles the major resources, some more apparent than real, available to non Catholic agencies. Perhaps because he had to rely on Anson, Kennerley found the explanation for the paucity of Catholic work in the composition of the Catholic Church in England: 'It must be remembered that the British Catholic community was only thinly endowed with monied middle class people, the key supporters of the protestant societies'. He emphasised the Catholic lack of a society dedicated to the mariner and any kind of national co-ordination. It is not easy to dismiss his explanation as his thesis offers a large amount of evidence relating to the funding of non Catholic agencies. Catholic seamen's work, even if it lacked middle class support, certainly enjoyed the support of some of the Catholic aristocracy; the efforts of the SVP represent something other than the working class; and to this may be added the Working Boys.

His reference to the lack of a 'monied middle class' could be misleading if the comparison is made between societies in the same year. The alternative adopted here, of comparing societies at similar stages of development, remains the better alternative. Before financial support, as in the reference to 'monied middle class', is discarded altogether, it should be noted that if all Catholic work is taken together, including the ŒdeM, financial comparisons become complicated. The ability of the ŒdeM to attract State funding adds to the equation a dimension which, for the BFSS and MtS, is lacking, except in the most marginal of instances. The introduction to the equation of the ŒdeM would require the work of the MDSF to be added on the protestant side, and at a time when the MDSF was attracting much financial support. Peripheral bodies, like the OSP, if added would compound the problem of comparison.

Nevertheless it is possible to suggest how Catholic work compared with other work after a similar number of years of foundation. The most satisfactory figures are those given for MtS. If allowance is made for the state of the founding church in each case, the Church of England established and post evangelical revival, the Church of Rome a minority in the United Kingdom and persecuted in France, the disparity between the figures becomes less obtrusive. Indeed, reflection suggests that, if better figures for the Working

19. Catholic Work 1900 - 14

Boys and the SVP were available, the Catholic Church might show a larger base of volunteers involved at the interface between Church and seafarer, and non Catholic societies advantaged with groups devoted to the provision of financial support. Without better figures for comparison it is a temptation to fall back upon impressions gained while studying the subject. Avoiding that temptation, what can be said with certainty is that the true position of the Catholic Church at this stage has consistently been understated: by Kennerley, because of limited figures; by Anson, for reasons which have to be guessed; by Toll, lacking information; by all three because the absence of a central body, something usually assumed of the Catholic Church, prevented the collection of proper statistics.

In short, attempts to organise or associate Catholic works for seamen before the 1914 – 18 war proved ephemeral. The outbreak of war was to render any discussion about relative figures nugatory. However, by chance, the consequent increase of naval work, and the recruitment of Anson to assist Miss Scott Murray, still faithfully working for Catholic Bluejackets, provided the means to extend greatly the Catholic ministry to the merchant seafarer. The death of Fr Goldie in 1913 and the recruitment of Anson in 1917 allow the war years to be seen as ones of transition rather than the regression which wartime closure of some Catholic works for seafarers might otherwise suggest.

For military reasons most docks were closed to ship-visitors in wartime. Chaplains were recruited for the RN. Clubs and hostels functioned where they could, but with difficulty. According to Anson's unpublished Church Maritime, the SVP's seamen's home by London's Victoria Docks, and the seamen's club in Genoa, run by the Italian Canons Regular of the Lateran, continued without interruption. In Liverpool, Fr Walker Hathersall, curate of St Alban's, Athol Street, aided local crews where possible, and Third Order Franciscan Sisters of St Mary of the Angels welcomed seafarers to their convent in Bugle Street. Sailor work continued in Montreal, New York and the few other United States centres. The ŒdeM's work was considerably curtailed. This record of limited continuity meant that the post-war period would require a fresh initiative from all agencies.

20. Peter Anson

The end of the Great War was followed by a period of adjustment for all the societies working among seamen. New ships had to be built and trade routes re-opened. The Catholic sea apostolate, not quite dead, and with seamen still active members of the AoS, required a revival, chronicled by the key figure of Peter Anson (Fig. 14) in his diaries, books and surviving letters.[1] If it is correct to describe him as the founder of the AoS, he is unusual among founders for the amount of information available about him far exceeds what remains of others in this book, Hopkins excepted. Anson was a man of contradictions; he could equally be engaging and courteous as vindictive; many remember him as a difficult man. This chapter will attempt to provide a chronology, with an accuracy lacking in Anson's books, using his diaries and letters, and the *Glasgow Observer* (the Glasgow diocesan newspaper), and show how the various pieces of the Catholic jigsaw became established as a united and world-wide organisation. The serious scholar wishing to follow Anson port by port, year by year, or in his personal life, is directed elsewhere.[2]

In his book *Harbour Head* Anson wrote of his upbringing and education. Richard (his baptismal name) was born on 22 August 1889; one of four children, having two sisters and a younger brother, Horatio. As his brother's name implies, the family was a naval one, their father an admiral. His mother's family was Scottish, which may explain the attraction of Scotland throughout his life. He referred to his brothers and sisters rarely, wrote little about his mother and less about his father. Diary entries suggest infrequent contact with his family. Like most naval childhoods, Anson's was a mobile one. Seldom precise about dates, he wrote that at a young age he was taken by his mother to join his father at Malta, with an early return to England forced by his mother's unspecified illness and his own Malta fever. At the age of eight he went to a day school in Ryde, on the Isle of Wight. His mother died when he was fourteen. He noted that she had suffered constantly from 'neuralgia, rheumatism and other ailments', and was 'highly strung' and 'a clever water colour painter'; characteristics found in her son, her influence on him stronger than his father's.

---

1 Two slight works on Anson have been published. Michael Yelton's, *Peter Anson: Monk, Writer and Artist*, mistaken in its title, is not interested in the AoS. S. Bruce and T. Harris, *Back to Sea*, contains Anson family pictures; the text has a number of mistakes.

2 Comprehensive details and sourcing are given in Miller, *Ship of Peter*, especially its Appendix Eleven.

21. Catholic Work after Anson

Peter Anson as a Caldey novice.
Reproduced with permission from The Abbot of Nunraw.

His teens were spent with a private tutor in Dorset. His father envisaging a diplomatic career for him, he crammed languages (certainly French), but failed to obtain a place at Oxford. Instead, and with little explanation, he spent two years as a student at the Architectural Association schools in Westminster.

From 1906 Anson was in touch with the Anglican Benedictine community on Caldey Island, off the south-west coast of Wales, where in 1910, aged twenty, he went to test his vocation. He later claimed that part of Caldey's appeal had lain in the community's maritime ethos. It is largely through his pen that the life of the Caldey community then survives. The abbot was often away, begging, particularly in America. Anson contrasted the comfort of the abbot's lodging with the Spartan life of the brethren. Details, such as nude bathing parties, confirm the impression that life on Caldey Island was not in every way similar to life in other communities. Perhaps Carlyle, erstwhile medical student, viewed it as a healthy option, much as his short-lived imposition of a vegetarian diet on the community.

Caldey had a profound effect on Anson's personal life, leading him to change his hand-writing, that most personal of expressions; his name, a potent symbol of identity, from Richard to Peter; and in 1913, when the community was reconciled with the Catholic Church, his denominational allegiance. The considerable confusion in his personal life which followed, touched on in his published writing, appear more fully in his letters and diaries.[1]

The period following Caldey's conversion to Rome was a time when Anson had a serious breakdown in health. A novice at the time, he reverted to oblateship with the rest of the brethren while their position as a Benedictine community was regularised by Rome. By 1916 confusion about his vocation raised serious questions about his future with the Caldey community. In an attempt to find an answer he went to stay with the Farnborough Benedictines. Benedictine communities vary in ethos; to go to another abbey while uncertainty about his vocation persisted was sensible. Surviving Farnborough letters, mostly undated though he was certainly there in March 1916, reveal him oscillating between a Farnborough vocation and a desire to be a naval chaplain. His letters are addressed to Fr Macdonald, the Catholic naval chaplain at Portsmouth.[2] Soon back at Caldey, Anson later had hopes of pursuing his vocation at Fort Augustus Abbey. He was to depend heavily on Benedictine hospitality as the sea apostolate developed.

At this time the AoS was unknown to him. He claimed thoughts of naval chaplaincy had led him to study naval history in 1915, but his first real involvement was through his recruitment to help Miss Scott Murray with her *List* of Catholic officers in the RN, and later in the provision of literature to ships. The burden of the WCB which she had carried for some thirty years from her home in Bournemouth, with little assistance, can only have been increased by the expansion of naval activity during the war. Anson's impression of her, now in her mid-sixties, was of a sick woman, though she lived another thirteen years. The WCB seems to have been replaced by the RNCA, linking her with its Secretary, Anson's friend, Fr Macdonald. Macdonald, aware of Anson's desire for naval work, mentioned so often in his letters, knew too that Anson had helped compile the *Catholic Directory* at Archbishop's House, Westminster while being treated by a London doctor for his mysterious collapses in health. Miss Scott Murray must have thought Anson, Benedictine oblate, son of a senior naval

---

[1] I have written in considerable detail about his health and his confusion about his vocation, as revealed in these, in *Ship of Peter*, 125ff.

[2] The late Fr John Maguire MHM, AoS Director, collected many of these letters and allowed me to see them. Their present whereabouts is uncertain.

officer, possessor of a patronym resonant in naval circles, and familiar with the ways of the printer, in every way suitable to assist her. The *Bournemouth Daily Echo,* reporting her funeral in April 1928, described her as a grand-daughter of Lady Lovat, revealing a distant relationship by marriage with Mrs Fraser, with whom she had sat when a member of the CTS Seamen's Sub Committee.

Anson's Caldey context would have added to his suitability as Miss Scott Murray's assistant. His Benedictine oblateship gave him considerable freedom to explore his interests and an opportunity to publish them. Why Caldey should have a maritime bias when other seaside or island abbeys did not is a mystery. It predated Anson's arrival, for there are occasional maritime references in the Caldey magazine *PAX* from as early as 1907, when an item referred to prayers for those at sea in the night office of the community. The largest bell on the island was inscribed *STELLA MARIA MARIS SUCCURRE PIISSIMA* (Mary, Star of the Sea, most loving one, lend us thy succour). There was mention, too, of the island's lighthouse and its keeper. More curiously, there was in 1911 a refutation of a rumour that the monks had refused to aid wrecked sailors at a time of prayer which noted:

> The whole feeling of the Community is with sailors in their difficult and tempted life. We pray for them specially every night at Matins, and if such a thing as a wreck did occur . . . all members of the Community would be out and doing . . .

Perhaps Abbot Carlyle saw Macdonald's request for Anson to assist Miss Scott Murray as part of the answer to the problem of his doubts about Anson's monastic vocation. Only Anson's version of his recruitment and the abbot's consent survives; it is confirmed by Anson's speedy involvement with the WCB. His first visit to Miss Scott Murray in Bournemouth, important because it establishes a major line of succession between pre and post war Catholic work for seafarers, effectively the date of his recruitment, was 31 July 1917. Other visits would follow. It would be odd if Miss Scott Murray did not tell Anson of the letter of Lord Archibald Douglas in the *Messenger of the Sacred Heart* and the work of the AoP it engendered; perhaps too she told him about the role of Fr Goldie SJ and the CTS, or the sailor work of the SVP and the GoR, familiar to her from her membership of the CTS Sub Committee.

Anson began his work for her by tackling the annual naval *List*, adding to this a list of ports with Catholic churches and their Mass times; both required much correspondence, checking and cross-checking, and business with printers. The service times would have been useful to naval officers responsible for arranging for Catholic personnel to attend Mass. Mailing a completed *List* was a considerable undertaking and occupied, his diaries reveal, much of the early part of each year. Miss Scott Murray appears to have begun to withdraw from WCB work in 1919, leaving it to Anson in 1920. The first available Anson diary, that of 1919, reveals frequent correspondence between the two, only beginning to dwindle in 1922, perhaps because of Anson's health, or because his work through the AoS had taken him far from the original WCB. His visit to Bournemouth in January 1919, probably his second, lasted three days and was spent mostly talking; five days followed at the end of July 1919; then, visits became brief and sporadic.

One of Anson's first actions was to contact the Catholic Reading Guild (CRG), perhaps prompted by Miss Scott Murray or Fr Macdonald; the purpose of the CRG was the 'diffusion of Catholic literature of all kinds'. Its limited maritime circulation has been mentioned in chapter nineteen. The CRG had developed considerably since its early association with the WCB though it may have ceased to provide Catholic literature to the Navy. A search for its records has proved nugatory. Anson took the opportunity when visiting London to see George E. Coldwell, on 21 January 1919, at 17, Red Lion Passage, Holborn, described as the CRG's 'Hon. Sec'. He was new in the post and might be supposed to be receptive to new ideas. Anson saw him again next day and later described their discussions about literature for the Navy as 'Quite satisfactory'.

Anson returned to Portsmouth, Macdonald's base, armed with a new *Navy List* which contained all the officers of the Navy (not to be confused with the *List* which listed Catholic officers). Here he received Miss Scott Murray's letter inviting him for that second Bournemouth visit, perhaps to discuss CRG involvement and the progress he had made. Coldwell, for his part, took the opportunity to place an article in the *Messenger of the Sacred Heart* explaining that the CRG had undertaken to 'carry on the branch work of the Apostleship of Prayer of enabling our Catholic seamen to get the right thing to read'. Significantly, for it indicates his understanding of the relationship, Coldwell wrote that 'Brother Anson . . . is giving us his valuable assistance'. He appealed for readers to volunteer to send papers to ships for at least three months, reminding them of the success of a similar campaign to send papers to the troops during the war, and stressing the peculiar isolation of the sailor. The AoP's willingness to publish the CRG's article suggests that the AoP authorities welcomed being relieved of further responsibility for circulating sailors with literature.

Anson's diary records a regular exchange of letters with Coldwell and suggests cordiality. Most of Coldwell's letters accompanied bundles of letters from volunteers forwarded to Anson, to be linked with appropriate ships, their movements gleaned from the *Navy List*. In return he sent Coldwell occasional bills. Sometimes they met. At some point in 1920 Anson began using CRG-headed paper describing him as Honorary Secretary of the Sailors' Branch of the CRG. He wrote to Macdonald (18 July 1920):

> The Reading Guild Work keeps me busy with correspondence. When the R[oyal] Navy is properly supplied with literature - i.e. about Easter - all my attention will be devoted to the Merchant Service and Fishermen.

Before pursuing this growing interest of Anson's in the MN, it is appropriate to consider the remainder of his connection with the CRG.

The point at which disenchantment set in between Anson and the CRG is revealed only in a contemporary letter, with an enclosure outlining the problem, sent by Anson to Cardinal Bourne at Westminster. Anson's disagreements work on two levels. There is the public reason. This usually appears entirely justified. Then there is another, usually personal, reason which by its nature suggests that the public reason is a presenting reason or pretext. This is well illustrated here. Anson's letter was written to the Cardinal from Rome on the 8th March,

1922. The Cardinal's reply of the 22nd March seems not to have survived. In the slight delay the Cardinal may have tried to discover for himself what was going on. Anson described the dispute as a 'silly little squabble', explaining that he was troubling the Cardinal with such a 'trivial matter' because 'I don't want to get into trouble with the CRG - nor do I want to make a [*sic*] enemy of such an excellent man as Mr Coldwell', a note of condescension maintained in the three-page accompanying memorandum. There was also archness: '. . . the regular scheme of distribution ought to be put under the direction of an organisation which is primarily interested in <u>sailors</u> and not in the "<u>conversion of England by books</u>"' [Anson's emphasis]. Anson bolstered his position by mentioning that Mgr Mackintosh (Rector of the Scots' College in Rome and Archbishop-designate of Glasgow) had invited him to remain at the College for as long as he liked and promised to accept him as a candidate for priesthood in the archdiocese of Glasgow. Mackintosh had also offered to obtain the blessing of the Holy Father upon the work of the AoS, Anson added, 'as the nucleus of an international society for the welfare of Catholic seafarers.'

Anson wrote in the memorandum that Miss Scott Murray had handed over to him her AoP work of thirty years for Catholic bluejackets and that he had attempted to give it permanency by arranging with the CRG Committee for the WCB to be conducted as a Sailors' Branch of the CRG, with himself as its Honorary Secretary. He had, he said, understood that a separate fund for this would be established. The Sailors' Branch had been formed in 1920, without his position being defined, after which he had set about expanding the work. At some point - his diary recording occasional expenses over which there seems to have been no problem - the CRG had declined to pay a claim for £5. 7s. 2d arising from the propaganda he had been producing; a refusal which had led to the discovery that no separate fund existed. Moreover, CRG funds were insufficient to meet the debt. Anson complained that he had not been given a place on nor invited to attend any meetings of the CRG Committee. By proceeding without committee approval, he had been acting as a freelance, and it is not difficult to imagine the reluctance of a committee to be responsible for his debts in consequence; added to which, on his own admission, since June 1921 Anson had diverted donations made to the Seamen's Branch to the Glasgow AoS Committee, of which he had become Honorary Secretary. Anson also objected that the CRG Annual Report had carried 'misleading statements' about the Sailors' Branch, written without any reference to him. The Cardinal's reply could justifiably, though it did not, accuse Anson of being disingenuous.

These differences, Anson told the Cardinal, had led him to realise the CRG's unsuitability as a vehicle for his plans for either RN or MN. After consulting Miss Scott Murray and the Glasgow AoS Committee the work had been placed in the care of the latter, which was being 'rapidly linked up with similar Catholic organisations in other parts of the world'. Coldwell 'seemed to think that Brother Anson had exploited the CRG and diverted many of its old supporters to a new organisation', a lack of precision which implies a moderate number of defections, sufficient for Coldwell to denounce, yet so few as to allow Anson a denial. The correspondence had been dragging on since June 1921, with the

CRG refusing to let go. Its Chairman, Dr Vaughan, with whom Anson's diaries record a number of contacts, was claimed to favour the transfer of the work to the AoS, but Secretary Coldwell, according to Anson, refused to surrender it, continuing to demand 'all papers, names of suppliers, and ships', while failing to understand that these changed constantly. The argument continued. Arthur Gannon in Glasgow, acting as AoS Secretary whilst Anson was in Rome, was held forth by Anson as one whose expenses the CRG refused to pay. This was the dispute which Anson offered for the Cardinal's arbitration.

The Cardinal's decision has to be guessed from the subsumption at an unknown date of the seamen's work of the CRG into the AoS. Hindsight allows a wisdom which could have predicted the disagreement; Anson had turned what had been a static secretariat, the part-time activity of an aging and ailing lady, into a roving commission, drawn others into the scheme, and tried to use the CRG as a platform to launch an organisation with world-wide potential. The CRG had never been intended to have that aim or degree of flexibility; nor was Anson's the kind of personality to accept the role envisaged for him by the CRG. What, if anything, the Cardinal did, prevented a complete rift between Anson and Coldwell, for they were still able to meet in 1923, by which time both must have been aware that the 'new and enlarged scheme' to which Anson had been giving 'valuable assistance', as Coldwell had put it in his 1920 *MSH* article, was turning out to be something rather different.

How did Anson proceed from assisting the WCB to Honorary Secretaryship of a world-wide organisation, which, it has to be said, in Anson's time never achieved the extent of Fr Goldie's pre war efforts, vestiges of which constituted the 'similar Catholic organisations in other parts of the world' mentioned? Being Miss Scott Murray's assistant was no small task in wartime, with the difficulty of compiling of lists exacerbated by demobilization. Her relief at having someone to whom the work could be handed can be imagined. The CRG link initially proved its worth in the number of people recruited to supply literature: by March 1920 these had increased from an unknown but modest base to around a hundred, its significance implicit in Anson's comment to Macdonald at Portsmouth that Miss Scott Murray 'is nearly off her head with delight and gratitude'. January 1920 seems the date of her surrender of the work to Anson, for on 2nd February he wrote that 'MSM [Miss Scott Murray] has sung her "Nunc Dimittis"'.

Anson's diaries show his enthusiasm for his new work. Operating in 1920 from Fort Augustus Abbey, the Honorary Secretary of the CRG Sailors' Branch was busy with the *List*. Its packing was completed by the 23rd January; chaplains' copies dispatched on the 24th, and officers' by the 27th. In February he started searching a complete run of *The Tablet* at Fort Augustus for references to Catholic work among seamen. He wrote to the major Protestant societies for information. *The Tablet* would have shown him Fr Goldie doing exactly the same a generation or so before. His diary noted receipt on 9th February, 1920 of "Reports . . . from Protestant Societies'. He was in touch with the Countess de Torre Diaz (perhaps another result of his *Tablet* search) who had continued her late husband's interest in the London Catholic Sailors' Home.

At this stage most of his work involved the use of his pen. He could be written to as well at Fort Augustus as anywhere. The advantage of Fort Augustus for Anson was that some of the monks had been Naval chaplains during the late war. On the 17th February he attended a lecture on the RN given by Fr Lawrence Mann OSB. He was also in touch with other Catholic agencies, including the SVP, perhaps prompted by Miss Scott Murray or by his *Tablet* search, or by the SVP's continuing connection with the London Catholic Sailors' Home.

By the third week of February 1920 Anson had drawn up a list of possible topics for articles to be written for the Catholic Press:
- Our Sailors and their Helpers
- Catholic Naval Chaplaincy
- Catholic Bluejackets from Ireland
- Don't destroy your old papers
- Our Deep Sea Fishermen
- Catholic Seamen's Clubs
- The Mission to Breton Fishermen

The titles indicate the contents. They were to be placed in such Catholic weeklies or monthlies as *The Month*, the *Universe, Catholic Gazette, Irish Catholic, Catholic Herald, Fireside,* and *Irish Rosary*. He already had access to Caldey's *PAX* and *Notes for the Month*. Letters to the editors of the *Universe, Tablet, Irish Catholic, America, Catholic Times* and *Glasgow Observer* drew attention to his work and asked for reduced rates, sometimes granted, for subscribers supplying literature to seamen. One article was to be given special attention, his 'Plea for Catholic Seamen'. At this time he was writing by hand. Later an arrangement would be made with the nuns at Talacre, close associates of Caldey, to type for him.

In March 1920 Anson sent Fr Macdonald a copy of his letter to editors (superscribed with an instruction to the typist for '8 copies' and enclosed with his letter of 14th March) headed CATHOLIC SEAMEN.

> SIR, - As assistant Secretary of the Catholic Reading Guild 'Seamen's Branch' - an appeal for which was made by Mr Geo. E Coldwell (Hon Secretary of the Guild) in a recent number of this paper - I am very anxious to obtain accurate information of any work being carried on among Catholic sailors, at home or abroad, at the present time, so that our efforts on their behalf may not overlap with any other society or private individual. We hope that before long we may be in a position to extend our activities to the Merchant Service and Deep Sea Fisheries as well as the Royal Navy.
> In view of this I specially wish to know:
> 1) Are there any Catholic Seamen's Homes or Institutes besides those of Victoria Docks (London), Genoa, Port Said, Montreal and New York?
> 2) Are there any societies or individuals (priests or laymen) who make regular visits to and distribute Catholic literature on ships of the mercantile marine in seaport towns? This work used to be done at various places in England by the SVP and the Guild of Ransom.
> 3) Whether there is any organised work now being carried on for or among Catholic Deep Sea Fishermen apart from the French '*Œuvres de Mer*' about

which I have obtained full details?
I shall be very glad to hear from anyone who can give me information on this subject.
Yours etc.
(Brother) Richard F Anson[1]
Caldey Island, Tenby, South Wales.

He told Fr Macdonald that this was appearing in 'all Catholic papers in Great Britain as well as in some American journals'. The interest of the letter is threefold: it indicates the extent of his research, reveals much of the Catholic work among seafarers which survived the war, and demonstrates his intention to expand the work of the CRG in a way which can hardly have been misunderstood by Coldwell and the CRG committee.

Anson's diaries give some idea of the timing of his contacts with the agencies mentioned in his letter. They coincide with the period of his *Tablet* searches. His first letter from the *Œuvres de Mer* appears to have been received on the 23rd February, from *Père* Yves Hamon. Letters to New York and London (SVP) were sent on the 27th February. The diaries show that his articles formed a background to his other writing throughout the year and that they were widely published. The ŒdeM particularly attracted his attention, with letters indicated on March the 2nd, 3rd, and 4th. On March the 5th he wrote to the ŒdeM President asking if he could join one of its ships, a wish never fulfilled. March the 6th and 7th were devoted to writing articles about the ŒdeM, probably revised in the light of letters received on the 8th and 9th, the latter including a pamphlet. It will be recalled that Anson spoke French.

Anson's articles produced a substantial response. Coldwell was forwarding him large bundles of letters. Correspondents around the world included a Mrs Solly, writing about Australian seamen; a Mr Bennett (of SVP?) writing about work in Poole, Dorset; others with information about the Dublin SVP, the New York Sailors' Home (from the famous Fr McGrath), and the SVP in New York and Philadelphia. Combined with the ports mentioned in Anson's newspaper appeal, here must be an almost complete list of surviving Catholic port work, the ghost of Fr Goldie walking in these pre war survivals. Other echoes of that earlier period came in letters from Lord Archibald Douglas and Mrs Fraser.

On the 2nd April, roughly two months into his campaign, Anson wrote to Macdonald:

> I am gradually collecting information about every sort of work for sailors in different parts of the world. The SVP in America have sent me exhaustive reports. They know how to do things 'over there'.

His daily correspondence was usually now in double figures. The CRG must have reimbursed some of his postage or Anson would have objected sooner. Caldey certainly picked up the bill at one stage. It is possible that Fort Augustus Abbey was helpful on occasion. Sometimes the diary mentions a donation. If Anson charged all his postage, stationary and travel to the CRG, the concern of the CRG would be easy to understand.

---

1   Anson's baptismal name was Richard. He adopted Peter as his name when admitted as a novice and kept it thereafter.

20. Peter Anson

Anson needed a system for organising his work, to record ships and correspondents. Perhaps it was for this purpose he bought card indices from Libraid. Diaries give names of correspondents, though with many gaps, and without details, leaving the reader to guess at many of his activities. Entries show that some letters contained invitations to visit this or that port; he wrote to Macdonald on 8th May to tell him he was about to enter Retreat to decide his future, after which he intended to begin a tour of the ports. The tour implies that he had already made up his mind about the work to be done in the immediate future in spite of his Retreat intention. His sailor-work was pointing him towards a major commitment to the seafarer and away from the part-time undertaking of his agreement to help Miss Scott Murray. In one sense that increase was of his own making. In another, he had, it seems, like Pandora, simply opened the box.

On 24 May 1920 Anson paid his bills and packed for departure, ready to travel the next day to the Scots fishing port of Buckie and the start of his first port tour. He was no longer confining himself to the postal despatch of literature; now, he was moving from information retrieval, by post and research, to personal observation. Diaries record with care train times and expenditure at least on port tours, presumably with an eye to reimbursement. The tour was intended to supplement the knowledge gleaned from *The Tablet* or from correspondents. That much is obvious. If it is asked why the port tour was undertaken at this time, the answer has to be deduced. When Anson had undertaken this work it was to assist Miss Scott Murray with the WCB, but its increase engendered by the link with the CRG had forced him to think on a larger scale, and, just possibly, the sort of scale envisaged by Fr Goldie. The gestation period seems to have been 1919, a time when wartime restriction made travel far from easy, and dock visits required special permits, a situation easing by 1920.

An examination of Anson's various itineraries reveals the journeys of 1920 as his most comprehensive. In later years most visits were supplementary ones. The 1920 visits were ones of discovery. His route, if the ports listed are traced on a map, was dictated by a combination of geographical proximity (or rail connection) and information or invitations received; otherwise, a pioneer's most obvious route would be to ports in order of commercial importance, for example, to London or Liverpool, rather than Buckie. In the event, although Anson seems not to have set off with the pioneer's agenda in mind, it is what he achieved, ferry ports excepted.

Port	% of trade	Anson visit 1920
Liverpool	31.7	18 Nov 1920
London	29.2	various
Manchester	6	
Hull	5	23 Jun 1920
Glasgow	4.6	4 Jun 1920
Southampton	2.6	17 Jul 1920
Bristol	2.1	1 Oct 1920

Port	% of trade	Anson visit 1920
Newcastle	2	14 Jun 1920
Dover (incl Folkestone)	1.8	(April 1923)
Grimsby	1.7	24 Jun 1920
Cardiff	1.7	22 Aug 1920
Goole	1.4	
Harwich	1.4	
Leith	1.3	5 Jun 1920
Newhaven	0.7	

Source: Gordon Jackson, *The History and Archaeology of Ports*, Tadworth, Surrey, 1983, 167.

Harwich, Dover, Folkestone, and Newhaven were primarily ferry ports; ferry crews were usually recruited locally, allowing a regular pattern of work at sea to alternate with time at home and access to parish and priest Anson conceived Catholic sailor-work at this stage primarily as a ministry to seamen tied to a port by a loading or discharging ship. Nevertheless it is odd that Anson did not call at Newhaven, at least when visiting Ditchling (below). In the case of Goole there seems to be a lacuna for it would have been hard to avoid Goole when visiting Hull or Grimsby. In short, and with speculation about Goole, in 1920 Anson visited at least ten of the top fifteen United Kingdom ports.

A typed summary headed 'Dates from Old Diaries' produced by Anson remained in the AoS archive. Its date uncertain, it listed those dates Anson believed in retrospect to be important in the history of the sea apostolate, perhaps produced as an *aide memoire* for one of his books. One of his significant dates was 30 April 1920, when the *Universe* printed his article (not letter) 'A Plea for Catholic Seamen'. He referred to it in his diary and later in *Harbour Head*. This article, perhaps deliberately timed, preceded his major tour of ports, meaning that Catholics meeting him would be more likely to be aware of the purpose of his visit. Anson seems to have ranked this article in the annals of the Catholic sea apostolate with Douglas's original 'Jack Wrecked at Sea' letter.

Starting in the north of Scotland at Buckie, Anson worked his way south, with a day or two in each place. A typical visit may stand for all visits. At Aberdeen his first day (the 31st May) was spent meeting local clergy and visiting the docks and fish market. The diary says, 'Walked round docks . . .' for he had yet to be initiated into the mystery of ship-visiting. Day two included discussions with local clergy, another visit to the docks, and one to a local seminary, with the evening spent writing letters and notes. On day three, after Mass at a local convent (probably an occasion he used to solicit, as the WCB organisers had before him, convent prayers for his work) he returned to the fish market before going on to Dundee. Day four was largely a repetition. Day five took him to Methil Docks, then to Edinburgh. Although Anson had an abiding interest in fishers he is seen here not to have been neglecting the MN or the RN during the tour: on the 7th June, for example, he made a foray from Edinburgh to the Royal Naval Barracks, lunching with a Fr Hannigan.

Anson's arrival in Glasgow on the 9th June was to prove a major step in his progress. His diary noted 'Long talk with Bro Shields SJ about sailor work'.[1] Shields took Anson to Queen's Dock in the afternoon, and to Prince's Dock for two hours after tea. 'Dates from Old Diaries' notes this day as specially significant: 'First meeting with Bro Shields at St Joseph's, N. Woodside Road'. In *Harbour Head* Anson said the meeting resulted from his *Universe* article and that several letters had preceded their meeting. The chronology does not bear close examination. A better version is that Shields's letters were prompted by Anson's general press appeal for information. Two diaries were in use for 1920. The diary Anson used one when writing *Harbour Head* gave their first meeting as the 24th July, the other as the 9th June. June the 9th is to be preferred and ties in with his series of visits to local clergy, churches, and the office of the *Glasgow Observer*.

The most significant part of the Glasgow visit, as Anson indicated, was his time spent in the docks with Shields. Previously Anson had visited docks in the sense of walking round and looking at ships. Shields, familiar with the docks from earlier days, approached them differently, for his purpose was to reach the men on the ships, to identify Catholics and point them to the local church, to offer counsel where appropriate, and to leave a parcel of Catholic and other books. This is what Anson would mean in future when referring to 'ship-visiting' rather than visiting the docks. He wrote later, 'Those days spent in Glasgow in June 1920 were an inspiration'. A typical afternoon with Shields (12th June) took the pair to the Prince's Dock where they went aboard the SS *War Power*, the *Krasiorarch*, and the *Clan Mcintosh*. The two men determined to revive the work in Glasgow, dormant since before the war, using largely the old methods, and launching an appeal through the *Glasgow Observer* for literature and *objets de pieté*. Shortly afterwards a committee was established.

The ship-visiting became part of the Anson port visit when on tour; in encouraging local people to initiate an approach to seamen he could now show them how to do it effectively. He continued south making similar port visits. In Sunderland he persuaded the SVP to revive its pre war work. Between his visits to Hull and Middlesbrough he broke his journey at Scarborough to have tea with Coldwell of the CRG where it is hard to believe that his ideas were not poured out at the table, for here was Anson in the middle of an exciting, perhaps exhilarating, tour, with old work being revived, the possibility of new being started, and the reader is expected to believe, on the strength of Coldwell's letter as quoted by Anson to the Cardinal at the time of Anson's disagreement with the CRG, that Coldwell could not or would not comprehend the scale of what was envisaged. This encourages caution in reading Anson's version to the Cardinal. It is just possible that Coldwell

---

[1] The Jesuit archive in London reveals that Shields returned to Glasgow, to St Joseph's, in 1919 and remained there until 1924.

could have thought that active port work was going to fall to the SVP.

Anson had used his CRG notepaper to write to Fr Macdonald that his Hull talks had aroused the interest of SVP and other laymen, mentioning their success, and the willingness of meetings to pass unanimously a resolution to begin work on the lines suggested by him, but, in an unusual instance of sensitivity, adding:

> What this tour has made me realize is that each seaport must be approached in a way suited to its individual needs and that it is useless to try to ram down a theoretical perfect scheme where the conditions are not suited . . .

He was having to recruit volunteers and encourage them to do what they could or would; a different model from the vertical approach of non Catholic societies which would send a chaplain to establish a Christian presence in the docks. What Anson was reviving here was to be organised horizontally, that is, each conducting his own work; he had no clear idea of a central authority and had probably yet to think out his own role as a link between ports.

Grimsby was the first major fishing port that Anson visited. Here his programme was unusually thorough, including a visit to the docks (with his friend Skipper McCarthy), the Trawler Owners' Federation, the Board of Trade, the 'Seamen's and Fishermen's Union', and the Church of England incumbent of St Andrew's church, Yarmouth, who was involved with the North Sea Church Mission (chapter eleven). It is likely to have been this man, Barton, whom Anson quoted as saying that Grimsby would benefit greatly if only the (Catholic) Bishop of Nottingham could send it Poor Clares or Carmelites. In *Harbour Head* Anson added a visit to the MDSF Institute.

Harbour Head places the Grimsby visit before the Yarmouth and Lowestoft visits on the way to London, with a return to Caldey via Alton Abbey, an abbreviated version. Here Anson is being careless; he connected The Rev. Paul Hopkins with Alton Abbey, stated clearly that Hopkins was dead, and added:

> The following year I wrote an article in the *Irish Monthly* dealing with the life and work of 'Father Paul', one of the most original and far-sighted sea apostles.

In reality, at the time of this tour (1920), Hopkins (chapter fourteen) whose name was Charles (or Michael in religion), was alive and living either in his Greenwich priory or in his St Mawes cottage. Anson did not visit Alton until Hopkins had died (March 1922), and wrote his article on Hopkins for the October 1922 issue of the *Irish Monthly*, using notes supplied by the brethren at Alton Abbey, which seem to have omitted Hopkins's union activity and 1911 strike involvement. His diary may lie behind the confusion, its first mention of Alton a letter of 23 July 1920 which Anson probably mistook as a note of a visit. His letter to Alton had been occasioned by a projected article on seamen's homes. Otherwise, the account of his tour is substantially correct. The same article also sourced material from the BFSS. To help him write more articles he subscribed to magazines like *Fishing World* and received books from the London Library. Anson's approach to written work was one of synthesis, and the prudent researcher always checks his sources.

An unnamed writer (probably Anson) reported Anson's progress in a

PAX article of November 1920, recalling that Brother Richard had taken over Miss Scott Murray's work, re-organising it under CRG auspices, based at Caldey. He had
> visited the chief seaports on the East Coast . . . to collect information about the actual condition of seamen . . . and to find out what is being done for the religious and social needs by Catholic and Protestant organisations.

He had found 'splendidly equipped non-Catholic Homes and Institutes' but nothing Catholic for the MN between Aberdeen and London. With the RN having its own Catholic organisation (the RNCA), the neglect of the MN meant that the 'actual need for some scheme . . . is even more imperative . . .'. Consequently, 'definite steps have already been taken in Glasgow, Hull and Sunderland to revive or start work for Catholic sailors'. In Glasgow the CYMS, and elsewhere the SVP, were giving their help. The article added that soon Anson would be visiting West Coast ports. Meanwhile, readers could obtain from Caldey a pamphlet about the London CSH, 'unfortunately the only institution of its kind in Great Britain', and assist by making donations:
> The expense of postage and travelling in connection with the development of the Movement are a heavy drain upon our resources. The Sailors' Branch of the Reading Guild has no endowment . . . [so we] are obliged to appeal to readers of *PAX*.

The implication is that Caldey was subsidising Anson despite, as his book *Abbot Extraordinary* reveals, the community's pecuniary embarrassment. Here too is contemporary evidence that as early as 1920 Anson was aware of the CRG's straightened circumstances despite his contrary claim when writing in 1922 to the Cardinal. The *PAX* article is a summary of what the tour had achieved, principally the revival of several pre war works; its failure to refer to work abroad is curious, for the diaries refer to letters from Canadian, American and Australian ports.

Anson's travel and correspondence constituted a tiring work load, and with the emotional strain of public speaking, cold-calling on clergy, and motivating reluctant supporters, explains Anson's appreciation of, indeed need for, periods of withdrawal and relative quiet, more so his trips to sea, where on board a trawler all would be left behind, while providing material for articles and speeches and adding to the nautical aura he was cultivating. As working trips, often in poor weather, they could hardly have been restful. His other consolations (his word) came 'in the shape of letters from Glasgow, Hull, Montreal and Grimsby - such grateful letters that seem exaggerated so warm is their gratitude for little done'. The same letter, to Fr Macdonald, asked for his *Navy List*, which suggests that Anson was working on the *List* of Catholic officers. This occupied much of his time at Fort Augustus, which might have been supposed to have its own copy of the *Navy List*. He was preparing for a 'rousing campaign in all the S. Wales coal ports in October'.

Anson's successor as AoS secretary, Arthur Gannon, first appears in the diaries in August 1920 when the receipt of a letter from Gannon is noted. Anson later described him as Secretary of the St John's, Portugal Street, CYMS in Glasgow, recruited by Shields to assist in the revival of the Glasgow

AoS following Anson's visit, according to Gannon. Shields had agreed to recruit members of the old Glasgow AoS, persuading Gannon to assist with recruiting colleagues from the CYMS. Whilst Anson was at sea on the trawler *Fiery Cross*, fishing in Mounts Bay, Gannon was writing to the archdiocesan newspaper, *Glasgow Observer*, his letter appearing on 2nd October, the day Anson's fishing trip ended with his return to Caldey. Gannon wrote as 'Pro tem. secy' from 58 Norfolk Street, Glasgow:

> Following upon the recent visits of Bro Anson OSB to Glasgow and the publicity given through your columns to the need for an organised effort to keep Catholic seamen who come into this port in touch with the Church, a small committee has been formed to reorganise the work which was carried on for so many years in Glasgow under the direction of the late Fr Egger SJ . . . an organisation for the visitation of ships by Catholic laymen is necessary, and we invite all who are willing to assist . . . to attend a meeting in the Catholic Institute . . . [1]

A front-page notice announced the meeting would take place on Monday, 4th October at 8.00 p.m., The Rev. Fr Bradley presiding.

This meeting is described in Anson's diary as 'first meeting of A.S. Glasgow'. Anson was not present. The continuing interest of the editor of the *Glasgow Observer* ensured a published report. The paper revived the AoS title for this article (later adding the newly designed AoS badge to its regular column) which was headed: MEETING IN GLASGOW; ACTIVE WORK COMMENCED. Its report was positive: 'At last steps are being taken . . .' and reminded readers that the Catholic seaman at sea was effectively cast adrift from religious practice, and ashore faced with a choice of welcomes from Protestant establishments. To remedy this deficiency the meeting formed a 'Central Committee' comprising Fr Bradley (of St John's), Fr Murphy, Messrs Barker, Fox, Dobbie, Nolan, McPartland, Darroch, McLaughlin, Murray, Donaghey, Gallagher, Reid, with Gannon as acting secretary. Shields was closely associated with the Committee. The Committee appointed delegates to wait upon local parish priests to obtain their assistance in forming parochial committees. Messrs Dobbie, Baker and Fox were charged with drawing up and having printed leaflets with directions to churches and service times. In the meantime, volunteers and subscribers were invited to assist in the visitation of ships in the docks.

This Committee met regularly, usually fortnightly. At the second meeting, on 13th October, officers were chosen:
- Chairman - Fr Bradley
- Vice-chairman - Mr D. Darroch
- Treasurer - Mr L. Nolan
- Secretary - Mr A. Gannon

It was agreed to print leaflets in English, French, Spanish and Italian. Ship-visiting was reported as begun in six riverside parishes, with arrangements made to entertain Catholic seamen in the halls of the parishes concerned.

The revival of past methods suggests a determination to maintain continuity

---

1   Not a seamen's institute.

with the past, confirmed by the press as a continuation of the work begun under Fr Egger. This is not just a matter of historic interest. It is a matter of succession. The attitude it represented would lead to problems involving Shields. Anson was to write later:

> It was this . . . loyalty to the memory of Fr Egger that led to considerable opposition on his part to the creation of a new organisation . . . It was only when he had finally been convinced, not without great difficulty, that this new body would function on practically the same lines as the one which he had been instrumental in helping to start in Glasgow some twenty-two years before, that he gave it his wholehearted support.

Those familiar with Anson's style will understand that Shields was, at least for a period, extremely awkward, something the conciliatory Gannon, a reliable witness as he was in close contact with Shields, confirmed when he wrote, 'As was to be expected, Brother Shields leaned towards preserving the Apostleship of Prayer ethos'. Shields's awkwardness would lead to a major public disagreement though to no delay in AoS development. It is mentioned here because tensions were potentially present from the day that old and new were combined.

Anson, meanwhile, continued his travels, ostensibly on behalf of the CRG. He spent some days in London, staying at the Catholic Sailors' Home, about which he had considerable correspondence with the Countess de Torre Diaz, and for which he seems to have produced some early publicity material, and visiting Archbishop's House, largely about sailor-work. There Mgr Jackman advised him to write to the Cardinal.

Anson wrote to the Cardinal from Grimsby on November the 15th and again on the 30th. Part of the Cardinal's reply survives in *Notes for the Month*. Official replies tend to reflect the content of the original letter so it is not hard to guess what Anson had written to the Cardinal:

> Dear Brother Anson, I am glad to know what you are proposing to do at Grimsby. I am keenly interested in the spiritual welfare of our Catholic merchant seamen and the deep sea fishermen. I beg God to bless your work, and I commend it to the clergy and laity who are in a position to assist you.

If any pattern can be detected in Anson's work, which at this stage appears more reactive than proactive, it is the need to achieve recognition, here at the national level. His Grimsby visit removed him from what appeared to him as the gloom of the London Catholic Sailors' Home and its East End setting; within days he was at sea with his friend skipper McCarthy, returning at the end of the month and travelling back to Caldey on 2nd December. His time on the steam trawler *Empyrean* ('hardly a pleasure . . . how she rolled!!!') soon became grist for another article on the maritime apostolate.

What can be said about 1920, Anson's first full year? He was now drawing support from a wide base, or, more prosaically, from where he could. His letters suggest that he was in touch with the Catholic Evidence Guild though nothing appears in CEG papers in Westminster Diocesan Archive. He had contacted - inexplicably - the Catholic Stage Guild and Sir Shane Leslie. His links with the SVP are clearer and more extensive. At least eighteen diary entries relate to the SVP, a minimum figure, for others may be hidden in the list of personal correspondents, one of whom is easily recognised: Major Wegg Prosser, member and subsequent chairman of the London SVP Superior Council, from a distinguished Hereford Catholic family, benefactors of Belmont Abbey and its Benedictines. SVP correspondence took several forms. Much of it was information in response to Anson's newspaper appeal, about New York, Philadelphia and Melbourne, for example, while some, relating to Sunderland, Newport and Hull, was to initiate or restart SVP sailor-work. Sometimes this meant that he, as Fr Goldie before him, had to address local groups. Then there are the Wegg Prosser letters. SVP records do not lack references to seamen at this time but reveal no Anson correspondence. Given the SVP system of reporting back, his letters may have been seeking central support for various port initiatives. Another possibility, depending upon ambiguous diary entries (the 20th August in each diary), hints at a connection with a publicity article. Of his other correspondents, Dr Atherton of Montreal featured regularly, as did the ŒdeM. Surviving Anson letters are nearly all on CRG paper.

1921

In just over twelve months Anson had turned Miss Scott Murray's legacy of WCB work into something potentially international with unlimited scope. Writing to Macdonald from Caldey (9 January 1921), illustrating his need for assistance, he mentioned that he had written 238 letters or postcards in one day. This is either a mistake or an extreme example: diary blanks for January give no clue. It might represent the current mailing of *Lists*, at the start of a new year, probably involving prepared labels. Whatever the explanation, his correspondence had increased dramatically, and was neither helping nor being helped by his collapses in health, or his need to travel. The Honorary Secretary, as Anson is described at this time, was the one person in contact with all the actual and potential manifestations of Catholic sailor-work. It was at this point that help seemed at hand in the guise of the Caldey novice, Michael Davies.

There are problems around this development but this seems to be the shape of things. Anson described Davies to Fr Macdonald as an Old Marlburian, a convert, 28 years old, tall and strong 'with a body that any artist would want to draw!' (9th January). A letter of the 23rd January also refers to Davies, its date confirmed by internal details, Anson writing to Fr Macdonald:

When I saw him on my return from Fort Augustus, I felt convinced that he was THE man I wanted as a fellow worker. We never spoke of the subject, but he wrote to Fr Abbot that he felt he must devote himself to this work . . . Just before Christmas Fr Prior [the abbot was in South America] suddenly told me what Michael Davies wanted and it gave me rather a shock . . . Permission having been given for us to talk - rather a wonderful half hour together was our first real introduction to each other . . . .[Anson's emphasis]

There is no doubt that Anson was given to this sort of response. Whatever may be made of the meeting of minds, the coincidence of needs was fortunate as January 1921 for Anson was marked by collapse and the need for bed rest. The release of Davies to assist him was timely, probably eased by that collapse; the more so as Anson's tour of Welsh coal ports was imminent. On 18th January the pair discussed what needed to be done during Anson's absence. Anson wrote to Macdonald:

> This new 'Michael' about whom I wrote . . . has now made up his mind that he wishes to devote himself to my work - as an oblate brother. So he is going to prepare for it by a year spent in the novitiate - a training of body and soul - which will do him much good. Meanwhile he is being allowed to act as my secretary and will answer all business letters while I am away from Caldey. I am so happy about it . . .

The diary confirms this role, 'Work with MD all a.m . . . .'. It notes on March the 4th a letter sent from Anson to 'MD'. Someone at Caldey was certainly forwarding Anson's mail, and a letter sent on 2nd March to Macdonald, from Anson while resting with the Benedictine nuns at Talacre, confirms that this was Davies: 'It is a relief to feel that I can leave certain things to him', from which point Davies disappears completely from letters, diaries, everything. By the summer, Gannon was acting as substitute secretary when Anson was absent. Davies seems to have left Caldey by the autumn.

Anson's 'Dates from Old Diaries' marked March 1921 as significant; on March the 3rd he had written to Macdonald:

> I have negotiated with the SJ folk to use the name <u>Apostleship of the Sea</u> for all my (I ought to say <u>OUR</u>) work which will give it an international scope - which is what I want. [Anson's emphasis]

There is no hint of Jesuit reluctance to agree to this request; they asked only that its use should be accompanied by a continuing commitment to saying the Morning Offering, and to enrolment in the AoP, both honoured at least in the first few years.[1]

On the 10th March Anson went to Glasgow, met there by Shields and Gannon; apparently his first meeting with Gannon. He spoke at the Catholic Institute on 'The Apostleship of the Sea' to local committee members and others at which, he claimed, he made for the first time the suggestion that this should be a world-wide organisation; a strange claim, for he was well aware that others had had similar plans, and his own activities had pointed in the same direction for some time. Perhaps the sense of occasion, following Jesuit permission to use the AoS title, led him to think of this as its first public expression. Fr Bradley, proposing the vote of thanks, assured Anson of the 'zealous support of Catholics in Glasgow in furtherance of this much needed apostolate'. Shields, more guarded, seconding, thanked Anson for his 'helpful interest shown in the Glasgow Apostleship of the Sea Committee'. For him the use of the AoS title was no novelty, nor requiring permission as Glasgow's was already an AoS Committee. Yet it is odd that he should couch his thanks thus. The international nature of the work was in no doubt; at this very time, the Glasgow committee was being furnished with French literature by a 'kindred association in France',

---

1 '. . . what is the 'Morning Offering? It consists of offering to the Sacred Heart each morning, the Prayers, Actions, and Sufferings of the rest of the day.' AoS, Seamen's Branch of the AoP, leaflet, 1895.

probably the ŒdeM, and there was the correspondence with Montreal.

Anson returned to Glasgow at the end of March for a further meeting with Gannon and then Shields. Back at Fort Augustus he wrote regularly to Gannon (with no sign of Michael Davies), and occupied himself with articles for the Press and his international correspondence. On St George's Day, 23rd April, he 'resolved to go to France as soon as possible', his interest again turning to the ŒdeM, and a visit now feasible with Gannon's secretarial support. *PAX* at this time described how within the year a complete system had been established on the Clyde, with Gannon as the 'capable and tireless secretary' of the Central Committee. (This Central Committee at this stage was central to the parish committees in Glasgow, requiring but a small step to become the Central Committee of a larger AoS). The article associated with it the work of the SVP in Dublin (SVP's Catholic Seamen's Institute) with the desire that 'similar work by the SVP might be found in Great Britain', and concluded by noticing the work of 'the French Society of the Œuvre *du Livre du Marin*'.

Another breakdown in health prevented Anson from going to France, according to the *Glasgow Observer*, which announced that for the next three months Gannon would have charge of Anson's work, whilst Anson, described as Honorary Secretary of both CRG and AoS, took a break on medical orders. Anson left for the north of Scotland armed with painting equipment, and an Edinburgh doctor's instruction to rest, with, if possible, a sea voyage. In July he was able to take a sea voyage, this time on the Buckie trawler *Morning Star*. Gannon's administration, usually credited as following Anson's resignation in 1924, then establishing it upon a firm foundation, actually predates Anson's resignation, for he was acting secretary while Anson was at sea, abroad or on sick leave, Gannon covering at least seven months' absence in 1921 and 1922.

In July Anson's diary entries reappeared after a two month gap. There had been sporadic letters to Gannon. Better health brought a return of interest: at the beginning of July Macdonald received a long letter discussing the appointment of Catholic chaplains to the MN and the RN, Anson fearing the bishops would regard MN chaplaincy as a 'dumping ground' for 'difficult cases'. He referred to 'my splendid and hard-working Secretary in Glasgow'. He discussed SVP work in various ports, particularly a real chance of a Catholic seamen's hostel in Salford. This return of interest is important because Anson was to claim that his visions of a world-wide organisation 'fell into their final shape' a few days later, on the 6th July, whilst trawling illegally, and very conveniently, on the 'Octave of SS Peter and Paul'. Anson liked his saints' days and was helped in their use by his Catholic diary which listed them all, day by day. It made a good story for a keen publicist. He meant that he had worked out how the world-wide scheme of the recent Glasgow speech could be effected.

How true was this account? The context of the idea 'in those hours soon after dawn when I was steering the *Morning Star*', or more prosaically, one morning at sea, is neither supported nor rendered impossible by diary entries, but however exciting the idea, it was not enough to drag him away from his rest cure until the end of the month, when he returned to Glasgow, took tea with Gannon, and resumed his duties as Secretary. If the context of his idea is a little suspect (there are echoes of the start of the ministries of G.C. Smith and John Ashley) it does seem as if Anson had finally worked out how the work of the AoS could be effected in one organisation, though detail is sparse at this date. Given Anson's Benedictine and Naval background the emergence of a vertical structure might have been expected. His experience of having to rely upon volunteer groups in a variety of ports probably accounts for the vague and horizontal structure which emerged. Equally it could have been sourced from Fr Goldie's enthusiasm for the structure of the SAWCM. His idea for organising internationally, such as it was, was not new. The novelty lay in its realization.

Anson spent August planning in the peace of Fort Augustus. On the 14th he began to read the SVP Rules. By the 17th he was able to record, 'Finished AS Rules', an entry accompanied without irony by a note that he was continuing his poaching article (actually an account of the recent fishing trip); the Rules written with more confidence after the Glasgow Committee's decision. Glasgow Committee members had not baulked at his latest proposal of an international association, because, although the committee was of recent formation, some of its members had worked for the old AoS; a significant factor was the conscientious way in the which the acting secretary, Gannon, had kept meetings regularly informed of world-wide developments by the reading of letters from overseas. Its active enthusiasm can be demonstrated: at a concert at St Paul's, Glasgow in July 1921, The Rev. Angus Mackintosh, presiding, voiced a widespread local feeling when calling 'for an extension of this form of Catholic sailor service to all large shipping ports . . . '. A letter from PROMOTER (not Mrs Howden, who had died in 1919; perhaps from Shields) in the *Glasgow Observer* commented: 'our Glasgow workers may be proud that their work is being copied in many seaports in Ireland, in England, and on the continent', adding to the experience of the committee and Gannon's careful nurture this note of pride in its being emulated. The Committee set about obtaining the approval of the hierarchy for its work.

The Rules envisaged by Anson seem to have involved the Glasgow Central Committee at the centre of a network, which he claimed later to be inspired by the structure of the BFSS. BFSS operated what may best be described as a system of franchises, a central committee furnishing the name, logo (flag) and basic guidance on organisation. In addition, Anson retained the saying of the Morning Offering by sailor members. The principal difference in the early rule of the AoS is that the sailor is seen as the primary agent of the association rather than the recipient of good works. It is possible that Anson's reference to the BFSS was intended to give the pot a stir; he had a mischievous side. He later claimed further inspiration from the OSP. One of its aims, reflected in Anson's earliest rules, which survive in French, was the provision of 'Healthy Recreation and Intercourse for the Men and Lads at its "Recreation Rooms"', though the omission of any reference by Anson to the industrial militancy found in *The Messenger* makes it difficult to say that Anson had any direct knowledge about the OSP's work at this time, or later when writing his *Call of the Cloister* (1964).

The OSP influence is likely to have been more subtle. In his accounts of the early days of the Catholic sea apostolate Anson refers in several places to the possibility of Catholics coming together to form a religious Order devoted to working with the sailor. The offer of the Augustinians of the Assumption, whose ŒdeM had been in part inspired by OSP, of the facility of their noviciate for anyone drawn to such a vocation, confirms that the question had been raised by someone at some time. It may be that Anson's enthusiasm for Michael Davies's assistance derived in part from an unexpressed thought that two Benedictine oblates might be the seed of such an Order. It is equally possible, by retaining the AoP foundation of prayer support by religious communities, that he expected one dedicated to the seafarer to emerge. Nothing emerged.

The principal source of the AoS Rules, he later acknowledged, was the SVP, whose Rules he had started reading on August 14th. Familiar with the SVP at all its levels, he now studied its Rules carefully. Of the AoS Rules summarised in Anson's *The Church and the Sailor*, the Object of the AoS finds a parallel in SVP's first Article; its organisation of Parochial, Central and Diocesan Committees copies the vertical structure of the SVP, even to the use of the term 'Superior Council' for its central committee; the officers of a Parochial AoS Committee, particularly that of Librarian, similarly match those of SVP. The grouping of parish committees into Central Committees is a renaming of SVP local Conferences, as is further grouping into Particular Councils; membership of both AoS and SVP, at least in the active class, required some 'active work of charity'; and the AoS honorary member (subscriber) also had its counterpart. In short, it is unnecessary to look beyond the SVP Rules to discover Anson's source of 'inspiration'.

It is likely that Anson had some sort of idea in his mind from a very early date, for he had done his research, knew of Fr Goldie's work, and must have encountered Goldie's dream of a world-wide federation, despite claiming his own vision as original. His familiarity with SVP would inevitably make its contribution. When the Glasgow Committee was restarted, however, the probability is that it adopted the old AoS way of organising, until it became necessary to distinguish between the Central Committee and the eight parish committees engaged in the Glasgow sea apostolate, and a year later to appoint a committee to run the new seamen's institute, when some sort of rules were required to clarify relationships. Gannon says these emerged 'midway in 1923'. His typescript history referred to an earlier set of 'Provisional rules' which through a typing error he ascribed to October 1931 (correctly, 1921). The Provisional Rules were those which had been printed and circulated when seeking the approval of the Catholic hierarchy of the British Isles (below) and met Anson's need for some sort of Rules to present when introducing the French to the AoS. They would also be what he would present in Rome.

Anson's ideas for organisation were not, therefore, original. If they had any novelty it lay in bringing the various bits together. He spent the next few days organising various members of the Glasgow Committee. After visiting Mr Quinn at the *Observer* office, he wrote to Macdonald: 'Big developments of an international character are now being discussed'. The Glasgow Committee accepted his ideas sufficiently for him to write a week later to Macdonald with the news that it had made him its honorary secretary 'and promise to pay all travelling expenses'. Actually, Gannon had used the title, honorary organising secretary, of Anson three months earlier.

In *Harbour Head* Anson said that his proposed Rules met with opposition from Shields, who feared the work might lose some of its spiritual nature; and from the Committee, reluctant to add to its responsibilities. Committee reluctance seems unlikely. Shields's opposition cannot be dismissed so easily as it is confirmed by Gannon; also by events in 1923. Memories are not always accurate. In Gannon's version, Anson, Shields and he exchanged drafts of the proposed Constitution by mail, with Anson writing to Gannon: 'I honestly prefer what you have written to my own elaborate production'; a correspondence absent from Anson's diaries at this time, which may point to a different date, as does Anson's presence in Glasgow in parts of August and September - otherwise, why write? The revised Rules were submitted to Bishop Toner, Apostolic Administrator of the vacant Glasgow archdiocese, for his approval. The Vicar General, Mgr Ritchie, conveyed Bishop Toner's approval in a letter read to the Committee at its meeting on 19th September. The Committee agreed to have printed five hundred copies of the Rules, also called the Constitution, in October.

Anson, meanwhile, had gone to London, writing from there to Macdonald that he was 'dashing around interviewing prelates and priests in high places' in the interest of AoS. He reported that the Cardinal and his private secretary were 'amazingly kind and complimentary'. He was planning a trip to France, for which he persuaded the Cardinal to write a letter of introduction. A visit to Archbishop's House on 12th October submitting AoS Rules for the Cardinal's approval prevented Anson's attendance at the Glasgow Committee's first Annual General Meeting (11th October). Those present heard that in Glasgow eight riverside parishes were involved in the apostolate, 833 ships had been visited, and contact made with 2,419 Catholic seamen. The Committee was in touch with Catholic Sailors' Clubs in Dublin, Belfast, London, and Montreal and *depôts* of the *Œuvres de Mer* in France. It was explained (the figure unsourced) that there were at least five hundred Protestant seamen's clubs - world-wide is implicit - but only eleven Catholic ones; a useful summary of Catholic post war development. Glasgow itself had an urgent need of such a club. How far Glasgow was intended to remain at the centre of things is a moot point for Anson was at this time planning to use the London Catholic Seamen's Home as his headquarters

... if the stodgy old committee of this Home think they can afford to pay my board and lodging without finding themselves in the bankruptcy court ...

This is a reminder both of the parlous state of the Home's finances, a perennial problem, and Anson's personal style, which sometimes hampered the maintenance of good relations with his hosts. A large abbey could probably carry a guest more easily than a small seamen's hostel.

Gannon, probably in his role as Glasgow's Committee Secretary, had written to Anson, now on Caldey Island, the week before Anson's London visit, asking him to design a badge for the AoS. Anson spent 31st September and 1st October working on various designs, one of which, the present badge, was adopted at a Glasgow Committee meeting on the 27th October and a quantity ordered. The same meeting, informed that all the British bishops had been sent copies of the Constitution, decided to extend the circulation to shipping companies. It considered Glasgow's need for a Catholic seamen's home (suitable premises would be obtained by March 1922), encouraged by a letter from Dr Atherton in Montreal. All of which suggests that the perception by Anson of any reluctance on the Committee's part lay in the eye of the beholder. The year had been marked by permission to use the AoS name, the drawing up of the Rules, the design of a corporate badge, and the approval of the British bishops, giving it a feeling of consolidation as Anson's ideas are tempered and shaped by those of Gannon and Shields, so that by the year's end the AoS had a definable structure and identity.

To France, 1921 - 22

With the Glasgow Committee working well, and Gannon to cover his absence, Anson was able to embark on his long-projected foreign tour. Anson had been impressed by what he had gleaned about the French sea apostolate; work among deep sea fishermen, led by a religious order with its own ships, clearly resonated with him. However, it was to Belgium that he went initially (accepting the offer of another Benedictine bed), leaving London for Bruges on 15 November 1921. He stayed for six weeks at the *Abbaye Saint-André*, apparently the guest of Dom Benedict Morrison, formerly of Caldey, and used the time to prepare a French translation of his English AoS material. The *Abbaye Saint-André* was strongly oriented towards mission, producing a bulletin, *Missions Benedictines*. The day after his arrival he noted in his diary, 'read article in *Études*', which can only mean the Grosjean article associated with the foundation of the ŒdeM (chapter eighteen). Anson's article for *Missions Benedictines* closely resembling Grosjean's, though with added contemporary material, and sharing Grosjean's conclusions, was printed in *Missions Benedictines* in 1923, when it had the advantage of being able to claim the support of the French hierarchy and include the AoS Rules.

Anson's French probably benefitted from his time at *Saint-André*. Soon he would be addressing Breton ears, for on 21st December he left Belgium to spend Christmas at Port en Bessin. On the afternoon of Christmas Day Mgr Lemonnier, Bishop of Bayeux, presided at a meeting of the Port en Bessin Fishermen's Union at which Anson gave an address on the present state of the AoS. Next day he lunched with the bishop before setting off for a 36-hour fishing trip on a French fishing boat. On New Year's Day he went to Caen to address the *Jeunesse Catholique*. A tour of French ports followed; his itinerary is not certain as there are contradictions in his diary and books. With him he carried Cardinal Bourne's letter of introduction, commending him

> très specialement à la bienveillance des autorités ecclésiastiques . . . le Frère Richard Anson s'occupé avec grand zèle des marins et pêcheurs catholiques.[1]

[1] 'specially to the kindness of the ecclesiastical authorities . . . Brother Richard

According to Anson, Mgr Lemonnier, on 2 January 1922, advised him to go to Rome to seek the Papal blessing on the AoS. There is no obvious reason why the same advice had not been given by Cardinal Bourne or any other British bishop. Anson continued his tour of ports and organisations, meeting on 1st February *Père* Eutrope Chardavoine of the AA, before spending time with the *Abbé* Bernard, parish priest of Port en Bessin, a man very familiar with the history of the French sea apostolate; as early as 1914 Bernard had envisaged some sort of seamen's association, the intervention of war perhaps the explanation of its failure to materialise. An article written by *M.* Bernard after Anson's visit summarised French work, mentioning most of the organisations which would later federate (chapter twenty-one), and which Anson included in his tour. Bernard wrote, too, in the July-December 1922 issue of *La Documentation Catholique*, of AoS work as it was understood in France, listing the *Œuvres de Mer, les abris* of *M.*de Thézac in Brittany, the *maison Jeanne d'Arc* in Toulon, twelve SVP port initiatives, and the revived work in Glasgow, which he attributed to Anson, assisted by *la Jeunesse Catholique* écossaise. The article appears to have been reprinted from the Port en Bessin parish magazine.

One of Anson's 1922 diaries contains some hard-to-decipher notes in French, written by another hand, unrelated to the days on the page, posing a series of questions for consideration, about details and numbers involved in the French system of compulsory naval service; one asking who in France could superintend the affiliation to the *Apostolat de la Mer*, followed by the comment: '*un officier inférieur*'; together with notes about Cardinal Dubois and *Père* Guerin. These are nowhere explained by Anson but their meaning seems clear enough; that even at this early stage, he, or whoever wrote them, had a clear intention of achieving a French federation linked with the AoS. Perhaps the suggestion of *un officier inférieur* was prompted by the knowledge that *M.* Bailly of the ŒdeM had been a naval officer, though as things turned out, it would be *Père* Chardavoine who achieved the federation in 1924 – 25.

Rome and 1922

Anson's original intention seems to have been to go to Rome on 22 February 1922. Instead, he left France on 1st March to stay at the Scots College in Rome. Its Rector, Mgr Mackintosh, had been announced to the archdiocese of Glasgow as its new bishop on 14th February. Anson's diary records receipt of Fr 500 from Glasgow on the 18th February, perhaps to cover his travel expenses. If the letter accompanying the money brought news of Mackintosh's appointment, it would suggest why now he should follow Lemonnier's advice to go to Rome. It would also give a bed at the Scots College a demonstrable utility beyond free accommodation.

Anson spent some of his Roman time sight-seeing and visiting old friends. He wrote to Cardinal Bourne of the 'silly little squabble' with CRG, perhaps

---

Anson has great zeal for sailors and catholic fishermen.'

because he felt the AoS needed, and was about to obtain, its independence. He visited the Benedictine Abbot Primate at Sant' Anselmo, possibly to regularise his increasingly anomalous position as a Benedictine oblate. His principal object in Rome, however, was to obtain papal approval. Several versions of how this was achieved exist. All involve Mackintosh. A diary note of 16th March says 'ordered Apostolic Blessings' but these were probably the printed sort freely obtainable by almost anyone. The many blank diary pages for the Rome visit make the clues in his March the 8th letter to Cardinal Bourne about the CRG valuable. He wrote that Mackintosh had promised

> to do his best to get the blessings of the Holy Father on the Apostleship of the Sea - as a nucleus of an international society for the spiritual welfare of Catholic seafarers.

To Mgr Jackman (21st March) he elaborated:

> Mgr Mackintosh has taken the matter of the Apostleship of the Sea with great enthusiasm and himself went to Cardinal Gasparri [Papal Secretary of State] to arrange about securing the necessary Blessings & Approval. So I have nothing more to do at present but to wait until this arrives!

Anson changed his story over the years, for example in 1951 when writing to *Père* Butel to clarify Mackintosh's relationship with the AoS, his letter concerned to explain that Mackintosh had been invited by the AoS and not by the Holy Father to be its President, an important point if a precedent was to be avoided, in the Autumn of 1922, and after Mackintosh had taken up his see. Giving the context, Anson emphasised that his visit to Rome had been at Lemonnier's and not Mackintosh's prompting, and continued:

> All that Mgr Mackintosh did do was to hand in the request from his guest to the right department at the Vatican when he happened to be going there on his own business. The Oblate-Brother [Anson] was staying at the Scots College, because the Abbot-Primate could not find a room for him at Sant'Anselmo . . . Incidentally, it was the French bulletin, *L'Apostolat de la Mer*, printed at their own expense by the Benedictines of Saint-André, which contained a translation of the rules and objects, that was submitted to the Papal Secretary of State. [Anson's emphasis]

Papal approval came in a letter signed by Cardinal Gasparri, Secretary of State and dated 17 April 1922. It includes the idea of something which would be world-wide. Gannon believed the text to have been arrived at after papal consultation with Mackintosh. The letter as it appears in Anson's *The Church and the Sailor* refers to the

> work which your Reverence has just brought to the notice of His Holiness . . . is such that it cannot be without the blessing of the Vicar of Jesus Christ, and also his approval and encouragement . . . With the certain knowledge that so noble an enterprise . . . will spread more and more along the sea coasts of both hemispheres . . . the Holy Father is pleased to invoke on it every Heavenly Grace . . .

A copy of the original Italian text survives in the Vatican archives. The letter marked a successful conclusion to Anson's Rome visit. He arrived back in England on April the 24th.

In his capacity as Honorary Organising Secretary, Anson went to Glasgow to attend the opening of its Catholic Seamen's Institute on 30th April. Anyone thinking this would be an occasion to make something of the newly received Papal approval would be mistaken; instead, Anson used it to appeal to Catholic bishops to 'deal with the scandal of neglect of the whole Merchant Marine' by appointing 'Catholic port missionaries in every large port'. It is hard to find any occasion when this apparently important recognition received an airing. As it is the Gasparri letter on which the present AoS hangs its date of foundation, this silence is a mystery. As a letter of good wishes it recognises the existence of the AoS. Its general terms may explain why it was not brandished in the later dispute with the SVP over which organisation would minister world-wide to seafarers (chapter twenty-one).

After the Glasgow meeting Anson returned to Fort Augustus, and the routine of organising by mail, and producing a new *List* of Catholic officers in the RN. A success at this time was the involvement of the Catholic Women's League which he persuaded to re-open a fisher-girls' club, closed by the war, at Lerwick, which he visited in July, expressing his hope of something similar being started at Grimsby, which received large seasonal migrations of 'fisher lassies'.

Mackintosh's consecration as bishop of Scotland's most populous Catholic diocese prompted the AoS Committee to invite him to be its President. Catholic organisations show official approval by naming a senior bishop as President; the role is largely honorific. This, rather than the Papal approval, and news of the increasing number of ports where sailor-work was being started or revived, occupied the agenda at the Annual General Meeting in Glasgow on the 24th October. The Council meeting following, on the 1st November, re-elected Gannon as Honorary Secretary, with an assistant, and Nolan as Honorary Treasurer, before appointing an Institute Treasurer and Trustees (who had financial functions). The Committee, effectively the old one re-elected, decided to present their new President with a replica of the AoS badge in gold.

In France it was reported, apparently in the Port en Bessin magazine *Le Pilote*, which Anson was receiving, that Mgr Lemonnier was expressing 'in cordial terms his desire to have this Apostolate made known', and was particularly interested in the International Union of Catholic Seafarers which was part of the AoS Constitution, effectively the sailor-members who undertook to say the Morning Offering. Lemonnier pointed out that almost every group except seafarers had been organised by the Church, and this Union, with its membership card as a kind of Catholic passport, he thought in some measure might meet that deficiency. The British AoS was still accepting membership cards issued in pre war days.

In England an increasing number of ports, most recently Barrow-in-Furness and Workington, was being organised. An institutional structure was being devised; perhaps in emulation of the protestant societies, whose annual reports were graced with lists of aristocratic Vice Presidents, in October 1922 the Duchess of Norfolk, the Countess de Torre Diaz, Hilaire Belloc, Admiral Sir Edward Charlton, and J. Cameron Head Esquire were announced in the *Glasgow Observer* as AoS Vice Presidents. Internal evidence suggests that these news items were sent to the paper by Anson, certainly by post for in October he had departed, apparently for private reasons, for *Saint-André*, thence to Rome at the beginning of December, again leaving the AoS in the hands of Arthur Gannon.

1923

Anson returned to the United Kingdom in January 1923. A few days were spent busily in London at important meetings, and staying at the Catholic Seamen's Home. Gone was the CRG notepaper; his letters were now on paper headed *L'Œuvre de l'Apostolat de la Mer*, perhaps to emphasise the international nature of his work, or because it looked rather splendid. His diaries record 22 January 1923 as spent, first at Archbishop's House, then with Major Wegg Prosser, before attending a full Committee Meeting of the SVP Superior Council. He returned to Glasgow for an AoS meeting on the 26th, followed by what seems to have been a meeting with a Miss M. Grahame of the Catholic Women's League regarding the Lerwick fisher lassies' club. In the next few days he met the AoS Treasurer and Secretary, and visited the Archbishop, an unusual pattern for Anson. It is tempting to see in it a sign of the trouble now brewing, especially as several meetings, with the Treasurer bore the comment: 'Further difficulties with Nolan'.

Anson discussed an imminent visit to Glasgow by Dr Atherton from Montreal, with whom he had had much correspondence, a star of the Catholic sea apostolate, but whom he had yet to meet. Atherton's lecture in Glasgow was to be the first of a tour, details of which have not survived. Although Anson was expected to attend the lecture his diary records his departure from Glasgow on the 1.30 p.m. train on the 30th January, for Aberdeen, thence to Buckie. Atherton gave his lecture on the next day when, in the presence of Mgr Ritchie (Vicar General and Administrator of the Cathedral), he spoke on 'Montreal and its Sailor Club'. It is curious that Anson's diary should extend to the detail of a train time on the 30th if he was intending to be at the talk on the 31st. If his absence is accepted, it may have been a temperamental reaction to his difficulties with Nolan. Nolan was one of the Glasgow AoS old guard. It is also known that Anson, having been ordered to take February as a month's rest because of overwork, fled north, perhaps this departure. If his flight was not a diplomatic withdrawal, it suggests another emotional collapse. Yet, although he was supposed to be resting, his diaries show, if anything, an increase in correspondence through February, perhaps the annual mailing of the *List*. He appears to have called briefly again at Glasgow *en route* for Caldey at the beginning of March, another month marked by heavy correspondence.

The looming trouble now broke in the correspondence column of the *Glasgow Observer*, apparently the culmination rather than the onset of a disagreement. The exact nature of the problem never appears but its drift is clear. On 3rd March a letter over the pseudonym JARL HIGG-CAMERON was published, purporting to be from a ship-visiting member familiar with the old AoS, which it claimed to have ceased in 1909.[1] It asked if this new AoS was

---

1 Around this time Mrs Howden's symptoms, which led to her entry into the Gartnavel Asylum as a voluntary patient, began to appear.

a revival of the old; indicated the lowly position of the prayers (especially the Morning Offering) in its Constitution; argued that its social side would be better left to other agencies; and quibbled at the tautology in the use of 'International' (as in the International Union of Catholic Seafarers) in the title of a Catholic body. It pressed for free AoS membership for sailors. Pointing to the original founders, Canon MacLuskey, Mr T. J. Nicholls, Mrs Catherine Howden, and Fr Egger SJ, it added

> It would be no compliment to Glasgow, if it were true, that they were unaware until Brother Anson OSB came and informed us that Catholic seamen came to our port in Glasgow....

A week later the paper printed SOME CRITICISMS ANSWERED from Gannon, as local Secretary, perhaps informed by Anson with whom he exchanged several letters at this time, rebutting the criticisms by indicating that various AoS publications of 1921 and 1922 paid tribute to former work; explaining the necessity to reduce the prayer commitment because the original rule required all ship-visitors to be AoP Promoters, where now more volunteers were necessary, and indicating the approval of the changes implied in the Papal Blessing and the Archbishop's Presidency. The membership fee was a single payment to cover the cost of badge and card. The word 'International' distinguished the Union from local Unions of Catholic Seafarers, as in Goa and France (of which no details were given). His conclusion referred to the 'anonymous contributor's interesting but ill-informed criticism', and paid tribute to Brother Shields 'than whom no-one has been more zealous in promoting this work', no longer a 'ferry-boat ... but an ocean-going liner'.

'Higg-Cameron' was undeterred. On March the 17th his reply complained that Gannon's letter had been written with neither mention nor approval at the recent Committee meeting. The thrust of this letter was against the priority of Anson, asking if he had invented ship-visiting, when he had first come to Glasgow, and where he had first heard the name of the AoS. Anson replied (31st March), calmly and at length to 'Mr Jarl Higg-Cameron's ... courteous and most reasonable criticisms of the method and organisation of the Apostleship of the Sea Society', pointing out that the AoS had been started, not by Fr Egger but Fr Dignam SJ, and referring Higg-Cameron to the (Jesuit) publication, *MSH*, of 1891. He mentioned Miss Scott Murray, Miss Margaret Stewart, and the provision of literature 'transferred to us by the original promoter herself'. AoS members were being recruited not just in Glasgow but in North Shields and in Cardiff. As to his own role, he emphasised that all work seemed to have stopped when he toured 'practically every seaport in Great Britain and Ireland' in 1920. Resulting from this tour and talks with

> one of the original band of early workers in Glasgow [i.e. Shields], with Miss Scott Murray ... and many other persons connected with the Catholic Truth Society's Seamen's Sub Committee (now defunct) - besides priests and laymen on the Continent - ... we eventually conceived of the idea of establishing a society with the object of promoting the Spiritual Welfare of seafarers....
>
> ... to revive the work, or rather create a new work which would be animated by the same spirit as the original Seamen's Branch of the Apostleship of Prayer.

Anson had talked with Fr Bliss SJ, the British AoP Director, and received his permission to use the AoS name, to which, and the prayers, was added the membership card so disliked by Higg-Cameron. Higg-Cameron's aversion to sailors' 'social interests' was questioned. Anson ended by noting that some changes had been unavoidable, citing Papal approval in defence. No more was heard from Higg-Cameron.

Is it possible to identify Higg-Cameron? The correspondence would explain Anson's and Gannon's memories of Shields's obstinacy if Shields were the author. There are clues: membership, or close association with a member, of the past and present committees, and close knowledge of the founders. Shields had a record of writing angry letters, as that of 1904, copied in 1905 to the Archbishop of Glasgow, regarding the CSH and its committee. Supposing Shields had wanted to succeed McNichol as manager of the original seamen's home, a general bitterness against anything beyond Fr Egger's pattern might be expected. Then there were Anson's recent problems with Nolan, a close associate of Shields. Shields is not mentioned in Higg-Cameron letters but is carefully named in each reply. The repeated invocation of Shields's name would have maximum usefulness if it was Shields himself who was the target, while his gentle treatment in the replies would reflect Shields's stature within the Glasgow AoS.

The storm subsided. Anson went to London in April to prepare for a tour of South East ports. Perhaps as a result of meeting with SVP officials on his previous visit to London, the Glasgow AoS Committee welcomed a Mr Moffat, from the London SVP, 'for the purpose of investigating the work here with a view to a similar start in London'. The months following form a period of consolidation. Anson's and Gannon's articles of the time are careful to mention Fr Egger's name as a nod in the direction of Higg-Cameron. Both were kept busy by correspondence and publicity, Gannon increasingly, as Anson began to pursue his own interests. Although the link with the CRG was a thing of the past, Anson was visited by Coldwell in August 1923, probably for social reasons. Another summer visitor, to Glasgow if not to Anson, was Professor Smith of Montreal, a colleague of Atherton and erstwhile Brother Alban of Caldey.

Anson's article on '*L'Apostolat des Marins*' for the *Missions Benedictines* was sent to *Saint-André* on the 12th May. It's publication in the second half of the year may explain the increase in Anson's foreign correspondence. Anson began to use details from the *Abbé* Bernard in contributions to the Catholic press, reporting in the *Glasgow Observer*:

> The project linking up the various Seafarer's Guilds and Confraternities which exist among the coastwise communities in France into a Union of Catholic Seafarers in affiliation with the Apostleship of the Sea is making headway.

This development will be considered in the next chapter.

At this time there is a definite, if difficult to define, change in Anson's attitude. The Higg-Cameron episode may have engendered a certain disenchantment but it was a characteristic of Anson that his enthusiasm would wane, despite his work for Catholic seamen outlasting any other enthusiasm before or after 1923; the title of one of his autobiographical volumes is *A Roving Recluse*. The AoS was beginning to assume a life of its own. There is a stage in the maturation process when an organisation begins to dictate the organiser's role, rather than the reverse. When at the beginning of October Gannon sent Anson an 'AS reorganisation scheme', the pioneer was beginning to be replaced by the settler. Diary entries imply something afoot, Anson visiting Cardinal Bourne (9th October), and writing to Archbishop Mackintosh and Shields; while Gannon appears to have had a meeting with Mackintosh which was other than routine. No details survive. An explanation might be that this was related to the imminent AGM, or perhaps concerns about Anson's health.

Anson attended the 1923 Glasgow AGM on 6th November at the Catholic Seamen's Institute to speak on AoS progress, and was introduced as one 'whose life is dedicated to the Apostleship of the Sea work'. He listed sailor-work of one sort or another at Leith, Dundee, South Shields, Sunderland, London, Ramsgate, Southampton, Bristol, Cardiff, Dublin, Belfast, Sydney, Buenos Aires, New York, Philadelphia, Montreal, Naples, Genoa and Gibraltar. If to his list are added the various French ventures, the modern shape of the AoS begins to appear. The work was beginning to provide its own impetus. A significant number of ports listed were in the care of the SVP. Anson's diaries continue to show considerable contact with the SVP at various levels, mainly by mail. The late Autumn is marked by an unusual number of diary references to meetings of AoS or SVP groups with the implication that they were attended by Anson.

1924

Diary entries suggest by the beginning of 1924 that Anson's commitment to the AoS was waning. Based at Quarr Abbey on the Isle of Wight for several months, he was able to travel more easily than from Caldey. Letters concerning AoS business are routine, but series of days are devoted to other activity: a few in London spent socially (unusual for Anson), others shared with the Quarr brethren, some discussing Caldey with Eric Gill. In February he set off for Scotland by sea, spending the month in the north. On 3rd March he arrived in Glasgow, spent the 4th with Shields, and then with the Archbishop, before attending an evening concert at the Catholic Seamen's Institute, and leaving Glasgow the next day. A letter to Miss Scott Murray followed on 7th March. All this was much as he had behaved in October.

Although Anson says in *Harbour Head* that he resigned his AoS position in 'the summer of 1924', his diary reveals otherwise. The situation was amplified in the *Glasgow Observer* of the 23rd March:

> Rev Brother Richard Anson, owing to constant ill-health and the inability to stand the strain of the rapidly growing work, has been obliged to resign the post of Honorary Organising Secretary of the AoS, to which he has devoted himself since 1919.

The paper added that future correspondence should be sent to the Honorary Secretary either at Liverpool or Glasgow, an indication of how the AoS had developed and matured. In the 1923 *Report* that maturation is illustrated with some statistics. The number of associates had grown to 500, with 150 active and 800 seafaring members of the International Union of Catholic Seafarers.

Anson had encouraged the SVP to ship-visit in twelve British ports and in others overseas, starting new groups and linking those which had survived the war. With such a record, what lay behind his resignation?

Two surviving contemporary letters add a little flesh to the bones. On 9 March 1924 Anson replied to Mgr Ritchie, answering a question about the cost of an organising secretary to the AoS or, given the Glasgow Vicar General's interest, the diocese. Anson thought the minimum would be £100 a year, of which £70 would cover board and lodging, assuming accommodation in a convent or institution, with £50 a year as a reasonable figure for travel costs. Stationery and postage would be drawn from AoS funds. In his own case he had made no inquiries about possible accommodation in the Liverpool archdiocese (Liverpool being the premier port) but thought the Benedictine Sisters at Talacre or the Superior at Quarr would accommodate him, Benedictine hospitality having kept him afloat for years. Implicit is the appointment of a single man. It is possible that Anson was being sounded for the job, effectively his present one but properly financed. Alternatively, given the state of his health, some of the uncertainties were being removed. It may also be that Ritchie was trying to avoid a repetition of the CRG fiasco by establishing clear lines of demarcation.

The second letter confirms that the interview with the Archbishop of Glasgow had been about Anson's future:

> Please do not take any further steps towards obtaining funds for my support as organising secretary of the AoS. I have been thinking over the matter since our meeting of a fortnight ago and I feel that I cannot conscientiously take on the work as a paid job. I have not got the strength to tackle it properly and it would mean spending practically all my time in an office at secretarial work, or else rushing about the country speaking or lecturing. And with the experience of the past few years the result would probably be another serious nervous breakdown in a month or so.
>
> If a whole time secretary is to be appointed he should be someone who is more reliable than myself.
>
> I have written to the Archbishop of Liverpool and to Arthur Gannon.
>
> Asking your blessing,
>
> I remain Your Grace's devoted son.

This letter was dated 15 March 1924. At this point Anson effectively disappears from the story, except to emerge as a guest of honour at the 1927 international conference; later as a self-appointed publicist and gadfly of the AoS; never again to control its fortunes. Nothing suggests that Anson was being got rid of, or that there had been a falling-out; a certain irony lies in his going on medical grounds just at the point when he seemed in better health than for some years.

The appointment of the first full-time paid secretary implies an organisation firmly established. The appointee would inherit the organisation, as described in the 1923 *Report*, and his legacy could be examined. A date for the foundation of the modern AoS, perhaps derived from the first meeting of the revived Glasgow Central Committee, or the date of issue of the Papal 'approval', would be equally convenient; yet the international guise of the

AoS was only properly assumed at the 1930 Conference. The departing secretary's mantle fell on Gannon. The problems it brought will be examined in the next chapter. Anson's work had made such an appointment possible and Shields's foresight had provided the person to fill it. Anson left more than problems; during his tenure the AoS had been reassembled, hindsight revealing a logical progression of information gathering, method (ship-visitation), official recognition, assumption of identity, international links, approval by Rome, and consolidation. In particular Anson - perhaps more properly, Gannon - had welded together a Central Committee.

As organising secretary Anson had been in touch world-wide with an increasing number of correspondents. It was he who had met the workers in France and Britain, making him the centre of an ever-widening circle; for many, he was the AoS. If his achievement is compared with that of Fr Goldie the similarity is obvious. The difference lay in Anson's creation of a means by which disparate agencies could coalesce in an international body whilst still allowing each bishop proper sway over the sea apostolate in his diocese. How that was achieved, and whether what it achieved was the best model for an apostolate which necessarily transcended parish structures will be examined in the conclusion.

There are strange versions of the founding of the AoS to be found in current AoS publicity material. One ascribes the foundation of the AoS to a 'group of dedicated lay people in Glasgow' in the 1920s, naming Anson, Gannon and Shields. It says that they wrote to Rome for a papal blessing on their work, and that Pius XI in his reply encouraged them to extend their work to all the ports throughout the world. A balanced account would say that the AoS was revived rather than founded by Anson, incorporating much earlier work, and that Papal encouragement followed rather than preceded its spread beyond Glasgow. It would ascribe to Anson the star role but one sustained with Gannon's loyal support; indeed, to speak of Gannon's support may be to undervalue that loyal service which allowed the AoS to survive during the long periods of Anson's absences. Shields can be credited with Anson's initiation and Gannon's recruitment, but the, almost certainly his, attempt to scupper the AoS in its modern form casts him in a rather different light. It was Anson who went to Rome to obtain the Papal approval, greatly assisted by Archbishop-designate Mackintosh, conveyed in Cardinal Gasparri's 1922 letter. Why that approval received so little attention remains a mystery. To suggest that the foundation of the modern AoS dates from this letter neglects the continuity of the AoS with Fr Goldie's legacy, Fr Dignam's creation of the original AoS, and the bringing together of the AoS and the Merchant Navy in Glasgow principally by Mrs Howden. Without the contribution of these people, it is impossible to guess what Peter Anson might have been doing between 1919 and 1924.

21. Catholic Work after Anson[1]

The Apostleship of the Sea assumed its present form after the departure of Peter Anson. Various national bodies had come into existence, for example the *Apostolaat ter Zee*, begun in Rotterdam in 1923, and the *Apostolaat des Meeres* in Germany later in the decade, but its international character was only properly assumed as the result of congresses held in France in 1927 and 1929, and the establishment of the *Apostolatus Maris International Concilium* (AMIC) in Liverpool in 1930. Why the initiative for an international congress was French can be explained in part by some of Arthur Gannon's problems on his formal assumption of the Secretary's job. Some of these were typical of any young organisation, others part of the Anson legacy. Gannon was dealing with domestic issues and the SVP's plans for sailor-work. The records are patchy but it is possible to make some sense of the evidence.

Gannon, writing in old age and sickness, gave an account of his early years as Secretary. The job was not new to him, but now he was no longer responsible to Anson; the two maintained a minimal correspondence. At some time in 1924 he gained the support of Fr Kerr McClement, a chaplain RN, who assumed the role of roving ambassador intending to spread the AoS method (ship-visitation, literature distribution etc.) to each port in which he found himself, and from Fr C. C. Martindale SJ, a famous preacher and missioner of his day, who publicised the work of the AoS nationally, writing a CTS pamphlet about the AoS, and producing for the SVP a new prayer book for sailors, also published by the CTS, which was widely translated, and ran into several editions. The two men supplied the desk-bound Gannon with some of the mobility and publicity lost to the AoS on Anson's departure.

In the matter of organisation Gannon had little to learn from Anson, but Anson had bequeathed him a number of pieces requiring assembly. A detailed account of his problems with finance, committee structure, and office siting, would be tedious. His most serious problem concerned the relationship of the AoS with the SVP, only finally resolved well into the 1930s, its roots extending beyond Anson to Goldie. It illustrates Gannon's problems well. The tendrils of SVP were intertwined with those of the AoS on both sides of Channel and Atlantic; how the SVP had been drawn into the sea apostolate in London, Montreal, Philadelphia, Dublin, Belfast and other ports has already been considered at length; of the work surviving the 1914 – 18 war, most involved the SVP. Anson's recognition of this is

---

1   Full references are given in Miller, *Ship of Peter*.

21. Catholic Work after Anson

demonstrated by his early contacts with the London Superior Council, and his visits to local conferences to revive work started by Goldie or initiate new work. SVP's French work is traceable to similar roots, Grosjean paying tribute to the SVP in his 1895 *Études* article, and noting that the President General of the SVP was a member of the ŒdeM committee.

SVP's post war work has received considerable attention in chapter twenty. From Anson's time it was supported at the highest level, Cardinal Bourne asking the London Superior Council to assume responsibility for London's ailing CSH in 1921. In the same year the Tyne Central Council 'in response to the Cardinal's desire' (perhaps his letter commending Anson) had begun ship-visiting. In 1922 SVP ship-visitors were to be found in Cardiff, Barry, Workington and Monkwearmouth; in 1923 in Southampton, Ramsgate, Salford, Manchester and Newport, prompted, most probably, by visits from Anson. His help with the London CSH had been acknowledged by SVP: 'The Propaganda Committee has the great advantage of the co-operation of the Rev. Richard Anson, whose untiring efforts in the Apostleship of the Sea are so well known'.

A few pertinent letters from the period survive.[1] They imply that Anson had proposed to the Superior Council that it take up its sailor-work again - 'again' referring to what it had been encouraged to do by Fr Goldie, much of which had fallen into abeyance between 1914 and 1918. To support this revival either Anson or Dr Atherton had offered the services of the latter, coming from Canada to lecture, perhaps as an extension of Atherton's pre-arranged tour. The Council thought the offer premature while Conferences were recovering from the war. Nothing indicates that this response was a tactful way of stalling. The SVP Council secretary hoped that a future visit from Atherton might be possible and that eventually the Council would 'be able to take up this grand work'. In the meantime, it was considering how best to accede to the Cardinal's wish that it assume responsibility for the London CSH. Anson's advice that the London CSH should employ a collector of funds met with an uncertain response. That he was involved in discussions about its financial future implies that the secretary of the AoS was not being kept at a distance by the SVP.

It is salutary to view the AoS through SVP eyes. Thus seen, it is a small and only partly organised body with a base in Glasgow, whereas the eyes that see belong to a well organised, international body with an office not only in Glasgow but a Superior[2] Council in London, and answerable to the Council General in Paris. Whether in 1924, with Anson's departure, the field was considered open for sailor-work is not clear, but it was the year in which the SVP began to show independence in the sea apostolate, claiming to believe that the AoS was just a diocesan society; a serious misunderstanding which raises questions about Anson's meetings with the Superior Council, with Wegg Prosser, the London CSH, and local SVPs around the country. Gannon knew of the SVP interest but seems to have overlooked its significance; though his memoir mentions the recruitment of Fr Martindale to the AoS interest

---

1 I am grateful to Dr Austin Fagan for access to SVP files.
2 Superior here means the one above, in the sense of another administrative layer.

in 1927 it says nothing of Martindale's dealings with the SVP. Gannon's contemporary correspondence, however, coupled the two: he wrote to Mgr Ritchie in March 1924 telling him that Fr Martindale had written to ask for AoS co-operation in connection with the sailor prayer book that the SVP Council had commissioned him to write. Gannon seems not to have asked why the SVP was ready to make this kind of investment in the sea apostolate.

The Superior Council was being pressed at this time (1924), according to its Minutes, by a Brother Short of Malta, lately its Plymouth secretary, who

> had drawn up a scheme for embracing all the Empire and other countries into a united work for seamen. It was agreed to accept the offer of Brother Short to provide a translation of the scheme to [send?] to the Council General and to send copies of the scheme to English speaking Councils of SVP which had ports.

Members could read in the SVP's July 1924 *English Bulletin* about Church neglect of seamen in an article explaining that the SVP, with the AoS, was remedying this state of affairs in twenty home and nineteen foreign ports, all listed, together with 'certain ports in Spain . . . considerable activity in the Royal Navy and in the ports of Brittany and Normandy . . .'. With almost all the home ports supplied the article suggested that it was the time to spread world-wide, a natural development for the world-wide SVP.

> There is not a harbour of importance in the world which has not its Conference of [SVP]. Why should not the sailor be handed from one Conference to another through an international chain of Institutes of the Society, with their ship-visitors? (. . . better results may be expected by the creation of special Conferences for this work for sailors than by the addition of such work to the activities of already existing Conferences.) The benefit to sailors of all nations could not be estimated were the Conferences of the Society in [the ports with sailor-work] asked to inaugurate work for Catholic seamen in conjunction with the Apostleship of the Sea.

The plan had been considered in detail, with attention to ships' arrivals and departures, the commendation of the names of Catholics to their next port of call, notices of churches and times of service to be readily available, as part of an international scheme. The plan's author, 'An Active Member of the Conference of the Holy Cross, Plymouth, England', was almost certainly Brother Short. The 1924 SVP *Report* added that his scheme to link up the Port Conferences of the world had been approved by the Council General in Paris. 'It is hoped to secure the cooperation of the Apostleship of the Sea in this great work'. How is not said nor what plan the SVP might have if the AoS failed to co-operate.

More details of the SVP plan appear in Superior Council Minutes. In May 1924 a brother returned from Malta reported that he had interviewed Brother Short and Fr McClement. The latter's role *vis à vis* either society is not clear, for the discussion had been about the possibility of establishing a SVP conference in the RN; also, the prospects for local ship-visiting in Malta ('not hopeful owing to local temperament'). Minutes (9th July) recorded the Council General's 'hearty agreement with the views set forth and which they have decided to communicate to other Superior Councils' but the detail of what was agreed was omitted. On the 8th October, when a letter from Short

21. Catholic Work after Anson

was read proposing the formation of conferences on HM Ships and in Naval ports abroad, he was invited to attend the Committee. Nothing about AoS was mentioned except receipt of a letter from Glasgow announcing the start of a magazine for sailors, probably *RECHT door ZEE*.

In January 1925 the SVP Committee received a further report on 'International Maritime Work', recording Short's view that Naval conferences should be established in the principal home ports, and the AoS encouraged. It is possible here to see a repetition of the 1890s' division of work between the WCB and the CTS, now between SVP and AoS, but with each working generally for the benefit of the seafarer, as in this instance: 'The Sup[erior] C[ouncil] agreed that co-operating with the AS should be encouraged, and assistance of Glasgow Committee be applied for the printing of the Prayer Book recently drawn up'. This was the prayer book about which Gannon had written to Mgr Ritchie in March 1924, perhaps then at its draft stage. Yet this Minute leaves no doubt about SVP's opinion of who was taking the initiative in sailor-work; the prayer book appears as a kind of barometer to be tapped to indicate the state of the relationship between SVP and AoS. It could have been this prayer book contact with Glasgow which caused the SVP's meeting of 25th February to delay its issue of a circular relating to the 'Empire Scheme . . . owing to possible amalgamation with the AoS, so as to avoid overlapping', a premature proposal as subsequent events would show. The meeting on the 11th March was told that Gannon had replied that the AoS could not help with the immediate cost of the prayer book, but would assist by purchasing copies; further, that he had consulted the Archbishop of Glasgow over the matter of co-operation.

This was not an enthusiastic reply. Gannon gave no clue about what the Archbishop's views might be. The SVP, seeing little point in further delay, decided to send its Special Circular to eighty Port Conferences about its proposed scheme. By the meeting of 10th June, half had replied in favour, four as 'unable to help'. Perhaps because of the extent to which its sailor-work was developing, the Superior Council minuted on 22 July 1925 its intention to establish two sub committees: the Seamen's Sub Committee and the Seamen's Home Sub Committee, meeting monthly. The former was deputed

> to deal with the work for seamen in all parts of the Empire, and keep in touch through the Superior Council and the Council General with this work in the remaining ports of the world. This committee to receive the reports of the Stella Maris conference and all isolated Conferences established in the R[oyal] Navy or, for work amongst men of the merchant service also, to keep in touch with the Apostleship of the Sea.

In July 1925 the Committee was told that a meeting had been called to discuss with Gannon and McClement the possibility of 'a closer co-operation on defined lines of the two Societies i.e. the AS and the SVP'. Publicly the SVP seemed to be looking away from the AoS, a paper being read at the English SVP's August Annual General Meeting, and then published, attempting to trace the ministry of the Church to seamen from medieval times to the work of the AoP and the CTS, and the commencement of SVP's ship-visitation in London in 1891. The unnamed author, President of the Port of London Conference, and familiar with the London CSH, had obviously given sailor-work some thought:

Homes should be situated in a quiet thoroughfare. There are obvious advantages to being off the beaten track. They should be made as comfortable as possible, and possess nothing to remind the seaman of his calling. Take down all pictures of the sea and send them in the sack to the Crusade of Rescue. Some years ago a generous soul reconditioned a house and had portholes made for lighting and ventilation purposes, thinking that the nautical flavour . . . would appeal to the sailor who, of course, never came . . .

He said nothing about the work of the AoS. He reported the recent establishment of two SVP Conferences in the Mediterranean Fleet under the direction of the Senior Naval Chaplain. Another report from 1925 told of a 'Seafarer's Sunday' arranged at Tilbury by the SVP, with a special sermon, and seamen as choir and servers. The SVP was clearly extending its work with both MN and RN.

In 1926 the two agencies had to work hard to achieve a *modus vivendi*. A key SVP Council member, Mr T. Scanlan, was given the task of resolving differences, making a number of trips to Glasgow. The documentation of this period is poor. Nothing satisfactorily explains the rivalry or lack of communication between the two societies, nor why the famous Papal Blessing was not produced to establish the priority of the AoS. Gannon knew how much the AoS depended upon SVP port work, but his expressed concerns were only that the AoS should be kept informed of SVP activities and seamen enrolled in the AoS, neither an unreasonable condition. The information required by the AoS of the SVP was claimed to be for statistical purposes, yet it took pressure, on the one side from the President General, on the other from Fr McClement, to obtain agreement over these apparently simple points. That small issues could be so divisive suggests that they were symbolic. Control of statistics may have represented control of the other or at least which organisation would take the credit. The interpretation of the affair is complicated because the President of the Superior Council in London was the Major Wegg Prosser with whom Anson had dealt so often, and the acting secretary of the SVP Seafarers' Sub Committee was the Mr Moffat who had gone to Glasgow in 1923 to acquaint himself with the work of the AoS. Each side should have been familiar not only with the other's work, but on a personal level as well. While Short's scheme seems to have been genuinely separate rather than an attempt to take over the AoS, both sides bear signs of having adopted a territorial attitude. Scanlan's discussions with Gannon led to a meeting between key AoS figures: Gannon, Tulloch (Director of Associations), the Archbishop of Glasgow, and Fr McLaughlin (HQ Chaplain) on 11th November, appropriately Armistice Day, when an agreement was reached that the AoS would co-operate with the SVP, in an attempt to obtain ship-visiting and other statistics, a strange situation when it was the SVP which was failing to provide the figures. Gannon wrote to the SVP in London and expressed this view as from the Archbishop. If this lacks clarity, what follows becomes labyrinthine.

On 8th December Wegg Prosser reported to his committee that, a letter being received from the President General on the subject of the AoS and

21. Catholic Work after Anson

SVP, he had invited the attendance of Moffat and Scanlan of the Seafarers' Sub Committee. The letter explained his discovery that the AoS had been founded 'some years ago' by the Archbishop of Glasgow, and placed under the protection of Cardinal van Rossum, which

> seemed to carry out the same work as Bro Short's scheme, and that if it had been known of, the C[ouncil] General would not have sanctioned the SVP scheme, as it is a custom ... not to clash with other works but to co-operate with them.

Wegg Prosser proposed a reply which would indicate that the AoS and SVP had worked in co-operation for some years, the SVP working 'before the existence of the AoS which is a Diocesan Society'; that Cardinal Bourne had given SVP the English work; and asking for time to present the SVP case before the Council General should make a final decision. Nothing suggests that Wegg Prosser's committee dissented from these views, which seem to have been founded on expediency. His first point, about co-operation, was probably intended as an emollient. His second, that the AoS was a diocesan society, suggests that several years of contact with Anson were conveniently forgotten in face of the President General's objection. The claim of English work as the Cardinal's gift was irrelevant to a world-wide scheme though may have excused an Empire one. The appeal for time indicated the general weakness of the case. Scanlan added that in Glasgow most of the AoS work was done by SVP brothers, the AoS lacking the resources even to consider a scheme such as Short's. Moffat was given the task of drawing up the case to present to the Council General.

The Council General had surprised the London Superior Council. There are clues about what had prompted its action. At a meeting on the 26th December the Brother President revealed

> that he had received from Br Scanlan the copy of a letter written by Admiral Auvert which showed that the AoS had been in communication with the Council General [in Paris] as far back as May quite unknown to the Superior Council of England which seemed hardly just and might make co-operation more difficult.

This suggests that Short's scheme had been circulated in France, prompting an approach to the SVP Council General by the French federation (below) through their joint member Admiral Auvert. In spite of the Superior Council's Minute (above) complaining of injustice, it was entirely proper that the international AoS should correspond with the international Council General; the London Superior Council's feeling that the AoS had gone behind its back was predictable. It was less proper that the SVP Superior Council in London, as a national body, should contemplate an international venture. Its claim that the AoS was a diocesan society, lacking credibility, suggests the Papal blessing which was supposed to have given world-wide authority to the AoS had yet to be produced, but provided a ladder to climb down should occasion require. The London Superior Council obtained Cardinal Bourne's approval for its reply to Paris. That reply's history of affairs showed SVP's sailor-work pre-dating that of the Glasgow AoS. It enclosed a letter from the Cardinal, perhaps a copy of his invitation to SVP to adopt the London

CSH, which may be supposed to have been sufficiently vague to allow an interpretation which included English sailor-work in general.

After an uneasy period, a reply to the Council General explained that London had misunderstood Short's scheme, failed to realise that it involved existing work, and not known that co-operation existed already with the AoS in the United Kingdom. It suggested there was room for both schemes. The London Committee was still being pressed by Gannon for a report on SVP's work among seamen for inclusion in the 1926 AoS *Report*. An unhappy Superior Council decided, 'Mr Gannon be simply informed that the reports he asked for would be furnished as soon as they were available...'. It received a letter from Fr Martindale expressing 'his view that by its progress and development of the work among seamen, the AS must be recognised as the organisation adapted for this one special work...'. Yet despite all this, an article on sailor-work was published in SVP's *English Bulletin* of June 1927 with no mention of the AoS, emphasising instead the world-wide nature of SVP sailor-work and telling readers exactly how to establish a Stella Maris Conference.

Discussions between the two were re-opened in July 1927 and progressed slowly. While the SVP insisted to Cardinal Bourne that its members were responsible for the bulk of AoS work, an exchange of information was agreed. Enrolment of sailors into the AoS took longer to agree. A meeting on 5 October 1927 considered the appointment of a joint Council, with equal membership; as Gannon took the idea back to Glasgow the suggestion may have originated with the SVP. However, as in London the SVP put forward a similar but alternative scheme, the proposal for a joint Council may have come from the Cardinal. Money seems to have been part of the AoS problem; when the joint Council was finally achieved, Gannon moved to London, opening an AoS office within the SVP offices, perhaps a necessary economy. Anson dated this as 1927s, Gannon more accurately as 1928. The matter continued to rumble into the 1930s.

The SVP saga is important, not because it provided Gannon with a series of headaches bequeathed as part of Anson's legacy, nor because the AoS could easily have been sunk by the might of the SVP; rather, the importance lies in SVP's continuing commitment to the seafarer which could have turned SVP into *the* organisation for Church work among seafarers, for had Short's scheme been implemented, an exponential growth in sailor-work might have resulted and chapter twenty of this book been devoted to Brother Short instead of Brother Anson.

Short's scheme had envisaged almost a mirror image of the AoS: a world-wide network of ship-visitors and institutes which in his description sounds more effective than anything then existing. It differed from Anson's scheme, and Goldie's before him, in its proposed central organisation, reflecting SVP's vertical structure. The source of Short's idea is not known. Goldie's articles on sailor-work in the various SVP publications, would be sufficient explanation, while the British attitude to Empire, and the size of its MN, would account for the London Superior Council's willingness to adopt his scheme. Alternatively, it may be wondered if Anson had managed to alienate

21. Catholic Work after Anson

the London SVP leadership, perhaps by giving the impression that the AoS was running SVP Conferences. It is difficult to understand the London Superior Council's ignorance of Anson's strong French connections which had brought so much to the AoS. By the time of this present confusion *Père* Chardavoine had succeeded in bringing French SVP sailor work, its connection with ŒdeM dating from 1894, into his federation (below). It is consistent with the records that Chardavoine intervened with the SVP Council General without Gannon's prompting, the most obvious conduit for his intervention being Admiral Auvert, who occupied senior positions in both organisations, neither a sinecure, from whom a word would suffice to cause London to retreat. An alternative explanation but involving the *Abbé* Bernard will be suggested below. The statistics and the AoS enrolment of sailors required of the SVP by the Glasgow AoS, seemingly trivial requests, are thus capable of being interpreted as symbolic of where lay the power.

Gannon's secretarial work has been glimpsed through his correspondence and meetings with SVP. A more general picture can be glimpsed in a memo of a meeting in 1926 between Gannon, the Archbishop of Glasgow and others. As well as the SVP problem the meeting considered the possible purchase of an institute which could double as a headquarters, the appointment of a ship-visiting director, the organisation of associates in parishes, and the obtaining of an indulgence for attachment to an AoS prayer. The meeting also considered Honorary Patrons and Honorary Council Members. Amongst those nominated may lie another indication of how pressure had been brought to bear upon the SVP in Paris: the *Abbé* Bernard, himself a Council Member, had included the Archbishop of Rouen, and *M.* de Verges, Vice President of the SVP Council General, as his nominees, Bernard and de Verges offering an alternative to Chardavoine and Admiral Auvert in the approach to the SVP Council General; in which case the nomination of de Verges as an Honorary Patron of the AoS would acknowledge his intervention.

Whoever intervened with the SVP Council General, there is no doubt that the French at this time had effectively seized the initiative in shaping the future of the AoS. While Gannon was preoccupied with the establishment of a proper secretariat and, in Glasgow, Tulloch proposing to the Archbishop a scheme for supporters in parishes to be organised by Commodores, Captains and Crews, the French, through *Père* Chardavoine's efforts to federate the various bodies in the French maritime apostolate, were providing a pattern to allow for the inclusion of a variety of national bodies working among seafarers within the AoS orbit.

Chardavoine's initiative may have started as early as 1923. It is certain that in 1924 ten French agencies at work in the maritime apostolate met regularly with the purpose of knowing each other better. On their behalf Chardavoine circulated a dozen existing missions (the additional two are not identified) on 27 June 1925 with the intention of retaining the identity of each but asking for nominated representatives to form a committee to produce a constitution and a financial structure for the proposed federation. Of the twelve circulated, the original ten agreed to membership and were sent on 12 August 1925 a notice of a meeting of nominated delegates; this took place on the 5th November at the office of the *Œuvre des Orphelins de Mer*, 5 Rue Bayard, Paris, home also of the ŒdeM. It was chaired by Admiral Auvert, provisional president and Chardavoine's co-signatory on the circular invitation.

The November meeting heard that the purpose of federating was not to form a new mission; rather it was in emulation of another grouping, one of agencies assisting war widows and orphans, which had found strength in working together. Its secretariat would exchange information, addresses, and anything else of common use. A series of statutes was agreed, together with a system of sharing the budget to take account of constituents' differing incomes. A committee was elected, one member of which, the *Abbé* Bernard, undertook to obtain information about *une œuvre anglaise trés intérèssante, l'Apostolat de la Mer*, with which several bodies already had contact. Bernard was present as Director of the *Union Catholique des gens de mer*. The success of the federation is testified by its decision in 1926 to organise *un premier Congrès d'apostolat maritime* for 1927.

The 1927 Congress was held at Port en Bessin, parish of the *Abbé* Bernard (*Curé*, 1907 – 51), with a Papal Blessing, and the advice and encouragement of Mgr Lemmonier, on 7th and 8th August.[1] Its principal purpose was to bring together every Catholic maritime agency. The AoS headquarters and Gannon had been in touch with Chardavoine, or he with them, since 1926. Anson had met him while still AoS Secretary. AoS was represented at the Congress by Anson, Gannon, and the AoS Chairman, Admiral Sir Edward Charlton. Bernard acknowledged in his opening speech the AoS as the international Catholic body at work among seamen. French federation members gave an account of their work and statutes. *Père* Ricard SJ, reporting on Catholic work among merchant fleets, paid tribute to the AoS and Anson. Charlton, Anson and Gannon each spoke about the work of AoS. Dom Odo Blundell OSB, Catholic port chaplain for Liverpool, appealed for a universal federation. Admiral Auvert spoke about the work of SVP, explaining that the Council General had charged him with the task of encouraging work for sailors; that the English Superior Council had proposed a scheme whereby port conferences of the SVP should pass on to the next port the names of Catholics among crews they visited; that it intended to serve ports throughout the British Empire; that the sailor-work of SVP in France had met with little success, whereas in England (*sic*) the SVP was able to work with the AoS in Glasgow. This was an interesting summary of both the Short scheme and the official SVP position.[2]

Before the Congress closed the hope was expressed that there would be a second congress. No formal decision was taken to federate, but that was the effect. It is from this Congress that the work of the AoS properly began to assume its modern form. A second French congress in 1929 was followed by an international one at Liverpool in 1930. The French had shown one way in which the disparate work for seafarers could be joined without loss

---

1   Gannon incorrectly gives the month as September.
2   Report of *Premier Congrès d'Apostolat Maritime*, Paris, 1927.

of identity, allowing the *Apostolatus Maris International Concilium* to be formed at Liverpool. Anson later described it as 'an *omnium gatherum* of diverse units of Catholic Maritime Action, drawn from many nations. . .'.

The south wall of the sanctuary of the parish church of Port en Bessin supports a plaque:

> En Souvenir
> du premier Congrès International
> d'Apostolat maritime
> tenu a Port en Bessin
> les 7 et 8 Aout 1927

In much of today's AoS publicity, Anson is credited as the founder of the AoS, making him equate with others who have founded (Smith, Ashley, Mather) or re-organised (Kingston) great sections of the maritime apostolate. If to allow this obscures the contribution of Fr Goldie SJ and those others upon whose work Anson built, to none would justice have been done. Overlooking or dismissing his ability to build on the work of others and render it an effective whole would indicate a failure to perceive him as an important link in the chain, while to acknowledge his achievements would not diminish the role of Fr Goldie, or the complementary roles of Mrs Fraser, Lady Amabel Kerr, Mrs Howden, Miss Scott Murray, Arthur Gannon or Daniel Shields SJ; all have their place in the history of the modern Catholic sea apostolate. It remains to thank God that others who followed were there to pick up the pieces which remained after Anson's departure.

Conclusion

Anson's *The Church and the Sailor* claimed to tell the story of the Church and the seafarer; particularly of the formative years of the Apostleship of the Sea, with which he had been so involved. Until Kverndal's *Seamen's Missions*, apart from a few minor publications produced by individual societies to encourage supporters, it was the only significant book on maritime missiology. It was the intention of the present book to bridge a few gaps, bringing to Anson academic rigor, and to Kverndal details of Anglican and Catholic work. Readers will be aware that this is not a definitive account of anything. Here is no mention of Toc H, for example, and little of the work of the Scandinavian churches; nor do the smaller societies listed by Kevrndal in his *Seamen's Mission* and by Friend in his thesis receive much attention. Nevertheless, enough has been covered to allow reflection about the changing patterns of the maritime apostolate over the centuries.

Missionary endeavours are usually associated with the Gospel imperative, the Lord's command to go out into all the world to preach the Good News. Throughout this book there has been another imperative, effectively a sub text, but important nonetheless, namely the economic one. At its most obvious, it has meant that missionary societies have done as much or as little as finances permitted; sailors' homes have opened and sailors' homes have closed. Less obvious, but of more significance, in every case the Church has followed trade in its efforts to extend the sea apostolate; no trade means no ships; no ships mean no seafarers; no seafarers mean no sea apostolate. In this way it can be said that the sea apostolate has been shaped by an economic imperative.

The earliest centuries had no dedicated ministry to seafarers, the Christians among them members rather than recipients. In the medieval period, while trade involved mostly short-sea shipping, the ministry to seafarers was local and parish-based; if the seafarer required special provision, it was likely to have been offered by the local church through special Masses, perhaps a guild, sometimes a *maison dieu*. There were good economic reasons, as well as spiritual ones, for providing hostels and lights. The Church until the Reformation, at least in the West, was homogenous, Catholic, allowing most Christians to find familiarity throughout, with the Mass much the same as in the parish church back home. As voyages lengthened, of Vasco da Gama to the South and Columbus to the West for example, there was no church at the other end to greet the sailor, or, indeed, certainty that there was an 'other end'. Of those voyages venturing into the unknown, those which returned are remembered as voyages of discovery. The parochial system had little to offer the crews of these ships. The establishment

22. Conclusion

of special, or even ordinary, facilities at distant destinations, where there were no settled communities, was feasible neither in terms of expense nor staffing. The long voyage remained the exception; the vast majority of voyages were short-sea, and for these a parochial ministry continued to suffice; for the extended voyage, a voyage chaplain avoided significant capital investment and long-term commitment of manpower, serving equally the voyager to new worlds and the Crusader travelling to Muslim lands. The Reformation reduced the number of ports at which a Catholic ministry was available to the traveller and the post Reformation Catholic ministry to seafarers, where it existed at all, presented a mixed and patchy response, with Vincent de Paul the shining, if not the only, light. For sailors in the Reformed mould the situation was equally patchy, with some liturgical provision on paper, but lacking even a Vincent de Paul. The wish to trade overcame most barriers, whether port or crew was Catholic, Protestant, even Muslim, though religious obstacles often took time to surmount.

Gospel transmission was shaped not only by economic activity as it reached new markets, but also by developing technology, that is, by the way in which those markets were reached. The need to deliver more goods over longer distances at lower prices led to the development of larger and faster vessels, combining to make an increasing number of sailors frequenters of a new world with the Church, fractured - at least physically - by the Reformation, poorly equipped to respond; that is to say, the Reformation broke up the old pattern of ministry to all, sailors included, just at a time when seafarers were becoming a significant economic force. In some countries the old methods of serving seafarers limped on, but by the 1800s, when the globe was shrinking and world travel was ceasing to be the exception, something more was required. The seafarer may not have been forgotten by the Church, but until that 'something more' was developed, its response made it appear so.

Before the Reformation a crew might include family members, was usually recruited from a single village or port, and could be expected to share a religious background. The Reformation made it possible to conceive of a lone Catholic or protestant in a crew. Church support for these scattered Christians, in place of the mutual comfort previously provided through that shared background, was hard to find. Cabantous could write:

> The first reality of maritime life is that mobility makes inadequate the parish groups, the missions, the brotherhoods, the school.[1]

It was for this reason that an entirely new means of meeting the needs of the seafarer became necessary in the nineteenth century, early recognised by Smith and those who followed. Goldie, Grosjean, Anson would accuse the Catholic Church of neglect and contrast it with this Protestant concern for seafarers; their efforts apparently prompted by Protestant work. In fact, of the Catholic Church, it could be argued that, as with the supertanker, its size slowed the change of course. The passage of time affords a perspective which allows us to see that it was not a case of Catholic imitating Protestant;

---

1 *Dix Mille Marins Face à l'Océan*, 469. *La première réalité maritime est bien celle de la mobilité qui rend obligatoirement inadéquats les cadres paroissiaux, les missions, les confréries, l'école*

rather, it was the need of each church to find a new method to meet a new situation. The new method found expression in the identifiable and specialized societies of the nineteenth century.

A significant factor in shaping the various Christian responses to the nineteenth-century seafarer was the understanding of authority in each church. It is another cause of the Catholic Church's apparent slowness in adopting the new response to seamen. Rome's problem, in the nineteenth century, as for the fifteenth-century Felix Fabri, who wrote that one reason Mass could not be celebrated at sea was the impossibility of knowing the name of the bishop in whose diocese the ship was sailing, was how the territorial jurisdiction of the bishop could be related to the extraterritorial mariner. A Catholic remains a Catholic through his or her relation to a bishop, the focal point around whose person gather those who share or want to share the Catholic faith. That is the essence of episcopacy and assures the individual Catholic of belonging to the Catholic Church. The bishops retain their own claim to Catholicity, that they hold the faith always and everywhere believed, by their relation to the Bishop of Rome, who binds them to each other; he is the sign that their faith is held in common, is not some private opinion, and is consistent with Apostolic tradition.

This matter of authority was a problem not only for Catholics. It concerned episcopal and non episcopal churches alike. For the non episcopal, for example the Baptist church, which lacked in the nineteenth century a common identity, and which produced G.C. Smith, founder of the BFSFSBU, there was an understanding that each local group of Christians formed a complete church. Thus, when Smith started to minister to seamen, his seamen's church was a complete church in itself, though his commission to minister came from another congregation. When he met groups of praying seamen, they formed in their places of work complete churches, prompting the question of how they related to each other, and what the position of the man who came to faith and then sailed alone as a believer. Smith, as other Baptists who discovered mission, had *mutatis mutandis* to reinvent the church as understood in the Catholic sense, that each is part of a single body, expressed through Smith's cobweb of individual missions, the sailor being passed from one to the next, the common logo of the BETHEL flag assuring a membership transcending the individual. Smith's foundations lacked, from the Catholic point of view, the features which make for unity, and his temperament increased their tendency to be fissile, but the network of protestant missions sharing a flag was in effect a rediscovery of the classical structure of the Church, that of dispersed authority with a focal point; essentially a horizontal structure. The language of the market allows some insight here. The Smith model has something in common with the concept of franchise, where the franchisee is responsible for his business locally, but trading with a common product under a common logo, precisely what Smith evolved in the BFSFSBU, each mission occupying a niche and drawing its strength from membership of the franchise. Its subsequent history as the BFSS has revealed that

22. Conclusion

originally dispersed authority increasingly being vested in its council to form a vertical (hierarchical would be the *mot juste* in an episcopal church) structure with a principal chaplain.

A Church of England solution to the problem, as manifested in the MtS, was different. Combining a number of small missions, the MtS was founded in 1856 as a centralised body, its staff were controlled from the centre. If a port needed an Anglican presence, the initiative to appoint would emanate from London, making for an administrative tidiness. It may well have been a reflection in the established church of a nation possessed of a fast-expanding and centrally-administered empire. If BFSS was a franchise, the MtS resembled a chain of stores. Though lacking a bishop it was effectively a monarchical episcopate, surprising to find in a church of the Reformation, but leaving its chaplains without the freehold which protected the English incumbent against improper decisions made monarchically. Though the want of a bishop was felt as the society grew in confidence, the campaign at successive Church Congresses for the supply of one was never successful.

Catholics in the Church of England believed that a centralised approach to the problem was at odds with the idea of episcopacy as generally understood; that is, that no ministry should be independent of the local bishop, and, at a lower level, no mission dissociated from the care of the parish priest; a horizontality differing from the vertical structure of the MtS, the Catholic understanding of episcopacy linking authority with territory. Accordingly, SAWCM, the second Church of England solution and representing its Catholic wing, founded in 1864 by a parish priest (The MtS being founded by a layman), used a system of dispersed authority. The head office of SAWCM provided the link, the encouragement, and grants when possible, but only to enable a local, parish-based ministry of missionary curates, each licensed by the local bishop to assist an incumbent in the service of seafarers. In due time SAWCM was absorbed into the MtS and the monarchical structure triumphed, but not before Fr Goldie had seen and adopted something of SAWCM's structure. In market language, the chain store, with central directorate and common products, prevailed over the franchise. Whether there is an inherent contradiction in the idea of a local ministry to the seafarer who is by definition other than local will be explored further.

It may seem anomalous that in the Catholic Church, which is perceived by many as hierarchical (from the Greek for priestly rule), the formation of the post 1922 AoS should be attributed to a group of lay people, just as the predecessors of Anson, Gannon and Shields, that earlier generation of Jesuit founders (Goldie, Gretton, Dignam, Egger), clergy all, were also dependent upon a group of laity (Mrs Fraser, Lady Amabel Kerr, Miss Scott Murray, Mrs Howden). The Catholic Church can also be perceived as androcentric, but here the problem lies in the perception rather than what is perceived, for it overlooks the importance of those women involved in the 1890s. It is the Protestant societies which were started mainly by males (Agnes Weston an exception), and ministers at that, which suggests there is something here which is important, though the explanation turns out to be simple enough. As a priest Goldie was part of the official Catholic structure, and to a certain extent constrained, in a way that the lay person was not, whereas Anson, Gannon and Shields through their lay status had relative freedom of action. The AoS offers a mirror image of the original BFSFSBU, for, although Kverndal has drawn attention to the lay nature of undenominational foundations, the BFSFSBU's founder was a minister. The Baptist laity were part of the local church, but a minister would have the necessary independence and recognition to act between churches. In an hierarchical church, it is the lay person who can move freely and establish new patterns, always saving his relationship with the episcopate. In the AoS (as in the original BFSFSBU) the authority continues to be dispersed, for it is the diocesan bishop who is responsible for the work in the ports in his diocese, while the banner under which it is conducted is that of the AoS; its National Director, in recent years a layman, in the United Kingdom exercising a role of encouragement and advice. This horizontal model is in strong contrast to the vertical one adopted by the Mission to Seafarers, and to an extent the British and International Sailors' Society (to use their current names), headed each by a minister and with more control from the centre. In recent years there have been signs of mutation. The BISS is not the monolith it once was, for in Canada, New Zealand and South Africa for example, its manifestations have chosen independence, while the Mission to Seafarers has acknowledged the provincial structure of Anglicanism in its appointment of a liaison bishop in each province. Whether the role of a liaison bishop is more than advisory is not clear.

Structures are important, especially as an organisation grows. The ŒdeM, catering for a niche market, the French deep sea fisheries, offered a model which was partly horizontal, through the industry, but mainly vertical through the line management of the Assumptionists; their problem with the Apostolic Prefect of St Pierre suggested a need for that management to be extended, duly supplied by the Instruction *Jam Inde*. The ŒdeM was a unitary body. By the 1920s the problem had become how the various French organisations could relate to each other nationally. Their solution of federation offered a model for other countries, allowing the AoS to be organised nationally, and internationally, while leaving the bishop responsible for the ports in his diocese. It is noteworthy that the French, with their experience of a vertical structure in the Catholic sea apostolate, should be the midwives of today's AoS horizontal structure.

It may be asked where the individual seafarer finds a place in all this. Just as a ship is seen as an extension of a country, through its registration, and rendered subject to a national framework of law, it can be argued that a seafarer can be seen as a parishioner away from home, and fitted into the framework of Canon Law. However, if it is posited that the seafarer is a transnational person, the ship his home sometimes for a very long time, the AoS system of national and diocesan structures appears in a different light. The parish system worked well for medieval seamen not far from home. Whilst it continues to work well for the land dweller, the contemporary circumstances are sufficiently

22. Conclusion

different for that to be no longer true for the seafarer. The sea is a geographical area, not in the care of a designated bishop and his clergy, served instead on its periphery by a ring of chaplains each answerable to a different bishop. A number of weaknesses follow. It offers no formal system, for example, for transferring expertise from one port to another, and minimal opportunity for the career development found in a more vertical structure. The nearest approach to a vertical structure lies in the advisory system of AoS regional directors, the whole administered by a titular archbishop who has no suffragans, ordains none, and cannot direct the clergy of other bishops upon whose ministry seafarers depend for the sacraments. When the seafarer is genuinely recognised as transnational, the structure of the AoS may alter, perhaps with a bishop appointed to this defined area and able to administer it canonically, something which already exists through personal prelatures, apostolic exarchates,[1] bishops to the forces, and ordinariates. But this is to overlook the problem of how it would be financed and how recruit its ministry. In the meantime, although from the Mission to Seafarers' structure the implication has been drawn that it erodes the traditional view of episcopal order, its quasi diocesan organisation may yet better recognise the seafarer's transnational status than implicitly seeing him or her as a parishioner away from home. The structure of the British and International Sailors' Society, conflicting with no concept of episcopacy in its supporting churches, may have a similar justification.

What other features emerge from this broadly historical account? One is the pattern which seems to repeat itself in the foundation of a number of societies involved in the maritime apostolate, beginning through letters to seamen, then tracts and other literature, followed by homes and institutes. This is as true of G.C. Smith, his Naval Correspondence Mission evolving into the BFSSFSBU, as of Agnes Weston, her letters preceding the Royal Sailors' Rests, and the letters and parcels of books of the WCB preceding the AoS. It is significant that those early letters were sent to members of the RN; its system for communicating with crews and ships kept regularly on station was unparalleled in the Merchant Navy. Those tracts and letters were made possible by the rise of cheap printing and increasingly efficient postal services, which is to say that nineteenth-century technology made it possible for the Church to reach out to nineteenth-century naval personnel economically and easily. Cheap printing was to the nineteenth century what the internet and all that it spawns are to the twenty-first; posing the question for the apostolate whether today's Christian seafarer is being supported in his faith as effectively as were those who received letters and tracts. There was a fashion in the 1970s for trying to encourage 'animators' on board ships. If Christians are to be helped, not only to live the Christian life, but to share it, then support is a necessity, and requires something other than welfare work. 'The primary thing that is asked of us ... is "presence", to be there, serving without ulterior motives, and for

---

1 Personal prelatures minister to distinct religious groups like *Opus Dei*. Exarchates minister to national groups, such as Poles resident in the UK.

the time being probably also without too many words'.[1] How 'presence' might be possible when those being served are at a distance occupied the early founders, long before Hoekendijk was writing, and occupies their successors in today's apostolate.

Almost the next step after the letters was encouragement for men to associate as Christians, in the very early days like the Methodist crews of the Thames Revival, later perhaps in a temperance union or some sort of guild, of which the SFSSP was an extreme example, or a pious confraternity; all economical ways of encouraging men to support each other and exercise the Christian influence which distance prevented the larger Christian body from exercising. The persistence of the guild idea is a reminder that the Church is here ministering to an industry rather than to nations, resurrecting the problem of geography versus industry, but reached by a different route. The religious guild evolved to serve the needs of religious craftsmen in the medieval period. Its revival might suggest that the founding fathers of the modern sea apostolate were backward looking, failing to recognise the drastic changes in the maritime industry, yet it is hard to see what other means of organisation could have been, indeed should now be, adopted so long as Christians are called to gather in Christ's name wherever they may be. It took little time for that gathered model to be replaced by a network of clubs and institutes. There is safety in buildings! The static ministry of the club room or hostel was a reasonable response while ships spent time alongside, but it is a response which has been overtaken by the rapid turn round of today's shipping. Buildings have largely gone the way of the hospital ships which served the fishing fleets, and for the same reason.

Whether the Catholic Church was copying the Protestants is a crude question sometimes asked, perhaps prompted by Goldie, Grosjean, Anson and others pointing to the large and growing ministry of contemporary Protestants to the seafarer, which they contrasted with Catholic neglect. In part it has been answered in the suggestion that the changes which peaked in the nineteenth-century shipping industry demanded equally radical changes of the denominations in their ministry to seafarers. Churches were effectively bankrupt by the nineteenth century in their approach to seafarers. What was evolving was a general and new approach, appearing first in the Protestant community, then in the Catholic. It could be that another shift in approach, in the wake of the container, will be observed when someone writes a history of the sea apostolate a century hence.

It is not possible to point to the start of Catholic work in the way that Protestant work can be said to have started, certainly post Reformation, and mainly at the end of the eighteenth or early nineteenth century. Kverndal's view, that in the preceding centuries the seaman was neglected, is as accurate as the idea that the Catholic sea apostolate started at worst in the 1920s, at best in the 1890s. Those whose roots precede the Reformation, and who pay attention to history, will want to consider the matter from the earliest centuries of the Church. The disruption of the Reformation changed the industry and

---

1 J.C. Hoekendijk, *The Church Inside Out*, 120.

destroyed many of the old ways of serving the seafarer, its shadow long hindering the re-emergence of an effective Christian ministry to seafarers. The view which considers the centuries suggests that seamen have always had some sort of place in the life of the Church; it is the societies, Catholic, Anglican, Protestant, in their present form which arrived late in the field.

The Church has changed. Small societies at work among seafarers have become large societies, just as small ships have become large ships. Where many of the early societies were either denominational or undenominational, today societies are learning to work ecumenically, that is to say, side by side, with the good of the seafarer as their primary purpose. As the Church has changed, so have its methods of bringing Christ to the world. The establishment of the World Council of Churches, the International Council of Seamen's Agencies, the International Christian Maritime Association, to name the most obvious bodies, and the developments of the Second Vatican Council, have all helped bring a spirit of fraternity to Christian ministry in the docks, while the International Transport Federation's policy of making a grant in a port only to a single agency has encouraged societies to learn how to work together.

The industry, too, has changed. Containerization, flags of convenience, the flagging out of the merchant navies of the developed world, and crewing from developing nations are a few of the issues which feature in that change. In his time Charles Hopkins's was a rare voice drawing attention to the injustices suffered by the seaman, and one given minimal support by his church. Today Christian seamen's welfare organisations readily join the International Labour Organisation and the International Maritime Organisation in drawing attention to such matters. Crews can still be found on board ships in poor condition, unpaid and unfed, their owners hidden in tax havens, but the modern system known as port-state control allows such ships to be detained in port and their crews repatriated. The Center for Seafarers' Rights of the SCI of New York/New Jersey has done much to publicise the need for justice and been greatly blessed in its Directors.[1]

What next? For the time being, great mobility is required of chaplains, where possible facilitated by trailer missions, minibuses, perhaps a dockside room offering basic necessities and access to telephones, email and the like. The shift in dock locations has rendered almost all the big institutes, and the smaller 'home missions' of the seventies, obsolete. Cheap and regular air travel, allowing crews to be flown quickly to their ships, has replaced the need for hostel accommodation. The seafarer who spends minutes ashore, hours if fortunate, rarely alongside for weeks, requires almost instant support, for families, for faith, for sanity. To say that chaplains and volunteers will need a flexibility previously unknown, better equipped to listen, and with the best possible support materials for Christian living, may sound daunting unless accompanied by the thought, illustrated repeatedly in this book, that God chooses unlikely people to do this work, puts them in the right place at the right time, and uses them, providing the while the necessary grace.

---

1 Douglas B. Stevenson, Seafarers and Justice, *The Way of the Sea*, 377-380. Paul K. Chapman, *Trouble on Board: The Plight of International Seafarers*, 1992.

Bibliography

Records held publicly
This list of sources was correct at the time of research. In some cases documentation seems to have disappeared.

Cambridge University Library: British and Foreign Bible Society Archive
Glasgow City Archives, Mitchell Library: Gartnavel Royal Lunatic Asylum papers (especially HB13/5/168).
Glasgow Diocesan Archives: AoS Papers (RI 18).
Greater London Records Office: FWA records.
Guildhall Library, London: *Lloyd's Captains' Register*.
Lambeth Palace Library: Archbishop Davidson's papers.
Moray District Council (Forres Central Museum Store), Scotland: Anson Diaries (all prefixed DFJ A79/-). (These may only be seen with the permission of the Abbot of Nunraw.)
The National Archive, Kew: Hopkins's application for British Citizenship; National Maritime Board papers.
Rhodes House Library, Oxford: USPG papers.
University of Liverpool, Special Collections Library: Glasier Papers.
University of Warwick Modern Records Centre: Seamen's Union and Shipping Federation papers.

Records held privately
Alton Abbey, Hampshire: Various papers, *The Messenger*.
AA (via San Pio V, 55, Rome). Papers and records relating the AA and the *Œuvres de Mer*. *Lettres à la Dispersion. L'Assomption et ses Œuvres*. Material is catalogued with the prefixes B, D, K, FK, SD, SE, SF, SG.
AoS - Glasgow   Gannon Papers, AoS Reports etc. (but refer to AoS London)
AoS - Rome   Anson correspondence, Anson, *Church Maritime*, (ts).
   Yzerman, *American Catholic Seafarers' Church* (ts).
   Benjamin, Roger et al, *L'Univers des Marins: Études Sociologique* etc.', Paris, ts, n.d.
AoS - London HQ   Anson papers, letters, books. (Some of these now seem to be missing.)
CTS, London   Minutes, Reports, publications, conference papers, *Superindex*.
Crusader Office (7 Edge Hill, London SW19 4LR): *Messenger of the Sacred Heart*.
Guild of Our Lady of Ransom (31 Southdown Road, London SW20 8QJ): *The Ransomer, Faith of Our Fathers*.
The Mission to Seafarers (St Michael Paternoster Royal, College Hill, London EC4R 2RL; older BCM, MtS, TCM, SAWCM records now at Hull History Centre, Worship Street, Hull, HU2 8BG.

Prinknash Abbey, Gloucestershire: *PAX, Notes for the Month.*
Salvation Army archives and museum, London.
Sint-Andriesabdij (*Abbaye Saint-André*), Belgium: *Bulletin des Missions.*
Society of Jesus - London *Apostleship of Prayer Papers* (48/7/4/1), *Letters and Notices, Our Dead.*
Society of Jesus - Paris - Records of brethren.
Society of St Vincent de Paul: Glasgow: Annual reports and journal.
London: Reports, *Minutes, Bulletin, English Bulletin.*
Westminster Diocesan Archives: AoS material in Bourne Papers (Bo 5/90(a)).Godfrey Papers (Go 2/26 (1961-2)).

Newspapers and journals

Place of publication is London unless stated by title or in brackets as otherwise
Acta Apostolica Sedis (Rome).
Acta Sancta Sedis (Rome).
All the World (Salvation Army).
The Anchor (Tilbury).
Anglican Sphere (Rotterdam).
Anglo-Norman Studies.
Annales de Normandie (St Malo).
Apostleship of the Sea Quarterly.
Archives de medecin navale (Paris)
Archaeologia Cantiana.
L'Assomption (Namur, Belgium).
L'Assomption et ses Œuvres (Seine et Oise).
L'Assomption et ses Œuvres (Paris).
Bournemouth Daily Echo.
Bristol Daily Post.
Bulletin (SVP).
Bulletin de l' Œuvres des Orphelins de la Mer (Paris).
Cardiff Shipping and Mercantile Gazette.
Cardiff Times.
Catholicism (Paris).
Catholic Magazine.
Catholic World.
Catholic Monthly.
Chronicle of Convocation.
Colonial Church Chronicle.
Communiques (Federation des Œuvres catholiques françaises pour marins) (Paris).
Daily News Overland Summary.
The Englishman (Weekly Summary) (Rangoon).
Études (Paris).
Faith of Our Fathers (Guild of Ransom).
Forth (PECUSA).
Glasgow Observer.
Hampshire Express.
Hastings and St Leonards News.
Hereford Times.
Indian Church Quarterly review.
Indian Daily News.

IJMH (St John's, Newfoundland).
Journal of Transport History.
Lloyd's List.
Medievalia et Humanistica (New Jersey).
Medieval Studies (Toronto).
The Messenger (Order of St Paul).
Messenger of the Sacred Heart (Wimbledon).
Missions Benedictines (*Saint-André*).
The Missionary Intelligencer.
The Missionary Register.
Mission Life or the Emigrant and the Heathen.
The Mission Field (SPG).
The Month (Wimbledon).
Nautical Guildsman.
New Sailors' Magazine.
Nineteenth Century.
Notes for the Month (Caldey Island).
The Officer (Salvation Army).
PAX (Caldey Island).
Questions Actuelles (Paris).
The Ransomer.
RECHT door ZEE (Rotterdam).
Sea Breezes (Liverpool).
The Seaman (NSFU).
Seaman's Chronicle.
Shields Daily Gazette.
Shipmates.
Soldiers' and Sailors' Magazine.
Southampton Times.
Stella Maris (Wimbledon 1901).
Stella Maris (Naples?, 1911).
Sunday Times (Calcutta).
The Tablet..
Toilers of the Deep (MDSF).
The Universe.
War Cry (Salvation Army).
Word on the Waters (The Missions to Seamen).

Papers and articles
Place of publication is London unless stated otherwise.

Abulafia, David, Pisan Commercial Colonies and Consulates in 12th century Sicily, *EHR*, XCIII, Jan 1978, 66-81.

Aelfric, The Will of the Archbishop of Canterbury, *Councils and Synods with Other Documents relating to the English Church, 871-1086*, D. Whitelock, M Brett and C.N.L. Brooke (eds), vol. I, Oxford, 1981

A.G., *Sur le Banc de Terre Neuve, L'Assomption et ses Œuvres*, vol 25, new series, Seine et Oise, 1 Jan 1899.

Allen, David, A Parish at Sea: Spiritual Concerns aboard the Order of St John's Galleys in the Seventeenth and Eighteenth Centuries, *The Military Orders*, Malcolm Barber (ed), Variorum, Aldershot 1994.

Allen, G.G., Hospital Church Ship *de HOOP*, *Anglican Sphere*, Rotterdam, May 1973.

Ambrose, On his Brother Satyrus I, *Funeral Orations by Saint Gregory Nazianzen and St Ambrose*, John J. Sullivan & Martin R. P. McGuire (trans), Fathers of the Church vol 22, Washington DC 1953.
Andrea, Alfred J., The Relationship of Sea Travellers and Excommunicated Captains under Thirteenth Century Law, *MM,* 68, May 1982.
Anon, Sailors' Homes and Refuges, *English Bulletin* XLVI(3) (published by SVP).
Anson, P.F., Brother Daniel Shields SJ, *The Anchor,* AoS Tilbury, Spring 1983, reprinted from *AoS Quarterly*, vol IX, No 36, May 1940.
Anson, Richard F (= P. F.), "Father" Hopkins - the Sky Pilot, *The Irish Monthly*, No 592, Oct 1922.
Apostolaat Maritime, L'Assomption, CXXXI (New Series), Namur, Belgium.
Assistance sur Mer etc., *Archives de médecine navale*, Paris, Nov 1901.
Balard, Michel, Coastal Shipping and Navigation in the Mediterranean, *Cogs, Caravels and Galleons*, Richard W. Unger (ed), 1994.
Bass, George F. & van Doorninck Jr, Frederick H., An 11th Century Shipwreck at Serçe Liman, Turkey, *International Journal of Nautical Archaeology*, 1978, 7(2).
Blue, L., Kentley, E., McGrail, S., Mishra, U., The Patia Fishing Boat of Orissa: A Case Study in Ethnoarchaeology, *South Asian Studies*, vol 13, 1997.
Bolster, W. Jeffrey, Roundtable: W. Jeffrey Bolster, *IJMH*, X(2), Dec 1998.
Bonaffy, Dr -, *Marins des Grand Pêche, Archives de médecine navale*, Paris, Feb 1898.
Boyle, Leonard E., Innocent III and Vernacular Versions of Scripture, *The Bible in the Medieval World*, Katherine Walsh & Diana wood (eds), Studies in Church History Subsidia 4, Ecclesiastical History Society, Oxford, 1985.
Bresc, G. & Bresc, H., *Les saints protecteurs de bateaux 1200-1460, Ethnologie Française*, IX(2), 1979.
Burton, Valerie, The Myth of Bachelor Jack, *Jack Tar in History*, Colin Howell and Richard Twomey (eds), New Brunswick, 1991.
Burton, V. C., Apprenticeship Regulation and Maritime Labour in the Nineteenth Century British Merchant Marine, *IJMH*, June 1989,
Cabantous, Alain, *Religion et monde maritime au Havre dans la seconde moitié du XVIIe siècle, Annales de Normandie*, St Malo, 1983.
Cabantous, Alain, On the Writing of the Religious History of Seafarers, *IJMH*, St John's, Newfoundland, III(1), 1991.
Carpenter-Turner, Mrs W. J., The Building of the *GRACE DIEU, VALENTINE* and *FALCONER* at Southampton 1416-1420, *MM*, vol 40 (1954).
Carus-Wilson, E., The Medieval Trade of the Ports of the Wash, *Medieval Archaeology*, vol 6-7, 1962-3.
Cederlund, Carl Oloff, Explaining a 13th century Cog Wreck near Småland, Sweden, *Medieval Ships and the Birth of Technological Societies*, vol i, Northern Europe, Christiane Villain-Gandossi, Salvini Busuttil, Paul Adam (eds), Malta, 1989
Cologan, W.H., The Magic Lantern as an Instrument of Religious Instruction, *The Tablet*, 27 Oct 1888.
Constable, Olivia Remie, The Problem of Jettison in Medieval Mediterranean Maritime Law, *Journal of Medieval History*, vol 20 (Sept 1994).
Dalbard, J., *La Societé des Œuvres de Mer de 1894 à 1939, Annales, (Societé d'Histoire et d'Archeologie*, St Malo, 1991.
Didache, Andrew Louth (ed), *Early Christian Writings*, 1987.
Dowker, George, Reculver Church, *Archaeologia Cantiana*, XII, 1878.
Driscoll, Michael S., Penance in Transition: Popular Piety and Practice, *Medieval Liturgy*, Lizette Larson-Miller (ed), 1997.

Edgar, The so-called "Canons of...", *Councils and Synods with other documents relating to the English Church*, I(i), D. Whitelock, M. Brett, C. N. L. Brooke (eds), Oxford 1981.

Ellmers, Detlev, Development and Usage of Harbour Cranes, *Medieval Ships and the Birth of Technological Societies*, vol I: Northern Europe, Christiane Villain-Gandossi, Salvini Busuttil, Paul Adam (eds), Malta 1989.

Field, J. E., The Beginning of Abingdon Abbey, *EHR*, XX (Oct 1905).

Fischer, Lewis R., Review of *Island Nation* (Frank Broeze), *MM*, 85(3), August 1999.

Fletcher, Philip, Ransom Chat, *Faith of Our Fathers*, IV(5), 1893.

Friedman, Ellen G., Trinitarian Hospitals in Algiers, *CHR*, LXVI(4), 1980.

Friel, Ian, Henry V's *GRACE DIEU* and the wreck in the River Hamble near Bursledon, Hampshire, *International Journal of Nautical Archaeology*, 22(i), 1993.

Friel, Ian, Ignorant of Nautical Matters?, *MM*, vol 97 (1), February 2011.

Friend, Stephen, Social and Spiritual Work Amongst Fishing Communities, *England's Sea Fisheries*, David J.Starkey, Chris Reid & Neil Ashcroft (eds), 2000.

Friend, Stephen, The North Sea Liquor Trade, c.1850-1893, *IJMH*, XV(2), December 2003.

Frijhof, Willem, *Barquettes Votives ou Maquettes Profanes?*, in *Foi Chrétienne et Milieux Maritimes*, Alain Cabantous & Françoise Hildesheimer (eds), Paris 1989.

Fulford, M. G., Rippon, S., Aalen, J. R., Hillam, J., Uncovering of 12th century Quay...' *Transactions*, Bristol & Gloucester Archaeological Society, vol 110, 1991.

Goldie, F., Our Sailors and their Helpers, *Month*, LXXX, Roehampton, 1894.

Goldie, F., What Our Neighbours are Doing, *Stella Maris*, Wimbledon, April 1901.

Goldie, F., Catholic Work for Merchant Seamen, *Bulletin*, p.p. SVP, LI(3), 1906.

Goldie, F., St Vincent de Paul, *CTS Publications*, XIII, 1909.

Goldie, F., Work for Catholic Sailors, *Catholic Social Year Book*, 1911.

Grosjean, Eugène, *Œuvres de Mer, Études*, LXIV, Paris 1895.

G.P.B.N. The *NAVIS DEI* of Hartlepool, *MM*, vol 26, 1940.

Harcourt, Freda, The High Road to India: The P&O Company and the Suez Canal, 1840-1874, *IJMH* XXII(2), Dec 2010.

Hawkins, L., The Mission Boats, *Sea Breezes*, Jan 1973.

Hollerich, Michael J., The Alexandrian Bishops and the Grain Trade: Ecclesiastical Commerce in late Roman Egypt, *Journal of the Economic and Social History of the Orient*, XXVI(ii), Leiden, 1982

Howse, Derek, Some Early Tidal Diagrams, *MM*, 79(1), 1993.

Hurley M. F., Topography and Development, *Late Viking and Medieval Waterford*, M. F. Hurley,.& O. M. B. Scully (eds), Waterford, 1997.

Illouze, Albert & Rigaud, Philippe, Grafitti, *Archaeologie Médiévale*, XXIV, Paris 1994.

Jacoby, David, Crusader Acre in the Thirteenth Century: Urban Layout and Topography, *Studi Medievali*, XX, Spoleto 1979.

Kedar, Benjamin Z., The Passenger List of a Crusader Ship, 1250, *Studi Medievali*, XIII, Spoleto 1972.

Kelley D.O., *History of the Diocese of California 1849-1914*, Bureau of Information and Supply, n.d.

Kelley H.H., The Early History of the Church's Work for Seamen in the United States, *Historical Magazine*, IX, 1940.

Kennerley, Alston, Seamen's Missions & Sailors' Homes: spiritual and social welfare provision to seafarers in British ports in the nineteenth century, with some reference to the South West, *Studies in British Privateering, Trading Enterprise & Seamen's Welfare*, Stephen Fisher (ed), Exeter, 1987.

Kennerley, Alston, The Seamen's Union, the National Maritime Board and Firemen: Labour Management in the British Mercantile Marine, *The Northern Mariner/Le Marin du Nord*, VII, No. 4 (Oct 1997)

Kennerley, Alston, Ratings for the Mercantile Marine: The Roles of Charity, the State and Industry in the Pre-Service Education and Training of Ratings for the Mercantile Marine, 1879-1939, *History of Education*, XXVIII (1), 1999.

Kennerley, Alston, The Shore Management of British Seafarers in the Twentieth Century, *Beyond Shipping and Shipbuilding*, David J. Starkey & H. Murphy (eds), Maritime Historical Studies Centre, University of Hull, 2007

Kennerley, Alston, Joseph Conrad at the London Sailors' Home, *The Conradian*, vol. 33, no. 1 (Spring 2008).

Kingsley, S. and Decker, M., New Rome, New Theories on Inter-Regional Exchange, *Economy and Exchange in the East Mediterranean during Late Antiquity*, Sean Kingsley and Michael Decker (eds), Oxford, 2001.

Knocker, Edward, On the Municipal Records of Dover, *Archaeologia Cantiana*, X(1876).

Laracy, Hugh, Marists as Mariners: The Solomon Islands Story, *IJMH*, III:1 (June 1991).

Loomis SJ, Albert J., Religion & Elizabethan Commerce with Spain, *CHR*, L(1), 1964.

Loomis SJ, Albert J., The Armadas & the Catholics of England, *CHR*, LIX(3), 1973.

Lowther Clarke, W.K., The Origins of Episcopacy, *Episcopacy Ancient and Modern*, C.Jenkins & K.D.Mackenzie(eds), 1930.

Lydon, James G., Thomas Jefferson and the Mathurins, *CHR*, XLIX(2), 1963.

Mango, Marlia Mundell, Beyond the Amphora: Non-Ceramic Evidence for Late Antiquity Industry and Trade, *Economy and Exchange in the East Mediterranean during Late Antiquity*, Sean Kingsley and Michael Decker (eds), Oxford, 2001.

Mango, Marlia Mundell, Byzantine Trade: local, regional, interregional and international, *Byzantine Trade, 4th-12th Centuries*, Marlia Mundell Mango (ed), Society for the Promotion of Byzantine Studies 14, 2009.

McClymont, Rev. Fr -, Catholics in the British Navy, *Glasgow Observer*, Jan-Apr, 1905.

McGrail, S., Renaissance and Romano-Celtic Ship Design and Shipbuilding Methods, *Between the Seas*, R. Bockius (ed), Mainz 2009.

McLynn, Neil B., Christian Controversy and Violence in the Fourth Century, *Christian Politics and Religious Culture in Late Antiquity*, Variorum CS928, Farnham, Surrey, 2009.

Miller, Robert (R.W.H.), The Salvation Navy, *MM*, 83(1), Feb 1997.

Miller, R.W.H., The *Apostolatus Maris*: Its Structural Development Including its 1997 Reorganisation - a Review, *Newsletter*, International Association for the Study of Maritime Mission, Spring/Summer 2000.

Miller, R (R.W.H.), The Early Medieval Seaman and the Church: contacts ashore, *MM*, 89(2), May 2003.

Miller, Robert (R.W.H.), Sea, Ship and Seaman in Early Christian Literature, *MM*, 96(iv), Nov. 2010.

Morant, A. W., Church of St Nicholas, Great Yarmouth, *Norfolk Archaeology*, VII, 1872.

Munch Thye, Birgitte, Early Christian Ship Symbols, *The Ship as Symbol*, Ole Crumlin-Pedersen & Birgitte Munch Thye (eds), Copenhagen 1995.

Murray, K. M. E., Dengemarsh and the Cinque Ports, *EHR*, LIV, 664ff.

Nicolle, David, Shipping in Islamic Art: Seventh Through Sixteenth Century AD, *American Neptune*, XLIX.

Œuvres de Mer, *Questions Actuelles*, XXVII(5), Paris, 1895.

Palmer, Sarah, Seamen Ashore in Late Nineteenth Century London: Protection from the Crimps, in Paul Adam (ed), *Seamen in Society*, Paris, 1980, 55-67..

Palmer, Sarah, The British Shipping Industry 1850-1914, *Change and Adaptation in Maritime History: the North Atlantic Fleets in the Nineteenth Century*, St John's, Lewis R. Fischer & G.E.Panting (eds), Newfoundland 1985.

Passamaneck, S. M., Traces of Rabbinical Maritime Law and Custom, *Tijdschrift voor Rechtsgeschiedenis XXXIV(iv)*, Groningen 1966.

Papacostas, Tassos, The Economy of Late Antique Cyprus, *Economy and Exchange in the East mediterranean during Late Antiquity*, S. Kingsley and M. Decker (eds), Oxford, 2001

Poulle, Emmanuel, *Les instruments astronomiques de l'Occident latin aux XIe et XIIe siècles*, *Cahiers de Civilisation Médiévale*, XV, Poitiers 1972.

Pryor, John H., & Bellabarba, Sergio, The Medieval Muslim Ships of the Pisan *Bacini*, *MM*, 76(2), May 1990.

Reynaud, Felix A., *Les ex-voto marins de Notre Dame de la Garde* etc., *Foi Chrétienne et Millieux Maritimes*, , Alain Cabantous & Françoise Hildesheimer (eds), Paris, 1989.

Richard, Jean, *Les Gens de Mer et le Croises*, *Croises, missionaires et voyageurs*, Jean Richard (ed), 1983.

Rigold, S. E., The St Nicholas or 'Boy Bishop' Tokens, *Proceedings*, XII, Suffolk Institute of Archaeology and Natural History, XXXIV, 1980.

Robbert, Louise Buenger, Venice and the Crusades,, *A History of the Crusades*, V, Kenneth M. Setton (ed),Wisconsin,

Roberts, Owain T., Descendants of Viking Boats, *Cogs, Caravels and Galleons*, Richard W. Unger (ed), 1994.

Rutledge, Elizabeth & Rutledge, Paul, King's Lynn and Great Yarmouth, Two Thirteenth Century Surveys, *Norfolk Archaeology*, XXXVII(i), 1978.

Slessarev, Vsevolod, *Ecclesiae Mercatorum* and the Rise of Merchant Colonies, *Business History Review*, XLI(2), Summer 1967, Harvard.

Smith, Julian A., Precursors to Peregrinus: the early history of magnetism and the mariner's compass in Europe, *Journal of Medieval History*, vol 18, 1992.

Springer, Otto, Medieval Pilgrim Routes from Scandinavia to Rome, *Medieval Studies*, XII, Toronto, 1950.

Stevenson, Douglas B. , Seafarers and Justice, *The Way of the Sea*, Roald Kverndal, Pasadena CA, 2008.

Sweet, Leonard I., Christopher Columbus and the Millennial Vision of the New World, *CHR*, LXXII(3), 1986

Tracy, James D., With and Without the Counter Reformation: the Catholic Church in the Spanish Netherlands and the Dutch Republic 1580-1650, *CHR*, LXXI(4), 1985.

van Rossum, Matthias, Lex Heerma van Voss, Jelle van Lottum & Jan Lucassen, National and International Labour Markets for Sailors in European, Atlantic and Asian Waters 1600-1850, *Maritime History as Global History*, IMEHA, St John's Newfoundland, 2010.

Wants of the Colonial and Missionary Church, SPG leaflet, May 1980.

William of Newburgh, The History of, Joseph Stevenson (ed & trans), *Church Historians of England* IV(ii), 1853.

Williams, David M. , Mid-Victorian Attitudes to Seamen and Maritime Reform: The Society for Improving the Condition of Merchant Seamen, 1867, *IJMH*, III(i), June 1991.

Williams, David M. & Armstrong, John, Changing Voyage Patterns in the Nineteenth Century, *IJMH*, XX(2), Dec 2010.

Williams, John Bryan, The Making of a Crusade, *Journal of Medieval History*, vol 23 (1997).

Wilson, F. R., On Wayside Chapels and Hermitages, with special reference to the

Chapel on the old Tyne Bridge, *Archaeologia Aeliana*, XIII(NS), 1889.
Wismeyer, J. M., The War Galleys of the Order of St John, *Sunday Times* (London), 8, 15, 22 Nov 1992.
Wormald, Francis, Bible Illustration in Medieval Manuscripts, G. W. H. Lampe (ed), *Cambridge History of the Bible*, vol 2, 1976.
Wright, R.F., The High Seas and the Church in the Middle Ages, *MM*, LIII, 1967.
Zanani OP, G., *Apostolaat de la Mer, Catholicism*, VIII, Paris, 1979.

Books and Pamphlets: a select list
Place of publication is London unless stated otherwise.
Abulafia, David, *Mediterranean Encounters, Economic, Religious, Political, 1100-1550*, Variorum (CS694), Aldershot (UK) & Burlington, Vermont, 2000.
Abu-Lughod, Janet L., *Before European Hegemony: the world system AD 1250-1350*, Oxford 1989 (paperback 1991).
Aikenhead, The Life and Work of Mary, by a member of the Congregation, Irish Sisters of Charity, London and New York, 1924.
Anderson, R. C. (ed), *Letters of the Fifteenth and Sixteenth Centuries from the Archives of Southampton*, Southampton Record Society, 1921.
Anderson's History of the Colonial Church, 1848.
Annals of Ulster (to AD 1131), Séan Mac Airt & Gearóid Mac Niocall (eds), Dublin, 1983
Anson, P.F., *List of Catholic Officers, RN, RM, RNR*, p.p.,1917.
Anson, P.F., *The Supply of Catholic Reading Matter to Seafarers*, tract, 1928.
Anson, P.F., *Harbour Head*, 1945.
Anson, P.F., *A Roving Recluse*, Cork, 1946.
Anson, P.F., *The Apostleship of the Sea*, tract, CTS, 1947.
Anson, P.F., *The Church and the Sailor*, 1949.
Anson, P.F., *Christ and the Sailor*, 1954.
Anson, P.F., *Abbot Extraordinary*, 1958.
Anson, P.F., *The Call of the Cloister*, 1964.
Anson, P.F., *Building Up the Waste Places*, Leighton Buzzard, 1973.
Arnold, T. (ed), *Memorial of St Edmund's Abbey*, RS, vol 1, 1890-6.
Ashburner, Walter (ed), *The Rhodian Sea-Law*, Oxford, 1909.
Atherton, W.H., *History of the Catholic Sailors' Club of Montreal*, Montreal, 1924.
Bailey, B., *Almshouses*, 1988.
Basil: Letters and Select Works, Nicene and Post-Nicene Fathers, 2nd series, Philip Schaff & Henry Wallace (eds), New York 2007
Beaver, Patrick, *A History of Lighthouses*, 1971.
Becket, Materials for a History of Thomas, James Craigie Robertson (ed), RS, vol i, 1875.
Becon, Works of Thomas, Parker Society, 1844.
Bishop, Journal and Letters of Captain Charles, Michael Roe (ed), Hakluyt Society 1967.
Black, A., *Guilds & Civil Society*, 1984.
Blake, Richard, *Evangelicals in the Royal Navy 1775-1815*, Woodbridge 2008.
Blunt, J. H. (ed), *Annotated Book of Common Prayer*, 1884.
Bolster, W. Jeffrey, *Black Jacks*, Cambridge (Mass.), 1997.
Boys, William, *Collection for a History of Sandwich, in Kent*, 1792.
Brandon, Peter & Short, Brian, *The South East from AD 1000*, 1990
Brewster, J.S. (ed), *Monumenta Franciscana*, 1858.
Brogan, D. W., *The Development of Modern France, 1943*.
Brooks, F.W. (ed), *The First Order Book of the Hull Trinity House*, York Archaeological

Bibliography

Society Record Series, vol 105, Beverley, 1942.
Brown, Peter, *The Rise of Western Christendom*, London, 1995
Bruce, S. & Harris, T. , *Back to Sea*, Banffshire Maritime & Heritage Association, 2009.
Bruijn, Jaap R., *The Dutch Navy of the Seventeenth and Eighteenth Centuries*, new edition 2011, St John's, Newfoundland, 2011.
Brundage, James A., *Medieval Canon Law and the Crusader*, 1969.
Brundage, James A., *Medieaval Canon Law*, 1995.
Bullen, F. T. , *With Christ at Sea*, 1900.
Bullock, F. W. B., *Voluntary Religious Societies 1520-1799*, 1963.
Burwash, Dorothy, *English Merchant Shipping 1460-1540*, 1947, reprint 1969.
Byrne, Eugene H., *Genoese Shipping in the Twelfth and Thirteenth Centuries*, Cambridge (Mass.), 1930.
Cabantous, Alain & Hildesheimer, Françoise (eds), *Foi Chrétienne et Milieux Maritimes*, Paris, 1989.
Cabantous, Alain, *Le Ciel dans la Mer*, Paris, 1990.
Cabantous, Alain, *Dix Mille Marins face à l'Océan*, Paris, 1991.
Cabantous, Alain, *Les citoyens du large*, Paris 1995.
Calendar of Documents preserved in France, vol I, 1899.
Calendar of Entries in Papal Registers relating to Great Britain and Ireland, vol 1, 1893.
Calendar of Inquisitions, 1910.
Calendar of Inquisitions Misc (Chancery), I, 1916.
Calendar of Liberate Rolls, vol IV, RS, 1959.
Calendar of Papal Registers: Papal Letters, IV, 1902.
Calendar of Patent Rolls, Henry III, vol IV, RS, 1908.
Calendar of State Papers, Domestic, 1651-2, 1877.
Calendar of State Papers Relating to English Affairs...in Venice etc., 1864.
Caliaro, Marco & Francesconi, Mario, *John Baptist Scalabrini*, New York, 1977.
Canton, W. , *The History of the BFBS*, 1904.
Carpentier, Vincent, *L'Église de Dives Sur-Mer*, Cabourg, France, 2011.
Carrothers, W. A. , *Emigration from the British Isles*, 1965.
Carte, Thomas, *A General History of England*, 1755.
Cassian, John, *Conferences*, Boniface Ramsey OP (trans), Ancient Christian Writers 57, NY, 1997.
Casson, L., *Ships and Seamanship in the Ancient World*, Princeton 1986.
Catholic Encyclopedia, 1908.
CTS, *Guide to Heaven, 1896.*
CTS, *Seamen's Branch of the CTS*, tract, 1894.
CTS, *Conference Papers*, various dates.
CTS, *Catholic Conference Report*, 1897.
CTS, *Catholic Conference 1902: Official Guide Book*, Newport, Mon., 1902.
Chapman, Paul K. , *Trouble on Board: The Plight of International Seafarers*, Ithaca NY, 1992.
Chaunu, H. & Chaunu, P., *Seville et l'Atlantique (1504-1650)*, 5 vols, Paris, 1955.
Chronicles of the Crusades, Joinville and Villehardouin, M. R. B. Shaw (trans), 1963.
Chronicles of Theophanes Confessor, Trans. Cyril Mango & Roger Scott, Oxford, 1997.
Clark, E. A. (trans & ed), *The Life of Melania the Younger*, Toronto 1985.
Clay, Rotha Mary, *The Medieval Hospitals of England*, 1909.
Clay, Rotha Mary, *Hermits and Anchorites of England*, 1914.
Clement of Alexandria, *Stromateis*, J Ferguson (trans), Washington DC, 1991.
Common Prayer, The Annotated Book of, J.H. Blunt (ed), 1888.
Cook, Godron C., *Disease in the Merchant Navy*, Oxford 2007.

Corbin, A., *The Lure of the Sea*, 1994.
Cornewall-Jones, R. J., *The British Merchant Service*, 1898.
Corpus Iuris Canonici, E. Friedberg (ed), Leipzig, 1879.
Coste CM, Pierre, *The Life and Works of St Vincent de Paul*, 3 vols, 1934.
Course, A.G., *The Merchant Navy: A Social History*, 1959.
Cownie, Emma, *Religious Patronage in Anglo-Norman England 1066-1135*, Royal Historical Society, 1998.
Crysafulli, V. S. & Nesbitt, J. W., *The Miracles of St Artemios*, Leiden 1997.
Cuming, G. J., *A History of Anglican Liturgy*, 1969.
Curia Regis Rolls, 9-10 Henry III, RS, 1957.
Cuthbert OSFC, The Rev Fr, *The Capuchins*, 1928.
Cyprian, *Letters*, trans. Sr Rose Bernard Donna CSJ, Fathers of the Church, Washington DC, 1964
Cyril of Jerusalem, *Works of*, L. P. MCauley & Stephenson, A. A. (trans), Washington DC, 1968.
Daley SJ, Brian E., *Gregory of Nazianzus*, 2006.
David, C.W. (trans), *De Expugantione Lyxbonensi*, New York, 1936.
David, C.W., *Robert Curthose*, Harvard, 1980.
Davies, Ralph, *The Rise of the Atlantic Economies*, 1973.
Davis, Robert C., *Christian Slaves, Muslim Masters: White Slaves in the Mediterranean, the Barbary Coast and Italy*, Houndmills 2003.
Dawes, Elizabeth & Baynes, Norman H.(trans), *Three Byzantine Saints*, Oxford 1977.
Dollinger, Philippe, *The German Hanse*, 1970.
Dugdale, W., *Monasticon Anglicanum*, edition 1849.
Eadmer, *History of Recent Events in England*, Geoffrey Bosanquet (trans), 1964.
The Early South-English Legendary, Carl Horstmann (ed), EETS, vol I, 1887.
Encyclopedia of Missions, New York and London 1904.
English Episcopal Acta: Norwich 1070-1214, Christopher Harper-Bill (ed), Oxford 1990.
English Historical Documents 1189-1327, Harry Rothwell (ed), vol III, 1975.
Every, E. F., *The Anglican Church in South America*, 1915.
Ewe, Herbert, *Schiffe auf Siegeln*, Berlin 1972.
Fabri, Felix, *The Book of the Wanderings of*, A. Stewart (trans), Palestine Pilgrim Text Society, 1892.
Falkus, H., *Master of Cape Horn*, 1982.
Fell, James, *British Merchant Shipping in San Francisco*, 1899.
Fenwick, Kenneth (ed), *Galley Slave: the autobiography of Jean Marteilhe*, 1957.
Fisheries Exhibition, *Handbooks issued in Connection with the Great Fisheries Exhibition*, 6 vols, 1883.
Fisheries Exhibition, *Papers of the Conferences held in Connection with the Great Fisheries Exhibition*, 45 vols, 1883.
Friel, Ian, *The Good Ship*, 1995.
Froude, J.A., *English Seamen in the Sixteenth Century*, 1930.
Fulcher of Chartres, *A History of the Expedition to Jerusalem 1095-1127*, Frances Rita Ryan (trans), Knoxville, Tennessee, 1969.
Furnivall, Frederick J., (ed), *The Stacions of Rome and the Pilgrim's Sea-Voyage*, EETS, OS 25, 1867.
Gabrieli, Francesco, *Arab Historians of the Crusades*, New York, 1989.
Gannon, Arthur, *Memoir: Apostolatus Maris 1920-1960*, p.p. New Orleans, 1964.
Gli Statuti Marittimi Veneziani fino al 1225, Riccardo Predelli & Adolfo Sacerdoti (eds), Venice, 1903.
Goldstein, Joshua S., *Long Cycles: Prosperity and War in the Modern Age*, Yale, 1988.

Gollock, G.A., *At the Sign of the Flying Angel*, 1930.
Gollwitzer, Heinz, *Europe in the Age of Imperialism 1880-1914*, 1969.
Goodman, Margaret, *Experiences of an English Sister of Mercy*, 1862.
Goodman, Margaret, *Sisterhoods in the Church of England*, 1863.
Gorman, W. Gordon, *Converts to Rome 1850-1910*, 1910.
Gotein, S. D., *A Mediterranean Society*, vol i, 1967.
Gregory of Nazianzen, St, Select Orations of, Charles Gordon Browne & James Edward Swallow, Nicene and Post Nicene Fathers, Second Series, vol VII, reprinted Michingan 1978.
Gregory of Nazianzus, St, : Three Poems, Denis Molaise Meehan (trans), The Fathers of the Church, 1987.
Gregory of Nazianzus: Autobiographical Poems, Caroline White (trans & ed), Cambridge 1996.
Gregory VII, Correspondence of, Ephraim Emerton (trans), New York, 1979.
Grenfell, W., *A Labrador Doctor*, 1931.
Grosjean, Eugène, *Adieu-va!*, Paris?, 1895 (AA Archive, Rome).
Hague, Douglas B. & Christie, Rosemary, *Lighthouses*, Gomer Press 1975.
Hakluyt, *Voyages of the Elizabethan Seamen*, E.J. Payne (ed), Oxford 1907.
Hambye SJ, le R.P., '*L'Aumônerie de la Flotte de Flandre au 17eme siècle*, Louvain, 1967.
Hampshire Registers, IV, CRS XLIX, Gosport and Portsea, n.d.
Hasted, E., *The History of Kent*, Canterbury, 1797.
Hayden, Roger, *English Baptist History and Heritage*, p.p. Baptist Union of Great Britain, 1990.
Heinrici Chronicon Lyvoniae, George Henry Pertz (ed), Hanover 1874.
Henningsen, Henning, *Somand og Somandskirke: Dansk Somandskirke i fremmede Havne 1867-1967*, Christiansfeld, 1967.
Henry of Huntingdon, Archdeacon, *Historia Anglorum*, Diana Greenway (ed), Oxford 1996.
Henry of Livonia, Chronicle of, James A. Brundage (trans), Madison (Wis), 1961.
Henson, Edwin (ed), *Record of the English College at Valladolid 1589-1863*, CRS XXIX, 1930.
Herbert de Losinga, Life, Letters and Sermons of, E. M. Goulburn & H. Symonds (eds), 2 vols, Oxford 1878.
Hoekendijk, J. C., *The Church Inside Out*, 1964.
Homilies, Book of, Oxford 1802.
Hope, Ronald, *A New History of British Shipping*, 1990.
Hopkins, C. P., *Altering Plimsoll's Mark*, 1913.
Hopkins, C. P., *National Service of British Seamen 1914-18*, 1920.
Horae de Beata Maria Virgine, Facsimiles of, E. S. Dewick (ed), HBS, 1902.
Hornell, James, *Water Transport*, Newton Abbot, 1970.
Hourani, George F., *Arab Seafaring*, Princeton NJ, 1995.
Hugill, Stan, *Shanties from the Seven Seas*, 1961.
Hugill, Stan, *Sailortown*, 1967.
Hubbard, G. E., *The Old Book of Wye*, 1951.
Hutchinson, Gillian, *Medieval Ships and Shipping*, 1994.
Ibn Jubayr, Travels of, R. J. C. Broadhurst, 1952
Ibn Shaddad, Baha' al-din, *The Rare and Excellent History of Saladin*, D. S. Richards (trans), Crusade Texts in Translation, Aldershot, 2001.
Ingram, Bruce S.(ed), *Three Sea Journals of Stuart Times*, 1936.
Israel, J.I., *Dutch Primacy in World Trade 1658-1740*, Oxford, 1989.
Jackson, Gordon, *The History and Archaeology of Ports*, Tadworth, Surrey, 1983.

Jacob, Edward, *History of Faversham*, Sheerness, 1974.
Jenkins, P., *The Lost History of Christianity*, 2008.
Joinville, *Histoire de S. Louis*, no date or editor, Lille.
John, Bishop of Ephesus, *The Third Part of the Ecclesiastical History*, R. Payne Smith (trans), Oxford, 1860.
John, Bishop of Nikiu, *The Chronicle of,* Charles, R. H., (trans), LXXXII(21), Text and Translation Society 1916
Jones, Gwynn (trans), *The Norse Atlantic Saga*, Oxford 1986.
Kentish Traveller's Companion, Anon, 2nd edition 1779.
Kerr, Lady Amabel, *Père de Clerc*, CTS Publications, XVIII, 1901.
Kerr, Lady Amabel, *Auguste Marceau 1806-1851*, CTS Publications, XXI, 1902.
Khalilieh, Hassan Salih, *Islamic Maritime Law - and Introduction*, Leiden, 1998.
Kingsford, M.R., *The Work and Influence of William Henry Giles Kingston*, Toronto, 1947.
Kingsford, M.R., *The Mersey Mission to Seamen 1856-1956*, Abingdon, 1957.
Knight, H. G., *The Law of the Sea*, typescript, Baton Rouge 1976 (Copy in Mystic Seaport Museum Library).
Knight, H. J. C., *The Diocese of Gibraltar*, 1917.
Knowles, David & Hadcock, R. Neville, *Medieval Religious Houses in England and Wales*, 1971.
Knowles, W. H., *The Priory Church of St Mary and St Oswin, Tynemouth, Northumberland*, 1910.
Kverndal, Roald, *Seamen's Missions: Their Origin and Early Growth*, Pasadena (CA), 1986.
Kverndal, Roald, *The Way of the Sea*, Pasadena (CA), 2008.
Kverndal, Roald, *George Charles Smith of Penzance*, Pasadena CA, 2012.
Lactantius, *Divine Institutes*, Mary Francis McDonald OP (trans), Fathers of the Church, Washington DC, 1968.
Landnámabók, Hermann Pálsson & Paul Edwards (trans), University of Manitoba Icelandic Studies 1, 1988.
Laxdaela Saga, M. Magnusson & H. Pálsson, 1969.
Lane, F. C., *Venice and History*, Baltimore, 1966.
Lane, F.C., *Venice - A Maritime Republic*, 1973.
Lapidge, Michael, *Anglo-Saxon Litanies of the Saints*, HBS, 1991.
Lea, H. C., *A History of Auricular Confession and Indulgences*, 1896.
Leland, J., *Itinerary*, 5 vols, reprinted 1964.
Leofric Missal, F. E. Warren (ed), Oxford 1883.
Libellus de vita et miraculis S. Godrici, heremitae Finchale by Reginald of Durham, J. Stevenson (ed), Surtees Society, vol 20, 1847
Liebeschuetz, J.H.W.G., *Barbarians and Bishops*, Oxford, 1990.
Littlehales, Henry, *A Layman's Prayer-Book in English*, 1890.
Liturgical Services of the Reign of Queen Elizabeth, Edward Keatinge (ed), Parker Society, 1847.
Lloyd, Christopher, *The British Seaman*, 1968.
Lopez, Robert S., *The Commercial Revolution of the MIddle Ages, 950-1350*, Cambridge, 1976.
Lubbock, Basil, *Round the Horn before the Mast*, 1903.
MacCarthy, Fiona, *Eric Gill*, 1989.
MacGregor, D. R., *The China Bird*, 1961.
Mackay, A., *Spain in the Middle Ages: From Frontier to Empire 1000-1500*, 1977.
MacKenzie, Compton, *My Life and Times: Octave Two*, 1963.

Bibliography

MacKinlay, James Murray, *Ancient Church Dedications in Scotland: Non Scriptural Dedications*, vol. 2, Edinburgh, 1914.
Magnus, Olaus, *Description of the Northern People*, Hakluyt Society, 1998.
Magnusson, Magnus, *Viking Expansion Westwards*, 1973.
Mango, C., and Scott, R. (trans), *The Chronicles of Theophanes Confessor*, Oxford 1997.
Mann, Tom, *Memoirs*, 1923.
Marsden, R. G., *Documents Relating to the Law and Custom of the Sea*, vol I, NRS, 1916.
Marsh, V. & Ryan, A., *The Seamen*, Oxford 1989.
Martindale SJ, C.C., *A Prayer Book for Catholic Seafarers*, CTS, 1925.
Martindale SJ, C.C., *The Sea and its Apostolate*, CTS, 1938.
Martyrology of Oengus the Culdee, Whitley Stokes (ed), HBS, 1918.
Mathews, Basil, *Wilfred Grenfell, the Master Mariner*, 1924.
Matthew, D. J. A., *The Norman Monasteries*, Oxford, 1962.
McDonaugh CSSR, Thomas A., untitled ts dated New Orleans, 1971, AoS Rome archive.
Memorandum and Articles of Association of the British Sailors' Society etc., 1905.
Messaien, Jacky, *Mission de la Mer*, Dunkirk, 1981.
Miller, Robert (R.W.H.), *From Shore to Shore*, p.p. Nailsworth, Glos, 1989.
Miller, R.W.H., *Priest in Deep Water*, Cambridge, 2010.
Milsom, C. H., *Guide to the Merchant Navy*, Glasgow 1968.
Montreal from 1535 to 1914: Biographical, anon, Montreal, 1914.
Moody, Robert, *John Benett of Pythouse*, p.p., Bristol 2003.
Moorman, J.R.H., *A History of the Franciscan Order*, Oxford, 1968.
Morison, Fynes, *Itinerary*, 1617.
Murray, K. M. E., *Constitutional History of the Cinque Ports*, Manchester, 1935.
Natkiel, Richard & Preston, Antony, *Atlas of Maritime History*, rev 1992.
Nibbs, C. A. J., *From the Bristol Channel to the Seven Seas*, The Missions to Seamen 1935.
Njal's Saga, M. Magnusson & H. Pálsson (trans), 1969.
Noonan, J. T., *The Scholastic Analysis of Usury*, Cambridge, 1957.
Norwich Cathedral Charters, Barbara Dodwell (ed), vol I, Pipe Rolls Society LXXVIII, NS XL, 1965-6, 1974.
Norwich Cathedral Priory, The First Register of, H. W. Saunders (trans), Norfolk Record Society, 1939.
Orderic Vitalis, The Ecclesiastical History of, Marjorie Chibnall (ed & trans), Oxford 1969.
Osbernus, *de Expugnatione Lyxbonensis, Chronicles and Memorials of the Reign of Richard I*, vol 1, 1864.
Owen, Dorothy M., *The Making of King's Lynn*, 1984.
Palliser, D. M., *The Age of Elizabeth 1547-1603*, 1992.
Parker, Vanessa, *The Making of King's Lynn*, 1984.
Parkhurst, P. G., *Ships of Peace*, vol i, p.p. 1962.
Pascoe, C. F., *Two Hundred Years of the S.P.G*, 1901.
Patterson, A. Temple, *A History of Southampton 1700-1914*, vol iii, Southampton 1975.
Platt, C. & Coleman Smith, R., *Excavations in Medieval Southampton 1963-1969*, Leicester 1975.
PECUSA, *Journal and Canons 1871*, Hartford CT, 1872.
Penfentenyo, H. de, *L'Industrie Morutière*, Paris, n.d.
Pérez-Mallaína, Pablo E., *Spain's Men of the Sea*, Carla Rahn Phillips (trans), Baltimore, 1998.
Peters, George, *The Plimsoll Line*, 1975.
Pharr, C. (trans), *The Theodosian Code*, Princeton 1952.

Pirenne, H., *Economic and Social History of Medieval Europe*, 1965.
Pollen, J. H., *The English Martyrs 1584-1603*, Catholic Record Society, 1907.
Prayer Book for Catholic Seamen, p.p. OSP, 1903.
Premier Congrès d'Apostolat Maritime: Report, Paris, 1927.
Prestage, E., *The Portuguese Pioneers*, 1966.
Prins, A. H. J., *In Peril on the Sea: Marine Votive Paintings on the Maltese Islands*, Valletta, Malta, 1989.
Proctor, David, *Music of the Sea*, 1992.
Proctor, F. & Frere, W. H., *A New History of the Book of Common Prayer*, 1911.
Prudentius, *Poems*, Sr Mary Clement Eagan (trans), Washington DC 1962.
The Prymer, Henry Littlehales (ed), pt ii, 1892.
Pryor, John H. & Elizabeth M. Jeffreys, *The Age of the ΔPOMΩN*, Leiden, 2006.
Purvis, J.S., *The York Cycle of Mystery Plays*, 1957.
Rahner, Hugo, *Greek Myths and Christian Mystery*, Brian Battershaw (trans), London 1963.
Ray, Himanshu P., *Monastery and Guild*, Oxford, 1986.
Rediker, Marcus, *Between the Devil and the Deep Blue Sea*, Cambridge, 1987.
Regesta Regum Anglo-Normanorrum 1066-1154, H. W. C. Davis (ed), vol. I, 1913.
Regesta Regum Anglo-Normanorrum 1066-1154, H. A. Cronne & R. H. C. Davis (eds), vol III, Oxford 1968.
Report of the Society for Improving the Condition of Merchant Seamen, 1867.
Richard of Chichester, St., David Jones (ed), Sussex Record Society, vol 79, Lewes 1993.
Richard of Cirencester, *Speculum Historiale*, John E. B. Mayor, vol II, RS, 1869.
Richard of Devizes (*Richardi Divisensis*), *Cronicon De Tempore Regis Richardi Primi*, John T. Appleby (ed), 1963.
Riemersma, Jelle C., *Religious Factors in Early Dutch Capitalism 1550-1650*, The Hague, 1967.
Rompkey, Ronald, *Terre-Neuve: Anthologie des vayageurs français, 1814-1914*, Rennes, 2005.
Ruddock, Alwyn A., *Italian Merchants and Shipping in Southampton, 1270-1600*, Southampton, 1951.
Ryan, Maxwell, *Year Book*, Salvation Army, 1977.
Saga of Grettir the Strong, G. A. Hight (trans), 1965.
Sandall, Robert, *History of the Salvation Army*, vol ii, 1950; vol iii, 1955.
Seaver, Kirsten, *The Frozen Echo*, Stanford (Con.), 1996.
Sěvčenko, I., & Sěvčenko, N. Patterson, *The Life of St Nicholas of Sion*, Brookline MA., 1984.
Smith, G. C., *Bethel or the Rag Unfurled*, 1819.
Smith, John, *Seaman's Grammar*, 1652.
Smith, Robert Sidney, *The Spanish Guild Merchant*, Durham, North Carolina, 1940.
Socrates, *Ecclesiastical History*, A. C. Zenos (ed), 1890.
Stanley, H.E.J. (trans), *The Three Sea Voyages of Vasco da Gama*, Hakluyt Society, First Series XLII, 1869.
Stevenson, D.A., *The World's Lighthouses before 1820*, Oxford, 1959.
Strömbäck, Dag, *The Conversion of Iceland*, Peter Foote (trans), Viking Society, vol VI, London 1975.
Strong, L.A.G., *Flying Angel: The Story of the Missions to Seamen*, 1956.
Strype, John, *The Life and Acts of Archbishop Parker*, Oxford 1821.
Sumption, Jonathan, *Pilgrimages*, 1975.

Bibliography

Taylor, E. G. R., *The Troublesome Voyage of Captain Edward Fenton*, Hakluyt Society 1957.
Taylor, Gordon, *The Sea Chaplains*, 1978.
Tengström, E., *Bread for the People*, Stockholm 1974.
Tertullian, *Against the Heathen*, Library of the Fathers, vol. 10, Oxford, 1842.
Tertullian, *De Anima*, Peter Holmes (trans), ANCL XV, Edinburgh 1870.
Tertullian, *On Repentance*, S. Thelwall (trans), ANCL IX, Edinburgh 1869.
Tertullian, *On the Resurrection of the Flesh*, Peter Holmes (trans), ANCL XV, *Tertullian*, vol ii, Edinburgh 1870.
Tertullian, *Answer to the Jews*, S. Thelwall (trans), ANCL XVIII, *Tertullian*, vol iii, Edinburgh 1870.
Tertullian, *On Idolatry*, S. Thelwall (trans), ANCL XI, *Tertullian*, vol i, Edinburgh 1869.
Theodoret, *The Ecclesiastical History, Dialogues and Letters*, B. Jackson (trans), Library of Nicene and Post Nicene Fathers, Second Series, vol 3, Oxford 1892.
Theodoret, *A History of the Monks of Syria*, Richard Price (trans), Kalamazoo 1985.
The Theodosian Code, Clyde Pharr (trans), Princeton, 1952.
Thómas Saga Erkibyskups, Eiríkr Magnússon (trans and ed), 1875.
Tolkowsky, Samuel, *They Took to the Sea*, 1964.
Toulmin Smith, L., *English Guilds: The Original Ordinances of More than One Hundred Early English Guilds*, Early English Text Society, 1870.
Tupper, Edward, *Seamen's Torch*, 1938.
Twiss, Sir Travers, (ed), *Black Book of the Admiralty*, 4 vols, Rolls Series, 1871.
Tyndale, William, *Doctrinal Treatises*, Parker Society, 1844.
Valence, Dr -, *Les Pêcheurs de la mer nord*, Paris, 1892.
Valtierra SJ, A., *Peter Claver, Saint of Slaves*, 1960.
Vauchez, André, *Sainthood in the Later Middle Ages*, Cambridge 1997.
Ville, Simon P., *Transport and Development of the European Economy 1750-1918*, 1990.
Vitry, Jacques de, *Exempla et sermones vulgares*, T. F. Crane (ed), Folk-Lore Society, CCVI, 1878.
Vitry, Lettres de Jacques de, R. B. C. Huygens, Leiden 1960.
Waldo, Fulleton L., *With Grenfell on the Labrador*, New York & Edinburgh 1920.
Walrond, Mary, *Launching Out Into the Deep*, 1904.
Wants of the Colonial and Missionary Church, SPG leaflet, May 1880
Waterton, Edmund, *Pietas Marianna Britannica*, 1879.
Webb, Adrian J. (ed), *A Maritime History of Somerset*, vol 1, Somerset Archaeological and Natural History Society, 2010.
Webster, G. S., *The Seamen's Friend*, New York 1932.
Westlake, H.F., *The Parish Guilds of Medieval England*, 1919.
Weston, Agnes, *My Life Among the Blue Jackets*, 1909.
White Jnr, Lynn, *Medieval Religion and Technology*, 1978.
Whyman, Henry C., *The Headstroms and the Bethel Ship Saga*, Southern Illinois U.P., 1992.
Wilkinson, John, *Jerusalem Pilgrims before the Crusades*, Warminster, 1977.
Willibrord, Calendar of, H.A. Wilson (ed), HBS 1918.
Wilson, J. Havelock, *My Stormy Voyage Through Life*, vol 1, 1925.
Winstedt, E. O., *The Christian Topography of Cosmas Indicopleustes*, Cambridge, 1909.
Winston-Allen, Anne, *Stories of the Rose*, Pennsylvania 1997.
Wood, Susan, *English Monasteries and their Patrons in the 13th Century*, Oxford 1955.
Woodruff, C. Eveleigh, *History of Fordwich*, Canterbury, n.d..
Woodward, Josiah, *An Account of the Rise and Progress of the Religious Societies in*

the City of London &c., 2nd edition 1698.
Wormald, Patrick, *The Making of English Law: King Alfred to the Twelfth Century*, vol I, Oxford 1999.
Wren, Wilfred J., *The Story of the 'Domus Dei' of Chichester with Statutes of St Mary's Hospital, Siena and Inventory of St Mary's Hospital, Dover*, Dover 1885.
Wren, Wilfred J., *Ports of the Eastern Counties*, Lavenham, Suffolk, 1976.
Wright, R. F., *Medieval Internationalism*, 1930.
Yenton, Michael, *Peter Anson: Monk, Writer and Artist*, Anglo-Catholic History Society, 2005.
Young, Robert, *From Cape Horn to Panama*, 1905.
Yzermans, Vincent A., *American Catholic Seafarer's Church*, 1992 (Library of Congress: 95-083201, other details are missing).

Unpublished theses

Carter, P. N., *An Edition of William of Malmesbury's Treatise on the Miracles of the Virgin Mary*, DPhil, University of Oxford, 1959.
Chatham, John, *British Seafarers: from opposition to collaboration, 1911-1927*, MA, Warwick University, 1981.
Friend, Stephen, *The Rise and Development of Christian Missions amongst British Fishing Communities during the 19th Century*, MPhil, University of Leeds, 1994.
Harris, G.G., *The History of Trinity House at Deptford 1540-1660*, MA, University of London, 1962.
Harrison, W.E.C., *Maritime Activity Under Henry VII*, MA, University of London, 1931.
Hayden, Roger, *Evangelical Calvinism among Eighteenth Century Bristol Baptists*, PhD, University of Keele, 1991.
Kennerley, Alston, *British Seamen's Missions and Sailors' Homes 1815-1970*, PhD, CNAA, 1989.
Kollar, Rene, *Abbot Aelred Carlyle and the Monks of Caldey Island: Anglo-Catholicism in the Church of England*, PhD, Ann Arbor, Michigan, 1981.
Miller, R.W.H., *Ship of Peter: The Catholic Sea Apostolate and the Apostleship of the Sea*, MPhil, University of Plymouth, 1995.
Miller, R.W.H., *The Man at the Helm: The Faith and Practice of the Medieval Seafarer etc*, PhD, University of London, 2002.
Oubré, Sinclair Kevin, *The Apostolatus Maris: Its Structural Development Including its 1997 Reorganization*, LCL, Catholic University of America, 1998.
Schaefer, Mary Martina, *Twelfth Century Latin Commentaries on the Mass*, Ann Arbor, Mi, PhD, 1983.

Artifacts

Mary Rose Inventory: The Mary Rose Trust, College Road, HM Naval Base, Portsmouth PO1 3LX.

Index

Abbeys
    Abingdon 45
    Battle 45, 46
    Caldey 294ff
    Canterbury, Christ Church 44
    Canterbury, St Augustine 44, 46
    Farnborough 294
    Fécamp 44f
    Fort Augustus 294, 299
    Melrose 45
    Mont St Michel 46, 48
    Mountebourg 45
    Osney 52
    Quarr 46, 321
    Ramsey 44f
    St André 314f
    St Georges de Bocherville 45
    St Mary des Dunes 45
    St Peter, Ghent 45
    Tintern 44, 71
    Val-Richer 48
    Waltham 47
Acre 50
Additional Curates Society 155
Alexandria 24, 31
Alfwold, Bp 46
Almsmen 56
American Seamen's Friend Society 187ff
Anson, P. F. 14, 43, 240, 292ff
Apostleship of Prayer 238, 252ff
Apostleship of the Sea 258ff, 306ff
Apostolaat des Meeres 324
Apostolaat ter Zee 324
Apprentices 200, 203, 245
Artemios, St 32

Ashley, John 121, 135ff
Athanasius of Alexandria 22f
Athanasius Pentaschoinites 22
Atherton, Dr W. H. 246, 308, 318
Augustine of Hippo 23
Augustinian Canons 47
Augustinians of the Assumption 238, 264ff, 312
Au Large 279
Auvert, Admiral 329, 332

Bacini 81
Bailly, M. Bernard 238, 268ff,
Bailly, Père Emmanuel 269
Baptists 122, 128ff, 336
Beaudoin, Abbé 237, 268
Becket, Thomas 64f, 89, 94
Becon, Thomas 107ff
Belin, *Abbé* 270
Bernard, Abbé 237, 268, 315, 332
BETHEL flag 121, 129, 188
Bibles
    confiscation 100, 102
    distribution 122ff
    oaths on 91f
    on board 90f, 102
Bishop, Captain Charles 115f
Bishop of the Seas 145ff
Bishops blessing 85f
Bishops at sea 85, 94
Bishop's Lydeard 54
Bonnafy, Dr 268
Boston (US) Marine Society 187
Bouchier, Rev. J. 143
Bourne, Cardinal 282, 296f, 307, 325

Brendan, St 58, 62, 197
Bridge Chapels 54
Bristol Channel Mission 121, 135ff, 160ff
Bristol Seamen's Institute 154
BFBS 116, 119, 163, 227
BFSFSBU 120f, 128f
BFSS 188ff, 311
British Ladies Female Emigration Society 142
British Reformation Society 132
British Sailors Relief Fund of Canada 175
British Sailors Society 132, 151
Britten, James 241, 256
Broadstairs 59
Brown, Alderman 129, 133

Calcutta Bible Association 126
Calendars 76, 98, 158
Canons Regular of the Lateran 283, 291
Canterbury Mission Society 171
Catholic Newspaper Guild 281
Catholic Reading Guild 281, 296
Catholic Reading Guild Sailors' Branch 297
Catholic Sailors' Home London 246
Catholic Sailors' Home Glasgow 259f
Catholic Sailors' Literature Committee 246
Catholic Truth Society 236ff, 256f, 284
Catholic Women's League 317
Catholic Young Men's Society 262, 306
Chaplains on board 100, 105, 114
    in port 51, 113
    naval 103, 111, 118, 122
Chardavoine, Père Eutrope 315, 331f
Childs, Rev. T. C. 138, 159
Christopher, St 43
Church Congresses
    Liverpool 1869 145
    Brighton 1869 146
    Stoke on Trent 1875 147
    Swansea 1879 148
    Newcastle 1881 149
    Portsmouth 1885 150
    Manchester 1888 150
    Cardiff 1889 154
    Norwich 1895 154
    Northampton 1902 166
Church Missionary Society 122
C of E Mission to the English in Spain ... 181ff
C of E Temperance Society 149, 227
Church Pastoral Aid Society 141
Cinque Ports 42, 61
Claver, Peter 112f
Clement of Alexandria 26, 27, 29
Clement of Rome 43, 58, 64
Coastguards 250f
Coldwell, George 296ff
Colonial Church & School Society 180ff
Colonization Society 159
Columbus 38
Committee on Spiritual Proviision 157ff
Common Prayer, Book of 104ff, 107ff, 115, 124, 127f
Communitatis navis 29
Confession (sacramental) 39, 48, 82, 106, 110, 114, 158
Confraternity of Notre Dame de la Mer 269
Confrérie du Saint-Sacrèment 114
Constantinople 182
Consular Advances Act 181
Conversion to Islam 40
Copers 227ff
Cork mission 142f
corpse-finder 71
corpus naviculorum 23
Cox, Lieutenant 124f
Crucifixes 42, 59
Cyprian 24, 27, 29
Cyril of Jerusalem 26

Daniel the Stylite 22, 33
Davies, Michael 308f
Dawson, Cdr 144ff
de Chambery, Sisters of St Joseph 271
de Courtney, John 90
de Thézac, M. 279, 315
de Torre Diaz, Count 282

Index

de Torre Diaz, Countess 298
de Vitry, Jacques 41, 79, 84
Deodand 73, 106
Diet 76, 80
Dignam SJ, Fr Augustus 239ff, 319
Directory of Public Worship 108f, 111
Dock St, St Paul's Seamen's Church 130, 132, 146, 161
Dock Strike 200, 205
Douglas, Rev. Lord Archibald 237f, 300
Dover 52, 59
Drake, Francis 104
Drummond, Lister 246
Dry Mass 59, 95, 97
Dublin, seamen's mission 142
Dutch Committee...for Fishermen 232
Dunwich 40, 43, 54

Easter Communion 39, 48, 80
East India Company 103, 107f, 116, 123
Ecclesia mercatorum 51, 91
Edmund, St 54
Egger SJ, Fr Joseph 259ff, 307
Elliott, Capt. R. 130f, 139
Episcopal Floating Church Society 131
Études 264f
Excommunication 70ff, 77ff

Fabri, Felix 39, 59, 95f
Fast days 76
Fell, Rev. James 193ff
Fenton, Edward 103ff
Flags 121, 129, 140, 170, 173, 183
Fletcher, Fr Philip 246
Floating chapel 129, 130, 133ff
Fordwich 44
Franciscans 36, 38, 53, 98, 100
Fraser, Hon. Mrs G. 238ff, 300
Frobisher 105
Fry, Elizabeth 115f

Gambier, George, 130f
Gambier, Lord 123, 129
Gannon, Arthur 298, 305ff, 325ff
Garnier, Abbé Theodore 269
Gasparri, Cardinal 316

Genoa, chaplaincy 48
Genoa 249f, 282
Gibraltar, Bishop of 180ff
Gibraltar, Diocesan Spiritual Aid Fund 180ff
Gibraltar Mission to Seamen 179ff
Gibraltar Seamen's Bethel Society 179
Glasgow AoS 259ff, 306
Glasgow, Archbishop of 261f, 297, 315
Glasgow CTS 259, 284
Glasgow CSI 259f, 281, 284, 316
Glasgow Central Committee 297, 311ff
Glass, clearing of 101, 104, 106
Goldie SJ, Fr Francis 118, 204, 236ff, 279, 280, 283
Gospels 72, 82, 92
Graffiti 53f
Gravesend 139ff, 168ff
Grenfell, Wilfred 279
Gretton, SJ, Fr 254ff
Grimsby fisher lads 243, 245
Grosjean SJ, Eugène 204, 265ff
Gregory Nazianzen 31
Guide to Heaven 214, 244f
Guild of Ransom 242, 246ff
Guild of Shipmasters 24
Guilds, medieval 56ff, 76

Hamon, Père Yves 270ff
Hanse 50, 101
Harlots 84, 112
Hartlepool, St Hilda 53
Hatherley, S.G. 15f
Hawkins, Canon (Grimsby) 245
Hay, Canon (Genoa) 249f, 282
Hebrides 89
Helgi the Lean 90
Herbert de Losinga 49f
Hermits 47
Hernias 32
Higg-Cameron, Jarl 318ff
Hills, Rev. G. 142
Holderness, Rev. W 141
Homilies, Book of 60, 107, 126ff
Hopkins, Rev. C. P. 198ff, 242, 304
Hospitals 43, 101
Hostels, see maisons dieu 43

Howden, Mrs K. 252, 260ff, 285
Hull Fishermen's Apprentices' Bethel 147

Icelandic hospital 271
Inquisition 90, 92, 102, 109
Intercontinental Church Society, see CCCS
Interdicts 96
International Committee of Seafarers' Unions 205ff, 214ff
Ireland, Island & Coast Society of 143
Islamic Law 68, 73

Jam Inde 264, 273-7
Jay, Rev. A. Osborne 200
Jesuits 100, 113
John the Almsgiver 24, 33
Julian, St 43, 58, 59, 62f, 64

Kerr, Lady Amabel 236ff
King George's Fund for Sailors 175
King's Lynn 43, 49f
Kingston, W. H. G. 121,142f, 159ff
Kingstown seamen's mission 142

Ladies Altar Guild (NY) 196
Lateran Councils 36, 39, 75, 77f
Lay Readers 152
Le Livre du Marin 279
Lemonnier, Bishop 314f
Letters on Christian Doctrine 256f, 281
Lichfield Diocesan Barge Mission 166
Lights 46ff
List of Catholic RN Officers 257, 282, 294f
Litany 84f
Liverpool MCS 134f, 145f
   Seamen's & Emigrants' Friend Society 135, 147, 166
London Episcopal Floating Church Society 129, 131, 133ff, 139, 165
London Missionary Society 115
Louis IX 84, 93, 95
Lucas, Edward 250f
Lynn chaplaincy 48
   seamen's church 48
Lyons, Councils 36

Macdonald, Fr Hamilton 282, 294ff

Mackintosh, Archbishop 297, 315ff
Madox, Richard 103ff
maisons dieu 43, 52f, 65
Marceau, Auguste 236, 243
Marcion 23, 24
Mare clausum 66f, 79
   Liberum 66f, 79
   nullius 66f, 79, 96
Marine Bible Society of NY 188
Mariners Church Society 134f, 165f
Marine Society 141, 187
Marten, R. H. 129, 133
Martindale SJ, Fr C. C. 245, 324, 326, 330
Mass at sea 59, 92ff
Mather, E. J. 225ff
Mathurins 53
Maude, The Hon. Francis 139
McClement, Fr Kerr 324, 326ff
Melania the Younger 22
Mercedarians 53
MSABS 120, 124, 141
Merchant Seamen's Orphan Asylum 130
Merchant Shipping Acts 200ff
Mersey Mission to Seamen 135, 165ff
Messenger of the Sacred Heart 237ff
Methodists 120, 157, 179
Missal Leofric 55
   Roman 55f
   Sarum 56
Missio navalis 114
MDSF 121, 153, 225ff, 276f
Mission to English Seamen in Spanish Ports 182
Mission to Seafarers 138
Missions to Galleys 113
Missions to Seamen 15, 121, 132, 138
Montreal 245f, 282
Morning Offering 258
Morton, The Rev. Thos. 140
Munus naviculorum 23
Muscovy Company 103

National Bible Society of America 126
National Maritime Board 220f.
NMBS 119, 122f, 141, 162
Naval Correspondence Mission 120,

128
New York Altar Guild 196
Nicholas of Myra 43, 60f
Nicholas of Sion 32
North & Central European Sailors' Mission 174f
North Sea Church Mission 155, 174, 304
Norwich, Bishop of 49
Oaths 70, 72, 82, 92
Œuvres de Mer 238, 264ff, 300
Œuvre des Bateliers 249
Œuvre des Orphelins de Mer 278
Olaf
 churches 50
 King/Saint 36, 62
Oleron, Laws of 59, 68ff
Order of St Paul 166, 200f, 204ff
Orthodox church Bristol 16
 Cardiff 15
Ospringe, Kent 54

P & O 145, 172
Papal Navy 105
Pilgrim badges 42
Pilgrims 54, 59, 76
Pilgrim ships 88, 95f
Pity, Our Lady of 59
Plaistow & Victoria Dock Mission 142, 169
Plimsoll, Samuel 15, 200ff
Port of London Society 120, 130, 189
Port Said 172
Prayer Book & Homily Society 120, 126f, 141f, 163
Prayer Book for Catholic Seamen 213f, 244f
Processions 84
PECUSA 190ff
Prymer 90f

Quakers 112

Reculver 59
Reformation of Manners, Societies for 110
Relics 70, 82
Religious Tract Society 119f, 123f
Reserved Sacrament 93, 95, 114
Revenue Cutters 124

Robinson, The Rev. C. E. R. 147, 164f, 168ff
Rogers, Zebedee 120
Rosary 42, 59
Royal Brunswick Maritime Establishment 130f
Royal Commission on Seamen, Report 146
RN Catholic Association 244, 282, 288
RN Scripture Readers' Society 145
Rules, AoS 311
Rye 42

Sailors' Snug Harbour 187
St George's College for Sailor Boys 198
Salvage 73f
Salvation Army 233
Salvation Navy 233ff
Sanctuary 74f
Sandwich, St Bartholomew's Hospital 52
San Francisco 155, 193ff
Satyrus 30
Scalabrinians 197
Scarborough 59
Scarth, Canon John 144ff
Scoresby, The Rev. W. 135
Scott Murray, Miss Mary 241ff, 251, 254ff, 282, 294ff, 319
Scribarius 51, 72, 91
Seals (port) 42, 61, 85
Seamen's Christian Friend Society 130, 147, 165
Seamen's Church Institutes 191ff
Seamen's Friendly Society of St Paul 208f
Sellon, Priscilla Lydia 197f
Shields SJ, Bro. Daniel 260ff, 284ff, 303, 320
Ship names 60
Shipping Federation 205
Ships
 America 196
 HMS Brazen 134, 139
 Carrack Of Rhodes 61
 Cassiope 199, 201
 HMS Curaçoa 253
 De Hoop 232
 Dolfijn 232

Edward Auriel 231
Eirene 135ff, 161
Ensign 227
Geologist 198
Goshawk 173
Grace Dieu 86
Helvetia 204
Kestrel 172f
Mary Rose 42, 61
Morning Star 310
Navis Dei 53
St Andrew The Fisherman 174
St Pierre 271f
Sapper 172f
Sir Edward P. Willis Ii 232
Swan 139
HMS Tees 135
Thessalia 16
United States 196
Water Kelpie 172
Shipwreck 23, 70f
Shipwrecked & Distressed Mariners' Society 129, 227
Short, Bro. (SVP) 326ff
Sick seamen 74
Silvanus, Bishop of Troas 22
Simeon Trustees 140
Slaves 112ff
Smith, G. C. 118, 120f, 128ff
SPCK 116, 119, 124, 141, 172
Society for the Propagation of the Gospel 116, 179ff
Society of St Paul 200
Society of St Raphael 243
Society of St Vincent de Paul 257, 283f, 286ff, 300ff, 318, 324ff
Soldiers' & Seamen's Evangelical Friend Society 130
South American Missionary Society 167
Southampton 43, 50, 59
Stella Maris (1901) 248, 281
Stella Maris (1911) 287
Stewart, Miss Margaret 241
Strike of 1911 216ff

Tertullian 23, 26, 28
Testicular problems 32f

Thames Church Mission 121, 139ff, 145ff, 160, 162ff, 225ff
Thames Revival 119
Theodore of Sykeon 31f
Theodosian Code 13, 24f
Theodosius 30
Tiberi, Mgr 270, 273f, 276
Tiverton, St Peter's Church 54
Toc H 334
Toll, Dr 287f
Tordesillas, Treaty of 66
Tracts 124, 127
Trinitarian Friars 46, 100
Trinity House 57, 58, 126
Tyndale, William 39
Tynemouth Priory 45f, 48

Union of Catholic Seafarers 317
Union, Seamen's 205ff
Usury 70

Victoria (BC) Harbour Mission 174
Vincent de Paul, St 113f
Votives 53-56
Vows 76, 107

Waldegrave, Capt. 139
Walker, John 104
Walrond, The Rev. T. A. 160ff
Watermen's Friend Society 129
Wegg Prosser, Major 328f
Weston, Agnes 150, 174
Wexford 47
William de Turbe 49
Wilson, J. Havelock 201f
Working Boys
　Pollokshaws 261
　St Aloysius 260ff
Work for Catholic Blue Jackets 252ff, 294
Wrecking 71, 73

Yarmouth
　Beach & Harbour Mission 142, 147
　seamen's church 48, 50
Youghal 47, 52, 53
Young Men's Christian Association 245